ESSENTIALS OF STATISTICS
for the
BEHAVIORAL SCIENCES

ESSENTIALS OF STATISTICS
for the
BEHAVIORAL SCIENCES

FREDERICK J GRAVETTER

State University of New York
College at Brockport

LARRY B. WALLNAU

State University of New York
College at Brockport

WEST PUBLISHING COMPANY
St. Paul / New York / Los Angeles / San Francisco

COPYEDITING	Linda Thompson
PROBLEM CHECKING	Roxy Peck
INTERIOR DESIGN	Kathi Townes
ART	Rolin Graphics
COMPOSITION	The Clarinda Company
INDEXING	Lois Oster
COVER ART	Leonardo da Vinci, ''Studies of a Woman's Head and Shoulders.'' Windsor Castle, Royal Library. © 1990. Her Majesty Queen Elizabeth II.

LIBRARY OF CONGRESS CATALOGING-IN-PUBLICATION DATA

Gravetter, Frederick J
  Essentials of statistics for the behavioral sciences / Frederick
J Gravetter, Larry B. Wallnau.
     p.   cm.
  Includes bibliographical references and index.
  ISBN 0-314-77291-X (soft)
  1. Social sciences—Statistical methods.   I. Wallnau, Larry B.
II. Title.
HA29.G726   1991
519.5'0243–dc20   90-49234
                                                   CIP

CONTENTS

PREFACE

Our intent in writing the *Essentials* statistics text is to provide a shorter, paperback textbook for the basic one-semester course in introductory statistics. The philosophy underlying this book (as with earlier editions of the standard Gravetter and Wallnau text, *Statistics for the Behavioral Sciences*) is that learning statistics requires more than simply memorizing a set of formulas. More specifically, we feel that students benefit from a complete, in-depth presentation of new topics, including analogies, and numerous examples demonstrating and explaining each statistical procedure. To accomplish our goals, we have included in this book only those topics that we feel are crucial to a basic understanding of statistical methods for behavioral sciences. We have attempted to provide complete coverage of the selected topics, rather than skim lightly over a wider range of areas in statistics. This book also reflects some organizational changes from our larger text, changes which we believe provide a smooth and logical development of hypothesis testing and related topics. Despite these changes, the goal of this book is the same as in previous editions: To go beyond the ''how-to'' presentation of statistics and help students gain a conceptual understanding of statistical methods and their applications.

We would like to thank the people at West Publishing who have assisted us with this project. We extend our gratitude to our editor Clark Baxter, developmental editor Nancy Hill-Whilton, production editor Jeff Carpenter, and promotion manager Ann Swift. They brought a great many professional and technical skills to this project, as well as their much appreciated encouragement and guidance. We thank Roxy Peck, who did an outstanding job checking our computations. We also thank the following people who provided thoughtful reviews and many helpful comments at various stages in the development of this book.

David L. Carpenter
Saint Bonaventure University

Ernest G. Davenport, Jr.
University of Minnesota

David Chiszor
University of Colorado at Boulder

George Domino
University of Arizona

Stephen S. Cooper
Glendale Community College

Freeman F. Elzey
San Francisco State University

Elliot Cramer
University of North Carolina

Nancy E. Furlong
Alfred University

Elizabeth L. Glisky
University of Arizona

James Hodgson
Middle Tennessee State University

Rick A. Lowe
Marshalltown Community College

Daniel D. Moriarty
University of San Diego

Lynn A. Phelps
Ohio University

Randall R. Robey
*Southern Illinois University—
Carbondale*

Mary Roznowski
The Ohio State University

Robert J. Schneider
Metropolitan State College

Elliott Schuman
Long Island University

Kathy Schwarz
Scottsdale Community College

Mark A. Shatz
The Ohio University

Michael Shirazi
*Mississippi County Community
College*

John J. Skowronski
The Ohio State University

Jim Snow
Pima Community College

Lynda Tompkins
Southwest Texas State University

Thomas W. Turnage
Iowa State University

Marion I. Upchurch
Southwest Texas State University

James A. Vail
Madison Community College

Rene E. Villa
Hillsborough Community College

Douglas Wallen
Mankato State University

Edward R. Whitson
*State University of New York College
at Geneseo*

Hilda Lee Williams
Drake University

Frank R. Yekovich
The Catholic University of America

Carolina Zingale
Rutgers University

The authors are grateful to the literary executor of the late Sir Ronald A. Fisher, F.R.S., to Dr. Frank Yates, F.R.S., and to Longman Group Ltd. (London) for permission to adapt Tables III and VI from their book *Statistical Tables for Biological, Agricultural, and Medical Research* (6th edition, 1974). We are also grateful to the people at Minitab, Inc. for their assistance with the material in Chapter 16.

Finally, the authors thank the following family and friends for their kind assistance, words of encouragement, and enduring patience: Justin, JoAnn, Naomi, Ed Berns, and the crew of *Anodyne*.

TO THE STUDENT

There is a common (and usually unfair) belief that visits to the dentist will be associated with fear and pain, even though dentists perform a service of great benefit to us. Although you initially may have some fears and anxieties about this course, we could argue that statistics courses also perform a beneficial service. This is evident when one considers that our world has become information-laden and information-dependent. The media informs us of the latest findings on oat bran and your health, global warming, economic trends, aging and memory, effects of educational programs, and so on. All these data-gathering efforts provide an enormous and unmanageable amount of information: Enter the statisticians, who use statistical procedures to analyze, organize, and interpret vast amounts of data. Having a basic understanding of a variety of statistical procedures will help you understand these findings, and even to examine them critically.

What about the fear of taking statistics? One way to deal with the fear is to get plenty of practice. You will notice that this book provides you with a number of opportunities to repeat the techniques you will be learning, in the form of Learning Checks, Examples, Demonstrations, and the end-of-chapter Problems. We encourage you to take advantage of these opportunities. Also, we encourage you to read the text, rather than just memorizing the formulas. We have taken great pains to present each statistical procedure in a conceptual context that explains why the procedure was developed and when it should be used. If you read this material and gain an understanding of the basic concepts underlying a statistical formula, you will find that learning the formula and how to use it will be much easier.

Over the years, our students in our classes have given us many helpful suggestions. We learn from them. If you have any suggestions or comments about this book, you can send a note to us at the Department of Psychology, SUNY College at Brockport, Brockport, NY 14420. We may not be able to answer every letter, but we always appreciate the feedback.

Frederick J Gravetter
Larry B. Wallnau

ESSENTIALS OF STATISTICS
for the
BEHAVIORAL SCIENCES

CHAPTER 1

INTRODUCTION TO STATISTICS

SECTION 1.1   **STATISTICS, SCIENCE, AND OBSERVATIONS**

The procedure is actually quite simple. First you arrange things into different groups depending on their makeup. Of course, one pile may be sufficient, depending on how much there is to do. If you have to go somewhere else due to lack of facilities, that is the next step; otherwise you are pretty well set. It is important not to overdo any particular endeavor. That is, it is better to do too few things at once than too many. In the short run this may not seem important, but complications from doing too many can easily arise. A mistake can be expensive as well. The manipulation of the appropriate mechanisms should be self-explanatory, and we need not dwell on it here. At first the whole procedure will seem complicated. Soon, however, it will become just another facet of life. It is difficult to foresee any end to the necessity for this task in the immediate future, but then one never can tell.*

The preceding paragraph was adapted from a psychology experiment reported by Bransford and Johnson (1972). If you have not read the paragraph yet, go back and read it now.

You probably find the paragraph a little confusing, and most of you probably think it is describing some obscure statistical procedure. Actually, this paragraph describes the everyday task of doing laundry. Now that you know the topic of the paragraph, try reading it again—it should make sense now.

Why did we begin a statistics textbook with a paragraph about washing clothes? Our goal is to demonstrate the importance of context—when not in the proper context, even the simplest material can appear difficult and confusing. In the Bransford and Johnson experiment people who knew the topic before reading the paragraph were able to recall 73% more than people who did not know that it was about doing laundry. When you have the appropriate background, it is much easier to fit new material into your memory and to recall it later. As you work through the topics in this book, remember that all statistical methods were developed to serve a purpose. The purpose for each statistical procedure provides a background or context for the details of the formulas and calculations. If you understand why a new procedure is needed, you will find it much easier to learn the procedure.

The objective for this first chapter is to provide an introduction to the topic of statistics and to give you some background for the rest of the book. We will discuss the role of statistics within the general field of scientific inquiry, and we will introduce some of the vocabulary and notation that are necessary for the statistical methods that follow.

Incidently, we cannot promise that statistics will be as easy as washing clothes. But if you begin each new topic within the proper context, you should eliminate some unnecessary confusion.

DEFINITIONS OF STATISTICS

Why study statistics? is a question countless students ask. One simple answer is that statistics have become a common part of everyday life and therefore deserve some attention. A quick glance at the newspaper yields statistics that deal with crime rates, birth rates, average income, average snowfall, and so on. By a common definition, therefore, statistics consist of facts and figures.

---

*Bransford, J. D., and Johnson, M. K. (1972), Contextual prerequisites for understanding: Some investigations of comprehension and recall. *Journal of Verbal Learning and Verbal Behavior, 11,* 717–726. Copyright by Academic Press. Reprinted by permission of the publisher and M. K. Johnson.

DEFINITION   *Statistics* are facts and figures.

These statistics generally are informative and time saving because they condense large quantities of information into a few simple figures or statements. For example, the average snowfall in Chicago during the month of January is based on many observations made over many years. Few people would be interested in seeing a complete list of day-by-day snowfall amounts for the past 50 years. Even fewer people would be able to make much sense of all those numbers at a quick glance. But nearly everyone can understand and appreciate the meaning of an average.

There is another definition of statistics that applies to many of the topics in this book. When statisticians use the word statistics, they are referring to a set of methods and procedures that help present, characterize, analyze, and interpret observations.

DEFINITION   *Statistics* consist of a set of methods and rules for organizing and interpreting observations.

These statistical procedures help ensure that the data (or observations) are presented and interpreted in an accurate and informative way. Although facts and figures can be interesting and important, this book will focus on methods and procedures of statistics.

STATISTICS AND SCIENCE

These observations should be public, in the sense that others are able to repeat the observations using the same methods to see if the same findings will be obtained.

It is frequently said that science is *empirical*. That is, scientific investigation is based on making observations. Statistical methods enable researchers to describe and analyze the observations they have made. Thus, statistical methods are tools for science. We might think of science as consisting of methods for making observations and of statistics as consisting of methods for analyzing them.

On one mission of the space shuttle Columbia, so much scientific data were relayed to computers on earth that scientists were hard pressed to convey, in terms the public could grasp, how much information had been gathered. One individual made a few quick computations on a pocket calculator and determined that if all the data from the mission were printed on pages, they would pile up as high as the Washington Monument. Such an enormous amount of scientific observation is unmanageable in this crude form. To interpret the data, many months of work have to be done by many people to statistically analyze them. Statistical methods serve scientific investigation by organizing and interpreting data.

SECTION 1.2 POPULATIONS AND SAMPLES

WHAT ARE THEY?

A *population* is the entire group of individuals that a researcher wishes to study. By entire group, we literally mean every single individual.

DEFINITION   A *population* consists of every member of a group that a researcher would like to study.

As you can well imagine, a population can be quite large—for example, the number of women on the planet earth. A researcher might be more specific, limiting the population for study to women who are registered voters in the United States. Perhaps the investigator would like to study the population consisting of women who are heads of state. Populations can obviously vary in size from extremely large to very small, depending on how the investigator defines the population. The population being studied should always be identified by the researcher. In addition, the population need not consist of people—it could be a population of rats, corporations, parts produced in a factory, or anything else an investigator wants to study. In practice, populations are typically very large, such as the population of fourth-grade children in the United States or the population of small businesses.

A *sample* is a subset of a population. It is a part of the population that is selected for study. A sample should always be identified in terms of the population from which it was selected.

DEFINITION   A *sample* is a portion of the population that is selected for observation.

Just as we saw with populations, samples can vary greatly in size. Imagine that you are about to conduct an opinion poll in a large city. You are going to ask people if they believe the mayor is doing a good job. Since the poll will be conducted by telephone, you define your population as people who live in the city and are listed in the telephone directory. Realizing that it would take more time than you can spend to call everyone in the phone book (the entire population), you call 100 people. Notice that it is often necessary to study a sample because the population is so large that it would be impractical to study every member of the population. If you are more ambitious, you could use a larger sample—for example, 1000 people. Later in this book we will examine the benefits of using large samples.

PARAMETERS AND STATISTICS

When describing data, it is necessary to distinguish whether the data come from a population or a sample. Any characteristic of a population, for example, its average, is called a population *parameter*. On the other hand, a characteristic of a sample is called a *statistic*. The average of the scores for a sample is a statistic. The range of scores for a sample is another type of statistic. As we shall see later, statisticians frequently use different symbols for a parameter and a statistic. By using different symbols, we can readily tell if a characteristic, such as an average, is describing a population or a sample.

DEFINITIONS   A *parameter* is a measurement that describes a characteristic of a population, such as a population average.

A *statistic* describes a characteristic of a sample.

DESCRIPTIVE AND INFERENTIAL STATISTICAL METHODS

There are two major types of statistical methods. The first type, *descriptive statistics,* is used to simplify and summarize data. Data typically consist of a set of scores called a *distribution*. These scores result from measurements taken during the course of making observations. For example, they may be IQ scores, ages, blood-alcohol levels, or number of correct responses. The original measurements or values in a distribution are called *raw scores*.

DEFINITIONS

Descriptive statistical methods summarize, organize, and simplify data.

A *distribution* is a set of scores.

A *raw score* is an original measurement or value in a distribution.

Descriptive statistics are techniques that take the raw scores from a distribution and summarize them in a form that is more manageable. There are many descriptive procedures, but a common technique is to compute an average. Note that even if the distribution has hundreds of scores, the average of those scores provides a single descriptive value for the entire distribution. Other descriptive techniques, including tables and graphs, will be covered in the next several chapters.

Inferential statistics are techniques that use sample data to make general statements about a population.

DEFINITION

Inferential statistics consist of techniques that allow us to study samples and then make generalizations about the population from which they were selected.

As we saw with the telephone survey, it is usually not practical to make observations of every member of the population of interest. Because the population is much too large to telephone every individual, a sample is selected. By analyzing the results for the sample, we hope to make general statements about the population. In this example, results from the telephone survey (a sample) can be used to draw inferences about the opinions of the general population.

Inferential statistics are a crucial part of conducting experiments. Suppose a researcher would like to test the effectiveness of a new therapy program for depression. It would be too costly and time-consuming to test the program on all depressed individuals. Therefore, the treatment is tested on a sample of depressed patients. Of course, the researcher would like to see these people overcome their misery, but keep in mind that one is not just interested in this sample of individuals. The investigator would like to generalize the findings to the entire population. If the treatment program is effective for the sample of depressed people, it would be great to be able to state with confidence that it will also work for others. It is important to note that inferential statistical methods will allow meaningful generalizations only if the individuals in the sample are representative of the population. One way to ensure that the sample is representative is to use *random selection*. In random sampling, every individual in the population has the same chance of being selected. There will be much more to say about this topic in later chapters.

DEFINITION

In *random selection*, every individual in the population has the same chance of being selected for the sample.

LEARNING CHECK

1. Science is empirical. This means that science is based on ___making observations___.

2. Science consists of methods for making observations, and statistics are methods for ___analyzing___ them.

3. A descriptive characteristic of a population is a *parameter.* A characteristic of a sample is called a *statistic.*

4. What are statistics?

5. What is the purpose of descriptive statistics?

6. Inferential statistics attempt to use _____ to make general statements about _____.

7. One way to ensure that a sample is representative of a population is to use _____ selection of the sample.

ANSWERS

1. observation

2. analyzing

3. parameter; statistic

4. By one definition, statistics are facts and figures. In this book, the term statistics refers to a set of methods for analyzing and interpreting data.

5. to simplify and summarize data

6. sample data; a population

7. random

SECTION 1.3

THE SCIENTIFIC METHOD AND THE DESIGN OF EXPERIMENTS

OBJECTIVITY

As noted earlier, science is empirical in that knowledge is acquired by observation. Another important aspect of scientific inquiry is that it should be *objective*. That is, theoretical biases of the researcher should not be allowed to influence the findings. Usually when a study is conducted, the investigator has a hunch about how it will turn out. This hunch, actually a prediction about the outcome of the study, is typically based on a theory that the researcher has. It is important that scientists conduct their studies in a way that will prevent these hunches or biases from influencing the outcome of the research. Experimenter bias can operate very subtly. Rosenthal and Fode (1963) had student volunteers act as experimenters in a learning study. The students were given rats to train in a maze. Half of the students were led to believe that their rats were "maze-bright," and the remainder were told their rats were "maze-dull." In reality they all received the same kind of rat. Nevertheless, the data showed real differences in the rats' performance for the two groups of experimenters. Somehow the students' expectations influenced the outcome of the experiment. Apparently there were differences between the groups in how the students handled the rats, and the differences accounted for the effect. For a detailed look at experimenter bias, you might read the review by Rosenthal (1963).

RELATIONSHIPS BETWEEN VARIABLES

Science attempts to discover orderliness in the universe. Even people of ancient civilizations noted regularity in the world around them—the change of seasons, changes in the moon's phases, changes in the tides—and they were able to make many observations to document these orderly changes. Something that can change or have different values is called a *variable*.

DEFINITION
A *variable* is something that can change or that can have different values for different individuals.

Variables are usually identified by a letter (usually X or Y) rather than a specific number. For example, the variable *height* could be identified by the letter X and *shoe size* could be identified by Y. It is reasonable to expect a consistent, orderly relation between these two variables: As X changes, Y also changes in a predictable way.

A value that does not change or vary is called a *constant*. For example, an instructor may adjust the exam scores for a class by adding 4 points to each student's score. Because every individual gets the same four points, this value is a constant.

DEFINITION
A *constant* is a value that does not vary but is the same for every individual.

A constant is usually identified by its numerical value, such as 4, or by the letter C. Adding a constant to each score, for example, could be represented by the expression $X + C$.

Science involves a search for relationships between variables. For example, there is a relationship between the amount of rainfall and crop growth. Rainfall is one of the variables. It varies from year to year and season to season. Crop growth is the other variable. Some years the corn stalks seem short and stunted; other years they are tall and full. When there is very little rainfall, the crops are short and shriveled. When rain is ample, the crops show vigorous growth. Note that in order to document the relationship, one must make observations—that is, measurements of the amount of rainfall and size of the crops.

The simplest way to look for relationships between variables is to make observations of changes in two variables. This is frequently called an *observational* or *correlational method*.

DEFINITION
In a *correlational method*, changes are observed in two variables to see if there is a relationship.

Suppose a researcher wants to examine whether or not a relationship exists between length of time in an executive position and assertiveness. A large sample of executives takes a personality test designed to measure assertiveness. Also, the investigator determines how long each person has served in an executive-level job. Suppose the investigator found that there is a relationship between the two variables—that the longer a person had an executive position, the more assertive that person tended to be. Naturally, one might jump to the conclusion that being an executive for a long time makes a person more assertive. The problem with the correlational method is that it provides no information about cause-and-effect relationships. An equally plausible explanation for the relationship is that assertive people choose to stay or survive longer in executive positions than less-assertive individuals. To determine the cause and the effect in a relationship, it is necessary to *manipulate and control* one of the variables being studied. This is accomplished by the experimental method.

Figure 1.1

Volunteers are randomly assigned to one of two treatment groups: massed practice or distributed practice. After memorizing a list of words using one of these methods, subjects are tested by having them write down as many words as possible from the list. A difference between the groups in performance is attributed to the treatment—the type of practice.

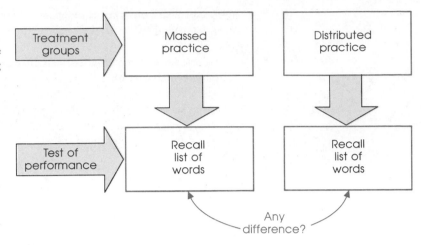

THE EXPERIMENTAL METHOD

A distinguishing characteristic of the *experimental method* is that the researcher manipulates and controls one of the variables under study. One then looks for the effect of this manipulation on the other variable.

DEFINITION

In the *experimental method,* one variable is controlled and manipulated while changes are observed in another variable.

By intentionally altering one variable while at the same time monitoring the other, a cause-and-effect relationship can be established. For example, suppose a psychologist would like to examine the effect of different methods of practice on learning performance. The psychologist solicits volunteers (often called *subjects*) to participate. One group of subjects memorizes a list of words by practicing for 30 minutes. This group is called the massed-practice condition. A second group of people practice for the same total amount of time but in three 10-minute sessions, with a 15-minute rest period between the practice sessions. This group is the distributed-practice condition. Shortly after practice is completed, both groups are tested for how many words were learned. The experiment is diagrammed in Figure 1.1. The experimenter is manipulating the type of practice the people have to use. The amount of learning is measured by the number of words they can jot down after practicing. If method of practice has an effect, these two groups should perform differently on the test. To determine if an effect did occur, the data from the experiment would have to be statistically analyzed.

THE INDEPENDENT AND DEPENDENT VARIABLES

Specific names are used for the two variables that are studied by the experimental method. The variable that is manipulated by the experimenter is called the *independent variable*. It can be identified as the treatment conditions to which subjects are assigned. For the example in Figure 1.1, the method of practice (massed or distributed) is the independent variable. The variable that is observed to assess a possible effect of the manipulation is the *dependent variable*.

DEFINITIONS

The *independent variable* is the variable that is manipulated or controlled by the researcher. In behavioral research, the independent variable usually consists of the two (or more) treatment conditions to which subjects are exposed.

The *dependent variable* is the one that is observed for changes in order to assess the effect of the treatment.

In psychological research, the dependent variable is typically a measurement or score obtained for each subject. For the practice experiment (Figure 1.1), the dependent variable is the number of words recalled on the learning test. Differences between groups in performance on the dependent variable suggest that the manipulation had an effect. That is, changes in the dependent variable *depend* on the independent variable.

Often we can identify one condition of the independent variable that receives no treatment. It is used for comparison purposes and is called the *control group*. The group that does receive the treatment is the *experimental group*.

DEFINITIONS

A *control group* is a condition of the independent variable that receives no treatment. It is used for the purpose of making comparisons.

An *experimental group* does receive a treatment.

Note that the independent variable always consists of at least two values. (Something must have at least two different values before you can say that it is "variable.") For the practice experiment (Figure 1.1), the independent variable is massed practice versus distributed practice. For an experiment with an experimental group and a control group, the independent variable would be treatment versus no treatment.

THEORIES AND HYPOTHESES

Theories are a very important part of psychological research. A psychological theory typically consists of a number of statements about the underlying mechanisms of behavior. Theories are important in that they help organize and unify many observations. They may try to account for very large areas of psychology, such as a general theory of learning. However, they may be more specific, such as a theory of the mechanisms involved in just avoidance learning. A theory is especially useful if it directs and promotes future research and provides specific predictions for the outcomes of that research.

When an investigator designs an experiment, there almost always is a specific hypothesis which is addressed. A *hypothesis* is a hunch about the result that will be obtained from the experiment.

DEFINITION

A *hypothesis* is a prediction about the outcome of an experiment. In experimental research, a hypothesis makes a prediction about how the manipulation of the independent variable will affect the dependent variable.

ecially helpful if it generates many testable hypotheses. By testable we mean the hypothesis can be confirmed or disconfirmed by making observations (conducting studies).

Hypotheses are often derived from the theory that the researcher is developing. An experimenter can state the hypothesis as a prediction—specifically, as a relationship between the independent and dependent variables. Simply stated, a hypothesis is a prediction about the effect of the treatment. Therefore, we can think of an experiment as a test of a hypothesis. A very important part of inferential statistics consists of the statistical analysis of hypothesis tests. Much of the book will focus on this topic.

CONSTRUCTS AND OPERATIONAL DEFINITIONS

Theories contain hypothetical concepts, which help describe the mechanisms that underlie behavioral phenomena. These concepts are called *constructs,* and they cannot be observed because they are hypothetical. For example, intelligence, personality types, and motives are hypothetical constructs. They are used in theories to organize observations in terms of underlying mechanisms. If constructs are hypothetical and cannot be observed, then how can they possibly be studied? The answer is that we have to *define* the construct so that it can be studied. An *operational definition* defines a construct in terms of an observable and measurable response. This definition should include the process and operations involved in making the observations. For example, an operational definition for emotionality might be stated as the amount of increase in heart rate after a person is insulted. An operational definition of intelligence might be the score on the Wechsler Adult Intelligence Scale.

DEFINITIONS

Constructs are hypothetical concepts that are used in theories to organize observations in terms of underlying mechanisms.

An *operational definition* defines a construct in terms of specific operations or procedures and the measurements that result from them. Thus an operational definition consists of two components: First, it describes a set of operations or procedures for measuring a construct. Second, it defines the construct in terms of the resulting measurements.

LEARNING CHECK

1. It is possible for a study to be objective even if the researcher's hypotheses or beliefs are allowed to influence the results. (True or false?)

2. Cause-and-effect relationships cannot be determined by a correlational method. (True or false?)

3. In a memory experiment, subjects memorize a list of words and then must recall as many words as possible after a 6-hour retention interval. One group sleeps during the retention interval, while people in the other group remain awake and go about their daily routine. The number of words recalled is measured for each subject. The experimenter wants to determine if type of activity during the retention interval has an effect on the number of words recalled. For this study, what is the independent variable? What is the dependent variable?

4. A hypothesis can be stated as a prediction about the effect of _____ on _____.

5. An operational definition defines a construct in terms of _____.

ANSWERS   1. false

2. true

3. the independent variable is type of activity during the retention interval; the dependent variable is the number of words recalled

4. an independent variable (or treatment); a dependent variable

5. a measurable response

SECTION 1.4   **SCALES OF MEASUREMENT**

WHAT IS A MEASUREMENT?   It should be obvious by now that data collection requires that we make measurements of our observations. Measurement involves either categorizing events (qualitative measurements) or using numbers to characterize the size of the event (quantitative measurement). There are several types of scales that are associated with measurements. The distinctions among the scales are important because they underscore the limitations of certain types of measurements and because certain statistical procedures are appropriate for data collected on some scales but not on others. If you were interested in people's heights, for example, you could measure a group of individuals by simply classifying them into three categories: tall, medium, and short. However, this simple classification would not tell you much about the actual heights of the individuals, and these measurements would not give you enough information to calculate an average height for the group. Although the simple classification would be adequate for some purposes, you would need more-sophisticated measurements before you could answer more-detailed questions. In this section we examine four different scales of measurement, beginning with the simplest and moving to the most sophisticated.

THE NOMINAL SCALE   A *nominal scale* of measurement labels observations so that they fall into different categories.

DEFINITION   In a *nominal scale* measurement, observations are labeled and categorized.

The word *nominal* means "having to do with names." Measurements that are made on this scale involve naming things. For example, if we wish to know the sex of a person responding to a questionnaire, it would be measured on a nominal scale consisting of two categories. A product warranty card might have you check the box that best describes your occupation, and it lists "sales," "professional," "skilled trade," "other (please specify)." Occupations are being measured in terms of categories; therefore, a nominal scale is being used. A researcher observing the behavior of a group of infant monkeys might categorize responses as playing, grooming, feeding, acting aggressive, or showing submissiveness. Again, this instance typifies a nominal scale of measurement. The nominal scale consists of qualitative distinctions. No attempt is made to measure the size of the event or response. The scales that follow do reflect an attempt to make quantitative distinctions.

THE ORDINAL SCALE In an *ordinal scale* of measurement, observations are ranked in terms of size or magnitude. As the word *ordinal* implies, the investigator simply arranges the observations in rank order.

DEFINITION An *ordinal scale* of measurement consists of ranking observations in terms of size or magnitude.

For example, a job supervisor is asked to rank employees in terms of how well they perform their work. The resulting data will tell us who the supervisor considers the best worker, the second best, and so on. However, the data provide no information about the amount that the workers differ in job performance. The data may reveal that Jan, who is ranked second, is viewed as doing better work than Joe, who is ranked third. However, the data do not reveal *how much* better. This is a limitation of measurements on an ordinal scale.

THE INTERVAL SCALE In an *interval scale* of measurement, intervals between numbers reflect differences in magnitude. That is, it allows you to measure differences in the size or amount of events. However, an interval scale does not have an absolute zero point that indicates complete absence of the variable being measured, so ratios of magnitude are not meaningful.

DEFINITION In an *interval scale,* the difference (or interval) between numbers on the scale reflects a difference in magnitude. However, ratios of magnitudes are not meaningful.

For example, if on June 1 the temperature is 80°F and on November 1 it is 40°, then we can say that the temperature on June 1 was 40° higher than on November 1. If Jim scored 160 on an IQ test and Sam scored 80, then Jim's is 80 points higher. Note that with an interval scale we can determine which observation is of greater magnitude and by *how much* it is greater. Also, measurements on an interval scale permit basic arithmetic operations. For example, you can *subtract* to determine how much difference there is between two measurements, or you can *add* to determine the sum for a set of measurements. However, measurements on an interval scale do not allow you to form ratios. For example, we cannot say that it was twice as hot on June 1st as on November 1st. A ratio is meaningful only when the scale of measurement has an absolute zero point that indicates the total absence of the quantity being measured. For example, zero on the Fahrenheit scale does not mean there is no temperature. It certainly can get colder than 0°F. This point becomes clearer if you consider both temperatures measured on the Celsius as well as the Fahrenheit scales. Table 1.1 shows the two Fahrenheit temperatures we have been

Table 1.1

Fahrenheit temperatures and equivalent Celsius temperatures for two days.

	TEMPERATURE IN °F	TEMPERATURE IN °C
Jun. 1	80°	27.3°
Nov. 1	40°	4.4°

considering and their equivalent Celsius temperatures. Although it may be tempting to view 80°F as being twice as hot as 40°F, it should be clear that 27.3°C does *not* appear to be twice as hot as 4.4°C. Without a true zero point, you cannot make ratio comparisons.

THE RATIO SCALE

A *ratio scale* of measurement has an absolute zero point, and thus ratios of numbers on this scale do reflect ratios of magnitudes.

DEFINITION

In a *ratio scale,* ratios of numbers do reflect ratios of magnitudes. Such a scale has an absolute zero point.

For example, two warehouse workers have a contest to see who can lift the heaviest carton. Bill lifts a 200-pound carton and John lifts a 100-pound box. It can be said that Bill is able to lift twice as much as John. Note that a ratio scale of measurement allows one to draw the same conclusions as with ordinal and interval scales, plus it allows one to form ratios to compare the magnitude of measurements. In a psychology laboratory, a researcher might measure people's reaction times to stimuli. For example, it takes Joan 500 milliseconds to respond to a stimulus, and Mary takes only 250 milliseconds. Therefore, Mary responds in half as much time as Joan.

Most dependent variables we will encounter can be measured on either an interval or a ratio scale. These scales allow basic arithmetic operations that permit us to calculate differences between scores, to sum scores, and to calculate average scores. However, you should know that the distinction between different scales of measurements is often unclear when considering specific measurements. For example, the scores resulting from an IQ test are usually treated as measurements on an interval scale, but many researchers believe that IQ scores are more accurately described as ordinal data. An IQ score of 105 is clearly greater than a score of 100, but there is some question concerning *how much* difference in intelligence is reflected in the 5-point difference between these two scores.

SECTION 1.5   DISCRETE AND CONTINUOUS VARIABLES

WHAT ARE THEY AND HOW DO THEY DIFFER?

The variables in a study can be characterized by the type of values that can be assigned to them. A *discrete variable* consists of separate, indivisible categories. For this type of variable there are no intermediate values between two adjacent categories. Consider the values displayed when dice are rolled. Between neighboring values—for example, seven dots and eight dots—no other values can ever be observed.

DEFINITION

A *discrete variable* consists of separate, indivisible categories. No values can exist between two neighboring categories.

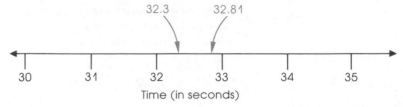

Figure 1.2

Representation of time as a continuous number line. Note that there are an infinite number of possible values with no gaps in the line.

A discrete variable is typically restricted to whole countable numbers—for example, the number of children in a family or the number of students attending class. If you observe class attendance from day to day, you may find 18 students one day and 19 students the next day. However, it is impossible ever to observe a value between 18 and 19. A discrete variable may also consist of observations that differ qualitatively. For example, a psychologist observing patients may classify some as having panic disorders, others as having dissociative disorders, and some as having psychotic disorders. The type of disorder is a discrete variable because there are distinct and finite categories that can be observed.

On the other hand, many variables are not discrete. Variables such as time, height, or weight are not limited to a fixed set of separate, indivisible categories. You can measure time, for example, in hours, minutes, seconds, or fractions of seconds. These variables are called *continuous* because they can be divided into an infinite number of fractional parts.

DEFINITION

For a *continuous variable,* there are an infinite number of possible values that fall between any two observed values. A continuous variable is divisible into an infinite number of fractional parts.

For example, subjects are given problems to solve, and a researcher records the amount of time it takes them to find the solutions. One person may take 31 seconds to solve the problems, whereas another may take 32 seconds. Between these two values it is possible to find any fractional amount—$31\frac{1}{2}$, $31\frac{1}{4}$, $31\frac{1}{10}$—provided the measuring instrument is sufficiently accurate. Time is a continuous variable. A continuous variable can be pictured as a number line that is continuous. That is, there are an infinite number of points on the line without any gaps or separations between neighboring points (see Figure 1.2).

LEARNING CHECK

1. An instructor records the order in which students complete their tests—that is, the first to finish, the second to finish, and so on. A(n) _____ scale of measurement is used in this instance.

2. The Scholastic Aptitude Test (SAT) most likely measures aptitude on a(n) _____ scale.

3. In a study on perception of facial expressions, subjects must classify the emotions displayed in photographs of people as either anger, sadness, joy, disgust, fear, or surprise. Emotional expression is measured on a(n) _____ scale.

4. A researcher studies the factors that determine how many children couples decide to have. The variable, number of children, is a _____ (discrete/continuous) variable.

5. An investigator studies how concept formation ability changes with age. Age is a _____ (discrete/continuous) variable.

ANSWERS   **1.** ordinal   **4.** discrete

                       2. interval   **5.** continuous

                       3. nominal

SECTION 1.6   STATISTICAL NOTATION

Measurements of behavior usually will provide data composed of numerical values. These numbers form the basis of the computations that are done for statistical analyses. There is a standardized notation system for statistical procedures, and it is used to identify terms in equations and mathematical operations. Some general mathematical operations, notation, and basic algebra are outlined in the review section of Appendix A. There is also a skills assessment exam (page A-1) to help you determine if you need the basic mathematics review. Here we will introduce some statistical notation that is used throughout this book. In subsequent chapters, additional notation will be introduced as it is needed.

SCORES   Making observations of a dependent variable in a study will typically yield values or scores for each subject. Raw scores are the original, unchanged set of scores obtained in the study. Scores for a particular variable are represented by the letter X. For example, if performance in your statistics course is measured by tests and you obtain a 35 on the first test, then we could state that $X = 35$. A set of scores can be presented in a column that is headed by X. For example, a list of quiz scores from your class might be presented as follows:

X
37
35
35
30
25
17
16

When observations are made for two variables, there will be two scores for each subject. The data can be presented as two lists labeled X and Y for the two variables. For example, observations for people's height in inches (variable X) and weight in pounds (variable Y) can be presented in the following manner. Each pair X, Y represents the observations made of a single subject.

X	Y
72	165
68	151
67	160
68	146
70	160
66	133

It is also useful to specify how many scores are in a set. The number of scores in a data set is represented by the letter N. For populations we will use an uppercase N, and for samples we will use a lowercase n. (Throughout the book, notational differences are used to distinguish between samples and populations.) For the height and weight data, $N = 6$ for both variables.

SUMMATION NOTATION

Many of the computations required in statistics will involve adding up a set of scores. Because this procedure is used so frequently, there is a special notation used to refer to the sum of a set of scores. The Greek letter sigma, or Σ, is used to stand for summation. The expression ΣX means to add all the scores for variable X. The summation sign Σ can be read as "the sum of." Thus ΣX is read "the sum of the scores." For the following set of quiz scores,

$$10, \quad 6, \quad 7, \quad 4$$

$\Sigma X = 27$ and $N = 4$. There are a number of rules of summation that help identify which scores are added together and which mathematical operation is performed first when several are required. These rules are summarized as follows.

1. When there are two variables X and Y, ΣX indicates the sum of the Xs, and ΣY refers to the sum of the Ys. For the following data, $\Sigma X = 16$, and $\Sigma Y = 34$:

X	Y	
3	10	$\Sigma X = 3 + 1 + 7 + 3 + 2 = 16$
1	4	
7	6	$\Sigma Y = 10 + 4 + 6 + 5 + 9 = 34$
3	5	
2	9	

2. When two variables (X and Y) are multiplied together, the product is represented by the symbols XY. Note that the multiplication sign is not written between the symbols ($X \times Y$ can cause confusion). The expression XY is understood to mean "X times Y." The following table shows scores for three individuals. For each person there is a score for variable X, a score for variable Y, and the product of the two scores, XY.

X	Y	XY
2	4	8
3	1	3
4	3	12

The total for the X values, $\Sigma X = 9$, is obtained by adding the scores in that column, and the sum of the Y values, $\Sigma Y = 8$, is obtained by adding the Y column. The expression ΣXY means "sum the products of X and Y." The first step is to compute the product for each pair of X and Y scores. These products are displayed in the column headed by XY. In the second step, the products are added together. For this example, the sum of the products is $\Sigma XY = 23$:

$$\Sigma XY = 8 + 3 + 12 = 23$$

It is very important to note that ΣXY *does not equal* $\Sigma X \Sigma Y$. The latter expression means "the sum of X times the sum of Y." For these data, it is easy to demonstrate that the two expressions are not the same:

$$\Sigma XY \neq \Sigma X \Sigma Y$$

$$23 \neq 9(8)$$

$$23 \neq 72$$

3. When a constant amount C is added to each score, the expression for the resulting scores is $X + C$. In the following example, the constant equals 4. If this value is added to every score, a column headed by $X + 4$ can be made.

X	X + 4
1	5
4	8
6	10

When a constant value is added to every score, it is necessary to use parentheses to represent the sum of these new scores, $\Sigma(X + 4)$. The calculations within the parentheses are always done first. Because the summation symbol is outside the parentheses, finding the sum is performed last. Therefore, to compute $\Sigma(X + 4)$, the constant 4 is first added to every score, creating the new $X + 4$ column of numbers. Then these new numbers are added together. For this example,

$$\Sigma(X + 4) = 5 + 8 + 10 = 23$$

A word of caution is necessary. The application of a summation sign *ends* at a plus (+) or minus (−) sign. For example, in the notation $\Sigma X + 4$, the

---

 1.1 **COMPUTING ΣX^2 WITH A CALCULATOR**

THE SUM of squared scores, ΣX^2, is a common expression in many statistical calculations. The following steps outline the most efficient procedure for using a typical, inexpensive hand calculator to find this sum. We assume that your calculator has one memory where you can store and retrieve information. *Caution:* The following instructions work for most calculators but not for every single model. If you encounter trouble, don't panic—check your manual or talk with your instructor.

1. Clear the calculator memory. You may press the memory-clear key (usually MC) or simply turn the calculator off then back on.

2. Enter the first score.

3. Press the multiply key ($\times$); then press the equals ($=$) key. The squared score should appear in the display. (Note you do not need to enter a number twice to square it. Just follow the sequence: number-times-equals.)

4. Put the squared value into the calculator memory. For most calculators, you press the key labeled M+.

5. Enter the next score, square it, and add it to memory (steps 2, 3, and 4). (Note you do not need to clear the display between scores.)

6. Continue this process for the full set of scores. Then retrieve the total (ΣX^2) from memory by pressing the memory-recall key (usually labeled MR).

Check this procedure with a simple set of scores such as: 1, 2, 3. You should find $\Sigma X^2 = 14$.

---

summation applies *only* to the X. To compute $\Sigma X + 4$, you first find the sum of the X values and then add 4 to this total:

$$\Sigma X + 4 = 11 + 4 = 15$$

In order for the symbol $X + 4$ to be treated as a single expression, you must use parentheses. In the notation $\Sigma(X + 4)$, the parentheses indicate that $(X + 4)$ has been created as a single variable and, therefore, the summation applies to the $(X + 4)$ values. Note that $\Sigma(X + C)$ *does not equal* $\Sigma X + C$.

> Remember, when a number is squared, it is multiplied by itself. A common mistake is to multiply a number by 2 instead of squaring it.

4. The squared value of a score is represented by the symbol X^2. If every score in the group is squared, then a new column of squared values can be listed:

X	X^2
3	9
1	1
4	16
2	4

The expression ΣX^2 means the sum of the squared scores. Each score is first squared, and then the sum is found for the squared values (see Box 1.1). In this example, adding the X^2 column reveals that

$$\Sigma X^2 = 9 + 1 + 16 + 4 = 30$$

Be careful! The symbol $(\Sigma X)^2$ represents a different order of operations, and the resulting value is not the same as that of ΣX^2. The operations inside the parentheses are performed first. Therefore, the sum of the Xs is determined first. The exponent is outside the parentheses, so the squaring is done last. The expression $(\Sigma X)^2$ means the *squared total*. In the example, this value is

$$(\Sigma X)^2 = (10)^2 = 100$$

Therefore, $(\Sigma X)^2$ is *not the same* expression as ΣX^2. It is very important to remember the order of operations for these two expressions. Later we will have to use statistical formulas that contain both of these expressions. It is imperative that you do not confuse them for each other.

LEARNING CHECK For the following data, find the values for the listed expressions

X	Y
3	1
3	2
1	1
2	3
4	5

1. ΣX **2.** ΣX^2 **3.** $(\Sigma X)^2$ **4.** $\Sigma(Y + 3)$ **5.** $(\Sigma Y)^2$ **6.** $\Sigma X \Sigma Y$
7. ΣXY **8.** N for the X scores

ANSWERS

1. 13 **2.** 39 **3.** 169 **4.** 27 **5.** 144 **6.** 156 **7.** 36 **8.** 5

SUMMARY

1. By common usage, the word *statistics* means facts and figures. In this book, the general use of the word is in reference to techniques and procedures for analyzing data.

2. Science is empirical in that it provides methods for making observations. Statistics consist of methods for organizing and interpreting data.

3. A population is composed of every individual from the group one wishes to study. A sample is a subset of the population. Samples are drawn from the population for study because the population in question is usually so large that it is not feasible to study every individual in it.

4. Descriptive statistics simplify and summarize data, so that the data are more manageable. Inferential statistics are techniques that allow one to use sample data to make general statements about a population. Meaningful generalizations are possible only if the sample is representative of the population from which it was drawn. Random sampling helps ensure that it is representative.

5. A correlational method looks for interrelationships between variables but cannot determine the cause-and-effect nature of the relationship. The experimental method is able to establish causes and effects in a relationship.

6. In the experimental method, one variable (the independent variable) is intentionally manipulated and controlled by the experimenter. Then changes are noted in another variable (the dependent variable) as a result of the manipulation.

7. A hypothesis is a prediction about the effect of an independent variable on a dependent variable. Hypotheses are usually derived from theories. Experiments basically involve the test of a hypothesis.

8. Constructs are hypothetical concepts used in theories to describe the mechanisms of behavior. Because they are hypothetical, they cannot be observed. Constructs are studied by providing operational definitions for them. An operational definition defines a construct in terms of an observable and measurable response or event.

9. A nominal scale labels observations so that they fall into different categories. A nominal scale involves making qualitative distinctions. No attempt is made to measure the magnitude of the event.

10. An ordinal scale involves ranking observations in terms of size or magnitude. Although this scale will tell us which observation is larger, it will not tell us how much larger it is.

11. In an interval scale, intervals between numbers reflect differences in magnitude of observations. It is possible to determine which event is of greater magnitude and how much larger it is.

12. A ratio scale has all of the characteristics of an interval scale, and ratios of measurements on this scale reflect ratios of magnitudes. Unlike the interval scale, a ratio scale has a meaningful zero point.

13. A discrete variable is one that can have only a finite number of values between any two values. It typically consists of whole numbers that vary in countable steps. A continuous variable can have an infinite number of values between any two values.

14. The letter X is used to represent scores for a variable. If a second variable is used, Y represents its scores. The letter N is used as the symbol for the number of scores in a set. The Greek letter sigma Σ is used to stand for summation. Therefore, the expression ΣX is read ''the sum of the scores.''

KEY TERMS

statistics	raw score	independent variable	nominal scale
population	inferential statistics	dependent variable	ordinal scale
sample	random selection	control group	interval scale
population parameter	variable	experimental group	ratio scale
sample statistic	constant	hypothesis	discrete variable
descriptive statistics	correlational method	construct	continuous variable
distribution	experimental method	operational definition	

FOCUS ON PROBLEM SOLVING

1. It may help to simplify summation notation if you observe that the summation sign is always followed by a symbol (or symbolic expression)—for example, ΣX or $\Sigma(X + 3)$. This symbol specifies which values you are to add. If you use the symbol as a column heading and list all the appropriate values in the column, your task is simply to add up the numbers in the column. To find $\Sigma(X + 3)$ for example, start a column headed with $(X + 3)$ next to the column of X's. List all the $(X + 3)$ values; then find the total for the column.

2. To use summation notation correctly you must be careful of two other factors:

a. When you are determining the "symbol" that follows the summation sign, remember that everything within parentheses is part of the same symbol, for example $\Sigma(X + 3)$, and a string of multiplied values is considered to be a single symbol, for example, ΣXY.

b. Often it is necessary to use several intermediate columns before you can reach the column of values specified by a particular symbol. To compute $\Sigma(X - 1)^2$, for example, you will need three columns: first the column of original scores, Xs; second, a column of $(X - 1)$ values; the third, a column of squared $(X - 1)$ values. It is the third column, headed by $(X - 1)^2$, that you should total.

DEMONSTRATION 1.1   SUMMATION NOTATION

A set of data consists of the following scores:

7 3 9 5 4

For these data find the following values:

  a. ΣX **b.** $(\Sigma X)^2$ **c.** ΣX^2 **d.** $\Sigma X + 5$ **e.** $\Sigma(X - 2)$

Compute ΣX. To compute ΣX, we simply add all of the scores in the group. For these data, we obtain:

$$\Sigma X = 7 + 3 + 9 + 5 + 4 = 28$$

Compute $(\Sigma X)^2$. The key to determining the value of $(\Sigma X)^2$ is the presence of parentheses. The rule is to perform the operations that are inside the paratheses first.
Step 1: Find the sum of the scores, ΣX.
Step 2: Square the total.
We have already determined that ΣX is 28. Squaring this total we obtain:

$$(\Sigma X)^2 = (28)^2 = 784$$

Compute ΣX^2. Calculating the sum of the squared scores, ΣX^2, involves two steps.
Step 1: Square each score.
Step 2: Sum the squared values.
These steps are most easily accomplished by constructing a computational table. The first column has the heading X and lists the scores. The second column is

labeled X^2 and contains the squared values for each score. For this example, the table is as follows:

X	X^2
7	49
3	9
9	81
5	25
4	16

To find the value for ΣX^2, we sum the X^2 column.

$$\Sigma X^2 = 49 + 9 + 81 + 25 + 16 = 180$$

Compute $\Sigma X + 5$. In this expression, there are no parentheses. Thus, the summation sign is applied only to the X values.
Step 1: Find the sum of X.
Step 2: Add the constant 5 to the total from Step 1.
In part (a) we found that the sum of the scores is 28. For $\Sigma X + 5$ we obtain the following:

$$\Sigma X + 5 = 28 + 5 = 33$$

Compute $\Sigma(X - 2)$. The summation sign is followed by an expression with parentheses. In this case, $X - 2$ is treated as a single expression and the summation sign applies to the $(X - 2)$ values.
Step 1: Subtract 2 from every score.
Step 2: Sum these new values.
This problem can be done by using a table with two columns, headed X and $X - 2$, respectively.

X	$X - 2$
7	5
3	1
9	7
5	3
4	2

To determine the value for $\Sigma(X - 2)$, we sum the $X - 2$ column.

$$\Sigma(X - 2) = 5 + 1 + 7 + 3 + 2 = 18$$

DEMONSTRATION 1.2   SUMMATION NOTATION WITH TWO VARIABLES

The following data consist of pairs of scores (X and Y) for four individuals.

X	Y
5	8
2	10
3	11
7	2

Determine the values for the following expressions:

a. $\Sigma X \Sigma Y$ **b.** ΣXY

Compute $\Sigma X \Sigma Y$. This expression indicates that we should multiply the sum of X by the sum of Y.

Step 1: Find the sum of X
Step 2: Find the sum of Y
Step 3: Multiply the results of Steps 1 and 2.

First, we find the sum of X.

$$\Sigma X = 5 + 2 + 3 + 7 = 17$$

Next, we compute the sum of Y.

$$\Sigma Y = 8 + 10 + 11 + 2 = 31$$

Finally, we multiply these two totals.

$$\Sigma X \Sigma Y = 17(31) = 527$$

Compute ΣXY. Now we are asked to find the sum of the products of X and Y.

Step 1: Find the XY products.
Step 2: Sum the products.

The computations are facilitated by using a third column labeled XY.

X	Y	XY
5	8	40
2	10	20
3	11	33
7	2	14

For these data, the sum of the XY products is

$$\Sigma XY = 40 + 20 + 33 + 14 = 107$$

PROBLEMS

*1. Scientific study is empirical and objective. What is meant by this statement?

2. Describe the purposes of descriptive and inferential statistical techniques.

3. What is the shortcoming of the correlational method of study?

4. Describe how the experimental method is conducted. What is the distinction between the two types of variables that are used?

5. A report states that insomniacs given a new sleeping drug fell asleep 20 minutes sooner than insomniacs given a placebo. For this report, what is the independent variable? What is the dependent variable?
   A placebo is an inactive or neutral substance (a sugar pill) that is given in place of a drug in psychological or medical research.

6. In a study of memory, the effect of retention interval length is examined. The first group memorizes a list of words. After a 20-minute retention interval, these subjects must write down as many words as they can remember. The second group memorizes the same list and must recall the words after a 1-hour interval. The last group studies the list of words and is tested for recall 2 hours later. The experimenter measures the number of words recalled for each subject. For this experiment, what is the independent variable? What is the dependent variable?

7. A researcher would like to determine whether or not office productivity is influenced by background music.
   a. Briefly describe how this researcher could gather data using the observational or correlational method.
   b. Briefly describe how data could be obtained using the experimental method.
   c. Identify the independent variable and the dependent variable for this experiment.

8. A researcher would like to examine the effect of the amount of sleep on performance of a vigilance task.

One group of subjects is allowed to sleep all night without interruptions. A second group of subjects is awakened six times during the night. In the morning, all the subjects are tested on a vigilance task. They are required to observe a radar screen display and respond anytime a small spot of light briefly flashes somewhere on the screen. The experimenter records the number of errors subjects make. For this experiment, what is the independent variable? What is the dependent variable?

9. Contrast the nominal scale of measurement to the ordinal scale. What type of scale is used in a list of the order of finish in a horse race? What type of scale is used when describing the sex of the jockeys?

10. Describe the difference between an ordinal scale of measurement and interval scale.

11. What is the difference between the interval scale and ratio scale of measurement?

12. What is the distinction between continuous and discrete variables?

13. What is the distinction between a construct and an operational definition?

14. For the following set of scores, calculate the value for each of the expressions listed:
   a. ΣX
   b. $\Sigma X + 5$
   c. $\Sigma(X + 5)$
   d. $\Sigma(X - 3)$
   e. $\Sigma X - 3$
   f. N

X
5
9
6
7
13

15. For the following set of scores, find the value for the expressions listed:
   a. ΣX
   b. ΣY
   c. $\Sigma X + \Sigma Y$
   d. $\Sigma(X + Y)$
   e. ΣXY
   f. $\Sigma X \Sigma Y$

X	Y
1	3
3	2
2	3
1	5
4	2

*Solutions for odd-numbered problems are provided in Appendix C.

16. For the following set of scores, calculate the value for the expressions:
a. ΣX
b. ΣX^2
c. $(\Sigma X)^2$

X
3
5
2
1
4

17. A student was asked to compute $\Sigma(X + 3)$ for a set of $N = 10$ scores. Rather than add 3 points to each score and find the new sum, the student simply added 30 points (10 times 3) to the old ΣX. Explain why this produced the correct answer.

18. For the following data, find each requested value:
a. ΣX^2
b. ΣY
c. ΣY^2
d. $\Sigma X \Sigma Y$
e. ΣXY
f. $(\Sigma X)^2$
g. $(\Sigma Y)^2$

X	Y
2.3	3.1
4.0	11.5
6.7	2.0
4.5	9.4
5.6	7.2
8.0	1.0
3.3	6.7

19. For the following data, calculate the values for the expressions:
a. ΣX
b. ΣX^2
c. ΣY
d. ΣY^2
e. ΣXY
f. $\Sigma X \Sigma Y$

X	Y
2	10
6	3
4	2
3	11
9	4

20. Use summation notation to express each of the following calculations:
a. The sum of the squared scores
b. The square of the sum of the scores

21. Use summation notation to represent each of the following calculations:
a. Add 3 points to each score and then sum the resulting values.

b. Square each score and subtract 1 point. Then sum the resulting values.
c. Subtract 2 points from each score and square the result. Add the squared values.
d. Add the scores and square the total. Then add 10 points to the squared total.

22. For the following set of scores, find the value of each expression:
a. ΣX
b. $\Sigma(X - 3)$
c. $\Sigma(X - 3)^2$
d. $(\Sigma X)^2 - \Sigma X^2$
e. $(\Sigma X + 2)^2 - \Sigma(X + 2)^2$

X
3
5
10
8
7

23. For the following set of scores find the value of each expression:
a. ΣX
b. $\Sigma(X + 2)$
c. ΣX^2

X
-2
5
-4
0
7
-1

24. For the following set of scores, find the value of each expression:
a. ΣX
b. ΣY
c. ΣXY
d. $\Sigma X \Sigma Y$

X	Y
-3	2
4	3
-6	-1
5	-2
-5	4

CHAPTER 2

FREQUENCY DISTRIBUTIONS

INTRODUCTION

When a researcher finishes the data collection phase of an experiment, the results usually consist of pages of numbers. The immediate problem for the researcher is to organize the scores into some comprehensible form so that any trends in the data can be seen easily and communicated to others. This is the job of descriptive statistics: to simplify the organization and presentation of data. One of the most common procedures for organizing a set of data is to place the scores in a frequency distribution.

DEFINITION

A *frequency distribution* is a record of the number of individuals located in each category on the scale of measurement.

A frequency distribution allows the researcher to see "at a glance" the entire set of scores. It shows whether the scores are generally high or low and whether they are concentrated in one area or spread out across the entire scale and generally provides an organized picture of the data. Frequency distributions can be structured either as tables or graphs, but both show the original measurement scale and the frequencies associated with each category. Thus, they present a picture of how the individual scores are distributed on the measurement scale—hence the name *frequency distribution*.

FREQUENCY DISTRIBUTION TABLES

It is customary to list scores from highest to lowest, but this is an arbitrary arrangement. Many computer programs will list scores from lowest to highest.

The simplest frequency distribution table presents the measurement scale by listing the individual scores in a column from highest to lowest. Beside each score, we indicate the frequency, or number of times the score occurred in the data. It is customary to use an X as the column heading for the scores and an f as the column heading for the frequencies. An example of a frequency distribution table follows.

EXAMPLE 2.1

The following set of $N = 20$ scores was obtained from a 10-point statistics quiz. We will organize these scores by constructing a frequency distribution table. Scores:

8, 9, 8, 7, 10, 9, 6, 4, 9, 8

7, 8, 10, 9, 8, 6, 9, 7, 8, 8

1. The highest score is $X = 10$, and the lowest score is $X = 4$. Therefore, the first column of the table will list scores (X values) from 10 down to 4. Notice that all of the possible values are listed in the table. For example, no one had a score of $X = 5$, but this value is included.

2. The frequency associated with each score is recorded in the second column. For example, two people had scores of $X = 6$, so there is a 2 in the f column beside $X = 6$.

X	f
10	2
9	5
8	7
7	3
6	2
5	0
4	1

Because the table organizes the scores, it is possible to see very quickly the general quiz results. For example, there were only two perfect scores, but most of the class had high grades (8s and 9s). With one exception (the score of $X = 4$) it appears that the class has learned the material fairly well.

You also should notice that the frequencies can be used to find the total number of scores in the distribution. By adding up the frequencies, you will obtain the total number of individuals:

$$\Sigma f = N$$

OBTAINING ΣX FROM A FREQUENCY DISTRIBUTION TABLE

There may be times when you need to compute the sum of the scores, ΣX, for data in a frequency distribution table. This procedure presents a problem because most students are tempted simply to add the scores listed in the X column of the table. However, this practice is incorrect because it ignores the information provided by the frequency (f) column. To calculate ΣX from a frequency distribution table, you must use both the X and f columns.

Consider the frequency distribution table for Example 2.1. It tells us that the distribution has two 10s, five 9s, and seven 8s, and so on. Therefore, you can obtain the total for X by first reconstructing the original distribution and then adding all the X values (compute ΣX): $10 + 10 + 9 + 9 + 9 + 9 + 9 + 8 + 8 + 8 + 8 + 8$ $+ 8 + 8 + \ldots$. For the data in Example 2.1, $\Sigma X = 158$. Try it yourself.

An alternative way to get ΣX from a frequency distribution table is to multiply each X value by its frequency and then add these products. This sum may be expressed in symbols as $\Sigma f X$. The computation is summarized as follows for the data in Example 2.1:

X	f	fX	
10	2	20	
9	5	45	
8	7	56	
7	3	21	
6	2	12	
5	0	0	(There are no 5s)
4	1	4	
		$\Sigma f X = 158$	

In using either method to find ΣX, by reconstructing the distribution or by computing ΣfX, the important point is that you must use the information given in the frequency column.

PROPORTIONS AND PERCENTAGES

In addition to the two basic columns of a frequency distribution, there are other measures that describe the distribution of scores and can be incorporated into the table. The two most common are proportion and percentage.

Proportion measures the fraction of the total group that is associated with each score. In Example 2.1, there were two individuals with $X = 6$. Thus, 2 out of 20 people had $X = 6$, so the proportion would be $2/20 = 0.10$. In general, the proportion associated with each score is

$$\text{proportion} = p = \frac{f}{N}$$

Because proportions describe the frequency (f) in relation to the total number (N), they often are called *relative frequencies*. Although proportions can be expressed as fractions (for example, 2/20), they more commonly appear as decimals. A column of proportions, headed with a p, can be added to the basic frequency distribution table (see Example 2.2).

In addition to using frequencies (f) and proportions (p), researchers often describe a distribution of scores with percentages. For example, an instructor might describe the results of an exam by saying that 15% of the class earned *A*s, 23% *B*s, and so on. To compute the percentage associated with each score, you first find the proportion (p) and then multiply by 100:

$$\text{percentage} = p(100) = \frac{f}{N}(100)$$

Percentages can be included in a frequency distribution table by adding a column headed with % (see Example 2.2).

EXAMPLE 2.2

The frequency distribution table from Example 2.1 is repeated here. This time we have added columns showing the proportion (p) and the percentage (%) associated with each score.

X	f	$p = f/N$	$\% = p(100)$
10	2	$2/20 = 0.10$	10%
9	5	$5/20 = 0.25$	25%
8	7	$7/20 = 0.35$	35%
7	3	$3/20 = 0.15$	15%
6	2	$2/20 = 0.10$	10%
5	0	$0/20 = 0$	0%
4	1	$1/20 = 0.05$	5%

GROUPED FREQUENCY DISTRIBUTION TABLES

The number of rows in the list of X values can be obtained by finding the difference between the highest and lowest score and adding 1:

rows = highest − lowest + 1

When a set of data covers a wide range of values, it is unreasonable to list all the individual scores in a frequency distribution table. For example, a set of exam scores ranges from a low of $X = 41$ to a high of $X = 96$. These scores cover a range of over 50 points.

If we were to list all the individual scores, it would take 56 rows to complete the frequency distribution table. Although this would organize and simplify the data, the table would be long and cumbersome. Additional simplification would be desirable. This is accomplished by dividing the range of scores into intervals and then listing these intervals in the frequency distribution table. For example, we could construct a table showing the number of students who had scores in the 90s, the number with scores in the 80s, etc. The result is called a *grouped frequency distribution table* because we are presenting groups of scores rather than individual values. The groups, or intervals, are called *class intervals*.

There are several rules that help guide you in the construction of a grouped frequency distribution table. These rules should be considered as guidelines rather than an absolute requirements, but they do help produce a simple, well-organized, and easily understood table.

RULE 1 The grouped frequency distribution table should have about 10 class intervals. If a table has many more than 10 intervals, it becomes cumbersome and defeats the purpose of a frequency distribution table. On the other hand, if you have too few intervals, you begin to lose information about the distribution of the scores. At the extreme, with only one interval, the table would not tell you anything about how the scores are distributed. Remember, the purpose for a frequency distribution is to help a researcher see the data. With too few or too many intervals, the table will not provide a clear picture. You should note that 10 intervals is a general guide. If you were constructing a table on a blackboard, for example, you probably would want only 5 or 6 intervals. If the table were to be printed in a scientific report, you may want 12 or 15 intervals. In each case your goal is to present a table that is relatively easy to see and understand.

RULE 2 The width of each interval should be a relatively simple number. For example, 2, 5, 10, or 20 would be good choices for the interval width. Notice that it is easy to count by 5s or 10s. These numbers are easy to understand and make it possible for someone to see quickly how you have divided the range.

RULE 3 The bottom score in each class interval should be a multiple of the width. If you are using a width of 10, for example, the intervals should start with 10, 20, 30, 40, etc. Again, this makes it easier for someone to understand how the table has been constructed.

RULE 4 All intervals should be the same width. They should cover the range of scores completely with no gaps and no overlaps, so that any particular score belongs in exactly one interval.

The application of these rules is demonstrated in Example 2.3.

EXAMPLE 2.3

An instructor has obtained the set of $N = 25$ exam scores shown here. To help organize these scores, we will place them in a frequency distribution table. Scores:

82,   75,   88,   93,   53,   84,   87,   58,   72,   94,   69,   84,   61,

91,   64,   87,   84,   70,   76,   89,   75,   80,   73,   78,   60

The first step is to examine the range of scores. For these data, the smallest score is $X = 53$ and the largest score is $X = 94$, so 42 rows would be needed for a table. Because it would require 42 rows to list each individual score in a frequency distribution table, we will have to group the scores into class intervals.

The best method for determining the appropriate interval width is to use Rules 1 and 2 simultaneously. According to Rule 1, we want about 10 intervals; according to Rule 2, we want the width to be a simple number. If we try a width of 2, how many intervals would it take to cover the range of scores? With each interval only 2 points wide, we would need 21 intervals to cover the range. This is too many. What about an interval width of 5? What about a width of 10? The following table shows how many intervals would be needed for each possible width:

WIDTH	NUMBER OF INTERVALS NEEDED TO COVER A RANGE OF 42 VALUES	
2	21	(too many)
5	9	(OK)
10	5	(too few)

Notice that an interval width of 5 will result in about 10 intervals, which is exactly what we want.

The next step is to actually identify the intervals. The lowest score for these data is $X = 53$, so the lowest interval should contain this value. Because the interval should have a multiple of 5 as its bottom score, the interval would be 50 to 54. Notice that this interval contains five values (50, 51, 52, 53, 54), so it does have a width of 5. The next interval would start at 55 and go to 59. The complete frequency distribution table showing all of the class intervals in presented in Table 2.1.

Once the class intervals are listed, you complete the table by adding a column of frequencies or proportions or percentages. The values in the frequency column indicate the number of individuals whose scores are located in that class interval. For this example, there were three students with scores in the 60-64 interval, so the frequency for this class interval is $f = 3$ (see Table 2.1).

CONTINUOUS VARIABLES AND REAL LIMITS

You should recall that a continuous variable has an infinite number of possible values. Therefore, it may be represented by a number line that is continuous and contains an infinite number of points. However, when a continuous variable is

Table 2.1

A Grouped Frequency Distribution Table Showing the Data from Example 2.3[a]

X	f
90–94	3
85–89	4
80–84	5
75–79	4
70–74	3
65–69	1
60–64	3
55–59	1
50–54	1

[a]The original scores range from a high of $X = 94$ to a low of $X = 53$. This range has been divided into nine intervals with each interval exactly five points wide. The frequency column (f) lists the number of individuals with scores in each of the class intervals.

measured, we typically do not assign our observation to a single point on the line. In practice, we assign the observation to an *interval* on the number line. For example, if you are measuring body weight to the nearest pound, weights of $X = 150.3$ and $X = 149.6$ pounds would both be rounded to scores of $X = 150$ (Figure 2.1). Note that a score of $X = 150$ is not a single point on the number line but instead represents an interval on the line. In this example, a score of 150 corresponds to an interval from 149.5 to 150.5. Any measurement that falls within this interval will be assigned a value of $X = 150$. The boundaries that form the interval are called the *real limits* of the interval. For this example, 149.5 in the *lower real limit* and 150.5 is the *upper real limit* of the interval that corresponds to $X = 150$.

Figure 2.1

When measuring weight to the nearest whole pound, 149.6 and 150.3 are assigned the value of 150 (top). Any value in the interval between 149.5 and 150.5 will be given the value of 150.

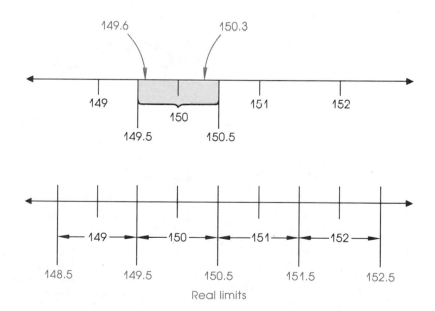

Real limits

DEFINITION   *Real limits* are the boundaries of intervals for scores that are represented on a continuous number line. The real limit separating two adjacent scores is located exactly halfway between the scores. Each score has two real limits. The *upper real limit* is at the top and the *lower real limit* is at the bottom of the interval.

In Figure 2.1, note that neighboring X values share a real limit. For example, the score of $X = 150$ has an upper real limit of 150.5. The value 150.5 is also the lower real limit for $X = 151$. Thus, on a continuous number line, such as Figure 2.1, there are no gaps between adjacent intervals.

The concept of real limits also applies to the class intervals of a grouped frequency distribution table. For example, a class interval of 40–49 contains scores from $X = 40$ to $X = 49$. These values are called the *apparent limits* of the interval because it appears that they form the upper and lower boundaries for the class interval. But $X = 40$ is actually an interval from 39.5 to 40.5. Similarly, $X = 49$ is an interval from 48.5 to 49.5. Therefore, the real limits of the interval are 39.5 (the lower real limit) and 49.5 (the upper real limit). Notice that the next higher class interval would be 50–59, which as a lower real limit of 49.5. Thus, the two intervals meet at the real limit 49.5, so there are no gaps in the scale. You also should notice that the width of each class interval becomes easier to understand when you consider the real limits of an interval. For example, the interval 50–54 has real limits of 49.5 and 54.5. The distance between these two real limits (5 points) is the width of the interval.

The concept of real limits will be used later for constructing graphs and for various calculations with continuous scales. For now, however, you should realize that real limits are a necessity whenever measurements are made of a continuous variable.

LEARNING CHECK   1. Place the following scores in a frequency distribution table showing proportion and percentage as well as the frequency for each score. Scores: 2, 3, 1, 2, 5, 4, 5, 5, 1, 4, 2, 2, 5, 5, 4, 2, 3, 1, 5, 4.

2. A set of scores ranges from a high of $X = 142$ to a low of $X = 65$. If these scores are to be placed in a grouped frequency distribution table, then

   a. What interval width should be used?

   b. What are the apparent limits of the bottom interval?

   c. What are the real limits of the bottom interval?

3. Explain why you should avoid having too many rows in a frequency distribution table. What is the problem with having too few rows?

ANSWERS   1.

X	f	p	%
5	6	0.30	30%
4	4	0.20	20%
3	2	0.10	10%
2	5	0.25	25%
1	3	0.15	15%

2. a. The range would require 78 rows for a frequency distribution table. With an interval width of 5 points, you would need 16 intervals to cover the range. With an interval width of 10, you would need 8 intervals. For most purposes, a width of 10 points probably is best.

   b. With a width of 10, the bottom interval would have apparent limits of 60–69.

   c. The real limits of the bottom interval would be 59.5 and 69.5.

3. With too many rows the table is not simple and, therefore, fails to meet the goal of descriptive statistics. With too few rows, you lose information about the distribution.

SECTION 2.3 **FREQUENCY DISTRIBUTION GRAPHS**

A frequency distribution graph is basically a picture of the information available in a frequency distribution table. We will consider several different types of graphs, but all start with two perpendicular lines called axes. The horizontal line is called the *X*-axis, or the abscissa. The vertical line is called the *Y*-axis, or the ordinate. The scores are listed along the *X*-axis in increasing value from left to right. The frequencies are listed on the *Y*-axis in increasing value from bottom to top. As a general rule, the point where the two axes intersect should have a value of zero for both the scores and the frequencies. A final general rule is that the graph should be constructed so that its height (*Y*-axis) is approximately three-quarters of its length (*X*-axis). Violating these guidelines can result in graphs that give a misleading picture of the data (see Box 2.1).

HISTOGRAMS AND BAR GRAPHS

The first type of graph we will consider is called either a histogram or a bar graph. For this type of graph, you simply draw a bar above each score so that the height of the bar corresponds to the frequency of the score. As you will see, the choice between using a histogram or a bar graph is determined by the scale of measurement.

When a frequency distribution graph is showing data from an interval or ratio scale, the bars are drawn so that adjacent bars touch each other. The touching bars produce a continuous figure which emphasizes the continuity of the variable. This type of frequency distribution graph is called a histogram. An example of a histogram is presented in Figure 2.2.

DEFINITION

For a *histogram*, vertical bars are drawn above each score so that

1. The height of the bar corresponds to the frequency.
2. The width of the bar extends to the real limits of the score.

A histogram is used when the data are measured on an interval or ratio scale.

When data have been grouped into class intervals, you can construct a frequency distribution histogram by drawing a bar above each interval so that the width of

Figure 2.2

An example of a frequency distribution histogram. The same set of data is presented in a frequency distribution table and in a histogram.

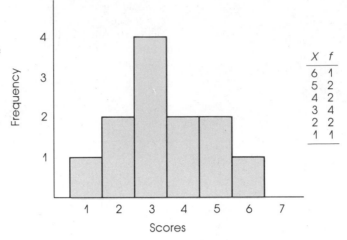

X	f
6	1
5	2
4	2
3	4
2	2
1	1

the bar extends to the real limits of the interval. This process is demonstrated in Figure 2.3.

When you are presenting the frequency distribution for data from a nominal or ordinal scale, the graph is constructed so that there is some space between the bars. In this case the separate bars emphasize that the scale consists of separate, distinct categories. The resulting graph is called a bar graph. An example of a frequency distribution bar graph is given in Figure 2.4.

DEFINITION   For a *bar graph*, a vertical bar is drawn above each score (or category) so that

1. The height of the bar corresponds to the frequency.

2. There is a space separating each bar from the next.

A bar graph is used when the data are measured on a nominal or ordinal scale.

Figure 2.3

An example of a frequency distribution histogram for grouped data. The same set of data is presented in a grouped frequency distribution table and in a histogram.

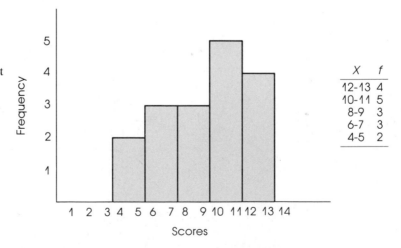

X	f
12-13	4
10-11	5
8-9	3
6-7	3
4-5	2

Figure 2.4

A bar graph showing the distribution of personality types in a sample of college students. Because personality type is a discrete variable measured on a nominal scale, the graph is drawn with space between the bars.

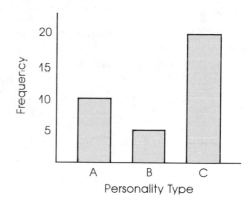

FREQUENCY DISTRIBUTION POLYGONS

Instead of a histogram, many researchers prefer to display a frequency distribution using a polygon.

DEFINITION

In a *frequency distribution polygon,* a single dot is drawn above each score so that

1. The dot is centered above the score.
2. The height of the dot corresponds to the frequency.

A continuous line is then drawn connecting these dots. The graph is completed by drawing a line down to the *X*-axis (zero frequency) at each end of the range of scores.

As with a histogram, the frequency distribution polygon is intended for use with interval or ratio scales. An example of a polygon is shown in Figure 2.5. A polygon also can be used with data that have been grouped into class intervals. In this case,

Figure 2.5

An example of a frequency distribution polygon. The same set of data is presented in a frequency distribution table and in a polygon. Note that these data are shown in a histogram in Figure 2.2.

X	f
6	1
5	2
4	2
3	4
2	2
1	1

Figure 2.6

An example of a frequency distribution polygon for grouped data. The same set of data is presented in a grouped frequency distribution table and in a polygon. Note that these data are shown in a histogram in Figure 2.3.

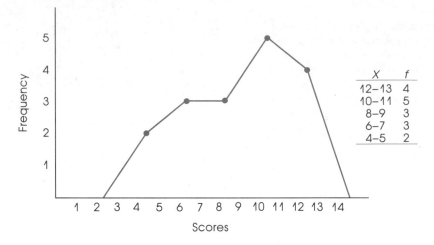

X	f
12–13	4
10–11	5
8–9	3
6–7	3
4–5	2

you position the dots directly above the midpoint of each class interval. The midpoint can be found by averaging the apparent limits of the interval or by averaging the real limits of the interval. For example, a class interval of 40–49 would have a midpoint of 44.5.

$$\text{apparent limits:} \quad \frac{40 + 49}{2} = \frac{89}{2} = 44.5$$

$$\text{real limits:} \quad \frac{39.5 + 49.5}{2} = \frac{89}{2} = 44.5$$

An example of a frequency distribution polygon with grouped data is shown in Figure 2.6.

RELATIVE FREQUENCIES AND SMOOTH CURVES

Often it is impossible to construct a frequency distribution for a population because there are simply too many individuals for a researcher to obtain measurements and frequencies for the entire group. In this case, it is customary to draw a frequency distribution graph showing *relative frequencies* (proportions) on the vertical axis. For example, a researcher may know that a particular species of animal has three times as many females as males in the population. This fact could be displayed in a bar graph by simply making the bar above ''female'' three times as tall as the bar above ''male.'' Notice that the actual frequencies are unknown but that the relative frequency of males and females can still be presented in a graph.

It also is possible to use a polygon to show relative frequencies for scores in a population. In this case, it is customary to draw a smooth curve instead of the series of straight lines that normally appears in a polygon. The smooth curve indicates that you are not connecting a series of dots (real frequencies) but rather are showing a distribution that is not limited to one specific set of data. One commonly occurring population distribution is the normal curve. The word *normal* refers to a specific shape that can be precisely defined by an equation. Less precisely, we can describe a normal distribution as being symmetrical, with the greatest frequency in the

Figure 2.7

The population distribution of IQ scores: an example of a normal distribution.

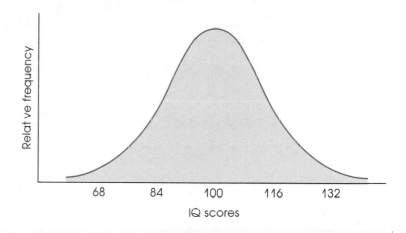

middle and relatively smaller frequencies as you move toward either extreme. A good example of a normal distribution is the population distribution for IQ scores shown in Figure 2.7. Because normal shaped distributions occur commonly and because this shape is mathematically guaranteed in certain situations, it will receive extensive attention throughout this book.

In the future we will be referring to *distributions of scores*. Whenever the term *distribution* appears, you should conjure up an image of a frequency distribution graph. The graph provides a picture showing exactly where the individual scores are located. To make this concept more concrete, you might find it useful to think of the graph as showing a pile of individuals. In Figure 2.7, for example, the pile is highest at an IQ score of around 100 because most people have "average" IQs. There are only a few individuals piled up at an IQ score of 130; it must be lonely at the top.

SECTION 2.4   # THE SHAPE OF A FREQUENCY DISTRIBUTION

Rather than drawing a complete frequency distribution graph, researchers often simply describe a distribution by listing its characteristics. There are three characteristics that completely describe any distribution: shape, central tendency, and variability. In simple terms, central tendency measures where the center of the distribution is located. Variability tells whether the scores are spread over a wide range or are clustered together. Central tendency and variability will be covered in detail in Chapters 3 and 4. Technically, the shape of a distribution is defined by an equation that prescribes the exact relation between each *X* and *Y* value on the graph. However, we will rely on a few less-precise terms that will serve to describe the shape of most distributions.

Nearly all distributions can be classified as being either symmetrical or skewed.

DEFINITIONS

In a *symmetrical distribution* it is possible to draw a vertical line through the middle so that one side of the distribution is an exact mirror image of the other (see Figure 2.8).

Figure 2.8

Examples of different shapes for distributions.

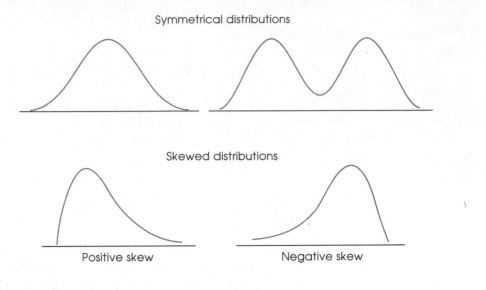

In a *skewed distribution* the scores tend to pile up toward one end of the scale and taper off gradually at the other end (see Figure 2.8).

The section where the scores taper off toward one end of a distribution is called the *tail* of the distribution.

A skewed distribution with the tail to the right-hand side is said to be *positively skewed* because the tail points toward the positive (above-zero) end of the X-axis. If the tail points to the left, the distribution is said to be *negatively skewed* (see Figure 2.8).

For a very difficult exam, most scores will tend to be low, with only a few individuals earning high scores. This will produce a positively skewed distribution. Similarly, a very easy exam will tend to produce a negatively skewed distribution, with most of the students earning high scores and only a few with low values.

LEARNING CHECK

1. Sketch a frequency distribution histogram and a frequency distribution polygon for the data in the following table:

X	f
5	4
4	6
3	3
2	1
1	1

2. Describe the shape of the distribution in exercise 1.

3. What type of graph would be appropriate to show the number of gold medals, silver medals, and bronze medals won by the United States during the 1984 Olympics?

Figure 2.9

Answers to Learning Check Exercise 1.

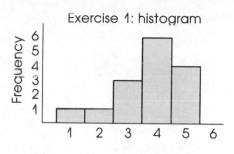

Exercise 1: histogram

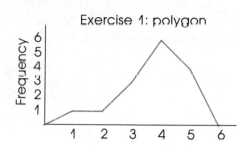

Exercise 1: polygon

4. What shape would you expect for the distribution of salaries for all employees of a major industry?

ANSWERS

1. The graphs are shown in Figure 2.9.

2. The distribution is negatively skewed.

3. A bar graph is appropriate for ordinal data.

4. The distribution probably would be positively skewed, with most employees earning an average salary and a relatively small number of top executives with vary large salaries.

SECTION 2.5 **OTHER TYPES OF GRAPHS**

In addition to displaying frequency distributions, graphs can be used to show relationships between variables. Perhaps the most common use is to show the results of an experiment by graphing the relation between the independent variable and the dependent variable. You should recall that the dependent variable is the score obtained for each subject and that the independent variable distinguishes the different treatment conditions or groups used in the experiment. For example, a researcher testing a new diet drug might compare several different dosages by measuring the amount of food that animals consume at each dose level. Figure 2.10

Figure 2.10

The relationship between an independent variable (drug dose) and a dependent variable (food consumption). Because drug dose is a continuous variable, a continuous line is used to connect the different dose levels.

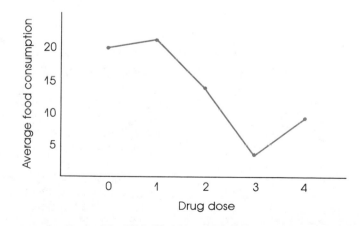

Figure 2.11

The relationship between an independent variable (brand of pain reliever) and a dependent variable (pain tolerance). The graph uses separate bars because the brand of pain reliever is measured on a nominal scale.

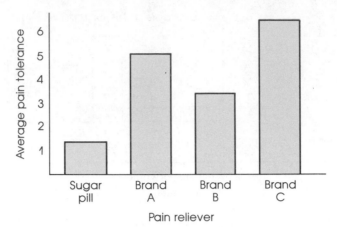

shows hypothetical data from this experiment. Notice that the four dose levels (the independent variable) are on the *X*-axis and that food consumption (the dependent variable) is shown on the *Y*-axis. The points in the graph represent the average food consumption for the group at each dose level. In this graph the points are connected with a line because the *X*-axis variable (drug dose) is continuous (measured on a ratio scale).

Figure 2.11 shows results from another experiment where the independent variable is discrete. In this graph, we have used separate bars for each position on the *X*-axis to indicate that we are comparing separate categories (measured on a nominal scale).

When constructing graphs of any type, you should recall the basic rules we mentioned earlier:

1. The height of a graph should be approximately three-quarters of its length.

2. Normally, you start numbering both the *X*-axis and the *Y*-axis with zero at the point where the two axes intersect.

More importantly, you should remember that the purpose of a graph is to give an accurate representation of the information in a set of data. Box 2.1 demonstrates what can happen when these basic principles are ignored.

LEARNING CHECK

1. In a study on stress, a researcher exposed groups of rats to either signaled shock, unsignaled shock, or no shock. The average size (in millimeters) of ulcers for each group was then determined. Construct a graph of the following data.

	Treatment Group		
	NO SHOCK	SIGNALED SHOCK	UNSIGNALED SHOCK
Average size of ulcers	0	3	7

THE USE AND MISUSE OF GRAPHS

ALTHOUGH GRAPHS are intended to provide an accurate picture of a set of data, they can be used to exaggerate or misrepresent a set of scores. These misrepresentations generally result from failing to follow the basic rules for graph construction. The following example demonstrates how the same set of data can be presented in two entirely different ways by manipulating the structure of a graph.

For the past several years, the city has kept records of the number of major felonies. The data are summarized as follows:

YEAR	NUMBER OF MAJOR FELONIES
1982	218
1983	225
1984	229

These same data are shown in two different graphs in Figure 2.12. In the first graph we have exaggerated the height, and we started numbering the Y-axis at 210 rather than at zero. As a result, the graph seems to indicate a rapid rise in the crime rate over the 3-year period. In the second graph, we have stretched out the X-axis and used zero as the starting point for the Y-axis. The result is a graph that shows no change in the crime rate over the 3-year period.

Which graph is correct? The answer is that neither one is very good. Remember that the purpose of a graph is to provide an accurate display of the data. The first graph in Figure 2.12 exaggerates the differences between years, and the second graph conceals the differences. Some compromise is needed. You also should note that in some cases a graph may not be the best way to display information. For these data, for example, showing the numbers in a table would be better than either graph.

Figure 2.12

Two graphs showing the number of major felonies in a city over a 3-year period. Both graphs are showing exactly the same data. However, the first graph gives the appearance that the crime rate is high and rising rapidly. The second graph gives the impression that the crime rate is low and has not changed over the 3-year period.

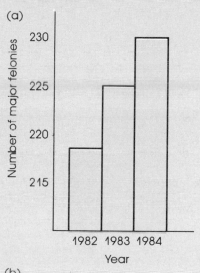

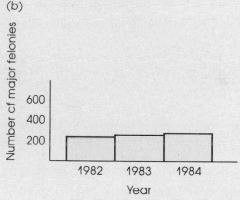

2. A psychologist studied the effect of sleep deprivation on mood. Groups of clinically depressed subjects were deprived of sleep for either 0, 1, 2, or 3 nights. After deprivation, the amount of depression was measured with a depression inventory. Construct a graph of the following data.

NIGHTS OF DEPRIVATION	AVERAGE DEPRESSION SCORE
0	22
1	17
2	9
3	7

ANSWERS 1.,   2. The graphs are shown in Figure 2.13.

Figure 2.13

Answers to Learning Check Exercises 1 and 2.

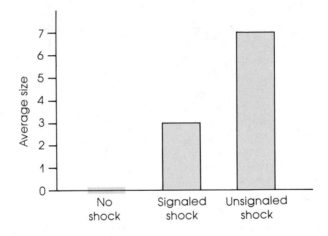

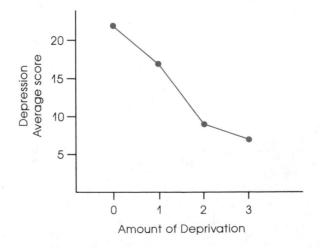

SUMMARY

1. The goal of descriptive statistics is to simplify the organization and presentation of data. One descriptive technique is to place data in a frequency distribution table or graph that shows how the scores are distributed across the measurement scale.

2. A frequency distribution table lists scores (from highest down to lowest) in one column and the frequency of occurrence for each score in a second column. The table may include a proportion column showing the relative frequency for each score:

$$\text{proportion} = p = \frac{f}{N}$$

   And the table may include a percentage column showing the percentage associated with each score:

$$\text{percentage} = \% = \frac{f}{N}(100)$$

3. When the scores cover a range that is too broad to list each individual value, it is customary to divide the range into sections called class intervals. These intervals are then listed in the frequency distribution table along with the frequency or number of individuals with scores in each interval. The result is called a grouped frequency distribution. The guidelines for constructing a grouped frequency distribution table are as follows:
   a. There should be about 10 intervals.
   b. The width of each interval should be a simple number (e.g., 2, 5, or 10).
   c. The bottom score in each interval should be a multiple of the width.
   d. All intervals should be the same width, and they should cover the range of scores with no gaps.

4. For a continuous variable, each score corresponds to an interval on the scale. The boundaries that separate intervals are called real limits. The real limits are located exactly halfway between adjacent scores.

5. A frequency distribution graph lists scores on the horizontal axis and frequencies on the vertical axis. The type of graph used to display a distribution depends on the scale of measurement used. For interval or ratio scales, you should use a histogram or a polygon. For a histogram, a bar is drawn above each score so that the height of the bar corresponds to the frequency. Each bar extends to the real limits of the score so that adjacent bars touch. For a polygon, a dot is placed above the midpoint of each score or class interval so that the height of the dot corresponds to the frequency; then lines are drawn to connect the dots. Bar graphs are used with nominal or ordinal scales. Bar graphs are similar to histograms except that gaps are left between adjacent bars.

6. Shape is one of the basic characteristics used to describe a distribution of scores. Most distributions can be classified as either symmetrical or skewed. A skewed distribution that tails off to the right is said to be positively skewed. If it tails off to the left, it is negatively skewed.

KEY TERMS

frequency distribution	upper real limit	bar graph	symmetrical distribution
grouped frequency distribution	lower real limit	polygon	positively skewed distribution
class interval	apparent limits	relative frequency	negatively skewed distribution
real limit	histogram		

FOCUS ON PROBLEM SOLVING

1. The reason for constructing frequency distributions is to transform a disorganized set of raw data into a comprehensible, organized format. Because several different types of frequency distribution tables and graphs are available, one problem is deciding which type should be used. Tables have the advantage of being easier to construct, but graphs generally give a better picture of the data and are easier to understand.

   To help you decide exactly which type of frequency distribution is best, consider the following points:

   a. What is the range of scores? With a wide range, you will need to group the scores into class intervals.

   b. What is the scale of measurement? With an interval or ratio scale you can use a polygon or a histogram.

With a nominal or ordinal scale, you must use a bar graph.

2. In setting up class intervals, a common mistake is to determine the interval width by finding the difference between the apparent limits. This is incorrect! To determine the interval width, you must take the difference for the *real limits*. For example, the width for the interval 70–79 is 10 because its real limits are 69.5 and 79.5, and

$$\text{width} = \text{upper real limit} - \text{lower real limit}$$

$$= 79.5 - 69.5 = 10$$

Resist the temptation to state the width is 9. You must use the real limits.

DEMONSTRATION 2.1   A GROUPED FREQUENCY DISTRIBUTION TABLE

For the following set of $N = 20$ scores, construct a grouped frequency distribution table. Use an interval width of 5 points and include columns for f and p.

Data: 14 8 27 16 10 22 9 13 16 12
       10 9 15 17 6 14 11 18 14 11

STEP 1 Set up the class intervals.

The largest score in this distribution is $X = 27$ and the lowest is $X = 6$. Therefore, a frequency distribution table for these data would have 22 rows and would be too large. A grouped frequency distribution table would be better. We have asked specifically for an interval width of 5 points, and the resulting table will have five rows:

X
25 – 29
20 – 24
15 – 19
10 – 14
5 – 9

Remember, the interval width is determined by the real limits of the interval. For example, the class interval 25 – 29 has an upper real limit of 29.5 and a lower real limit of 24.5. The difference between these two values is the width of the interval, namely 5.

STEP 2   Determine the frequencies for each interval.

Examine the scores and count how many fall into the class interval of 25 − 29. Cross out each score that you have already counted. Record the frequency for this class interval. Now repeat this process for the remaining intervals. The result is the following table:

X	f	
25 − 29	1	(the score X − 27)
20 − 24	1	(X = 22)
15 19	5	(the scores X = 16, 16, 15, 17, and 18)
10 − 14	9	(X = 14, 10, 13, 12, 10, 14, 11, 14, and 11)
5 − 9	4	(X = 8, 9, 9, and 6)

STEP 3   Compute the proportions.

The proportion (p) of scores contained in an interval is determined by dividing the frequency (f) of that interval by the number of scores (N) in the distribution. Thus, for each interval, we must compute the following:

$$p = f/N$$

This is demonstrated in the following table.

X	f	p
25−29	1	$f/N = 1/20 = 0.05$
20−24	1	$f/N = 1/20 = 0.05$
15−19	5	$f/N = 5/20 = 0.25$
10−14	9	$f/N = 9/20 = 0.45$
5−9	4	$f/N = 4/20 = 0.20$

PROBLEMS

1. A set of scores covers a range of 15 points. Should these scores be presented in a regular table or a grouped table? Explain the advantages and disadvantages of each.

2. A set of $N = 7$ scores ranges from a high of $X = 96$ to a low of $X = 61$. Explain why it would *not* be a good idea to display this set of data in a frequency distribution table.

3. A researcher collected personality scores from a sample of 100 students and organized the scores in a grouped frequency distribution table. That evening the researcher took the table home in order to use a home computer to do more-detailed calculations. However, the researcher soon found that the table did not provide enough information to do even the simplest arithmetic—for example, it was impossible to find ΣX for the scores. Explain why.

4. What is the difference between a histogram and a bar graph? Under what circumstances is a bar graph appropriate? When is a histogram preferable?

5. Place the following set of scores in a frequency distribution table, and draw a polygon showing the distribution of scores. Scores: 6, 1, 3, 5, 5, 4, 5, 6, 3, 4, 2, 5, 4.

6. For the set of scores shown in the following frequency distribution table,
   a. How many scores are in the distribution? ($N = ?$)
   b. Find ΣX for this set of scores.

X	f
4	6
3	1
2	3
1	2

7. Sketch a histogram and a polygon showing the distribution of scores in the following table:

X	f
10–11	2
8–9	4
6–7	5
4–5	3
2–3	1

8. For the following set of scores,
   a. Construct a frequency distribution table to organize the quiz scores.
   b. Draw a frequency distribution histogram for these data.

   3, 5, 4, 6, 2, 3, 4, 1, 4, 3

   7, 7, 3, 4, 5, 8, 2, 4, 7, 10

9. Use a frequency distribution table to organize the following set of scores:

   206, 350, 590, 473, 450, 483

   112, 380, 584, 620, 743, 816

   685, 592, 712, 727, 686, 592

   542, 490, 684, 491, 520, 380

10. Sketch a frequency distribution histogram for the following data.

X	f
10	1
9	3
8	5
7	6
6	3
5	2

11. Place the following 28 scores in a grouped frequency distribution table using
    a. An interval width of 2
    b. An interval width of 5

    23, 12, 16, 16, 17, 19, 28

    20, 14, 21, 18, 24, 29, 24

    18, 21, 22, 27, 21, 25, 19

    22, 23, 21, 30, 27, 23, 18

12. Five sets of data are described. For each set the range of scores (lowest to highest) is given. Describe how each set should be presented in a grouped frequency distribution. That is, give the interval width that you would suggest and the number of intervals needed.

    a. 3–24   d. 132–207
    b. 41–93   e. 161–786
    c. 11–18

13. The following two sets of scores are from two different sections of an introductory statistics class:

SECTION I						SECTION II					
70	83	60	68	58	85	93	57	83	70	86	76
73	76	70	67	83	65	85	67	72	82	77	87
77	75	93	89	76	75	69	87	89	91	77	94
92	63	62	79	86	80	97	92	62	85	72	87
74	81	69	78	80	71	65	81	75	90		

    a. Organize the scores from each section into a grouped frequency distribution polygon using an interval width of 5 for each graph.
    b. Describe the similarities and differences between the two sections.

14. A psychologist would like to examine the effects of diet on intelligence. Two groups of rats are selected with 12 rats in each group. One group is fed the regular diet of Rat Chow, whereas the second group has special vitamins and minerals added to their food. After 6 months each rat is tested on a discrimination problem. The psychologist records the number of errors each animal makes before it solves the problem. The data from this experiment are as follows:

    regular diet scores: 13, 11, 12, 13, 11, 9
                          12, 10, 12, 14, 10, 12

    special diet scores: 9, 8, 7, 8, 9, 10
                          7, 8, 9, 6, 8, 10

a. Identify the independent variable and the dependent variable for this experiment.

b. Sketch a frequency distribution polygon for the group of rats with the regular diet. On the same graph (in a different color), sketch the distribution for the rats with the special diet.

c. From looking at your graphs, would you say that the special diet had any effect on intelligence? Explain your answer.

15. For the following scores, construct a frequency distribution table using
a. An interval width of 5
b. An interval width of 10

64, 75, 50, 67, 86, 66, 62, 64, 71, 47

57, 74, 63, 67, 56, 65, 70, 87, 48, 50

41, 66, 73, 60, 63, 45, 78, 68, 53, 75

16. College officials recently conducted a survey to determine student's attitudes toward extending the library hours. Four different groups of students were surveyed, representing the four major subdivisions of the college. The average score for each group was as follows:

humanities: 7.25
sciences: 5.69
professions: 6.85
fine arts: 5.90

Use a graph to present the results of this survey.

17. A recent study reports the effect of alcohol on simple reaction time. The relation between reaction time and blood alcohol level is shown in the following table:

BLOOD ALCOHOL LEVEL	REACTION TIME
0.06	205
0.08	214
0.10	232
0.12	230
0.14	241

Construct a graph showing these data.

18. A researcher examined the effect of amount of relaxation training on insomnia. Four treatment groups were used. Subjects received relaxation training for 2, 4, or 8 sessions. A control group received no training (0 sessions). Following training, the researcher measured how long it took the subjects to fall asleep. The average times for each group are presented in the following table:

TRAINING SESSIONS	AVERAGE TIME (IN MINUTES)
0	72
2	58
4	31
8	14

Present these data in a graph.

19. Place the following set of scores in a frequency distribution table:

1, 3, 1, 1, 4, 1, 4, 5, 6, 2, 1, 1, 5

1, 3, 2, 1, 6, 2, 4, 5, 2, 3, 2, 3

Compute the proportion and the percentage of individuals with each score. From your frequency distribution table, you should be able to identify the shape of this distribution.

20. For the past several weeks a bored statistician has kept records for the post position of the winning horse for each race at a local track. The following data represent all races with exactly eight horses:

POST POSITION OF THE WINNING HORSE						
1	3	3	7	4	5	1
3	2	8	5	3	6	1
4	7	1	2	5	8	5
3	4	8	1	8	3	2
6	7	3	4	2	6	5
4	8	2	6	4	7	2

a. Construct a frequency distribution graph showing the number of winners for each of the eight post positions.

b. Describe the shape of this frequency distribution.

c. On the basis of these data, if you were betting on a race where you knew nothing about the horses or the jockeys, which post position would you choose? Explain your answer.

CHAPTER 3

CENTRAL TENDENCY

SECTION 3.1 INTRODUCTION

The goal in measuring central tendency is to describe a group of individuals (more accurately, their scores) with a single measurement. Ideally, the value we use to describe the group will be the single value that is most representative of all the individuals.

DEFINITION

Central tendency is a statistical measure that identifies a single score as a representative for an entire distribution.

Usually, we want to choose a value in the middle of the distribution because central scores are often the most representative. In everyday language, the goal of central tendency is to find the "average" or "typical" individual. This average value can then be used to provide a simple description of the entire population or sample. For example, archeological discoveries indicate that the average height for men in the ancient Roman city of Pompeii was 5 feet and 7 inches. Obviously, not all the men were exactly 5 feet and 7 inches, but this average value provides a general description of the population. Measures of central tendency also are useful for making comparisons between groups of individuals or between sets of figures. For example, suppose that weather data indicate that during the month of December, Seattle averages only 2 hours of sunshine per day, whereas Miami averages over 6 hours. The point of these examples is to demonstrate the great advantage of being able to describe a large set of data with a single, representative number. Central tendency characterizes what is typical for a large population and in doing so makes large amounts of data more digestible. Statisticians sometimes use the expression "number crunching" to illustrate this aspect of data description. That is, we take a distribution consisting of many scores and "crunch" them down to a single value that describes them all.

Unfortunately, there is no single, standard procedure for determining central tendency. The problem is that no single measure will always produce a typical, representative value in every situation. Therefore, there are three different ways to measure central tendency: the mean, the median, and the mode. They are computed differently and have different characteristics. To decide which of the three measures is best for any particular distribution, you should keep in mind that the general purpose of central tendency is to find the single most representative score. Each of the three measures we shall present has been developed to work best in a specific situation. We will examine this issue in more detail after we define the three measures.

SECTION 3.2 THE MEAN

The mean, commonly known as the arithmetic average, is computed by adding all the scores in the distribution and dividing by the number of scores. The mean for a population will be identified by the Greek letter mu, μ (pronounced "myoo"), and the mean for a sample will be identified by $\overline{X}$ (read "x-bar").

DEFINITION   The *mean* for a distribution is the sum of the scores divided by the number of scores.

The formula for the population mean is

$$\mu = \frac{\Sigma X}{N} \tag{3.1}$$

First, sum all the scores in the population and then divide by N. For a sample, the computation is done the same way, but the formula uses symbols that signify sample values:

$$\text{sample mean} = \overline{X} = \frac{\Sigma X}{n} \tag{3.2}$$

In general, we will use Greek letters to identify characteristics of a population and letters of our own alphabet to stand for sample values. If a mean is identified with the symbol $\overline{X}$, you should realize that we are dealing with a sample. Also note that n is used as the symbol for the number of scores in the sample.

EXAMPLE 3.1 For a population of $N = 4$ scores,

$$3, \quad 7, \quad 4, \quad 6$$

the mean is

$$\mu = \frac{\Sigma X}{N} = \frac{20}{4} = 5$$

Although the procedure of adding the scores and dividing by the number provides a useful definition of the mean, there are two alternative definitions that may give you a better understanding of this important measure of central tendency.

The first alternative is to think of the mean as the amount each individual would get if the total (ΣX) were divided equally among all the individuals (N) in the distribution. This somewhat socialistic viewpoint is particularly useful in problems where you know the mean and must find the total. Consider the following example.

EXAMPLE 3.2 A group of six students decided to earn some extra money one weekend picking vegetables at a local farm. At the end of the weekend the students discovered that their average income was $\mu = \$30$. If they decide to pool their money for a party, how much will they have?

You don't know how much money each student earned. But you do know that the mean is $30. This is the amount that each student would have if the total were divided equally. For each of six students to have $30, you must start with $6 \times \$30 = \$180$. The total, ΣX, is $180. To check this answer, use the formula for the mean:

$$\mu = \frac{\Sigma X}{N} = \frac{\$180}{6} = \$30$$

The second alternative definition of the mean is to describe the mean as a balance point for a distribution. Consider the population consisting of $N = 4$ scores (2, 2, 6, 10). For this population, $\Sigma X = 20$ and $N = 4$, so $\mu = \frac{20}{4} = 5$.

Imagine that the frequency distribution histogram for this population is drawn so that the X-axis, or number line, is a seesaw, and the scores are boxes of equal weight that are placed on the seesaw (see Figure 3.1). If the seesaw is positioned so that it pivots at the value equal to the mean, it will be balanced and will rest level.

The reason the seesaw is balanced over the mean becomes clear when we measure the distance of each box (score) from the mean:

SCORE	DISTANCE FROM THE MEAN
$X = 2$	3 points below the mean
$X = 2$	3 points below the mean
$X = 6$	1 point above the mean
$X = 10$	5 points above the mean

Notice that the mean balances the distances. That is, the total distance below the mean is the same as the total distance above the mean:

3 points below + 3 points below = 6 points below

1 point above + 5 points above = 6 points above

Figure 3.1

The frequency distribution shown as a seesaw balanced at the mean.

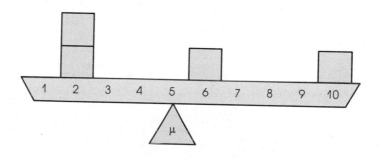

THE WEIGHTED MEAN   Often it is necessary to combine two sets of scores and then find the overall mean for the combined group. For example, an instructor teaching two sections of introductory psychology obtains an average quiz score of $\overline{X} = 6$ for the 12 students in one section and an average of $\overline{X} = 7$ for the 8 students in the other section. If the two sections are combined, what is the mean for the total group?

The solution to this problem is straightforward if you remember the definition of the mean:

$$\overline{X} = \frac{\Sigma X}{n}$$

To find the overall mean we must find two values: the total number of students (n) for the combined group, and the overall sum of scores for the combined group (ΣX). Finding the number of students is easy. If there are $n = 12$ in one group and $n = 8$ in the other, then there must be $n = 20$ $(12 + 8)$ in the combined group. To find the sum of scores for the combined group, we will use the same method: First find the sum for one group, then find the sum for the other, and then add the two sums together.

We know that the first section has $n = 12$ and $\overline{X} = 6$. Using these values in the equation for the mean gives

$$\overline{X} = \frac{\Sigma X}{n}$$

$$6 = \frac{\Sigma X}{12}$$

$$12(6) = \Sigma X$$

$$72 = \Sigma X$$

The second section has $n = 8$ and $\overline{X} = 7$, so ΣX must be equal to 56. When these two groups are combined, the sum of all 20 scores will be

$$72 + 56 = 128$$

Finally, the mean for the combined group is

$$\overline{X} = \frac{\Sigma X}{n} = \frac{128}{20} = 6.4$$

Notice that this value is not obtained by simply averaging the two means. (If we had simply averaged $\overline{X} = 6$ and $\overline{X} = 7$, we would obtain a mean of 6.5.) Because the samples are not the same size, one will make a larger contribution to the total group and, therefore, will carry more weight in determining the overall mean. For this reason, the overall mean we have calculated is called the *weighted mean*. In this example, the overall mean of $\overline{X} = 6.4$ is closer to the value of $\overline{X} = 6$ (the larger sample) than it is to $\overline{X} = 7$ (the smaller sample).

COMPUTING THE MEAN FROM A   Table 3.1 shows the scores on a quiz for a section of statistics students. Instead of
FREQUENCY DISTRIBUTION TABLE   listing all of the individual scores, these data are organized into a frequency

Table 3.1

Statistics quiz scores for a section of $n = 8$ students

QUIZ SCORE (X)	f	fX
10	1	10
9	2	18
8	4	32
7	0	0
6	1	6

distribution table. To compute the mean for this sample, you must use all the information in the table, the *f* values as well as the *X* values.

To find the mean for this sample, we will need the sum of the scores (ΣX) and the number of scores *(n)*. The number *n* can be found by summing the frequencies:

$$n = \Sigma f = 8$$

It is very common for people to make mistakes when determining ΣX from a frequency distribution table. Often the column labeled *X* is summed, while the frequency column is ignored. Be sure to use the information in the *f* column when determining ΣX. (See Chapter 2, p. 29.)

Note that there is one 10, two 9s, four 8s, and one 6 for a total of $n = 8$ scores. To find ΣX, you must be careful to add all eight scores:

$$\Sigma X = 10 + 9 + 9 + 8 + 8 + 8 + 8 + 6 = 66$$

This sum also can be found by multiplying each score by its frequency and then adding up the results. This is done in the third column *(fX)* in Table 3.1. Note, for example, that the two 9s contribute 18 to the total.

Once you have found ΣX and *n*, you compute the mean as usual:

$$\overline{X} = \frac{\Sigma X}{n} = \frac{\Sigma fX}{\Sigma f} = \frac{66}{8} = 8.25$$

LEARNING CHECK

1. Compute the mean for the sample of scores shown in the following frequency distribution table:

X	f
4	2
3	4
2	3
1	1

2. Two samples were obtained from a population. For sample A, $n = 8$ and $\overline{X} = 14$. For sample B, $n = 20$ and $\overline{X} = 6$. If the two samples are combined, will the overall mean be closer to 14 than to 6, closer to 6 than to 14, or halfway between 6 and 14? Explain your answer.

3. A sample of $n = 20$ scores has a mean of $\overline{X} = 5$. What is ΣX for this sample?

ANSWERS 1. $\overline{X} = \frac{27}{10} = 2.7$

2. The mean will be closer to 6. The larger sample will carry more weight in the combined group.

3. $\Sigma X = 100$

CHARACTERISTICS OF THE MEAN

The mean has many characteristics that will be important in future discussions. In general, these characteristics result from the fact that every score in the distribution contributes to the value of the mean. Specifically, every score must be added into the total in order to compute the mean. Three of the more important characteristics will now be discussed.

1. **Changing a Score or Introducing a New Score.** Changing the value of any score, or adding a new score to the distribution, will change the mean. For example, the quiz scores for a psychology lab section consist of

   9, 8, 7, 5, and 1

   The mean for this sample is

   $$\overline{X} = \frac{\Sigma X}{n} = \frac{30}{5} = 6.00$$

   Suppose that the student who received the score of $X = 1$ returned a few days later and explained that she was ill on the day of the quiz. In fact, she went straight to the infirmary after class and was admitted for two days with the flu. Out of the goodness of the instructor's heart, the student was given a makeup quiz, and she received an 8. By having changed her score from 1 to 8, the distribution now consists of

   9, 8, 7, 5, and 8

   The new mean is

   $$\overline{X} = \frac{\Sigma X}{n} = \frac{37}{5} = 7.40$$

   Changing a single score in this sample has given us a different mean.

2. **Adding or Subtracting a Constant from Each Score.** If a constant value is added to every score in a distribution, the same constant will be added to the mean. Similarly, if you subtract a constant from every score, the same constant will be subtracted from the mean.

   Consider the feeding scores for a sample of $n = 6$ rats. See Table 3.2. These scores are the amounts of food (in grams) they ate during a 24-hour testing session. The $\Sigma X = 26$ for $n = 6$ rats, so $\overline{X} = 4.33$. On the following day, each rat is given an experimental drug that reduces appetite. Suppose that this drug has the effect of reducing the meal size by 2 grams for each rat. Note that the effect of the drug is to subtract a constant (two points) from each rat's feeding score. The new distribution is shown in Table 3.3. Now $\Sigma X = 14$ and n is still 6, so the mean amount of food consumed is $\overline{X} = 2.33$. Subtracting two points from each score has

Table 3.2

Amount of food (in grams) consumed
during baseline session

RAT'S IDENTIFICATION	AMOUNT (X)
A	6
B	3
C	5
D	3
E	4
F	5

$\Sigma X = 26$

$n = 6$

$\bar{X} = 4.33$

Table 3.3

Amount of food (in grams) consumed
after drug injections

RAT	BASELINE SCORE MINUS CONSTANT	DRUG SCORE (X)
A	6 − 2	4
B	3 − 2	1
C	5 − 2	3
D	3 − 2	1
E	4 − 2	2
F	5 − 2	3

$\Sigma X = 14$

$n = 6$

$\bar{X} = 2.33$

changed the mean by the same constant, from $\bar{X} = 4.33$ to $\bar{X} = 2.33$. (It
is important to note that experimental effects are practically never so simple as the adding or subtracting of a constant. Nonetheless, the principle of
this characteristic of the mean is important and will be addressed in later
chapters when we are using statistics to evaluate the effects of experimental manipulations.)

3. **Multiplying or Dividing Each Score by a Constant.** If every score in a
distribution is multiplied by (or divided by) a constant value, the mean will
be changed in the same way.

Suppose a yardstick is used to measure five pieces of wood, resulting in
the five scores shown in Table 3.4. Notice that each score is a measurement in yards. Now, suppose we want to convert these measurements from
yards to feet. To accomplish this conversion, we simply multiply each of
the original measurements by 3. Again, the resulting values are shown in
Table 3.4. Notice that multiplying by 3 (changing from yards to feet) did

Table 3.4

Measurement of five pieces of wood

ORIGINAL MEASUREMENT IN YARDS	CONVERSION TO FEET (MULTIPLY BY 3)
10	30
9	27
12	36
8	24
11	33
$\Sigma X = 50$	$\Sigma X = 150$
$\bar{X} = 10$ yards	$\bar{X} = 30$ feet

not change any of the lengths. It simply changes the unit of measurement. Also note that the average of $\bar{X} = 30$ feet is identical in length to the original average of $\bar{X} = 10$ yards. In general, multiplying (or dividing) each score by a constant will also cause the mean to be multiplied (or divided) by the same constant.

LEARNING CHECK

1. a. Compute the mean for the following sample of scores:

   6,   1,   8,   0,   5

b. Add four points to each score and then compute the mean.

c. Multiply each of the original scores by 5 and then compute the mean.

2. After every score in a distribution is multiplied by 3, the mean is calculated to be $\bar{X} = 60$. What was the mean for the original distribution?

ANSWERS

1. a. $\bar{X} = \frac{20}{5} = 4$ **b.** $\bar{X} = \frac{40}{5} = 8$ **c.** $\bar{X} = \frac{100}{5} = 20$

2. The original mean was $\bar{X} = 20$.

SECTION 3.3

THE MEDIAN

The second measure of central tendency we will consider is called the *median*. The median is the score that divides a distribution exactly in half. Exactly one-half of the scores are less than or equal to the median, and exactly one-half are greater than or equal to the median.

DEFINITION

The *median* is the score that divides a distribution exactly in half. Exactly 50% of the individuals in a distribution have scores at or below the median.

By midpoint of the distribution we mean that the area in the graph is divided into two equal parts. We are not locating the midpoint between the highest and lowest *X* values.

The goal of the median is to determine the precise midpoint of a distribution. The commonsense goal is demonstrated in the following three examples. The three examples are intended to cover all of the different types of data you are likely to encounter.

METHOD 1: WHEN *N* IS AN ODD NUMBER

With an odd number of scores, you list the scores in order (lowest to highest), and the median is the middle score in the list. Consider the following set of $N = 5$ scores, which have been listed in order:

   3,   5,   8,   10,   11

The middle score is $X = 8$, so the median is equal to 8.0. In a graph, the median divides the space or area of the graph in half (Figure 3.2). The amount of area above the median consists of $2\frac{1}{2}$ ''boxes,'' the same as the area below the median (shaded portion).

Figure 3.2

The median divides the area in the graph exactly in half.

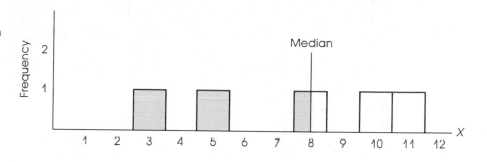

METHOD 2: WHEN *N* IS AN EVEN NUMBER

With an even number of scores in the distribution, you list the scores in order (lowest to highest), and then locate the median by finding the point halfway between the middle two scores. Consider the following population:

$$3, \quad 3, \quad 4, \quad 5, \quad 7, \quad 8$$

Now we select the middle pair of scores (4 and 5), add them together, and divide by 2:

$$\text{median} = \frac{4 + 5}{2} = \frac{9}{2} = 4.5$$

In terms of a graph, we see again that the median divides the area of the distribution exactly in half (Figure 3.3). There are three scores (or boxes) above the median and three below the median.

METHOD 3: WHEN THERE ARE SEVERAL SCORES WITH THE SAME VALUE IN THE MIDDLE OF THE DISTRIBUTION

In most cases, one of the two methods already outlined will provide you with a reasonable value for the median. However, when you have more than one individual at the median, these simple procedures may oversimplify the computations. Consider the following set of scores:

$$1, \quad 2, \quad 2, \quad 3, \quad 4, \quad 4, \quad 4, \quad 4, \quad 4, \quad 5$$

Figure 3.3

The median divides the area of the graph exactly in half.

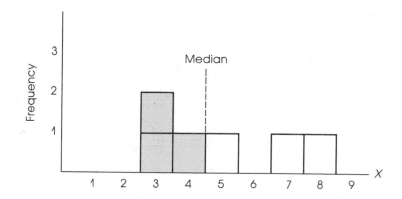

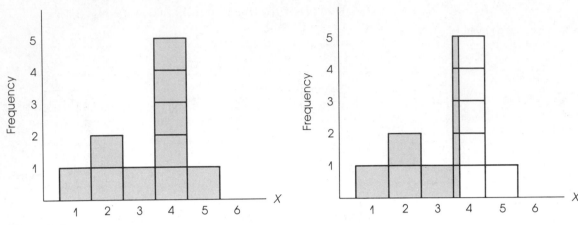

Figure 3.4

A distribution with several scores clustered at the median.

There are 10 scores (an even number), so you normally would use method 2 and average the middle pair to determine the median. By this method, the median would be 4.

In many ways this is a perfectly legitimate value for the median. However, when you look closely at the distribution of scores (see Figure 3.4(a)), you probably get the clear impression that $X = 4$ is not in the middle. The problem comes from the tendency to interpret the score of 4 as meaning exactly 4.00 instead of meaning an interval from 3.5 to 4.5. The simple method of computing the median has determined that the value we want is located in this interval. To locate the median with greater precision, it is necessary to use a process called *interpolation*. Although it is possible to describe the interpolation process in general mathematical terms, we will use a simple graphic presentation to demonstrate how this procedure can be used to find the median.

E X A M P L E   3 . 3   For this example we will use the data shown in Figure 3.4(a). Notice that the figure shows a population of $N = 10$ scores, with each score represented by a block in the histogram. To find the median, we must locate the position of a vertical line that will divide the distribution exactly in half, with 5 blocks on the left-hand side and 5 blocks on the right-hand side.

To begin the process, start at the left-hand side of the distribution and move up the scale of measurement (the *X*-axis), counting blocks as you go along. The vertical line corresponding to the median should be drawn at the point where you have counted exactly 5 blocks (50% of the total of 10 blocks). By the time you reach a value of 3.5 on the *X*-axis, you will have gathered a total of 4 blocks, so that only one more block is needed to give you exactly 50% of the distribution. The problem is that there are 5 blocks in the next interval. The solution is to take only a fraction of each of the 5 blocks so that the fractions combine to give you one more block. If you take $\frac{1}{5}$

of each block, the five fifths will combine to make one whole block. This solution is shown in Figure 3.4(b).

Notice that we have drawn a line separating each of the four blocks so that $\frac{1}{5}$ is on the left-hand side of the line and $\frac{4}{5}$ is on the right-hand side. Thus, the line should be drawn exactly $\frac{1}{5}$ of the way into the interval containing the five blocks. This interval extends from a lower real limit of 3.5 to an upper real limit of 4.5 on the X-axis and has a width of 1.00 point. One fifth of the interval would be 0.20 points ($\frac{1}{5}$ of 1.00). Therefore, the line should be drawn at the point where $X = 3.70$ (the lower real limit of 3.5 + $\frac{1}{5}$ of the interval, or 0.20). This value, $X = 3.70$, is the median and divides the distribution exactly in half.

The interpolation process demonstrated in Example 3.3 can be summarized in the following four steps which can be generalized to any situation where several scores are tied at the median.

STEP 1: Count the number of scores (boxes in the graph) below the tied value.

STEP 2: Find the number of additional scores (boxes) needed to make exactly one half of the total distribution.

STEP 3: Form a fraction:

$$\frac{\text{number of boxes needed (Step 2)}}{\text{number of tied boxes}}$$

STEP 4: Add the fraction (Step 3) to the lower real limit of the interval containing the tied scores.

LEARNING CHECK 1. Find the median for each distribution of scores:

a. 3, 10, 8, 4, 10, 7, 6

b. 13, 8, 10, 11, 12, 10

c. 3, 4, 3, 2, 1, 3, 2, 4

2. A distribution can have more than one median (true or false).

3. If you have a score of 52 on an 80-point exam, then you definitely scored above the median (true or false).

ANSWERS 1. a. The median is $X = 7$.

b. The median is $X = 10.5$.

c. The median is $X = 2.83$ (by interpolation).

2. False

3. False. The value of the median would depend on where the scores are located.

Table 3.5

Favorite restaurants named by a sample of $n = 100$ students

Caution: The mode is always a score or category, not a frequency. For this example, the mode is Luigi's, not $f = 42$.

RESTAURANT	f
College Grill	5
George & Harry's	16
Luigi's	42
Oasis Diner	18
Roxbury Inn	7
Sutter's Mill	12

SECTION 3.4   THE MODE

The final measure of central tendency that we will consider is called the mode. In its common usage, the word *mode* means "the customary fashion" or "a popular style." The statistical definition is similar in that the mode is the most common observation among a group of scores.

DEFINITION

In a frequency distribution, the *mode* is the score or category that has the greatest frequency.

The mode can be used to describe what is typical for any scale of measurement (see Chapter 1). Suppose, for example, you ask a sample of 100 students on campus to name their favorite restaurants in town. Your data might look like the results shown in Table 3.5. These are nominal data because the scale of measurement involves separate, unordered categories (restaurants). For these data, the modal response is Luigi's. This restaurant was named most frequently as a favorite place.

In a frequency distribution graph, the greatest frequency will appear as the tallest part of the figure. To find the mode, you simply identify the score located directly beneath the highest point in the distribution.

It is possible for a distribution to have more than one mode. Figure 3.5 shows the number of fish caught at various times during the day. There are two distinct peaks in this distribution, one at 6 A.M. and one at 6 P.M. Each of these values is a mode

Figure 3.5

The relationship between time of day and number of fish caught.

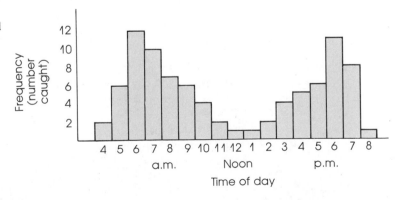

in this distribution, one at 6 A.M. and one at 6 P.M. Each of these values is a mode in the distribution. Note that the two modes do not have identical frequencies. Twelve fish were caught at 6 A.M., and 11 were caught at 6 P.M. Nonetheless, both of these points are called modes. The taller peak is called the *major mode,* and the shorter one is the *minor mode.* Of course, it also is possible to have a distribution with two (or more) separate peaks that are exactly the same height. A distribution with two modes is said to be *bimodal.* When a distribution has more than two modes, it is called *multimodal.* It also is common for a distribution with several equally high points to be described as having no mode.

1. Find the mode for the set of scores shown in the following frequency distribution table:

X	f
5	2
4	6
3	4
2	2
1	1

2. In a recent survey comparing picture quality for three brands of color televisions, 63 people preferred brand A, 29 people preferred brand B, and 58 people preferred brand C. What is the mode for this distribution?

3. What is the reason for computing a measure of central tendency?

ANSWERS

1. The mode is $X = 4$.

2. The mode is brand A.

3. The goal of central tendency is to identify a single value to represent an entire distribution.

SECTION 3.5 **SELECTING A MEASURE OF CENTRAL TENDENCY**

How do you decide which measure of central tendency to use? The answer to this question depends on several factors. Before we discuss these factors, however, it should be noted that with many sets of data it is possible to compute two or even three different measures of central tendency. Often the three measures will produce similar results, but there are situations where they will be very different (see Section 3.6). Also, it should be noted that the mean is most often the preferred measure of central tendency. Because the mean uses every score in the distribution, it usually is a good representative value. Remember, the goal of central tendency is to find the single value that best represents the entire distribution. Besides being a good representative, the mean has the added advantage of being closely related to variance and standard deviation, the most common measures of variability (Chapter 4). This relationship makes the mean a valuable measure for purposes of inferential

Figure 3.6

Major field of study for *n* = 9 students enrolled in an experimental psychology laboratory section.

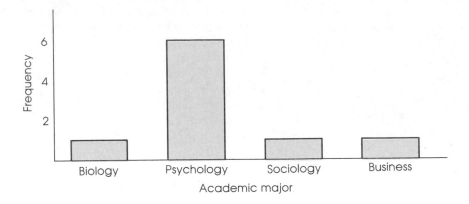

statistics. For these reasons, and others, the mean generally is considered to be the best of the three measures of central tendency. But there are specific situations where it either is impossible to compute a mean or where the mean is not particularly representative. It is in these situations that the mode and the median are used.

WHEN TO USE THE MODE

The mode has two distinct advantages over the mean. First, it is easy to compute. Second, it can be used with any scale of measurement (nominal, ordinal, interval, ratio; see Chapter 1).

It is a bit misleading to say that the mode is easy to calculate because actually no calculation is required. When the scores are arranged in a frequency distribution, you identify the mode simply by finding the score with the greatest frequency. Because the value of the mode can be determined ''at a glance,'' it is often included as a supplementary measure along with the mean or median as a no-cost extra. The value of the mode (or modes) in this situation is to give an indication of the shape of the distribution as well as a measure of central tendency. For example, if you are told that a set of exam scores has a mean of 72 and a mode of 80, you should have a better picture of the distribution than would be available from the mean alone (see Section 3.6).

The fact that the mode can be used with any scale of measurement makes it a very flexible value. When scores are measured on a nominal scale, it is impossible or meaningless to calculate either a mean or a median, so the mode is the only way to describe central tendency. Consider the frequency distribution shown in Figure 3.6. These data were obtained by recording the academic major for each student in a psychology lab section. Notice that ''academic major'' forms a nominal scale that simply classifies individuals into discrete categories.

You cannot compute a mean for these data because it is impossible to determine ΣX. (How much is one biologist plus six psychologists?) Also note that there is no natural ordering for the four categories in this distribution. It is a purely arbitrary decision to place biology on the scale before psychology. Because it is impossible to specify any order for the scores, you cannot determine a median. The mode, on the other hand, provides a very good measure of central tendency. The mode for this

Figure 3.7

Frequency distribution of errors committed before reaching learning criterion.

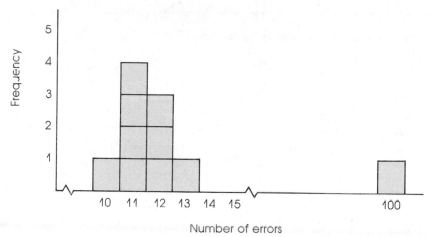

Notice that the graph in Figure 3.7 shows two *breaks* in the X-axis. Rather than listing all the scores from 0 to 100, the graph jumps directly to the first score, which is $X = 10$, and then jumps directly from $X = 15$ to $X = 100$. The breaks shown in the X-axis are the conventional way of notifying the reader that some values have been omitted.

sample is psychology. This category describes the typical, or most representative, academic major for the sample.

Because the mode identifies the most typical case, it often produces a more sensible measure of central tendency. The mean, for example, will generate conclusions such as "the average family has 2.4 children and a house with 5.33 rooms." Many people would feel more comfortable saying "the typical, or modal, family has 2 children and a house with 5 rooms" (see Box 3.1).

WHEN TO USE THE MEDIAN

There are four specific situations where the median serves as a valuable alternative to the mean. These occur when (1) there are a few extreme scores in the distribution, (2) some scores have undetermined values, (3) there is an open-ended distribution, and (4) when the data are measured on an ordinal scale.

Extreme scores or skewed distributions When a distribution has a few extreme scores, scores that are very different in value from most of the others, then the mean will not be a good representative of the majority of the distribution. The problem comes from the fact that one or two extreme values can have a large influence and cause the mean to be displaced. In this situation, the fact that the mean uses all of the scores equally can be a disadvantage. For example, suppose a sample of $n = 10$ rats is tested in a T-maze for food reward. The animals must choose the correct arm of the T (right or left) to find the food in the goal box. The experimenter records the number of errors each rat makes before it solves the maze. Hypothetical data are presented in Figure 3.7.

The mean for this sample is

$$\bar{X} = \frac{\Sigma X}{n} = \frac{203}{10} = 20.3$$

Notice that the mean is not very representative of any score in this distribution. Most of the scores are clustered between 10 and 13. The extreme score of $X = 100$ (a slow learner) inflates the value of ΣX and distorts the mean.

3.1   WHAT IS THE "AVERAGE"?

THE WORD *average* is used in everyday speech to describe what is typical and commonplace. Statistically, averages are measured by the mean, median, or mode. U.S. Government agencies frequently characterize demographic data, such as average income or average age, with the median. Winners of elections are determined by the mode, the most frequent choice. Scholastic Aptitude Test (SAT) scores for large groups of students usually are described with the mean. The important thing to remember about these measures of central tendency (or the "average") is that they describe and summarize a group of individuals rather than any single person. In fact, the "average person" may not actually exist. Figure 3.8 shows data which

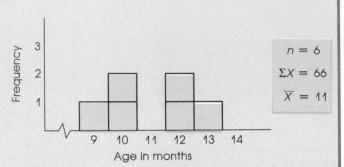

$$n = 6$$
$$\Sigma X = 66$$
$$\overline{X} = 11$$

Figure 3.9

Frequency distribution showing the age at which each infant in a sample of $n = 6$ uttered his or her first word.

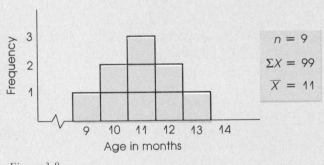

$$n = 9$$
$$\Sigma X = 99$$
$$\overline{X} = 11$$

Figure 3.8

Frequency distribution showing the age at which each infant in a sample of $n = 9$ uttered his or her first word.

were gathered from a sample of $n = 9$ infants. The age at which each infant said his/her first word was recorded by the parents. Note that the mean for this group is $\overline{X} = 11$ months and that there are three infants who uttered their first intelligible words at this age.

Now look at the results of a different study using a sample of $n = 6$ infants (Figure 3.9). Note that the mean for this group is also $\overline{X} = 11$ months but that the "average infant" does not exist in this sample.

The mean describes the group, not a single individual. It is for this reason that we find humor in statements like "the average American family has 2.4 children," fully knowing that we never will encounter this family.

The median, on the other hand, is not easily affected by extreme scores. For this sample, $n = 10$, so there should be five scores on either side of the median. The median is 11.50. Notice that this is a very representative value. Also note that the median would be unchanged even if the slow learner made 1000 errors instead of only 100. The median commonly is used when reporting the average value for a skewed distribution. For example, the distribution of personal incomes is very skewed, with a small segment of the population earning incomes that are astronomical. These extreme values distort the mean, so that it is not very representative of the salaries that most of us earn. As in the previous example, the median is the preferred measure of central tendency when extreme scores exist.

Undetermined values   Occasionally, you will encounter a situation where an individual has an unknown or undetermined score. In psychology, this often occurs

Table 3.6

Amount of time to complete puzzle

PERSON	TIME (MIN.)
1	8
2	11
3	12
4	13
5	17
6	Never finished

in learning experiments where you are measuring the number of errors (or amount of time) required for an individual to solve a particular problem. For example, suppose a sample of $n = 6$ people were asked to assemble a wooden puzzle as quickly as possible. The experimenter records how long (in minutes) it takes each individual to arrange all the pieces to complete the puzzle. Table 3.6 presents the outcome of this experiment.

Notice that person 6 never completed the puzzle. After an hour, this person still showed no sign of solving the puzzle, so the experimenter stopped him or her. This person has an undetermined score. (There are two important points to be noted. First, the experimenter should not throw out this individual's score. The whole purpose for using a sample is to gain a picture of the population, and this individual tells us that part of the population cannot solve the puzzle. Second, this person should not be given a score of $X = 60$ minutes. Even though the experimenter stopped the individual after 1 hour, the person did not finish the puzzle. The score that is recorded is the amount of time needed to finish. For this individual, we do not know how long this would be.)

It is impossible to compute the mean for these data because of the undetermined value. We cannot calculate the ΣX part of the formula for the mean. However, it is possible to compute the median. For these data the median is 12.5. Three scores are below the median, and three scores (including the undetermined value) are above the median.

Open-ended distributions A distribution is said to be *open-ended* when there is no upper limit (or lower limit) for one of the categories. The following table provides an example of an open-ended distribution, showing the number of children in each family for a sample of $n = 20$ households.

NUMBER OF CHILDREN (X)	f
5 or more	3
4	2
3	2
2	3
1	6
0	4

The top category in this distribution shows that three of the families have "5 or more" children. This in an open-ended category. Notice that it is impossible to compute a mean for these data because you cannot find ΣX (the total number of children for all 20 families). However, you can find the median. For these data, the median is 1.5 (exactly 50% of the families have fewer than 1.5 children).

Ordinal scale   Many researchers believe that it is not appropriate to use the mean to describe central tendency for ordinal data. When scores are measured on an ordinal scale, the median is always appropriate and is usually the preferred measure of central tendency. The following example demonstrates that although it is possible to compute a "mean rank," the resulting value can be misleading.

EXAMPLE 3.4   Three children held a basketball competition to see who could hit the most baskets in 10 attempts. The contest was held twice; the results are shown in the following table.

	FIRST CONTEST			SECOND CONTEST	
CHILD	RANK	NUMBER OF BASKETS	CHILD	RANK	NUMBER OF BASKETS
A	1st	10	C	1st	7
B	2nd	4	B	2nd	6
C	3rd	2	A	3rd	5

According to the data, child A finished first in one contest and third in the other, for a "mean rank" of 2. Child C also finished first one time and third one time and also has a mean rank of 2. Although these two children are identical in terms of mean rank, they are different in terms of the total number of baskets: Child A hit a total of 15 baskets and child C hit only 9. The mean rank does not reflect this difference.

SECTION 3.6   **CENTRAL TENDENCY AND THE SHAPE OF THE DISTRIBUTION**

We have identified three different measures of central tendency, and often a researcher will calculate all three for a single set of data. Because the mean, the median, and the mode are all trying to measure the same thing (central tendency), it is reasonable to expect that these three values should be related. In fact there are some consistent and predictable relationships among the three measures of central tendency. Specifically, there are situations where all three measures will have exactly the same value. On the other hand, there are situations where the three measures are guaranteed to be different. In part, the relationship between the mean, median, and mode is determined by the shape of the distribution. We will consider two general types of distributions.

Figure 3.10

Measures of central tendency for three symmetrical distributions: normal, bimodal, and rectangular.

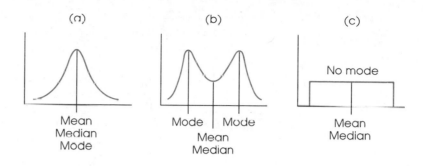

SYMMETRICAL DISTRIBUTIONS

For a *symmetrical distribution*, the right-hand side of the graph will be a mirror image of the left-hand side. By definition, the median will be exactly at the center of a symmetrical distribution because exactly half of the area in the graph will be on either side of the center. The mean also will be exactly at the center of a symmetrical distribution, because each individual score in the distribution has a corresponding score on the other side (the mirror image), so that the average of these two values is exactly in the middle. Because all the scores can be paired in this way, the overall average will be exactly at the middle. For any symmetrical distribution, the mean and the median will be the same (Figure 3.10.).

If a symmetrical distribution has only one mode, then it must be exactly at the center so that all three measures of central tendency will have the same value (see Figure 3.10). On the other hand, a bimodal distribution that is symmetrical [Figure 3.10(b)] will have the mean and median together in the center with the modes on each side. A rectangular distribution [Figure 3.10(c)] has no mode because all X values occur with the same frequency. Still, the mean and the median will be in the center of the distribution and equivalent in value.

SKEWED DISTRIBUTIONS

Distributions are not always symmetrical. In fact, quite often they are lopsided, or *skewed*. For example, Figure 3.11(a) shows a *positively skewed distribution*. In this distribution, the peak (highest frequency) is on the left-hand side. This is the position of the mode. If you examine Figure 3.11(a) carefully, it should be clear that the vertical line drawn at the mode does not divide the distribution into two equal parts. In order to have exactly 50% of the distribution on each side, the median must be located to the right of the mode. Finally, the mean will be located to the right of median because it is influenced most by extreme scores and will be displaced farthest to the right by the scores in the tail. Therefore, in a positively skewed distribution, the mean will have the largest value, followed by the median and then the mode [see Figure 3.11(a)].

Negatively skewed distributions are lopsided in the opposite direction, with the scores piling up on the right-hand side and the tail tapering off to the left. The grades on an easy exam, for example, will tend to form a negatively skewed distribution [see Figure 3.11(b)]. For a distribution with negative skew, the mode is on the right-hand side (with the peak), while the mean is displaced on the left by the extreme scores in the tail. As before, the median is located between the mean the

Figure 3.11

Measures of central tendency for skewed distributions.

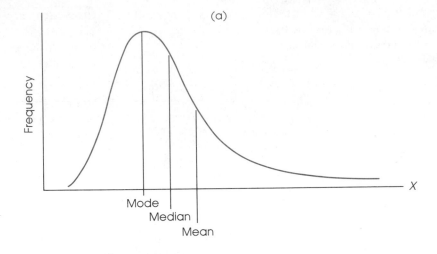

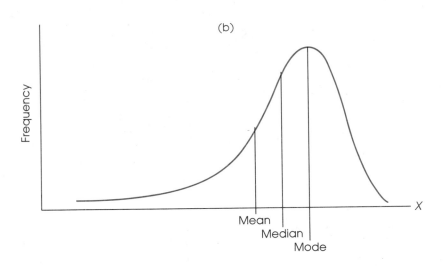

mode. In order from highest value to lowest value, the three measures of central tendency will be the mode, the median, and the mean.

SUMMARY

1. The purpose of central tendency is to determine the single value that best represents the entire distribution of scores. The three standard measures of central tendency are the mode, the median, and the mean.

2. The mean is the arithmetic average. It is computed by adding all the scores and then dividing by the number of scores. Changing any score in the distribution will cause the mean to be changed. When a constant value is added to (or subtracted from) every score in a distribution, the same constant value is added to (subtracted from) the mean. If every score is multiplied by a constant, the mean will be multiplied by the same con-

stant. In nearly all circumstances, the mean is the best representative value and is the preferred measure of central tendency.

3. The median is the value that divides a distribution exactly in half. The median is the preferred measure of central tendency when a distribution has a few extreme scores that displace the value of the mean. The median also is used when there are undetermined (infinite) scores that make it impossible to compute a mean.

4. The mode is the most frequently occurring score in a distribution. It is easily located by finding the peak in a frequency distribution graph. For data measured on a nominal scale, the mode is the appropriate measure of central tendency. It is possible for a distribution to have more than one mode.

5. For symmetrical distributions, the mean will equal the median. If there is only one mode, then it will have the same value too.

6. For skewed distributions, the mode will be located toward the side where the scores pile up, and the mean will be pulled toward the extreme scores in the tail. The median will be located between these two values.

KEY TERMS

central tendency	mode	bimodal distribution	skewed distribution
mean	major mode	multimodal distribution	positive skew
weighted mean	minor mode	symmetrical distribution	negative skew
median			

FOCUS ON PROBLEM SOLVING

1. Because there are three different measures of central tendency, your first problem is to decide which one is best for your specific set of data. Usually the mean is the preferred measure, but the median may provide a more representative value if you are working with a skewed distribution. With data measured on a nominal scale, you must use the mode.

2. Although the three measures of central tendency appear to be very simple to calculate, there is always a chance for errors. The most common sources of error are listed next.

   a. Many students find it very difficult to compute the mean for data presented in a frequency distribution table. They tend to ignore the frequencies in the table and simply average the score values listed in the X column. You must use the frequencies and the scores! Remember, the number of scores is found by $N = \Sigma f$, and the sum of all N scores is found by ΣfX.

   b. The median is the midpoint of the distribution of scores, not the midpoint of the scale of measurement. For a 100-point test, for example, many students incorrectly assume that the median must be $X = 50$. To find the median you must have the *complete set* of individual scores. The median separates the individuals into two equal-sized groups.

   c. The most common error with the mode is for students to report the highest frequency in a distribution rather than the score with the highest frequency. Remember, the purpose of central tendency is to find the most representative score. Therefore, for the following data the mode is $X = 3$, not $f = 8$.

X	f
4	3
3	8
2	5
1	2

DEMONSTRATION 3.1   COMPUTING MEASURES OF CENTRAL TENDENCY

For the following sample data, find the mean, median, and mode.

Scores: 5   6   9   11   5   11   8   14   2   11

Compute the mean. Calculating the mean involves two steps:

1. Obtain the sum of the scores, ΣX
2. Divide the sum by the number of scores, n

For these data, the sum of the scores is as follows:

$$\Sigma X = 5 + 6 + 9 + 11 + 5 + 11 + 8 + 14 + 2 + 11 = 82$$

We can also observe that $n = 10$. Therefore, the mean of this sample is obtained by

$$\bar{X} = \frac{\Sigma X}{n} = \frac{82}{10} = 8.2$$

Find the median. The median divides the distribution in half, in that half of the scores are above or equal to the median and half are below or equal to it. In this demonstration, $n = 10$. Thus, the median should be a value that has 5 scores above it and 5 scores below it.

Step 1: Arrange the scores in order.

2   5   5   6   8   9   11   11   11   14

Step 2: With an even number of scores, locate the midpoint between the middle two scores. The middle scores are $X = 8$ and $X = 9$. The median is the midpoint between 8 and 9.

$$\text{median} = \frac{8 + 9}{2} = \frac{17}{2} = 8.5$$

Find the mode. The mode is the X value that has the highest frequency. Looking at the data, we can readily determine that $X = 11$ is the score that occurs most frequently.

DEMONSTRATION 3.2   COMPUTING THE MEAN FROM A FREQUENCY DISTRIBUTION TABLE

Compute the mean for the data in the following table.

X	f
6	1
5	0
4	3
3	3
2	2

To compute the mean from a frequency distribution table, you must use the information in *both* the X and *f* columns.

STEP 1   Multiply each X value by its frequency.
You can create a third column labeled *fX*. For these data,

fX
6
0
12
9
4

STEP 2   Find the sum of the *fX* values.

$$\Sigma fX = 6 + 0 + 12 + 9 + 4 = 31$$

STEP 3   Find *n* for these data.
Remember, $n = \Sigma f$.

$$n = \Sigma f = 1 + 0 + 3 + 3 + 2 = 9$$

STEP 4   Divide the sum of *fX* by *n*.

$$\bar{X} = \frac{\Sigma fX}{n} = \frac{31}{9} = 3.44$$

PROBLEMS

1. What is meant by the following statement: The mean is the balance point of the distribution?

2. A sample has a mean of $\bar{X} = 20$. If each X value is multiplied by 6, then what is the value of the new mean?

3. A set of scores has a total of $\Sigma X = 400$ and has a mean of $\mu = 50$. How many scores are in this population?

4. A population of $N = 10$ scores has a mean of $\mu = 50$. If one of the scores is changed from $X = 60$ to $X = 80$, what will happen to the mean? Find the value for the new mean.

5. A sample of $n = 18$ children took a reading test and showed a mean score of $\bar{X} = 24$. A few days later, two children who had previously been absent took the test. Their scores were $X = 36$ and $X = 32$. What will the mean be if their scores are included with the original data?

6. A psychologist has measured how much time is required to solve a problem for each person in a sample of $n = 30$. The average time was $\bar{X} = 330$ seconds. If the psychologist converted all of the scores from seconds to minutes, what value would be obtained for the mean?

7. What is meant when it is said that the median is the *midpoint* of the distribution?

8. Describe three situations where the median is preferred over the mean as the measure of central tendency. Explain why the median is a better measure in each case.

9. Under what circumstances should the mode be used

as the measure of central tendency rather than the mean or the median.

10. For the following set of scores, sketch a frequency distribution histogram and calculate the mean, median and mode.

    10, 8, 14, 7, 10, 11,

    13, 15, 12, 9, 11, 10

11. Find the mean, median, and mode for the set of scores in the following frequency distribution table:

X	f
6	1
5	2
4	1
3	1
2	2
1	3

12. a. Find the mean, median, and mode for the scores in the following frequency distribution table. Note that you must use interpolation to find the median.
    b. Looking at the values you obtained for the mean, median, and mode, is the distribution positively or negatively skewed?

X	f
8	1
7	1
6	1
5	2
4	2
3	4
2	1

13. A distribution has a mean of 50 and a median of 43. Is it more likely that this distribution is positively skewed or negatively skewed? Explain your answer.

14. For sample of scores, $n = 6$ and $\overline{X} = 20$. If one of the scores, $X = 40$, is removed from this sample, what value will be obtained for the mean of the remaining scores?

15. Find the mean, median, and mode for the following set of scores: 2, 4, 3, 4, 1, 5, 4, 2.

16. If you change the value of a single score in a distribution, you will sometimes change the median and sometimes leave the median unaffected. Describe the circumstances where the median would change and where the median would not change.

17. The following data are quiz scores for an introductory psychology class.

    18, 21, 16, 21, 20, 17, 15

    21, 18, 22, 20, 17, 21, 19

    a. Compute the mean, median, and mode for these data.
    b. Based on the results of part a, is this distribution positively or negatively skewed?
    c. Draw a frequency distribution histogram for the data. Note the shape of distribution and compare it to your answer in part b. If parts b and c do not agree, check your computations in part a.

18. A psychologist would like to determine how many errors are made, on the average, before rats can learn a particular maze. A sample of $n = 10$ rats is obtained, and each rat is tested on the maze. The scores for the first 9 rats are as follows: 6, 2, 4, 5, 3, 7, 6, 2, 1.
    a. Calculate the mean and the median for these data. On the average, how many errors does each rat make?
    b. The tenth rat in the sample committed 100 errors before mastering the maze. When this rat is included in the sample, what happens to the mean? What happens to the median? What general conclusion can be drawn from this result?

19. In a problem-solving experiment with $n = 100$ children, 5 of the children failed to complete the problem within 10 minutes and were simply marked as "failed." If the experimenter wanted to find a measure of central tendency to describe the "average" amount of time needed to complete the problem, what measure should be used? Explain your answer.

20. Four students have part-time jobs in the same store. The mean weekly pay for these students is $30, and the median weekly pay is $25.
    a. If one of the students gets a $10 raise, what is the new mean?
    b. If one of the students gets a $10 raise, what is the new median? (Be careful and explain your answer.)

c. If one student gets a $10 raise and another gets a $20 raise, what is the new mean?

d. If the student with the highest salary gets a $10 raise, what is the new median?

21. The final exam grades for two sections of the same course are reported as follows:

Section I: $n = 30, \bar{X} = 63$

Section II: $n = 70, \bar{X} = 78$

If both sections are combined, what is the average grade for the entire set of students?

22. A 20-point quiz is given to each of two sections of an introductory statistics class. The scores for each section are as follows:

Section I: 6,   5,   5,   7,   17,   5,   6,   5

Section II: 9,   8,   10,   7,   8,
9,   1,   0,   9,   9

a. Sketch a histogram showing the distribution of scores for section I.

b. Sketch a histogram showing the distribution for section II.

c. Looking at your graphs, which section would you say had better scores?

d. Calculate the mean and the median for each section. Which measure of central tendency best describes the difference between these two distributions?

23. To evaluate teaching effectiveness, a professor measures each student's attitude toward psychology at the beginning of the course and again at the end. For each person, the change in attitude is computed. A positive score means that the person's opinion of psychology went up; a negative score means that the person's opinion went down. The scores are as follows:

−12,   31,   20,   1,   4,   12,   13,
−6,   7,   −9,   11,   −4,   10,   0,
3,   6,   2,   −18,   −2,   21,   9

a. Compute the mean change for this sample of $n = 21$ students.

b. Because the professor does not like to work with negative numbers, 20 points are added to each score and then the mean is calculated. How should

this mean compare with the value you obtained in part a? Exactly what value should be obtained?

24. A school psychologist has computed the average IQ for a sample of $n = 99$ children and obtained a mean of $\bar{X} = 104$. If one additional student with an IQ of 133 is included in this sample, what will the average IQ be for the entire group of 100 students?

25. A professor teaches a morning class of $n = 61$ students and an afternoon class of $n = 34$. The same test is given to both classes. The mean for the morning group is $\bar{X} = 44.1$, and the mean for the afternoon group is $\bar{X} = 50.3$. If the two classes are combined, what is the mean for the entire group of students?

26. A psychologist is collecting attitude scores for high school students as part as an experiment. Because the testing room will hold only 15 people, the students are tested in three separate groups. The data for these three groups are as follows:

Group 1: $n = 15, \bar{X} = 46.5$

Group 2: $n = 14, \bar{X} = 43.2$

Group 3: $n = 11, \bar{X} = 50.9$

Find the overall mean for the entire group of high school students.

27. Reaction time data for a sample of $n = 15$ subjects are as follows:

1.0,   .9,   1.2,   1.3,   .9,   .8,   1.0,

.7,   .9,   1.1,   .7,   1.2,   1.0,   1.1,   .8

Find the mean and the median for these scores. (*Hint:* If you first multiply each score by 10, you will get rid of the decimals.)

28. The Jones & Jones Corporation is currently involved in negotiations with the employees' labor union. The hourly wages for the 20 employees at Jones & Jones are as follows:

HOURLY WAGES			
8.50	7.40	7.25	12.00
7.50	8.00	8.55	7.30
7.00	11.00	9.50	7.25
8.20	7.10	10.50	9.00
9.50	7.10	7.25	8.50

The union and the company both have access to these figures. The statewide average hourly wage for this type of industry is $8.25.

a. Calculate the mean and the median hourly wage for the Jones & Jones employees.

b. If you were a company official arguing that the present salaries are reasonable, which measure of central tendency would you prefer? Using this measure, how does the ''average'' wage at Jones & Jones compare with the statewide average?

c. If you were a union official arguing for a salary increase, which measure of central tendency would you prefer? How does this ''average'' compare with the statewide average?

29. On a standardized reading achievement test, the nationwide average for seventh grade children is $\mu = 7.00$. A seventh-grade teacher is interested in comparing class reading scores with the national average. The scores for 16 students are as follows:

6.5, 7.2, 7.8, 7.2, 6.8, 7.1, 8.3, 6.9

8.2, 7.4, 6.2, 6.8, 7.3, 6.2, 8.1, 7.0,

Calculate the mean for this class. On the average, how does this class compare with the national norm?

CHAPTER 4

VARIABILITY

SECTION 4.1 **INTRODUCTION**

The term *variability* has much the same meaning in statistics as it has in everyday language; to say that things are variable means that they are not all the same. In statistics our goal is to measure the amount of variability for a particular set of scores, a distribution. In simple terms, if the scores in a distribution are all the same, then there is no variability. If there are small differences between scores, then the variability is small, and if there are big differences between scores, then the variability is large.

DEFINITION   *Variability* provides a quantitative measure of the degree to which scores in a distribution are spread out or clustered together.

The purpose of measuring variability is to determine how spread out a distribution of scores is. Are the scores all clustered together, or are they scattered over a wide range of values? A good measure of variability should provide an accurate picture of the spread of the distribution. Variability, along with central tendency and shape, is one of the three basic descriptive indices that are used to describe distributions of scores.

In addition to providing a description of the distribution, a good measure of variability also serves two other valuable purposes. First, variability gives an indication of how accurately the mean describes the distribution. If the variability is small, then the scores are all close together, and each individual score is close to the mean. In this situation, the mean is a good representative of all the scores in the distribution. On the other hand, when variability is large, the scores are all spread out, and they are not necessarily close to the mean. In this case, the mean may be less representative of the whole distribution. To make this point more concrete, consider the two ''games of chance'' described in Box 4.1.

The second valuable purpose served by a good measure of variability is to give an indication of how well an individual score (or group of scores) represents the entire distribution. For example, there are occasions when the population mean is unknown. In these situations, a sample is selected from the population, and the sample is then used to represent the entire distribution. This is particularly important in the area of inferential statistics where relatively small samples are used to answer general questions about large populations. If the scores in a distribution are all clustered together (small variability), then any individual score will be a reasonably accurate representative of the entire distribution. But if the scores are all spread out, then a single value selected from the distribution often will not be representative of the rest of the group. This point also is illustrated in Box 4.1.

In this chapter we will consider three different measures of variability: the range, the interquartile range, and the standard deviation. Of these three, the standard deviation (and the related measure of variance) is by far the most important.

SECTION 4.2 **THE RANGE**

The range is the distance between the largest score (X_{max}) and the smallest score in the distribution (X_{min}). In determining this distance, you must also take into account

4.1 AN EXAMPLE OF VARIABILITY

TO EXAMINE the role of variability, we will consider two games of chance.

For the first game you pay $1 to play, and you get back 90 cents every time. That's right, you pay me $1, and I give you back 90¢. Notice that this game has no variability; exactly the same thing happens every time. On the average, you lose 10¢ each time you play, and, in this case, the average gives a perfect description of the outcome of the game.

For the second game the rules are a little different. It still costs $1 to play, but this time you have a 1-out-of-10 chance of winning $9. The rest of the time you win nothing. For this second game we have added variability; the outcomes are not all the same. Notice, however, that in the long run you still lose 10¢ each time you play. In 10 games, for example, you would expect to win once ($9), but you would have paid $10 to play. You expect to lose $1 during 10 games, for an average loss of 10¢ per game.

On the average these two games are identical. But in one case the average perfectly describes every single outcome, and in the other case the average is not at all representative of what actually happens on any single trial. The difference between these two games is the variability.

You also should notice the number of times you would need to watch each game in order to understand it. For the first game, any individual outcome (pay $1 and get back 90¢) gives a complete description of the game. After only one observation, you know the entire game. For the second game, however, you would need to watch a long time before the nature of the game became clear. In this case it would take a large sample to provide a good description of the game.

the real limits of the maximum and minimum X values. The range, therefore, is computed as the difference between the upper real limit (URL) for X_{max} and the lower real limit (LRL) for X_{min}.

$$\text{range} = \text{URL } X_{max} - \text{LRL } X_{min}$$

DEFINITION

The *range* is the difference between the upper real limit for the largest (maximum) X value and the lower real limit of the smallest (minimum) X value.

For example, consider the following data:

3   7   12   8   5   10

For these data, $X_{max} = 12$ with an upper real limit of 12.5, and $X_{min} = 3$ with a lower real limit of 2.5. Thus the range equals

When the distribution consists of whole numbers, the range also can be obtained as follows: range = highest X − lowest X + 1.

$$\text{range} = \text{URL } X_{max} - \text{LRL } X_{min}$$
$$= 12.5 - 2.5 = 10$$

The range is perhaps the most obvious way of describing how spread out the scores are—simply find the distance between the maximum and minimum scores. The problem with using the range as a measure of variability is that it is completely determined by the two extreme values and ignores the other scores in the distribution. For example, the following two distributions have exactly the same range; 10 points in each case. However, the scores in the first distribution are clustered together at one end of the range, whereas the scores in the second distribution are spread out over the entire range.

Distribution 1:   1,   8,   9,   9,   10,   10

Distribution 2:   1,   2,   4,   6,   8,   10

If, for example, these were scores on a 10-point quiz for two different class sections, there are clear differences between the two sections. Nearly all the students in the first section have mastered the material, but there is a wide range of different abilities for students in the second section. A good measure of variability should show this difference.

Because the range does not consider all the scores in the distribution, it often does not give an accurate description of the variability for the entire distribution. For this reason, the range is considered to be a crude and unreliable measure of variability.

SECTION 4.3

THE INTERQUARTILE RANGE AND SEMI-INTERQUARTILE RANGE

In Chapter 3 we defined the median as the score that divides a distribution exactly in half. In a similar way, a distribution can be divided into four equal parts using quartiles. By definition, the first quartile ($Q1$) is the score that separates the lower 25% of the distribution from the rest. The second quartile ($Q2$) is the score that has exactly two quarters, or 50%, of the distribution below it. Notice that the second quartile and the median are the same. Finally, the third quartile ($Q3$) is the score that divides the bottom three-fourths of the distribution from the top quarter. The interquartile range is defined as the distance between the first and third quartiles. The semi-interquartile range is one-half of the interquartile range. It provides a descriptive measure of the "typical" distance of scores from the median ($Q2$).

DEFINITIONS

The *interquartile range* is the distance between the first quartile and the third quartile:

$$\text{interquartile range} = Q3 - Q1$$

When the interquartile range is used to describe variability, it commonly is transformed into the *semi-interquartile range*. The semi-interquartile range is simply one-half of the interquartile range:

$$\text{semi-interquartile range} = \frac{(Q3 - Q1)}{2}$$

EXAMPLE 4.1

Figure 4.1 shows a frequency distribution histogram for a set of 16 scores. For this distribution the first quartile is $Q1 = 4.5$. Exactly 25% of the scores (4 out of 16) are located below $X = 4.5$. Similarly, the third quartile is $Q3 =$

Figure 4.1

Frequency distribution for a population of $N = 16$ scores. The first quartile is $Q1 = 4.5$. The third quartile is $Q3 = 8.0$. The interquartile range is 3.5 points. Note that the third quartile ($Q3$) divides the two boxes at $X = 8$ exactly in half, so that a total of 4 boxes are above $Q3$ and 12 boxes are below it.

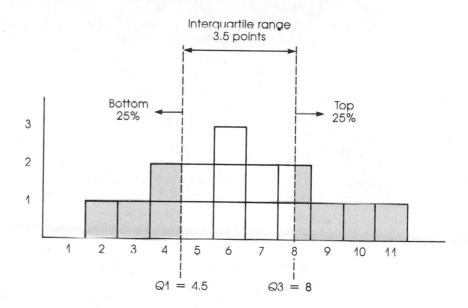

8.0. Note that this value separates the bottom 75% of the distribution (12 out of 16 scores) from the top 25%. For this set of scores the interquartile range is

$$Q3 - Q1 = 8.0 - 4.5 = 3.5$$

The semi-interquartile range is simply one-half of this distance:

$$\text{semi-interquartile range} = \frac{3.5}{2} = 1.75$$

Because the semi-interquartile range focuses on the middle 50% of a distribution, it is less likely to be influenced by extreme scores and, therefore, gives a better and more stable measure of variability than the range. Nevertheless, the semi-interquartile range does not take into account the actual distances between individual scores, so it does not give a complete picture of how scattered or clustered the scores are. Like the range, the semi-interquartile range is considered to be a somewhat crude measure of variability. In chapter 6 we will introduce another method to determine the semi-interquartile range for normal distributions.

LEARNING CHECK **1.** For the following data, find the range and the semi-interquartile range.

3,   4,   5,   7,   9,   10,   11,   13

2. Consider the distribution of exercise 1, except replace the score of 13 with a score of 100. What are the new values for the range and the semi-interquartile range? In comparing the answer to the one of the previous problem, what can you conclude about these measures of variability?

1. Range = URL X_{max} − LRL X_{min} = 13.5 − 2.5 = 11; Semi-interquartile range = $(Q3 − Q1)/2 = (10.5 − 4.5)/2 = 3$.

2. Range = 98, semi-interquartile range = 3. The range is greatly affected by extreme scores in the distribution.

S E C T I O N   4 . 4   **STANDARD DEVIATION AND VARIANCE FOR A POPULATION**

The standard deviation is the most commonly used and the most important measure of variability. Standard deviation uses the mean of the distribution as a reference point and measures variability by considering the distance between each score and the mean. It determines whether the scores are generally near or far from the mean. That is, are the scores clustered together or scattered? In simple terms, the standard deviation approximates the average distance from the mean.

Although the concept of standard deviation is straightforward, the actual equations will appear complex. Therefore, we will begin by looking at the logic that leads to these equations. If you remember that our goal is to measure the standard or typical, distance from the mean, then this logic and the equations that follow should be easier to remember.

STEP 1 The first step in finding the standard distance from the mean is to determine the deviation, or distance from the mean, for each individual score. By definition, the deviation for each score is the difference between the score and the mean.

DEFINITION   *Deviation* is distance from the mean:

$$\text{deviation score} = X − \mu$$

A deviation score occasionally is identified by a lowercase letter x.

For a distribution of scores with $\mu = 50$, if your score is $X = 53$, then your deviation score is

$$X − \mu = 53 − 50 = 3$$

If your score were $X = 45$, then your deviation score would be

$$X − \mu = 45 − 50 = −5$$

Notice that there are two parts to a deviation score: the sign (+ or −) and the number. The sign tells the direction from the mean, that is, whether the score is located above (+) or below (−) the mean. The number gives the actual distance from the mean. For example, a deviation score of −6 corresponds to score that is below the mean by six points.

STEP 2 Because our goal is to compute a measure of the standard distance from the mean, the obvious next step is to calculate the mean of the deviation scores. To compute this mean, you first add up the deviation scores and then divide by N. This process is demonstrated in the following example.

EXAMPLE 4.2 We start with the following set of $N = 4$ scores. These scores add up to $\Sigma X = 12$, so the mean is $\mu = \frac{12}{4} = 3$. For each score we have computed the deviation.

X	$X - \mu$
8	+5
1	−2
3	0
0	−3
	$0 = \Sigma(X - \mu)$

Remember, the mean is the balancing point for the distribution.

Notice that the deviation scores add up to zero. This should not be surprising if you remember that the mean serves as a balance point for the distribution. The distances above the mean are equal to the distances below the mean (see page 53). Logically, the deviation scores must *always* add up to zero.

Because the mean deviation is always zero, it is of no value as a measure of variability. It is zero whether the scores are grouped together or are all scattered out. The mean deviation score provides no information about variability. (You should note, however, that the constant value of zero can be useful in other ways. Whenever you are working with deviation scores, you can check your calculations by making sure that the deviation scores add up to zero.)

STEP 3 The reason that the average of the deviation scores will not work as a measure of variability is that it is always zero. Clearly, this problem results from the positive and negative values canceling each other out. The solution is to get rid of the signs (+ and −). The standard procedure for accomplishing this is to square each deviation score. Using these squared values, you then compute the average squared deviation, which is called variance.

DEFINITION *Population variance* = average squared deviation. Variance is the mean of the squared deviation scores.

Note that the process of squaring deviation scores does more than simply get rid of plus and minus signs. It results in a measure of variability based on *squared* distances. Although variance is valuable for some of the *inferential* statistical methods covered later, the average squared distance is not the best *descriptive* measure for variability.

STEP 4 Remember that our goal is to compute a measure of the standard distance from the mean. Variance, the average squared deviation, is not exactly what we want. The final step simply makes a correction for having squared all the distances. The new measure, the standard deviation, is the square root of the variance.

DEFINITION *Standard deviation* $= \sqrt{\text{variance}}$.

Technically, standard deviation is the square root of the mean squared deviation. But conceptually, standard deviation is easier to understand if you think of it as describing the typical distance of scores from the mean (that is, the typical $X - \mu$). As the name implies, standard deviation measures the standard, or typical, deviation score.

The concept of standard deviation (or variance) is the same for a sample as for a population. However, the details of the calculations differ slightly, depending on whether you have sample data or a complete population. Therefore, we will first consider the formulas for measures of population variability.

SUM OF SQUARED DEVIATIONS (SS)

Variance, you should recall, is defined as the mean squared deviation. This average is computed exactly the same way you compute any mean: First find the sum; then divide by the number of scores:

$$\text{variance} = \text{average squared deviation} = \frac{\text{sum of squared deviations}}{\text{number of scores}}$$

The value in the numerator of this equation, the sum of the squared deviations, is a basic component of variability, and we will focus on it. To simplify things, it is identified by the notation SS (for sum of squared deviations), and it generally is referred to as the *sum of squares*.

DEFINITION SS, or *sum of squares*, is the sum of the squared deviation scores.

There are two formulas you will need to know in order to compute SS. These formulas are algebraically equivalent (they always produce the same answer), but they look different and are used in different situations.

The first of these formulas is called the definitional formula because the terms in the formula literally define the process of adding up the squared deviations:

$$\text{Definitional formula:} \quad SS = \Sigma(X - \mu)^2 \tag{4.1}$$

Note that the formula directs you to square each deviation score $(X - \mu)^2$ and then add them. The result is the sum of the squared deviations, or SS. Following is an example using this formula.

EXAMPLE 4.3

We will compute SS for the following set of $N = 4$ scores. These scores have a sum of $\Sigma X = 8$, so the mean is $\mu = \frac{8}{4} = 2$. For each score, we have computed the deviation and the squared deviation. The squared deviations add up to $SS = 22$.

Caution: The definitional formula requires that you first square the deviations and then add them.

X	$X - \mu$	$(X - \mu)^2$	
1	-1	1	$\Sigma X = 8$
0	-2	4	$\mu = 2$
6	$+4$	16	
1	-1	1	
		$\overline{22} = \Sigma(X - \mu)^2$	

The second formula for SS is called the computational formula (or the machine formula) because it works directly with the scores (X values) and, therefore, is generally easier to use for calculations, especially with an electronic calculator:

$$\text{Computational formula:} \quad SS = \Sigma X^2 - \frac{(\Sigma X)^2}{N}$$

(4.2)

The first part of this formula directs you to square each score and then add them up (ΣX^2). The second part requires you to add up the scores (ΣX) and then square this total and divide the result by N (see Box 4.2). The use of this formula is shown in Example 4.4 with the same set of scores we used for the definitional formula.

EXAMPLE 4.4 The computational formula is used to calculate SS for the same set of $N = 4$ scores we used in Example 4.3. First, compute ΣX. Then square each score and compute ΣX^2. These two values are used in the formula.

X	X^2	
1	1	$\Sigma X = 8$
0	0	
6	36	$\Sigma X^2 = 38$
1	1	

$$SS = \Sigma X^2 - \frac{(\Sigma X)^2}{N}$$

$$= 38 - \frac{(8)^2}{4}$$

$$= 38 - \frac{64}{4}$$

$$= 38 - 16$$

$$= 22$$

Notice that the two formulas produce exactly the same value for SS. Although the formulas look different, they are in fact equivalent. The definitional formula should be very easy to learn if you simply remember that SS stands for the sum of the squared deviations. If you use notation to write out "the sum of" (Σ) "squared deviations" $(X - \mu)^2$, then you have the definitional formula. Unfortunately, the terms in the computational formula do not translate directly into "sum of squared deviations," so you simply need to memorize this formula.

The definitional formula for SS is the most direct way of calculating sum of squares, but it can be awkward to use for most sets of data. In particular, if the mean is not a whole number, then the deviation scores will all be fractions or decimals, and the calculations become difficult. In addition, calculations with decimals or fractions introduce the opportunity for rounding error, which makes the results less

4.2　COMPUTING *SS* WITH A CALCULATOR

THE COMPUTATIONAL formula for *SS* is intended to simplify calculations, especially when you are using an electronic calculator. The following steps outline the most efficient procedure for using a typical, inexpensive hand calculator to find *SS*. (We assume that your calculator has one memory, where you can store and retrieve information.) The computational formula for *SS* is presented here for easy reference.

$$SS = \Sigma X^2 - \frac{(\Sigma X)^2}{N}$$

STEP 1: The first term in the computational formula is ΣX^2. The procedure for finding this sum is described in Box 1.1 on page 18. Once you have calculated ΣX^2, write this sum on a piece of paper so you don't lose it. Leave ΣX^2 in the calculator memory and go to the next step.

STEP 2: Now you must find the sum of the scores, ΣX. We assume that you can add a set of numbers with your calculator—just be sure to press the equals key (=) after the last score. Write this total on your paper.

　(*Note:* You may want to clear the calculator display before you begin this process. It is not necessary, but you may feel more comfortable starting with zero.)

STEP 3: Now you are ready to plug the sums into the formula. Your calculator should still have the sum of the scores, ΣX, in the display. If not, enter this value.

1. With ΣX in the display, you can compute $(\Sigma X)^2$ simply by pressing the multiply key ($\times$) and then the equals key (=).

2. Now you must divide the squared sum by N, the number of scores. Assuming that you have counted the number of scores, just press the divide key ($\div$), enter N, and then press the equals key.

Your calculator display now shows $(\Sigma X)^2/N$. Write this number on your paper.

3. Finally, you subtract the value of your calculator display from ΣX^2, which is in the calculator memory. You can do this by simply pressing the memory subtract key (usually M−). The value for *SS* is now in memory, and you can retrieve it by pressing the memory recall key (MR).

Try the whole procedure with a simple set of scores such as 1, 2, 3. You should obtain *SS* = 2 for these scores.
　We asked you to write values at several steps during the calculation in case you make a mistake at some point. If you have written the values for ΣX^2, ΣX, and so on, you should be able to compute *SS* easily even if the contents of memory were lost.

---

accurate. For these reasons, the computational formula is used most of the time. If you have a small group of scores and the mean is a whole number, then the definitional formula is fine; otherwise, use the computational formula.

FORMULAS FOR POPULATION STANDARD DEVIATION AND VARIANCE

In the same way that sum of squares, or *SS*, is used to refer to the sum of squared deviations, the term *mean square*, or *MS*, is often used to refer to variance which is the mean squared deviation.

With the definition and calculation of *SS* behind you, the equations for variance and standard deviation become relatively simple. Remember, variance is defined as the average squared deviation. The average is the sum divided by N, *so the equation* for variance is

$$variance = \frac{SS}{N}$$

　Standard deviation is the square root of variance, so the equation for standard deviation is

$$\text{standard deviation} = \sqrt{\frac{SS}{N}}$$

There is one final bit of notation before we work completely through an example computing SS, variance, and standard deviation. Like the mean (μ), variance and standard deviation are parameters of a population and will be identified by Greek letters. To identify the standard deviation, we use the Greek letter sigma (the Greek letter s, standing for standard deviation). The capital letter sigma (Σ) has been used already, so we now use the lowercase sigma, σ:

$$\text{population standard deviation} = \sigma = \sqrt{\frac{SS}{N}} \qquad (4.3)$$

The symbol for population variance should help you remember the relation between standard deviation and variance. If you square the standard deviation, you will get the variance. The symbol for variance is sigma squared, σ^2:

$$\text{population variance} = \sigma^2 = \frac{SS}{N} \qquad (4.4)$$

EXAMPLE 4.5 The following population of scores will be used to demonstrate the calculation of SS, variance, and standard deviation:

$$1, \quad 9, \quad 5, \quad 8, \quad 7$$

These five scores add up to $\Sigma X = 30$, so the mean is $\frac{30}{5} = 6$. Before we do any other calculations, remember that the purpose of variability is to determine how spread out the scores are. Standard deviation accomplishes this by providing a measurement of the standard distance from the mean. The scores we are working with have been placed in a frequency distribution histogram in Figure 4.2 so you can see the variability more easily. Note that the score closest to the mean is $X = 5$ or $X = 7$, both of which are only 1 point away. The score farthest from the mean is $X = 1$, and it is 5 points away. For this distribution, the biggest distance from the mean is five points, and the small-

Figure 4.2

A frequency distribution histogram for a population of $N = 5$ scores. The mean for this population is $\mu = 6$. The smallest distance from the mean is one point, and the largest distance is 5 points. The standard distance (or standard deviation) should be between 1 and 5 points.

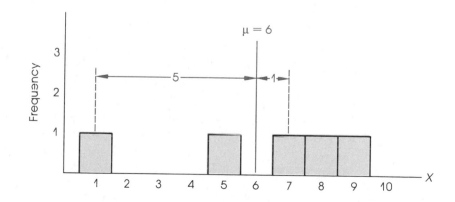

est distance is one point. The typical, or standard, distance should be somewhere between 1 and 5. By looking quickly at a distribution in this way, you should be able to make a rough estimate of the standard deviation. In this case, the standard deviation should be between 1 and 5, probably around 3 points. Making a preliminary judgment of standard deviation can help you avoid errors in calculation. If, for example, you worked through the formulas and ended up with a value of $\sigma = 12$, you should realize immediately that you have made an error. (If the biggest deviation is only 5 points, then it is impossible for the standard deviation to be 12.)

Now we will start the calculations. The first step is to find SS for this set of scores.

Because the mean is a whole number ($\mu = 6$), we can use the definitional formula for SS:

X	$X - \mu$	$(X - \mu)^2$	
1	−5	25	$\Sigma X = 30$
9	+3	9	$\mu = 6$
5	−1	1	
8	+2	4	
7	+1	1	
		$40 = \Sigma(X - \mu)^2 = SS$	

$$\sigma^2 = \frac{SS}{N}$$

$$= \frac{40}{5} = 8$$

$$\sigma = \sqrt{8} = 2.83$$

For this set of scores, the variance is $\sigma^2 = 8$, and the standard deviation is $\sigma = \sqrt{8} = 2.83$. Note that the value for the standard deviation is in excellent agreement with our preliminary estimate of the standard distance from the mean.

LEARNING CHECK

1. Write brief definitions of variance and standard deviation.

2. Find SS, variance, and standard deviation for the following population of scores: 10, 10, 10, 10, 10. (*Note:* You should be able to answer this question without doing any calculations.)

3. **a.** Sketch a frequency distribution histogram for the following population of scores: 1, 3, 3, 9. Using this histogram, make an estimate of the standard deviation (i.e., the standard distance from the mean.)

   b. Calculate SS, variance, the standard deviation for these scores. How well does your estimate from part a compare with the real standard deviation?

ANSWERS **1.** Variance is the average squared distance from the mean. Standard deviation is the square root of variance and provides a measure of the standard distance from the mean.

2. Because there is no variability in the population, *SS*, variance, and standard deviation are all equal to zero.

3. a. Your sketch should show a mean of $\mu = 4$. The score closest to the mean is $X = 3$, and the farthest score is $X = 9$. The standard deviation should be somewhere between one point and five points.

b. For this population, $SS = 36$; the variance is $\frac{36}{4} = 9$; the standard deviation is $\sqrt{9} = 3$.

GRAPHIC REPRESENTATION OF THE MEAN AND STANDARD DEVIATION

In frequency distribution graphs we will identify the position of the mean by drawing a vertical line and labeling it with μ or $\overline{X}$ (see Figure 4.3). Because the standard deviation measures distance from the mean, it will be represented by a line drawn from the mean outward for a distance equal to the standard deviation (see Figure 4.3). For rough sketches, you can identify the mean with a vertical line in the middle of the distribution. The standard deviation line should extend approximately halfway from the mean to the most extreme score.

SECTION 4.5 STANDARD DEVIATION AND VARIANCE FOR SAMPLES

The goal of inferential statistics is to use the limited information from samples to draw general conclusions about populations. The basic assumption of this process is that samples should be representative of the populations from which they come. This assumption poses a special problem for variability because samples consistently tend to be less variable then their populations. An example of this general tendency is shown in Figure 4.4. The fact that a sample tends to be less variable than its population means that sample variability gives a *biased* estimate of population variability. This bias is in the direction of underestimating the population value rather than being right on the mark. To correct for this bias, it is necessary to make an adjustment in the calculation of variability when you are working with sample data. The intent of the adjustment is to make the resulting value for sample variability a more accurate estimate of the population variability.

A sample statistic is said to be *biased* if, on the average, it does not provide an accurate estimate of the corresponding population parameter.

Figure 4.3

The graphic representation of a population with a mean of $\mu = 40$ and a standard deviation of $\sigma = 4$.

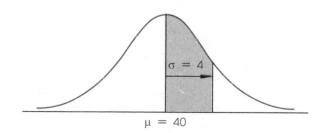

$\sigma = 4$

$\mu = 40$

Figure 4.4

The population of adult heights forms a normal distribution. If you select a sample from this population, you are most likely to obtain individuals who are near average in height. As a result, the scores in the sample will be less variable (spread out) than the scores in the population.

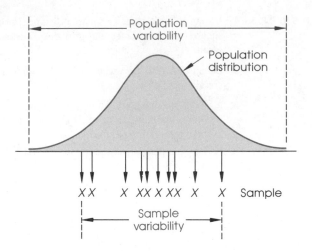

To compute sample variability, we begin by defining the deviation for each score in the sample. As before, deviation measures the distance from the mean, but now we are using the sample mean in place of the population mean:

$$\text{sample deviation score} = X - \overline{X} \tag{4.5}$$

The deviation scores will have a sign and a magnitude. The sign tells the direction from the mean ($+$ for above, $-$ for below), and the magnitude tells the distance from the mean. The deviation scores always add up to zero.

Variance and standard deviation for sample data have the same basic definitions as they do for populations: Variance measures the average squared distance from the mean, and standard deviation is the square root of variance. To compute the values, we first will need to find *SS,* the sum of squared deviations. The formulas we use to compute sample *SS* are essentially identical to the formulas used for populations:

$$\text{Definitional formula:}\quad SS = \Sigma(X - \overline{X})^2 \tag{4.6}$$

$$\text{Computational formula:}\quad SS = \Sigma X^2 - \frac{(\Sigma X)^2}{n} \tag{4.7}$$

Note that the only difference between these formulas and the population formulas is a minor change in notation. We have substituted $\overline{X}$ in place of μ and n in place of N. For all practical purposes the population and sample formulas for *SS* are interchangeable. The difference in notation will have no effect on the calculations.

After you compute *SS,* however, it becomes critical to differentiate between samples and populations. To correct for the bias in sample variability, it is necessary to make an adjustment in the formulas for sample variance and standard deviation. With this in mind, sample variance (identified by the symbol s^2) is defined as

$$\text{sample variance} = s^2 = \frac{SS}{n - 1} \tag{4.8}$$

Sample standard deviation (identified by the symbol s) is simply the square root of the variance.

$$\text{sample standard deviation} = s = \sqrt{\frac{SS}{n - 1}} \tag{4.9}$$

Figure 4.5

The frequency distribution histogram for a sample of $n = 7$ scores. The sample mean is $\overline{X} = 5$. The smallest distance from the mean is 1 point, and the largest distance from the mean is 4 points. The standard distance (standard deviation) should be between 1 and 4 points.

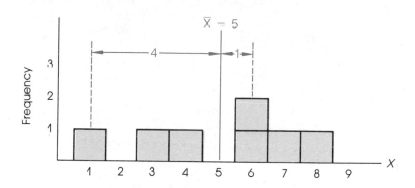

Remember, sample variability tends to underestimate population variability unless some correction is made.

Notice that these sample formulas use $n - 1$ instead of n. This is the adjustment that is necessary to correct for the bias in sample variability. The effect of the adjustment is to increase the value you will obtain. Dividing by a smaller number ($n - 1$ instead of n) produces a larger result and makes sample variability an accurate, or unbiased, estimator of population variability.

A complete example showing the calculation of sample variance and standard deviation will now be worked out.

EXAMPLE 4.6 We have selected a sample of $n = 7$ scores from a population. The scores are 1, 6, 4, 3, 8, 7, 6. The frequency distribution histogram for this sample is shown in Figure 4.5. Before we begin any calculations, you should be able to look at the sample distribution and make a preliminary estimate of the outcome. Remember that standard deviation measures the standard distance from the mean. For this sample the mean is $\overline{X} = 5$ ($\frac{35}{7} = 5$). The scores closest to the mean are $X = 4$ and $X = 6$, both of which are exactly 1 point away. The score farthest from the mean is $X = 1$, which is 4 points away. With the smallest distance from the mean equal to 1 and the largest distance equal to 4, we should obtain a standard distance somewhere around 2.5 (between 1 and 4).

Now let's begin the calculations. First, we will find SS for this sample. Because there are only a few scores and the mean is a whole number, the definitional formula will be easy to use. You should try this formula for practice. Meanwhile, we will work with the computational formula.

X	X^2	
1	1	$\Sigma X = 35$
6	36	$\Sigma X^2 = 211$
4	16	
3	9	
8	64	
7	49	
6	36	

Caution: For sample variance, you use $n - 1$ after calculating SS. Do not use $n - 1$ in the formula for SS.

$$SS = \Sigma X^2 - \frac{(\Sigma X)^2}{n}$$

$$= 211 - \frac{(35)^2}{7}$$

$$= 211 - \frac{1225}{7}$$

$$= 211 - 175$$

$$= 36$$

SS for this sample is 36. You should obtain exactly the same answer using the definitional formula. Continuing the calculations,

$$\text{sample variance} = s^2 = \frac{SS}{n - 1} = \frac{36}{7 - 1} = 6$$

Finally, the standard deviation is

$$s = \sqrt{s^2} = \sqrt{6} = 2.45$$

Note that the value we obtained is in excellent agreement with our preliminary prediction.

Remember that the formulas for sample variance and standard deviation were constructed so that the sample variability would provide a good estimate of population variability. For this reason, sample variance is often called *estimated population variance,* and the sample standard deviation is called *estimated population standard deviation.* When you have only a sample to work with, the sample variance and standard deviation provide the best possible estimates of the population variability.

LEARNING CHECK

1. **a.** Sketch a frequency distribution histogram for the following sample of scores: 1, 1, 9, 1. Using your histogram, make an estimate of the standard deviation for this sample.

   b. Calculate SS, variance, and standard deviation for this sample. How well does your estimate from part a compare with the real standard deviation?

2. If the scores in the previous exercise were a population, what value would you obtain for SS?

3. If the scores in exercise 1 were a population, would you obtain a larger or smaller value for the standard deviation? Explain your answer.

ANSWERS

1. **a.** Your graph should show a sample mean of $\bar{X} = 3$. The score farthest from the mean is $X = 9$, and the closest score is $X = 1$. You should estimate the standard deviation to be between two points and six points.

   b. For this sample, $SS = 48$; the sample variance is $\frac{48}{3} = 16$; the sample standard deviation is $\sqrt{16} = 4$.

2. $SS = 48$ whether the data are from a sample or a population.

3. Smaller. The formulas for sample data increase the size of variance and standard deviation by dividing by $n - 1$ instead of N. The population formulas will produce smaller values.

SAMPLE VARIABILITY AND DEGREES OF FREEDOM

Although the concept of a deviation score and the calculation of SS are almost exactly the same for samples and populations, the minor differences in notation are really very important. When you have only a sample to work with, you must use the sample mean as the reference point for measuring deviations. Using $\overline{X}$ in place of μ places a restriction on the amount of variability in the sample. The restriction on variability comes from the fact that you must know the value of $\overline{X}$ before you can begin to compute deviations or SS. Notice that if you know the value of $\overline{X}$, then you also must know the value of ΣX. For example, if you have a sample of $n = 3$ scores and you know that $\overline{X} = 10$, then you also know that ΣX must be equal to 30 ($\overline{X} = \Sigma X/n$).

The fact that you must know $\overline{X}$ and ΣX before you can compute variability implies that not all of the scores in the sample are free to vary. Suppose, for example, that you are taking a sample of $n - 3$ scores and you know that $\Sigma X = 30$ ($\overline{X} = 10$). Once you have identified the first two scores in the sample, the value of the third score is restricted. If the first scores were $X = 0$ and $X = 5$, then the last score would have to be $X = 25$ in order for the total to be $\Sigma X = 30$. Note that the first scores in this sample could have any values but that the last score is restricted. As a result, the sample is said to have $n - 1$ degrees of freedom; that is, only $n - 1$ of the scores are free to vary.

DEFINITION

Degrees of freedom, or *df,* for a sample are defined as

$$df = n - 1$$

where n is the number of scores in the sample.

The $n - 1$ degrees of freedom for a sample is the same $n - 1$ that is used in the formulas for sample variance and standard deviation. Remember that variance is defined as the average squared deviation. As always, this average is computed by finding the sum and dividing by the number of scores:

$$\text{average} = \frac{\text{sum}}{\text{number}}$$

To calculate sample variance (average squared deviation), we find the sum of the squared deviations (SS) and divide by the number of scores that are free to vary. This number is $n - 1 = df$.

$$s^2 = \frac{\text{sum of squared deviations}}{\text{number of scores free to vary}} = \frac{SS}{df} = \frac{SS}{n - 1}$$

Later in this book we will use the concept of degrees of freedom in other situations. For now, you should remember that knowing the sample mean places a restriction on sample variability. Only $n - 1$ of the scores are free to vary; $df = n - 1$.

PROPERTIES OF THE STANDARD DEVIATION

Because standard deviation requires extensive calculations, there is a tendency for many students to get lost in the arithmetic and forget what standard deviation is and why it is useful. As a measure of variability, standard deviation has the general purpose of describing the extent to which a set of scores is spread out or clustered together. As the name implies, standard deviation measures the standard distance from the mean—are the scores all clustered close to μ, or are the scores all spread out at great distances from the mean?

Figure 4.6 shows two distributions of quiz scores. Both distributions have $\mu = 20$, but one distribution has small variability, $\sigma = 2$, and the other has larger varibility, $\sigma = 6$. For one group, the students are all very similar in terms of their quiz performance. For the second group, there are huge differences in performance from one student to the next. You also should recognize that the same score (X value) can have very different meanings in these two distributions. For example, a score of $X = 22$ is one of the highest scores in the low variability group, but it is only average in the high variability distribution.

Standard deviation also helps researchers make predictions about sample data. Referring to the two distributions in Figure 4.6, if you were to select a single score from the low-variability population, you could be very confident of obtaining a value close to $\mu = 20$. On the other hand, you have a much greater chance of obtaining an extreme score if you are picking from the high-variability distribution.

Figure 4.6

Two hypothetical distributions of test scores for a statistics class. For both distributions, $N = 16$ and $\mu = 20$. In distribution A, where there is little variability, a score of 22 is nearly the top score. In distribution B there is more variability, and the same score occupies a more central position in the distribution.

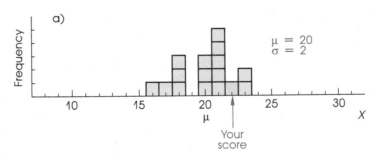

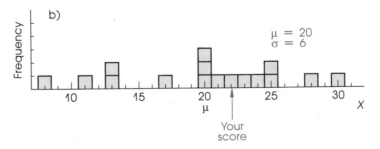

In later chapters you will see that standard deviation plays a valuable role in inferential statistics. You should recall that inferential statistics use sample data to draw inferences about populations. If a sample comes from a population with low variability, you can be reasonably confident that the sample provides a good representation of the general population. But when the standard deviation is large, extreme samples are possible, and any single sample may not accurately reflect the population.

In summary, you should realize that standard deviation is a valuable measure. It will appear repeatedly throughout the remainder of this book.

TRANSFORMATIONS OF SCALE

Occasionally it is convenient to transform a set of scores by adding a constant to each score or by multiplying each score by a constant value. This is done, for example, when you want to "curve" a set of exam scores by adding a fixed amount to each individual's grade or when you want to change the scale of measurement (to convert from minutes to seconds, multiply each X by 60). What happens to the standard deviation when the scores are transformed in this manner?

The easiest way to determine the effect of a transformation is to remember that the standard deviation is a measure of distance. If you select any two scores and see what happens to the distance between them, you also will find out what happens to the standard deviation.

1. **Adding a constant to each score will not change the standard deviation.** If you begin with a distribution that has $\mu = 40$ and $\sigma = 10$, what happens to σ if you add 5 points to every score? Consider any two scores in this distribution: Suppose, for example, that these are exam scores and that you had $X = 41$ and your friend had $X = 43$. The distance between these two scores is $43 - 41 = 2$ points. After adding the constant, 5 points, to each score, your score would be $X = 46$, and your friend would have $X = 48$. The distance between scores is still 2 points. Adding a constant to every score will not affect any of the distances and, therefore, will not change the standard deviation. This fact can be seen clearly if you imagine a frequency distribution graph. If, for example, you add 10 points to each score, then every score in the graph would be moved 10 points to the right. The result is that the entire distribution is shifted to a new position 10 points up the scale. Note that the mean moves along with the scores and is increased by 10 points. However, the variability does not change because each of the deviation scores $(X - \mu)$ does not change.

2. **Multiplying each score by a constant causes the standard deviation to be multiplied by the same constant.** Consider the same distribution of exam scores we looked at earlier. If $\mu = 40$ and $\sigma = 10$, what would happen to σ if each score were multiplied by 2? Again we will look at two scores, $X = 41$ and $X = 43$, with a distance between them equal to 2 points. After all the scores have been multiplied by 2, these scores would become $X = 82$ and $X = 86$. Now the distance between scores is 4 points, twice the original distance. Multiplying each score causes each distance to be multiplied, and so the standard deviation also is multiplied by the same amount.

RELATIONSHIP WITH OTHER STATISTICAL MEASURES   You should notice that variance and standard deviation have a direct relation to the mean—namely, they are based on deviations from the mean. Therefore, when data are described, the mean and standard deviation tend to be reported together. Because the mean is the most commonly reported measure of central tendency, the standard deviation will be the most common measure of variability.

Because the median and the semi-interquartile range are both based on quartiles (remember, median = $Q2$), they share a common foundation and tend to be associated. Whenever the median is used to report central tendency, the semi-interquartile range is commonly used to report variability.

The range, however, has no direct relationship to any other statistical measure. For this reason, it is rarely used in conjunction with other statistical techniques.

SUMMARY

1. The purpose of variability is to determine how spread out the scores are in a distribution. There are four basic measures of variability: the range, the semi-interquartile range, the variance, and the standard deviation.

   The range is the distance between the upper real limit of the largest X and the lower real limit of the smallest X in the distribution. The semi-interquartile range is one-half the distance between the first quartile and the third quartile. Variance is defined as the average squared deviation. Standard deviation is the square root of the variance.

   Standard deviation and variance are by far the most commonly used measures of variability.

2. The logical steps leading to the formulas for variance and standard deviation are summarized as follows. Remember that the purpose of standard deviation is to provide a measure of the standard distance from the mean.
   a. A deviation score is defined as $X - \mu$ and measures the direction and distance from the mean for each score.
   b. Because of the plus and minus signs, the sum of the deviation scores and the average of the deviation scores will always be zero.
   c. To get rid of the signs, we square each deviation and then compute the average squared deviation, or the variance.
   d. Finally, we correct for having squared all the deviations by taking the square root of the variance. The result is the standard deviation, and it gives a measure of the standard distance from the mean.

3. To calculate either variance or standard deviation, you first need to find the sum of the squared deviations, SS. There are two formulas for SS:

   $$\text{Definitional formula:} \quad SS = \Sigma(X - \mu)^2$$

   $$\text{Computational formula:} \quad SS = \Sigma X^2 - \frac{(\Sigma X)^2}{N}$$

4. Variance is the average squared deviation and is obtained by finding the sum of squared deviations and then dividing by the number. For a population, variance is

   $$\sigma^2 = \frac{SS}{N}$$

   For a sample, only $n - 1$ of the scores are free to vary (degrees of freedom or $df = n - 1$), so sample variance is

   $$s^2 = \frac{SS}{n - 1}$$

5. Standard deviation is the square root of the variance. For a population this is

   $$\sigma = \sqrt{\frac{SS}{N}}$$

   Sample standard deviation is

   $$s = \sqrt{\frac{SS}{n - 1}}$$

Using $n - 1$ in the sample formulas makes sample variance and sample standard deviation accurate and unbiased estimates of the corresponding population parameters.

6. Adding a constant value to every score in a distribution will not change the standard deviation. Multiplying every score by a constant, however, will cause the standard deviation to be multiplied by the same constant.

KEY TERMS

variability	semi interquartile range	variance	sum of squares (SS)
range	deviation score	standard deviation	degrees of freedom (df)
interquartile range			

FOCUS ON PROBLEM SOLVING

1. The purpose of variability is to provide a measure of how spread out the scores are in a distribution. Usually this is described by the standard deviation. Because the calculations are relatively complicated, it is wise to make a preliminary estimate of the standard deviation before you begin. Remember, standard deviation provides a measure of the typical, or standard, distance from the mean. Therefore, the standard deviation must have a value somewhere between the largest and the smallest deviation scores. As a rule of thumb, the standard deviation should be about one-fourth of the range.

2. Rather than trying to memorize all the formulas for SS, variance, and standard deviation, you should focus on the definitions of these values and the logic that relates them to each other:

   SS is the sum of squared deviations.
   Variance is the average squared deviation.
   Standard deviation is the square root of variance.

   The only formula you should need to memorize is the computational formula for SS.

3. If you heed the warnings in the following list, you may avoid some of the more common mistakes in solving variability problems.

   a. Because the calculation of standard deviation requires several steps of calculation, students often get lost in the arithmetic and forget what they are trying to compute. It helps to examine the data before you begin and make a rough estimate of the mean and the standard deviation.

   b. The standard deviation formulas for populations and samples are slightly different. Be sure that you know whether the data come from a sample or a population before you begin calculations.

   c. A common error is to use $n - 1$ in the computational formula for SS when you have scores from a sample. Remember, the SS formula always uses n (or N). After you compute SS for a sample, you must correct for the sample bias by using $n - 1$ in the formulas for variance and standard deviation.

DEMONSTRATION 4.1   COMPUTING MEASURES OF VARIABILITY

For the following sample data, compute the variance and standard deviation.

Scores: 10   7   6   10   6   15

Compute sum of squares. For *SS*, we will use the definitional formula:

$$SS = \Sigma(X - \bar{X})^2$$

STEP 1 Calculate the sample mean for these data.

$$\bar{X} = \Sigma X/n = 54/6 = 9$$

STEP 2 Compute the deviation scores, $(X - \bar{X})$, for every X value. This is facilitated by making a table listing the scores in one column and the deviation scores in another column.

X	$X - \bar{X}$
10	$10-9=+1$
7	$7-9=-2$
6	$6-9=-3$
10	$10-9=+1$
6	$6-9=-3$
15	$15-9=+6$

STEP 3 Square the deviation scores. This is shown in a new column labeled $(X - \bar{X})^2$.

X	$X - \bar{X}$	$(X - \bar{X})^2$
10	$+1$	1
7	-2	4
6	-3	9
10	$+1$	1
6	-3	9
15	$+6$	36

STEP 4 Sum the squared deviation scores to obtain the value for *SS*.

$$SS = \Sigma(X - \bar{X})^2 = 1 + 4 + 9 + 1 + 9 + 36 = 60$$

Compute the sample variance. For sample variance, we divide *SS* by $n - 1$ (also known as degrees of freedom).

STEP 1 Compute degrees of freedom, $n - 1$.

$$\text{degrees of freedom} = df = n - 1 = 6 - 1 = 5$$

STEP 2 Divide *SS* by *df*.

$$s^2 = \frac{SS}{n - 1} = \frac{60}{5} = 12$$

Compute the sample standard deviation. The sample standard deviation is simply the square root of the sample variance.

$$s = \sqrt{\frac{SS}{n-1}} = \sqrt{\frac{60}{5}} = \sqrt{12} = 3.46$$

PROBLEMS

1. Briefly define or explain each of the following:
   a. *SS*
   b. Variance
   c. Standard deviation

2. For the following population of scores, calculate the mean and then compute the deviation score for each individual. Show that the sum of the deviation scores is zero. Scores: 4, 3, 7, 0, 1, 9.

3. Calculate the range, the semi-interquartile range, and the standard deviation for the following sample:

   2, 8, 5, 9, 1, 6, 6, 3, 6, 10, 4, 12

4. For the sample data in problem 3, add 2 points to every score in the distribution.
   a. Find the range, the semi-interquartile range, and the standard deviation the new distribution.
   b. Compare the results to the previous problem. What happens to the values of these measures of variability when a constant is added to every score?

5. a. Using the computational formula, calculate *SS* for the following population of scores: 0, 1, 9.
   b. Calculate *SS* for these scores using the definitional formula. You should notice that the computational formula is much easier to use and that it probably will produce a more accurate answer because it does not require that you constantly round off decimal values.

6. The quiz scores for a class of $N = 6$ students are as follows: 1, 3, 8, 5, 0, 1.
   a. Using the definitional formula, compute *SS* and variance for these scores (assume that the set of scores is a population).
   b. The instructor would like to "curve" this distribution by adding two points to each score so that the mean becomes $\mu = 5$. Add two points to each score and then recalculate *SS* and variance.

(You should find that adding a constant does not change any of the deviation scores.)

7. Two samples are as follows:

   Sample A: 7, 9, 10, 8, 9, 12

   Sample B: 13, 5, 9, 1, 17, 9

   a. Just by looking at these data, which sample has more variability? Explain your answer.
   b. Compute the mean and standard deviation for each sample.
   c. In which sample is the mean more representative (more "typical") of its scores? How does the standard deviation affect the interpretation of the mean?

8. Two sets of data are presented here. Each set is a population.

   Data set A: 3, 5, 7, 3, 5, 6, 4, 7, 4, 6

   Data set B: 6, 4, 5, 3, 7

   a. Sketch a frequency distribution histogram for each population.
   b. Looking at your graphs, does it appear that one population is more variable than the other?
   c. Compute *SS* for each population. You should get different values. Does this mean that one population is more variable than the other?
   d. Compute variance for each population. The two values should be the same.
   e. Explain why variance is a better measure of variability than *SS*.

9. If a population of scores has $\mu = 0$, then $SS = \Sigma X^2$.
   a. Make up a set of $N = 4$ scores so that $\mu = 0$.
   b. Using the definitional formula, compute *SS* for your scores.
   c. Explain why $SS = \Sigma X^2$ whenever $\mu = 0$.

10. A population has $\mu = 100$ and $\sigma = 20$. If you select a single score from this population, on the average, how close would it be to the population mean? Explain your answer.

11. A researcher is measuring student opinions using a standard 7-point scale (1 = "strongly agree" and 7 = "strongly disagree"). For one question, the researcher reports that the student responses averaged $\overline{X} = 5.8$ with a standard deviation of $s = 8.4$. It should be obvious that the researcher has made a mistake. Explain why.

12. The following scores are brain weights in grams for a sample of $n = 5$ fish. Calculate the mean and variance for these data. (*Hint:* Multiply each score by 100 to get rid of the decimal places. Remember to correct for this multiplication before you report your answer.) Scores: .08, .09, .08, .11, .09.

13. Calculate *SS*, variance, and standard deviation for the following sample of scores. (*Hint:* The calculations will be easier if you first subtract 430 from each score. For example, $431 - 430 = 1$, and $436 - 430 = 6$. (Remember, subtracting a constant will not affect these measures of variability.) Scores: 431, 432, 435, 432, 436, 431, 434.

14. For the following set of scores, calculate *SS* using the definitional formula and then using the computational formula. (You should get the same answer for each method.) Scores: 2, 6, 3, 7, 6, 1, 3

15. For the data in the following sample,

$$1, \quad 4, \quad 3, \quad 6, \quad 2, \quad 7, \quad 18, \quad 3, \quad 7, \quad 2, \quad 4, \quad 3$$

   a. Sketch a frequency distribution histogram.
   b. Compute the mean and standard deviation.
   c. Find the median and the semi-interquartile range.
   d. Which measures of central tendency and variability provide a better description of the sample? Explain your answer.

16. A population of scores has $\mu = 50$ and $\sigma = 0$.
   a. What value would be obtained for *SS* for this population?
   b. What value would be obtained for the population variance?
   c. Describe the scores in the population. (What are the scores)

17. Can *SS* ever have a value less than zero? Explain your answer.

18. A set of $n = 20$ quiz scores has a mean of $\overline{X} = 20$. One person is selected from the class to be the "mystery person." If the deviation scores for the other 19 students in the class add up to +6, what score did the mystery person have?

19. Two sets of scores are presented here:

   Set A: 4,   1,   3,   2

   Set B: 9,   6,   8,   9

   a. Calculate the mean for each set.
   b. If you had to calculate *SS* for each set of scores, which formula would you prefer to use for set A? Which formula would you prefer for set B?

   (Try both formulas on both sets of data until you are sure which is easier to use. In general, when should you use the definitional formula and when should you use the computational formula for *SS?*)

20. Two populations are presented here:

   Population A: 53,   58,   52,   55,   57

   Population B: 31,   47,   53,   71,   79

   a. Just looking at these data, which population will have the larger standard deviation? Explain your answer.
   b. Without precisely calculating the mean, *SS*, and so on, make an estimate of the standard deviation for each population. (First make a rough estimate of the mean. Then judge the average distance from the mean to the rest of the scores.)
   c. Compute the standard deviation for each population.

21. People are most accurate at remembering and describing other individuals when they share some characteristics with the person being described. This fact can be very important in eye-witness testimony. A typical experiment examining this phenomenon is presented here.

   Two groups of subjects are used: The first group consists of college students, all 18–20 years old. The second group consists of businesspeople aged 38–40. Each group views a short film of a bank robbery. The criminal in the film is a 40 year-old man wearing a suit and tie. After viewing the film, each subject is asked to describe the bank robber. This description includes an estimate of the robber's age. The data, showing each witness's estimate of age, are as follows:

College students: 35, 30, 55, 40, 40
50, 45, 28, 33, 50

Business people: 40, 45, 40, 42, 40
40, 35, 40, 41, 38

a. Calculate the mean for each sample. Based on the two means, does it appear that one group is more accurate than the other?
b. Calculate the standard deviation for each sample. Based on these values, does it appear that one group is more accurate than the other? Explain your answer.

22. The following data are from an experiment comparing two treatment conditions:

TREATMENT A	TREATMENT B
6	12
0	2
4	8
13	14
1	3
4	12
0	5

a. Sketch a histogram showing the distribution of scores for the two treatment conditions. Show both treatments in the same histogram, using different colors to differentiate the two treatment conditions.
b. Looking at your graph, does it appear that there is a difference between the two treatments? Are the scores in treatment A noticeably different from the scores in treatment B?
c. Calculate the mean and standard deviation for each treatment condition. Is there a mean difference between the treatments?

Note: You should find a 4-point difference between the treatment means. However, the large variability makes the 4-point difference hard to see in the data or in the graph.

23. For the scores in the following sample,

19, 22, 25, 60, 16, 21, 22, 27,
26, 22, 20, 15, 17, 21, 23, 29

a. Sketch a histogram showing the distribution of scores.
b. Calculate the mean and standard deviation for this sample. Calculate the median and the semi-interquartile range for this sample.
c. Which measures of central tendency and variability seem to provide the better description of the sample? Why?

CHAPTER 5

z-SCORES: LOCATION OF SCORES AND STANDARDIZED DISTRIBUTIONS

SECTION 5.1 **z-SCORES AND LOCATION IN A DISTRIBUTION**

WHAT IS A z-SCORE?

Suppose you received a score of $X = 76$ on a statistic exam. How did you do? It should be clear that you need more information to predict your grade. Your score of $X = 76$ could be one of the best scores in the class, or it might be the lowest score in the distribution. To find the location of your score, you must have information about the other scores in the distribution. It would be useful, for example, to know the mean for the class. If the mean were $\mu = 70$, you would be in a much better position than if the mean were $\mu = 85$. Obviously, your position relative to the rest of the class depends on the mean. However, the mean by itself is not sufficient to tell you the exact location of your score. Suppose you know that the mean for the statistics exam is $\mu = 70$, and your score is $X = 76$. At this point, you know that your score is above the mean, but you still do not know exactly where it is located. You may have the highest score in the class, or you may be only slightly above average. Figure 5.1 shows two possible distributions of exam scores. Both distributions have $\mu = 70$, but for one distribution $\sigma = 3$ and for the other $\sigma = 12$. Notice that the location of $X = 76$ is very different for these two distributions.

The purpose of the opening example is to demonstrate that a score *by itself* does not necessarily provide much information about its position within a distribution. These original, unchanged scores that are the direct result of measurement are often called *raw scores*. To make raw scores more meaningful, they are often transformed or standardized so that the resulting values contain more information. For example, IQ tests are commonly standardized so that the mean is 100 and the standard deviation is 15. Because the distribution of IQ scores is standardized, most people have a good understanding of where IQ scores such as 130 or 90 are located.

The goal of z-scores is to provide a simple procedure for standardizing *any distribution*. A z-score takes information about the population mean and standard

Figure 5.1

Two distributions of exam scores. For both distributions, $\mu = 70$, but for one distribution $\sigma = 3$ and for the other, $\sigma = 12$. The position of $X = 76$ is very different for these two distributions.

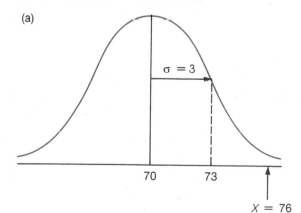

(a)

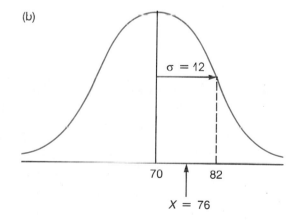

(b)

Figure 5.2

The relationship between *z*-score values
and locations in a population distribution.

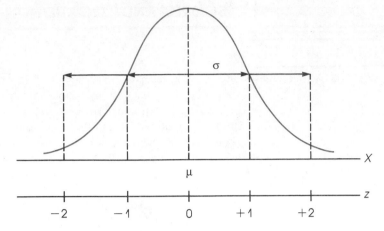

deviation and uses this information to produce a single numerical value that
specifies the location of any raw score within any distribution. The *z*-score
accomplishes this by transforming a raw score into a signed number (+ or −) so that

1. The *sign* tells whether the score is located above (+) or below (−) the
   mean, and
2. The *number* tells the distance between the score and the mean in terms of
   the number of standard deviations.

Thus, in a distribution of standardized IQ scores with $\mu = 100$ and $\sigma = 15$, a score
of $X = 130$ would be transformed into $z = +2.00$. The *z* value tells that the score
is located above the mean (+) by a distance of 2 standard deviations (30 points).

DEFINITION

A *z-score* specifies the precise location of each *X* value within a distribution. The sign of the *z*-score (+ or −) signifies whether the score is above
the mean (positive) or below the mean (negative). The numerical value of
the *z*-score specifies the distance from the mean by counting the number of
standard deviations between *X* and μ.

Notice that a *z*-score always consists of two parts: a sign (+ or −) and a
magnitude. Both parts are necessary to describe completely where a raw score is
located within a distribution.

Figure 5.2 shows a population distribution with various positions identified by
their *z*-score values. Notice that all *z*-scores above the mean are positive and all
z-scores below the mean are negative. The sign of a *z*-score tells you immediately
whether the score is located above or below the mean. Also, note that a *z*-score of
$z = +1.00$ corresponds to a position above the mean by exactly 1 standard
deviation. A *z*-score of $z = +2.00$ is always located above the mean by exactly 2
standard deviations. The numerical value of the *z*-score tells you the number of
standard deviations from the mean (see Box 5.1). Now suppose that the scores from
your statistics exam are reported as *z*-scores and you receive a score of $z = -0.50$.
How did you do? From this single value you should be able to locate your exact

Whenever you are working with *z*-scores
you should imagine or draw a picture
similar to Figure 5.2. Although you
should realize that not all distributions are
normal, we will use the normal shape as
an example when showing *z*-scores.

5.1 RELATIVE POSITION WITHIN A DISTRIBUTION: THE ROLE OF STANDARD DEVIATION

WE HAVE now seen that the standard deviation is an essential part of converting any X value to a z-score. Therefore, in a general sense, the amount of variability in a distribution and the relative position of a particular score are interrelated. This can be demonstrated with a simple example of two distributions.

Suppose that in Caribou, Maine, the average snowfall per year is $\mu = 110$ inches with $\sigma = 30$. In Boston, however, let us assume that the yearly average is only $\mu = 24$ inches with $\sigma = 5$. Last year Caribou enjoyed 125 inches of snow, while Boston was blessed with 39 inches. In which city was the winter much worse than average for its residents?

We are essentially asking a question about the relative position of a raw score in its distribution. In particular, we wish to locate the relative position of last year's accumulation for each city. Thus, in the distribution of annual accumulations for Caribou, where does X = 125 fall? Similarly, where does X = 39 fall within the distribution for Boston?

If we simply consider deviation scores $(X - \mu)$, the snowfall last year was 15 inches above average for both cities. But does this tell the whole story? In

this case, it does not. The distributions for each city differ in terms of variability ($\sigma = 30$ for Caribou, $\sigma = 5$ for Boston). Again, the amount of variability affects the relative standing of a score. Therefore, it is misleading to simply look at deviation scores. When determining the position of a score in a distribution, we should measure distance of a score from the mean in terms of standard deviation units (see the definition of a z-score).

If we look at Caribou, we find that $\mu = 110$ and $\sigma = 30$. A winter with X = 125 inches of snow is 15 points above the mean, or 0.5 standard deviations away. For Boston, the distribution has $\mu = 24$ with $\sigma = 5$. Its winter with X = 39 inches is also 15 points above the mean, but this is a distance equal to 3 standard deviation units. When we consider the variability in each distribution, we see that it was not an unusual winter for Caribou. Its snowfall was only $\frac{1}{2}$ standard deviation above the mean ($z = +0.5$), close to what we would expect for that town. On the other hand, Boston had an extreme winter. Its snowfall was 3 standard deviations above the mean ($z = +3.0$), much more snow than its residents would expect.

position within the distribution. In this case ($z = -0.50$), you are below the mean by one-half of the standard deviation. Find this position in Figure 5.2.

The definition of a z-score indicates each X value has a corresponding z-score. The following examples demonstrate the relation between X values and z-scores within a distribution.

EXAMPLE 5.1 A distribution of exam scores has a mean (μ) of 50 and a standard deviation (σ) of 8.

a. For this distribution, what is the z-score corresponding to X = 58? Because 58 is *above* the mean, the z-score has a positive sign. The score is 8 points greater than the mean. This distance is exactly 1 standard deviation (because $\sigma = 8$), so the z-score is

$$z = +1$$

This z-score indicates that the raw score is located one standard deviation above the mean.

b. What is the z-score corresponding to $X = 46$? The z-score will be negative because 46 is *below* the mean. The X value is 4 points away from the mean. This distance is exactly one-half of the standard deviation; therefore, the z-score is

$$z = -\tfrac{1}{2}$$

This z-score tells us that the X value is one-half of a standard deviation below the mean.

c. For this distribution, what raw score corresponds to a z-score of $+2$? This z-score indicates that the X value is 2 standard deviations above the mean. One standard deviation is 8 points, so two standard deviations would be 16 points. Therefore, the score we are looking for is 16 points above the mean. The mean for the distribution is 50, so the X value is

$$X = 50 + 16 = 66$$

THE z-SCORE FORMULA

The relation between X values and z-scores can be expressed symbolically in a formula. The formula for transforming raw scores into z-scores is

$$z = \frac{X - \mu}{\sigma} \tag{5.1}$$

The numerator of the equation, $X - \mu$, is a *deviation score* (Chapter 4, page 82) and measures the distance in points between X and μ and whether X is located above or below the mean. We divide this difference by σ because we want the z-score to measure distance in terms of standard deviation units. Remember, the purpose of a z-score is to specify an exact location in a distribution. The z-score formula provides a standard procedure for determining a score's location by calculating the direction and distance from the mean.

EXAMPLE 5.2

A distribution of general psychology test scores has a mean of $\mu = 60$ and a standard deviation of $\sigma = 4$. What is the z-score for a student who received a 66?

Looking at a sketch of the distribution (Figure 5.3), we see that the raw score is above the mean by at least 1 standard deviation but not quite by 2. Judging from the graph, 66 appears to be $1\tfrac{1}{2}$ standard deviations from the mean. The computation of the z-score with the formula confirms our estimate:

$$z = \frac{X - \mu}{\sigma} = \frac{66 - 60}{4} = \frac{+6}{4} = +1.5$$

EXAMPLE 5.3

The distribution of SAT verbal scores for high school seniors has a mean of $\mu = 500$ and a standard deviation of $\sigma = 100$. Joe took the SAT and scored

Figure 5.3

For the population of general psychology test scores, $\mu = 60$ and $\sigma = 4$. A student whose score is 66 is 1.5σ above the mean or has a z-score of $+1.5$.

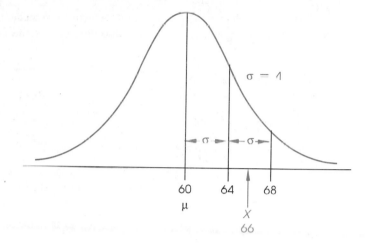

430 on the verbal subtest. Locate his score in the distribution by using a z-score.

Joe's score is 70 points below the mean, so the z-score will be negative. Because 70 points is less than 1 standard deviation, the z-score should have a magnitude that is less than 1. Using the formula, his z-score is

$$z = \frac{X - \mu}{\sigma} = \frac{430 - 500}{100} = \frac{-70}{100} = -0.70$$

DETERMINING A RAW SCORE FROM A z-SCORE

There may be situations in which you have an individual's z-score and would like to determine the corresponding raw score. When you start with a z-score , you can compute the X value by using a different version of the z-score formula. Before we introduce the new formula, let us look at the logic behind converting a z-score back to a raw score.

EXAMPLE 5.4

A distribution has a mean of $\mu = 40$ and a standard deviation of $\sigma = 6$.

What raw score corresponds to $z = +1.5$? The z-score indicates that the X value is located 1.5 standard deviations *above* the mean. Because 1 standard deviation is 6 points, 1.5 standard deviations equal 9 points. Therefore, the raw score is 9 points above the mean, or $X = 49$.

In Example 5.4 we used the z-score and the standard deviation to determine the deviation for an X value; that is, how much distance lies between the raw score and the mean. The deviation score was then added to or subtracted from the mean (depending on the sign of z) to yield the X value. These steps can be incorporated into a formula so that the X value can be computed directly. This formula is obtained by solving the z-score formula for X:

$$z = \frac{X - \mu}{\sigma}$$

$z\sigma = X - \mu$ (multiply both sides by σ)

$X - \mu = z\sigma$ (transpose the equation)

$X = \mu + z\sigma$ (Add μ to both sides)   (5.2)

Notice that the third equation in this derivation contains the expression $X - \mu$, the definition for a deviation score (Chapter 4, page 82). Therefore, the deviation score for any raw score can also be found by multiplying the z-score by the standard deviation ($z\sigma$). Essentially, this is the method we used in Example 5.4. If $z\sigma$ provides a deviation score, then we may rewrite equation 5.2 as:

raw score = mean + deviation score

In using formula 5.2, always remember that the sign of the z-score ($+$ or $-$) will determine whether the deviation score is added to or subtracted from the mean.

EXAMPLE 5.5 A distribution has a mean of $\mu = 60$ and a standard deviation of $\sigma = 12$.

a. What raw score has $z = +0.25$?

$X = \mu + z\sigma$

$= 60 + 0.25(12)$

$= 60 + 3$

$= 63$

b. What X value corresponds to $z = -1.2$?

$X = \mu + z\sigma$

$= 60 + (-1.2)(12)$

$= 60 - 14.4$

$= 45.6$

THE CHARACTERISTICS OF A
z-SCORE DISTRIBUTION

It is possible to describe the location of every raw score in the distribution by assigning z-scores to all of them. The result would be a transformation of the distribution of raw scores into a distribution of z-scores. That is, for each and every X value in the distribution of raw scores, there would be a corresponding z-score in the new distribution. This new distribution has specific characteristics—characteristics which make a *z-score transformation* a very useful tool in statistics. If every X value is transformed into a z-score, then the distribution of z-scores will have the following properties:

1. **Shape.** The shape of the z-score distribution will be the same as the origi-

Figure 5.4

Following a z-score transformation, the X-axis is relabeled in z-score units. The distance that is equivalent to one standard deviation on the X-axis ($\sigma = 10$ points in this example) corresponds to 1 point on the z-score scale.

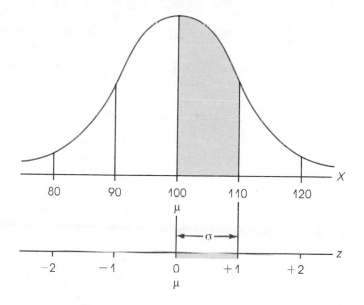

nal distribution of raw scores. If the original distribution is negatively skewed, for example, then the z-score distribution will also be negatively skewed. If the original distribution was normal, the distribution of z-scores will also be normal. Transforming raw scores into z-scores does not change anyone's location in the distribution. For example, any raw score that is above the mean by 1 standard deviation will be transformed to a z-score of $z = +1.00$, which is still above the mean by one standard deviation. Transforming a distribution from X values to z values does not move scores from one location to another; the procedure simply relabels each score (see Figure 5.4). Because each individual score stays in its same position within the distribution, the overall shape of the distribution does not change.

2. **The Mean.** When raw scores are transformed into z-scores, the resulting z-score distribution will *always* have a mean of zero. This is the case regardless of the value of μ for the raw score distribution. Suppose a population of scores has $\mu = 100$ and $\sigma = 10$. What is the z-score for the value $X = 100$? Notice that the X value equals the mean of the distribution, so its z-score will also be the z-score for the mean (see Figure 5.4).

$$z = \frac{X - \mu}{\sigma} = \frac{100 - 100}{10} = \frac{0}{10} = 0$$

The mean of the distribution has a z-score of zero. You will remember that raw scores that fall below the mean have negative z-scores (that is, z-scores *less than zero*) and that X values above the mean have positive z-scores (*greater than zero*). This fact makes the mean a convenient reference point.

3. **The Standard Deviation.** When a distribution of X values is transformed

into a distribution of z-scores, the new distribution will have a standard deviation of 1. For example, a distribution of raw scores has $\mu = 100$ and $\sigma = 10$. In this distribution a raw score of 110 will have a z-score of $+1$ (1 standard deviation above the mean). When X is 90, the z will be -1 (or 1 standard deviation below the mean). When X is 120, z is $+2$, and so on. The distribution in Figure 5.4 is labeled in terms of both X values and their corresponding z-scores. Note that 10 points on the X scale is the equivalent of 1 standard deviation. Furthermore, the distance of 1 standard deviation on the X scale corresponds to 1 point on the z-score scale. That is, the X scale has merely been relabeled following a z transformation, so that 1 point on the z scale corresponds to one standard deviation unit on the X scale. This relabeling will give the z-score distribution a standard deviation of 1 point.

LEARNING CHECK

1. What information does a z-score provide?

2. A population of scores has $\mu = 45$ and $\sigma = 5$. Find the z-scores for the following raw scores:

   a. $X = 47$ **c.** $X = 40$ **e.** $X = 52$ **g.** $X = 45$
   b. $X = 48$ **d.** $X = 44$ **f.** $X = 39$ **h.** $X = 56$

3. For the same population, determine the raw scores that correspond to the following z-scores:

   a. $z = +1.3$ **c.** $z = -3.0$ **e.** $z = +2.8$
   b. $z = -0.4$ **d.** $z = -1.5$ **f.** $z = 0$

4. What is the advantage of having $\mu = 0$ for a distribution of z-scores?

ANSWERS

1. A z-score identifies a precise location in a distribution. The sign indicates whether the location is above or below the mean, and the magnitude of z indicates the number of standard deviations from the mean.

2. **a.** $+0.4$ **c.** -1.0 **e.** $+1.4$ **g.** 0
   b. $+0.6$ **d.** -0.2 **f.** -1.2 **h.** $+2.2$

3. **a.** 51.5   **b.** 43   **c.** 30   **d.** 37.5   **e.** 59   **f.** 45

4. With $\mu = 0$ you know immediately that any positive value is above the mean and any negative value is below the mean.

SECTION 5.2   **USING z-SCORES FOR MAKING COMPARISONS**

See Box 5.2 for other examples of how z-scores are useful in statistics.

The transformation of raw scores into z-scores is very useful when we want to compare scores from two different distributions. For example, Bob received a 60 on a psychology exam. For this class, the mean was 50 and $\sigma = 10$. In biology, Bob's test score was 56, and for this class $\mu = 48$ with $\sigma = 4$. In which course does Bob have a higher standing? First, you should notice that Bob's psychology score is higher than his score in biology ($X = 60$ versus $X = 56$). Also, if you look at deviation scores, Bob is 10 points above the mean in psychology and only 8 points

5.2 WHY ARE *z*-SCORES IMPORTANT?

WE HAVE introduced *z*-scores as a statistical method for describing a specific location within a distribution. As you have seen, *z*-scores can be used to determine the precise location of an individual score, and *z*-scores can be used to compare the relative positions of two or more scores. The ability to describe a location in a distribution is of great value for other statistical purposes. The following is a brief outline of some of the ways that *z* scores will be used in later chapters.

1. *Probability*. One of the basic goals for statistics is to determine the probability or likelihood of particular events. Often it is possible to use *z*-scores as a starting point for finding probabilities. In many situations, the most likely outcomes are those that are "typical," or average. In other words, observing an individual with a *z*-score near zero (in the middle of the distribution) is much more likely than observing an individual with a *z*-score of +3.00. In Chapter 6, we examine the relation between *z*-scores and probability.

2. *Evaluating Treatment Effects*. Many experiments are done to determine whether or not a particular treatment has any effect on a dependent variable. For example, a researcher testing a new stimulant drug would like to know if the drug affects heart rate. One simple test would be to look at the heart rates of individuals who have taken the drug. If these individuals have heart rates that are still aver-age or typical (i.e., *z*-scores around zero), the researcher could conclude that drug does not seem to influence heart rate. On the other hand, if the individuals had heart rates that were extremely high (i.e., *z*-scores of +3.00 or +4.00), the researcher might conclude that the drug does increase heart rate. In general, *z*-scores provide an easy method for determining whether an individual score is average or extreme. We take a closer look at this inferential procedure in Chapter 8.

3. *Measuring Relationships*. Some statistical methods are intended to describe and measure the relationship between two variables. For example, a psychologist might be interested in the relation between physical development and mental development for 5-year-old children. Are children who are unusually large also unusually bright? In order to examine the relation, it is first necessary to find the location of each child in the distribution of heights and in the distribution of IQs. Extremely tall children will have large positive *z*-scores, those of average height will have *z*-scores near zero, and small children will have negative *z*-scores. Similarly, each child's IQ can be described as a *z*-score. The researcher can then determine whether there is a consistent relation between the *z*-scores for height and the *z*-scores for IQ. We examine statistical methods for measuring relationships in Chapter 14.

above the mean in biology. Does this mean that he performed better in psychology than in biology? Not necessarily! The problem is that we cannot simply compare his psychology score to his biology score because these scores come from *different distributions*. Any comparisons between these two test scores would be like the proverbial comparison of apples to oranges.

To make a meaningful comparison of Bob's scores, we must standardize the distributions of both classes to make them similar. Remember, a *z*-score transformation will always produce a distribution that has $\mu = 0$ and $\sigma = 1$. Therefore, if every raw score in the psychology and biology classes is transformed into a *z*-score, the resulting distributions for both classes would have $\mu = 0$ and $\sigma = 1$. All we need to do is compare Bob's *z*-score for psychology with his *z*-score for biology to determine which exam score is better. When data transformations are used to make distributions comparable, we are using *standardized distributions*. The *z*-scores in this instance are often called *standard scores*.

DEFINITIONS

A *standardized distribution* is composed of transformed scores that result in predetermined values for μ and σ, regardless of their values for the raw score distribution. Standardized distributions are used to make dissimilar distribution comparable.

A *standard score* is a transformed score that provides information of its location in a distribution. A z-score is an example of a standard score.

In practice it is not necessary to transform every score in a distribution to make comparisons between two scores. We need to transform only the two scores in question. In Bob's case, we must find the z-scores for his psychology and biology scores. For psychology, Bob's z-score is

Be sure to use the μ and σ values for the distribution to which X belongs.

$$z = \frac{X - \mu}{\sigma} = \frac{60 - 50}{10} = \frac{10}{10} = +1.0$$

For biology, Bob's z-score is

$$z = \frac{56 - 48}{4} = \frac{8}{4} = +2.0$$

Note that Bob's z-score for biology is +2.0, which means that his test score is 2 standard deviations above the class mean. On the other hand, his z-score is +1.0 for psychology, or 1 standard deviation above the mean. In terms of relative class standing. Bob is doing much better in the biology class. Unlike the absolute size of the raw scores, the z-scores describe *relative* positions within a distribution.

LEARNING CHECK

1. Why is it possible to compare scores from different distributions after each distribution is transformed into z-scores?

2. For distribution A, μ = 20 and σ = 7. Distribution B has μ = 23 and σ = 2. In which distribution will a raw score of 27 have a higher standing?

ANSWERS

1. Comparisons are possible because both distributions will have the same μ and σ (μ = 0, σ = 1) following a z-score transformation.

2. For distribution A, a raw score of 27 has a z-score of +1.0. For distribution B, a score of 27 corresponds to a z-score of +2.0. Therefore, a raw score of 27 has a higher relative standing in distribution B.

SECTION 5.3 ## OTHER STANDARDIZED DISTRIBUTIONS BASED ON z-SCORES

TRANSFORMING z-SCORES TO A PREDETERMINED μ AND σ

Although z-score distributions have distinct advantages, many people find them cumbersome because they contain negative values and decimals. For these reasons, it is common to standardize a distribution by transforming z-scores to a distribution with a predetermined mean and standard deviation that are whole round numbers.

The goal is to create a new (standardized) distribution that has "simple" values for the mean and standard deviation but does not change any individual's location within the distribution. Standardized scores of this type are frequently used in psychological testing. For example, raw scores of the Scholastic Aptitude Test (SAT) are transformed to a standardized distribution that has $\mu = 500$ and $\sigma = 100$. For intelligence tests, raw scores are frequently converted to standard scores that have a mean of 100 and a standard deviation of 15. If the same standardized scale is used for several types of intelligence tests, then the exam scores on different tests can be more readily compared because the distributions will have the same mean and standard deviation. Basically, two steps are involved in standardizing a distribution so that it has a prespecified μ and σ: (1) Each of the raw scores is transformed into a z-score, and (2) each of the z-scores is then converted into a new X value so that a particular μ and σ are achieved. This process assures that each individual has exactly the same z-score (location) in the new distribution as in the original distribution.

EXAMPLE 5.6   An instructor gives an exam to a psychology class. For this exam, the distribution of raw scores has a mean of $\mu = 57$ with $\sigma = 14$. The instructor would like to simplify the distribution by transforming all scores into a new, standardized distribution with $\mu = 50$ and $\sigma = 10$. To demonstrate this process, we will consider what happens to two specific students: Joe, who has a raw score of $X = 64$ in the original distribution, and Maria, whose original raw score is $X = 43$.

STEP 1   Transform each of the original, raw scores into z-scores. For Joe, $X = 64$, so his z-score is

$$z = \frac{X - \mu}{\sigma} = \frac{64 - 57}{14} = +0.5$$

Remember, the values of μ and σ are for the distribution from which X was taken.

For Maria, $X = 43$, and her z-score is

$$z = \frac{X - \mu}{\sigma} = \frac{43 - 57}{14} = -1.0$$

STEP 2   Change the z-scores to the new standardized scores. The instructor wants to create a standardized distribution with $\mu = 50$ and $\sigma = 10$. Joe's z-score, $z = +0.50$, indicates that he is above the mean by exactly one-half standard deviation. In the new distribution, this position would be above the mean by 5 points (½ of 10), so his standardized score would be 55. Maria's score is located one standard deviation below the mean ($z = -1.00$). In the new standardized distribution, Maria is located 10 points ($\sigma = 10$) below the mean ($\mu = 50$), so her new score would be $X = 40$.

The results of this two-step transformation process are summarized in Table 5.1. Notice that Joe, for example, has exactly the same z-score ($z = +0.50$) in both the original, raw score distribution and the new, standardized distribution. This means that Joe's position relative to the other students in the class has not been changed. Similarly, *all* the students stay in the same position relative to the rest of the class. Thus, standardizing a distribution does not

Table 5.1

	JOE	MARIA
Raw score	$X = 64$	43
Step 1: compute *z*-score	$z = +0.5$	-1.0
Step 2: standard score	55	40

change the shape of the overall distribution and it does not move individuals around within the distribution—the process simply changes the mean and standard deviation.

A FORMULA FOR FINDING THE STANDARDIZED SCORE

Earlier in the chapter, we derived a formula [Formula (5.2)] to find the raw score that corresponds to a particular *z*-score:

$$X = \mu + z\sigma$$

For purposes of computing the new standardized score, we can rewrite the equation:

$$\text{standard score} = \mu_{new} + z\sigma_{new} \qquad (5.3)$$

The standard score equals the mean of the new standardized distribution plus its *z*-score times the standard deviation of the new standardized distribution. The *z*-score in the formula is the one computed for the original raw score (step 1). Notice that $z\sigma$ is the deviation score of the standard score. If the raw score is below the mean, then its *z*-score and $z\sigma$ will be negative. For scores above the mean, $z\sigma$ is positive.

EXAMPLE 5.7 A psychologist has developed a new intelligence test. For years the test has been given to a large number of people; for this population $\mu = 65$ and $\sigma = 10$. The psychologist would like to make the scores of his subjects comparable to scores on other IQ tests, which have $\mu = 100$ and $\sigma = 15$. If the test is standardized so that it is comparable (has the same μ and σ) to other tests, what would be the standardized scores for the following individuals?

PERSON	X
1	75
2	45
3	67

STEP 1 Compute the *z*-score for each individual. Remember, the original distribution has $\mu = 65$ and $\sigma = 10$.

STEP 2 Compute the standardized score for each person. Remember that the standardized distribution will have $\mu = 100$ and $\sigma = 15$. Table 5.2 summarizes the computations for these steps and the results.

Table 5.2

	COMPUTATIONS	
	STEP 1: $z = \dfrac{X - \mu}{\sigma}$	STEP 2: $X = \mu + z\sigma$
Person 1	$z = \dfrac{75 - 65}{10} = +1.0$	$X = 100 + 1(15)$ $= 100 + 15 = 115$
Person 2	$z = \dfrac{45 - 65}{10} = -2.0$	$X = 100 - 2(15)$ $= 100 - 30 = 70$
Person 3	$z = \dfrac{67 - 65}{10} = +0.2$	$X = 100 + 0.2(15)$ $= 100 + 3 = 103$

		SUMMARY	
PERSON	X	z	STANDARDIZED SCORE
1	75	+1.00	115
2	45	−2.00	70
3	67	+0.20	103

LEARNING CHECK

1. A population has $\mu = 37$ and $\sigma = 2$. If this distribution is transformed into a new distribution with $\mu = 100$ and $\sigma = 20$, what new values will be obtained for each of the following scores: 35, 36, 37, 38, 39?

2. For the following population, $\mu = 7$ and $\sigma = 4$. Scores: 2, 4, 6, 10, 13.

   a. Transform this distribution so $\mu = 50$ and $\sigma = 20$.

   b. Compute μ and σ for the new distribution. (You should obtain $\mu = 50$ and $\sigma = 20$.)

ANSWERS

1. The five scores 35, 36, 37, 38, and 39 are transformed to 80, 90, 100, 110, and 120, respectively.

2. a. The original scores 2, 4, 6, 10, and 13 are transformed to 25, 35, 45, 65, and 80, respectively.

   b. The new scores add up to $\Sigma X = 250$ so the mean is $\frac{250}{5} = 50$. SS for the transformed scores is 2000, the variance is 400, and the new standard deviation is 20.

SUMMARY

1. Each X value can be transformed into a z-score that specifies the exact location of X within the distribution. The sign of the z-score indicates whether the location is above (positive) or below (negative) the mean. The numerical value of the z-score specifies the number of standard deviations between X and μ.

2. The z-score formula is used to transform X values into z-scores:

$$z = \frac{X - \mu}{\sigma}$$

3. To transform z-scores back into X values, solve the z-score equation for X:

$$X = \mu + z\sigma$$

4. When an entire distribution of X values is transformed into z-scores, the result is a distribution of z-scores. The z-score distribution will have the same shape as the distribution of raw scores, and it always will have a mean of 0 and a standard deviation of 1.

5. When comparing raw scores from different distributions, it is necessary to standardize the distributions with a z-score transformation. The distributions will then be comparable because they will have the same parameters ($\mu = 0$, $\sigma = 1$). In practice, it is necessary to transform only those raw scores that are being compared.

6. In certain situations, such as in psychological testing, the z-scores are converted into standardized distributions that have a particular mean and standard deviation.

KEY TERMS

raw score

z-score

deviation score

z-score transformation

standardized distribution

standard score

FOCUS ON PROBLEM SOLVING

1. When you are converting an X value to a z-score (or vice versa), do not rely entirely on the formula. You can avoid careless mistakes if you use the definition of a z-score (sign and numerical value) to make a preliminary estimate of the answer before you begin computations. For example, a z-score of $z = -0.85$ identifies a score located *below* the mean by almost one standard deviation. When computing the X value for this z-score, be sure that your answer is smaller than the mean, and check that the distance between X and μ is slightly less than the standard deviation.

   A common mistake when computing z-scores is to forget to include the sign of the z-score. The sign is determined by the deviation score ($X - \mu$) and should be carried through all steps of the computation. If, for example, the correct z-score is $z = -2.0$, then an answer of $z = 2.0$ would be wrong. In the first case, the raw score is 2 standard deviations *below* the mean. But the second (and incorrect) answer indicates that the X value is 2 standard deviation *above* the mean. These are clearly different answers, and only one can be correct. What is the best advice to avoid careless errors? Sketch the distribution, showing the mean and the raw score (or z-score) in question. This way you will have a concrete frame of reference for each problem.

2. When comparing scores from distributions that have different standard deviations, it is important to be sure that you use the correct value for σ in the z-score formula. Use the σ value for the distribution from which the raw score in question was taken.

3. Remember, a z-score specifies a relative position within the context of a specific distribution. A z-score is a relative value, not an absolute value. For example, a z-score of $z = -2.0$ does not necessarily suggest a very low raw score—it simply means that the raw score is among the lowest within that specific group.

DEMONSTRATION 5.1 TRANSFORMING X VALUES TO z-SCORES

A distribution of scores has a mean of $\mu = 60$ with $\sigma = 12$. Find the z-score for $X = 75$.

STEP 1 Determine the sign of the z-score.

First determine whether X is above or below the mean. This will determine the sign of the z-score. For this demonstration, X is larger than (above) μ so the z-score will be positive.

STEP 2 Find the distance between X and μ.

The distance is obtained by computing a deviation score.

$$\text{deviation score} = X - \mu = 75 - 60 = 15$$

Thus, the score, $X = 75$, is 15 points above μ.

STEP 3 Convert to the distance to standard deviation units.

Converting the distance from Step 2 to σ units is accomplished by dividing the distance by σ. For this demonstration,

$$\frac{15}{12} = 1.25$$

Thus, $X = 75$ is 1.25 standard deviations from the mean.

STEP 4 Combine the sign from Step 1 with the number from Step 2

The raw score is above the mean, so the z-score must be positive (Step 1). For these data,

$$z = +1.25.$$

In using the z-score formula, the sign of the z-score will be determined by the sign of the deviation score, $X - \mu$. If X is larger than μ, then the deviation score will be positive. However, if X is smaller than μ, then the deviation score will be negative. For this demonstration, formula 5.1 is used as follows:

$$z = \frac{X - \mu}{\sigma} = \frac{75 - 60}{12} = \frac{+15}{12} = +1.25$$

DEMONSTRATION 5.2 CONVERTING z-SCORES TO X VALUES

For a population with $\mu = 60$ and $\sigma = 12$, what is the X value corresponding to $z = -0.50$?

Notice that in this situation we know the z-score and must find X.

STEP 1 Locate X in relation to the mean.

The sign of the z-score is negative. This tells us that the X value we are looking for is below μ.

STEP 2   Determine the distance from the mean (deviation score).

The magnitude of the z-score tells us how many standard deviations there are between X and μ. In this case, X is one-half a standard deviation from the mean. In this distribution, one standard deviation is 12 points ($\sigma = 12$). Therefore, X is one-half of 12 points from the mean, or

$$(0.5)(12) = 6 \text{ points}$$

STEP 3   Find the X value.

Starting with the value of the mean, use the direction (Step 1) and the distance (Step 2) to determine the X value. For this demonstration, we want to find the score that is 6 points below $\mu = 60$. Therefore,

$$X = 60 - 6 = 54$$

Formula 5.2 is used to convert a z-score to an X value. For this demonstration, we obtain the following using the formula:

$$X = \mu + z\sigma$$
$$= 60 + (-0.50)(12)$$
$$= 60 + (-6) = 60 - 6$$
$$= 54$$

Notice that the sign of the z-score determines whether the deviation score is added or subtracted from the mean.

PROBLEMS

1. Describe exactly what information is provided by a z-score.

2. Describe the characteristics of a distribution following a z transformation.

3. At the beginning of the semester the instructor for developmental psychology gave the class an exam to determine how much the students already knew about the topic. The exam results were reported as z-scores, and Tom received a score of $z = +2.40$. Is Tom correct in concluding that he already knows a lot about developmental psychology? Explain your answer.

4. Suppose that two different distributions of raw scores have the same mean, $\mu = 200$. For both distributions a score of $X = 250$ is above the mean by 50 points. In which case would the score be a more extreme value: in the first distribution where the variability is small, $\sigma = 20$; or in the second distribution where the variability is large, $\sigma = 100$? Explain your answer.

5. For a distribution of raw scores, the mean is $\mu = 45$. The z-score for $X = 55$ is computed and a value of $z = -2.00$ is obtained. Regardless of the value for the standard deviation, why must this z-score be incorrect?

6. For a population of scores with $\mu = 100$ and $\sigma = 16$,
   a. Find the z-scores that corresponds to each of the following X values:

$X = 108$	$X = 104$
$X = 132$	$X = 92$
$X = 100$	$X = 120$
$X = 124$	$X = 84$

   b. Find the raw scores for each of the following z-scores:

$z = -1.00$	$z = +\frac{1}{2}$
$z = +1.50$	$z = -1.25$
$z = 0$	$x = +0.25$
$z = +2.00$	$z = -2.00$

7. A population has a mean of $\mu = 25$ with $\sigma = 5$.
   a. Compute the z-scores for the following X values.

   27, 31, 29, 17, 15
   28, 34, 33, 19, 22

   b. Compute the X values for the following z-scores.

   +0.4, +1, −3, +2.8, +1.4, 0.4,
   −1.4, +2

8. A population is composed of the following scores:

   13, 7, 12, 15, 5, 10, 11, 11, 10, 6

   a. Compute μ and σ.
   b. Find the z-score for each raw score in the population.

9. A population consists of the following scores:

   14, 11, 1, 4, 12, 5, 8, 7, 3, 5

   a. Compute μ and σ for this population.
   b. Find the z-score for each raw score in the population.

10. A population of scores has $\mu = 80$ and $\sigma = 20$. Find the z-score corresponding to each of the following X values:

    85, 90, 110, 75, 60, 45

    130, 82, 68, 80, 95, 30

11. A population has $\mu = 50$ and $\sigma = 6$. Find the raw score for each of the following z-scores:

    2.50, 1, −3, −1.33, −1.5, $+\frac{1}{2}$, −2, 0, $-\frac{1}{2}$

12. For a population with $\mu = 50$, a raw score of 43 corresponds to a z-score of −1.00. What is the standard deviation of this population?

13. For a population with $\sigma = 40$, a score of $X = 320$ corresponds to a z-score of +2.00. What is the mean for this population?

14. The grades from a physics exam were reported in X values and in corresponding z-scores. For this exam, a raw score of 65 corresponds to a z-score of +2.00. Also, when $X = 50$, $z = −1.00$. Find the mean and standard deviation for the distribution of exam scores. (*Hint:* Sketch the distribution, and locate the positions

for the two scores. How many standard deviations fall between the two X values?)

15. A population has a mean of $\mu = 115$. A raw score of $X = 145$ has a corresponding z-score of $z = +1.5$. What is the standard deviation for the population?

16. On a statistics quiz you obtain a score of 7. Would you rather be in section A where $\sigma = 2$ or in section B where $\sigma = 1$? Assume that $\mu = 6$ for both sections.

17. Answer the same question in problem 16, but assume that $\mu = 8$ for both sections. Explain your answer.

18. Suppose you have a score of $X = 60$ in a distribution with $\mu = 55$. Explain how the standard deviation could make your score appear to be either "close to" the mean or "far from" the mean.

19. In psychology, you received an exam score of 37, whereas the mean for the class is $\mu = 28$ with $\sigma = 6$. In another general psychology section, your friend received a 46. The distribution for this class has $\mu = 35$ and $\sigma = 10$. Who has a higher standing in the class?

20. A distribution of exam scores has a mean of $\mu = 75$ and a standard deviation of 8. On this exam, Mary has a score of $X = 82$, Bill has a z-score of $z = +0.75$, and Susan scored at the mean. List these three students in order from highest to lowest score.

21. The mean of a distribution after a z-score transformation is always zero because $\Sigma z = 0$. Explain why Σz must always equal zero. (*Hint:* Examine the z-score formula.)

22. The Wechsler Adult Intelligence Scale is composed of a number of subtests. Each subtest is standardized so that $\mu = 10$ and $\sigma = 3$. For one subtest, the raw scores have $\mu = 35$ and $\sigma = 6$. Following are some raw scores for this subtest. What will these scores be when standardized?

    41, 32, 39, 44, 45, 24, 37, 27

23. A population of $N = 5$ scores consists of

    1, 3, 5, 6, 7

    a. Compute μ and σ for this population.
    b. Find the z-score for each raw score in the distribution.

  c. Compute the mean and standard deviation for the set of z-scores (round off all calculations to two decimal places). What is demonstrated about z-score transformations?

  d. Explain the advantages of the characteristics of z transformations.

24. For a distribution, $\mu = 20$ and $\sigma = 2$. The raw scores from this distribution are as follows:

16,   17,   18,   18,   18,   20,   20,   20

21,   21,   21,   21,   21,   22,   23,   23

  a. Transform this distribution so that $\mu = 50$ and $\sigma = 10$.

  b. Compute the values of μ and σ for the new distribution. They should equal 50 and 10, respectively.

CHAPTER 6

PROBABILITY

TOOLS YOU WILL NEED

The following items are considered essential background material for this chapter. If you doubt your knowledge of any of these items, you should review the appropriate chapter or section before proceeding.

- Proportions (math review, Appendix A)
  - Fractions
  - Decimals
  - Percentages
- Basic algebra (math review, Appendix A)
- Upper and lower real limits (Chapter 2)
- z Scores (Chapter 5)

SECTION 6.1   **INTRODUCTION TO PROBABILITY**

Relations between samples and populations most often are described in terms of probability. Suppose, for example, you are selecting a sample of 1 marble from a jar that contains 50 black and 50 white marbles. Although you cannot guarantee the exact outcome of your sample, it is possible to talk about the potential outcomes in terms of probabilities. In this case, you have a fifty-fifty chance of getting either color. Now consider another jar (population) that has 90 black and only 10 white marbles. Again, you cannot specify the exact outcome of a sample, but now you know that the sample probably will be a black marble. By knowing the makeup of a population, we can determine the probability of obtaining specific samples. In this way, probability gives us a connection between populations and samples.

You may have noticed that the preceding examples begin with a population and then use probability to describe the samples that could be obtained. This is exactly backward from what we want to do with inferential statistics. Remember, the goal of inferential statistics is to begin with a sample and then answer general questions about the population. We will reach this goal in a two-stage process. In the first stage, we develop probability as a bridge from population to samples. This stage involves identifying the types of samples that probably would be obtained from a specific population. Once this bridge is established, we simply reverse the probability rules to allow us to move from samples to populations (see Figure 6.1). The process of reversing the probability relation can be demonstrated by considering again the two jars of marbles we looked at earlier. (One jar has 50 black and 50 white marbles; the other jar has 90 black and only 10 white marbles.) This time, suppose that you are blindfolded when the sample is selected and that your task is to use the sample to help you to decide which jar was used. If you select a sample of $n = 4$ marbles and all are black, where did the sample come from? It should be clear that it would be relatively unlikely (low probability) to obtain this sample from jar 1; in four draws, you almost certainly would get at least 1 white marble. On the

Figure 6.1

The role of probability in inferential statistics. The goal of inferential statistics is to use the limited information from samples to draw general conclusions about populations. The relationship between samples and populations usually is defined in terms of probability. Probability allows you to start with a population and predict what kind of sample is likely to be obtained. This forms a bridge between populations and samples. Inferential statistics uses the *probability bridge* as a basis for making conclusions about populations when you have only sample data.

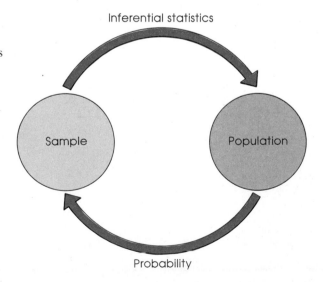

other hand, this sample would have a high probability of coming from jar 2 where nearly all the marbles are black. Your decision, therefore, is that the sample probably came from jar 2. Notice that you now are using the sample to make an inference about the population.

PROBABILITY DEFINITION

Probability is a huge topic that extends far beyond the limits of introductory statistics, and we will not attempt to examine it all here. Instead, we will concentrate on the few concepts and definitions that are needed for an introduction to inferential statistics. We begin with a relatively simple definition of probability.

DEFINITION
In a situation where several different outcomes are possible, we define the *probability* for any particular outcome as a fraction or proportion. If the possible outcomes are identified as *A, B, C, D,* etc., then

$$\text{probability of } A = \frac{\text{number of outcomes classified as } A}{\text{total number of possible outcomes}}$$

For example, when you toss a balanced coin, the outcome will be either heads or tails. Because heads is one of two possible outcomes, the probability of heads is $p = \frac{1}{2}$.

If you are selecting 1 card from a complete deck, there are 52 possible outcomes. The probability of selecting the king of hearts is $p = \frac{1}{52}$. The probability of selecting an ace is $p = \frac{4}{52}$ because there are four aces in the deck.

To simplify the discussion of probability, we will use a notation system that eliminates a lot of the words. The probability of a specific outcome will be expressed with a capital P (for probability) followed by the specific outcome in parentheses. For example, the probability of selecting a king from a deck of cards will be written as $P(\text{king})$. The probability of obtaining heads for a coin toss will be written as $P(\text{heads})$.

You should note that probability is defined as a proportion. This definition makes it possible to restate any probability problem as a proportion problem. For example, the probability problem "What is the probability of obtaining a king from a deck of cards?" can be restated as "Out of the whole deck, what proportion are kings?" In each case, the answer is $\frac{4}{52}$, or "four out of fifty-two." This translation from probability to proportion may seem trivial now, but it will be a great aid when the probability problems become more complex. In most situations we are concerned with the probability of obtaining a particular sample from a population. The terminology of *sample* and *population* will not change the basic definition of probability. For example, the whole deck of cards can be considered as a population, and the single card we select is the sample.

The definition we are using identifies probability as a fraction or a proportion. If you work directly from this definition, the probability values you obtain will be expressed as fractions. For example, if you are selecting a card,

$$P(\text{spade}) = \frac{13}{52} = \frac{1}{4}$$

Or if you are tossing a coin,

$$P(\text{heads}) = \frac{1}{2}$$

You should be aware that these fractions can be expressed equally well as either decimals or percentages:

If you are unsure how to convert from fractions to decimals or percentages, you should review the section on proportions in the math review, Appendix A.

$$p = \tfrac{1}{4} = 0.25 = 25\%$$

$$p = \tfrac{1}{2} = 0.50 = 50\%$$

By convention, probability values most often are expressed as decimal values. But you should realize that any of these three forms is acceptable.

You also should note that all the possible probability values are contained in a limited range. At one extreme, when an event never occurs, the probability is zero or 0% (see Box 6.1). At the other extreme, when an event always occurs, the probability is 1, or 100%. For example, suppose you have a jar containing 10 white marbles. The probability of randomly selecting a black marble would be

$$P(\text{black}) = \tfrac{0}{10} = 0$$

The probability of selecting a white marble would be

$$P(\text{white}) = \tfrac{10}{10} = 1$$

RANDOM SAMPLING

For the preceding definition of probability to be accurate, it is necessary that the outcomes be obtained by a process called random sampling.

DEFINITION

A *random sample* must satisfy two requirements:

1. Each individual in the population has an *equal chance* of being selected.
2. If more than one individual is to be selected for the sample, there must be *constant probability* for each and every selection.

Each of the two requirements for random sampling has some interesting consequences. The first assures that there is no bias in the selection process. For a population with N individuals, each individual must have the same probability, $p = 1/N$, of being selected. This means, for example, that you would not get a random sample of people in your city by selecting names from the yacht club membership list. Similarly, you would not get a random sample of college students by selecting individuals from your psychology classes. You also should note that the first requirement of random sampling prohibits you from applying the definition of probability to situations where the possible outcomes are not equally likely. Consider, for example, the question of whether or not there is life on Mars. There are only two possible alternatives.

1. There is life on Mars.
2. There is no life on Mars.

However, you cannot conclude that the probability of life on Mars is $p = \tfrac{1}{2}$.

The second requirement also is more interesting than may be apparent at first glance. Consider, for example, the selection of $n = 2$ cards from a complete deck. For the first draw, what is the probability of obtaining the jack of diamonds?

$$P(\text{jack of diamonds}) = \tfrac{1}{52}$$

6.1   ZERO PROBABILITY

AN EVENT that never occurs has a probability of zero. However, the opposite of this statement is not always true: A probability of zero does not mean that the event is guaranteed never to occur. Whenever there is an extremely large number of possible events, the probability of any specific event is assigned the value zero. This is done because the probability value tends toward zero as the number of possible events gets large. Consider, for example, the series

$$\frac{1}{10} \quad \frac{1}{100} \quad \frac{1}{1000} \quad \frac{1}{10,000} \quad \frac{1}{100,000}$$

Note that the value of the fraction is getting smaller and smaller, headed toward zero. At the far extreme, when the number of possible events is so large that it cannot be specified, the probability of a single, specific event is said to be zero.

$$\frac{1}{\text{infinite number}} = 0$$

Consider, for example, the fish in the ocean. If there were only 10 fish, then the probability of selecting any particular one would be $p = \frac{1}{10}$. Note that if you add up the probabilities for all 10 fish, you get a total of 1.00. Of course, there really are billions of fish in the ocean, and the probability of catching any specific one would be 1 out of billions; for all practical purposes, $p = 0$. However, this does not mean that you are doomed to fail whenever you go fishing. The zero probability simply means that you cannot predict in advance which fish you will catch. Note that each individual fish has a probability of zero, but there are so many fish that when you add up all the zeros you still get a total of 1.00. In probability, a value of zero doesn't mean never. But, practically speaking, it does mean very, very close to never.

Now, for the second draw, what is the probability of obtaining the jack of diamonds? Assuming you still are holding the first card, there are two possibilities.

$$P(\text{jack of diamonds}) = \tfrac{1}{51} \text{ if the first card was not the jack of diamonds}$$

or

$$P(\text{jack of diamonds}) = 0 \text{ if the first card was the jack of diamonds}$$

In either case, the probability is different from its value for the first draw. This contradicts the requirement for random sampling which says that the probability must stay constant. To keep the probabilities from changing from one selection to the next, it is necessary to replace each sample before you make the next selection. This is called *sampling with replacement*. The second requirement for random samples (constant probability) demands that you sample with replacement. (*Note:* The definition we are using defines one type of random sampling, often called a *simple random sample* or an *independent random sample*. Other types of random sampling are possible. You also should note that the requirement for replacement becomes relatively unimportant with very large populations. With large populations the probability values stay essentially constant whether or not you use replacement.)

PROBABILITY AND FREQUENCY DISTRIBUTIONS

The situations where we are concerned with probability usually will involve a population of scores that can be displayed in a frequency distribution graph. If you think of the graph as representing the entire population, then different portions of

Figure 6.2

A frequency distribution histogram for a population that consists of $N = 10$ scores. The shaded part of the figure indicates the portion of the whole population that corresponds to scores greater than $X = 4$. The shaded portion is two-tenths ($p = \frac{2}{10}$) of the whole distribution.

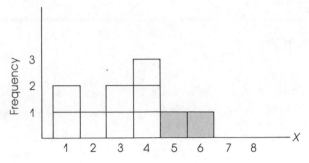

the graph will represent different portions of the population. Because probability and proportion are equivalent, a particular proportion of the graph corresponds to a particular probability in the population. Thus, whenever a population is presented in a frequency distribution graph, it will be possible to represent probabilities as proportions of the graph. The relationship between graphs and probabilities is demonstrated in the following example.

EXAMPLE 6.1   We will use a very simple population that contains only $N = 10$ scores with values 1, 1, 2, 3, 3, 4, 4, 4, 5, 6. This population is shown in the frequency distribution graph in Figure 6.2. If you are taking a random sample of $n = 1$ score from this population, what is the probability of obtaining a score greater than 4? In probability notation.

$$P(X > 4) = ?$$

Using the definition of probability, there are 2 scores that meet this criterion out of the total group of $N = 10$ scores, so the answer would be $p = \frac{2}{10}$. This answer can be obtained directly from the frequency distribution graph if you recall that probability and proportion measure the same thing. Looking at the graph (Figure 6.2), what proportion of the population consists of scores greater than 4? The answer is the shaded part of the distribution, that is, 2 squares out of the total of 10 squares in the distribution. Notice that we now are defining probability as proportion of *area* in the frequency distribution graph. This provides a very concrete and graphic way of representing probability.

Using the same population once again, what is the probability of selecting a score less than 5? In symbols,

$$P(X < 5) = ?$$

Going directly to the distribution in Figure 6.2, we now want to know what part of the graph is not shaded. The unshaded portion consists of 8 out of the 10 blocks ($\frac{8}{10}$ of the area of the graph), so the answer is $p = \frac{8}{10}$.

LEARNING CHECK

1. The animal colony in the psychology department contains 20 male rats and 30 female rats. Of the 20 males, 15 are white and 5 spotted. Of the 30 females, 15 are white and 15 are spotted. Suppose you randomly select 1 rat from this colony

   a. What is the probability of obtaining a female?
   b. What is the probability of obtaining a white male?
   c. Which selection is more likely, a spotted male or a spotted female?

2. What is the purpose of sampling with replacement?

3. Suppose you are going to select a random sample of $n = 1$ score from the distribution in Figure 6.2. Find the following probabilities.

   a. $P(X > 2)$
   b. $P(X > 5)$
   c. $P(X < 3)$

ANSWERS

1. a. $P = 30/50 = 0.60$
   b. $P = 15/50 = 0.30$
   c. A spotted female ($P = 0.30$) is more likely than a spotted male ($P = 0.10$)

2. Sampling with replacement is necessary to maintain constant probabilities for each and every selection.

3. a. $P = 7/10 = 0.70$
   b. $P = 1/10 = 0.10$
   c. $P = 3/10 = 0.30$

SECTION 6.2 **PROBABILITY AND THE NORMAL DISTRIBUTION**

The normal distribution was first introduced in Chapter 2 as an example of a commonly occurring shape for population distributions. An example of a normal distribution is shown in Figure 6.3. Although the exact shape for the normal distribution is precisely defined by an equation (see Figure 6.3), we can easily describe its general characteristics: It is a symmetrical distribution, with the highest frequency in the middle (mode = mean = median) and the frequencies tapering off gradually as the scores get farther and farther from the mean. In simple terms, in a normal distribution most individuals are around average, and extreme scores are relatively rare. This shape describes many common variables such as adult heights, intelligence scores, personality scores, and so on.

The normal shape also can be defined by the proportions of area contained in each section of the distribution. For instance, all normal shaped distributions will have exactly 34.13% of their total area in the section between the mean and the point that is one standard deviation above the mean (see Figure 6.3). By this definition, a distribution is normal if and only if it has all the right proportions.

Because the normal distribution is a good model for many naturally occurring distributions and because this shape is guaranteed in some circumstances (as you

Figure 6.3

The normal distribution. The exact shape of the normal distribution is specified by an equation relating each *X* value (score) with each *Y* value (frequency). The equation is

$$Y = \frac{1}{\sqrt{2\pi\sigma^2}}\, e^{-(X-\mu)^2/2\sigma^2}$$

(π and *e* are mathematical constants.) In simpler terms, the normal distribution is symmetrical with a single mode in the middle. The frequency tapers off as you move farther from the middle in either direction.

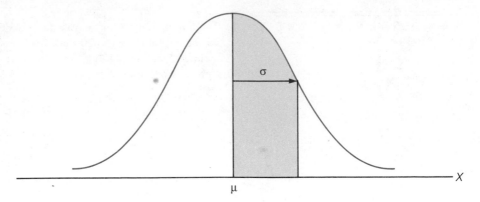

will see in Chapter 7), we will devote considerable attention to this particular distribution.

The process of answering probability questions about a normal distribution is introduced in the following example.

EXAMPLE 6.2 Adult heights form a normal shaped distribution with a mean of 68 inches and a standard deviation of 6 inches. Given this information about the population, our goal is to determine the probability associated with specific samples. For example, what is the probability of randomly selecting an individual who is taller than 6 feet (6 feet = 72 inches)? Restating this question in probability notation, we get

$$P(X > 72) = ?$$

We will follow a step-by-step process to find the answer to this question.

1. First, the probability question is translated to a proportion question: Out of all the possible adult heights, what proportion is greater than 72 inches?

2. You know that "all the possible adult heights" is simply the population distribution. This population is shown in Figure 6.4(a).

3. We want to find what portion of the distribution (what area) consists of values greater than 72. This part is shaded in the figure.

4. Looking at Figure 6.4(a), it appears that we have shaded in approximately 0.25 (or 25%) of the distribution. This is the answer we wanted.

THE UNIT NORMAL TABLE Obviously, the probability answer we obtained for the preceding example was just a rough approximation. To make the answer more precise, we need a way to

(a) *X* values

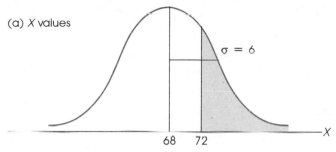

(b) *z* values

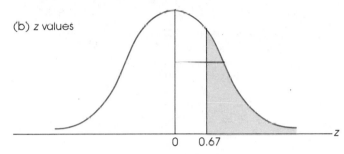

Figure 6.4

(a) The distribution of adult heights. This is a normal distribution with $\mu = 68$ and $\sigma = 6$. The portion of the distribution corresponding to scores greater than 72 has been shaded. (b) The distribution of adult heights after being transformed into *z*-scores.

The mean is changed to $z = 0$, and the value of $X = 72$ is transformed to $z = +0.67$. The portion of the distribution corresponding to *z*-scores greater than +0.67 has been shaded.

measure accurately the area in the normal distribution. Conceivably, you could do this by very carefully drawing the distribution on graph paper and then precisely measuring the amount of area in each section. Fortunately, this work already has been done, and the results are available in a table. The table, called the *unit normal table,* lists areas, or proportions, for all the possible sections of the normal distribution.

To use the unit normal table, you first need to transform the distribution of adult heights into a distribution of *z*-scores. Remember, changing from *X* values to *z*-scores will not change the shape of the distribution (it still will be normal), but it will transform the mean from $\mu = 68$ to $z = 0$ and will transform the standard deviation to 1. This is called *standardizing* the distribution. You should note that standardizing any normal distribution will produce the same result. No matter what mean or standard deviation you begin with, the standardized distribution (of *z*-scores) will be normal, with $\mu = 0$ and $\sigma = 1$. Because all normal distributions transform to this single standardized normal distribution, it is possible to have a single table that serves for every normal distribution.

Our distribution of adult heights is redrawn and standardized in Figure 6.4(b). Note that we have simply converted *X* values to *z*-scores. The value of $X = 72$ corresponds to a *z*-score of $z = \frac{4}{6}$, or 0.67. Our problem now is to determine what proportion of the normal distribution corresponds to *z*-scores greater than +0.67. The answer can be found in the unit normal table. This table lists the proportion of area corresponding to every possible *z*-score for the normal distribution.

A complete unit normal table is provided in Appendix B on page A-22, and a portion of the table is reproduced in Figure 6.5. The table lists *z*-score values and two proportions associated with each *z*-score in the normal distribution. The *z*-scores are listed in column A of the table. Column B lists the proportion of the distribution that is located between the mean and each *z*-score. Column C lists the proportion of the distribution that lies in the tail beyond each *z*-score.

To change from a decimal value to a percentage, you multiply by 100 or simply move the decimal point two places to the right.

For a *z*-score of $z = 0.25$, for example, the table lists 0.0987 in column B and 0.4013 in column C. Of the entire normal distribution 0.0987 (9.87%) is located between the mean and a *z*-score of +0.25 (see Figure 6.5). Similarly, the tail of the distribution beyond $z = +0.25$ contains 0.4013 (40.13%) of the distribution (see

Figure 6.5

A portion of the unit normal table. This table lists proportions of the normal distribution corresponding to each *z*-score value. Column A of the table lists *z*-scores. Column B lists the proportion of the normal distribution that is located between the mean and the *z*-score value. Column C lists the proportion of the normal distribution that is located in the tail of the distribution beyond the *z*-score value.

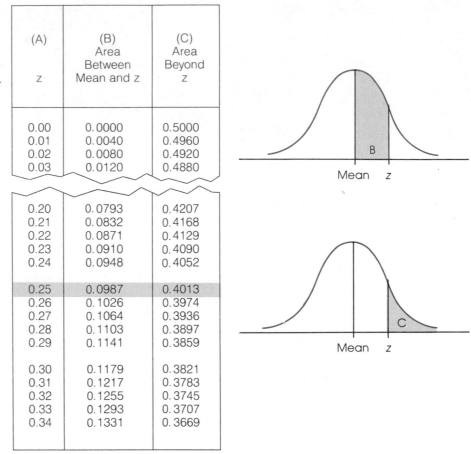

(A) z	(B) Area Between Mean and z	(C) Area Beyond z
0.00	0.0000	0.5000
0.01	0.0040	0.4960
0.02	0.0080	0.4920
0.03	0.0120	0.4880
0.20	0.0793	0.4207
0.21	0.0832	0.4168
0.22	0.0871	0.4129
0.23	0.0910	0.4090
0.24	0.0948	0.4052
0.25	0.0987	0.4013
0.26	0.1026	0.3974
0.27	0.1064	0.3936
0.28	0.1103	0.3897
0.29	0.1141	0.3859
0.30	0.1179	0.3821
0.31	0.1217	0.3783
0.32	0.1255	0.3745
0.33	0.1293	0.3707
0.34	0.1331	0.3669

Figure 6.5). Notice that these two values account for exactly one-half or 50% of the distribution:

$$0.0987 + 0.4013 = 0.5000$$

The following examples demonstrate several different ways the table can be used to find proportions or probabilities. Later we will return to the problem on adult heights.

EXAMPLE 6.3A Occasionally, the answer to a proportion problem can be found directly in the table. For example, what proportion of the normal distribution corresponds to *z*-scores greater than *z* = 1.00? The portion we want has been shaded in the normal distribution shown in Figure 6.6(a).

In this case, the shaded portion is the tail of the distribution beyond *z* = 1.00. To find this proportion, you simply look up *z* = 1.00 in the table and read the answer directly from column C. The answer is 0.1587 (or 15.87%).

(a)

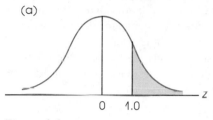

0   1.0

(b)

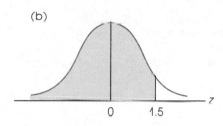

0   1.5

(c)

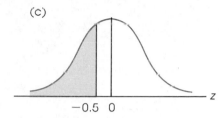

−0.5 0

Figure 6.6

Proportions of the normal distribution. (a) The portion consisting of z values greater than +1.00. (b) The portion consisting of z values less than +1.50. (c) The portion consisting of z values less than −0.50.

EXAMPLE 6.3B

Sometimes the table will provide only a part of the required proportion. Suppose, for example, that you want the proportion of the normal distribution corresponding to z-scores less than z = 1.50. This portion has been shaded in Figure 6.6(b).

In this example, the shaded area consists of two sections:

1. The section between the mean and the z-score

2. The entire left half of the distribution

To find the area between the mean and the z-score, look up z = 1.50 in the table and read the proportion from column B. You should find 0.4332 in the table. The rest of the shaded area consists of the section to the left of the mean. Because the normal distribution is symmetrical, exactly one-half (0.5000, or 50%) is on each side of z = 0. Thus, the shaded area left of the mean is exactly 0.5000. You add the two sections to obtain the total shaded area:

$$0.5000 + 0.4332 = 0.9332$$

(*Note:* You could solve this problem by looking up z = 1.50 and reading the column C value of 0.0668 from the table. This proportion corresponds to the unshaded tail of the distribution—precisely the portion of the distribution that you don't want. To find the rest of the distribution, you simply subtract from 1.00: 1.0000 − 0.0668 = 0.9332.)

EXAMPLE 6.3C

Many problems will require that you find proportions for negative z-scores. For example, what proportion of the normal distribution corresponds to z-scores less than z = −0.5? This portion has been shaded in Figure 6.6(c).

To answer questions with negative z-scores, simply remember that the distribution is symmetrical with a z-score of zero in the middle, positive values to the right, and negative values to the left. The proportion in the left-hand tail beyond z = −0.50 is exactly the same as the area in the right-hand tail beyond z = +0.50. To find this proportion, look up z = 0.50 in the table and find the proportion in column C. You should get an answer of 0.3085.

As a general rule when working probability problems with the normal distribution, you should always sketch a distribution, locate the mean with a vertical line, and shade in the portion you are trying to determine. Before you start work, look at your sketch and make an estimate of the answer. (Does the shaded portion look like 20% or like 60% of the total distribution?) If you make a habit of drawing sketches and estimating answers, you will avoid careless errors.

LEARNING CHECK

To help avoid mistakes, always sketch a normal distribution and shade in the portion you want.

1. Find the proportion of a normal distribution that is located in the tail beyond each z-score listed:

   a. $z = +1.00$ **b.** $z = +0.80$ **c.** $z = -2.00$ **d.** $z = -0.33$

2. Find the proportion of a normal distribution that is located between the mean and each z-score listed:

   a. $z = -0.50$ **b.** $z = -1.50$ **c.** $z = +0.67$ **d.** $z = +2.00$

3. Find the proportion of a normal distribution that is located between the z-score boundaries listed:

   a. Between $z = -0.50$ and $z = +0.50$

   b. Between $z = -1.00$ and $z = +1.00$

   c. Between $z = -1.96$ and $z = +1.96$

ANSWERS

1. **a.** 0.1587 (15.87%)   **b.** 0.2119 (21.19%)   **c.** 0.0228 (2.28%)   **d.** 0.3707 (37.07%)

2. **a.** 0.1915 (19.15%)   **b.** 0.4332 (43.32%)   **c.** 0.2486 (24.86%)   **d.** 0.4772 (47.72%)

3. **a.** 0.3830 (38.30%)   **b.** 0.6826 (68.26%)   **c.** 0.9500 (95.00%)

ANSWERING PROBABILITY QUESTIONS WITH THE UNIT NORMAL TABLE

The unit normal table provides a listing of proportions or probability values corresponding to every possible z-score in a normal distribution. To use this table to answer probability questions, it is necessary that you first transform the X values into z-scores (standardize the distribution) and then use the table to look up the probability value. This process is discussed in Box 6.2.

EXAMPLE 6.4

We now can use the unit normal table to get a precise answer to the probability problem we started earlier in the chapter (see Example 6.2). The goal is to find the probability of randomly selecting an individual who is taller than 6 feet (72 inches). We know that the distribution of adult heights is normal with $\mu = 68$ and $\sigma = 6$. In symbols, we want

$$P(X > 72) = ?$$

Restated as a proportion question, we want to find the proportion of the whole distribution that corresponds to values greater than 72. The whole distribution is drawn in Figure 6.4, and the part we want has been shaded (see page 129).

6.2

FINDING PROBABILITIES FROM A NORMAL DISTRIBUTION

WORKING WITH probabilities for a normal distribution involves two steps: (1) using a *z*-score formula and (2) using the unit normal table. However, the order of the steps may vary, depending on the type of probability question you are trying to answer.

   In one instance, you may start with a known *X* value and have to find a probability that is associated with it (as in Example 6.4). First you must convert the *X* value to a *z*-score using formula 5.1 (page 106). Then you consult the unit normal table to get the probability associated with the particular area of the graph. *Note:* you cannot go directly from the *X* value to the unit normal table. You must find the *z*-score first.

   However, suppose you begin with a known probability value and want to find the *X* value associated with it (as in Example 6.5). In this case you use the unit normal table first, to find the *z*-score that corresponds with the probability value. Then you convert the *z*-score into an *X* value using formula 5.2 (page 108).

   Figure 6.7 illustrates the steps you must take when moving from an *X* value to a probability or from a probability back to an *X* value. This chart, much like a map, guides you through the essential steps as you "travel" between *X* values and probabilities.

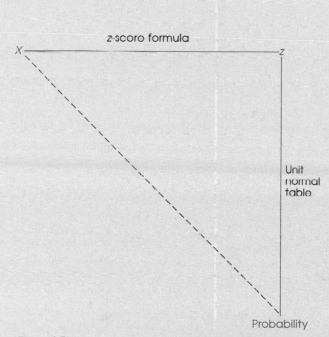

Figure 6.7

This map shows how to find a probability value that corresponds to any specific score, or how to find the score that corresponds to any specific probability value.

You cannot go directly from a score to the unit normal table. You always must go by way of *z*-scores.

The first step is to change the *X* values to *z*-scores. Specifically, the score of *X* = 72 is changed to

$$z = \frac{X - \mu}{\sigma} = \frac{72 - 68}{6} = \frac{4}{6} = 0.67$$

Next, you look up this *z*-score value in the unit normal table. Because we want the proportion of the distribution that is located beyond *z* = 0.67, the answer will be found in column C. A *z*-score of 0.67 corresponds to a proportion of 0.2514.

   The probability of randomly selecting someone taller than 72 inches is 0.2514, or about 1 out of 4:

$$P(X > 72) = 0.2514 \quad (25.14\%)$$

In the previous example we started with an *X* value and used the table to find the corresponding probability value. Looking at the map in Box 6.2, we started at *X* and moved to *P*. Like most maps, this one can be used to guide travel in either direction; that is, it is possible to start at *P* and move to *X*. To move in this direction means that you start with a specific probability value and then find the corresponding score. The following example demonstrates this type of problem.

EXAMPLE   6.5   Scores on the Scholastic Appitude Test (SAT) form a normal distribution with $\mu = 500$ and $\sigma = 100$. What is the minimum score necessary to be in the top 15% of the SAT distribution? This problem is shown graphically in Figure 6.8.

In this problem, we begin with a proportion (15% = 0.15) and we are looking for a score. According to the map in Box 6.2, we can move from *P* (proportion) to *X* (score) by going via *z*-scores. The first step is to use the unit normal table to find the *z*-score that corresponds to a proportion of 0.15. Because the proportion is located beyond *z* in the tail of the distribution, we will look in column C for a proportion of 0.1500. Note that you may not find 0.1500 exactly, but locate the closest value possible. In this case, the closest value in the table is 0.1492, and the *z*-score that corresponds to this proportion is $z = 1.04$.

The next step is to determine whether the *z*-score is positive or negative. Remember, the table does not specify the sign of the *z*-score. Looking at the graph in Figure 6.8, you should realize that the score we want is above the mean, so the *z*-score is positive, $z = +1.04$.

Now you are ready for the last stage of the solution, that is, changing the *z*-score into an *X* value. Using *z*-score formula 5.2 (page 108) and the known values of μ, σ, and *z*, we obtain

$$X = \mu + z\sigma$$
$$= 500 + 1.04(100)$$
$$= 500 + 104$$
$$= 604$$

Figure 6.8

The distribution of SAT scores. The problem is to locate the score that separates the top 15% from the rest of the distribution. A line is drawn to divide the distribution roughly into 15% and 85% sections.

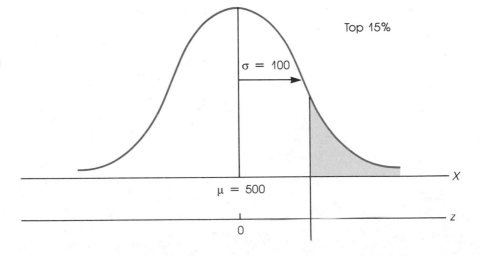

The conclusion for this example is that you must have an SAT score of at least 604 to be in the top 15% of the distribution.

EXAMPLE 6.6

This example demonstrates the process of determining a probability associated with a specified range of scores in a normal distribution. Once again, we will use the distribution of SAT scores which is normal with $\mu = 500$ and $\sigma = 100$. For this distribution, what is the probability of randomly selecting an individual with a score between $X = 600$ and $X = 650$? In probability notation, the problem is to find

$$P(600 < X < 650) = ?$$

Figure 6.9 shows the distribution of SAT scores with the relevant portion shaded. Remember, finding the probability is the same as finding the proportion of the distribution located between 600 and 650.

The first step is to transform each of the X values into a z-score:

$$\text{For } X = 600: \quad z = \frac{X - \mu}{\sigma} = \frac{600 - 500}{100} = \frac{100}{100} = 1.00$$

$$\text{For } X = 650: \quad z = \frac{X - \mu}{\sigma} = \frac{650 - 500}{100} = \frac{150}{100} = 1.50$$

The problem now is to find the proportion of the distribution that is located between $z = +1.00$ and $z = +1.50$. There are several different ways this problem can be solved using the information in the unit normal table. One technique is described here.

Using column C of the table, we find that the area beyond $z = 1.00$ is 0.1587. This includes the portion we want, but it also includes an extra por-

---

Figure 6.9

The distribution of SAT scores. The problem is to find the proportion of this distribution located between the values $X = 600$ and $X = 650$. This portion is shaded in the figure.

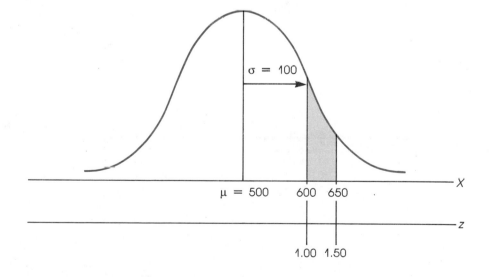

tion in the tail. This extra portion is the area beyond $z = 1.50$, and according to the table (column C), it is 0.0668 of the total distribution. Subtracting out the extra portion, we obtain a final answer of

$$P(600 < X < 650) = 0.1587 - 0.0668$$
$$= 0.0919$$

Thus, the probability of randomly selecting an individual with a SAT score between 600 and 650 is $p = 0.0919$ (9.19%).

LEARNING CHECK

1. For a normal distribution with a mean of 80 and a standard deviation of 10, find each probability value requested.
   a. $P(X > 85) = ?$ **c.** $P(X > 70) = ?$
   b. $P(X < 95) = ?$ **d.** $P(75 < X < 100) = ?$

2. For a normal distribution with a mean of 100 and a standard deviation of 20, find each value requested.
   a. What score separates the top 40% from the bottom 60% of the distribution?
   b. What is the minimum score needed to be in the top 5% of this distribution?
   c. What scores form the boundaries for the middle 60% of this distribution?

3. What is the probability of selecting a score greater than 45 from a positively skewed distribution with $\mu = 40$ and $\sigma = 10$?

ANSWERS

1. **a.** $p = 0.3085$ (30.85%)   **c.** $p = 0.8413$ (84.13%)
   b. $p = 0.9332$ (93.32%)   **d.** $p = 0.6687$ (66.87%)

2. **a.** $z = +0.25$; $X = 105$
   b. $z = +1.64$; $X = 132.8$
   c. $z = \pm 0.84$; boundaries are 83.2 and 116.8

3. You cannot obtain the answer. The unit normal table cannot be used to answer this question because the distribution is not normal.

SECTION 6.3 **PERCENTILES AND PERCENTILE RANKS**

Another useful aspect of the normal distribution is that we can determine the standing of an individual score in the distribution. For example, if you had a score of $X = 43$ on a test, we could determine what percent of the individuals scored lower than you. This would give us information about your standing relative to others that took the test. We will use percentiles and percentile ranks to answer questions about relative standing.

DEFINITIONS

The *percentile rank* of a particular score is defined as the percentage of individuals in the distribution with scores at or below that particular score.

The particular score associated with a percentile rank is called a *percentile*.

Suppose, for example, that you have a score of $X = 43$ on an exam and that you know that exactly 60% of the class had scores of 43 or lower. Then your score $X = 43$ has a percentile rank of 60% and your score would be called the 60th percentile. Notice that *percentile rank* refers to a percentage of the distribution, and *percentile* refers to a score.

FINDING PERCENTILE RANKS

Finding percentile ranks for normal distributions is straightforward if you visualize the distribution. Because a percentile rank is the percentage of the individuals that fall below a particular score, we will need to find the proportion of the distribution to the left of the score. When finding percentile ranks, we will always be concerned with the percentage on the *left-hand* side of some X value, or, in terms of symbols, $P(X < \text{some value})$.

EXAMPLE 6.7A

A population is normally distributed with $\mu = 100$ and $\sigma = 10$. What is the percentile rank for $X = 114$?

Because a percentile rank indicates one's standing relative to all lower scores, we must focus on the area of the distribution to the *left* of $X = 114$. The distribution is shown in Figure 6.10, and the area of the curve containing all scores below $X = 114$ is shaded. The proportion for this shaded area will give us the percentile rank.

Because the distribution is normal, we can use the unit normal table to find this proportion. The first step is to compute the z-score for the X value we are considering.

Figure 6.10

The distribution for Example 6.7a. The proportion for the shaded area provides the percentile rank for $X = 114$.

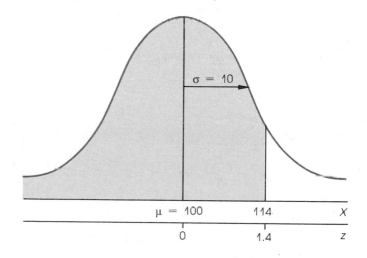

$$z = \frac{X - \mu}{\sigma} = \frac{114 - 100}{10} = \frac{14}{10} = 1.40$$

The next step is to consult the unit normal table. Note that the shaded area in Figure 6.10 is made up of two sections: (1) the section below the mean and (2) the section between the mean and the z-score. The area below the mean is exactly one-half ($p = 0.5000$, or 50%) of the distribution (remember the mean equals the median in a normal distribution). The area between the mean and the z-score is represented in column B of the unit normal table. Adding the proportions for these two sections gives us the entire shaded area. For $z = 1.40$, column B indicates proportion to $p = 0.4192$. Therefore, the proportion of the distribution below $X = 114$ is

$$P = 0.5000 + 0.4192 = 0.9192$$

The percentile rank for $X = 114$ is 91.92%.

EXAMPLE 6.7B For the distribution in Example 6.7a, what is the percentile rank for $X = 92$?
  This example is diagramed in Figure 6.11. The score $X = 92$ is placed in the left side of the distribution because it is below the mean. Again, percentile ranks deal with the area of the distribution below the score in question. Therefore, we have shaded the area to the left of $X = 92$.
  First the X-value is transformed to a z-score:

$$z = \frac{X - \mu}{\sigma} = \frac{92 - 100}{10} = \frac{-8}{10} = -0.80$$

Now the unit normal table can be consulted. The proportion in the left-hand tail beyond $z = -0.80$ can be found in column C. According to the unit nor-

Figure 6.11

The distribution for Example 6.7b. The proportion for the shaded area provides the percentile rank for $X = 92$.

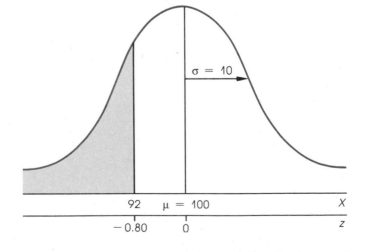

Remember, the normal distribution is symmetrical. Therefore, the proportion in the right-hand tail beyond $z = 0.80$ is identical to that in the left-hand tail beyond $z = -0.80$.

mal table, for $z = 0.80$ the proportion in the tail is $p = 0.2119$. This also is the area beyond $z = -0.80$. Thus the percentile rank for $X = 92$ is 21.19%. That is, a score of 92 is greater than 21.19% of the scores in the distribution.

FINDING PERCENTILES

The process of finding a particular percentile is very similar to the process used in Example 6.5. You are given a percentage (this time a percentile rank) and you must find the corresponding X value (the percentile). You should recall that finding a X value from a percentage requires the intermediate step of determining the z-score for that proportion of the distribution. The following example demonstrates this process for percentiles.

EXAMPLE 6.8

A population is normally distributed with $\mu = 60$ and $\sigma = 5$. For this population, what is the 34th percentile?

In this example we are looking for an X value (percentile) that has 34% (or $p = 0.3400$) of the distribution below it. This problem is illustrated in Figure 6.12. Note that 34% is roughly equal to one-third of the distribution, so the corresponding shaded area in Figure 6.12 is located entirely on the left-hand side of the mean. In this problem, we begin with a proportion (34% = 0.3400) and we are looking for a score (the percentile). The first step in moving from a proportion to a score is to find the z score (Box 6.2). You must look at the unit normal table to find the z-score that corresponds to a proportion of 0.3400. Because the proportion is in the tail beyond z, you must look in column C for a proportion of 0.3400. However, there is no entry in the table for the proportion of exactly 0.3400. Instead we use the closest value, which you will find to be $p = 0.3409$. The z-score corresponding to this value is $z = -0.41$. Note that it is a negative z-score because it is below the mean (Figure 6.12). Thus the X value for which we are looking has a z of -0.41.

Figure 6.12

The distribution for Example 6.8.

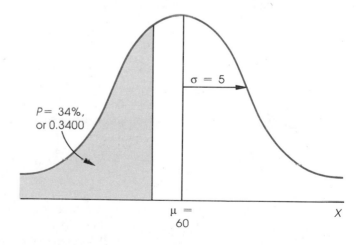

$P = 34\%$, or 0.3400

$\sigma = 5$

$\mu = 60$

X

The next step is to convert the z-score to an X value. Using the z-score formula solved for X, we obtain

$$X = \mu + z\sigma$$
$$= 60 + (-0.41)(5)$$
$$= 60 - 2.05$$
$$= 57.95$$

The 34th percentile for this distribution is $X = 57.95$. This answer makes sense because the 50th percentile for this example is 60 (the mean and median). Therefore, the 34th percentile has to be a value less than 60.

QUARTILES   Percentiles divide the distribution into 100 equal parts, each corresponding to 1% of the distribution. The area in a distribution can also be divided into four equal parts called quartiles, each corresponding to 25%. We first looked at quartiles in Chapter 4 (page 80) in considering the semi-interquartile range. The first quartile (Q1) is the score that separates the lowest 25% of the distribution from the rest. Thus the first quartile is the same as the 25th percentile. Similarly, the second quartile (Q2) is the score that has 50% (two quarters) of the distribution below it. You should recognize the Q2 is the median or 50th percentile of the distribution. Finally, the third quartile (Q3) is the X value that has 75% (three quarters) of the distribution below it. The Q3 for a distribution is also the 75% percentile.

For a normal distribution, the first quartile always corresponds to $z = -0.67$, the second quartile corresponds to $z = 0$ (the mean), and the third quartile corresponds to $z = +0.67$ (Figure 6.13). These values can be found by consulting the unit normal table and are true of any normal distribution. This makes finding quartiles and the semi-interquartile range straightforward for normal distributions. The following example demonstrates the use of quartiles.

EXAMPLE 6.9   A population is normally distributed and has a mean of $\mu = 50$ with a standard deviation of $\sigma = 10$. Find the first, second, and third quartile, and compute the semi-interquartile range.

The first quartile, Q1, is the same as the 25th percentile. The 25th percentile has a corresponding z-score of $z = -0.67$. With $\mu = 50$ and $\sigma = 10$, we can determine the X value of Q1.

$$X = \mu + z\sigma$$
$$= 50 + (-0.67)(10)$$
$$= 50 - 6.7$$
$$= 43.3$$

The second quartile, Q2, is also the 50th percentile, or median. For a normal distribution, the median equals the mean, so Q2 is 50. By the formula, with a z-score of 0, we obtain

Figure 6.13

The z-scores corresponding to the first, second, and third quartiles in a normal distribution.

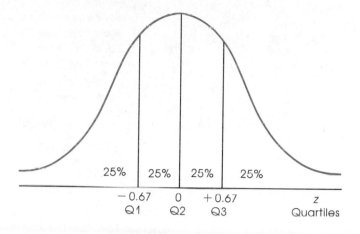

Figure 6.13

The z-scores corresponding to the first, second, and third quartiles in a normal distribution.

$$X = \mu + z\sigma$$
$$= 50 + 0(10)$$
$$= 50$$

The third quartile, Q3, is also the 75th percentile. It has a corresponding z-score of $z = +0.67$. Using the z-score formula solved for X, we obtain

$$X = \mu + z\sigma$$
$$= 50 + 0.67(10)$$
$$= 50 + 6.7$$
$$= 56.7$$

In Chapter 4 (page 80), the semi-interquartile range was defined as one-half the distance between the first and third quartile, or

$$\text{semi-interquartile range} = \frac{(Q3 - Q1)}{2}$$

For this example, the semi-interquartile range is

$$\text{semi-interquartile range} = \frac{(Q3 - Q1)}{2}$$
$$= \frac{(56.7 - 43.3)}{2}$$
$$= \frac{13.4}{2}$$
$$= 6.7$$

Notice that Q1 and Q3 are the same distance from the mean (6.7 points in the previous example). Q1 and Q3 will always be equidistant from the mean for normal

Remember, $z\sigma$ is a deviation score, or distance from the mean (Chapter 5).

distributions because normal distributions are symmetrical. Therefore, one-half of the distance between Q1 and Q3 (the semi-interquartile range by definition) will also equal the distance of Q3 from mean (see Figure 6.13). The distance of Q3 from the mean can be obtained simply by multiplying the z-score for Q3 ($z = 0.67$) times the standard deviation. Using this shortcut greatly simplifies the computation. For a normal distribution.

$$\text{semi-interquartile range} = 0.67\sigma \qquad (6.1)$$

Remember, this simplified formula is used *only* for normal distributions.

LEARNING CHECK

1. A population is normally distributed and has a mean of $\mu = 90$ with $\sigma = 8$. Find the following values.
   a. The percentile rank for $X = 100$
   b. The percentile rank for $X = 88$
   c. The 85th percentile
   d. The 10th percentile

2. For the population in example 1, find Q1, Q3, and the semi-interquartile range.

ANSWERS

1. a. 89.44%   b. 40.13%   c. $X = 98.32$ d. $X = 79.76$

2. Q1 = 84.64, Q2 = 95.36, semi-interquartile range = 5.36

SUMMARY

1. The probability of a particular event A is defined as a fraction or proportion:

$$P(A) = \frac{\text{number of outcomes classified as A}}{\text{total number of possible outcomes}}$$

2. This definition is accurate only for a random sample. There are two requirements that must be satisfied for a random sample:
   a. Every individual in the population has an equal chance of being selected.
   b. When more than one individual is being selected, the probabilities must stay constant. This means there must be sampling with replacement.

3. All probability problems can be restated as proportion problems. The "probability of selecting a king from a deck of cards" is equivalent to the "proportion of the deck that consists of kings." For frequency distribu-

tions, probability questions can be answered by determining proportions of area. The "probability of selecting an individual with an IQ greater than 108" is equivalent to the "proportion of the whole population that consists of IQs above 108."

4. For normal distributions, these probabilities (proportions) can be found in the unit normal table. This table provides a listing of the proportions of a normal distribution that corresponds to each z-score value. With this table it is possible to move between X values and probabilities using a two-step procedure:
   a. The z-score formula (Chapter 5) allows you to transform X to z or to change z back to X.
   b. The unit normal table allows you to look up the probability (proportion) corresponding to each z-score or the z-score corresponding to each probability.

5. A percentile rank measures the relative standing of a score in a distribution. Expressed as a percent, it indicates the proportion of individuals with scores at or below a particular X value. For a normal distribution, you must determine the proportion (percent) of the distribution that falls to the left of the score in question. This percent of the distribution is the percentile rank of that score.

6. A percentile is the X value that is associated with a percentile rank. For example, if 80% of the scores in a distribution are less than 250, then X − 250 is the 80th

percentile. Note that the 50th percentile is the median of the distribution.

7. Quartiles are the scores that divide the distribution into four areas that make up one-quarter of the distribution in each area. Thus, the first quartile (Q1) is equivalent to the 25th percentile. The second quartile (Q2) is also the 50th percentile (the median), and the third quartile is the same as the 75th percentile. For a normal distribution, the semi-interquartile range can be obtained by a special formula,

$$\text{semi-interquartile range} - 0.67\sigma$$

KEY TERMS

probability	sampling with replacement	percentile rank	percentile
random sample	unit normal table		

FOCUS ON PROBLEM SOLVING

1. We have defined probability as being equivalent to a proportion, which means that you can restate every probability problem as a proportion problem. This definition is particularly useful when you are working with frequency distribution graphs where the population is represented by the whole graph and probabilities (proportions) are represented by portions of the graph. When working problems with the normal distribution, you always should start with a sketch of the distribution. You should shade the portion of the graph that reflects the proportion you are looking for.

2. When using the unit normal table you must remember that the proportions in the table correspond (columns B and C) to specific portions of the distribution. This is important because you will often need to translate the proportions from a problem into specific proportions provided in the table. Also, remember that the table allows you to move back and forth between z-scores and proportions. You can look up a given z to find a proportion, or you can look up a given proportion to find the corresponding z-score. However, you cannot go directly from an X value to a probability in the unit normal table. You must first compute the z-score for X.

Likewise, you cannot go directly from a probability value to a raw score. First you have to find the z-score associated with the probability (see Box 6.2).

3. Remember, the unit normal table shows only positive z-scores in column A. However, since the normal distribution is symmetrical, the probability values in columns B and C also apply to the half of the distribution that is below the mean. To be certain that you have the correct sign for z, it helps to sketch the distribution showing μ and X.

4. A common error for students to to use negative values for proportions on the left-hand side of the normal distribution. Proportions (or probabilities) are always positive: 10% is 10% whether it is in the left or right tail of the distribution.

5. The proportions in the unit normal table are accurate only for normal distributions. If a distribution is not normal, you cannot use the table.

6. When determining percentile ranks, it helps to sketch the distribution first. Remember, shade in the area to the left of the particular X value. Its percentile rank

will be the proportion of the distribution in the shaded area. You will need to compute the z-score for the X value to find the proportion in the unit normal table. Percentile ranks are always expressed as a percent (%) of the distribution.

7. Percentiles are *X* values. When asked to find the 90th percentile, you are looking for the *X* value that has 90% (or 0.9000) of the distribution below (to the left of) it. The procedure of finding a percentile requires that you go from a proportion to a *z*-score, then from *z*-score to *X* value (Box 6.2).

DEMONSTRATION 6.1 FINDING PROBABILITY FROM THE UNIT NORMAL TABLE

A population is normally distributed with a mean of $\mu = 45$ and a standard deviation of $\sigma = 4$. What is the probability of randomly selecting a score that is greater than 43? In other words, what proportion of the scores in this distribution is greater than 43?

STEP 1 Sketch the distribution.

You should always start by sketching the distribution, identifying the mean and standard deviation ($\mu = 45$ and $\sigma = 4$ in this example). You should also find the approximate location of the specified score and draw a vertical line through the distribution at that score. The score of $X = 43$ is lower than the mean and therefore it should be placed somewhere to the left of the mean. Figure 6.14a shows the preliminary sketch.

STEP 2 Shade in the distribution.

Read the problem again to determine whether you want the proportion greater than the score (to the right of your vertical line) or less than the score (to the left of the line). Then shade in the appropriate portion of the distribution. In this demonstration, we are considering scores greater than 43. Thus, we shade in the distribution to the right of this score (Figure 6.14b). Notice that if the shaded area covers more than one-half of the distribution, then the probability should be greater than 0.5000.

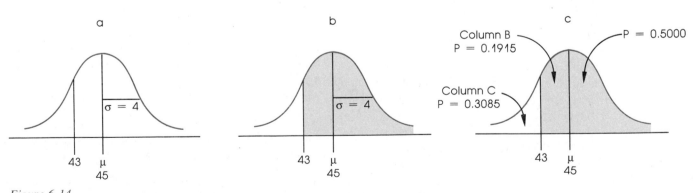

Figure 6.14

Sketches of the distribution for Demonstration 6.1.

STEP 3   Transform the X value to a z-score.

Remember, to get a probability from the unit normal table, we must first convert the X value to a z-score.

$$z = \frac{X - \mu}{\sigma} = \frac{43 - 45}{4} = \frac{-2}{4} = -0.5$$

STEP 4   Consult the unit normal table.

Look up the z-score (ignoring the sign) in the unit normal table. Find the two proportions in the table that are associated with the z-score and write the two proportions in the appropriate regions on the figure. Remember, column B gives the proportion of area between μ and z, and column C gives the area in the tail beyond z. Figure 6.14c shows the proportions for different regions of the normal distribution. For the tail beyond $z = -0.5$, $p = 0.3085$ (column C). Between z and μ the proportion is $p = 0.1915$ (column B). The entire right side of the distribution (everything above μ) makes up one-half of the distribution, or $p = 0.5000$.

STEP 5   Determine the probability.

If one of the proportions in Step 4 corresponds exactly to the entire shaded area, then that proportion is your answer. Otherwise, you will need to do some additional arithmetic. Looking at the sketch of the distribution (Figure 6.14c), take note of the proportions that correspond to the shaded region of the graph and add these proportions. The result is the proportion for the entire shaded area. This is the probability we are looking for.

$$P(X > 43) = 0.1915 + 0.5000 = 0.6915$$

PROBLEMS

1. In a psychology class of 60 students there are 15 males and 45 females. Of the 15 men, only 5 are freshmen. Of the 45 women, 20 are freshmen. If you randomly sample an individual from this class,
   a. What is the probability of obtaining a female?
   b. What is the probability of obtaining a freshman?
   c. What is the probability of obtaining a male freshman?

2. A jar contains 10 black marbles and 20 white marbles. If you are taking random sample of three marbles from this jar and the first two marbles are both white, what is the probability that the third marble will be black?

3. Find the proportion of the normal distribution that lies in the tail beyond each of the following z-scores:
   a. $z = 0.50$ c. $z = -1.50$
   b. $z = 1.75$ d. $z = -0.25$

4. Find the proportion of the normal distribution that is located between the following z-score boundaries:
   a. Between $z = 0.25$ and $z = 0.75$
   b. Between $z = -1.00$ and $z = +1.00$
   c. Between $z = 0$ and $z = 1.50$
   d. Between $z = -0.75$ and $z = 2.00$

5. For a normal distribution with a mean of $\mu = 80$ and $\sigma = 12$,
   a. What is the probability of randomly selecting a score greater than 83?
   b. What is the probability of randomly selecting a score greater than 74?
   c. What is the probability of randomly selecting a score less than 92?
   d. What is the probability of randomly selecting a score less than 62?

6. One question on a multiple-choice test asked for the

probability of selecting a score greater than $X = 50$ from a normal population with $\mu = 60$ and $\sigma = 20$. The answer choices were:

a. 0.1915   **b.** 0.3085   **c.** 0.6915

Sketch a distribution showing this problem, and without looking at the unit normal table, explain why answers a and b cannot be correct.

7. A normal distribution has a mean of 120 and a standard deviation of 20. For this distribution,

   a. What score separates the top 40% (highest scores) from the rest?
   b. What score corresponds to the 90th percentile?
   c. What range of scores would form the middle 60% of this distribution?

8. It takes Tom an average of $\mu = 30$ minutes to drive to work. The distribution of driving times is nearly normal with $\sigma = 10$ minutes. If Tom leaves home at 9:05, what is the probability that he will be late for a 9:30 meeting at work?

9. A normal distribution has a mean of 80 and a standard deviation of 10. For this distribution, find each of the following probability values:

   a. $P(X > 75) = ?$ **c.** $P(X < 100) = ?$
   b. $P(X < 65) = ?$ **d.** $P(65 < X < 95) = ?$

10. IQ scores form a normal distribution with $\mu = 100$ and $\sigma = 15$.

   a. IQ scores between 90 and 110 are designated "average." What proportion of the population is average?
   b. IQ scores between 120 and 130 are designated "superior." What proportion of the population is superior?

11. The scores on a psychology exam form a normal distribution with $\mu = 80$ and $\sigma = 8$. On this exam, Tom has a score of $X = 84$. Mary's score is located at the 60th percentile. John's score corresponds to a z-score of $z = 0.75$. If these three students are listed from highest score to lowest score, what is the correct ordering?

12. Scores on the college entrance exam are normally distributed with $\mu = 500$ and $\sigma = 100$.

   a. What is the minimum score needed to be in the top 2% on this exam?
   b. What is the 70th percentile on this exam?
   c. John has an exam score of $X = 630$. What is his percentile rank?

   d. What scores (X values) form the boundaries for the middle 95% of this distribution?
   e. Find the semi-interquartile range.

13. A positively skewed distribution has a mean of 100 and a standard deviation of 12. What is the probability of randomly selecting a score greater than 106 from this distribution? (Be careful; this is a trick problem.)

14. A normal distribution has a mean of 60 and a standard deviation of 10.

   a. Find the semi-interquartile range for this distribution.
   b. If the standard deviation were 20, what would be the value for the semi-interquartile range?
   c. In general, what is the relation between the standard deviation and the semi-interquartile range for a normal distribution?

15. A mathematics instructor teaches the same algebra course to a section of humanities students and to a section of pre-engineering students. The results of the final exam for each section are summarized as follows. Assume that both distributions are normal.

HUMANITIES	ENGINEERING
$\mu = 63$	$\mu = 72$
$\sigma = 12$	$\sigma = 8$

   a. Bill is in the humanities section and earned a grade of $X = 74$ on the final. What is his percentile rank in this section? What would his rank be if he were in the pre-engineering section?
   b. Tom is in the pre-engineering section. His grade on the final exam corresponds to a percentile rank of 40%. What rank would he have if he were in the humanities section?
   c. Mary scored at the 60th percentile in the humanities section, and Jane scored at the 31st percentile in the pre-engineering section. Who had the better exam score (X value)?

16. All entering freshmen are required to take an English proficiency placement exam (EPPE). Based on these exam scores, the college assigns students to different sections of introductory English. The top 25% of the class goes into the advanced course, the middle 50% goes into the regular English course, the students in the bottom 25% are assigned to a remedial English course. For this year's class the distribution of EPPE scores was approximately normal with $\mu = 68$ and $\sigma = 7.5$. What scores should be used as the cutoff values for assigning students to the three English courses?

17. The scores on a civil service exam form a normal distribution with $\mu = 100$ and $\sigma = 20$. Only those individuals scoring in the top 20% on this exam are interviewed for jobs.
    a. What is the minimum score needed to qualify for an interview?
    b. Because there was an unusually high demand for new employees this year, the civil service board offered job interviews to everyone scoring above $X = 108$. What percentage of the individuals taking the exam were offered interviews?

18. A social psychologist has developed a new test designed to measure social aggressiveness. The scores on this test form a normal distribution with $\mu = 60$ and $\sigma = 9$. Based on these test scores, the psychologist wants to classify the population into five categories of aggressiveness:

    I: The meek (the lowest 5%)

    II: The mild (the next 20%)

    III: The average (the middle 50%)

    IV: The aggressive (the next 20%)

    V: The dangerous (the top 5%)

    What scores should be used to form the boundaries for these categories?

19. The college admissions office reports that applicants for last year's freshman class had an average SAT score of $\mu = 480$ with $\sigma = 90$. The minimum SAT required for admission last year was $X = 450$. The distribution of SAT scores for this year's applicants has $\mu = 500$ with $\sigma = 80$. This year's cutoff for ad-

mission is $X = 470$. Assume that both distributions are normal.
    a. What proportion of last year's applicants were offered admission?
    b. What proportion of this year's applicants were offered admission?
    c. Of the students who were admitted last year, what proportion would have been rejected if the college had been using this year's cutoff?
    d. Of the students who were rejected this year, what proportion would have been accepted if the college were still using last year's standards?

Caution: For parts c and d of Problem 19 you are asked for a proportion of a proportion.

20. A normal distribution has $\mu = 60$ and $\sigma = 8$. Find the following.
    a. The percentile rank for $X = 70$
    b. The percentile rank for $X = 53$
    c. The percentile rank for $X = 79$

21. For the distribution in problem 20, find the following values.
    a. The 85th percentile
    b. The 60th percentile
    c. The 20th percentile

22. For the distribution in problem 20, find
    a. Q1, Q2, Q3
    b. The semi-interquartile range

23. A normal distribution has a mean of $\mu = 120$ with $\sigma = 15$. Find the following values.
    a. The 15th percentile
    b. The 88th percentile
    c. The percentile rank for $X = 142$
    d. The percentile rank for $X = 102$
    e. The percentile rank for $X = 120$
    f. The semi-interquartile range

SECTION 7.1 **SAMPLES AND SAMPLING ERROR**

The purpose of this chapter is to establish the set of rules that relate samples to populations. These rules, which are of great importance to later topics in inferential statistics, will be based on probabilities. In contrast to Chapter 6, in which we looked at the probability of obtaining a certain score, we will now be looking at samples of more than one score. Therefore, the focus will shift to probability questions involving sample means.

The difficulty of working with samples is that samples generally are not identical to the populations from which they come. More precisely, the statistics calculated for a sample will differ from the corresponding parameters for the population. For example, the sample mean may differ from the population mean. This difference, or *error*, is referred to as *sampling error*.

DEFINITION   *Sampling error* is the discrepancy, or amount of error, between a sample statistic and its corresponding population parameter.

Furthermore, samples are variable; they are not all the same. If you take two separate samples from the same population, the samples will be different. They will contain different individuals, they will have different scores, and they will have different sample means. How can you tell which sample is giving the best description of the population? Can you even predict how well a sample will describe its population? What is the probability of selecting a sample that has a certain sample mean? These questions can be answered once we establish the set of rules that relate samples to populations.

SECTION 7.2 **THE DISTRIBUTION OF SAMPLE MEANS**

As noted, two separate samples probably will be different even though they are taken from the same population. The samples will have different individuals, different scores, different means, and the like. In most cases, it is possible to obtain thousands of different samples from one population. With all these different samples coming from the same population, it may seem hopeless to try to establish some simple rules for the relations between samples and populations. But fortunately the huge set of possible samples does fall into a relatively simple, orderly, and predictable pattern that makes it possible to accurately predict the characteristics of a sample if you know about the population it is coming from. These general characteristics are specified by the distribution of sample means.

DEFINITION   *The distribution of sample means* is the collection of sample means for all the possible random samples of a particular size *(n)* that can be obtained from a population.

You should notice that the distribution of sample means is different from distributions we have considered before. Until now we always have discussed distributions of scores; now the values in the distribution are not scores, they are statistics (sample means). Because statistics are obtained from samples, a distribution of statistics is referred to as a sampling distribution.

DEFINITION

A sampling distribution is a distribution of statistics obtained by selecting all the possible samples of a specific size from a population.

Thus, the distribution of sample means is an example of a sampling distribution. In fact, it often is called the sampling distribution of $\overline{X}$.

Before we consider the general rules concerning this distribution, we will look at a simple example that provides an opportunity to examine the distribution in detail.

EXAMPLE 7.1

Consider a population that consists of only four scores: 2, 4, 6, 8. This population is pictured in the frequency distribution histogram in Figure 7.1.

We are going to use this population as the basis for constructing the distribution of sample means for $n = 2$. Remember, this distribution is the collection of sample means from all the possible random samples of $n = 2$ from this population. We begin by looking at all the possible samples. Each of the 16 different samples is listed in Table 7.1.

Remember, random sampling requires sampling with replacement.

Next, we compute the mean, $\overline{X}$, for each of the 16 samples (see the last column of Table 7.1). The 16 sample means form the distribution of sample means. These 16 values are organized in a frequency distribution histogram in Figure 7.2.

Notice that the distribution of sample means has some predictable and some very useful characteristics:

1. The sample means tend to pile up around the population mean. For this example, the population mean is $\mu = 5$, and the sample means are clustered around a value of 5. It should not surprise you that the sample means tend to approximate the population mean. After all, samples are supposed to be representative of the population.

2. The distribution of sample means is approximately normal in shape. This is a characteristic that will be discussed in detail later and will be extremely useful because we already know a great deal about probabilities and the normal distribution (Chapter 6).

Remember, our goal in this chapter is to answer probability questions about samples with $n > 1$.

3. Finally, you should notice that we can use the distribution of sample means to answer probability questions about sample means. For example, if you take a sample of $n = 2$ scores from the original popu-

Figure 7.1

Frequency distribution histogram for a population of four scores: 2, 4, 6, 8.

Table 7.1

All the possible samples of $n = 2$ scores that can be obtained from the population presented in Figure 7.1[a].

| | SCORES | | SAMPLE MEAN |
SAMPLE	FIRST	SECOND	$\bar{X}$
1	2	2	2
2	2	4	3
3	2	6	4
4	2	8	5
5	4	2	3
6	4	4	4
7	4	6	5
8	4	8	6
9	6	2	4
10	6	4	5
11	6	6	6
12	6	8	7
13	8	2	5
14	8	4	6
15	8	6	7
16	8	8	8

[a]Notice that the table lists *random samples*. This requires sampling with replacement, so it is possible to select the same score twice. Also note that samples are listed systematically. The first four samples are all the possible samples that have $X = 2$ as the first score; the next four samples all have $X = 4$ as the first score; etc. This way we are sure to have all the possible samples listed, although the samples probably would not be selected in this order.

lation, what is the probability of obtaining a sample mean greater than 7? In symbols, $P(\bar{X} > 7) = ?$

Because probability is equivalent to proportion, the probability question can be restated as follows: Of all the possible sample means, what proportion have values greater than 7? In this form the question is easily answered by looking at the distribution of sample means. All the possible sample means

Figure 7.2

The distribution of sample means for $n = 2$. This distribution shows the 16 sample means from Table 7.1.

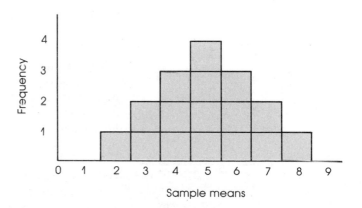

are pictured (Figure 7.2), and only 1 out of the 16 means has a value greater than 7. The answer, therefore, is 1 out of 16, or $p = \frac{1}{16}$.

THE CENTRAL LIMIT THEOREM

Example 7.1 demonstrates the construction of the distribution of sample means for a relatively simple, specific situation. In most cases, however, it will not be possible to list all the samples and compute all the possible sample means. Therefore, it is necessary to develop the general characteristics of the distribution of sample means that can be applied in any situation. Fortunately, these characteristics are specified in a mathematical proposition known as the *central limit theorem*. This important and useful theorem serves as a cornerstone for much of inferential statistics. Following is the essence of the theorem:

DEFINITION

Central Limit Theorem: For any population with mean μ and standard deviation σ, the distribution of sample means for sample size n will approach a normal distribution with a mean of μ and a standard deviation of $\sigma/\sqrt{n}$ as n approaches infinity.

The value of this theorem comes from two simple facts. First, it describes the distribution of sample means for *any population,* no matter what shape, or mean, or standard deviation. Second, the distribution of sample means "approaches" a normal distribution very rapidly. By the time the sample size reaches $n = 30$, the distribution is almost perfectly normal.

Notice that the central limit theorem describes the distribution of sample means by identifying the three basic characteristics that describe any distribution: shape, central tendency, and variability. Each of these will be examined.

THE SHAPE OF THE DISTRIBUTION OF SAMPLE MEANS

It has been observed that the distribution of sample means tends to be a normal distribution. In fact, this distribution will be almost perfectly normal if either one of the following two conditions is satisfied.

1. The population from which the samples are selected is a normal distribution.
2. The number of scores *(n)* in each sample is relatively large, around 30 or more.

(As *n* gets larger, the distribution of sample means will closely approximate a normal distribution. With $n > 30$ the distribution is almost perfectly normal regardless of the shape of the original population.)

The fact that the distribution of sample means tends to be normal should not be surprising. Whenever you take a sample from a population, you expect the sample mean to be near to the population mean. When you take lots of different samples, you expect the sample means to "pile up" around μ, resulting in a normal shaped distribution.

THE MEAN OF THE DISTRIBUTION OF SAMPLE MEANS: THE EXPECTED VALUE OF $\overline{X}$

You probably noticed in Example 7.1 that the distribution of sample means is centered around the mean of the population from which the samples were obtained. In fact, the average value of all the sample means is exactly equal to the value of the population mean. This fact should be intuitively reasonable; the sample means are expected to be close to the population mean, and they do tend to pile up around μ. The formal statement of this phenomenon is that the mean of the distribution of sample means always will be identical to the population mean. This mean value is called the *expected value of* $\overline{X}$.

DEFINITION

The expected value of $\overline{X}$ is often identified by the symbol $\mu_{\overline{X}}$, signifying the "mean of the sample means." However, $\mu_{\overline{X}}$ is always equal to μ, so we will continue to use the symbol μ to refer to the mean for the population of scores and the mean for the distribution of sample means.

The mean of the distribution of sample means will be equal to μ (the population mean) and is called the *expected value of* $\overline{X}$.

In commonsense terms, a sample mean is "expected" to be near its population mean. When all of the possible sample means are obtained, the average value will be identical to μ.

THE STANDARD ERROR OF $\overline{X}$

So far we have considered the shape and the central tendency of the distribution of sample means. To completely describe this distribution, we need one more characteristic, variability. The value we will be working with is the standard deviation for the distribution of sample means, and it is called the *standard error of* $\overline{X}$.

DEFINITION

The standard deviation of the distribution of sample means is called the *standard error of* $\overline{X}$.

Like any measure of standard deviation, the standard error defines the standard, or typical, distance from the mean. In this case, we are measuring the standard distance between a single sample mean $\overline{X}$ and the population mean μ.

The notation that is used to identify the standard error is $\sigma_{\overline{X}}$. The σ indicates that we are measuring a standard deviation or a standard distance from the mean. The subscript $\overline{x}$ indicates that we are measuring standard deviation for sample means.

$$\text{standard error} = \sigma_{\overline{X}} = \text{standard distance between } \overline{X} \text{ and } \mu$$

The standard error is an extremely valuable measure because it specifies precisely how well a sample mean estimates its population mean, that is, how much error you should expect, on the average, between $\overline{X}$ and μ. Remember, one basic reason for taking samples is to use the sample data to answer questions about the population. Specifically, we can use the sample mean as an estimate of the population mean. Although we do not expect a sample mean to be exactly the same as the population mean, it should provide a good estimate. The standard error tells how good the estimate will be.

The numerical value of the standard error is determined by two characteristics: (1) the variability of the population from which the sample is selected and (2) the size of the sample. We will examine each of these separately.

1. *Standard Deviation of the Population.* The accuracy with which a sample mean represents its population mean is determined in part by the individual

scores in the sample. If the sample contains extreme scores (far from μ), then the sample mean is likely to be very different from μ. On the other hand, if all the individual scores are close to μ, then the sample mean will certainly give an accurate representation of the population mean. Standard deviation measures the standard distance between an individual score (X) and the population mean (μ). When σ is small, each individual score is close to μ, and the average score ($\overline{X}$) is also close to μ. With a large standard deviation, you are likely to obtain extreme scores that can increase the distance between $\overline{X}$ and μ.

2. *The Sample Size.* As a general rule, the larger the sample, the more accurately the sample represents its population. This rule is also known as the *law of large numbers* (see Box 7.1).

DEFINITION   The *law of large numbers* states that the larger the sample size *(n)*, the more probable it is that the sample mean will be close to the population mean.

If you were assigned the job of estimating the average IQ for freshmen at your college, you would expect to get a more accurate measure from a group of $n = 100$ than from a sample of $n = 2$. The larger the sample, the smaller the standard error.

These two characteristics are combined in the formula for the standard error:

$$\text{standard error} = \sigma_{\overline{X}} = \frac{\sigma}{\sqrt{n}} \tag{7.1}$$

Notice that when the population standard deviation (σ) is small, the standard error will be small. Also, if the sample size *(n)* is increased, the standard error will get smaller.

LEARNING CHECK   1. What is the difference between a distribution of raw scores and a sampling distribution?

2. Under what circumstances is the distribution of sample means guaranteed to be normal?

3. A population of scores is normal with $\mu = 50$ and $\sigma = 12$. Describe the distribution of sample means for samples of size $n = 16$ selected from this population. (Describe shape, central tendency, and variability for the distribution.)

4. A population of scores is normal with $\mu = 100$ and $\sigma = 16$.
   a. If you randomly select one score from this population, then, on the average, how close should the score be to the population mean?
   b. If you selected a random sample of $n = 4$ scores, how much error would you expect, on the average, between the sample mean and the population mean?

7.1   THE LAW OF LARGE NUMBERS

CONSIDER THE following problem:

> Imagine an urn filled with balls. Two-thirds of the balls are one color, and the remaining one-third are a second color. One individual selects 5 balls from the urn and finds that 4 are red and 1 is white. Another individual selects 20 balls and finds that 12 are red and 8 are white. Which of these two individuals should feel more confident that the urn contains two-thirds red balls and one-third white balls rather than the opposite?*

When Tversky and Kahneman presented this problem to a group of experimental subjects, they found that most people felt that the first sample (4 out of 5) provided much stronger evidence and therefore should give more confidence. At first glance, it may appear that this is the correct decision. After all, the first sample contained 4/5 = 80% red balls, and the second sample contained only 12/20 = 60% red balls.

However, you should also notice that the two samples differ in another important aspect: the sample size. One sample contains only $n = 5$ scores, and the other sample contains $n = 20$. The correct answer to the problem is that the larger sample (12 out of 20) gives a much stronger justification for concluding that the balls in the urn are predominately red. It appears that most people tend to focus on the sample proportion and pay very little attention to the sample size.

The importance of sample size may be easier to appreciate if you approach the urn problem from a different perspective. Suppose that you are the individual assigned the responsibility for selecting a sample and then deciding which color is in the majority. Before you select your sample, you are offered a choice of selecting a sample of $n = 5$ balls or a sample of $n = 20$ balls. Which would you prefer? It should be clear that the larger sample would be better. The larger sample is much more likely to provide an accurate representation of the population. This is an example of the law of large numbers, which states that large samples will be representative of the population from which they are selected.

*Adapted from Tversky, A. and Kahneman, D. (1974). Judgments under uncertainty: Heuristics and biases. *Science, 185,* 1125–1131. Copyright 1974 by the AAAS.

c. If you selected a random sample of $n = 64$ scores, how much error, on the average, should there be between the sample mean and the population mean?

ANSWERS   1. A distribution of raw scores is composed of original measurements, and a sampling distribution is composed of statistics.

2. The distribution of sample means will be normal if the original population is normal or if the sample size is at least 30.

3. The distribution of sample means will be normal because the population is normal. It will have an expected value of $\mu = 50$ and a standard error of $\sigma_{\bar{X}} = 12/\sqrt{16} = 3$.

4. **a.** Standard deviation, $\sigma = 16$, measures standard distance from the mean.

   b. For a sample of $n = 4$ the standard error would be $16/\sqrt{4} = 8$ points.

   c. For a sample of $n = 64$ the standard error would be $16/\sqrt{64} = 2$ points.

MORE ABOUT THE STANDARD ERROR

The concept of standard error is probably the most important new idea in this chapter. The following two examples will demonstrate some important aspects of standard error.

EXAMPLE 7.2

Consider a population consisting of $N = 3$ scores: 1, 8, 9. The mean for this population is $\mu = 6$. Using this population, try to find a random sample of $n = 2$ scores with a sample mean $(\overline{X})$ exactly equal to the population mean. (Try selecting a few samples—write down the scores and the sample mean for each of your samples.)

You may have guessed that we constructed this example so that it is impossible to obtain a sample mean that is identical to μ. The point of the example is to emphasize the notion of sampling error. Samples are not identical to their populations, and a sample mean generally will not provide a perfect estimate of the population mean. The purpose of standard error is to provide a quantitative measure of the difference between sample means and the population mean. Standard error is the standard distance between $\overline{X}$ and μ.

EXAMPLE 7.3

Sample size is a critical factor in determining how well a sample represents its population—the larger the sample, the more accurately the sample represents the population. Suppose you would like to find the average IQ for students at your college. Rather than obtaining IQ scores for the entire population, your job is to get a sample and use the sample mean to estimate μ.

You know that IQ scores form a normal distribution with $\sigma = 15$. For the general population $\mu = 100$, but you want to find μ for your fellow students. Would you rather have a sample $n = 9$, $n = 25$, or $n = 100$ students? Clearly, the larger your sample, the better you can estimate μ. Standard error tells you exactly how much better.

Figure 7.3 shows distributions of sample means based on $n = 9$, $n = 25$, and $n = 100$. Each distribution shows the collection of all the possible sample

Figure 7.3

The distribution of sample means for samples of size $n = 9$ (left), $n = 25$ (center), and $n = 100$ (right). In each case the original population is normal with $\sigma = 15$ and an unknown mean, $\mu = ?$. Notice that the standard error gets smaller as the sample size gets larger.

(a)

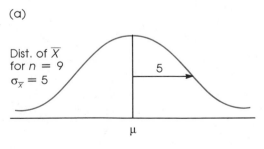

Dist. of $\overline{X}$
for $n = 9$
$\sigma_{\overline{X}} = 5$

5

μ

(b)

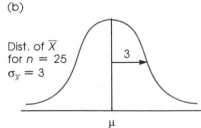

Dist. of $\overline{X}$
for $n = 25$
$\sigma_{\overline{X}} = 3$

3

μ

(c)

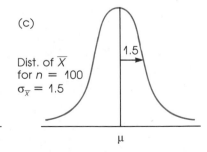

Dist. of $\overline{X}$
for $n = 100$
$\sigma_{\overline{X}} = 1.5$

1.5

μ

means that you could obtain for that particular sample size. Notice that all three sampling distributions are normal because the population of IQ scores is a normal distribution. All three distributions have the same mean, which is the unknown population mean that you are trying to estimate. However, the distributions are very different with respect to variability. With the smallest sample size, $n = 9$, the standard error is

$$\sigma_{\overline{X}} = \frac{\sigma}{\sqrt{n}} = \frac{15}{\sqrt{9}} = \frac{15}{3} = 5$$

With $n = 9$, you expect— on the average—a 5-point error between $\overline{X}$ and μ. Although some samples will give you an $\overline{X}$ very close to μ, it is likely that you will obtain a sample mean that is 5 points or even 10 points different from the population mean that you are trying to estimate.

With larger samples, however, the standard error gets smaller. For $n = 25$, the standard error is

$$\sigma_{\overline{X}} = \frac{\sigma}{\sqrt{n}} = \frac{15}{\sqrt{25}} = \frac{15}{5} = 3$$

And with $n = 100$, the standard error is

$$\sigma_{\overline{X}} = \frac{\sigma}{\sqrt{n}} = \frac{15}{\sqrt{100}} = \frac{15}{10} = 1.5$$

A sample of $n = 100$ scores should provide a much better description of the population than you would obtain with a sample of only $n = 9$ scores or a sample of $n = 25$. This fact is clearly seen when you compare the distributions of sample means (Figure 7.3). With $n = 100$, the sample means are clustered very close to the population mean, and there is very little error between $\overline{X}$ and μ. On the average, with $n = 100$, you expect only a 1.5-point difference between $\overline{X}$ and μ. It is almost impossible to obtain a sample of $n = 100$ with a mean that is more than 5 points different from μ.

This is another example of the law of large numbers.

As sample size increases, the sample becomes a better representative of the population. Standard error defines the relation between the sample size and the accuracy with which $\overline{X}$ represents μ.

SECTION 7.3 **PROBABILITY AND THE DISTRIBUTION OF SAMPLE MEANS**

The primary use of the distribution of sample means is to find the probability associated with any specific sample. You should recall that probability is equivalent to proportion. Because the distribution of sample means presents the entire set of all possible $\overline{X}$s, we can use proportions of this distribution to determine probabilities. The following example demonstrates this process.

EXAMPLE 7.4 The population of scores on the SAT forms a normal distribution with $\mu = 500$ and $\sigma = 100$. If you take a random sample of $n = 25$ students, what is the probability that the sample mean would be greater than $\overline{X} = 540$?

First, you can restate this probability question as a proportion question: Out of all the possible sample means, what proportion have values greater than 540? You know about "all the possible sample means"; this is simply the distribution of sample means. The problem is to find a specific portion of this distribution. The parameters of this distribution are the following:

Caution: Whenever you have a probability question about a sample mean, you must use the distribution of sample means.

a. The distribution is normal because the population of SAT scores is normal.

b. The distribution has a mean of 500 because the population mean is $\mu = 500$.

c. The distribution has a standard error of $\sigma_{\overline{X}} = 20$:

$$\sigma_{\overline{X}} = \frac{\sigma}{\sqrt{n}} = \frac{100}{\sqrt{25}} = \frac{100}{5} = 20$$

This distribution of sample means is shown in Figure 7.4.

We are interested in sample means greater than 540 (the shaded area in Figure 7.4), so the next step is to use a z-score to locate the exact position of $\overline{X} = 540$ in the distribution. The value 540 is located above the mean by 40 points, which is exactly two standard deviations (in this case, exactly two standard errors). Thus, the z-score for $\overline{X} = 540$ is $z = +2.00$.

Because this distribution of sample means is normal, you can use the unit normal table to find the probability associated with $z = +2.00$. The table indicates that 0.0228 of the distribution is located in the tail of the distribution beyond $z = +2.00$. Our conclusion is that it is very unlikely, $p = 0.0228$

Figure 7.4

The distribution of sample means for $n = 25$. Samples were selected from a normal population with $\mu = 500$ and $\sigma = 100$.

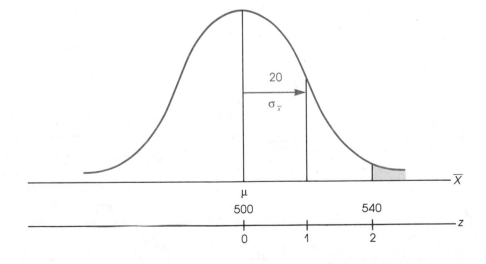

7.2 **THE DIFFERENCE BETWEEN STANDARD DEVIATION AND STANDARD ERROR**

A CONSTANT source of confusion for many students is the difference between standard deviation and standard error. You should remember that standard deviation measures the standard distance between a *score* and the population mean, $X - \mu$. Whenever you are working with a distribution of scores, the standard deviation is the appropriate measure of variability. Standard error, on the other hand, measures the standard distance between a *sample mean* and the population mean, $\overline{X} - \mu$. Whenever you have a question concerning a sample, the standard error is the appropriate measure of variability.

If you still find the distinction confusing, there is a simple solution. Namely, if you always use standard error, you always will be right. Consider the formula for standard error:

$$\text{standard error} = \sigma_{\overline{X}} = \frac{\sigma}{\sqrt{n}}$$

If you are working with a single score, then $n = 1$, and the standard error becomes

$$\text{standard error} = \sigma_{\overline{X}} = \frac{\sigma}{\sqrt{n}} = \frac{\sigma}{\sqrt{1}}$$
$$= \sigma = \text{standard deviation}$$

Thus standard error always measures the standard distance from the population mean, whether you have a sample of $n = 1$ or $n = 100$.

(2.28%), to obtain a random sample of $n = 25$ students with an average SAT score greater than 540.

As demonstrated in Example 7.4, it is possible to use a z-score to describe the position of any specific sample within the distribution of sample means. The z-score tells exactly where a specific sample is located in relation to all the other possible samples that could have been obtained. A z-score of $z = +2.00$, for example, indicates that the sample mean is much larger than usually would be expected: It is greater than the expected value of $\overline{X}$ by twice the standard distance. The z-score for each sample mean can be computed by using the standard z-score formula with a few minor changes. First, the value we are locating is a sample mean rather than a score, so the formula uses $\overline{X}$ in place of X. Second, the standard deviation for this distribution is measured by the standard error, so the formula uses $\sigma_{\overline{X}}$ in place of σ (see Box 7.2). The resulting formula, giving the z-score value corresponding to any sample mean, is

$$z = \frac{\overline{X} - \mu}{\sigma_{\overline{X}}}$$

(7.2)

Every sample mean has a z-score that describes its position in the distribution of sample means. Using z-scores and the unit normal table, it is possible to find the probability associated with any specific sample mean (as in Example 7.4). The following example demonstrates that it also is possible to make quantitative predictions about the kinds of samples that should be obtained from any population.

EXAMPLE 7.5

Suppose you simply wanted to predict the kind of value that would be expected for the mean SAT score for a random sample of $n = 25$ students. For example, what range of values would be expected for the sample mean 80% of the time? The simplest way of answering this question is to look at the distribution of sample means. Remember, this distribution is the collection of all the possible sample means, and it will show which samples are likely to be obtained and which are not.

As demonstrated in Example 7.4, the distribution of sample means for $n = 25$ will be normal, will have an expected value of $\mu = 500$, and will have a standard error of $\sigma_{\bar{X}} = 20$. Looking at this distribution, shown again in Figure 7.5, it is clear that the most likely value to expect for a sample mean is around 500. To be more precise, we can identify the range of values that would be expected 80% of the time by locating the middle 80% of the distribution. Because the distribution is normal, we can use the unit normal table. To find the middle 80%, we need exactly 40% (or 0.40) between the mean and the z-score on each side. Looking up a proportion of 0.40 in the unit normal table (column B) gives a z-score of $z = 1.28$. By definition, a z-score of 1.28 indicates that the score is 1.28 standard error units from the mean. This distance is $1.28 \times 20 = 25.6$ points. The mean is 500, so 25.6 points either direction would give a range from 474.4 to 525.6. This is the middle 80% of all the possible sample means, so you can expect any particular sample mean to be in this range 80% of the time.

Remember, when answering probability questions, it always is helpful to sketch a distribution and shade in the portion you are trying to find.

LEARNING CHECK

1. A normal population has $\mu = 80$ and $\sigma = 10$. A sample of $n = 25$ scores has a mean $\bar{X} = 83$. What is the z-score corresponding to this sample mean?

2. A random sample of $n = 9$ scores is selected from a normal population with $\mu = 40$ and $\sigma = 6$.

   a. What is the probability of obtaining a sample mean greater than 41?

   b. What is the probability of obtaining a sample mean less than 46?

Figure 7.5

The middle 80% of the distribution of sample means for $n = 25$. Samples were selected from a normal population with $\mu = 500$ and $\sigma = 100$.

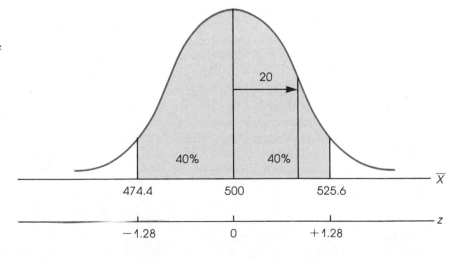

3. A skewed distribution has $\mu = 60$ and $\sigma = 8$.

    a. What is the probability of obtaining a sample mean greater than $\overline{X} = 62$ for a sample of $n = 4$? (Be careful.)

    b. What is the probability of obtaining a sample mean greater than $\overline{X} = 62$ for a sample of $n = 64$?

ANSWERS   **1.** The standard error is 2. $z = -\frac{3}{2} = 1.5$.

    2. a. $\overline{X} = 41$ corresponds to $z = +.50$. The probability is 0.3085 (30.85%).

    b. $\overline{X} = 46$ corresponds to $z = +3.0$. The probability is 0.9987 (99.87%).

    3. a. Cannot answer because the distribution of sample means is not normal.

    b. With $n = 64$ the distribution of sample means will be normal. $\overline{X} = 62$ corresponds to $z = +2.0$. The probability is 0.0228 (2.28%).

SUMMARY

1. The distribution of sample means is defined as the set of all the possible $\overline{X}s$ for a specific sample size (n) that can be obtained from a given population. The parameters of the distribution of sample means are as follows:

    a. *Shape*. The distribution of sample means will be normal if either one of the following two conditions is satisfied:

      (1) The population from which the samples are selected is normal.

      (2) The size of the samples is relatively large (around $n = 30$ or more).

    b. *Central Tendency*. The mean of the distribution of sample means will be identical to the mean of the population from which the samples are selected. The mean of the distribution of sample means is called the expected value of $\overline{X}$.

    c. *Variability*. The standard deviation of the distribution of sample means is called the standard error of $\overline{X}$ and is defined by the formula

$$\sigma_{\overline{X}} = \frac{\sigma}{\sqrt{n}}$$

Standard error measures the standard distance between a sample mean $\overline{X}$ and the population mean μ.

2. One of the most important concepts in this chapter is the standard error. The standard error is the standard deviation of the distribution of sample means. It measures the standard distance between a sample mean ($\overline{X}$) and the population mean (μ). The standard error tells how much error to expect if you are using a sample mean to estimate a population mean.

3. The location of each $\overline{X}$ in the distribution of sample means can be specified by a z score:

$$z = \frac{\overline{X} - \mu}{\sigma_{\overline{X}}}$$

Because the distribution of sample means tends to be normal, we can use these z-scores and the unit normal table to find probabilities for specific sample means. In particular, we can identify which sample means are likely and which are very unlikely to be obtained from any given population. This ability to find probabilities for samples is the basis for the inferential statistics in the chapters ahead.

KEY TERMS

sampling error

distribution of sample
means

sampling distribution

central limit theorem

expected value of $\overline{X}$

standard error of $\overline{X}$

law of large numbers

FOCUS ON PROBLEM SOLVING

1. Whenever you are working probability questions about sample means, you must use the distribution of sample means. Remember, every probability question can be restated as a proportion question. Probabilities for sample means are equivalent to proportions of the distribution of sample means.

2. When computing probabilities for sample means, the most common error is to use standard deviation (σ) instead of standard error ($\sigma_{\overline{X}}$) in the z-score formula. Standard deviation measures the typical deviation (or "error") for a single score. Standard error measures the typical deviation (or error) for a sample. Remem-

ber, the larger the sample, the more accurately the sample represents the population—that is, the larger the sample, the smaller the error.

$$\text{standard error} = \sigma_{\overline{X}} = \frac{\sigma}{\sqrt{n}}$$

3. Although the distribution of sample means is often normal, it is not always a normal distribution. Check the criteria to be certain the distribution is normal before you use the unit normal table to find probabilities (see 1a of the Summary). Remember, all probability problems with the normal distribution are easier if you sketch the distribution and shade in the area of interest.

DEMONSTRATION 7.1   PROBABILITY AND THE DISTRIBUTION OF SAMPLE MEANS

For a normally distributed population with $\mu = 60$ and $\sigma = 12$, what is the probability of selecting a random sample of $n = 36$ scores with a sample mean greater than 64?

In symbols, for $n = 36$, $P(\overline{X} > 64) = ?$

Notice that we may rephrase the probability question as a proportion question. Out of all the possible sample means for $n = 36$, what proportion have values greater than 64?

STEP 1 Sketch the distribution.

We are looking for a specific proportion of *all possible sample means*. Therefore, we will have to sketch the distribution of sample means. We should include the expected value, the standard error, and the specified sample mean.

The expected value for this demonstration is $\mu = 60$. The standard error is

$$\sigma_{\overline{X}} = \frac{\sigma}{\sqrt{n}} = \frac{12}{\sqrt{36}} = \frac{12}{6} = 2$$

Remember, we must use the standard error, *not* standard deviation, because we are dealing with the distribution of sample means.

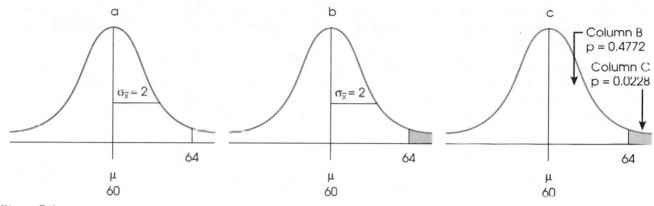

Figure 7.6

Sketches of the distribution for Demonstration 7.1.

Find the approximate location of the sample mean and place a vertical line through the distribution. In this demonstration, the sample mean is 64. It is larger than the expected value of $\mu = 60$ and therefore is placed on the right side of the distribution. Figure 7.6a depicts the preliminary sketch.

STEP 2   Shade the appropriate area of the distribution.

Determine whether the problem asks for a proportion greater than ($>$) or less than ($<$) the specified sample mean. Then shade the appropriate area of the distribution. In this demonstration, we are looking for the area greater than $\overline{X} = 64$ so we shade the area on the right-hand side of the vertical line (Figure 7.6b).

STEP 3   Compute the z-score for the sample mean.

Use the z-score formula for sample means. Remember that it uses standard error in the denominator.

$$z = \frac{\overline{X} - \mu}{\sigma_{\overline{X}}} = \frac{64 - 60}{2} = \frac{4}{2} = 2.00$$

STEP 4   Consult the unit normal table.

Look up the z-score in the unit normal table and note the two proportions in columns B and C. Jot them down in the appropriate areas of the distribution (Figure 7.6c). For this demonstration, the value in column C (the tail beyond z) corresponds exactly to the proportion we want (shaded area). Thus, for $n = 36$,

$$P(\overline{X} > 64) = P(z > +2.00) = 0.0228$$

PROBLEMS

1. Briefly define each of the following:
   a. The distribution of sample means
   b. Expected value of $\overline{X}$
   c. Standard error of $\overline{X}$

2. A population consists of exactly three scores: $X = 0$, $X = 2$, and $X = 4$.
   a. List all the possible random samples of $n = 2$ scores from this population. (You should obtain 9 different samples—see Example 7.1.)

b. Compute the sample mean for each of the 9 samples, and draw a histogram showing the distribution of sample means.

3. Two samples are randomly selected from a population. One sample has $n = 5$ scores and the second has $n = 30$. Which sample should have a mean $(\overline{X})$ that is closer to μ? Explain your answer.

4. You have a population with $\mu = 100$ and $\sigma = 30$.
   a. If you randomly select a single score from this population, then, on the average, how close would you expect the score to be to the population mean?
   b. If you randomly select a sample of $n = 100$ scores, then, on the average, how close would you expect the sample mean to be to the population mean?

5. The distribution of SAT scores is normal with $\mu = 500$ and $\sigma = 100$.
   a. If you selected a random sample of $n = 4$ scores from this population, how much error would you expect between the sample mean and the population mean?
   b. If you selected a random sample of $n = 25$ scores, how much error would you expect between the sample mean and the population mean?
   c. How much error would be expected for a sample of $n = 100$ scores?

6. A population has $\mu = 200$ and $\sigma = 50$. Find the z-score for each of the following sample means:
   a. A sample of $n = 25$ with $\overline{X} = 220$.
   b. A sample of $n = 100$ with $\overline{X} = 190$.
   c. A sample of $n = 4$ with $\overline{X} = 230$.

7. On an immediate memory test, 10-year-old children can correctly recall an average of $\mu = 7$ digits. The distribution of recall scores is normal with $\sigma = 2$.
   a. What is the probability of randomly selecting a child with a recall score less than 6?
   b. What is the probability of randomly selecting a sample of $n = 4$ children whose average recall score is less than 6?

8. Simple reaction times for college students form a normal distribution with $\mu = 200$ milliseconds and $\sigma = 20$.
   a. What is the probability of randomly selecting a student whose reaction time is less than 190?
   b. What is the probability of randomly selecting a sample of $n = 4$ students with an average reaction time less than 190?

c. What is the probability of randomly selecting a sample of $n = 25$ students with an average reaction time less than 190?

9. If you select a random sample of $n = 36$ scores from a population with $\mu = 80$ and $\sigma = 24$, then
   a. What is the probability of obtaining a sample mean greater than 84?
   b. What is the probability of obtaining a sample mean less than 72?

10. A sample is selected from a population with $\sigma = 10$. If the standard error for this sample is $\sigma_{\overline{X}} = 2$, how many scores are in the sample?

11. If you are taking a random sample from a normal population with $\mu = 100$ and $\sigma = 12$, which of the following outcomes is more likely?
   a. A sample mean greater than 106 for a sample of $n = 4$
   b. A sample mean greater than 103 for a sample of $n = 36$ scores

12. IQ scores form a normal distribution with $\mu = 100$ and $\sigma = 15$.
   a. What is the probability of randomly selecting a sample of $n = 9$ students so that their average IQ is different by more than one point from the population mean? (What is the probability of obtaining a sample mean greater than 101 or less than 99?)
   b. What is the probability of randomly selecting a sample of $n = 100$ individuals so that their average IQ is more than one point away from the population mean?

13. Standard error measures the standard distance between a sample mean and the population mean. For a population with $\sigma = 20$,
   a. How large a sample would be needed to obtain a standard error of less than 10 points?
   b. How large a sample would be needed to have a standard error smaller than 5 points?
   c. If you wanted your sample mean to be within 1 point of the population mean (on the average), how large a sample should you use?

14. A population is normally distributed with $\mu = 100$ and $\sigma = 20$.
   a. Find the z-score corresponding to each of the following samples:

Sample 1: $n = 4; \overline{X} = 110$

Sample 2: $n = 25; \overline{X} = 105$

Sample 3: n 100; $\overline{X} = 104$

b. Which of the samples in part a is least likely to be obtained by random sampling?

15. a. Calculate the mean and standard deviation for the population of digits 0 through 9.

b. If you took a random sample of $n = 8$ digits from this population, what is the probability that the digits in your sample would total 50 or more? (*Note:* For 8 digits to total 50, they must average 6.25 each.) Assume the distribution of sample means is normal even though $n = 8$.

c. If you took a random sample of 12 digits, what is the probability that they would total 50 or more? Assume the distribution of sample means is normal even though $n = 12$.

16. The 27 freshmen in Tower Dormitory finished their first semester with a mean grade point average of 2.61. They consider this to be a remarkable achievement because the mean GPA for the entire freshman class was only $\mu = 2.35$. If GPAs are normally distributed with $\sigma = .27$, what is the probability that a random sample of $n = 27$ would have an average GPA of 2.61 or higher? Are the freshmen in Tower Dorm justified in being proud?

17. The local hardware store sells screws in 1-pound bags. Because the screws are not identical, the number of screws per bag varies with $\mu = 115$ and $\sigma = 6$. A carpenter needs a total of 600 screws for a particular project. What is the probability that he will have enough screws if he buys five bags? (Assume the distribution is normal.)

18. The average age for registered voters in the county is $\mu = 39.7$ years with $\sigma = 11.8$. The distribution of ages is approximately normal. During a recent jury trial in the county courthouse, a statistician noted that the average age for the 12 jurors was $\overline{X} = 51.4$ years.

a. How likely is it to obtain a jury this old or older by chance?

b. Is it reasonable to conclude that this jury is not a random sample of registered voters?

19. At the beginning of this chapter we noted that the law of large numbers says that the larger the sample, the more likely that the sample mean will be close to the population mean. This law can be demonstrated using IQ scores which form a normal distribution with $\mu = 100$ and $\sigma = 16$.

a. What is the probability of randomly selecting one individual whose IQ is within 5 points of the population mean?

b. If you select a sample of five people, how likely is it that their average IQ will be within 5 points of the population mean?

c. How likely is it for a sample of 10 people to have an average IQ within 5 points of the population mean?

20. A manufacturer of flashlight batteries claims that its batteries will last an average of $\mu = 34$ hours of continuous use. Of course, there is some variability in life expectancy with $\sigma = 1$ hour. During consumer testing, a sample of 30 batteries lasted an average of only $\overline{X} = 31.5$ hours. How likely is it to obtain a sample that performs this badly if the manufacturer's claim is true?

21. Error scores for laboratory rats on a standardized discrimination problem form a normal distribution with $\mu = 85$ and $\sigma = 15$.

a. Sketch the distribution of sample means for samples of size $n = 10$.

b. Find the range of values corresponding to the middle 95% of this distribution. Note that 95% of all the possible samples will have a mean in this range.

c. What is the range of sample means that would contain 99% of all the possible samples of $n = 10$ rats?

INTRODUCTION TO HYPOTHESIS TESTING

SECTION 8.1 **THE LOGIC OF HYPOTHESIS TESTING**

It is usually impossible or impractical for a researcher to observe every individual in a population. Therefore, researchers usually collect data from a sample. Hypothesis testing is a statistical procedure that allows scientists to use sample data to draw inferences about the population of interest.

DEFINITION   *Hypothesis testing* is an inferential procedure that uses sample data to evaluate the credibility of a hypothesis about a population.

In very simple terms the logic underlying the hypothesis-testing procedure is as follows:

1. First, we state a hypothesis about a population. Usually, the hypothesis concerns the value of a population parameter. For example, we might hypothesize that the mean IQ for registered voters in the United States is $\mu = 110$.

2. Next, we obtain a random sample from the population. For example, we select a random sample of $n = 200$ registered voters.

3. Finally, we compare the sample data with the hypothesis. If the data are consistent with the hypothesis, we will conclude that the hypothesis was reasonable. But if there is a big discrepancy between the data and the hypothesis, we will decide that the hypothesis was wrong.

Although the general logic of hypothesis testing is relatively simple, there are many details involved in standardizing and quantifying the hypothesis testing procedure. In this chapter we will examine these details and develop the general technique of hypothesis testing.

The hypothesis-testing procedure usually begins with an unknown population, specifically, a population with an unknown mean. Often this situation arises after a treatment is administered to a known population (see Figure 8.1). In this case, the researcher begins with an original population with known parameters. For example, suppose the original population is known to be normal with $\mu = 26$ and $\sigma = 4$. The researcher's question concerns what effect the treatment will have on this

Figure 8.1

The basic experimental situation for hypothesis testing. It is assumed that the parameter μ is known for the population before treatment. The purpose of the experiment is to determine whether or not the treatment has an effect on the population mean.

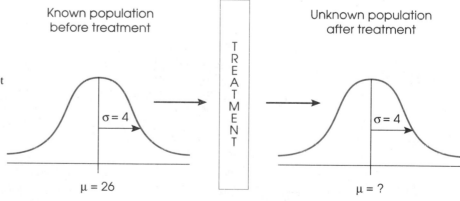

population. Will the treatment cause the scores to increase, or decrease, or will the treatment have no effect whatsoever? The specific question is, What happens to the population mean after treatment? Hypothesis testing is a procedure that will help the researcher determine whether or not a treatment effect occurred. This situation is illustrated in Figure 8.1.

To simplify the hypothesis-testing situation, one basic assumption is made about the effect of the treatment: If the treatment has any effect, it is simply to add (or subtract) a constant amount to each individual's score. You should recall from Chapters 3 and 4 that adding (or subtracting) a constant will not change the shape of the population, nor will it change the standard deviation. Thus we will assume that the population after treatment has the same shape as the original population, and has the same standard deviation as the original population. This assumption is incorporated into the situation shown in Figure 8.1.

The first step in the hypothesis-testing procedure involves stating a hypothesis about the unknown population mean. We could, for example, hypothesize that the treatment has no effect, so that the population mean after treatment is the same as the mean for the original population. Or, we might hypothesize that the treatment will increase each individual's score by 10 points so that the mean for the treated population will be 10 points higher than the mean for the original population. Notice that the hypothesis concerns the entire population.

Next, the researcher would collect sample data. A sample of individuals is selected from the treated population. That is, the researcher obtains a sample of individuals who have received the treatment. The sample data are then used to evaluate the hypothesis. Specifically, the researcher must determine whether the sample data are consistent with the hypothesis or if the sample data contradict the hypothesis. Notice that the researcher is using the information from a sample to evaluate a hypothesis about a population. This is the basis of inferential statistics: using sample data to draw inferences about populations.

In this overview of the hypothesis-testing procedure, you can think of the researcher as a police detective gathering evidence. The sample is the evidence that the researcher uses to build a case for or against the hypothesis. Sometimes the evidence is overwhelming, and the researcher can make confident conclusions about the hypothesis. Often the evidence is not very convincing, and the researcher is uncertain about a conclusion. There is always a possibility that the evidence is misleading and the researcher will reach the wrong conclusion.

Because the process of hypothesis testing involves some uncertainty and can lead to errors, the procedure has been formalized to a standard series of operations. In this way, the researcher has a standardized method for evaluating the evidence from an experiment. Other researchers will recognize and understand exactly how the data were evaluated and how conclusions were reached. In addition, the hypothesis-testing procedure is developed so that a researcher can identify and partially control the risk of an error. Throughout this book we will present hypothesis testing as a four-step procedure.

The following example will be used to provide a concrete foundation for introducing the hypothesis-testing procedure. Psychologists have noted that stimulation during infancy can have profound effects on the development of infant rats. It has been demonstrated that stimulation (for example, increased handling) and even stress (mild electric shock) result in eyes opening sooner, more rapid brain maturation, decreases in emotionality, faster growth, and larger body weight (see

Levine, 1960). Based on the data, one might theorize that increased stimulation and possibly occasional mild stress early in life can be beneficial. Suppose a researcher who is interested in this developmental theory would like to determine whether or not stimulation during infancy also has an effect on human development.

STEP 1: STATING THE HYPOTHESES

Suppose our researcher knows from national health statistics that the average weight for 2-year-olds who are not receiving any special treatment is $\mu = 26$ pounds. To determine whether increased handling has any effect, the researcher must compare the weights from the sample data with this national average. To begin this process, the researcher states two opposing hypotheses. Note that both hypotheses are stated in terms of population parameters.

The first is the *null hypothesis,* or H_0. This hypothesis states that the treatment has no effect. (The null hypothesis always says that there is no effect, no change, no difference, nothing happened—hence the name *null.*) In this example, the null hypothesis states that additional handling during infancy will have *no effect* on body weight for the population of infants. In symbols, this hypothesis would be

$$H_0 : \mu_{\text{infants handled}} = 26 \text{ pounds}$$

(Even with extra handling, the mean weight at 2 years is still 26 pounds.)

The goal of inferential statistics is to make general statements about the population by using sample data. Therefore, when testing hypotheses, we make our predictions about the population parameters.

DEFINITION

The *null hypothesis* (H_0) predicts that the independent variable (treatment) has no effect on the dependent variable for the population.

The second hypothesis is simply the opposite of the null hypothesis, and it is called the *scientific* or *alternative hypothesis* (H_1). This hypothesis states that the treatment will have an effect on the dependent variable. For this example, it predicts that handling does alter growth for the population. In symbols, it is represented as

$$H_1 : \mu_{\text{infants handled}} \neq 26$$

(With handling, the mean will be different from 26 pounds.)

DEFINITION

The *alternative hypothesis* (H_1) predicts that the independent variable (treatment) will have an effect on the dependent variable for the population.

Notice that the alternative hypothesis simply states that there will be some type of change. It does not specify whether the effect will be increased or decreased growth. In some circumstances it is appropriate to specify the direction of the effect in H_1. For example, the researcher might hypothesize that increased handling will increase growth ($\mu > 26$ pounds). This type of hypothesis results in a directional hypothesis test, which will be examined in detail later in this chapter. For now we will concentrate on nondirectional tests, where the hypotheses always state that the treatment has some effect (H_1) or has no effect (H_0). A nondirectional hypothesis test is always appropriate, even when a researcher has a definite prediction that the treatment will increase (or decrease) scores. For this example, we are examining whether handling in infancy does alter growth in some way (H_1) or has no effect (H_0). You should also note that both hypotheses refer to a population whose mean is unknown—namely, the population of infants who receive extra handling early in life.

STEP 2: SETTING THE CRITERIA FOR A DECISION

The researcher will eventually use the data from the sample to evaluate the credibility of the null hypothesis. For this example, the null hypothesis states that the mean for the treated population will still be $\mu = 26$ (the same as the original population). Thus, if our sample of treated infants showed a mean weight close to 26 pounds, we could conclude that the treatment (increased handling) does not seem to have any effect. On the other hand, if our sample weighed much more (or less) than 26 pounds, we could conclude that the increased handling does seem to have an effect on development.

Notice that the final decision is based on a comparison of the sample data versus the null hypothesis. Whenever there is a big discrepancy between the data and the hypothesis, we can conclude that the hypothesis is wrong. However, you should also notice that we are comparing a sample (the data) versus a population (the null hypothesis). You should recall from Chapter 7 that a sample generally will not be identical to its population. There will almost always be some discrepancy between a sample and its population due to sampling error. The problem for the researcher is to determine whether the difference between the sample data and the null hypothesis is the result of the treatment effect or is simply due to sampling error. When does the sample provide sufficient evidence to conclude that the treatment really does have an effect? To solve this problem, the researcher must establish criteria that define precisely how much difference must exist between the data and the null hypothesis to justify a decision that the null hypothesis is false. The procedure for establishing criteria is considered in Section 8.2. For now, you should recognize that criteria are essential for a researcher to make an objective decision about the hypotheses.

STEP 3: COLLECTING SAMPLE DATA

The next step in hypothesis testing is to obtain the sample data. A random sample of infants would be selected and parents would be trained to provide additional daily handling during the first few months of infancy. Then the body weight of the infants would be measured when they reach 2 years of age. Usually the raw data from the sample are summarized in a single statistic, such as the sample mean or a z-score. Of course, selecting a sample randomly is important because it helps ensure that the sample is representative of the population. For example, it would help avoid the selection of a group of infants that would be unusually small or large, regardless of the treatment.

You also should note that the data are collected only after the researcher has stated hypotheses and established criteria for making a decision. This sequence of events helps ensure that a researcher makes an honest, objective evaluation of the data and does not tamper with the decision criteria after the experiment outcome is known.

STEP 4: EVALUATING THE NULL HYPOTHESIS

In the final step, the researcher compares the data ($\overline{X}$) with the null hypothesis (μ) and makes a decision according to the criteria that were established in step 2. There are two possible decisions, and both are stated in terms of the null hypothesis.

REJECTING THE NULL HYPOTHESIS VERSUS PROVING THE ALTERNATIVE HYPOTHESIS

IT MAY seem awkward to pay so much attention to the null hypothesis. After all, the purpose of most experiments is to show that a treatment does have an effect, and the null hypothesis states that there is no effect. The reason for focusing on the null hypothesis rather than the alternative hypothesis comes from the limitations of inferential logic. Remember, we want to use the sample data to draw conclusions, or inferences, about a population. Logically, it is much easier to demonstrate that a universal (population) hypothesis is false than to demonstrate that it is true. This principle is shown more clearly in a simple example. Suppose you make the universal statement "all dogs have four legs" and you intend to test this hypothesis by using a sample of one dog. If the dog in your sample does have four legs, have you proved the statement? It

should be clear that one four-legged dog does not prove the general statement to be true. On the other hand, suppose the dog in your sample has only three legs. In this case, you have proved the statement to be false. Again, it is much easier to show that something is false than to prove that it is true.

Hypothesis testing uses this logical principle to achieve its goals. It would be difficult to state "the treatment has an effect" as the hypothesis and then try to prove that this is true. Therefore, we state the null hypothesis, "the treatment has no effect," and try to show that it is false. The end result still is to demonstrate that the treatment does have an effect. That is, we find support for the alternative hypothesis by disproving (rejecting) the null hypothesis.

One possibility is that the researcher decides to *reject the null hypothesis*. This decision is made whenever the sample data are substantially different from what the null hypothesis predicts. In this case, the data provide strong evidence that the treatment does have an effect.

The second possibility occurs when the data do not provide convincing evidence of a treatment effect. In this case the sample data are consistent with the null hypothesis, and the statistical decision is to *fail to reject the null hypothesis*. The term *fail to reject* is used because the experiment failed to produce evidence that H_0 is wrong. (See Box 8.1.)

ERRORS IN HYPOTHESIS TESTING

The problem in hypothesis testing is deciding whether or not the sample data are consistent with the null hypothesis. In the second step of the hypothesis-testing procedure, we identify the kind of data that are expected if the null hypothesis is true. If the outcome of the experiment is consistent with this prediction, then there is no need to be suspicious about the credibility of the null hypothesis. If, on the other hand, the outcome of the experiment is very different from this prediction, then we would reject the null hypothesis because the evidence is overwhelmingly against it. In either case, it is possible that the data obtained from a single experiment can be misleading and cause a researcher to make an incorrect decision. The two possibilities are presented here and in Box 8.2.

Type I errors It is possible to reject the null hypothesis when in reality the treatment has no effect. The outcome of the experiment could be different from what H_0 predicted just by chance. After all, unusual events do occur. For example, it is possible, although unlikely, to toss a balanced coin five times and have it turn

A SUMMARY OF STATISTICAL ERRORS

Definitions:

A Type I error is rejecting a true null hypothesis.
A Type II error is failing to reject a false null hypothesis.

Interpretation:

Type I error: The researcher concludes that the treatment does have an effect when, in fact, there is no treatment effect.

Type II error: The researcher concludes that there is no evidence for a treatment effect when, in fact, the treatment does have an effect.

How Does it Happen?:

Type I error: By chance, the sample consists of individuals with extreme scores. As a result, the sample looks different from what we would have expected according to H_0. Note that the treatment has not actually affected the individuals in the sample—they were different from average from the start of the experiment.

Type II error: Although there are several explanations for a type II error, the simplest is that the treatment effect was too small to have a noticeable effect on the sample. As a result, the sample does not appear to have been affected by the treatment. It is also possible that, just by chance, the sample was extreme to start with and in the opposite direction for the treatment effect. The treatment effect, in turn, restores the sample to the average that is expected by H_0. A treatment effect does not appear to have occurred even though it did.

Consequences:

Type I error: Because the sample data appear to demonstrate a treatment effect, the researcher may claim in a published report that the treatment has an effect. This is a false report and can have serious consequences. For one, other researchers may spend precious time and resources trying to replicate the findings to no avail. In addition, the false report creates a false data base upon which other workers develop theories and plan new experiments. In reality, they may be taking a journey down an experimental and theoretical dead end.

Type II error: In this case, the sample data do not provide sufficient evidence to say that the treatment has any effect—that is, the experiment has failed to detect the treatment effect. The researcher can interpret this finding in two different ways:

First, the researcher can conclude that the treatment probably does have an effect but the experiment was not good enough to find it. Perhaps an improved experiment (larger sample, better measurement, more potent treatment, etc.) would be able to demonstrate the treatment effect. The consequence is that refined experiments may be capable of detecting the effect.

Second, the researcher may believe that the statistical decision is correct. Either the treatment has no effect, or the effect is too small to be important. In this case, the experiment is abandoned. Note that this interpretation can have serious consequences. It means that the researcher is giving up a line of research that could have otherwise provided important findings.

up heads every time. In the experiment we have been considering, it is possible just by chance to select a sample of exceptional infants who display unusual (much less or much greater than normal) growth patterns even though the handling treatment has no effect. In this situation the data would lead us to reject the null hypothesis even though it is correct. This kind of mistake is called a *Type I error* (see Table 8.1), and in psychology it is very serious mistake. A Type I error results in the investigator making a false report of a treatment effect. In the handling experiment, the researcher would claim that handling during infancy alters growth when in fact no such effect exists.

DEFINITION   A *Type I error* consists of rejecting the null hypothesis when H_0 is actually true.

Table 8.1

Possible outcomes of a statistical decision

		ACTUAL SITUATION	
		No Effect, H_0 True	Effect Exists, H_0 False
Experimenter's decision	Reject H_0	Type I error	Decision correct
	Retain H_0	Decision correct	Type II error

Type II errors It also is possible for the data to be consistent with the null hypothesis even when H_0 is false. Suppose that handling has a small effect on growth so that even with early handling our sample averages slightly above 26 pounds at 2 years of age. However, the difference between the sample and the predicted (H_0) data is too small to reject H_0 confidently. Another possibility is that the sample of infants was exceptionally small at the start. Handling increases their growth but only to the extent that they reach the expected weight of 26 pounds at 2 years. In these cases, we would decide to retain a null hypothesis when in reality it is false, a *Type II error* (Table 8.1). That is, we conclude that the treatment has no effect when in fact it does.

DEFINITION

In a *Type II error*, the investigator fails to reject a null hypothesis that is really false.

LEARNING CHECK

1. What does the null hypothesis predict about a population?

2. Why do we evaluate (decide to reject or not reject) the null hypothesis instead of evaluating the alternative hypothesis?

3. What is a Type I error? A Type II error?

4. Is it possible to commit a Type II error when H_0 is rejected? Explain your answer.

5. Why do we state hypotheses in terms of population parameters?

ANSWERS

1. The null hypothesis predicts that the treatment will have no effect on the dependent variable for the population.

2. It is much easier to disprove a universal (population) statement than to prove one. Therefore, to find support for a treatment effect in the population, we must obtain sample data that suggest we should reject H_0. That is, we support the presence of a treatment effect when we disprove the null hypothesis.

3. A Type I error occurs when the experimenter rejects a null hypothesis that is actually true. An effect is reported when none exists. A Type II error occurs when the decision is "fail to reject H_0" but the null hypothesis is really false. One fails to report an effect that does exist.

4. No. A Type II error results from *failing to reject* a false H_0. Therefore, it cannot result from rejecting the null hypothesis.

5. We make predictions about the population because the goal of inferential statistics is to make general statements about the *population* based on the sample data.

SECTION 8.2 **EVALUATING HYPOTHESES**

As previously noted, there is always the possibility for error in making an inference. As a result, we can never be absolutely positive that a hypothesis test has produced the correct decision. Although we cannot know for certain if our decision is right or wrong, we can know the probabilities for being right or wrong. Specifically, the hypothesis testing procedure is structured so that a researcher can specify and control the probability of making a Type I error. By keeping this probability small, a researcher can be confident that the risk of error is very low whenever the null hypothesis is rejected.

ALPHA LEVEL: MINIMIZING THE RISK OF A TYPE I ERROR

The final decision in a hypothesis test is based on a comparison of the sample data versus the null hypothesis. Specifically, a big discrepancy between the data ($\overline{X}$) and the null hypothesis (μ) will lead us to reject the null hypothesis. To formalize this decision process, it is necessary to determine what data are expected if H_0 is true and what data are very unlikely. This is accomplished by examining the distribution of all possible outcomes if the null hypothesis is true. Usually, this is the distribution of sample means for the sample size (n) that was used in the experiment. This distribution is then separated into two parts:

1. Those sample means that are expected (high probability) if H_0 is true— that is, sample data that are consistent with the null hypothesis.
2. Those sample means that are very unlikely (low probability) if H_0 is true— that is, sample data that are very different from the null hypothesis.

In using statistical symbols and notation for hypothesis testing, we will follow APA style as outlined in the *Publication Manual of the American Psychological Association*. The APA style does not use a leading zero in a decimal value for an alpha level. The expression $\alpha = .05$ is traditionally read ''alpha equals point oh-five.''

The *level of significance,* also called the *alpha level,* is simply a probability value that is used to define the term ''very unlikely.'' By convention, alpha (α) levels are very small probabilities, commonly .05 (5%), .01 (1%), or .001 (0.1%). With an alpha level of $\alpha = .05$, for example, the extreme 5% of the distribution of sample means (''very unlikely'' outcomes) would be separated from the rest of the distribution (see Figure 8.2). Thus the alpha level is used to divide the distribution of sample means into two sections: (1) sample means that are compatible with the null hypothesis (the center of the distribution), and (2) sample means that are significantly different from the null hypothesis (the very unlikely values in the extreme tails). Whenever we obtain sample data in the extreme tails of the distribution, we will conclude that there is a significant discrepancy between the data and the hypothesis, and we will reject the null hypothesis.

Although extreme data, as defined by alpha, are very unlikely to be obtained if H_0 is true, there is still a slim probability (equal to α) that such data will be obtained. That is, when the null hypothesis is true, it is still possible to obtain extreme data that will lead us to reject the null hypothesis. Thus it is possible to reject a true null hypothesis and thereby commit a Type I Error. However, the

Figure 8.2

The alpha level separates the extreme and unlikely sample means from the rest of the distribution.

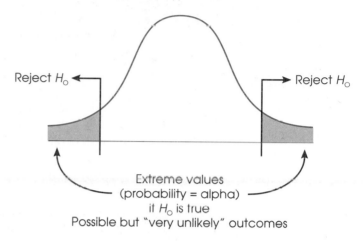

The distribution of sample means
(all possible experimental outcomes)
if the null hypothesis is true

Reject H_0 ← → Reject H_0

Extreme values
(probability = alpha)
if H_0 is true
Possible but "very unlikely" outcomes

probability of this error occurring is determined by the alpha level. With $\alpha = .05$, for example, there is a 5% chance of obtaining extreme sample data that will lead us to reject H_0 even when H_0 is true. Thus, with $\alpha = .05$, there is a 5% risk of committing a Type I Error.

DEFINITION

The *alpha level,* or *level of significance,* is a probability value that defines the very unlikely sample outcomes when the null hypothesis is true. Whenever an experiment produces very unlikely data (as defined by the alpha level), we will reject the null hypothesis. Thus the alpha level also defines the probability of a Type I Error—that is the probability of rejecting H_0 when it is actually true.

We will examine the role that alpha plays in the hypothesis-testing procedure by returning to the example of the effects of increased handling during infancy.

PROCEDURE AND STEPS

Recall that the study examines the effect of extra handling during infancy on growth. We will assume that the researcher intends to conduct this experiment using a sample of $n = 16$ infants. Each set of parents is instructed in how to provide additional handling during the first few months of their infant's life, and then the child's weight is measured at 2 years of age. Let us assume that weights are normally distributed with $\mu = 26$ pounds and $\sigma = 4$ for the population of untreated (did not receive additional handling) children. There are four steps to hypothesis testing: (1) state the hypotheses and select an alpha level, (2) use the alpha level to define what kind of sample data would warrant rejection of H_0, (3) analyze the sample data, and (4) make a decision about H_0. We will use these steps to assess the effect of additional handling during infancy on growth.

STEP 1

We must state the hypotheses and select an alpha level. The null hypothesis predicts that no effect will occur. That is, even with additional handling during infancy, the population mean weight for 2-year-olds will still be 26 pounds. In symbols, this hypothesis is stated as follows:

$$H_0 : \mu_{\text{handling in infancy}} = 26 \text{ pounds}$$

The alternative hypothesis states that early handling will change the mean weight for the population. In symbols, this hypothesis would state the following:

$$H_1 : \mu_{\text{handling}} \neq 26 \text{ pounds}$$

We will select an alpha level of 5%, or in terms of a proportion, $\alpha = .05$. This means that in order to reject the null hypothesis, the sample data must be extremely convincing—the data must be in the most extreme 5% of the distribution. By setting α to this level, we are limiting the probability of a Type I error to only 5%.

STEP 2   We establish criteria that define what kind of sample data would warrant rejection of the null hypothesis. We begin by looking at all the possible data that could be obtained if the null hypothesis were true. Our researcher is taking a random sample of $n = 16$. If the null hypothesis is true, it is possible to examine the distribution of all the possible sample means that could be obtained from this experiment. This distribution is the distribution of sample means based on samples of $n = 16$. It will be normal and have an expected value of $\mu = 26$ if H_0 is true. Furthermore, this distribution will have a standard error of

$$\sigma_{\bar{X}} = \frac{\sigma}{\sqrt{n}} = \frac{4}{\sqrt{16}} = \frac{4}{4} = 1$$

This distribution is shown in Figure 8.3.

If H_0 is true we expect to obtain a sample mean near the population mean, $\mu = 26$. Extreme values in the tails of the distribution would be extremely unlikely.

We have selected the value of $\alpha = .05$ for the level of significance. This proportion is divided evenly between the two tails of the distribution (see Figure 8.3). It is very unlikely that we would obtain a sample mean from this area of the distribution if H_0 is true. The area between the tails is the middle 95% of the distribution. The area contains the most likely sample means, and it is very likely that we would obtain a sample from this region if H_0 is true.

Notice that the boundaries that separate the middle 95% from the extreme 5% (2.5% in each tail) are located at the z-score values of $+1.96$ and -1.96 (from the unit normal table in Appendix B). A z-score of 1.96 indicates that the corresponding sample mean is 1.96 standard errors away from μ. For this example, the standard error is $\sigma_{\bar{X}} = 1$, so the z-score of $+1.96$ corresponds to a sample mean of 27.96 and the z-score of -1.96 corresponds to a sample mean of 24.04. These values mark off the boundaries between the middle 95% and the extreme tails of the distribution (see Figure 8.3).

If the treatment has no effect (H_0 is true), then we would expect to observe a sample mean near 26 pounds. Most of the time (95% to be exact) we would expect the sample to be in the middle section of the distribution. It is very improbable that we would obtain a sample mean that is out in the extreme tails of the distribution if H_0 is true. These extreme tails, the shaded areas in Figure 8.3, are

Figure 8.3

The distribution of all the possible sample means for $n = 16$ that could be obtained if H_0 is true. The boundaries separate the middle 95% from the most extreme 5% ($\alpha = .05$).

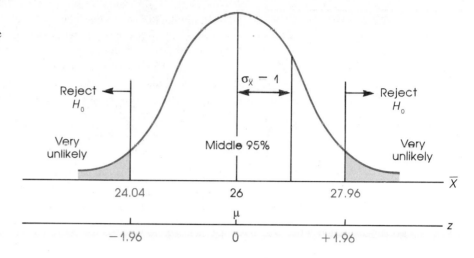

called the *critical region* of the distribution. If H_0 were true, then it would be extremely unlikely to obtain a sample in the critical region. Notice that we have defined "extremely unlikely" as meaning "having a probability less than alpha." For this example, the H_0 is rejected only when the sample data are really extreme—when the probability of our sample observation is less than the alpha level ($p < .05$). In other words, H_0 is rejected when the sample data fall in the critical region. Thus it may be helpful to consider critical regions as "regions of rejection."

APA style does not use a leading zero in a probability value that refers to a level of significance.

DEFINITION   The *critical region* is composed of extreme sample values that are very unlikely to be obtained if the null hypothesis is true. The size of the critical region is determined by the alpha level. Sample data that fall in the critical region will warrant the rejection of the null hypothesis.

STEP 3   We now turn our attention to the sample data. The researcher selects a sample of $n = 16$ infants, trains each set of parents to administer extra handling, and then records each child's weight at age 2. Suppose the average weight for this sample is $\overline{X} = 31$ pounds. What can we conclude about the relationship between handling in infancy and growth?

STEP 4   We must make a decision about the null hypothesis. The result we obtained from the sample, $\overline{X} = 31$, lies in the critical region (Figure 8.3). The sample is not what we expected if the null hypothesis is true. It is an extremely unlikely outcome ($p < .05$) if H_0 is true. Therefore, we decide to reject the null hypothesis and conclude that extra handling during infancy did have a statistically significant effect on growth. With this statistical decision, we are risking a Type I error. That is, we could be rejecting a true null hypothesis. It is possible that the handling had no effect on growth and that the infants we sampled would have averaged 31 pounds anyway. However, this is very unlikely. If H_0 is true, the probability of obtaining any sample in the critical region is less than 5%, the alpha level we selected. The maximum probability of committing a Type I error is equal to alpha.

Always state your conclusion in terms of the independent variable and the dependent variable for the particular experiment being examined.

z-SCORES AND HYPOTHESIS TESTING

In the handling example, our decision to reject H_0 was based on the obtained sample mean of $\overline{X} = 31$, which falls within the critical region. We could have based this decision entirely on z-scores. For this example, the critical region consists of any z value greater than $+1.96$ or less than -1.96 (figure 8.3). We can simply convert the obtained $\overline{X}$ value into a z-score to determine its location. That is, we determine whether or not it is in the critical region. For the obtained sample,

$$z = \frac{\overline{X} - \mu}{\sigma_{\overline{X}}} = \frac{31 - 26}{1} = 5.00$$

The obtained z-score is greater than $+1.96$ and thus lies in the critical region. The statistical decision would be the same, H_0 is rejected. Notice that the z-score is being used to test a hypothesis. In this use, the z-score is often called a *test statistic*. We will examine other types of test statistics which are used in hypothesis testing in later chapters.

THE STRUCTURE OF THE z-SCORE FORMULA

It is useful to define the z-score formula

$$z = \frac{\overline{X} - \mu}{\sigma_{\overline{X}}}$$

in terms of the important steps and elements of hypothesis testing. The null hypothesis is represented in the formula by μ. The value of μ that we use in the formula is the value predicted by H_0. We test H_0 by collecting sample data, which are represented by the sample mean ($\overline{X}$) in the formula. Thus the numerator of the z formula can be rewritten as

$$\overline{X} - \mu = \text{sample data} - \text{population hypothesis}$$

You should recall that the standard error ($\sigma_{\overline{X}}$) measures the standard distance between a sample mean and the population mean. Thus standard error measures the expected difference (due to chance) between $\overline{X}$ and μ. Now we can restate the entire z-score test statistic as

$$z = \frac{\text{sample data} - \text{population hypothesis}}{\text{standard error between } \overline{X} \text{ and } \mu}$$

Notice that the difference between the sample data and the null hypothesis must be substantially larger than would be expected by chance in order to obtain a z-score that is large enough to fall in the critical region. The structure of this z-score formula will form the basis for some of the test statistics to follow in later chapters.

LEARNING CHECK

1. Define alpha.

2. If H_0 is rejected when alpha is .05, will it necessarily be rejected when alpha has been set at .01?

3. What is the critical region? How is it used?

4. Experimenter 1 typically sets alpha to .10, whereas experimenter 2 always uses an alpha level of .05. In the long run, which experimenter will make more Type I errors?

ANSWERS
1. Alpha is the risk an investigator takes of committing a Type I error. The alpha level determines the level of significance of a statistical test.

2. Not necessarily. The data may be extreme enough to warrant rejecting H_0 at the 5% level of significance but not extreme enough for the same decision at the 1% level.

3. The critical region consists of extreme sample values that are very unlikely to be obtained (probability less than α) if the null hypothesis is true. If sample data fall in the critical region, we reject H_0.

4. Experimenter 1 is taking a greater risk (10%) of committing a Type I error.

FAILURES TO REJECT THE NULL HYPOTHESIS

Using the handling example again, let us suppose that we obtained a sample of $n = 16$ infants that attained an average weight of $\bar{X} = 27.5$ pounds at 2 years. Steps 1 and 2 (stating the hypotheses and locating the critical region) remain the same. For Step 3, we can compute the z-score for this sample mean. If $\bar{X} = 27.5$, then

$$z = \frac{\bar{X} - \mu}{\sigma_{\bar{X}}} = \frac{27.5 - 26}{1} = 1.50$$

Limitations in the logic of inference make it easier to disprove a hypothesis about the population (Box 8.1).

In the final step, the statistical decision is made. The z-score for the obtained sample score is not in the critical region. This is the kind of outcome we would expect if H_0 were true. It is important to note that we have not proved that the null hypothesis is true. The sample provides only limited information about the entire population, and, in this case, we did not obtain sufficient evidence to claim that additional handling early in life does or does not have an effect on growth. For this reason, researchers avoid using the phrase ''accepting the null hypothesis,'' opting instead for ''failing to reject the null hypothesis.'' The latter phrase is more consistent with the logic of hypothesis testing. When the data are not overwhelmingly contrary to H_0, at best all we can say is that the data do not provide sufficient evidence to reject the null hypothesis.

Our decision to ''fail to reject'' H_0 means that we are risking a Type II error. For this example, a Type II error would mean that the extra handling actually did have some effect and yet we failed to discover it. A Type II error generally is not as serious a mistake as a Type I error. The consequences of a Type II error would be that a real effect is not reported. If a researcher suspects that a Type II error has occurred, there is always the option of repeating the experiment, usually with some refinements or modifications.

α is for Type I, and β is for Type II.

Unlike Type I errors where the exact amount of risk is specified by the alpha level (α), there is no simple way to determine the probability of a Type II error. In fact, this probability is not a single value but rather depends on the size of the treatment effect. Although the exact probability of committing a Type II error is not easily calculated, it is identified by the Greek letter *beta*, β.

WORD

REPORTING THE RESULTS OF THE STATISTICAL TEST

There is a special jargon and notational system that is used in published reports of hypothesis tests. When you are reading a scientific journal, for example, you will not be told explicitly that the researcher evaluated the data using a z-score as a test statistic with an alpha level of .05. Instead, you will see a statement like

"The treatment effect was significant, $z = 3.85$, $p < .05$".

Let us examine this statement part by part. First, what is meant by the term *significant?* In statistical tests, this word indicates that the result is different from what would be expected by chance. A significant result means that the null hypothesis has been rejected. That is, the data are in the critical region and not what we would have expected to obtain if H_0 were true.

Next, what is the meaning of $z = 3.85$? The z indicates that the data were used to compute a z-score for a test statistic and that its value was 3.85. Finally, what is meant by $p < .05$? This part of the statement is the conventional way of specifying the alpha level that was used for the hypothesis test. More specifically, we are being told that the result of the experiment would occur by chance with a probability (p) that is less than .05.

In circumstances where the statistical decision is to fail to reject H_0, the report might state that "There was no evidence for an effect, $z = 1.30$, $p > .10$." In this case, we are saying that the obtained result, $z = 1.30$, is not unusual (not in the critical region) and is relatively likely to occur by chance (the probability is greater than .10).

MORE ABOUT ALPHA—THE LEVEL OF SIGNIFICANCE

As you have seen, the alpha level for a hypothesis test serves two very important functions. First, alpha determines the risk of a Type I error. Second, alpha helps determine the boundaries for the critical region. As you might expect, these two functions interact with each other. When you lower the alpha level—for example, from .05 to .01—you reduce the risk of a Type I error. To gain this extra margin of safety, you must demand more evidence from the data before you are willing to reject H_0. This is accomplished by moving the boundaries for the critical region. With $\alpha = .05$ for example, the z-score boundaries are located at ± 1.96. For $\alpha = .01$, the boundaries move to $z = \pm 2.58$, and with $\alpha = .001$, the boundaries move all the way out to $z = \pm 3.30$ (see Figure 8.4). With $\alpha = .001$, it would take a huge difference between the data and the hypothesis to be significant. In general, as you lower the alpha level, the critical boundaries move farther away from the population mean, and it becomes increasingly more difficult to obtain a sample that is located in the critical region. Thus, sample data that are sufficient to reject H_0 at the .05 level of significance may not provide sufficient evidence to reject H_0 at the .01 level. If you push alpha to an extremely low level, it can become essentially impossible for an experiment ever to demonstrate a significant treatment effect.

Where do you set the critical boundaries so that your experiment has some chance of being successful and (at the same time) minimize your risk of a Type I error? Historically, the answer is to use an alpha level of .05. This value was first suggested in 1925 by a well-known statistician named Sir Ronald A. Fisher. Fisher noted that it is convenient to use the .05 level as a limit in judging whether a result is considered to be significant or not, and he suggested that researchers ignore all results that fail to reach this limit. Although Fisher selected $\alpha = .05$ as a personal,

Figure 8.4

The location of the critical region boundaries for three different levels of significance: $\alpha = .05$, $\alpha = .01$, and $\alpha = .001$.

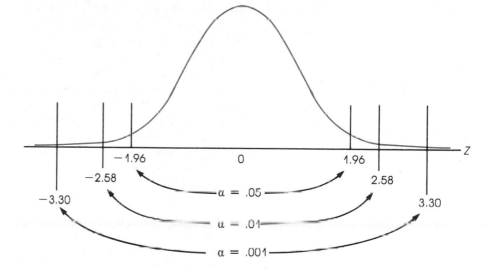

arbitrary standard, it has become recognized as the minimum level of significance that is acceptable for publication of research in many journals. In fact, some of the more prestigious journals require an alpha level of .01 for their published results. For most research an alpha level of .05 is appropriate and is generally defined as *statistically significant*. The .01 level of significance is used in situations where you have special reason to fear a Type I error or where you want to make an exceptionally strong demonstration of a treatment effect. The .01 alpha level is generally defined as *highly statistically significant*. (For more information on the origins of the .05 level of significance, see the excellent short article by Cowles and Davis, 1982.)

ASSUMPTIONS FOR HYPOTHESIS TESTS WITH z-SCORES

It will become evident in later chapters that certain conditions must be present for each type of hypothesis test to be an appropriate and accurate procedure. These conditions are assumed to be satisfied when the results of a hypothesis test are interpreted. However, the decisions based on the test statistic (that is, rejecting or not rejecting H_0) may be compromised if these assumptions are not satisfied. In practice, researchers are not overly concerned with the conditions of a statistical test unless they have strong suspicions that the assumptions have been violated. Nevertheless, it is crucial to keep in mind the fundamental conditions that are associated with each type of statistical test to ensure that it is being used appropriately. The assumptions for hypothesis tests with z-scores which involve one sample are summarized below.

Random sampling   It is assumed that the subjects used to obtain the sample data were selected randomly. Remember, we wish to generalize our findings from the sample to the population. This task is accomplished when we use sample data to test a hypothesis about the population. Therefore, the sample must be representative of the population from which it has been drawn. Random sampling helps to ensure that it is representative.

The value of σ is unchanged by the treatment   The general purpose of hypothesis testing is to determine whether or not a treatment (independent variable) produces a change in the population mean. The null hypothesis, the critical region, and the z-score statistic all are concerned with the treated population. In the z-score formula we use $\bar{X}$ from the treated sample, a hypothesized value of μ for the treated population and a standard error that indicates how close $\bar{X}$ should be to μ. However, you may have noticed that when we compute the standard error, we use the standard deviation from the untreated population. Thus, the z-score appears to be using values from two different populations: $\bar{X}$ and μ for the treated population and σ from the untreated population. To justify this apparent contradiction we must make an assumption. Specifically, we must assume that the value of σ is the same after treatment as it was before treatment.

Actually, this assumption is the consequence of a more general assumption that is part of many statistical procedures. This general assumption states that the effect of the treatment is to add (or subtract) a constant amount to every score in the population. You should recall that adding (or subtracting) a constant will change the mean but will have no effect on the standard deviation. You also should note that this assumption is a theoretical ideal. In actual experiments a treatment generally will not show a perfect and consistent additive effect.

Normal sampling distribution   To evaluate hypotheses with z-scores, we have used the unit normal table to identify the critical region. This table can be used only if the distribution of sample means is normal.

LEARNING CHECK   1. An instructor has been teaching large sections of general psychology for the past 10 semesters. As a group, final exam scores are normally distributed with $\mu = 42$ and $\sigma = 9$. With the current class of $n = 100$ students, the instructor tries a different teaching format. Once a week the class breaks down into smaller groups that meet with the instructor for discussion of recent lecture and reading material. At the end of the semester, the instructor notes that the mean for this section on the final exam was $\bar{X} = 46.5$. Did the teaching format have a significant effect on performance on the final exam? Test with alpha set at .05.

    a. State the hypotheses.

    b. Locate the critical region.

    c. Compute the test statistic.

    d. Make a decision regarding H_0.

    e. For this example, identify the independent and dependent variables.

ANSWERS   1. **a.** $H_0 : \mu_{\text{discussion groups}} = 42; H_1 : \mu_{\text{discussion groups}} \neq 42$.

    b. The critical region consists of z-score values greater than $+1.96$ or less than -1.96.

    c. $\sigma_{\bar{X}} = 0.9; z = +5.0$.

    d. Reject H_0 and conclude that teaching format does affect scores on the final exam. The small-group sessions improve final test performance.

    e. The independent variable is teaching format. The dependent variable is the score on the final exam.

DIRECTIONAL (ONE-TAILED) HYPOTHESIS TESTS

The hypothesis testing procedure presented in Section 8.2 was the standard, or *two-tailed*, test format. The *two-tailed* comes from the fact that the critical region is located in both tails of the distribution. This format is by far the most widely accepted procedure for hypothesis testing. Nonetheless, there is an alternative that will be discussed in this section.

Usually, a researcher begins an experiment with a specific prediction about the direction of the treatment effect. For example, a special training program is expected to *increase* student performance, or alcohol consumption is expected to *slow* reaction times. In these situations, it is possible to state the statistical hypotheses in a manner that incorporates the directional prediction into the statement of H_0 and H_1. The result is a directional test, or what commonly is called a *one-tailed test*.

DEFINITION

In a *directional hypothesis test*, or a *one-tailed test*, the statistical hypotheses (H_0 and H_1) specify either an increase or a decrease in the population mean score.

Suppose, for example, a researcher is using a sample of $n = 16$ laboratory rats to examine the effect of a new diet drug. It is known that under regular circumstances these rats eat an average of 10 grams of food each day. The distribution of food consumption is normal with $\sigma = 4$. The expected effect of the drug is to reduce food consumption. The purpose of the experiment is to determine whether or not the drug really works.

THE HYPOTHESES FOR A DIRECTIONAL TEST

Because there is a specific direction expected for the treatment effect, it is possible for the researcher to perform a directional test. The first step (and the most critical step) is to state the statistical hypotheses. Remember that the null hypothesis states that there is no treatment effect and that the alternative hypothesis says that there is an effect. For directional tests, it is easier to begin with the alternative hypothesis. In words, this hypothesis says that with the drug the mean food consumption is *less than* 10 grams per day; that is, the drug does reduce food consumption. In symbols, H_1 would say the following:

$$H_1 : \mu_{\text{with drug}} < 10 \quad \text{(mean food consumption is reduced)}$$

The null hypothesis states that the treatment did not work (the opposite of H_1). In this case, H_0 states that the drug does not reduce food consumption. That is, even with the drug the rats still will eat at least 10 grams per day. In symbols, H_0 would say the following:

$$H_0 : \mu_{\text{with drug}} \geq 10 \quad \text{(the mean is at least 10 grams per day)}$$

THE CRITICAL REGION FOR DIRECTIONAL TESTS

The critical region is determined by sample values that are very unlikely if the null hypothesis is true. That is, sample values that refute H_0 and provide evidence that the treatment really does work. In this example, the treatment is intended to reduce food consumption. Therefore, only sample values that are substantially less than μ

Figure 8.5

The distribution of sample means for $n = 16$ if H_0 is true. The null hypothesis states that the diet pill has no effect, so the population mean will be $\mu = 10$ or larger.

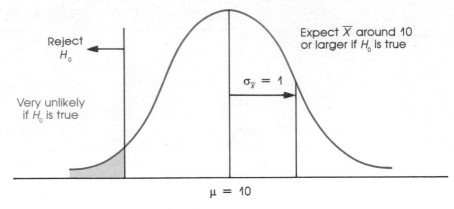

= 10 would indicate that the treatment worked and thereby lead to rejecting H_0. Thus the critical region is located entirely in one tail of the distribution (see Figure 8.5). This is why the directional test commonly is called one-tailed.

A complete example of a one-tailed test is presented next. Once again, the experiment examining the effect of extra handling on the physical growth of infants will be used to demonstrate the hypothesis-testing procedure.

EXAMPLE 8.1   It is known that under regular circumstances the population of 2-year-old children has an average weight of $\mu = 26$ pounds. The distribution of weights is normal with $\sigma = 4$. The researcher selects a random sample of $n = 4$ newborn infants, instructs the parents to provide each child with extra handling, and then records the weight of each child at age 2 years. The average weight for the sample is $\overline{X} = 29.5$ pounds.

STEP 1   *State the hypotheses:* Because the researcher is predicting that extra handling will produce an increase in weight, it is possible to do a directional test. It usually is easier to begin with H_1, the alternative hypothesis, which states that the treatment does have an effect. In symbols,

$$H_1 : \mu > 26 \quad \text{(there is an increase in weight)}$$

The null hypothesis states that the treatment does not have an effect. In symbols,

$$H_0 : \mu \leq 26 \quad \text{(there is no increase)}$$

Simply because you can do a directional test does not mean that you must use a directional test. A two-tailed test is always acceptable and generally preferred.

STEP 2   *Locate the critical region.* To find the critical region, we look at all the possible sample means for $n = 4$ that could be obtained if H_0 were true. This is the distribution of sample means. It will be normal (because the population is normal), it will have a standard error of $\sigma_{\overline{X}} = 4/\sqrt{4} = 2$, and it will have a mean of $\mu = 26$ if the null hypothesis is true. The distribution is shown in Figure 8.6.

If H_0 is true and extra handling does not increase weight, we would expect the sample to average around 26 pounds or less. Only large sample means

Figure 8.6

Critical region for Example 8.1.

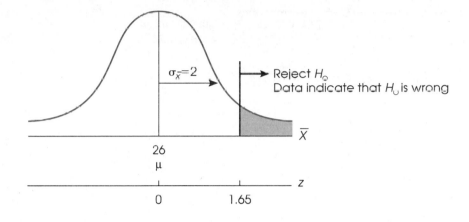

would provide evidence that H_0 is wrong and that extra handling actually does increase weight. Therefore, it is only large values that comprise the critical region. With $\alpha = .05$, the most likely 95% of the distribution is separated from the most unlikely 5% by a z-score of $z = +1.65$ (see Figure 8.6).

STEP 3 *Obtain the sample data:* The mean for the sample is $\overline{X} = 29.5$. This value corresponds to a z-score of

$$z = \frac{\overline{X} - \mu}{\sigma_{\overline{X}}} = \frac{29.5 - 26}{2} = \frac{3.5}{2} = 1.75$$

STEP 4 *Make a statistical decision.* A z-score of $z = +1.75$ indicates that our sample mean is in the critical region. This is a very unlikely outcome if H_0 is true, so the statistical decision is to reject H_0. The conclusion is that extra handling does result in increased growth for infants.

COMPARISON OF ONE-TAILED VERSUS TWO-TAILED TESTS

The general goal of hypothesis testing is to determine whether or not a particular treatment has any effect on a population. The test is performed by selecting a sample, administering the treatment to the sample, and then comparing the result with the original population. If the treated sample is noticeably different from the original population, then we conclude that the treatment has an effect, and we reject H_0. On the other hand, if the treated sample is still similar to the original population, then we conclude that there is no evidence for a treatment effect, and we fail to reject H_0. The critical factor in this decision is the *size of the difference* between treated sample and the original population. A large difference is evidence that the treatment worked; a small difference is not sufficient to say that the treatment has any effect.

The major distinction between one-tailed and two-tailed tests is in the criteria they use for rejecting H_0. A one-tailed test allows you to reject the null hypothesis when the difference between the sample and the population is relatively small, provided the difference is in the specified direction. A two-tailed test, on the other hand, requires a relatively large difference independent of direction. This point is illustrated in the following example.

EXAMPLE 8 . 2   Consider again the experiment examining extra handling and infant growth (see Example 8.1). If we had used a standard two-tailed test, then the hypotheses would have been

$$H_0 : \mu = 26 \text{ pounds} \qquad \text{(no treatment effect)}$$

$$H_1 : \mu \neq 26 \text{ pounds} \qquad \text{(handling does affect growth)}$$

With $\alpha = .05$, the critical region would consist of any z-score beyond the $z = \pm 1.96$ boundaries.

If we obtained the same sample data, $\overline{X} = 29.5$ pounds, which corresponds to a z-score of $z = 1.75$, our statistical decision would be "fail to reject H_0."

Notice that with the two-tailed test (Example 8.2), the difference between the data ($\overline{X} = 29.5$) and the hypothesis ($\mu = 26$) is not big enough to conclude that the hypothesis is wrong. In this case, we are saying that the data do not provide sufficient evidence to justify rejecting H_0. However, with the one-tailed test (Example 8.1), the same data led us to reject H_0.

All researchers agree that one-tailed tests are different from two-tailed tests. However, there are several ways to interpret the difference. One group of researchers (the present authors included) contends that one-tailed tests make it too easy to reject H_0 and, therefore, too easy to make a Type I error. According to this position, a two-tailed test requires strong evidence to reject H_0 and thus provides a convincing demonstration that a treatment effect has occurred. A one-tailed test, on the other hand, can result in rejecting the null hypothesis even when the evidence is relatively weak. For this reason, you usually will find two-tailed tests used for research that is published in journal articles for scrutiny by the scientific community. In this type of research, it is important that the results be convincing, and it is important to avoid a Type I error (publishing a false report). The two-tailed (nondirectional) test satisfies these criteria.

Another group of researchers focuses on the advantages of one-tailed tests. As we have noted, one-tailed tests can lead to rejecting H_0 when the evidence is relatively weak. The statement can be rephrased by saying that one-tailed tests are more sensitive in detecting a treatment effect. If you think of a hypothesis test as a detection device that is used to seek out a treatment effect, then the advantages of a more-sensitive test should be obvious. Although a more-sensitive test will generate more false alarms (Type I errors), it also is more likely to find a significant treatment effect. Thus, one-tailed tests can be very useful in situations where a researcher does not want to overlook any possible significant outcome and where a Type I error is not very damaging. A good example of this situation is in exploratory research. The intent of exploratory research is to investigate a new area or to try an approach that is new and different. Instead of producing publishable results, exploratory research is directed toward generating new research possibilities. In this atmosphere, a researcher is willing to tolerate a few false alarms (Type I errors) in exchange for the increased sensitivity of a one-tailed test.

For the reasons we have outlined, most researchers do not use one-tailed tests except in very limited situations. Even though most experiments are designed with

Remember, you risk a Type I error every time H_0 is rejected.

an expectation that the treatment effect will be in a specific direction, the directional prediction is not included in the statement of the statistical hypothesis. Nevertheless, you will probably encounter one-tailed tests and you may find occasion to use them, so you should understand the rationale and the procedure for conducting directional tests.

LEARNING CHECK

1. A researcher predicts that a treatment will lower scores. If this researcher uses a one-tailed test, will the critical region be in the right- or left-hand tail of the distribution?

2. A psychologist is examining the effects of early sensory deprivation on the development of perceptual discrimination. A sample of $n = 9$ newborn kittens is obtained. These kittens are raised in a completely dark environment for 4 weeks, after which they receive normal visual stimulation. At age 6 months, the kittens are tested on a visual discrimination task. The average score for this sample is $\overline{X} = 32$. It is known that under normal circumstances cats score an average of $\mu = 40$ on this task. The distribution of scores is normal with $\sigma = 12$. The researcher is predicting that the early sensory deprivation will reduce the kittens' performance on the discrimination task. Use a one-tailed test with $\alpha = .01$ to test this hypothesis.

ANSWERS

1. The left-hand tail.

2. The hypotheses are $H_0 : \mu \geq 40$ and $H_1 : \mu < 40$. The critical region is determined by z-scores less than -2.33. The z-score for these sample data is $z = -2.00$. Fail to reject H_0.

SUMMARY

1. Hypothesis testing is an inferential procedure for using the limited data from a sample to draw a general conclusion about a population. It begins with hypothesizing values for the mean of an unknown population, generally a population that has received a treatment (Figure 8.1).

2. The null hypothesis (H_0) states that the treatment has not changed the mean. That is, it is the same as the mean for a known and untreated population. At this stage we also select an alpha level, usually $\alpha = .05$ or $.01$, which sets the risk of committing a Type I error. Alpha determines the level of significance of a statistical test.

3. The second step involves locating the critical region. We examine all the possible experimental outcomes if the null hypothesis is true and then identify the most unlikely values. We define "unlikely according to H_0" as the outcomes with a probability less than alpha. Thus, the selected alpha level determines the critical z-scores that are associated with the critical region. Sample data that produce a z-score that falls within the critical region would imply that H_0 is not tenable.

4. The sample data are collected. Specifically, the sample mean $\overline{X}$ is used to test a hypothesis about μ. To determine how unlikely the obtained sample mean is, we must locate it within the distribution of sample means. This is accomplished by computing a z-score for $\overline{X}$:

$$z = \frac{\overline{X} - \mu}{\sigma_{\overline{X}}}$$

When a z-score is used in the test of a hypothesis, it is called a test statistic.

5. The z-score equation can be expressed as

$$z = \frac{\text{sample mean} - \text{hypothesized population mean}}{\text{standard error between } \overline{X} \text{ and } \mu}$$

That is, the difference between the sample mean and the hypothesized population mean (according to H_0) is compared to (divided by) the amount of error we would expect between $\overline{X}$ and μ.

6. In the fourth step, we compare the obtained data to the set of possible results that were outlined in the second step. That is, if the obtained z-score falls in the critical region, we reject H_0 because it is very unlikely that these data would be obtained if H_0 were true. We would conclude that a treatment effect occurred. If the data are not in the critical region, then there is not sufficient evidence to reject H_0. The statistical decision is "fail to reject H_0." We conclude that we failed to find sufficient evidence for an effect.

7. Whatever decision is reached in a hypothesis test, there is always a risk of making the incorrect decision. There are two types of errors that can be committed.

A Type I error is defined as rejecting a true H_0. This is a serious error because it results in falsely reporting a treatment effect. The risk of a Type I error is determined by the alpha level and, therefore, is under the experimenter's control.

A Type II error is defined as failing to reject a false H_0. In this case, the experiment fails to report an effect that actually occurred. The probability of a Type II error cannot be specified as a single value and depends in part on the size of the treatment effect. It is identified by the symbol β (beta).

8. When a researcher predicts that a treatment effect will be in a particular direction (increase or decrease), it is possible to do a directional or one-tailed test. The first step in this procedure is to state the alternative hypothesis (H_1). This hypothesis states that the treatment works and, for directional tests, specifies the direction of the predicted treatment effect. The null hypothesis is the opposite of H_1. To locate the critical region, you must identify the kind of experimental outcome that refutes the null hypothesis and demonstrates that the treatment works. These outcomes will be located entirely in one tail of the distribution. The entire critical region (5% or 1%, depending on α) will be in one tail.

9. Directional tests should be used with caution because they may allow the rejection of H_0 when the experimental evidence is relatively weak. Even though a researcher may have a specific directional prediction for an experiment, it is generally safer and never inappropriate to use a nondirectional (two-tailed) test.

KEY TERMS

hypothesis testing	Type I error	alpha level	beta
null hypothesis	Type II error	critical region	directional test
alternative hypothesis	level of significance	test statistic	one-tailed test

FOCUS ON PROBLEM SOLVING

1. Hypothesis testing involves a set of logical procedures and rules that enable us to make general statements about a population when all we have are sample data. This logic is reflected in the four steps that have been used throughout this chapter. Hypothesis-testing problems will become easier to tackle when you learn to follow the steps.

STEP 1   State the hypotheses and set the alpha level.

STEP 2   Locate the critical region.

STEP 3   Compute the z-score for the sample data.

STEP 4 Make a decision about H_0 based on the result of Step 3.

A nice benefit of mastering these steps is that all hypothesis tests that will follow use the same basic logic outlined in this chapter.

2. Students often ask, "What alpha level should I use?" Or a student may ask, "Why is an alpha of .05 used?" as opposed to something else. There is no single correct answer to either of these questions. Keep in mind the idea of setting an alpha level in the first place: *to reduce the risk of committing a Type I error*. Therefore, you would not want to set α to something like .20. In that case, you would be taking a 20% risk of committing a Type I error—reporting an effect when one actually does not exist. Most researchers would find this level of risk unacceptable. Instead, researchers generally agree to the convention that $\alpha = .05$ is the greatest risk one should take in making a Type I error. Thus, the .05 level of significance is frequently used and has become the "standard" alpha level. However, some researchers prefer to take even less risk and use alpha levels of .01 and smaller.

3. Take time to consider the implications of your decision about the null hypothesis. The null hypothe-

sis states that there is no effect. Therefore, if your decision is to reject H_0, you should conclude that the sample data provide evidence for a treatment effect. However, it is an entirely different matter if your decision is to fail to reject H_0. Remember, that when you fail to reject the null hypothesis, the results are inconclusive. It is impossible to *prove* that H_0 is correct; therefore, you cannot state with certainty that "there is no effect" when H_0 is not rejected. At best, all you can state is that "there is insufficient evidence for an effect" (see Box 8.1).

4. It is very important that you understand the structure of the z-score formula (page 178). It will help you understand many of the other hypothesis tests that will be covered later.

5. When you are doing a directional hypothesis test, read the problem carefully and watch for key words (such as increase or decrease, raise or lower, and more or less) that tell you which direction the researcher is predicting. The predicted direction will determine the alternative hypothesis (H_1) and the critical region. For example, if a treatment is expected to *increase* scores, H_1 would contain a *greater than* symbol and the critical region would be in the tail associated with high scores.

DEMONSTRATION 8.1 HYPOTHESIS TEST WITH z

A researcher begins with a known population, in this case scores on a standardized test that are normally distributed with $\mu = 65$ and $\sigma = 15$. The researcher suspects that special training in reading skills will produce a change in the scores for the individuals in the population. Because it is not feasible to administer the treatment (the special training) to everyone in the population, a sample of $n = 25$ individuals is selected and the treatment is given to this sample. Following treatment, the average score for this sample is $\bar{X} = 70$. Is there evidence that the training has an effect on test scores?

STEP 1 State the hypotheses and select an alpha level.
Remember, the goal of hypothesis testing is to use sample data to make general conclusions about a population. The hypotheses always concern an unknown population. For this demonstration, the researcher does not know what would happen if the entire population were given the treatment. Nevertheless, it is possible to make hypotheses about the treated population.

Specifically, the null hypothesis says that the treatment has no effect. According to H_0, the unknown population (after treatment) is identical to the original population (before treatment). In symbols,

$$H_0 : \mu = 65 \text{ (After special training, the mean is still 65)}$$

The alternative hypothesis states that the treatment does have an effect which causes a change in the population mean. In symbols,

$$H_1 : \mu \neq 65 \text{ (After special training, the mean is different from 65)}$$

At this time you also select the alpha level. Traditionally, α is set at .05 or .01. If there is particular concern about a Type I Error, or if a researcher desires to present overwhelming evidence for a treatment effect, a smaller alpha level can be used (such as $\alpha = .001$). For this demonstration, we will set alpha to .05. Thus, we are taking a 5% risk of committing a Type I error.

STEP 2 Locate the critical region.

You should recall that the critical region is defined as the set of outcomes that is very unlikely to be obtained if the null hypothesis is true. Therefore, obtaining sample data from this region would lead us to reject the null hypothesis and conclude there is an effect. Remember, the critical region is a region of rejection.

We begin by looking at all possible outcomes that could be obtained, then use the alpha level to determine the outcomes that are unlikely. For this demonstration, we look at the distribution of sample means for samples of $n = 25$; that is, all possible sample means that could be obtained if H_0 were true. The distribution of sample means will be normal because the original population is normal. It will have an expected value of $\mu = 65$ and a standard error of

$$\sigma_{\overline{X}} = \frac{\sigma}{\sqrt{n}} = \frac{15}{\sqrt{25}} = 15/5 = 3$$

With $\alpha = .05$, we want to identify the most unlikely 5% of this distribution. The most unlikely part of a normal distribution is in the tails. Therefore, we divide our alpha level evenly between the two tails, 2.5% or $p = .0250$ per tail. In column C of the Unit Normal table, find $p = .0250$. Then find its corresponding z-score in column A. The entry is $z = 1.96$. The boundaries for the critical region are -1.96 (on the left side) and $+1.96$ (on the right side). The distribution with its critical region is shown in Figure 8.7.

STEP 3 Obtain the sample data and compute the test statistic.

For this demonstration, the researcher obtained a sample mean of $\overline{X} = 70$. This sample mean corresponds to a z-score of

$$z = \frac{\overline{X} - \mu}{\sigma_{\overline{X}}} = \frac{70 - 65}{3} = \frac{5}{3} = +1.67$$

STEP 4 Make a decision about H_0 and state the conclusion.

The z-score we obtained is not in the critical region. This indicates that our sample mean of $\overline{X} = 70$ is not an extreme or unusual value to be obtained from

Figure 8.7

The critical region for Demonstration 8.1 consists of the extreme tails with boundaries of $z = -1.96$ and $z = +1.96$.

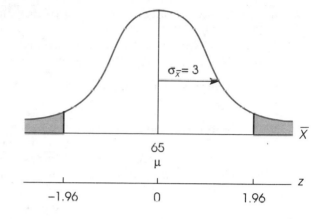

a population with $\mu = 65$. Therefore our statistical decision is to *fail to reject* H_0. Our conclusion for the study is that the data do not provide sufficient evidence that the special training changes test scores.

PROBLEMS

1. After several years of studying human performance in flight simulators, a psychologist knows that reaction times to an overhead emergency indicator form a normal distribution with $\mu = 200$ milliseconds and $\sigma = 20$. The psychologist would like to determine if placing the indicator in front of the person at eye level has any effect on reaction time. A random sample of $n = 25$ people is selected, they are tested in a simulator with the indicator light at eye level, and their reaction times are recorded.
   a. Identify the dependent variable and the independent variable.
   b. State the null hypothesis using a sentence that includes the dependent and independent variables.
   c. Using symbols, state the hypotheses (H_0 and H_1) that the psychologist is testing.
   d. Sketch the appropriate distribution and locate the critical region for the .05 level of significance.
   e. If the psychologist obtained an average reaction time of $\overline{X} = 195$ milliseconds for this sample, then what decision would be made about the null hypothesis?
   f. If the psychologist had used a sample of $n = 100$ subjects and obtained an average reaction time of $\overline{X} = 195$, then what decision would be made about the effects of the position of the indicator? Explain

   why this conclusion is different from the one in part e.

2. Suppose that scores on the Scholastic Aptitude Test form a normal distribution with $\mu = 500$ and $\sigma = 100$. A high school counselor has developed a special course designed to boost SAT scores. A random sample of $n = 16$ students is selected to take the course and then the SAT. The sample had an average score of $\overline{X} = 554$. Does the course have an effect on SAT scores?
   a. What are the dependent and independent variables for this experiment?
   b. Perform the hypothesis test using the four steps outlined in the chapter. Use $\alpha = .05$.
   c. If $\alpha = .01$ were used instead, what z-score values would be associated with the critical region?
   d. For part c, what decision should be made regarding H_0? Compare to part b and explain the difference.

3. Explain the structure of the z-score formula as it is used for hypothesis testing.
   a. What does $\overline{X} - \mu$ tell us in a hypothesis-testing situation?
   b. What does the standard error indicate?

4. Discuss the errors that can be made in hypothesis testing.
   a. What is a Type I error? Why might it occur?
   b. What is a Type II error? How does it happen?

5. Why do we test H_0 to establish an effect instead of H_1?

6. Patients recovering from an appendix operation normally spend an average of $\mu = 6.3$ days is the hospital. The distribution of recovery times is normal with $\sigma = 1.2$ days. The hospital is trying a new recovery program that is designed to shorten the time patients spend in the hospital. The first 10 appendix patients in this new program were released from the hospital in an average of 5.5 days. On the basis of these data, can the hospital conclude that the new program has a significant effect on recovery time. Test at the .05 level of significance.

7. For the past 2 years the vending machine in the psychology department has charged 40¢ for a soft drink. During this time, company records indicate that an average of $\mu = 185$ cans of soft drinks were sold each week. The distribution of sales is approximately normal with $\sigma = 23$. Recently, the company increased the price to 50¢ a can. The weekly sales for the first 8 weeks after the price increase are as follows: 148, 135, 142, 181, 164, 159, 192, 173. Do these data indicate that there was a significant change in sales after the price increase? Test at the .05 level of significance.

8. IQ scores for the general population form a normal distribution with $\mu = 100$ and $\sigma = 15$. However, there are data that indicate that children's intelligence can be affected if their mothers have German measles during pregnancy. Using hospital records, a researcher obtained a sample of $n = 20$ school children whose mothers all had German measles during their pregnancies. The average IQ for this sample was $\overline{X} = 97.3$. Do these data indicate that German measles have a significant effect on IQ? Test with $\alpha = .05$.

9. In 1965 a nationwide survey revealed that U.S. grade school children spent an average of $\mu = 8.4$ hours per week doing homework. The distribution of homework times was normal with $\sigma = 3.3$. Last year a sample of $n = 200$ student was given the same survey. For this sample, the average number of homework hours was $\overline{X} = 7.1$.

a. Do these data indicate a significant change in the amount of homework hours for American grade school children? Test at the .01 level of significance.
b. If there had been only $n = 20$ students in the sample, would the data still indicate a significant change? Use the same sample mean, $\overline{X} = 7.1$, and use $\alpha = .01$.

10. The following sample of $n = 10$ scores was obtained from a normal population with $\sigma = 12$:

    78, 90, 54, 77, 71, 99, 85, 74, 93, 84.

a. Use these data to test the hypothesis that the population mean is $\mu = 75$. Use $\alpha = .05$ for your test.
b. Use these data to test the hypothesis that the population mean is $\mu = 85$. Use $\alpha = .05$ for your test.
c. In parts a and b of this problem you should find that $\mu = 75$ and $\mu = 85$ are both acceptable hypotheses. Explain how two different values can both be acceptable.

11. A researcher is trying to assess some of the physical changes that occur in addicts during drug withdrawal. For the population, suppose the average body temperature is $\mu = 98.6°F$ with $\sigma = 0.56$. The following data consist of the body temperatures of a sample of heroin addicts during drug withdrawal: 98.6, 99.0, 99.4, 100.1, 98.7, 99.3, 99.9, 101.0, 99.6, 99.5, 99.4, 100.3. Is there a significant change in body temperature during withdrawal? Test at the .01 level of significance. Show all four steps of the hypothesis test.

12. A researcher would like to know if oxygen deprivation at the time of birth has a permanent effect on IQ. It is known that scores on a standard intelligence exam are normally distributed for the population with $\mu = 100$ and $\sigma = 15$. The researcher takes a random sample of individuals for whom complications at birth indicate moderate oxygen deprivation. The sample data are as follows: 92, 100, 106, 78, 96, 94, 98, 91, 83, 81, 86, 89, 87, 91, 89. Is there evidence for an effect?
a. Test the hypothesis using the four-step method with alpha set at .05.
b. What would the decision be if the .01 level of significance is used instead of the .05 level?

13. A psychologist develops a new inventory to measure depression. Using a very large standardization group

of "normal" individuals, the mean score on this test is $\mu = 55$ with $\sigma = 12$, and the scores are normally distributed. To determine if the test is sensitive in detecting those individuals that are severely depressed, a random sample of patients who are described as depressed by a therapist is selected and given the test. Presumably, the higher the score on the inventory, the more depressed the patient is. The data are as follows: 59, 60, 60, 67, 65, 90, 89, 73, 74, 81, 71, 71, 83, 83, 88, 83, 84, 86, 85, 78, 79. Do patients score significantly different on the test? Test with the .01 level of significance.

14. On a vocational/interest inventory that measures interest in several categories, a very large standardization group of adults has an average score on the "literary" scale of $\mu = 22$ with $\sigma = 4$. A researcher would like to determine if scientists differ from the general population in terms of writing interests. A random sample of scientists is selected from the directory of a national scientific society. The scientists are given the inventory, and their test scores on the literary scale are as follows: 21, 20, 23, 28, 30, 24, 23, 19. Do scientists differ from the general population in their writing interests? Test at the .05 level of significance.

15. Suppose that the average birth weight for the population is $\mu = 2.9$ kilograms with $\sigma = 0.65$. An investigator would like to see if the birth weights of infants are significantly different for mothers that smoked cigarettes throughout their pregnancy. A random sample of women who smoke is selected, and the birth weight of their infants is recorded. The data (in kilograms) are as follows: 2.3, 2.0, 2.2, 2.8, 3.2, 2.2, 2.5, 2.4, 2.4, 2.1, 2.3, 2.6, 2.0, 2.3. What should the scientist conclude? Use the .01 level of significance.

16. A developmental psychologist has prepared a training program that, according to a psychological theory, should improve problem-solving ability. For the population of 6-year-olds, the average score on a standardized problem-solving test is known to be $\mu = 80$ with $\sigma = 10$. To test the effectiveness of the training program, a random sample of $n = 18$ 6-year-old children is selected. After training, the average score for this sample is $\overline{X} = 84.44$. Can the experimenter conclude that the program has an effect? Test with alpha set at .05.

a. Perform the hypothesis test showing all four steps. When you state the hypotheses, explain what they predict in terms of the independent and dependent variables used in this experiment.

b. Would the same decision have been made about H_0 if a one-tailed had been used.

17. A researcher did a one-tailed hypothesis test using an alpha level of .01. For this test, H_0 was rejected. A colleague analyzed the same data but used a two-tailed test with $\alpha = .05$. In this test H_0 was *not* rejected. Can both analyses be correct? Explain your answer.

18. Performance scores on a motor skills task form a normal distribution with $\mu = 20$ and $\sigma = 4$. A psychologist is using this task to determine the extent to which increased self-awareness affects performance. The prediction for this experiment is that increased self-awareness will reduce a subject's concentration and result in lower performance scores. A sample of $n = 16$ subjects is obtained, and each subject is tested on the motor skills task while seated in front of a large mirror. The purpose of the mirror is to make the subjects more self-aware. The average score for this sample is $\overline{X} = 15.5$. Use a one-tailed test with $\alpha = .05$ to test the psychologist's prediction.

19. A psychological theory predicts that individuals who grow up as an only child will have above-average IQs. A sample of $n = 64$ people from single-child families is obtained. The average IQ for this sample is $\overline{X} = 104.9$. In the general population, IQs form a normal distribution with $\mu = 100$ and $\sigma = 15$. Use a one-tailed test with $\alpha = .01$ to evaluate the theory.

20. A psychologist is interested in the long-term effects of a divorce on the children in a family. A sample is obtained of $n = 10$ children whose parents were divorced at least 5 years ago. Each child is given a personality questionnaire measuring depression. In the general population, the scores on this questionnaire form a normal distribution with $\mu = 80$ and $\sigma = 12$. The scores for this sample are as follows: 83, 81, 75, 92, 84, 107, 63, 112, 92, 88. The psychologist is predicting that children from divorced families will be more depressed than children in the general population. Use a one-tailed test with $\alpha = .05$ to test this hypothesis.

CHAPTER 9

INTRODUCTION TO THE *t* STATISTIC

TOOLS YOU WILL NEED

The following items are considered essential background material for this chapter. If you doubt your knowledge of any of these items, you should review the appropriate chapter or section before proceeding.

- Sample standard deviation (Chapter 4)
- Degrees of freedom (Chapter 4)
- Hypothesis testing (Chapter 8)

SECTION 9.1 **INTRODUCTION**

In the previous chapter we presented the statistical procedures that permit researchers to use a sample mean to test hypotheses about a population. These statistical procedures were based on a few basic notions, which we summarize as follows:

Remember, the expected value of the distribution of sample means is μ, the population mean.

1. A sample mean $\overline{X}$ is expected more or less to approximate its population mean μ. This permits us to use the sample mean to test a hypothesis about the population mean.

2. The standard error provides a measure of how well a sample mean approximates the population mean.

$$\sigma_{\overline{X}} = \frac{\sigma}{\sqrt{n}}$$

3. To quantify our inferences about the population, we convert each sample mean to a z-score using the formula

$$z = \frac{\overline{X} - \mu}{\sigma_{\overline{X}}}$$

When the z-scores form a normal distribution, we are able to use the unit normal table (Appendix B) to find the critical region for the hypothesis test.

The shortcoming of using the z-score as an inferential statistic is that the z-score formula requires more information than is usually available. Specifically, z-scores require that we know the value of the population standard deviation, which is needed to compute the standard error. Most often the standard deviation of the population is not known, and the standard error of sample means cannot be computed. Without the standard error, we have no way of quantifying the expected amount of distance (or error) between $\overline{X}$ and μ. We have no way of making precise, quantitative inferences about the population based on z-scores.

THE t STATISTIC—A SUBSTITUTE FOR z

Fortunately, there is a relatively simple solution to the problem of not knowing the population standard deviation. When the value of σ is not known, we use the sample standard deviation in its place. In Chapter 4, the sample standard deviation was developed specifically to be an unbiased estimate of the population standard deviation. You should recall that the formula for the sample standard deviation is

$$s = \sqrt{\frac{SS}{n-1}}$$

Using this sample statistic, we can now estimate the standard error. The estimated standard error $s_{\overline{X}}$ is obtained by the formula

$$s_{\overline{X}} = \frac{s}{\sqrt{n}}$$

(9.1)

Notice that we have substituted the sample standard deviation (*s*) in place of the unknown population standard deviation (σ). Also notice that the symbol for the estimated standard error is $s_{\overline{X}}$ instead of $\sigma_{\overline{X}}$, indicating that the value is computed from sample data rather than from the population parameter.

DEFINITION   *The estimated standard error* ($s_{\overline{X}}$) *is used as an estimate of* $\sigma_{\overline{X}}$ *when the value of* σ *is unknown. It is computed from the sample standard deviation and provides an estimate of the standard distance between a sample mean* $\overline{X}$ *and the population mean* μ

Now we can substitute the estimated standard error in the denominator of the *z*-score formula. This new test statistic is called a *t statistic:*

$$t = \frac{\overline{X} - \mu}{s_{\overline{X}}} \tag{9.2}$$

The only difference between the *t* formula and the *z*-score formula is that the *z*-score formula uses the actual population standard deviation (σ) and the *t* statistic uses the sample standard deviation as an estimate when σ is unknown:

$$z = \frac{\overline{X} - \mu}{\sigma_{\overline{X}}} = \frac{\overline{X} - \mu}{\sigma/\sqrt{n}} \qquad t = \frac{\overline{X} - \mu}{s_{\overline{X}}} = \frac{\overline{X} - \mu}{s/\sqrt{n}}$$

Structurally, these two formulas have the same form:

$$z \text{ or } t = \frac{\text{sample mean} - \text{population mean}}{\text{(estimated) standard error}}$$

Because both *z*, and *t* formulas are used for hypothesis testing, there is one rule to remember:

RULE   When you know the value of σ, use a *z*-score. If σ is unknown, use the *t* statistic.

DEFINITION   The *t statistic* is used to test hypotheses about μ when the value for σ is not known. The formula for the *t* statistic is similar in structure to the *z*-score, except that the *t* statistic uses estimated standard error.

DEGREES OF FREEDOM AND THE *t* STATISTIC

In this chapter we have introduced the *t* statistic as a substitute for a *z*-score. The basic difference between these two is that the *t* statistic uses sample standard deviation (*s*), and the *z*-score uses the population standard deviation (σ). To determine how well a *t* statistic approximates a *z*-score, we must determine how well the sample standard deviation approximates the population standard deviation.

In Chapter 4 we introduced the concept of degrees of freedom. Reviewing briefly, you must know the sample mean before you can compute sample standard deviation. This places a restriction on sample variability such that only $n - 1$ scores in a sample are free to vary. The value $n - 1$ is called the *degrees of freedom* (or *df*) for the sample standard deviation.

$$\text{degrees of freedom} = df = n - 1 \tag{9.3}$$

DEFINITION

Degrees of freedom describe the number of scores in a sample that are free to vary. Because the sample mean places a restriction on the value of one score in the sample, there are $n - 1$ degrees of freedom for the sample (see Chapter 4).

The greater the value of *df* for a sample, the better *s* represents σ, and the better the *t* statistic approximates the *z*-score. This should make sense because the larger the sample (n), the better the sample represents its population. Thus, the degrees of freedom associated with *s* also describe how well *t* represents *z*.

THE *t* DISTRIBUTIONS

Every sample from a population can be used to compute a *z*-score or a *t* statistic. If you select all the possible samples of a particular size (n), then the entire set of resulting *z*-scores will form a *z*-score distribution. In the same way, the set of all possible *t* statistics will form a *t* *distribution*. As we saw in Chapter 7, the distribution of *z*-scores computed from sample means tends to be a normal distribution. For this reason, we consulted the unit normal table to find the critical region when using *z*-scores to test hypotheses about a population. The *t* distribution, on the other hand, is generally not normal. However, the *t* distribution will approximate a normal distribution in the same way that a *t* statistic approximates a *z*-score. How well a *t* distribution approximates a normal distribution is determined by degrees of freedom. In general, the greater the sample size (n), the larger the degrees of freedom ($n - 1$), and the better the *t* distribution approximates the normal distribution (see Figure 9.1).

THE SHAPE OF THE *t* DISTRIBUTION

The exact shape of a *t* distribution changes with degrees of freedom. In fact, statisticians speak of a "family" of *t* distributions. That is, there is a different sampling distribution of *t* (a distribution of all possible sample *t* values) for each

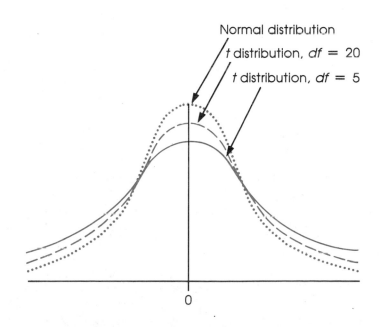

Figure 9.1

Distributions of the *t* statistic for different values of degrees of freedom are compared to a normal *z*-score distribution. Like the normal distribution, *t* distributions are bell-shaped and symmetrical and have a mean of zero. However, *t* distributions have more variability, indicated by the flatter and more spread-out shape. The larger the value of *df*, the more closely the *t* distribution approximates a normal distribution.

9.1

THE CRITICAL VALUES IN A NORMAL *z* DISTRIBUTION AND A *t* DISTRIBUTION: THE INFLUENCE OF DEGREES OF FREEDOM

AS PREVIOUSLY noted, a *t* distribution approximates a normal *z* distribution. How well it approximates a normal distribution depends on the value of *df*. This can be seen by simply comparing critical values for *z* with critical values of *t* at various degrees of freedom. For example, if we test a hypothesis with a *z*-score using a two-tailed test and $\alpha = .05$, the critical *z*-scores will be $+1.96$ and -1.96. However, suppose the population standard deviation were not known and we conducted this hypothesis test with a *t* statistic. For a sample of $n = 4$, the *t* statistic would have $df = 3$. For three degrees of freedom, the critical values of *t* would be $+3.182$ and -3.182 (with alpha still set a .05). When *df* is small, the *t* distribution is flatter and more spread out. Consequently, the tails have a greater area for the *t* distribution compared to a normal distribution (see Figure 9.1). The extreme 5% of the distribution will be farther from the mean and have a larger critical value in the *t* distribution. If, however, we use a sample of $n = 31$, then $df = 30$, and the critical *t* values will be $+2.042$ and -2.042. These values are very close to the critical *z*-score values (± 1.96). If the sample is made even larger, say $n = 121$, the critical values get even closer to the *z* values. For 120 degrees of freedom, the critical values of *t* are $+1.980$ and -1.980 when $\alpha = .05$. Thus, the difference between a *t* distribution and a normal *z*-distribution becomes negligible when a sample of more than 30 individuals is used. (Note: Determining critical values for *t* is discussed on page 199.)

possible number of degrees of freedom. As *df* gets very large, the *t* distribution gets closer in shape to a normal *z*-score distribution (see Box 9.1). A quick glance at Figure 9.1 reveals that distributions of *t* are bell-shaped and symmetrical and have a mean of zero. However, the *t* distribution has more variability than a normal *z* distribution, especially when *df* values are small (Figure 9.1). The *t* distribution tends to be flatter and more spread out, whereas the normal *z* distribution has more of a central peak.

Why is the *t* distribution flatter and more variable than a normal *z* distribution? For a particular population, the top of the *z*-score formula, $\overline{X} - \mu$, can take on different values because $\overline{X}$ will vary from one sample to another. However, the value of the bottom of the *z*-score formula, $\sigma_{\overline{X}}$, is constant. The standard error will not vary from sample to sample because it is derived from the population standard deviation. The implication is that samples which have the same value for $\overline{X}$ should also have the same *z*-score.

On the other hand, the standard error in the *t* formula is not a constant because it is estimated. That is, $s_{\overline{X}}$ is based on the sample standard deviation, which will vary in value from sample to sample. The result is that samples can have the same value for $\overline{X}$ yet different values of *t* because the estimated error will vary from one sample to another. Therefore, a *t* distribution will have more variability than the normal *z* distribution. It will look flatter and more spread out. When the value of *df* increases, the variability in the *t* distribution decreases, and it more closely resembles the normal distribution, because with greater *df*, $s_{\overline{X}}$ will more closely estimate $\sigma_{\overline{X}}$, and when *df* is very large, they are nearly the same.

DETERMINING PROPORTIONS AND PROBABILITIES FOR *t* DISTRIBUTIONS

Just as we used the unit normal table to locate proportions associated with *z*-scores, we will use a *t* distribution table to find proportions for *t* statistics. The complete *t* distribution table is presented in Appendix B, page A-26, and a portion of this table is reproduced in Table 9.1. The two rows at the top of the table show proportions

Table 9.1

A portion of the *t* distribution table

			PROPORTION IN ONE TAIL			
	0.25	0.10	0.05	0.025	0.01	0.005
			PROPORTION IN TWO TAILS			
df	0.50	0.20	0.10	0.05	0.02	0.01
1	1.000	3.078	6.314	12.706	31.821	63.657
2	0.816	1.886	2.920	4.303	6.965	9.925
3	0.765	1.638	2.353	3.182	4.541	5.841
4	0.741	1.533	2.132	2.776	3.747	4.604
5	0.727	1.476	2.015	2.571	3.365	4.032
6	0.718	1.440	1.943	2.447	3.143	3.707

The numbers in the table are the values of *t* that separate the tail from the main body of the distribution. Proportions for one or two tails are listed at the top of the table and *df* values for *t* are listed in the first column.

of the *t* distribution contained in either one or two tails, depending on which row is used. The first column of the table lists degrees of freedom for the *t* statistic. Finally, the numbers in the body of the table are the *t* values that mark the boundary between the tails and the rest of the *t* distribution.

For example, with $df = 3$, exactly 5% of the *t* distribution is located in the tail beyond $t = 2.353$ (see Figure 9.2). To find this value, you locate $df = 3$ in the first column and locate 0.05 (5%) in the one-tail proportion row. When you line up these two values in the table, you should find $t = 2.353$. Similarly, 5% of the *t* distribution is located in the tail beyond $t = -2.353$ (see Figure 9.2). Finally, you should notice that a total of 10% is contained in the two tails beyond $t = \pm2.353$ (check the proportion value in the "two-tails" row at the top of the table).

LEARNING CHECK

1. A hypothesis test with a *z*-score can be performed only when the population standard deviation is known. (true/false)

2. To compute estimated standard error, $s_{\bar{X}}$, you must know the value for the population standard deviation. (true/false)

Figure 9.2

The *t* distribution with $df = 3$. Note that 5% of the distribution is located in the tail beyond $t = 2.353$. Also, 5% is in the tail beyond $t = -2.353$. Thus, a total proportion of 10% (0.10) is in the two tails beyond $t = \pm2.353$.

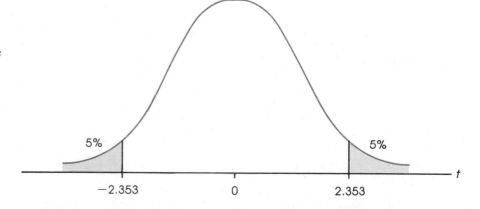

3. As the value for *df* gets smaller, the *t* distribution resembles a normal distribution more and more. (true/false)

4. As the value for *df* gets larger, *s* provides a better estimate of σ. (true/false)

5. For *df* = 10, what *t* value(s) are associated with
   a. The top 1% of the *t* distribution?
   b. The bottom 5% of the *t* distribution?
   c. The most-extreme 1% of the distribution?

ANSWERS   1. True. (With large samples, *z*-scores and *t* statistics are very similar. For this reason, some statisticians allow the use of a *z*-score instead of *t* when the sample size is at least *n* = 30. However, there is always some difference between *z* and *t*, so we recommend that you use a *z*-score only when the population standard deviation is known.)

2. false   3. false   4. true

5. a. + 2.764   b. −1.812   c. +3.169 and −3.169

SECTION 9.2   HYPOTHESIS TESTS WITH THE *t* STATISTIC

The *t* statistic formula is used in exactly the same way that the *z*-score formula is used to test a hypothesis about a population mean. Once again, the *t* formula and its structure are

$$t = \frac{\overline{X} - \mu}{s_{\overline{X}}} = \frac{\text{sample mean} - \text{population mean}}{\text{estimated standard error}}$$

In the hypothesis-testing situation, we have a population with an unknown mean, often a population that has received some treatment (Figure 9.3). The goal is to use a sample from the treated population as the basis for determining whether or not the treatment has any effect. As always, the null hypothesis states that the treatment has

---

Figure 9.3

The basic experimental situation for using the *t* statistic or the *z*-score is presented. It is assumed that the parameter μ is known for the population before treatment. The purpose of the experiment is to determine whether or not the treatment has an effect. We ask, is the population mean after treatment the same as or different from the mean before treatment? A sample is selected from the treated population to help answer this question.

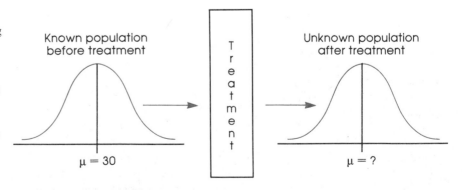

no effect. Specifically, H_0 predicts that the population mean is unchanged. The hypothesized value for the population mean is put into the *t* formula along with the sample mean (from the obtained data) and the estimated standard error (also computed from the sample data). When the resulting *t* statistic is near zero, we can conclude that the sample mean is not significantly different from the hypothesized value and the decision is "fail to reject H_0." In other words, there is no support for a treatment effect. If there is a substantial difference between the sample mean and the hypothesized μ, we will obtain a large value for *t* (large positive or large negative value). In this case, we would conclude that the data are not consistent with the null hypothesis and our decision would be to "reject H_0." The evidence suggests the existence of a treatment effect. The basic steps of the hypothesis-testing procedures will now be reviewed.

STEPS AND PROCEDURES

For hypothesis tests with a *t* statistic, we use the same steps that were used with *z*-scores (Chapter 8). The major difference is that we are now required to estimate standard error because σ is unknown. Consequently, we compute a *t* statistic rather than a *z*-score and consult the *t* distribution table rather than the unit normal table to find the critical region.

STEP 1 The hypotheses are stated and the alpha level is set. The experimenter states the null hypothesis, that is, what should happen if no treatment effect exists. On the other hand, the alternative hypothesis predicts the outcome if an effect does occur. These hypotheses are always stated in terms of the population parameter, μ.

STEP 2 Locate the critical region. The exact shape of the *t* distribution, and therefore the critical *t* values, vary with degrees of freedom. Thus, to find a critical region in a *t*-distribution, it is necessary to determine the value for *df*. Then the critical region can be located by consulting the *t* distribution table (Appendix B).

STEP 3 The sample data are collected and the test statistic is computed. When σ is unknown, the test statistic is a *t* statistic (Formula 9.2).

STEP 4 The null hypothesis is evaluated. If the *t* statistic we obtained in step 3 falls within the critical region (exceeds the value of a critical *t*), then H_0 is rejected. It can be concluded that a treatment effect exists. However, if the obtained *t* value does not lie in the critical region, then we fail to reject H_0, and we conclude that we failed to observe evidence for an effect in our study (see Box 9.2).

HYPOTHESIS-TESTING EXAMPLE

Let us look at research on aversion to eyelike patterns to demonstrate the procedures of hypothesis testing. Studies have shown that direct eye contact and eyelike patterns are avoided by many animals. Some insects, such as moths, have even evolved large eye-spot patterns on their wings to ward off predators. The following experiment will look at the effect of exposure to eye-spot patterns on the behavior of moth-eating birds, using procedures similar to Scaife's (1976) study.

EXAMPLE 9.1 To test the effectiveness of eye-spot patterns in deterring predation, a sample of $n = 16$ insectivorous birds is selected. The animals are tested in a box that

9.2   A RECIPE FOR MAKING *t* STATISTICS

THE **t** statistic formula, like any formula, can be thought of as a recipe. If you follow the instructions and use all the right ingredients, the formula will always produce a *t* statistic. In hypothesis testing situations, however, you do not have all the necessary ingredients. Specifically, you do not know the value for the population mean (μ), which is one component (or ingredient) in the formula.

This situation is similar to trying to follow a cake recipe where one of the ingredients is not clearly listed. For example, a cake recipe may call for flour but not specify exactly how much flour is needed. In this situation, you could proceed with the recipe and just add whatever amount of flour you think is appropriate. Your "hypoth-esis" about the amount of flour would be confirmed or rejected depending on the outcome of the cake. If the cake was good you could reasonably assume that your hypothesis was correct. But if the cake was horrid, you would conclude that your hypothesis was wrong.

In a hypothesis test with the *t* statistic, you do not know the value for μ. Therefore, you take a hypothesized value from H_0, plug it into the *t* formula, and see how it works. If your hypothesized value produces a reasonable outcome (a *t* statistic near zero), you conclude that the hypothesis was acceptable. But if the formula produces an extreme *t* statistic (in the critical region), you conclude that the hypothesis was wrong.

has two separate chambers. The birds are free to roam from one chamber to another through a doorway in a partition. On the wall of one chamber, two large eye-spot patterns have been painted. The other chamber has plain walls. The birds are tested one at a time by placing them in the doorway in the center of the apparatus. Each animal is left in the box for 60 minutes, and the amount of time spent in the plain chamber is recorded. Suppose that the sample of $n = 16$ birds spent an average of $\overline{X} = 35$ minutes in the plain side, with $SS = 1215$. Can we conclude that eye-spot patterns have an effect on behavior? Note that while it is possible to predict a value for μ, we have no information about the population standard deviation.

STEP 1   State the hypotheses and select an alpha level. If the null hypothesis were true, then the eye-spot patterns would have no effect on behavior. The animals should show no preference for either side of the box. That is, they should spend half of the 60-minute test period in the plain chamber. In symbols the null hypothesis would state that

$$H_0 : \mu_{\text{plain side}} = 30 \text{ minutes}$$

Directional hypotheses could be used and would specify whether the average time on the plain side is more or less than 30 minutes.

The alternative hypothesis would state that the eye patterns have an effect on behavior. There are two possibilities: (1) The animals may avoid staying in the chamber with the eye spots as we suspect, or (2) maybe for some reason the animals may show a preference for the patterns painted on the wall. A nondirectional hypothesis (for a two-tailed test) would be represented in symbols as follows:

$$H_1 : \mu_{\text{plain side}} \neq 30 \text{ minutes}$$

We will set the level of significance at $\alpha = .05$ for two tails.

Figure 9.4

The critical region in the *t* distribution for $\alpha = .05$ and $df = 15$.

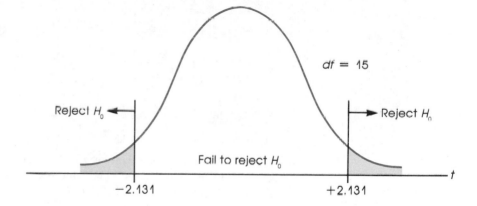

S T E P 2   Locate the critical region. The test statistic is a *t* statistic because the population standard deviation is not known. The exact shape of the *t* distribution and therefore the proportions under the *t* distribution depend on the number of degrees of freedom associated with the sample. To find the critical region, *df* must be computed:

$$df = n - 1 = 16 - 1 = 15$$

For a two-tailed test at the .05 level of significance and with 15 degrees of freedom, the critical region consists of *t* values greater than $+2.131$ or less than -2.131. Figure 9.4 depicts the critical region in this *t* distribution.

S T E P 3   Calculate the test statistic. To obtain the value for the *t* statistic, we first must compute s and then $s_{\overline{X}}$. The sample standard deviation is

$$s = \sqrt{\frac{SS}{n-1}}$$
$$= \sqrt{\frac{1215}{15}}$$
$$= \sqrt{81}$$
$$= 9$$

The estimated standard error is

$$s_{\overline{X}} = \frac{s}{\sqrt{n}}$$
$$= \frac{9}{\sqrt{16}}$$
$$= 2.25$$

Finally, we can compute the *t* statistic for these sample data:

$$t = \frac{\overline{X} - \mu}{s_{\overline{X}}}$$

$$= \frac{35 - 30}{2.25}$$

$$= \frac{5}{2.25}$$

$$= 2.22$$

STEP 4 Make a decision regarding H_0. The obtained t statistic of 2.22 falls into the critical region on the right-hand side of the t distribution (Figure 9.4). Our statistical decision is to reject H_0 and conclude that the presence of eye-spot patterns does influence behavior. As can be seen from the sample mean, there is a tendency for animals to avoid the eyes and spend more time on the plain side of the box. For this example, alpha was set at .05. Therefore, the probability that a Type I error has been committed is $p < .05$. It is common practice in scientific literature to report the results of the t test in the following manner:

> The data suggest that the birds spend significantly more time in the chamber without eye-spot patterns; $t(15) = +2.22$, $p < .05$, two-tailed.

Note that the degrees of freedom are reported in parentheses right after the symbol t. The value for the obtained t statistic follows (2.22) and next is the probability of committing a Type I error (less than 5%). Finally, the type of test (one- versus two-tailed) is noted.

DIRECTIONAL HYPOTHESES AND ONE-TAILED TESTS

As we noted in Chapter 8, the nondirectional (two-tailed) test is commonly used for research that is intended for publication in a scientific journal. On the other hand, a directional (one-tailed) test may be used in some research situations, such as exploratory investigations or pilot studies. Although one-tailed tests are used occasionally, you should remember that the two-tailed test is preferred by most researchers. Even though a researcher may have a specific directional prediction for an experiment, it is generally safer and always appropriate to use a nondirectional (two-tailed) test. The following example demonstrates a directional hypothesis test with a t statistic, using the same experimental situation that was presented in Example 9.1.

EXAMPLE 9.2 The research question is whether eye-spot patterns will affect the behavior of birds placed in a special testing box. The researcher is expecting the birds to avoid the eye-spot patterns. Therefore, the researcher predicts that the birds will spend most of the hour on the plain side of the box.

STEP 1 State the hypotheses and select an alpha level. With most directional tests it is easier to begin by stating the alternative hypothesis. Remember, H_1 states that

Figure 9.5

The critical region in the *t* distribution for $\alpha = .05$, $df = 15$, one-tailed test.

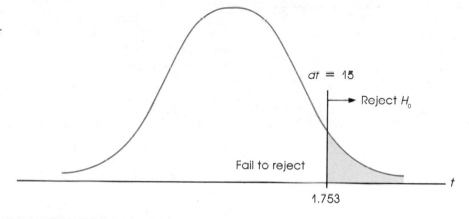

$df = 15$

Reject H_0

Fail to reject

1.753

the treatment does have an effect. For this example, the eye patterns should cause the birds to spend most of their time on the plain side. In symbols,

$$H_1 : \mu_{\text{plain side}} > 30 \text{ minutes}$$

The null hypothesis states that the treatment will not have the predicted effect. In this case, H_0 says that the eye patterns will not cause the birds to spend more time on the plain side. In symbols,

$$H_0 : \mu_{\text{plain side}} \leq 30 \text{ minutes} \qquad \text{(not greater than 30 minutes)}$$

We will set the level of significance at $\alpha = .05$.

STEP 2 Locate the critical region. In this example, the researcher is predicting that the sample mean ($\overline{X}$) will be greater than 30. The null hypothesis states that the population mean is $\mu = 30$ (or less). If you examine the structure of the *t* statistic formula, it should be clear that a positive *t* statistic would support the researcher's prediction and refute the null hypothesis.

$$t = \frac{\overline{X} - \mu}{s_{\overline{X}}}$$

The problem is to determine how large a positive value is necessary to reject H_0. To find the critical value you must look in the *t* distribution table using the one-tail proportions. With a sample of $n = 16$, the *t* statistic will have *df* $= 15$; using $\alpha = .05$, you should find a critical *t* value of 1.753. Figure 9.5 depicts the critical region in the *t* distribution.

STEP 3 Calculate the test statistic. The computation of the *t* statistic is the same for either a one-tailed or a two-tailed test. Earlier (in Example 9.1), we found that the data for this experiment produce a test statistic of $t = 2.22$.

STEP 4 Make a decision. The test statistic is in the critical region, so we reject H_0. In terms of the experimental variables, we have decided that the birds spent significantly more time on the plain side of the box than on the side with eye-spot patterns.

ASSUMPTIONS OF THE *t* TEST

As noted earlier (Chapter 8), for each statistical test it is assumed that a certain set of conditions exists. Severe violations of one or more of these assumptions may compromise the validity of the statistical test. Of course, for a *t* test it is assumed that the sample has been randomly selected. This condition helps to ensure that the sample is representative of the population so that valid generalizations can be made from sample to population. Another important assumption for the *t* test is that the population distribution of scores is normal. If this condition is not met, the *t* distribution table cannot be used to locate the critical region. It is difficult to determine the exact *t* distribution that will be appropriate for the test when the population is not normally distributed.

Some statisticians have suggested that the *t* test is "robust." By robust, they mean the *t* test will still be a valid statistical test even when there are departures from the assumption of normality. However, the *t* statistic is more likely to be robust to violations of normality when large samples (for example, $n > 30$) are used. It should be noted that the assumption of normality is a condition that applies to all types of *t* tests that follow in later chapters.

THE VERSATILITY OF THE *t* TEST

The obvious advantage of hypothesis testing with the *t* statistic (as compared to *z*-scores) is that you do not need to know the value of the population standard deviation. This means that we still can do a hypothesis test even though we have little or no information about the population. One result of this extra versatility is that it is possible to do *t* tests in circumstances where hypothesis tests with *z*-scores would not even allow for the statement of a null hypothesis.

Both the *t* statistic and *z*-score tests have been introduced as a means of determining whether or not a treatment has any effect on the dependent variable. Recall that the null hypothesis states that the treatment has no effect. That is, the population mean after treatment has the same value that it had before treatment. Notice that this experimental situation requires that we know the value of the population mean before the treatment. This requirement is often unrealistic and limits the usefulness of *z*-score tests. Although the *t* statistic often is used in this before-and-after type of experiment (Figure 9.3), the *t* test also permits hypothesis testing in situations where we do not have a "known" population to serve as a before-treatment standard. Specifically, the *t* test can be used in situations where the value for the null hypothesis can come from a theory, a prediction, or just wishful thinking. Some examples follow. Notice in each example that the hypothesis is not dependent on knowing the actual population mean before treatment and that the rest of the *t* statistic can be computed entirely from the obtained sample data.

1. A researcher would like to examine the accuracy of people's judgment of time when they are distracted. Individuals are placed in a waiting room where many distracting events occur for a period of 12 minutes. The researcher then asks each person to judge how much time has passed. The null hypothesis would state that distraction has no effect and that time judgments are accurate. That is,

   $H_0: \mu = 12$ minutes

2. A local fund-raising organization has set a goal of receiving $25 per contributor. After 1 week, a sample of contributions is selected to see if they deviate significantly from the goal. The null hypothesis would state that the

contributions do not deviate from the goal of the organization. In symbols, it is

$$H_0: \mu = \$25.00$$

3. A soft-drink company has developed a new, improved formula for its product and would like to determine how consumers respond to the new formula. A sample is obtained, and each individual is asked to taste the original soft drink and the new formula. After tasting, the subjects are required to state whether the new formula is better or worse than the original formula using a 7-point scale. A rating of 4 indicates no preference between the old and new formulas. Ratings above 4 indicate that the new formula is better (5 = slightly better, 6 = better, and 7 = much better). Similarly, ratings below 4 indicate that the new formula tastes worse than the old formula. The null hypothesis states that there is no perceived difference between the two formulas. In symbols, the new formula would receive an average rating of

$$H_0: \mu = 4$$

LEARNING CHECK

1. A professor of philosophy hypothesizes that an introductory course in logic will help college students with their other studies. To test this hypothesis, a random sample of $n = 25$ freshmen is selected. These students are required to complete a logic course during their freshman year. At the time of graduation, the final grade point average is computed for each of these students. The mean GPA for this sample is $\overline{X} = 2.83$ with $SS = 6$. Can the professor conclude that the grades for the sample were significantly different from the rest of the graduating class, which had an average GPA of $\mu = 2.58$? Test with a two-tailed test at $\alpha = .05$.

   a. State the hypotheses.

   b. Determine the value for df and locate the critical region.

   c. Compute the test statistic.

   d. Make a decision regarding H_0.

ANSWERS

1. a. $H_0: \mu_{\text{with logic course}} = 2.58$ (even with the logic course, the population mean GPA will still be 2.58)

   $H_1: \mu_{\text{with logic course}} \neq 2.58$ (for the population, the logic course has an effect on GPA)

   b. $df = 24$; the critical region begins at t values of $+2.064$ and -2.064.

   c. $s = 0.5$; $s_{\overline{X}} = 0.1$; $t = |2.5|$.

   d. Reject H_0.

SUMMARY

1. When σ is unknown, the standard error cannot be computed, and a hypothesis test based on a z-score is impossible.

2. In order to test a hypothesis about μ when σ is unknown, σ must first be estimated using the sample standard division s:

$$s = \sqrt{\frac{SS}{n-1}}$$

Next, the standard error is estimated by substituting s for σ in the standard error formula. The estimated standard error ($s_{\overline{X}}$) is calculated in the following manner:

$$s_{\overline{X}} = \frac{s}{\sqrt{n}}$$

Finally, a t statistic is computed using the estimated standard error. The t statistic serves as a substitute for a z-score, which cannot be computed because σ is unknown.

$$t = \frac{\overline{X} - \mu}{s_{\overline{X}}}$$

3. The structure of the t formula is similar to that of the z-score in that

$$z \text{ or } t = \frac{\text{sample mean} - \text{population mean}}{\text{(estimated) standard error}}$$

4. The t distribution is an approximation of the normal z distribution. To evaluate a t statistic that is obtained for a sample mean, the critical region must be located in a t distribution. There is a family of t distributions, with the exact shape of a particular distribution of t values depending on degrees of freedom ($n-1$). Therefore, the critical t values will depend on the value for df associated with the t test. As df increases, the shape of the t distribution approaches a normal distribution.

KEY TERMS

estimated standard error t statistic   degrees of freedom t distribution

FOCUS ON PROBLEM SOLVING

1. The first problem we confront in analyzing data is determining the appropriate statistical test. Remember, you can use a z-score for the test statistic only when the value for σ is known. If the value for σ is not provided, then you must use the t statistic.

2. For a t test, students sometimes use the unit normal table to locate the critical region. This, of course, is a mistake. The critical region for a t test is obtained by consulting the t distribution table. Notice that to use

this table you first must compute the value for degrees of freedom (df).

3. For the t test, the sample standard deviation is used to find the value for estimated standard error. Remember, when computing the sample standard deviation use $n-1$ in the denominator (see Chapter 4). When computing estimated standard error, use $\sqrt{n}$ in the denominator.

DEMONSTRATION 9.1   A HYPOTHESIS TEST WITH THE *t* STATISTIC

A psychologist has prepared an "Optimism Test" that is administered yearly to graduating college seniors. The test measures how each graduating class feels about its future—the higher the score, the more optimistic the class. Last year's class had a mean score of $\mu = 15$. A sample of $n = 9$ seniors from this year's class was selected and tested. The scores for these seniors are as follows:

$$7 \quad 12 \quad 11 \quad 15 \quad 7 \quad 8 \quad 15 \quad 9 \quad 6$$

On the basis of this sample, can the psychologist conclude that this year's class has a different level of optimism than last year's class?

Note that this hypothesis test will use a *t* statistic because the population standard deviation (σ) is not known.

STEP 1 State the hypotheses and select an alpha level.

The statements for the null hypothesis and the alternative hypothesis follow the same form for the *t* statistic and the *z*-score test.

$$H_0: \mu = 15 \text{ (there is no change)}$$
$$H_1: \mu \neq 15 \text{ (this year's mean is different)}$$

For this demonstration we will use $\alpha = .05$, two tails.

STEP 2 Locate the critical region.

Remember, for hypothesis tests with the *t* statistic, we must now consult the *t* distribution table to find the critical *t* values. With a sample of $n = 9$ students, the *t* statistic will have degrees of freedom equal to

$$df = n - 1 = 9 - 1 = 8$$

For a two-tailed test with $\alpha = .05$ and $df = 8$, the critical *t* values are $t = \pm 2.306$. These critical *t* values define the boundaries of the critical region. The obtained *t* value must be more extreme that either of these critical values to reject H_0.

STEP 3 Obtain the sample data and compute the test statistic.

For the *t* formula, we need to determine the values for the following:
1. the sample mean, $\overline{X}$
2. the estimated standard error, $s_{\overline{X}}$

We will also have to compute sums-of-squares (*SS*) and the standard deviation (*s*) for the sample in order to get the estimated standard error.

The sample mean. For these data, the sum of the scores is

$$\Sigma X = 7 + 12 + 11 + 15 + 7 + 8 + 15 + 9 + 6 = 90$$

Therefore, the sample mean is

$$\overline{X} = \frac{\Sigma X}{n} = \frac{90}{9} = 10$$

Sum-of-squares. We will use the definitional formula for sums-of-squares,

$$SS = \Sigma(X - \overline{X})^2$$

The following table summarizes the steps in the computation of *SS*.

X	$X - \bar{X}$	$(X - \bar{X})^2$
7	$7 - 10 = -3$	9
12	$12 - 10 = +2$	4
11	$11 - 10 = +1$	1
15	$15 - 10 = +5$	25
7	$7 - 10 = -3$	9
8	$8 - 10 = -2$	4
15	$15 - 10 = +5$	25
9	$9 - 10 = -1$	1
6	$6 - 10 = -4$	16

For this demonstration problem, sums-of-squares is

$$SS = \Sigma(X - \bar{X})^2 = 9 + 4 + 1 + 25 + 9 + 4 + 25 + 1 + 16$$
$$= 94$$

Sample standard deviation. The sample standard deviation is the square root of *SS* divided by degrees of freedom.

$$s = \sqrt{\frac{SS}{n-1}} = \sqrt{\frac{94}{8}} = \sqrt{11.75} = 3.43$$

Estimated standard error. The estimated standard error for these data is

$$s_{\bar{X}} = \frac{s}{\sqrt{n}} = \frac{3.43}{\sqrt{9}} = \frac{3.43}{3} = 1.14$$

The t statistic. Now that we have the estimated standard error and the sample mean, we can compute the *t* statistic. For this demonstration,

$$t = \frac{\bar{X} - \mu}{s_{\bar{X}}} = \frac{10 - 15}{1.14} = \frac{-5}{1.14} = -4.39$$

STEP 4 Make a decision about H_0 and a conclusion.

The *t* statistic we obtained ($t = -4.39$) is in the critical region. Thus our sample data are unusual enough to reject the null hypothesis at the .05 level of significance. We can conclude that there is a significant difference in level of optimism between this year's and last year's graduating classes, $t(8) = -4.39$, $p < .05$, two tailed.

PROBLEMS

1. When a *t* statistic is used, why is it necessary to estimate the standard error?

2. Why is the *t* statistic more versatile for inferential statistics than the *z*-score?

3. What assumptions (or set of conditions) must be satisfied for a *t* test to be valid?

4. Why is a *t* distribution generally more variable than a normal distribution?

5. What is the relationship between the value for degrees of freedom and the shape of the t distribution? What happens to the critical value of t for a particular alpha level when df increases in value?

6. A distribution is known to be normal with $\mu = 50$ and $\sigma = 12$. A researcher would like to evaluate the effect of a particular treatment on this population. A sample of $n = 4$ individuals is selected, and the treatment is administered. After treatment, this sample yielded an average score of $\overline{X} = 64$ with $SS = 300$.

   a. Because σ is known, you can use a z-score hypothesis test. Also you could ignore the fact that σ is known and just use the sample data to compute a t statistic. Which of these two tests do you think is more likely to produce a correct decision? Explain your answer.

   b. Using the fact that $\sigma = 12$ is known, do a z-score test with $\alpha = .05$ to determine whether or not the treatment has a significant effect.

   c. Ignoring the fact that σ is known, use the sample data to compute an estimated standard error and do the t statistic test with $\alpha = .05$ to determine whether or not the treatment has a significant effect.
   (Note that the same data can lead to different conclusions depending on which test you use.)

7. For a standard set of discrimination problems that have been used for years in primate research, it is known that monkeys require an average of $\mu = 20$ trials before they can successfully reach the criterion (five consecutive correct solutions). A psychologist hypothesizes that the animals can learn the task vicariously—that is, simply by watching other animals perform the task. To test this hypothesis, the researcher selects a random sample of $n = 4$ monkeys. These animals are placed in neighboring enclosures from which they can watch another animal learn the task. After a week of viewing other animals, the four monkeys in the sample are tested on the problem. These animals require an average of $\overline{X} = 15$ trials to solve the problem, with $SS = 300$. On the basis of these data, can the psychologist conclude that there is evidence that the animals perform significantly better after viewing others. Use a one-tailed test at the .01 level of significance

   a. State the hypotheses using symbols. Explain what they predict for this experiment.

   b. Sketch the distribution and locate the critical region.

   c. Calculate the test statistic.

   d. Make a decision regarding H_0 and state your conclusion.

8. A group of students recently complained that all of the statistics classes are offered early in the morning. They claim that they "think better" later in the day and therefore would do better in the course had it been offered in the afternoon. To test this claim, the instructor scheduled the course this past semester for 3 P.M. The afternoon class was given the same final exam that has been used in previous semesters. The instructor knows that for previous students the scores are normally distributed with a mean of 70. The afternoon class with 16 students had an average score on the final of $\overline{X} = 76$ with $SS = 960$. Do the students perform significantly better in the afternoon section?

   a. Test with alpha set at .05 and with a one-tailed test.

   b. Identify the independent and dependent variables.

9. A recent national survey reports that the general population gives the president an average rating of $\mu = 62$ on a scale of 1 to 100. A researcher suspects that college students are likely to be more critical of the president than people in the general population. To test these suspicions, a random sample of college students is selected and asked to rate the president. The data for this sample are as follows: 44, 52, 24, 45, 39, 57, 20, 38, 78, 74, 61, 56, 49, 66, 53, 49, 47, 88, 38, 51, 65, 47, 35, 59, 23, 41, 50, 19. On the basis of this sample, can the researcher conclude that college students rate the president differently? Test at the .01 level of significance, two tails.

10. A fund raiser for a charitable organization has set a goal of averaging $20 per donation. To see if the goal is being met, a random sample of recent donations is selected. The data from this sample are as follows: 20, 5, 10, 15, 25, 5, 8, 10, 30, 10, 15, 24, 50, 10, 7, 15, 10, 5, 5, 15.

   a. Do the contributions differ significantly from the goal of the fund raiser? Test at the .05 level of significance.

   b. Would you reach the same conclusion had the .01 level of significance been used?

11. A researcher would like to examine the effect of labor unions on the average pay of workers. The investiga-

tor obtains information from the National Carpenters Union, which states that the average pay for union carpenters is $\mu = \$7.80$ per hour. The researcher then obtains a random sample of eight carpenters who do not belong to a union and records the pay for each. The data from this sample are as follows: 6.25, 7.50, 6.75, 6.90, 7.10, 7.15, 8.00 6.15.

Does the average pay of nonunion carpenters differ significantly from union members? Test at the .01 level of significance.

12. After many studies of memory, a psychologist has determined that when a standard list of 40 words is presented at a rate of 2 words per second, college students can recall an average of $\mu = 17.5$ words from the list. The psychologist would like to determine if the rate of presentation affects memory. A random sample of $n = 15$ students is selected, and each is given the standard list of words at a rate of only 1 word per second. At the end of the presentation of the list, each student is tested for recall. The number of words recalled is as follows: 14, 21, 23, 19, 17, 20, 24, 16, 27, 17, 20, 21, 18, 20, 19.
   a. Is there evidence for an effect of presentation rate? Test at the .05 level of significance and with two tails.
   b. Would you arrive at the same conclusion had the .01 level of significance been used?

13. A researcher knows that the average weight of American men between the ages of 30 and 50 is $\mu = 166$ pounds. The researcher would like to determine if men who have heart attacks between those ages are heavier than the average male. For a random sample of heart patients, body weights are recorded. The data are as follows: 153, 176, 201, 188, 157, 182, 208, 186, 163, 187, 230, 196, 167, 193, 171, 198, 191, 193, 233, 197, 196.

Are these patients significantly heavier than expected? Use a one-tailed test at the .01 level of significance.

14. A psychologist assesses the effect of distraction on time perception. Subjects are asked to judge the length of time between signals given by the experimenter. The actual interval of time is 10 minutes. During this period, the subjects are distracted by noises, conversation between the experimenter and his assistant, and questions from the assistant. The experimenter expects that the subjects' judgments will aver-

age around 10 minutes if the distraction has no effect. The data are as follows:

11	9.5	14	8
8	14	15	15
12	7.5	15	18
15	12	11	10
20	10	9	14

Is there a significant effect? Test at the .05 level of significance. What conclusion can be made?

15. A researcher would like to determine whether humidity can have an effect on eating behavior. It is known that under regular circumstances laboratory rats eat an average of $\mu = 10$ grams of food each day. The researcher selects a random sample of $n = 15$ rats and places them in a controlled atmosphere room where the relative humidity is maintained at 90%. The daily food consumption for each of these rats is as follows:

FOOD CONSUMPTION				
9.1	8.3	7.6	10.2	8.4
6.9	9.3	10.7	11.2	9.8
8.5	12.1	8.4	7.7	9.2

On the basis of these data, can the researcher conclude that humidity affects eating behavior? Test with $\alpha = .05$.

16. A manufacturer of office furniture is designing a new computer table. Although it is known that the standard height for typing tables is 26 inches, the manufacturer is concerned that the best height for a computer might be different. A sample of $n = 18$ computer operators is obtained, and each is asked to position the height of an adjustable table at its most comfortable level. The heights for this sample are as follows:

HEIGHTS (INCHES)		
27.50	26.25	25.75
29.50	26.50	29.00
27.25	26.00	28.25
26.25	28.00	26.25
26.75	27.00	27.50
28.00	26.25	25.75

On the basis of this sample, should the company conclude that the best height for a computer table is different from 26 inches? Test with $\alpha = .05$.

17. Recently the college newspaper conducted a survey to assess student attitudes toward spending student government money to help support college athletic teams. Student responses were recorded on a scale from 0 (totally opposed) to 10 (completely in favor). A value of 5 on this scale represented a neutral point. The results from $n = 327$ students gave an average opinion score of $\overline{X} = 6.3$ with $SS = 1343$. Do these data indicate that the general student opinion is significantly different from neutral. Test with $\alpha = .01$.

18. For several years the members of the faculty in the department of psychology have been teaching small sections of the introductory statistics course because they believe that students learn better in small classes. For these small classes, the average score on the standardized final exam is $\mu = 73.5$. This year, for the first time, the department offered one large section. For the 81 students in this large class, the scores on the final exam averaged $\overline{X} = 71.2$ with $SS = 9647$. The psychologist would like to use these data to determine whether there is any difference between students' performance in large versus small classes. Perform the appropriate test with $\alpha = .05$.

CHAPTER 10

HYPOTHESIS TESTS WITH TWO INDEPENDENT SAMPLES

SECTION 10.1 **INTRODUCTION**

Until this point, all the inferential statistics we have considered have involved using one sample as the basis for drawing conclusions about one population. Although these *single-sample* techniques are used occasionally in real research, most of the interesting experiments require two (or more) sets of data in order to compare two (or more) populations. For example, a social psychologist may want to compare men and women in terms of their attitudes toward abortion, or an educational psychologist may want to compare two methods for teaching mathematics. In both of these examples, the basic question concerns a mean difference between two populations or between two treatments. Is the average attitude for men any different from the average attitude for women? Do children who are taught math by method A score higher than children who are taught by method B?

In most experimental situations, a researcher will not have prior knowledge about either of the two populations being compared. This means that the researcher has a question about two unknown populations. One way to examine two unknown populations is to take two separate samples (see Figure 10.1). In this chapter we will present the statistical techniques that permit a researcher to examine the data obtained from two separate samples. More specifically, our goal is to use the data from two samples as the basis for evaluating the mean difference between two populations.

DEFINITION An experiment that uses a separate sample for each treatment condition (or each population) is called an *independent-measures* experimental design.

The term *independent-measures* comes from the fact that the experimental data consist of two *independent* sets of measurements, that is, two separate samples. On occasion, you will see an independent measures experiment referred to as a

Figure 10.1

Do the achievement scores for children taught by method A differ from the scores for children taught by method B? In statistical terms, are the two population means the same or different? Because neither of the two population means is known, it will be necessary to take two samples, one from each population. The first sample will provide information about the mean for the first population, and the second sample will provide information about the second population.

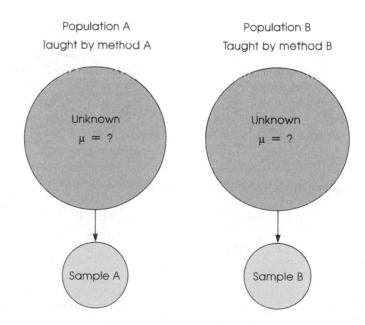

between-subjects or a *between-groups* design. This terminology reflects the fact that an independent-measures design evaluates differences between treatments by looking at differences between the groups of subjects.

SECTION 10.2 ## THE *t* STATISTIC FOR AN INDEPENDENT-MEASURES EXPERIMENT

Because an independent-measures experiment involves two separate samples, we will need some special notation to help specify which data go with which sample. This notation involves the use of subscripts, which are small numbers written beside each sample statistic. For example, the number of scores in the first sample would be identified by n_1; for the second sample, the number of scores would be n_2. The sample means would be identified by $\overline{X}_1$ and $\overline{X}_2$. The sums of squares would be SS_1 and SS_2.

Recall that our goal is to evaluate the mean difference between two populations (or between two treatment conditions). In symbols, the mean difference between the two populations can be written as $\mu_1 - \mu_2$. For hypothesis tests we will hypothesize a value for this mean difference. Generally, the null hypothesis says there is no difference between the two population means: $\mu_1 - \mu_2 = 0$.

The basis for the hypothesis test will be a *t* statistic. The formula for this *t* statistic will have the same general structure as the single-sample *t* formula that was introduced in Chapter 9.

$$t = \frac{\overline{X} - \mu}{s_{\overline{X}}} = \frac{\text{sample data} - \text{population parameter}}{\text{estimated standard error}}$$

However, the details of the formula must be modified to accommodate the independent-measures experimental design. Now the population parameter of interest is the difference between the two population means $(\mu_1 - \mu_2)$. The corresponding sample data would be the difference between the two sample means $(\overline{X}_1 - \overline{X}_2)$. The standard error in the denominator of the formula measures the standard distance between the sample data $(\overline{X}_1 - \overline{X}_2)$ and the population parameter $(\mu_1 - \mu_2)$. As always, standard error tells how well a sample value is expected to approximate the corresponding population value. In this case, the standard error tells how well the sample mean difference should approximate the population mean difference. The symbol for this standard error is $s_{\overline{X}_1 - \overline{X}_2}$. The *s* indicates an estimated standard distance and the subscript $\overline{X}_1 - \overline{X}_2$ simply indicates that our sample value is the difference between two sample means. Substituting these values into the general *t* formula gives

$$t = \frac{(\overline{X}_1 - \overline{X}_2) - (\mu_1 - \mu_2)}{s_{\overline{X}_1 - \overline{X}_2}}$$

This is the *t* formula that will be used with data from an independent-measures experiment. You should note that this is still a *t* statistic; it has the same basic structure as the original *t* formula that was introduced in Chapter 9. However, to distinguish between these two *t* formulas, we will occasionally refer to the original formula as the *single-sample t statistic* and this new formula as the *independent-measures t statistic*. To complete the independent-measures *t* formula, we must define more precisely the calculations needed for the standard error $s_{\bar{X}_1 - \bar{X}_2}$.

POOLED VARIANCE

The purpose of standard error is to provide a measure of how well a sample statistic represents the corresponding population parameter. In general, standard error is determined by two factors:

1. The variability of the scores
2. The size of the sample

To calculate the standard error for the independent-measures *t* statistic, we will begin by determining the variability of the scores.

You should recall that the original *t* statistic was developed to be used in situations where the population variability is unknown. The general strategy of the *t* statistic is to use the sample data to compute an estimate of the variability in the population. With an independent-measures experiment, we have two samples which are combined to obtain a single estimate of population variance. The result is called the *pooled variance* because it is obtained by averaging, or "pooling", the two sample variances. To compute this pooled variance, we will find the average of the two sample variances, but we will allow the bigger sample to carry more weight in determining the average. This process is demonstrated in the following example.

EXAMPLE 10.1

Suppose we have two samples from the same population. The first sample has $n = 4$ scores and $SS = 36$. For the second sample, $n = 8$ and $SS = 56$. From these data, we can compute a variance for each sample.

For sample 1,

$$s^2 = \frac{SS}{n-1} = \frac{36}{3} = 12$$

For sample 2,

$$s^2 = \frac{SS}{n-1} = \frac{56}{7} = 8$$

Because these two samples are from the same population, each of the sample variances provides an estimate of the same population variance. Therefore, it is reasonable somehow to average these two estimates together in order to get a better estimate. Before we average the two variances, however, you should notice that one of the samples is much bigger than the other. Because bigger samples tend to give better estimates of the population, we would expect the sample variance based on $n = 8$ to be a better value than the variance based on $n = 4$. When we pool the two variances, we will let the "better" value carry more weight.

To compute the pooled variance, we will weight each of the sample variances by its degrees of freedom ($df = n - 1$). The degrees of freedom indicate how well the sample variance approximates the population variance (the bigger the sample, the bigger the *df*, and the better the estimate). To find the pooled variance, or the weighted mean for two sample variances, you follow two steps:

1. Multiply each s^2 by its *df* and then add the results together (this weights each variance).
2. Divide this total by the sum of the two *df* values.

The equation for this process is

$$\text{pooled variance} = s_p^2 = \frac{df_1 s_1^2 + df_2 s_2^2}{df_1 + df_2} \qquad (10.1)$$

For this example, the calculation can be described in words as follows: You take 3 of the first variance ($df = 3$) and 7 of the second variance ($df = 7$). This gives you a total of 10 variances ($df_1 + df_2 = 10$). To find the average, you must divide by 10. For example,

$$\text{pooled variance} = \frac{3(12) + 7(8)}{3 + 7} = \frac{36 + 56}{10} = 9.2$$

Notice that the value we obtained is not halfway between the two sample variances. Rather it is closer to $s^2 = 8$ (the big sample) than it is to $s^2 = 12$ (the small sample), because the larger sample carried more weight in computing the average.

You may have noticed that the calculation of the pooled variance in Example 10.1 can be simplified greatly. In the numerator of the formula, each sample variance is multiplied by its *df*. When you do this, you always obtain *SS:*

$$df(s^2) = df \frac{SS}{df} = SS$$

Therefore, we can use *SS* in place of $df(s^2)$ in the formula. The simplified result is

$$\text{pooled variance} = s_p^2 = \frac{SS_1 + SS_2}{df_1 + df_2} \qquad (10.2)$$

THE STANDARD ERROR FOR A SAMPLE MEAN DIFFERENCE

In general, the purpose of standard error is to provide a measure of how accurately a sample statistic approximates the population parameter. In the independent measures *t* formula, the sample statistic consists of two sample means, and the population parameter consists of two population means. We expect the sample data $(\overline{X}_1 - \overline{X}_2)$ to be close to the population parameter $(\mu_1 - \mu_2)$, but there will be some error. Our goal is to determine how much error. To develop the formula for this standard error, we will consider two points:

1. First, we know that each of the two sample means provides an estimate of its own population mean:

$\overline{X}_1$ approximates μ_1 with some error.

$\overline{X}_2$ approximates μ_2 with some error.

10.1

IN CHAPTER 7 we first introduced standard error as a measure of how well a sample mean ($\overline{X}$) represents its population mean (μ). Formula 7.1 defined standard error as $\sigma_X = \sigma/\sqrt{n}$. Later, in Chapter 9, we introduced the estimated standard error, $s_{\overline{X}}$, which is used with the *t* statistic. Estimated standard error was defined by formula 9.1 as $s_{\overline{X}} = s/\sqrt{n}$. Notice that in both equations, standard error is determined by two values:

1. The variability of the scores, either σ or s

2. The sample size, n

In the independent-measures *t* statistic, these two values are again used to compute standard error, but now the standard error equation for each sample appears as $\sqrt{s_p^2/n}$. Although this equation *looks* different from the equations in Chapters 7 and 9, it actually is the same thing. This fact can be demonstrated by starting with Formula 9.1 and then (1) squaring the standard error and (2) taking the square root of the squared value.

original standard error	squared standard error	square root of squared value
$\dfrac{s}{\sqrt{n}}$	$\dfrac{s^2}{n}$	$\sqrt{\dfrac{s^2}{n}}$

Note that by squaring and then taking the square root, we are right back where we started. The value of the standard error is the same, but the appearance of the formula has changed. In the independent-measures *t* formula, standard error has a new appearance but it is really the same standard error you learned in Chapters 7 and 9, and it still provides a measure of how accurately a sample mean ($\overline{X}$) represents it population mean (μ).

Finally, you should remember that in the independent-measures formula we now have two sample means, so the formula shows two errors, one from each sample.

The amount of error from each sample is defined by the standard error of $\overline{X}$.

2. We want to know the total amount of error involved in using two sample means to approximate two population means. To do this, we will find the error from each sample separately and then add the two errors together.

The resulting formula for the independent-measures standard error is

$$s_{\overline{X}_1 - \overline{X}_2} = \sqrt{\frac{s_p^2}{n_1} + \frac{s_p^2}{n_2}}$$

(10.3)

In this formula, s_p^2/n_1 represents the error from the first sample and s_p^2/n_2 is the error from the second sample (see Box 10.1). Because we now have two sample means approximating two population means, we now have two sources of error. The formula for the standard error for the independent-measures *t* statistic simply adds together the two sources of error. Also note that the standard error formula uses the pooled variance, s_p^2, as the measure of variability for the scores.

THE FINAL FORMULA AND DEGREES OF FREEDOM

The complete equation for the independent measures *t* statistic is as follows:

$$t = \frac{(\overline{X}_1 - \overline{X}_2) - (\mu_1 - \mu_2)}{s_{\overline{X}_1 - \overline{X}_2}} = \frac{(\overline{X}_1 - \overline{X}_2) - (\mu_1 - \mu_2)}{\sqrt{\dfrac{s_p^2}{n_1} + \dfrac{s_p^2}{n_2}}}$$

(10.4)

with the pooled variance s_p^2 defined by either formula 10.1 or formula 10.2.

The degrees of freedom for this t statistic are determined by the df values for the two separate samples:

Remember, we pooled the two sample variances to compute the t statistic. Now we combine the two df values to obtain the overall df for the t statistic.

$$df = df \text{ for first sample} + df \text{ for second sample}$$
$$= df_1 + df_2 \tag{10.5}$$

Occasionally, you will see degrees of freedom written in terms of the number of scores in each sample:

$$df = (n_1 - 1) + (n_2 - 1)$$
$$= n_1 + n_2 - 2 \tag{10.6}$$

This t formula will be used for hypothesis testing. We will use the sample data $(\bar{X}_1 - \bar{X}_2)$ as the basis for testing hypotheses about the population parameter $(\mu_1 - \mu_2)$.

LEARNING CHECK

1. Describe the general experimental situation in which an independent-measures statistic would be used.

2. Identify the two sources of error that are reflected in the standard error for the independent-measures t statistic.

3. Sample 1 of an experiment has dozens of subjects, and $s_1^2 = 32$. On the other hand, sample 2 has fewer than 10 subjects, and its variance is $s_2^2 = 57$. When these variances are pooled, which sample variance will s_p^2 more closely resemble?

ANSWERS

1. Independent-measures statistics are used whenever an experiment uses separate samples to represent the different treatment conditions or populations being compared.

2. The two sources of error come from the differences between the means of both samples and their respective population means. That is, $\bar{X}_1$ approximates μ_1 with some error and $\bar{X}_2$ approximates μ_2 with some error.

3. The value for s_p^2 will be closer to $s_1^2 = 32$ because the size of sample 1 is larger.

SECTION 10.3

HYPOTHESIS TESTS WITH THE INDEPENDENT-MEASURES t STATISTIC

The independent-measures t statistic can be used to test a hypothesis about the mean difference between two populations (or between two treatments). As always, the null hypothesis states that there is no difference:

$$H_0: \mu_1 - \mu_2 = 0$$

The alternative hypothesis says that there is a mean difference:

$$H_1: \mu_1 - \mu_2 \neq 0$$

Figure 10.2

The *t* distribution with $df = 18$. The critical region for $\alpha = .05$ is shown.

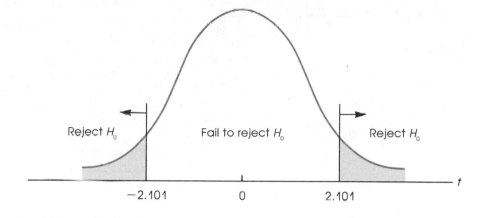

Reject H_0 Fail to reject H_0 Reject H_0

-2.101 0 2.101 t

The hypothesis test procedure will determine whether or not the data provide evidence for a mean difference between the two populations. At the conclusion of the hypothesis test, we will decide either to

a. Reject H_0: We conclude that the data indicate a significant difference between the two populations, or to

b. Fail to reject H_0: The data do not provide sufficient to evidence to conclude that a difference exists.

For hypothesis tests, we will use the *t* formula as follows:

$$t = \frac{\text{sample data} - \text{hypothesized population parameter}}{\text{estimated standard error}}$$

Notice that we simply take the value from the null hypothesis ($\mu_1 - \mu_2 = 0$) and use it in the formula along with the data from the experiment. When the sample data are close to the hypothesis, we should get a *t* statistic near zero, and our decision will be to fail to reject H_0 (see Figure 10.2). On the other hand, when the data are very different from the hypothesis, we should obtain a large value for *t* (large positive or large negative), and we will reject H_0.

A complete example of a hypothesis test with two independent samples follows. Notice that the hypothesis testing procedure follows the same four steps that we have used before.

STEP 1   State the hypotheses H_0 and H_1 and select an alpha level. For the independent measures *t* test, the hypotheses concern the difference between two population means.

STEP 2   Locate the critical region. The critical region is defined as sample data that would be extremely unlikely ($p < \alpha$) if the null hypothesis were true. In this case, we will be locating extremely unlikely *t* values.

STEP 3   Get the data and compute the test statistic. Here we compute the *t* value for our data using the value from H_0 in the formula.

STEP 4   Make a decision. If the *t* statistic we compute is in the critical region, we reject H_0. Otherwise we conclude that the data do not provide sufficient evidence that the two populations are different.

EXAMPLE 10.2

In recent years psychologists have demonstrated repeatedly that using mental images can greatly improve memory. A hypothetical experiment, designed to examine this phenomenon, is presented here.

The psychologist first prepares a list of 40 pairs of nouns (for example, dog/bicycle, grass/door, lamp/piano). Next, two groups of subjects are obtained (two separate samples). Subjects in the first group are given the list for 5 minutes and instructed to memorize the 40 noun pairs. Subjects in the second group receive the same list of words, but in addition to the regular instructions these people are told to form a mental image for each pair of nouns (imagine a dog riding a bicycle, for example). Notice that the two samples are identical except that the second group is using mental images to help learn the list.

Remember, an independent-measures design means that there are separate samples for each treatment condition.

Later each group is given a memory test, and the psychologist records the number of words correctly recalled for each individual. The data from this experiment are as follows. On the basis of these data, can the psychologist conclude that mental images affected memory?

DATA (NUMBER OF WORDS RECALLED)			
GROUP 1 (NO IMAGES)		GROUP 2 (IMAGES)	
24	13	18	31
23	17	19	29
16	20	23	26
17	15	29	21
19	26	30	24
$n = 10$		$n = 10$	
$\bar{X} = 19$		$\bar{X} = 25$	
$SS = 160$		$SS = 200$	

STEP 1 State the hypothesis and select α.

Directional hypotheses could be used and would specify whether imagery should increase or decrease recall scores.

$H_0: \mu_1 - \mu_2 = 0$ (no difference; imagery has no effect)

$H_1: \mu_1 - \mu_2 \neq 0$ (imagery produces a difference)

We will set $\alpha = .05$.

STEP 2 This is an independent-measures design. The t statistic for these data will have degrees of freedom determined by

$$df = df_1 + df_2$$
$$= (n_1 - 1) + (n_2 - 1)$$
$$= 9 + 9$$
$$= 18$$

The t distribution for $df = 18$ is presented in Figure 10.2. For $\alpha = .05$, the critical region consists of the extreme 5% of the distribution and has boundaries of $t = +2.101$ and $t = -2.101$.

STEP 3 Obtain the data and compute the test statistic. The data are as given, so all that remains is to compute the *t* statistic. Because the independent measures *t* formula is relatively complex, the calculations can be simplified by dividing the process into three parts.

First, find the pooled variance for the two samples:

Caution: The pooled variance combines the two samples to obtain a single estimate of variance. In the formula the two samples are combined in a single fraction.

$$s_p^2 = \frac{SS_1 + SS_2}{df_1 + df_2}$$

$$= \frac{160 + 200}{9 + 9}$$

$$= \frac{360}{18}$$

$$= 20$$

Second, use the pooled variance to compute the standard error:

Caution: The standard error adds the errors from two separate samples. In the formula these two errors are added as two separate fractions.

$$s_{\overline{X}_1 - \overline{X}_2} = \sqrt{\frac{s_p^2}{n_1} + \frac{s_p^2}{n_2}}$$

$$= \sqrt{\frac{20}{10} + \frac{20}{10}}$$

$$= \sqrt{4}$$

$$= 2$$

Third, compute the *t* statistic:

$$t = \frac{(\overline{X}_1 - \overline{X}_2) - (\mu_1 - \mu_2)}{s_{\overline{X}_1 - \overline{X}_2}} = \frac{(19 - 25) - 0}{2}$$

$$= \frac{-6}{2}$$

$$= -3.00$$

STEP 4 Make a decision. The obtained value ($t = -3.00$) is in the critical region. This result is very unlikely if H_0 is true. Therefore, we reject H_0 and conclude that using mental images produced a significant difference in memory performance. More specifically, the group using images recalled significantly more words than the group with no images.

In the scientific literature it is common to report the results of a hypothesis test in a concise, standardized format. For the test described in Example 10.2, the report would state the following: $t(18) = -3.00, p < .05$. This statement indicates that the *t* statistic has $df = 18$, the value obtained from these sample data is $t = -3.00$, and this value is in the critical region with $\alpha = .05$.

THE t STATISTIC AS A RATIO

You should note that the magnitude of the t statistic is determined not only by the mean difference between the two samples but also by the sample variability. The bigger the difference between the sample means (the numerator of the t formula), the bigger the t value. This relation is reasonable because a big difference between the samples is a clear indication of a difference between the two populations. However, the sample variability (in the denominator of the t formula) is just as important. If the variability is large, t will tend to be small. The role of variability becomes clearer if you consider a simplified version of the t formula:

$$t = \frac{\text{sample mean difference}}{\text{variability}}$$

Notice that we have left out the population mean difference because the null hypothesis says that this is zero. Also, we have used the general term *variability* in place of standard error. In this simplified form, t becomes a ratio involving only the sample mean difference and the sample variability. It should be clear that large variability will make the t value smaller (or small variability will make t larger). Thus, variability plays an important role in determining whether or not a t statistic is significant. When variability is large, even a big difference between the two sample means may not be enough to make the t statistic significant. On the other hand, when variability is low, even a small difference between the two sample means may be enough to produce a significant t statistic.

DIRECTIONAL HYPOTHESES AND ONE-TAILED TESTS

When planning an independent-measures experiment, a researcher usually has some expectation or specific prediction for the outcome. For the memory experiment described in Example 10.2, the psychologist clearly expects the group using images to have higher memory scores than the group without images. This kind of directional prediction can be incorporated into the statement of the hypotheses, resulting in a directional, or one-tailed, test. You should recall from Chapter 8 that one-tailed tests are used only in limited situations, where a researcher wants to increase the chances of finding a significant difference. In general, a nondirectional (two-tailed) test is preferred, even in research situations where there is a definite directional prediction. The following example demonstrates the procedure for stating hypotheses and locating the critical region for a one-tailed test using the independent-measures t statistic.

EXAMPLE 10.3

We will use the same experimental situation that was described in Example 10.2. The researcher is using an independent-measures design to examine the effect of mental images on memory. The prediction is that the imagery group will have higher memory scores.

STEP 1 State the hypotheses and select α. As always, the null hypothesis says that there is no effect, and H_1 says that there is a difference between the treatments. With a one-tailed test, it usually is easier to begin with the statement of H_1.

Figure 10.3

The critical region in the *t* distribution for $\alpha = .05$, *df* = 18, one tailed test.

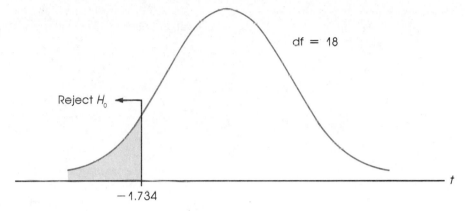

Reject H_0

df = 18

t

-1.734

For this example, we will identify the no-imagery condition as treatment 1 and the imagery condition as treatment 2. Because images are expected to produce higher scores, the alternative hypothesis would be

$$H_1: \mu_1 - \mu_2 < 0 \qquad \text{(imagery produces higher scores)}$$

The null hypothesis states that the treatment does not work. For this example,

$$H_0: \mu_1 - \mu_2 \geq 0 \qquad \text{(imagery scores are not higher)}$$

We will set $\alpha = .05$.

STEP 2   Locate the critical region. The researcher predicts that the imagery group (sample 2) will have higher scores. If this is correct, then $\overline{X}_2$ will be greater than $\overline{X}_1$, and the data will produce a negative *t* statistic.

$$t = \frac{(\overline{X}_1 - \overline{X}_2) - (\mu_1 - \mu_2)}{s_{\overline{X} - \overline{X}}}$$

The table lists critical values without signs. You must determine whether the sign is positive or negative.

Thus, a negative value for *t* will tend to support the researcher's prediction and refute H_0. The question is, How large a negative *t* value is needed to reject H_0? With $n = 10$ scores in each sample, the data will produce an independent-measures *t* statistic with *df* = 18. To find the critical value, look in the *t* distribution table with *df* = 18 and $\alpha = .05$ for a one-tailed test. You will find a critical *t* value of 1.734, and this value should be negative. Figure 10.3 shows the one-tailed critical region in the *t* distribution. The data from this example produce a test statistic of $t = -3.00$ (see Example 10.2). This value is in the critical region, so we reject H_0 and conclude that recall is significantly better in the imagery condition than in the no-imagery condition.

LEARNING CHECK   1. A development psychologist would like to examine the difference in mathematical skills for 10-year-old boys versus 10-year-old girls. A sample of 10 boys and 10 girls is obtained, and each child is given a standardized mathematical abilities test. The data from this experiment are as follows:

BOYS	GIRLS
$\bar{X} = 37$	$\bar{X} = 31$
$SS = 150$	$SS = 210$

Do these data indicate a significant different in mathematical skills for boys versus girls? Test at the .05 level of significance.

2. A psychologist is interested in the effect of aging on memory. A sample of 10 college graduates is obtained. Five of these people are between 30 and 35 years old. The other 5 are between 60 and 65 years old. Each person is given a list of 40 words to memorize. A week later each person is asked to recall ·as many of the words as possible. The data from this experiment are as follows:

30-YEARS-OLDS	60-YEAR-OLDS
$\bar{X} = 21$	$\bar{X} = 16$
$SS = 130$	$SS = 190$

Do these data provide evidence for a significant change in recall ability with age? Test at the .05 level of significance.

ANSWERS **1.** Pooled variance $= 20$; standard error $= 2$; $t = 3.00$. With $df = 18$, this value is in the critical region, so the decision is to reject H_0: There is a significant difference.

2. Pooled variance $= 40$; standard error $= 4$; $t = 1.25$. With $df = 8$, this value is not in the critical region, so the decision is to fail to reject H_0. These data do not provide evidence for a significant difference.

SECTION 10.4 **ASSUMPTIONS UNDERLYING THE t FORMULA**

In addition to random sampling, there are two assumptions that should be satisfied before you use the independent-measures t formula for hypothesis testing:

1. The distribution of the sample mean differences should be normal.
2. The two populations from which the samples are selected must have the same variances.

The first assumption should be very familiar by now. In both the z-score formula and the single-sample t formula, it was necessary that the sample data come from a normal distribution. For an independent measures experiment, the sample data consist of a mean difference $(\bar{X}_1 - \bar{X}_2)$, and, once again, these data should form a normal distribution. To satisfy this assumption, it is necessary that the distribution of sample means for both samples $(\bar{X}_1$ and $\bar{X}_2)$, be normal. You should recall from

Chapter 7 that these sampling distributions do tend to be normal. Specifically, these distributions will be normal and the assumption will be satisfied if either

a. The two populations are normal or

b. The samples are relatively large (*n* around 30 or more).

In general, this assumption is satisfied easily and is not a cause for concern in most research. When there is reason to suspect that the populations are far from normal in shape, you should compensate by ensuring that samples are relatively large.

The second assumption is referred to as *homogeneity of variance* and states that the two populations being compared must have the same variance. You may recall a similar assumption for both the *z*-score and the single-sample *t*. For those tests, we assumed that the effect of the treatment was to add (or subtract) a constant amount to each individual score. As a result, the population standard deviation after treatment was the same as it had been before treatment. We now are making essentially the same assumption but phrasing it in terms of variances.

You should recall that the pooled variance in the *t* statistic formula is obtained by averaging together the two sample variances. It makes sense to average these two values only if they both are estimating the same population variance—i.e., if the homogeneity of variance assumption is satisfied. If the two sample variances represent different population variances, then the average would be meaningless. (*Note:* There is no meaning to the value obtained by averaging two unrelated numbers. For example, what is the significance of the number obtained by averaging your shoe size and the last two digits of your social security number?)

The homogeneity of variance assumption is quite important because violating this assumption can negate any meaningful interpretation of the data from an independent-measures experiment. Specifically, when you compute the *t* statistic in a hypothesis test, all the numbers in the formula come from the data except for the population mean difference which you get from H_0. Thus, you are sure of all the numbers in the formula except for one. If you obtain an extreme result for the *t* statistic (a value in the critical region), you conclude that the hypothesized value was wrong. But consider what happens when you violate the homogeneity of variance assumption. In this case, you have two questionable values in the formula (the hypothesized population value and the meaningless average of the two variances). Now if you obtain an extreme *t* statistic, you do not know which of these two values is responsible. Specifically, you cannot reject the hypothesis because it may have been the pooled variance that produced the extreme *t* statistic. Without satisfying the homogeneity of variance requirement, you cannot accurately interpret a *t* statistic, and the hypothesis test becomes meaningless.

How do you know whether or not the homogeneity of variance requirement is satisfied? There are statistical tests that can be used to determine if the two population variances are the same or different (see Box 10.2), but there is a simple rule of thumb that works most of the time. If the two population variances are the same, then the two sample variances should be very similar. You can just look at the two sample variances to see whether or not they are close. If one of the sample variances is more than four times larger than the other, you probably have violated the homogeneity of variance requirement. Otherwise the two population variances are close enough to proceed with the hypothesis test.

Remember, adding (or subtracting) a constant to each score does not change the standard deviation.

10.2 HARTLEY'S *F*-MAX TEST FOR HOMOGENEITY OF VARIANCE

ALTHOUGH THERE are many different statistical methods for determining whether or not the homogeneity of variance assumption has been satisfied, Hartley's *F*-max test is one of the simplest to compute and to understand. An additional advantage is that this test can be used to check homogeneity of variance with two or more independent samples. In Chapter 13 we will examine statistical methods involving several samples, and Hartley's test will be useful again.

The *F*-max test is based on the principle that a sample variance provides an unbiased estimate of the population variance. Therefore, if the population variances are the same, the sample variances should be very similar. The procedure for using the *F*-max test is as follows:

1. Compute the sample variance, $s^2 = SS/df$, for each of the separate samples.

2. Select the largest and the smallest of these sample variances and compute

$$F\text{-max} = \frac{s^2(\text{largest})}{s^2(\text{smallest})}$$

A relatively large value for *F*-max indicates a large difference between the sample variances. In this case, the data suggest that the population variances are different and that the homogeneity assumption has been violated. On the other hand, a small value of *F*-max (near 1.00) indicates that the sample variances are similar and that the homogeneity assumption is reasonable.

3. The *F*-max value computed for the sample data is compared with the critical value found in Table B3 (Appendix B). If the sample value is larger than the table value, then you conclude that the variances are different and that the homogeneity assumption is not valid.

To locate the critical value in the table, you need to know

a. k = number of separate samples. (For the independent measures *t* test, $k = 2$.)

b. $df = n - 1$ for each sample variance. The Hartley test assumes that all samples are the same size.

c. The α level. The table provides critical values for $\alpha = .05$ and $\alpha = .01$. Generally, a test for homogeneity would use the larger alpha level.

Example: Two independent samples each have $n = 10$. The sample variances are 12.34 and 9.15. For these data,

$$F\text{-max} = \frac{s^2(\text{largest})}{s^2(\text{smallest})} = \frac{12.34}{9.15} = 1.35$$

With $\alpha = .05$, $k = 2$, and $df = n - 1 = 9$, the critical value from the table is 4.03. Because the obtained *F*-max is smaller than this critical value, you conclude that the data do not provide evidence that the homogeneity of variance assumption has been violated.

SUMMARY

1. The independent measures *t* statistic is used to draw inferences about the mean difference between two populations or between two treatment conditions. The term *independent* is used because this *t* statistic requires data from two separate (or independent) samples.

2. The formula for the independent measures *t* statistic has the same structure as the original *z*-score or the single-sample *t:*

$$t = \frac{\text{sample data} - \text{population parameter}}{\text{estimated standard error}}$$

For the independent measures statistic, the data consist of the difference between the two sample means $(\bar{X}_1 - \bar{X}_2)$. The population parameter of interest is the difference between the two population means $(\mu_1 - \mu_2)$. The standard error is computed by combining the errors for the two sample means. The resulting formula is

$$t = \frac{(\bar{X}_1 - \bar{X}_2) - (\mu_1 - \mu_2)}{s_{\bar{X}_1 - \bar{X}_2}}$$

$$= \frac{(\bar{X}_1 - \bar{X}_2) - (\mu_1 - \mu_2)}{\sqrt{\dfrac{s_p^2}{n_1} + \dfrac{s_p^2}{n_2}}}$$

The pooled variance in the formula, s_p^2, is the weighted mean of the two sample variances:

$$s_p^2 = \frac{SS_1 + SS_2}{df_1 + df_2}$$

This t statistic has degrees of freedom determined by the sum of the df values for the two samples:

$$df = df_1 + df_2$$
$$= (n_1 - 1) + (n_2 - 1)$$

3. For hypothesis testing, the formula has the following structure:

$$t = \frac{\text{sample data} - \text{hypothesized population parameter}}{\text{estimated standard error}}$$

The null hypothesis normally states that there is no difference between the two population means:

$$H_0: \mu_1 = \mu_2 \quad \text{or} \quad \mu_1 - \mu_2 = 0$$

4. Appropriate use and interpretation of the t statistic requires that the data satisfy the homogeneity of variance assumption. This assumption stipulates that the two populations have equal variances. An informal test of this assumption can be made by simply comparing the two sample variances: If the two sample variances are approximately equal, the t test is justified. Hartley's F-max test provides a statistical technique for determining whether or not the data satisfy the homogeneity assumption.

KEY TERMS

independent-measures experimental design

between-subjects experimental design

pooled variance

homogeneity of variance

FOCUS ON PROBLEM SOLVING

1. As you learn more about different statistical methods, one basic problem will be deciding which method is appropriate for a particular set of data. Fortunately, it is easy to identify situations where the independent-measures t statistic is used. First, the data will always consist of two separate samples (two ns, two $\bar{X}$s, two SSs, and so on). Second, this t statistic always is used to answer questions about a mean difference: On the average, is one group different (better, faster, smarter) than the other group? If you examine the data and identify the type of question that a researcher is asking, you should be able to decide whether or not an independent-measures t is appropriate.

2. When computing an independent-measures t statistic from sample data, we suggest that you routinely divide the formula into separate stages rather than trying to do all the calculations at once. First, find the pooled variance. Second, compute the standard error. Third, compute the t statistic.

3. One of the most common errors for students involves confusing the formulas for pooled variance and standard error. When computing pooled variance, you are "pooling" the two samples together into a single variance. This variance is computed as a *single fraction*, with two SS values in the numerator and two df values in the denominator. When computing the standard error, you are adding the error from the first sample and the error from the second sample. These two separate errors add as *two separate fractions* under the square root symbol.

DEMONSTRATION 10.1   THE INDEPENDENT MEASURES *t* TEST

In a study of jury behavior, two samples of subjects were provided details about a trial in which the defendant was obviously guilty. Although group 2 received the same details as group 1, the second group was also told that some evidence had been withheld from the jury by the judge. Later the subjects were asked to recommend a jail sentence. The length of term suggested by each subject is presented below. Is there a significant difference between the two groups in their responses?

$$\text{Group 1 scores:} \quad 4 \quad 4 \quad 3 \quad 2 \quad 5 \quad 1 \quad 1 \quad 4$$
$$\text{Group 2 scores:} \quad 3 \quad 7 \quad 8 \quad 5 \quad 4 \quad 7 \quad 6 \quad 8$$

There are two separate samples in this study. Therefore, the analysis will use the independent-measures *t* test.

STEP 1 State the hypotheses and select an alpha level.

$H_0: \mu_1 - \mu_2 = 0$ For the population, knowing evidence has been withheld has no effect on the suggested sentence.

$H_1: \mu_1 - \mu_2 \neq 0$ For the population, knowledge of withheld evidence has an effect on the jury's response.

We will set the level of significance to $\alpha = .05$, two tails.

STEP 2 Identify the critical region.

For the independent-measures *t* statistic, degrees of freedom are determined by

$$df = n_1 + n_2 - 2$$
$$= 8 + 8 - 2$$
$$= 14$$

The *t* distribution table is consulted, for a two-tailed test with $\alpha = .05$, and $df = 14$. The critical *t* values are $+2.145$ and -2.145.

STEP 3 Compute the test statistic.

We are computing an independent-measures *t* statistic. To do this, we will need the mean and *SS* for each sample, pooled variance, and estimated standard error. *Sample means and sum-of-squares.* The mean ($\overline{X}$) and sums-of-squares (*SS*) for the samples are computed as follows.

SAMPLE 1		SAMPLE 2	
X	X^2	X	X^2
4	16	3	9
4	16	7	49
3	9	8	64
2	4	5	25
5	25	4	16
1	1	7	49
1	1	6	36
4	16	8	64
$\Sigma X = 24$	$\Sigma X^2 = 88$	$\Sigma X = 48$	$\Sigma X^2 = 312$

$$n_1 = 8 \qquad\qquad n_2 = 8$$

$$\overline{X}_1 = \frac{\Sigma X}{n} = \frac{24}{8} = 3 \qquad\qquad \overline{X}_2 = \frac{\Sigma X}{n} = \frac{48}{8} = 6$$

$$SS_1 = \Sigma X^2 - \frac{(\Sigma X)^2}{n} \qquad\qquad SS_2 = \Sigma X^2 - \frac{(\Sigma X)^2}{n}$$

$$= 88 - \frac{(24)^2}{8} \qquad\qquad = 312 - \frac{(48)^2}{8}$$

$$= 88 - \frac{576}{8} \qquad\qquad = 312 - \frac{2304}{8}$$

$$= 88 - 72 \qquad\qquad = 312 - 288$$

$$SS_1 = 16 \qquad\qquad SS_2 = 24$$

Pooled variance. For these data, the pooled variance equals

$$s_p^2 = \frac{SS_1 + SS_2}{df_1 + df_2} = \frac{16 + 24}{7 + 7} = \frac{40}{14} = 2.86$$

Estimated standard error. Now we can calculate the estimated standard error for mean differences.

$$s_{\overline{X}_1 - \overline{X}_2} = \sqrt{\frac{s_p^2}{n_1} + \frac{s_p^2}{n_2}} = \sqrt{\frac{2.86}{8} + \frac{2.86}{8}} = \sqrt{0.358 + 0.358}$$

$$= \sqrt{0.716} = 0.85$$

The t statistic. Finally, the t statistic can be computed.

$$t = \frac{(\overline{X}_1 - \overline{X}_2) - (\mu_1 - \mu_2)}{s_{\overline{X}_1 - \overline{X}_2}} = \frac{(3 - 6) - 0}{0.85} = \frac{-3}{0.85}$$

$$= -3.53$$

STEP 4 Make a decision about H_0 and state a conclusion.

The obtained t value of -3.53 falls in the critical region of the left tail (critical $t = \pm 2.145$). Therefore the null hypothesis is rejected. The subjects that were informed about the withheld evidence gave significantly longer sentences, $t(14) = -3.53$, $p < .05$, two tails.

PROBLEMS

1. For each situation described, decide whether the appropriate statistic is a single-sample t or an independent-measures t.

   a. A researcher would like to compare the average weight of 6-week-old rats with neurological damage to the known μ for the population of healthy 6-week-old rats.

   b. A researcher would like to know whether there is any difference in mathematical aptitude for 6-year-old boys versus 6-year-old girls.

c. A researcher would like to compare subjects in a behavior-modification program versus subjects in a control group to determine how much effect behavior modification has on the eating habits of obese people.

2. What is measured by the estimated standard error that is used for the independent-measures t statistic?

3. Describe the homogeneity of variance assumption, and explain why it is important for the independent measures hypothesis test.

4. A psychologist would like to compare the amount of information that people get from television versus newspapers. A random sample of 20 people is obtained. Ten of these people agree to get all of their news information from TV (no newspapers) for 4 weeks. The other 10 people agree to get all of their news information from newspapers. At the end of 4 weeks all 20 people are given a test on current events. The average score for the TV group was $\overline{X} = 41$ with $SS = 200$. The average for the newspaper group was $\overline{X} = 49$ with $SS = 160$. On the basis of these data, can the psychologist conclude that there is a significant difference between TV news and newspapers? Test at the .05 level of significance.

5. A local politician would like to compare the political attitudes for the older people and the younger people in his district. He develops a questionnaire which measures political attitude on a scale from 0 (very conservative) to 100 (very liberal) and administers this questionnaire to a sample of 10 young voters and a sample of 10 elderly voters. The data from these two samples are as follows:

OLD	YOUNG
$\overline{X} = 39$	$\overline{X} = 52$
$SS = 4200$	$SS = 4800$

On the basis of these data, should the politician conclude that there is a significant difference between political attitudes for younger voters and older voters? Test with $\alpha = .05$.

6. The following data are from two separate independent-measures experiments. Without doing any calculation, which experiment is more likely to demonstrate a significant difference between treatments A and B? Explain your answer. *Note:* You do not need to compute the t statistics; just look carefully at the data.

EXPERIMENT I		EXPERIMENT II	
TREATMENT A	TREATMENT B	TREATMENT A	TREATMENT B
$n = 10$	$n = 10$	$n = 10$	$n = 10$
$\overline{X} = 42$	$\overline{X} = 52$	$\overline{X} = 61$	$\overline{X} = 71$
$SS = 180$	$SS = 120$	$SS = 986$	$SS = 1042$

7. A researcher selects two random samples from a population with $\mu = 60$. Sample 1 is given treatment A, and sample 2 is given treatment B. The resulting data for these two samples are as follows:

SAMPLE 1	SAMPLE 2
$n = 9$	$n = 9$
$\overline{X} = 58$	$\overline{X} = 62$
$SS = 72$	$SS = 72$

a. Do the data from sample 1 indicate that the treatment A has a significant effect? Use a single-sample t statistic with $\alpha = .05$.

b. Do the data from sample 2 indicate that treatment B has significant effect? Use a single-sample t statistic with $\alpha = .05$.

c. Use an independent-measure t statistic to determine whether there is a significant difference between treatment A and treatment B. Test at the .05 level of significance.

d. The results from parts a and b should indicate that neither treatment has a significant effect. However, the results from the independent-measures test should show a significant difference between the two treatments. Are these results contradictory? Explain your answer.

8. In an experiment designed to examine the effect that personality can have on practical decisions, a psychologist selects a random sample of $n = 5$ people who are classified as ''impulsive'' and a sample of $n = 10$ people who are classified as ''reflective.'' Each person is given a brief description of a crime and then is asked for his or her judgment of a reasonable prison sentence for the criminal. The impulsive people gave an average sentence of 14 years with $SS = 130$, and the reflective people gave an average sentence of 12.5 years with $SS = 260$. On the basis of these samples, can the psychologist conclude that there is a signifi-

cant difference in the harshness of judgment for impulsive versus reflective people? Test with $\alpha = .01$.

9. A researcher has done a series of experiments to determine whether there is any significant difference between two treatments. The data from three of these experiments are as follows:

EXPERIMENT I	
A	B
$n = 5$	$n = 5$
$\bar{X} = 40$	$\bar{X} = 35$
$SS = 36$	$SS = 44$

EXPERIMENT II	
A	B
$n = 5$	$n = 5$
$\bar{X} = 40$	$\bar{X} = 35$
$SS = 120$	$SS = 200$

EXPERIMENT III	
A	B
$n = 5$	$n = 5$
$\bar{X} = 40$	$\bar{X} = 38$
$SS = 36$	$SS = 44$

a. Use the data from each experiment to determine whether there is any significant difference between treatment A and treatment B. Test at the .05 level of significance.

b. How do you explain the fact that the results of experiments I and II lead to different conclusions? Notice that the sample means are identical for these two experiments.

c. How do you explain that experiments I and III lead to different conclusions? Note that the sample SS values are identical for these two experiments.

10. A local hospital is planning a fund-raising campaign to raise money for the expansion of their pediatrics ward. Part of the campaign will involve visits to local industries to present their case to employees and to solicit contributions. One factory is selected as a test site to compare two different campaign strategies. Within this factory the employees are randomly divided into two groups. The individuals in one group are presented the "hard facts" (number of people served, costs, and the like) about the hospital. The

individuals in the second group receive an "emotional appeal" that describes in detail the personal histories of two children recently treated at the hospital. The average contribution for the 20 employees in the hard-facts group was $21.50 with $SS = 970$. The average for the 20 employees in the emotional group was $29.80 with $SS = 550$.

a. On the basis of these sample data, should the hospital conclude that one strategy is significantly better than the other? Test at the .05 level of significance.

b. Use Hartley's F-max test to determine whether these data satisfy the homogeneity of variance assumption.

11. A psychologist would like to examine the effects of fatigue on mental alertness. An attention test is prepared which requires subjects to sit in front of a blank TV screen and press a response button each time a dot appears on the screen. A total of 110 dots are presented during a 90-minute period, and the psychologist records the number of errors for each subject. Two groups of subjects are selected. The first group ($n = 5$) is tested after they have been kept awake for 24 hours. The second group ($n = 10$) is tested in the morning after a full night's sleep. The data for these two samples are as follows:

AWAKE 24 HOURS	RESTED
$\bar{X} = 35$	$\bar{X} = 24$
$SS = 120$	$SS = 270$

On the basis of these data, can the psychologist conclude that fatigue significantly increases errors on an attention task? Use a one-tailed test with $\alpha = .05$.

12. A school psychologist would like to examine cheating behavior for 10-year-old children. A standardized achievement test is used. One sample of $n = 8$ children is given the test under unsupervised conditions where cheating is possible. A second sample of 8 children receives the same test under very strict supervision. The test scores for these children are summarized as follows:

UNSUPERVISED	SUPERVISED
$\bar{X} = 78$	$\bar{X} = 65$
$SS = 3000$	$SS = 2600$

Can the psychologist conclude that the unsupervised (cheating?) group did significantly better than the strictly supervised group? Test at the .05 level of significance.

13. A psychologist would like to measure the effects of air pollution on life expectancy. Two samples of newborn rats are selected. The first sample of 10 rats is housed in cages where the atmosphere is equivalent to the air in a severely polluted city. The second sample with $n = 20$ is placed in cages with clean air. The average life span for the first group is $\overline{X} = 478$ days with $SS = 5020$ and for the second group $\overline{X} = 511$ with $SS = 10,100$. Does pollution cause a difference in life expectancy? Test with $\alpha = .01$.

14. A psychologist studying human memory would like to examine the process of forgetting. One group of subjects is required to memorize a list of words in the evening just before going to bed. Their recall is tested 10 hours later in the morning. Subjects in the second group memorize the same list of words in the morning, and then their memories are tested 10 hours later after being awake all day. The psychologist hypothesizes that there will be less forgetting during sleep than during a busy day. The recall scores for two samples of college students are as follows:

ASLEEP SCORES				AWAKE SCORES			
15	13	14	14	15	13	14	12
16	15	16	15	14	13	11	12
16	15	17	14	13	13	12	14

a. Sketch a frequency distribution polygon for the "asleep" group. On the same graph (in a different color) sketch the distribution for the "awake" group. Just by looking at these two distributions, would you predict a significant difference between the two treatment conditions?

b. Use the independent measures t statistic to determine whether there is a significant difference between the treatments. Conduct the test with $\alpha = .05$.

15. The experiment described in Problem 14 was repeated using samples of 6-year-old children. The data for this experiment are as follows:

ASLEEP SCORES				AWAKE SCORES			
15	13	8	10	6	8	5	8
7	10	6	9	4	7	12	9
14	11	5	12	3	10	13	11

a. Again, sketch a frequency distribution polygon for each group on the same graph. Does there appear to be a significant difference between the two treatments?

b. Use the independent measures t statistic to test for significance with $\alpha = .05$

c. Note that the data from Problem 14 and the data here show the same mean difference. Explain why the statistical analysis produces different conclusions for these two problems.

16. An instructor would like to evaluate the effectiveness of a new programmed learning course in statistics. The class is randomly divided in half. One group gets the regular lecture series and textbook, while the other group takes the programmed course. At the end of the semester all students take the same final exam. The scores are as follows:

REGULAR COURSE GRADES			PROGRAMMED COURSE GRADES		
82	73	93	92	82	97
61	89	99	81	80	62
73	91	84	72	74	68
71	68	81	84	81	71
75	72	69	63	65	73

Use these data to determine whether there is any significant difference between the programmed course and the regular course. Test at the .05 level.

17. Although the instructor from Problem 16 found no significant difference in grades for the two different statistics courses, it is possible that the students preferred one teaching method over the other. At the end of the course, each student was given a course-evaluation questionnaire that included a question about how much he or she enjoyed the course. The response range from 1 (not at all) to 5 (very much). The data for the two sections of students are as follows:

REGULAR COURSE				PROGRAMMED COURSE			
4	4	3	4	3	4	2	3
4	2	4	5	4	4	2	2
3	4	5	5	4	3	2	2
4	5	5		3	2	5	

Do these data indicate a significant preference between the two teaching methods? Test with $\alpha = .05$.

18. A researcher is interested in testing the opinions of college students concerning the value of their college education. She suspects that seniors will place more value on their education than will sophomores. A sample of 20 seniors and 20 sophomores is selected, and each subject is given an opinion questionnaire. The data for each sample are as follows:

SOPHOMORES				SENIORS			
18	21	24	21	25	19	23	22
20	19	23	26	23	21	21	18
19	24	19	28	27	18	28	21
22	17	27	18	26	25	22	16
25	22	14	17	21	29	18	20

Using a one-tailed test with $\alpha = .05$, do these data indicate that seniors have significantly higher value scores?

19. A principal for a city high school would like to determine parents' attitudes toward a proposed sex education program. A sample of 15 families is selected, and each set of parents is requested to fill out an opinion questionnaire. Part of this questionnaire requires the parents' names and occupations. Looking over the data, the principal noticed that the opinions seemed to be a lot more favorable than had been expected. The principal suspected that the parents might have felt "forced" into stating a favorable opinion because they were required to identify themselves. They might have responded more honestly if the questionnaire had been anonymous. Therefore, a second sample of 15 families was selected, and they were requested to complete the same questionnaire without reporting their names or occupations. The data from both questionnaires are as follows:

FIRST QUESTIONNAIRE				
60	56	54	58	63
61	52	49	57	58
65	59	42	51	67

SECOND QUESTIONNAIRE				
51	50	53	48	42
62	57	47	49	50
51	43	48	53	41

Use these data to test the principal's hypothesis. Set $\alpha = .05$.

20. a. Sketch a frequency distribution polygon showing the following samples. Use a different color for each set of scores.

SAMPLE 1			SAMPLE 2		
14	18	12	15	21	16
11	18	15	22	14	12
15	17	16	19	20	18
15	18	14	20	21	17
16	14	15	22	19	20
16	17	13	20	19	18

b. By just looking at your polygon, does it appear that these two samples came from different populations or from the same population?

c. Calculate the independent-measures t statistic for these data. Does the t statistic indicate that the samples came from different populations? Set $\alpha = .05$.

21. The following data came from an independent-measures experiment comparing two different treatment conditions. The score for each subject is the amount of time (measured in minutes) required to complete a set of math problems.

TREATMENT 1 (SAMPLE 1)		TREATMENT 2 (SAMPLE 2)	
2.5	3.2	1.8	2.1
3.4	2.9	2.0	1.6
2.4	2.6	1.9	2.3
2.5	3.0	2.2	2.5
2.7	3.1	1.8	2.1

a. Use an independent-measures t statistic to determine whether or not there is a significant difference between the two treatments. Use $\alpha = .05$.

b. The experimenter would like to convert each subject's score from minutes to seconds. To do this, each value must be multiplied by 60. After each value is multiplied, what will happen to the sample means? What will happen to the sample standard deviations? What do you expect will happen to the t statistic for these data?

c. Multiply each of the original scores by 60 (i.e., change them from minutes to seconds). Now compute the independent-measures t statistic for the new scores? How does this t statistic compare with the t statistic for the original data?

CHAPTER 11

HYPOTHESIS TESTS WITH RELATED SAMPLES

TOOLS YOU WILL NEED

The following items are considered essential background material for this chapter. If you doubt your knowledge of any of these items, you should review the appropriate chapter or section before proceeding.

- Introduction to the *t* statistic (Chapter 9)
  - Estimated standard error
  - Degrees of freedom
  - *t* distribution
  - Hypothesis tests with the *t* statistic
- Independent-measures design (Chapter 10)

SECTION 11.1 **INTRODUCTION TO RELATED SAMPLES**

Previously we discussed inferential techniques using two separate samples to examine the mean difference between two populations. Usually, our goal was to evaluate the difference between two treatment conditions. For example, if a researcher would like to assess the effect of a new drug on depression, he or she might use two treatment conditions: a drug treatment and a no-drug treatment. With an independent-measures design (Chapter 10), one sample of patients receives the drug, and the other sample receives an ineffective placebo. Depression can be measured by the subjects' scores on a depression inventory. Differences in the severity of depression between these two samples may then be used to test the effectiveness of the new drug. This independent-measures design can be recognized by the assignment of separate, or "independent," samples of subjects for each treatment condition.

It should be obvious that there is a different experimental technique that could be used to evaluate the drug. Specifically, you could use a single sample of subjects and measure their depression scores before they receive the drug and then repeat the measurements after they have received the drug. This experimental design is called a *repeated-measures* study. By repeating measurements on a single sample of subjects, we are looking for differences *within* the same subjects from one measurement to the next. Sometimes this type of study is also called a *within-subjects* design.

DEFINITION

A *repeated-measures* study is one in which a single sample of individuals is tested more than once on the dependent variable. The same subjects are used for every treatment condition.

The main advantage of a repeated-measures experiment is that it uses exactly the same subjects in all treatment conditions. Thus, there is no risk that the subjects in one treatment are substantially different from the subjects in another. With an independent-measures design, on the other hand, there is always a risk that the results are biased by the fact that one sample was much different (smarter, faster, more extroverted, and so on) than the other.

Occasionally, researchers will try to approximate the advantages of a repeated-measures experiment by using a technique known as *matched subjects*. For example, suppose a researcher is testing the effectiveness of a special reading program. One sample of fourth graders takes the reading course, and a second sample serves as the control group. The researcher plans to compare these two groups in terms of reading comprehension. However, the researcher is concerned that there might be differences in intelligence between the two samples, which could confound the results. Therefore, the researcher matches the subjects in terms of IQ. That is, if a person assigned to the control group has an IQ of 120, the researcher assigns another individual with the same IQ to the treatment group (see Table 11.1). The result is called a *matched-subjects* experiment.

DEFINITION

In a *matched-subjects* experiment, each individual in one sample is matched with a subject in the other sample. The matching is done so that the two individuals are equivalent (or nearly equivalent) with respect to a specific variable that the researcher would like to control.

Table 11.1

Group assignment of subjects matched for IQ.

	Control		Reading Program	
Subject	IQ		Subject	IQ
A	120		E	120
B	105		F	105
C	110		G	110
D	95		H	95

A matched-subjects experiment occasionally is called a *matched-samples design.* But the subjects in the samples must be matched one-to-one before you can use the statistical techniques in this chapter.

In a repeated-measures, or a matched-subjects, design all the subjects in one treatment are directly related, one-to-one, with the subjects in another treatment. For this reason, these two experimental designs are often called *related-samples* experiments (or correlated-samples experiments). In this chapter we will focus our discussion on repeated-measures experiments because they are overwhelmingly the more common example of related-groups designs. However, you should realize that the statistical techniques used for repeated-measures experiments can be applied directly to data from a matched-subjects experiment.

Now we will examine the statistical techniques that allow a researcher to use the sample data from a repeated-measures experiment to draw inferences about the general population.

DIFFERENCE SCORES

Table 11.2 presents hypothetical data for a drug evaluation study. The first score for each person (X_1) is the score obtained on the depression inventory before the drug treatment. The second score (X_2) was obtained after the drug treatment. Because we are interested in how much change occurs as a result of the treatment, each person's scores are summarized as a single difference score. This is accomplished by subtracting the first score (before treatment) from the second score (after treatment) for each person:

$$\text{difference score} = D = X_2 - X_1 \tag{11.1}$$

In a matched-subjects design, D is the difference between scores for two matched subjects.

The difference scores, or D values, are shown in the last column of the table. Note that the sign of each D score tells you the direction of change. For example, person A showed a decrease in depression, as indicated by the negative difference score.

Table 11.2

Scores on a depression inventory before and after treatment.

Person	Before Treatment, X_1	After Treatment, X_2	D
A	72	64	−8
B	68	60	−8
C	60	50	−10
D	71	66	−5
E	55	56	+1
			$\Sigma D = -30$

$$\bar{D} = \frac{\Sigma D}{n} = \frac{-30}{5} = -6$$

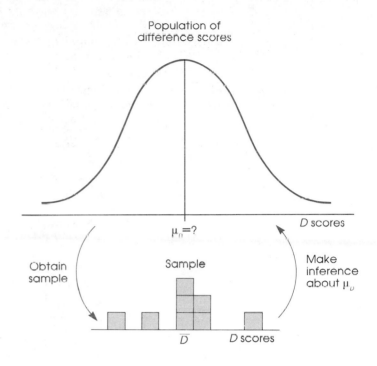

Figure 11.1

Because populations are usually too large to test in a study, the researcher selects a random sample from the population. The sample data are used to make inferences about the population mean μ_D. The data of interest in the repeated-measures study are difference scores (D scores) for each subject.

The researcher's goal is to use this sample of difference scores to answer questions about the general population. Notice that we are interested in a population of *difference scores*. More specifically, we are interested in the mean for this population of difference scores. We will identify this population mean difference with the symbol μ_D (using the subscript letter D to indicate that we are dealing with D values rather than X scores). Because populations usually are too large to test in an experiment, investigators must rely on the data from samples. Do these data indicate that the drug has a significant effect (more than chance)? Our problem is to use the limited data from a sample to test hypotheses about the population. This problem is diagrammed in Figure 11.1.

Notice that the problem we are facing here is essentially identical to the situation we encountered in Chapter 9. We have a single sample of scores that must be used to test hypotheses about a single population. In Chapter 9 we introduced a t statistic that allowed us to use the sample mean as a basis for testing hypotheses about the population mean. This t statistic formula will be used again here to develop the repeated-measures t test.

THE t STATISTIC FOR RELATED SAMPLES

To refresh your memory, the single-sample t statistic (Chapter 9) is defined by the formula

$$t = \frac{\overline{X} - \mu}{s_{\overline{X}}}$$

The sample mean $\overline{X}$ comes from the data. The standard error $s_{\overline{X}}$ (also computed from the sample data) gives a measure of the error between the sample mean and the population mean μ.

For the repeated-measures experiment, the sample data are difference scores and are identified by the letter D rather than X. Therefore, we will substitute D's in the formula in place of Xs to emphasize that we are dealing with difference scores instead of X values. Also, the population mean that is of interest to us is the population mean difference (the mean amount of change for the entire population), and we identify this parameter with the symbol μ_D. With these simple changes, the *t formula for the repeated-measures design* becomes

$$t = \frac{\overline{D} - \mu_D}{s_{\overline{D}}} \qquad (11.2)$$

In this formula, the estimated standard error for $\overline{D}$, $s_{\overline{D}}$, is computed exactly as it was in the original single-sample t statistic. First, we compute the standard deviation for the sample (this time a sample of D scores):

$$s = \sqrt{\frac{SS}{n - 1}}$$

Then we divide this value by the square root of the sample size:

$$s_{\overline{D}} = \frac{s}{\sqrt{n}} \qquad (11.3)$$

Notice that the sample data we are using consist of the D scores. Also, there is only one D value for each subject in a repeated-measures study or for each matched pair of subjects in a matched-subjects study. Because there are only n difference scores in the sample, our t statistic will have degrees of freedom equal to

$$df = n - 1 \qquad (11.4)$$

Note that this formula is identical to the df equation used for the single-sample t statistic (Chapter 9). However, n refers to the number of D scores, not the number of X values.

SECTION 11.2 **HYPOTHESIS TESTS FOR THE REPEATED-MEASURES DESIGN**

In a repeated-measures experiment we are interested in whether or not any change occurs between scores in the first treatment and scores in the second treatment. In statistical terms, we are interested in the population mean difference μ_D. Is the population mean difference equal to zero (no change), or has a change occurred? As always, the null hypothesis states that there is no treatment effect. In symbols, this is

$$H_0 : \mu_D = 0$$

PROCEDURES AND STEPS   As a statistician, your job is to determine whether the sample data support or refute the null hypothesis. In simple terms, we must decide whether sample mean difference is close to zero (indicating no change) or far from zero (indicating there

As we saw in previous tests, the level of significance defines what values are sufficiently "far away" to reject H_0

is a change). The t statistic helps us determine if the sample data are "close to" or "far from" zero.

The repeated-measures t test procedure follows the same outline we have used in other situations. The basic steps for hypothesis testing are reviewed here.

STEP 1 The hypotheses are stated, and an alpha level is selected. For the repeated-measures experiment, the null hypothesis is stated symbolically as

$$H_0: \mu_D = 0$$

Directional hypotheses can be used as well and would predict whether μ_D is greater or smaller than zero. A one-tailed test is used in those instances.

The alternative hypothesis states that here is a difference between the treatments. In symbols, this is

$$H_1: \mu_D \neq 0$$

STEP 2 The critical region is located. As before, the critical region is defined as values that would be very unlikely (probability less than alpha) if H_0 is true. Because the repeated-measures test uses a t statistic with $df = n - 1$, we simply compute df and look up the critical values in the t distribution table.

STEP 3 Compute the test statistic, in this case, the t statistic for repeated measures. We first must find the sample mean $\overline{D}$ and SS for the set of difference scores. From SS we compute the estimated standard error $s_{\overline{D}}$. These values are then put into the t formula along with the hypothesized value of μ_D from H_0.

STEP 4 If the obtained value falls in the critical region, we reject H_0 and conclude that there is a significant treatment effect. Remember, it is very unlikely for the t value to be in the critical region if H_0 is true. On the other hand, if the obtained t is not in the critical region, then we fail to reject H_0 and conclude that the sample data do not provide sufficient evidence for a treatment effect.

The complete hypothesis testing procedure is demonstrated in Example 11.1.

EXAMPLE 11.1 A researcher in behavioral medicine believes that stress often makes asthma symptoms worse for people who suffer from this respiratory disorder. Because of the suspected role of stress, the investigator decides to examine the effect of relaxation training on the severity of asthma symptoms. A sample of five patients is selected for the study. During the week before treatment, the investigator records the severity of their symptoms by measuring how many doses of medication are needed for asthma attacks. Then the patients receive relaxation training. For the week following training, the researcher once again records the number of doses required by each patient. Table 11.3 shows the data and summarizes the findings. Do these data indicate that relaxation training alters the severity of symptoms?

STEP 1 State hypotheses and select alpha:

$$H_0: \mu_D = 0 \quad \text{(no change in symptoms)}$$

$$H_1: \mu_D \neq 0 \quad \text{(there is a change)}$$

The level of significance is set at $\alpha = .05$ for a two-tailed test.

Table 11.3

The number of doses of medication needed for asthma attacks before and after relaxation training

PATIENT	WEEK BEFORE TRAINING	WEEK AFTER TRAINING	D	D^2
A	9	4	-5	25
B	4	1	-3	9
C	5	5	0	0
D	4	0	-4	16
E	5	1	-4	16

$$\Sigma D = -16 \qquad \Sigma D^2 = 66$$

$$\overline{D} = \frac{\Sigma D}{n} = \frac{-16}{5} = -3.2$$

$$SS = \Sigma D^2 - \frac{(\Sigma D)^2}{n} = 66 - \frac{(-16)^2}{5}$$

$$= 66 - 51.2 = 14.8$$

STEP 2 Locate the critical region. For this example, $n = 5$, so the t statistic will have $df = n - 1 = 4$. From the t distribution table, you should find that the critical values are $+2.776$ and -2.776. These values are shown in Figure 11.2.

STEP 3 Calculate the t Statistic. The mean for this example is $\overline{D} = -3.2$. To compute the SS for the D scores, we will use the computational formula (see Chapter 4, page 85):

$$SS = \Sigma X^2 - \frac{(\Sigma X)^2}{n}$$

Because we are using difference scores (D values) in place of X scores, this formula can be rewritten as

Remember, the computations for SS and s are based on the D scores for the subjects in the sample.

$$SS = \Sigma D^2 - \frac{(\Sigma D)^2}{n}$$

For our data, the SS is

$$SS = 66 - \frac{(-16)^2}{5}$$

$$= 66 - 51.2$$

$$= 14.8$$

Next, use the SS value to compute the sample standard deviation:

$$s = \sqrt{\frac{SS}{n-1}} = \sqrt{\frac{14.8}{4}} = \sqrt{3.7} = 1.92$$

Finally, the estimated standard error is computed:

$$s_{\overline{D}} = \frac{s}{\sqrt{n}} = \frac{1.92}{\sqrt{5}} = \frac{1.92}{2.24} = .86$$

Figure 11.2

The critical regions with $\alpha = .05$ and $df = 4$ begin at $+2.776$ and -2.776 in the t distribution. Obtained values of t that are more extreme than these values will lie in a critical region. In that case, the null hypothesis would be rejected.

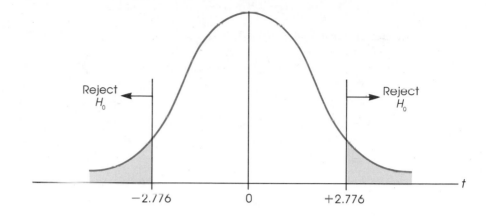

Reject H_0

Reject H_0

-2.776 0 $+2.776$ t

Now these values are used to calculate the value of t:

$$t = \frac{\overline{D} - \mu_D}{s_{\overline{D}}} - \frac{-3.2 - 0}{.86} = -3.72$$

STEP 4   The t value we obtained falls in the critical region (see Figure 11.2). The investigator rejects the null hypothesis and concludes that relaxation training does affect the amount of medication needed to control the asthma symptoms. For this example, a journal report might summarize the conclusion as follows:

> Relaxation training resulted in a significant reduction in the dose of medication needed to control asthma symptoms, $t(4) = -3.72$, $p < .05$, two tails.

As is customary, the number of degrees of freedom is contained in parentheses after the t, followed by the obtained value. The probability of a Type I error (the alpha level) and the type of test (one or two tails) also are reported.

DIRECTIONAL HYPOTHESES AND ONE-TAILED TESTS

In many repeated-measures and matched-subjects experiments, the researcher has a specific prediction concerning the direction of the treatment effect. For example, in the study described in Example 11.1, the researcher expects relaxation training to reduce the severity of asthma symptoms and, therefore, to reduce the amount of medication needed for asthma attacks. This kind of directional prediction can be incorporated into the statement of hypotheses, resulting in a directional, or one-tailed, hypothesis test. You should recall that directional tests should be used with caution. The standard two-tailed test usually is preferred and is always appropriate, even in situations where the researcher has a specific directional prediction. The following example demonstrates how the hypotheses and critical region are determined in a directional test.

EXAMPLE 11.2   We will re-examine the experiment presented in Example 11.1. The researcher is using a repeated-measures experiment to investigate the effect of relaxation training on the severity of asthma symptoms. The researcher pre-

Figure 11.3

The one-tailed critical region for $\alpha = .05$ in the t distribution with $df = 4$.

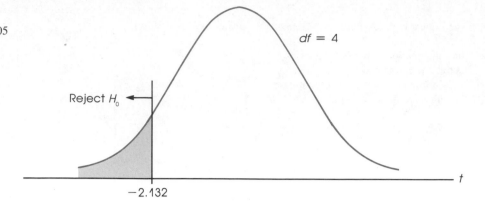

dicts that people will need less medication after training than before, which will produce negative difference scores.

$$D = X_2 - X_1 = \text{after} - \text{before}$$

STEP 1 State the hypotheses and select α. With most one-tailed tests, it is easiest to incorporate the researcher's prediction directly into H_1. In this example, the researcher predicts a negative difference, so

$H_1: \mu_D < 0$ (medication is reduced after training)

The null hypothesis states that the treatment does not have the predicted effect. In this example,

$H_0: \mu_D \geq 0$ (medication is not reduced after training)

STEP 2 Locate the critical region. The researcher is predicting negative difference scores if the treatment works. Hence, a negative t statistic would tend to support the experimental prediction and refute H_0. With a sample of $n = 5$ subjects, the t statistic will have $df = 4$. Looking in the t distribution table for $df = 4$ and $\alpha = .05$ for a one-tailed test, we find a critical value of 2.132. Thus, a t statistic that is more extreme than -2.132 would be sufficient to reject H_0. The t distribution with the one-tailed critical region is shown in Figure 11.3. For this example, the data produce a t statistic of $t = -3.72$ (see Example 11.1). Therefore, we reject H_0 and conclude that the relaxation training did significantly reduce the amount of medication needed for asthma attacks.

LEARNING CHECK 1. A researcher would like to examine the effect of hypnosis on cigarette smoking. A sample of smokers ($n = 4$) is selected for the study. The number of cigarettes smoked on the day prior to treatment is recorded. The subjects are then hypnotized and given the posthypnotic suggestion that each time they light a cigarette they will experience a horrible taste and feel nauseous. The data are as follows.

The number of cigarettes smoked before and after hypnosis

SUBJECT	BEFORE TREATMENT	AFTER TREATMENT
1	19	13
2	35	37
3	20	14
4	31	25

a. Find the difference scores (D values) for this sample.

b. The difference scores have $\overline{D} = -4$ and $SS = 48$. Do these data indicate that hypnosis has a significant effect on cigarette smoking? Test with $\alpha = .05$.

ANSWER 1. a. The difference scores are $-6, 2, -6, -6$.

b. For these data $s - 4$, $s_{\overline{D}} = 2$, and $t - -2.00$. With $\alpha = .05$, we fail to reject H_0; these data do not provide sufficient evidence to conclude that hypnosis has a significant effect on cigarette smoking.

SECTION 11.3
HYPOTHESIS TESTING WITH A MATCHED-SUBJECTS DESIGN

As noted in the introduction, matched-subjects experiments involve two related samples. Each subject in the second sample has been matched to a subject in the first sample on some variable that the researcher wishes to control. In this way, the researcher attempts to make the groups equivalent at the start of the experiment, so that any differences observed can be attributed to the treatment (independent variable). As noted earlier, data from the matched-subjects design may be analyzed using the related-samples t test. The following example illustrates this analysis.

EXAMPLE 11.3 A psychologist studies the effectiveness of a newly developed reading program. One sample of students takes the new reading course. A second sample serves as a control group and takes the regular coursework. The groups are later tested in reading comprehension to assess the effectiveness of the new program. However, the researcher is concerned with the possibility that differences in intelligence between the two groups (rather than the new reading program) will cause differences in reading comprehension. Therefore, when assigning subjects to treatment groups, each subject in the first group is matched to one in the second group in terms of IQ score. That is, if a child in the first group has an IQ of 110, then another child with the same IQ would be assigned to the second group. Thus the study consists of matched pairs of children, with one child of each pair serving in the control group and the other

Table 11.4

Reading comprehension scores for children in a matched samples study of a new reading program

	CONTROL	READING PROGRAM	D	D^2
Matched pair A	6	15	+9	81
Matched pair B	5	15	+10	100
Matched pair C	11	17	+6	36
Matched pair D	6	13	+7	49

$$\Sigma D = +32 \quad \Sigma D^2 = 266$$

$$\bar{D} = \frac{\Sigma D}{n} = \frac{+32}{4} = +8$$

$$SS = \Sigma D^2 - \frac{(\Sigma D)^2}{n} = 266 - \frac{(32)^2}{4}$$

$$= 266 - \frac{1024}{4} = 266 - 256 = 10$$

participating in the reading program. The data are summarized in Table 11.4. Is there evidence for a significant effect of the new reading program?

STEP 1 State the hypotheses and select an alpha level.

$$H_0: \mu_D = 0 \qquad \text{(no effect on reading comprehension)}$$

$$H_1: \mu_D \neq 0 \qquad \text{(there is an effect)}$$

We will set the alpha level to .01 for a two-tailed test.

STEP 2 Locate the critical region. For this example, $df = n - 1 = 3$. The t distribution table indicates the critical values are $+5.841$ and -5.841.

STEP 3 Calculate the t statistic. This study used a matched-samples design; thus a related-samples t statistic is appropriate. The values for SS and D were calculated in Table 11.4. Now, the standard deviation is computed:

$$s = \sqrt{\frac{SS}{n-1}} = \sqrt{\frac{10}{4-1}} = \sqrt{\frac{10}{3}}$$

$$= \sqrt{3.33} = 1.82$$

Next, the estimated standard error is computed:

$$s_{\bar{D}} = \frac{s}{\sqrt{n}} = \frac{1.82}{\sqrt{4}} = 0.91$$

Finally, the value for the t statistic can be determined:

$$t = \frac{\bar{D} - \mu_D}{s_{\bar{D}}} = \frac{8 - 0}{0.91} = \frac{8}{0.91} = 8.79$$

STEP 4 The obtained t value of $t = 8.79$ is more extreme than the critical value of $+5.841$. Therefore, it falls within the critical region on the right side of the t

distribution. The null hypothesis can be rejected and it can be concluded that the new reading program has a significant effect on reading comprehension, $t(3) = 8.79$, $p < .01$, two tails.

SECTION 11.4 **USES AND ASSUMPTIONS FOR RELATED-SAMPLES t TESTS**

USES OF RELATED-SAMPLE STUDIES

The repeated-measures experiment differs from an independent-measures study in a fundamental way. In the latter type of study, a separate sample is used for each treatment. In the repeated-measures design, only one sample of subjects is used, and measurements are repeated for the same sample in each treatment. There are many situations where it is possible to examine the effect of a treatment by using either type of study. However, there are situations where one type of experimental design is more desirable or appropriate than the other. For example, if a researcher would like to study a particular type of subject (a rare species, people with an unusual illness, etc.) that is not commonly found, a repeated-measures study will be more economical in the sense that fewer subjects are needed. Rather than selecting several samples for the study (one sample per treatment), a single sample can be used for the entire experiment.

Another factor in determining the type of experimental design is the specific question being asked by the experimenter. Some questions are better studied with a repeated-measures design, especially those concerning changes in response across time. For example, a psychologist may wish to study the effect of practice on how well a person performs a task. To show that practice is improving a person's performance, the experimenter would typically measure the person's responses very early in the experiment (when there is little or no practice) and repeat the measurement later when the person has had a certain amount of practice. Most studies of skill acquisition examine practice effects by using a repeated-measures design. Another situation where a repeated-measures study is useful is in developmental psychology. By repeating observations of the same individuals at various points in time, an investigator can watch behavior unfold and obtain a better understanding of developmental processes.

There are situations where a repeated-measures design cannot or should not be used. Specifically, when you are comparing two different populations (men versus women, first-born versus last-born children, and the like), you must use an independent-measure design with separate samples from each population.

Finally, it should be noted that there are certain statistical advantages to repeated-measures designs, particularly when you are studying a population with large differences from one individual to the next. One of the sources of variability that contributes to the standard error is due to these individual differences—that is, subjects all respond differently because they enter the experiment with different abilities, experiences, and the like. Large individual differences would produce larger standard errors, which might mask a mean difference. A repeated-measures design reduces the amount of this error variability in the analysis by using the same subjects for every treatment. The result is that the size of the standard error is reduced, and the t test will be more likely to detect the presence of a treatment effect.

It should be noted that a matched-subjects design also reduces *individual differences*. This is accomplished by matching subjects from each group with respect to some variable the researcher wants to control. If the matching variable (for example, intelligence in Example 11.3) would otherwise contribute to variability in the experiment, then the using a matched-subjects design will reduce the standard error. Once again, the related-measures t test will be more sensitive in detecting a treatment effect.

ASSUMPTIONS OF THE RELATED-SAMPLES t TEST

As in the previous statistical tests, it is required that the sample of individuals is randomly selected from the population. This requirement helps ensure that the sample is representative of the population from which it was selected. There is also an assumption of normality for the repeated-measures t test. Specifically, the population distribution of difference scores (D) should be normal. Ordinarily, researchers do not worry about this assumption unless there is ample reason to suspect a violation of this requirement of the test. In the case of severe departure from normality, the validity of the t test may be compromised. However, as noted before, the t statistic is robust to violations of normality when large samples ($n > 30$) are used.

LEARNING CHECK

1. What assumptions must be satisfied for the repeated-measures t tests to be valid?

2. Describe some situations for which a repeated-measures design is well suited?

3. How is a matched-subjects design similar to a repeated-measures design? How do they differ?

ANSWERS

1. The sample must be randomly selected from the population. The population distribution of D scores is assumed to be normal.

2. The repeated-measures design is suited to situations where a particular type of subject is not readily available for study. This design is helpful because it uses fewer subjects (only one sample is needed). Certain questions are addressed more adequately by a repeated-measures design—for example, anytime one would like to study changes across time in the same individuals. Also, when individual differences are large, a repeated-measures design is helpful because it reduces the amount of this type of error in the statistical analysis.

3. They are similar in that the role of individual differences in the experiment is reduced. They differ in that there are two samples in a matched-subjects design and only one in a repeated-measures study.

SUMMARY

1. In a repeated-measures experiment, a single sample of subjects is randomly selected, and measurements are repeated on this sample for each treatment condition. This type of experiment may take the form of a before-and-after study.

2. The data analysis for a repeated-measures t test is done on the basis of the difference between the first and second measurement for each subject. These difference scores (D scores) are obtained by

$$D = X_2 - X_1$$

3. The formula for the repeated-measures t statistic is

$$t = \frac{\overline{D} - \mu_D}{s_{\overline{D}}}$$

where the sample mean is

$$\overline{D} = \frac{\Sigma D}{n}$$

the estimated standard error is

$$s_{\overline{D}} = \frac{s}{\sqrt{n}}$$

and the value of degrees of freedom is obtained by

$$df = n - 1$$

4. A repeated-measures design may be more useful than an independent-measures study when one wants to observe changes in behavior in the same subjects, as in learning or developmental studies. The repeated-measures design has the advantage of reducing error variability due to individual differences.

5. A related-samples study may consist of two samples in which subjects have been matched on some variable. The repeated measures t test may be used in this situation.

KEY TERMS

repeated-measures design	matched-subjects design	repeated measures t statistic	individual differences
within-subjects design	difference scores	estimated standard error for $\overline{D}$	

FOCUS ON PROBLEM SOLVING

1. Once data have been collected, we must then select the appropriate statistical analysis. How can you tell if the data call for a repeated-measures t test? Look at the experiment carefully. Is there only one sample of subjects? Are the same subjects tested a second time? If your answers are yes to both of these questions, then a repeated-measures t test should be done. There is only one situation in which the repeated-measures t can be used for data from two samples, and that is for *matched-subjects* experiments (page 245).

2. The repeated-measures t test is based on difference scores. In finding difference scores, be sure you are consistent with your method. That is, you may use either $X_2 - X_1$ or $X_1 - X_2$ to find D scores, but you must use the same method for all subjects.

DEMONSTRATION 11.1   A REPEATED-MEASURES t TEST

A major oil company would like to improve its tarnished image following a large oil spill. Its marketing department develops a short television commercial and tests it on a sample of $n = 7$ subjects. People's attitudes about the company are measured with a short questionnaire, both before and after viewing the commercial. The data are as follows:

PERSON	X_1 (BEFORE)	X_2 (AFTER)
A	15	15
B	11	13
C	10	18
D	11	12
E	14	16
F	10	10
G	11	19

Was there a significant change?

Note that subjects are being tested twice − once before and once after viewing the commercial. Therefore, we have a repeated-measures experiment.

STEP 1   State the hypotheses and select an alpha level.

The null hypothesis states that the commercial has no effect on people's attitude, or in symbols,

$$H_0: \mu_D = 0 \text{ (the mean difference is zero)}$$

The alternative hypothesis states that the commercial does alter attitudes about the company, or

$$H_1: \mu_D \neq 0 \text{ (there is a mean change in attitudes)}$$

For this demonstration we will use an alpha level of .05 for a two-tailed test.

STEP 2   Locate the critical region.

Degrees of freedom for the repeated measures t test is obtained by the formula

$$df = n - 1$$

For these data, degrees of freedom equal

$$df = 7 - 1 = 6$$

The t distribution table is consulted for a two-tailed test with $\alpha = .05$ for $df = 6$. The critical t values for the critical region are $t = \pm 2.447$.

STEP 3   Obtain the sample data and compute the test statistic.

To compute the repeated measures t statistics, we will have to determine the values for the difference (D) scores, $\overline{D}$, SS for the D scores, the sample standard deviation for the D scores, and the estimated standard error for $\overline{D}$.

The difference scores. The following table illustrates the computations of the D values for our sample data. Remember, $D = X_2 - X_1$.

X_1	X_2	D
15	15	15−15= 0
11	13	13−11=+2
10	18	18−10=+8
11	12	12−11=+1
14	16	16−14=+2
10	10	10−10= 0
11	19	19−11=+8

The sample mean of D values. The sample mean for the difference scores is equal to the sum of the D values divided by n. For these data,

$$\Sigma D = 0 + 2 + 8 + 1 + 2 + 0 + 8 = 21$$

$$\overline{D} = \frac{\Sigma D}{n} = \frac{21}{7} = 3$$

Sum-of-squares for D scores. We will use the computational formula for SS. The following table summarizes the calculations.

D	D^2
0	0
2	4
8	64
1	1
2	4
0	0
8	64

$\Sigma D = 21$

$\Sigma D^2 = 0 + 4 + 64 + 1 + 4 + 0 + 64 = 137$

$$SS = \Sigma D^2 - \frac{(\Sigma D)^2}{n} = 137 - \frac{(21)^2}{7}$$

$$= 137 - \frac{441}{7} = 137 - 63 = 74$$

Standard deviation for D scores. The standard deviation for the sample of D values equals

$$s = \sqrt{\frac{SS}{n-1}} = \sqrt{\frac{74}{7-1}} = \sqrt{\frac{74}{6}} = \sqrt{12.33} = 3.51$$

Estimated standard error for $\overline{D}$. The estimated standard error for sample mean difference is computed as follows:

$$s_{\overline{D}} = \frac{s}{\sqrt{n}} = \frac{3.51}{\sqrt{7}} = \frac{3.51}{2.646} = 1.33$$

The repeated measures t statistic. We now have the information required to calculate the t statistic.

$$t = \frac{\overline{D} - \mu_D}{s_{\overline{D}}} = \frac{3 - 0}{1.33} = \frac{3}{1.33} = 2.26$$

STEP 4   Make a decision about H_0 and state the conclusion.

The obtained t value is not extreme enough to fall in the critical region. Therefore, we fail to reject the null hypothesis. We conclude that there is no evidence that the commercial will change people's attitudes, $t(6) = 2.26$, $p > .05$, two tailed. (Note that we state that p is *greater than* .05 because we failed to reject H_0.)

PROBLEMS

1. For the following studies, indicate whether or not a repeated-measures t test is the appropriate analysis. Explain your answers.

   a. A researcher examines the effect of relaxation training on test anxiety. One sample of subjects receives relaxation training for 3 weeks. A second sample serves as a control group and does not receive the treatment. The researcher then measures anxiety levels for both groups in a test-taking situation.

   b. Another researcher does a similar study. Baseline levels of test anxiety are recorded for a sample of subjects. Then all subjects receive relaxation training for 3 weeks and their anxiety levels are measured again.

   c. In a test-anxiety study, two samples are used. Subjects are assigned to groups so that they are matched for self-esteem and for grade-point average. One sample receives relaxation training for 3 weeks and the second serves as a no-treatment control group. Test anxiety is measured for both groups at the end of 3 weeks.

2. What is the advantage of a matched-subjects design over an independent-measures design?

3. A psychologist would like to know if there are any changes in personality during imprisonment. She selects a random sample of $n = 25$ people who have been sentenced to at least 5 years of prison. The psychologist interviews each of these people during their first week in prison and administers a personality test which measures introversion/extroversion on a scale from 0 to 50 (low scores indicate introversion). After 1 year, the investigator returns for a second interview with the prisoners and again administers the personal-

ity test. For each person, she calculates the difference between their initial score and the score after 1 year of confinement. The average for this sample of difference scores is $\overline{D} = -5$ with $SS = 2400$.

   a. Test the hypothesis that imprisonment changes personality variables. Set alpha at .05.

   b. Would the same decision be made had alpha been set at .01?

4. A researcher arguing for stricter laws for drunk driving argues that even one can of beer an produce a significant effect on reaction time. In an attempt to prove his claim, he selects a random sample of $n = 4$ people and measures their baseline reaction times. This is accomplished by having the subjects view a stimulus display and press a button as fast as they can when a light flashes on. The subjects then consume a 12-ounce can of beer. After 30 minutes, they are tested again on the task. The researcher computed the difference scores and determined that for this sample $\overline{D} = 32$ milliseconds. That is, on average it took the group of subjects 32 milliseconds longer to respond. Also, the sample had $SS = 1200$. Do the data support the investigator's claim? Test at the .05 level of significance.

5. For the experiment described in Problem 4, the researcher probably expects reaction times to increase following beer consumption. If a one-tailed test were performed, how would H_0 and H_1 be expressed in symbols? (Assume that difference scores are computed by $D = X_2 - X_1$.)

6. A college professor performed a study to assess the effectiveness of computerized exercises in teaching mathematics. She decides to use a *matched-subjects*

design. One group of subjects is assigned to a regular lecture section of introductory mathematics. A second group must attend a computer laboratory in addition to the lecture. These students work on computerized exercises for additional practice and instruction. Both samples are matched in terms of general mathematics ability, as measured by mathematical SAT scores. At the end of the semester, both groups are given the same final exam. For $n = 16$ matched pairs of subjects, the professor found a mean improvement of $\overline{D} = 9.3$ points for the computer group. The SS for the D values was 2160. Does the computerized instruction lead to a significant improvement? Test at the .01 level of significance.

7. A researcher tested a new medication to see if it would be effective in lowering blood pressure. Two samples of subjects were matched for initial blood pressure readings and medical history. For $n = 15$ matched pairs, one member of each pair received a placebo and the remaining member got the drug. The researcher recorded their diastolic blood pressure. Subjects receiving the drug showed lower blood pressure, $\overline{D} = -12.8$, with $SS = 4536$. Did the drug produce a significant change? Use a one-tailed test with $\alpha = .01$.

8. A psychologist for NASA examines the effect of cabin temperature on reaction time. A random sample of $n = 10$ astronauts and pilots is selected. Each person's reaction time is measured in a simulator, where the cabin temperature is maintained at 70°F, and again the next day at 95°F. The subjects are run through a launch simulation. Their reaction time (in milliseconds) is measured when an emergency indicator flashes and they must quickly press the appropriate switch. The data from this experiment are as follows:

EXPERIMENT 1		
70°	95°	D
180	190	10
176	201	25
204	220	16
216	240	24
194	217	23
183	206	23
207	228	21
229	255	26
231	245	14
210	228	18

a. Using the results from this experiment, can the psychologist conclude that temperature has a significant effect on reaction time? Test at the .05 level of significance.

b. To verify the results of the first experiment, the psychologist repeats the experiment with another sample of $n = 10$. The data for the replication are as follows:

EXPERIMENT 2		
70°	95°	D
178	252	74
194	244	50
217	200	−17
186	231	45
242	218	−24
212	214	2
221	201	−20
194	236	42
187	247	60
219	207	−12

Again, test for a significant difference at the .05 level of significance.

c. Both experiments showed reaction times that were on average 20 milliseconds longer with the hotter cabin temperature. Why are the results of one experiment significant and of the other not significant? (*Hint:* Compare the two experiments in terms of the consistency of the effect for all subjects. How does the consistency (or inconsistency) of the effect affect the analysis?)

9. A high school counselor has developed a course designed to help students with the mathematics portion of the SAT. A random sample of students is selected for the study. These students take the SAT at the end of their junior year. During the summer, they take the SAT review course. When they begin their senior year, they all take the SAT again. The data for the sample are as follows:

SAT SCORES (MATHEMATICS)	
BEFORE	AFTER
402	468
486	590
543	625
516	553
475	454
403	447
522	543
480	416
619	652
493	495
485	496
551	585
573	610
437	491
472	544
409	492

Did the students perform significantly better on the SAT after taking the special course? Use a one-tailed test with alpha at .05.

10. A researcher assessed the role of routine walking in physical fitness. In this experiment, $n = 7$ pairs of subjects were matched for age, sex, and weight. However, one member of each pair typically walked to work, whereas the other typically drove. Subjects were given a physical fitness test. Their fitness scores are summarized as follows. Is there a significant difference in fitness between walkers and drivers? Test with $\alpha = .05$, two tails.

DRIVERS	WALKERS
9	8
14	17
10	17
11	10
12	15
9	13
10	14

11. A psychologist tests a new drug for its pain-killing effects. Pain threshold is measured for a sample of subjects by determining the intensity (in milliamperes) of electric shock that causes discomfort. After the initial baseline is established, subjects receive the drug, and their thresholds are once again measured. The data are as follows:

PAIN THRESHOLDS (MILLIAMPERES)	
BEFORE	AFTER
2.1	3.2
2.3	2.9
3.0	4.6
2.7	2.7
1.9	3.1
2.1	2.9
2.9	2.9
2.7	3.4
3.2	5.3
2.5	2.5
3.1	4.9

Is there an effect of the drug treatment? Test with alpha of .05.

12. A researcher examines the effects of sensitization on cigarette smoking in habitual smokers. A random sample of $n = 12$ smokers is selected. The number of cigarettes smoked per day is first determined for these people. The subjects are then sensitized to the effects of smoking by having them view a film that graphically shows the harm caused by cigarette smoke. A week later, the subjects are asked to count the number of cigarettes they smoke that day. The data are as follows:

NUMBER OF CIGARETTES SMOKED	
BEFORE	ONE WEEK LATER
19	15
22	7
32	31
17	10
37	28
20	12
23	23
24	17
28	19
21	24
15	11
18	16

Did sensitization cause a reduction in smoking? Use the .05 level of significance.

13. A researcher tests the effectiveness of a drug called Ritalin on hyperkinetic children. The researcher uses a sample of $n = 12$ hyperkinetic children ranging in age from 8 to 9 years of age. The children are told several brief stories. After each story, the experimenter asks the children questions about the story. The total number of questions answered correctly for all the stories is recorded as the child's score. Because hyperkinetic children have attentional deficits, they should not perform well on this task when they are not treated. The researcher tests all of the children under two conditions: following administration of a sugar pill (placebo condition) and after receiving Ritalin. For the following data, determine if the drug treatment has an effect on performance. Use an alpha level of .01.

SUBJECT	PLACEBO	RITALIN
A	10	15
B	8	15
C	11	13
D	6	17
E	7	8
F	9	17
G	6	18
H	8	3
I	5	14
J	10	20
K	7	18
L	2	19

14. A psychologist studied cognitive ability in children whose mothers drank alcohol during pregnancy. The psychologist attempted to control several variables by matching subjects in both groups for sex, weight at birth, and socioeconomic status of parents. In each pair of subjects, one child had a mother who drank during pregnancy, whereas the other child did not. The psychologist measured the children's IQ. For $n = 18$ pairs of matched subjects, the children of nondrinkers scored on average $\overline{D} = 10.5$ points higher than the children of drinkers, with $SS = 2448$. Is there a difference between the children of drinkers and those of nondrinkers? Use the .01 level of significance and a two-tailed test.

15. A statistics instructor was unable to decide between two potential textbooks. To help with this decision, a random sample of 12 students was obtained, and each student was to rate both books using a scale from 1

(very bad) to 10 (excellent). The data from these 12 students are as follows:

STUDENT	BOOK 1	BOOK 2
1	3	5
2	6	7
3	8	7
4	7	8
5	5	6
6	3	5
7	8	6
8	6	3
9	2	5
10	5	6
11	7	5
12	4	7

Do these data indicate that students perceive a significant difference between the books? Test at the .05 level of significance.

16. Although psychologists do not completely understand the phenomenon of dreaming, it does appear that people need to dream. One experiment demonstrating this fact shows that people who are deprived of dreaming one night will tend to have extra dreams the following night, as if they were trying to make up for the lost dreams. In a typical version of this experiment, the psychologist first records the number of dreams (by monitoring rapid eye movements (REMs)) during a normal night's sleep. The next night, each subject is prevented from dreaming by being awakened as soon as he or she begins a dream. During the third night, the psychologist once again records the number of dreams. Hypothetical data from this experiment are as follows:

SUBJECT	FIRST NIGHT	NIGHT AFTER DEPRIVATION
1	4	7
2	5	5
3	4	8
4	6	7
5	4	10
6	5	7
7	4	7
8	4	6

Do these data indicate a significant increase in dreams after one night of dream deprivation? Test at the .05 level of significance.

17. A pharmaceutical company would like to test the effectiveness of a new antidepressant drug. A sample of 15 depressed patients is obtained, and each patient is given a mood inventory questionnaire before and after receiving the drug treatment. The data for this experiment are as follows:

PATIENT	BEFORE	AFTER
1	18	23
2	21	20
3	16	17
4	19	20
5	14	13
6	23	22
7	16	18
8	14	18
9	21	21
10	18	16
11	17	19
12	14	20
13	16	15
14	14	15
15	20	21

On the basis of these data, can the company conclude that the drug has a significant effect on mood? Test with $\alpha = .01$.

18. A consumer protection agency is testing the effectiveness of a new gasoline additive that claims to improve gas mileage. A sample of 10 cars is obtained, and each car is driven over a standard 100-mile course with and without the additive. The researchers carefully record the miles per gallon for each test drive. The results of this test are as follows:

CAR	WITH ADDITIVE	WITHOUT ADDITIVE
1	23.0	21.6
2	20.2	19.8
3	17.4	17.5
4	19.6	20.7
5	22.8	23.1
6	20.4	19.8
7	26.8	26.4
8	23.7	24.0
9	17.2	15.9
10	18.5	18.3

Does the new gasoline additive have a significant effect on gas mileage? Test at the .05 level of significance.

ESTIMATION

SECTION 12.1   **AN OVERVIEW OF ESTIMATION**

In Chapter 8 we introduced hypothesis testing as a statistical procedure that allows researchers to use sample data to draw inferences about populations. Hypothesis testing is probably the most frequently used inferential technique, but it is not the only one. In this chapter we will examine the process of estimation, which provides researchers with an additional method for using samples as the basis for drawing general conclusions about populations.

The basic principle underlying all of inferential statistics is that samples are representative of the populations from which they come. The most direct application of this principle is the use of sample values as estimators of the corresponding population values; that is, using statistics to estimate parameters. This process is called estimation.

DEFINITION   The inferential process of using sample data to estimate population parameters is called *estimation*.

The use of samples to estimate populations is quite common. For example, you often hear news reports such as ''Sixty percent of the general public approves of the president's new budget plan.'' Clearly, the percentage that is reported was obtained from a sample (they don't ask everyone's opinion), and this sample statistic is being used as an estimate of the population parameter.

We already have encountered estimation in earlier sections of this book. For example, the formula for sample standard deviation (Chapter 4) was developed so that the sample value would give an accurate and unbiased estimate of the population. Now we will examine the process of using sample means as the basis for estimating population means.

PRECISION AND CONFIDENCE IN ESTIMATION

Before we begin the actual process of estimation, there are a few general points that should be kept in mind. First, a sample will not give a perfect picture of the whole population. A sample is expected to be representative of the population, but there always will be some differences between the sample and the entire population. These differences are referred to as *sampling error*. Second, there are two distinct ways of making estimates. Suppose, for example, you are asked to estimate the weight of this book. You could pick a single value (say, 2 pounds), or you could choose a range of values (say, between 1.5 pounds and 2.5 pounds). The first estimate, using a single number, is called a *point estimate*. Point estimates have the advantage of being very precise; they specify a particular value. On the other hand, you generally do not have much confidence that a point estimate is correct. You would not bet on it, for example.

DEFINITION   For a *point estimate*, you use a single number as your estimate of an unknown quantity.

The second type of estimate, using a range of values, is called an *interval estimate*. Interval estimates do not have the precision of point estimates, but they do give you more confidence. You would feel more comfortable, for example, saying

Figure 12.1

The basic experimental situation for estimation. The purpose is to use the sample data to obtain an estimate of the population mean after treatment.

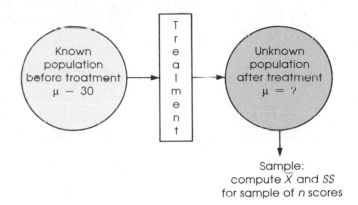

Known population before treatment $\mu - 30$

Treatment

Unknown population after treatment $\mu = ?$

Sample: compute $\overline{X}$ and SS for sample of n scores

that this book weighs "around 2 pounds." At the extreme, you would be very confident in estimating that this book weighs between 0.5 and 10 pounds. Notice that there is a trade-off between precision and confidence. As the interval gets wider and wider, your confidence grows. But, at the same time, the precision of the estimate gets worse. We will be using samples to make both point and interval estimates of a population mean. Because the interval estimates are associated with confidence, they usually are called *confidence intervals*.

DEFINITIONS

For an *interval estimate*, you use a range of values as your estimate of an unknown quantity.

When an interval estimate is accompanied with a specific level of confidence (or probability), it is called a *confidence interval*.

Estimation is used in the same general situations in which we have already used hypothesis testing. In fact, there is an estimation procedure that accompanies each of the hypothesis tests we presented in the preceding four chapters. Although the details of the estimation process will differ from one experiment to the next, the general experimental situation is shown in Figure 12.1. The figure shows a population with an unknown mean (the population after treatment). A sample is selected from the unknown population. The goal of estimation is to use the sample data to obtain an estimate of the unknown population mean.

COMPARISON OF HYPOTHESIS TESTS AND ESTIMATION

You should recognize that the situation shown in Figure 12.1 is the same situation in which we have used hypothesis tests in the past. In many ways hypothesis testing and estimation are similar. They both make use of sample data and either z-scores or t statistics to find out about unknown populations. But these two inferential procedures are designed to answer different questions. Using the situation shown in Figure 12.1 as an example, we could use a hypothesis test to evaluate the effect of the treatment. The test would determine whether or not the treatment has any effect. Notice that this is a yes-no question. The null hypothesis says, "No, there is no treatment effect." The alternative hypothesis says, "Yes, there is a treatment effect."

The goal of estimation, on the other hand, is to determine the value of the population mean after treatment. Essentially, estimation will determine *how much* effect the treatment has. If, for example, we obtained a point estimate of $\mu = 38$ for the population after treatment, we could conclude that the effect of the treatment is to increase scores by an average of 8 points (from the original mean of $\mu = 30$ to the posttreatment mean of $\mu = 38$).

WHEN TO USE ESTIMATION

There are three situations where estimation commonly is used.

1. Estimation is used after a hypothesis test where H_0 is rejected. Remember that when H_0 is rejected, the conclusion is that the treatment does have an effect. The next logical question would be, How much effect? This is exactly the question that estimation is designed to answer.

2. Estimation is used when you already know that there is an effect and simply want to find out how much. For example, the city school board probably knows that a special reading program will help students. However, they want to be sure that the effect is big enough to justify the cost. Estimation is used to determine the size of the treatment effect.

3. Estimation is used when you simply want some basic information about an unknown population. Suppose, for example, you want to know about the political attitudes of students at your college. You could use a sample of students as the basis for estimating the population mean.

THE LOGIC OF ESTIMATION

The logic underlying the general process of estimation is as follows:

1. Each set of sample data has a corresponding z-score or t-statistic. For example, the data from a single sample can be used to compute either

$$z = \frac{\overline{X} - \mu}{\sigma_{\overline{X}}} \quad or \quad t = \frac{\overline{X} - \mu}{s_{\overline{X}}}$$

Remember that the z formula is used when the population standard deviation, σ, is known. The t formula is for situations where σ is unknown.
   In general, the z-score or t-statistic has the structure

$$z \text{ or } t = \frac{\text{sample data} - \text{population parameter}}{\text{standard error}}$$

2. For hypothesis testing we used the z or t formula to evaluate a hypothesis about the unknown population parameter. Now, our goal is to determine the value for the unknown population parameter. Therefore, we will solve the z (or t) equation for this unknown value

$$\begin{array}{l} \text{population} \\ \text{parameter} \end{array} = \begin{array}{l} \text{sample} \\ \text{data} \end{array} - (z \text{ or } t)(\text{standard error}) \tag{12.1}$$

This is the basic structure of the equation we will use for estimation.

3. In formula 12.1, the values for the sample mean and the standard error can be computed directly from the sample data. Only the value for the

z-score (or *t*) is unknown. If we can determine this missing value, then the equation can be used to compute the unknown population parameter.

4. Although the specific value for the z-score (or *t* statistic) is not known, you do know what the entire distribution of z-scores (or *t* statistics) looks like. For example, the z-scores will tend to form a normal-shaped distribution with a mean of zero, and the *t* statistics will form a *t*-distribution, also with a mean of zero and with a shape that depends on the value of *df* for the sample data.

Remember, t is used when the value of σ is unknown.

5. You still do not know the specific value for the z-score (or *t*-statistic) for the sample data, but you do know that the value is located somewhere in the entire distribution. The key to the estimation process involves *estimating* the location of the sample data in the distribution.

For a point estimate, your best bet is to predict that the sample statistic is located in the exact center of the distribution at $z = 0$ (or $t = 0$). This is the most likely location because z-scores or *t* statistics become increasingly unlikely as you move toward the tails of the distribution.

For an interval estimate, your best bet is to predict that the sample statistic is in the middle section of the distribution. To be 90% confident, for example, you would simply predict that the sample statistic is in the middle 90% of the distribution. The unit normal table or the *t*-distribution table can be used to determine the precise z-scores or *t* values, respectively, that correspond to the middle 90%.

Notice that in Step 5 you are estimating the location of your sample data in the distribution. This estimate provides specific values for the z-score or *t* statistic corresponding to your sample data. Once these values are obtained, they can be used in the estimation equation (formula 12.1) along with the sample mean and the standard error to compute the value of the unknown population parameter. However, because the z-score or *t* statistic is based on an estimate, the value you obtain for the population parameter is also an estimate.

The details of the estimation procedure will now be demonstrated for each of the experimental situations we have considered thus far: the z-score statistic, the single-sample *t*, the independent-measures *t*, and the repeated-measures *t*.

SECTION 12.2   **ESTIMATION WITH z-SCORES**

The z-score statistic is used in situations where the population standard deviation is known but the population mean is unknown. Often this is a population that has received some treatment. Suppose you are examining the effect of a special summer reading program for grade school children. Using a standard reading achievement test, you know that the scores for second-graders in the city school district form a normal distribution with $\mu = 80$ and $\sigma = 10$. It is reasonable to assume that a special reading program would increase the students' scores. The questions is, How much?

The example we are considering is shown graphically in Figure 12.2. Notice that we have assumed that the effect of the treatment (the special program) is to add a

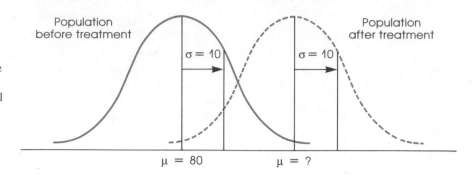

Figure 12.2

A population distribution before the treatment is administered and the same population after treatment. Note that the effect of the treatment is to add a constant amount to each score. The goal of estimation is to determine how large the treatment effect is; i.e., what is the new population mean $\mu = ?$

If the treatment simply adds a constant to each score, the standard deviation will not be changed. Although it is common practice to assume that a treatment will add a constant amount, you should realize that in most real-life situations there is a general tendency for variability to increase when the mean increases.

constant amount to each student's reading score. As a result, after the summer reading program the entire distribution would be shifted to a new location with a larger mean. This new mean is what we want to estimate.

Because it would not be reasonable to put all the students in the special program, we cannot measure this mean directly. However, we can get a sample and use the sample mean to estimate the population value for μ. For this example, assume that a random sample of $n = 25$ students is selected to participate in the summer program. At the end of the summer, each student takes the reading test and we compute a mean reading score of $\overline{X} = 88$. Note that this sample represents the population after the special program. The goal of estimation is to use this sample mean as the basis for estimating the unknown population mean.

The procedure for estimating μ is based on the distribution of sample means (see Chapter 7). You should recall that this distribution is the set of all the possible $\overline{X}$ values for a specified sample size (n). The parameters of this distribution are the following:

1. The mean (called expected value) is equal to the population mean.
2. The standard deviation for this distribution (called standard error) is equal to $\sigma/\sqrt{n}$.
3. The distribution of sample means will be normal if either
   a. The population is normal, or
   b. The sample size is at least $n = 30$.

For the example we are considering, the distribution of sample means for $n = 25$ will be normal (because the population is normal), it will have a standard error of $\sigma/\sqrt{n} = 10/\sqrt{25} = 10/5 = 2$, and it will have a mean that is equal to the unknown population mean ($\mu = ?$). This distribution is shown in Figure 12.3.

Our sample mean, $\overline{X} = 88$, is somewhere in this distribution; that is, we have one value out of all the possible sample means. Unfortunately, we do not know where our sample mean is located in the distribution. Nonetheless, we can specify different locations by using z-scores. The z-score values and their locations have been identified in Figure 12.3.

Our sample mean, $\overline{X} = 88$, has a z-score given by the formula

$$z = \frac{\overline{X} - \mu}{\sigma_{\overline{X}}}$$

Figure 12.3

The distribution of sample means based on $n = 25$. Samples were selected from the unknown population (after treatment) shown in Figure 12.2.

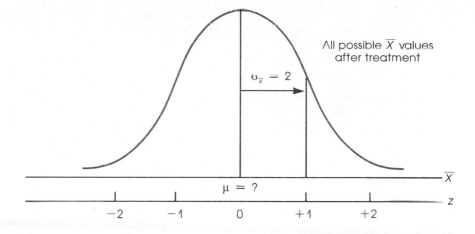

Because our goal is to find the population mean (μ), we will solve this z-score equation for μ. The algebra in this process is as follows:

$$z\sigma_{\overline{X}} = \overline{X} - \mu \quad \text{(Multiply both sides of the equation by } \sigma_{\overline{X}})$$

$$\mu + z\sigma_{\overline{X}} = \overline{X} \quad \text{(Add } \mu \text{ to both sides of the equation.)}$$

$$\mu = \overline{X} - z\sigma_{\overline{X}} \quad \text{(Subtract } z\sigma_{\overline{X}} \text{ from both sides of the equation.)} \qquad \textbf{(12.2)}$$

To use this equation, we begin with the values we know: $\overline{X} = 88$ and $\sigma_{\overline{X}} = 2$. To complete the equation we must obtain a value for z. The value we will use for z is determined by estimating the z-score for our sample mean. More precisely, we are estimating the location of our sample mean within the distribution of sample means. The estimated position will determine a z-score value which can be used in the equation to compute μ. It is important to note that the z-score value we will be using is an *estimate;* therefore, the population mean that we compute will also be an estimate.

POINT ESTIMATES
For a point estimate, you must select a single value for the z-score. It should be clear that your best bet is to select the exact middle of the distribution—that is, $z = 0$. It would be unwise to pick an extreme value such as $z = 2$ because there are relatively few samples that far away from the population mean. Most of the sample means pile up around $z = 0$, so this is your best choice. When this z-value is used in the equation, we get

$$\mu = \overline{X} - z\sigma_{\overline{X}}$$

$$\mu = 88 - 0(2)$$

$$= 88$$

This is our point estimate of the population mean. You should notice that we simply have used the sample mean $\overline{X}$ to estimate the population mean μ. The sample is the *only* information we have about the population, and you should recall from Chapter 7 that sample means tend to approximate μ (central limit theorem). Our conclusion is that the special summer program will increase reading scores from an average of $\mu = 80$ to an average of $\mu = 88$. We are estimating that the program will have an 8-point effect on reading scores.

INTERVAL ESTIMATES

To make an interval estimate, you select a range of z-score values rather than a single point. Looking again at the distribution of sample means in Figure 12.3, where would you estimate our sample mean is located? Remember, you now can pick a range of values. As before, your best bet is to predict that the sample mean is located somewhere in the center of the distribution. There is a good chance, for example, that our sample mean is located somewhere between $z = +1$ and $z = -1$. You would be almost certain that $\overline{X}$ is between $z = +3$ and $z = -3$. How do you know what range to use? Because several different ranges are possible and each range has its own degree of confidence, the first step is to determine the amount of confidence we want and then use this value to determine the range. Commonly used levels of confidence start at about 60% and go up. For this example, we will use 90%. This means that we want to be 90% confident that our interval estimate of μ is correct.

There are no strict rules for choosing a level of confidence. Researchers must decide how much precision and how much confidence are needed in each specific situation.

To be 90% confident, we simply estimate that our sample mean is somewhere in the middle 90% of the distribution of sample means. This section of the distribution is bounded by z-scores of $z = +1.65$ and $z = -1.65$ (check the unit normal table). We are 90% confident that our particular sample mean ($\overline{X} = 88$) is in this range because 90% of all the possible means are there.

The next step is to use this range of z-score values in the estimation equation. We use the two ends of the z-score range to compute the two ends of the interval estimate for μ.

At one extreme, $z = +1.65$, which gives

$$\mu = \overline{X} - z\sigma_{\overline{X}}$$
$$= 88 - 1.65(2)$$
$$= 88 - 3.30$$
$$= 84.70$$

At the other extreme, $z = -1.65$, which gives

$$\mu = \overline{X} - z\sigma_{\overline{X}}$$
$$= 88 - (-1.65)(2)$$
$$= 88 + 3.30$$
$$= 91.30$$

The result is an interval estimate for μ. We are estimating that the population mean after the special summer program is between 84.70 and 91.30. If the mean is as small as 84.70, then the effect of the special program would be to increase reading scores by an average of 4.70 points (from $\mu = 80$ to $\mu = 84.70$). If the mean is as large as 91.30, the program would have increased score by an average of 11.30 points (from $\mu = 80$ to $\mu = 91.30$). Thus, we conclude that the special summer program will increase reading scores, and we estimate that the magnitude of the increase will be between 4.7 and 11.3 points. We are 90% confident that this estimate is correct because the only thing that was estimated was the z-score range, and we were 90% confident about that. Again, this interval estimate is called a confidence interval. In this case, it is the 90% confidence interval for μ.

Notice that the confidence interval sets up a range of values with the sample mean in the middle. As with point estimates, we are using the sample mean to estimate the population mean, but now we are saying that the value of μ should be *around* $\overline{X}$ rather than exactly equal to $\overline{X}$. Because the confidence interval is built around $\overline{X}$, adding in one direction and subtracting in the other, we will modify the estimation equation in order to simplify the arithmetic.

$$\mu = \overline{X} \pm z\sigma_{\overline{X}} \qquad\qquad (12.3)$$

To build the confidence interval, start with the sample mean and add $z\sigma_{\overline{X}}$ to get the boundary in one direction; then subtract $z\sigma_{\overline{X}}$ to get the other boundary. Translated into words, the formula says that

population mean = sample mean $\pm$ some error

The sample mean is expected to be representative of the population mean with some margin of error. Although it may seem obvious that the sample mean is used as the basis for estimating the population mean, you should not overlook the reason for this result. Sample means, on the average, provide an accurate, unbiased representation of the population mean. You should recognize this fact as one of the characteristics of the distribution of sample means: The mean (expected value) of the distribution of sample means is μ.

LEARNING CHECK 1. A cattle rancher is interested in using a newly developed hormone to increase the weight of beef cattle. Before investing in this hormone, the rancher would like to obtain some estimate of its effect. Without the hormone, the cattle weigh an average of $\mu = 1250$ pounds when they are sold at 8 months. The distribution of weights is approximately normal with $\sigma = 80$. A sample of 16 calves is selected to test the hormone. At age 8 months, the average weight for this sample is $\overline{X} = 1340$ pounds.

  a. Use these data to make a point estimate of the population mean weight if all the cattle were given the hormone.

  b. Make an interval estimate of the population mean so that you are 95% confident that the true mean is in your interval.

ANSWERS 1. **a.** For a point estimate, use the sample mean: $\overline{X} = 1340$ pounds.

  b. For the 95% confidence interval, $z = \pm1.96$ and $\sigma_{\overline{X}} = 20$. The interval would be

$$\mu = 1340 \pm 39.20$$

The interval ranges from 1300.80 to 1379.20 pounds.

SECTION 12.3   **ESTIMATION WITH THE SINGLE-SAMPLE _t_ STATISTIC**

The single-sample _t_ statistic is used in situations where you have a population with an unknown mean (μ = ?) and an unknown standard deviation (σ = ?). The goal of estimation is to use the sample data to obtain an estimate of the unknown population mean. As you will see, the process of estimation with _t_ statistics is nearly identical to the process described for _z_-scores in Section 12.2. However, in situations where σ is unknown, we must use a _t_ statistic instead of a _z_-score.

Because the purpose of estimation is to find the approximate value for the population mean μ, we begin with the _t_ statistic.

$$t = \frac{\overline{X} - \mu}{s_{\overline{X}}}$$

Solving for μ we obtain

$$\mu = \overline{X} - ts_{\overline{X}}$$

Because _t_ can have a positive or negative value in interval estimates, we can simplify the arithmetic of the formula:

$$\mu = \overline{X} \pm ts_{\overline{X}} \tag{12.4}$$

This is the basic formula for estimation using the _t_ statistic. You should notice that this formula is very similar to the _z_-score formula used for estimation (formula 12.3). Also note that either formula (using _t_ or _z_) can be expressed conceptually in words as

$$\text{population mean} = \text{sample mean} \pm \text{some error}$$

PROCEDURES OF ESTIMATION USING A _t_ STATISTIC

To obtain an estimate of μ using formula 12.4, we first find the value for the sample mean (from the sample data) and calculate the estimated standard error (also computed from the sample data). Next, we must obtain a value for _t_. Remember that you cannot calculate _t_ because you do not know the population mean μ. However, you know that every sample has a corresponding _t_ value, and this _t_ value is located somewhere within the _t_ distribution. Therefore, the next step is to estimate where your particular sample is located in the _t_ distribution. For a point estimate you use the most likely value in the distribution, namely, _t_ = 0. For an interval estimate you use a range of _t_ values determined by the level of confidence you have selected (for example 95% or 99%). Because the _t_ value in the formula is an estimate, the result we obtain is an estimate for the value of μ. The process of estimation is demonstrated in the following example.

EXAMPLE 12.1

In this example we are simply trying to estimate the value of μ. Because no particular treatment is involved here, we are not trying to determine the size of a treatment effect.

A marketing researcher for a major U.S. jeans manufacturer would like to estimate the mean age for the population of people who buy its products. This information will be valuable in making decisions about how to spend advertising dollars. For example, should the company place more advertisements in _Seventeen_ magazine or in _Cosmopolitan?_ These represent publications that are directed at different age groups. It would be too costly and time consuming to record the age of every person in the population of their consumers, so a random sample is taken to estimate the value of μ. A sample of $n = 30$ people is drawn from the consumers who purchase the jeans from several major clothing outlets. The mean age of this sample is $\overline{X} = 30.5$ years, with $SS = 709$. The marketing researcher wishes to make a point estimate and to determine the 95% confidence interval for μ.

Notice that nothing is known about the population parameters. Estimation of the value for μ will be based solely on the sample data. Because σ is unknown, a t statistic will be used for the estimation. The confidence level has been selected (95%), and the sample data have been collected. Now we can turn our attention to the computational steps of estimation.

Compute s and $s_{\overline{X}}$ The population standard deviation is not known; therefore, to estimate μ, it is necessary to use the estimated standard error. To obtain $s_{\overline{X}}$, we must first compute the sample standard deviation. Using the information provided, we obtain

$$s = \sqrt{\frac{SS}{n-1}}$$
$$= \sqrt{\frac{709}{29}}$$
$$= \sqrt{24.45}$$
$$= 4.94$$

For estimated standard error we obtain

$$s_{\overline{X}} = \frac{s}{\sqrt{n}}$$
$$= \frac{4.94}{\sqrt{30}}$$
$$= \frac{4.94}{5.48}$$
$$= 0.90$$

Compute the point estimate The value for t that is used depends on the type of estimate being made. A single t value is used for a point estimate and an interval of values is used for the confidence interval. Just as we observed with the z-score distribution, t values are symmetrically distributed with a mean of zero. Therefore, we will use $t = 0$, the center of the distribution, as the best choice for the point estimate. Using the sample data, the estimation formula yields a point estimate of

$$\mu = \overline{X} \pm ts_{\overline{X}}$$
$$= 30.5 \mid 0(0.90)$$
$$= 30.5 + 0$$
$$= 30.5$$

Figure 12.4

The 95% confidence interval for *df* = 29 will have boundaries that range from *t* = −2.045 to +2.045. Because the *t* distribution table presents proportions in both tails of the distribution, for the 95% confidence interval you find the *t* values under *p* = 0.05 (proportions of *t*-scores in two tails) for *df* = 29.

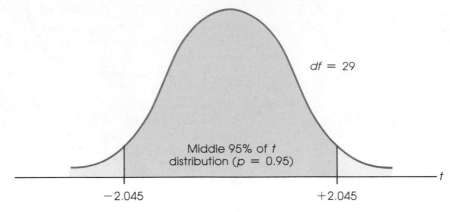

As noted before, the sample mean is the most appropriate point estimate of the population mean.

We do not know the actual *t* value associated with the $\bar{X}$ we obtained. For that information, we would need the value for μ—which we are trying to estimate. So we use values of *t*, just as we did with *z*, to define an interval around $\bar{X}$ that probably contains the value of μ.

Construct an interval estimate For an interval estimate of μ we construct an interval around the sample mean in which the value for μ probably falls. We now use a range of *t* values to define this interval. For example, there is a good chance that the sample has a *t* value somewhere between *t* = +2 and *t* = −2 and even a much better chance it is between *t* = +4 and *t* = −4. The level of confidence (percent confidence) will determine the *t* values that mark off the boundaries of this interval. However, unlike the normal *z* distribution, there is a family of *t* distributions in which the exact shape of the distribution depends on the value of degrees of freedom. Therefore, the value of *df* that is associated with the sample is another determining factor of the *t* values to be used in the interval estimate. For this example,

$$df = n - 1 = 30 - 1 = 29$$

The marketing researcher selected the 95% confidence interval. Figure 12.4 depicts the *t* distribution for *df* = 29. To obtain the *t* values associated with the 95% confidence interval, we must consult the *t* distribution table. We look under the heading of proportions in *two tails*. If the middle 95% of the distribution is of interest to us, then both tails outside of the interval together will contain 5% of the *t* values. Therefore, to find the *t* values associated with the 95% confidence interval, we look for the entry under *p* = 0.05, two tails, for *df* = 29. The values of *t* used for the boundaries of this confidence interval are −2.045 and +2.045 (Figure 12.4). Using these values in the formula for μ, we obtain, for one end of the confidence interval,

$$\mu = \bar{X} - ts_{\bar{X}}$$
$$= 30.5 - 2.045(0.90)$$
$$= 30.5 - 1.84$$
$$= 28.66$$

For the other end of the interval

$$\mu = \bar{X} + ts_{\bar{X}}$$
$$= 30.5 + 2.045(0.90)$$
$$= 30.5 + 1.84$$
$$= 32.34$$

Therefore, the marketing researcher can be 95% confident that the population mean age for consumers of his product is between 28.66 and 32.34 years. The confidence level (%) determines the range of *t* values used in constructing the interval. As long as the obtained sample really does have a *t* value that falls within the estimated range of *t* values, the population mean will be included in the confidence interval.

LEARNING CHECK

1. A professor of philosophy hypothesizes that an introductory course in logic will help college students with their other studies. To test this hypothesis, a random sample of $n = 25$ freshmen is selected. These students are required to complete a logic course during their freshman year. At the time of graduation, the final grade point average is computed for each of these students. The mean GPA for this sample is $\bar{X} = 2.83$ with $SS = 6$. Using the sample data, estimate how much of an effect the professor can expect. Specifically, make a point estimate and an interval estimate for the mean GPA of the population of students that take the course. Use a confidence level of 99%.

2. Suppose the same data consisted of $\bar{X} = 2.83$, $SS = 6$, and $n = 16$. Make a point estimate and construct the 99% confidence interval.

ANSWERS

1. Point estimate: $\mu = 2.83$. 99% confidence interval: μ is between 3.11 and 2.55.

2. Point estimate: $\mu = 2.83$. 99% confidence interval: $s - 0.63$; $s_{\bar{X}} = 0.16$; μ is between 3.30 and 2.36.

SECTION 12.4 ESTIMATION WITH THE INDEPENDENT-MEASURES *t* STATISTIC

The independent-measures *t* statistic can be used for estimation as well as for hypothesis testing. In either case, the *t* statistic provides a means for using sample data to draw inferences about the difference between two population means. For the hypothesis test, the goal is to answer a yes-no question: Is there any mean difference between the two populations? For estimation, the goal is to determine *how much* difference.

Recall that the basic structure of the independent-measures *t* formula is the same as we observed for the initial *z*-score or single-sample *t*:

$$t = \frac{\text{sample data} - \text{population parameter}}{\text{estimated standard error}}$$

Because we are interested in finding the population parameter, we will rewrite this equation as follows:

population parameter = sample data $\pm$ t(estimated standard error)

This is the basic formula for estimation. With an independent-measures experimental design, we must solve formula 10.4 for $\mu_1 - \mu_2$. The formula we obtain for estimation is

$$\mu_1 - \mu_2 = (\overline{X}_1 - \overline{X}_2) \pm ts_{\overline{X}_1 - \overline{X}_2}$$

(12.5)

In words, we are using the sample mean difference, plus or minus some error, to estimate the population mean difference. To use this equation to estimate $\mu_1 - \mu_2$ requires two steps:

1. Use the sample data to compute the sample mean difference $(\overline{X}_1 - \overline{X}_2)$ and the standard error $(s_{\overline{X}_1 - \overline{X}_2})$.

2. Estimate the t value that is associated with the sample data. This is accomplished by selecting a t value that is appropriate for the type of estimate we are using. That is, we can either make a point estimate, in which case $t = 0$, or we select a level of confidence and use a range of t values for the estimate. With 90% confidence, for example, you would estimate that the t statistic for $\overline{X}_1 - \overline{X}_2$ is located somewhere in the middle 90% of the t distribution.

Remember, we are not simply choosing a t value but are estimating the location of our sample data within the t distribution.

At this point you have all the values on the right-hand side of the equation (formula 12.5), and you can compute the value for $\mu_1 - \mu_2$. If you have used a single number to estimate the location of t, you will get a single, point estimate for $\mu_1 - \mu_2$. If you have used a range of values for t, you will compute a confidence interval for $\mu_1 - \mu_2$. A complete example of this estimation procedure follows.

EXAMPLE 12.2 Recent studies have allowed psychologists to establish definite links between specific foods and specific brain functions. For example, lecithin (found in soybeans, eggs, liver) has been shown to increase the concentration of certain brain chemicals that help regulate memory and motor coordination. This experiment is designed to demonstrate the importance of this particular food substance.

The experiment involves two separate samples of newborn rats (an independent-measures experiment). The 10 rats in the first sample are given a normal diet containing standard amounts of lecithin. The 5 rats in the other sample are fed a special diet, which contains almost no lecithin. After 6 months, each of the rats is tested on a specially designed learning problem that requires both memory and motor coordination. The purpose of the experiment is to demonstrate the deficit in performance that results from lecithin deprivation. The score for each animal is the number of errors before the learning problem was solved. The data from this experiment are as follows:

Regular Diet	No-Lecithin Diet
$n = 10$	$n = 5$
$\overline{X} = 25$	$\overline{X} = 33$
$SS = 250$	$SS = 140$

Because we fully expect that there will be a significant difference between these two treatments, we will not do the hypothesis test (although you should be able to do it). We want to use these data to obtain an estimate of the size of the difference between the two population means; that is, how much does lecithin affect learning performance? We will use a point estimate and the 80% confidence interval.

The basic equation for estimation with an independent measures experiment is

$$\mu_1 - \mu_2 = (\bar{X}_1 - \bar{X}_2) \pm t s_{\bar{X}_1 - \bar{X}_2}$$

The first step is to obtain the known values from the sample data. The sample mean difference is easy; one group averaged $\bar{X} = 25$, and the other averaged $\bar{X} = 33$, so there is an 8-point difference. Notice that it is not important whether we call this a +8 or a −8 difference. In either case the size of the difference is 8 points, and the regular diet group scored lower. Because it is easier to do arithmetic with positive numbers, we will use

$$\bar{X}_1 - \bar{X}_2 = 8$$

Compute the standard error   To find the standard error, we first must pool the two variances:

$$s_p^2 = \frac{SS_1 + SS_2}{df_1 + df_2} = \frac{250 + 140}{9 + 4}$$

$$= \frac{390}{13}$$

$$= 30$$

Next, the pooled variance is used to compute the standard error:

$$s_{\bar{X}_1 - \bar{X}_2} = \sqrt{\frac{s_p^2}{n_1} + \frac{s_p^2}{n_2}} = \sqrt{\frac{30}{10} + \frac{30}{5}} = \sqrt{3 + 6} = \sqrt{9} = 3$$

You should recall that this standard error combines the error from the first sample and the error from the second sample. Because the first sample is much larger, $n = 10$, it should have less error. This difference shows up in the formula. The larger sample contributes an error of 3 points, and the smaller sample contributes 6 points, which combine for a total error of 9 points under the square root.

Sample 1 had $df = 9$, and sample 2 has $df = 4$. The *t* statistic has $df = 9 + 4 = 13$.

The final value needed on the right-hand side of the equation is *t*. The data from this experiment would produce a *t* statistic with $df = 13$. With 13 degrees of freedom, we can sketch the distribution of all the possible *t* values. This distribution is shown in Figure 12.5. The *t* statistic for our data is somewhere in this distribution. The problem is to estimate where. For a point estimate, the best bet is to use $t = 0$. This is the most likely value, located exactly in the middle of the distribution. To gain more confidence in the estimate, you can select a range of *t* values. For 80% confidence, for example, you would estimate that the *t* statistic is somewhere in the middle 80% of

Figure 12.5

The distribution of t values with $df = 13$. Note that t values pile up around zero and that 80% of the values are between $+1.350$ and -1.350.

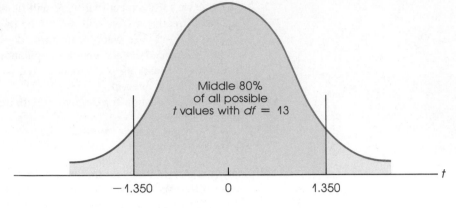

Middle 80%
of all possible
t values with $df = 13$

-1.350 0 1.350 t

the distribution. Checking the table, you find that the middle 80% is bounded by values of $t = +1.350$ and $t = -1.350$.

Using these t values and the sample values computed earlier, we now can estimate the magnitude of the performance deficit caused by lecithin deprivation.

Compute the point estimate   For a point estimate, use the single-value (point) estimate of $t = 0$:

$$\mu_1 - \mu_2 = (\bar{X}_1 - \bar{X}_2) \pm ts_{\bar{X}_1 - \bar{X}_2}$$
$$= 8 \pm 0(3)$$
$$= 8$$

Notice that the result simply uses the sample mean difference to estimate the population mean difference. The conclusion is that lecithin deprivation produces an average of 8 more errors on the learning task. (Based on the fact that the normal animals averaged around 25 errors, an 8-point increase would mean a performance deficit of approximately 30%.)

Construct the interval estimate   For an interval estimate, or confidence interval, use the range of t values. With 80% confidence, at one extreme,

$$\mu_1 - \mu_2 = (\bar{X}_1 - \bar{X}_2) + ts_{\bar{X}_1 - \bar{X}_2}$$
$$= 8 + 1.350(3)$$
$$= 8 + 4.05$$
$$= 12.05$$

and at the other extreme,

$$\mu_1 - \mu_2 = (\bar{X}_1 - \bar{X}_2) - ts_{\bar{X}_1 - \bar{X}_2}$$
$$= 8 - 1.350(3)$$
$$= 8 - 4.05$$
$$= 3.95$$

This time we are concluding that the effect of lecithin deprivation is to increase errors with an average increase somewhere between 3.95 and 12.05 errors. We are 80% confident of this estimate because the only thing estimated was the location of the *t* statistic, and we used the middle 80% of all the possible *t* values.

Note that the result of the point estimate is to say that lecithin deprivation will increase errors by exactly 8. To gain confidence, you must lose precision and say that errors will increase by around 8 (for 80% confidence, we say that the average increase will be $8 + 4.05$).

LEARNING CHECK   1. In families with several children, the first-born children tend to be more reserved and serious, whereas the last-born children tend to be more outgoing and happy-go-lucky. A psychologist is using a standardized personality inventory to measure the magnitude of this difference. A sample of eight first-born and eight last-born children is obtained. Each child is given the personality test. The results of this test are as follows:

FIRST-BORN	LAST-BORN
$\bar{X} = 11.4$	$\bar{X} = 13.9$
$SS = 26$	$SS = 30$

a. Use these sample data to make a point estimate of the population mean difference in personality for first-born versus last-born children.

b. Make an interval estimate of the population mean difference so that you are 80% confident that the true mean difference is in your interval.

ANSWERS   1. a. For a point estimate, use the sample mean difference: $\bar{X}_1 - \bar{X}_2 = 2.5$ points.

b. With $df = 14$, the middle 80% of all possible *t* statistics is bounded by $t = +1.345$ and $t = -1.345$. For these data the pooled variance is 4, and the standard error is 1. The 80% confidence interval is 1.155 to 3.845.

SECTION 12.5   **ESTIMATION WITH THE REPEATED-MEASURES *t* STATISTIC**

In a repeated-measures experiment, a single sample of subjects is measured in two different treatment conditions. For each subject a difference score is computed by subtracting the first score (treatment 1) from the second score (treatment 2).

$$D = X_2 - X_1$$

The resulting sample of difference scores can be used to draw inferences about the mean difference for the general population, μ_D. The repeated-measures *t* statistic allows researchers to use the sample mean difference, $\overline{D}$, to estimate the value of μ_D. Once again, the repeated-measures t formula is

$$t = \frac{\overline{D} - \mu_D}{s_{\overline{D}}}$$

Because we want to estimate the value of the population mean difference, this formula is solved for μ_D:

$$\mu_D = \overline{D} \pm ts_{\overline{D}} \qquad (12.6)$$

In words, this formula may be stated as

population mean difference = sample mean difference ± some error

That is, to estimate the mean difference for the population, we use the sample mean difference plus or minus some error.

PROCEDURE FOR ESTIMATION OF μ_D

The process of estimation with the repeated-measures t statistic follows the same steps that were used for estimation with the single-sample t statistic. First you calculate the sample mean ($\overline{D}$) and the estimated standard error ($s_{\overline{D}}$) using the sample of difference scores. Next, you determine the appropriate values for t ($t = 0$ for a point estimate or a range of values from the t distribution for an interval estimate). Finally, these values are used in the estimation formula (12.6) to compute an estimate of μ_D. The following example demonstrates this process.

EXAMPLE 12.3

A school psychologist has determined that a remedial reading course increases scores on a reading comprehension test. The psychologist now would like to estimate how much improvement might be expected for the whole population of students in his city. A random sample of $n = 16$ children is obtained. These children are first tested for level of reading comprehension and then enrolled in the course. At the completion of the remedial reading course, the students are tested again, and the difference between the second score and the first score is recorded for each child. For this sample, the average difference was $\overline{D} = +21$, and the SS for the difference scores was $SS = 1215$. The psychologist would like to use these data to make a point estimate and a 90% confidence interval estimate of μ_D.

The formula for estimation requires that we know the values of $\overline{D}$, $s_{\overline{D}}$, and t. We know that $\overline{D} = +21$ points for this sample, so all that remains is to compute $s_{\overline{D}}$ and look up the value of t in the t distribution table.

Compute the standard error   To find the standard error, we first must compute the sample standard deviation:

$$s = \sqrt{\frac{SS}{n-1}} = \sqrt{\frac{1215}{15}} = \sqrt{81} = 9$$

Figure 12.6

The *t* values for the 90% confidence interval are obtained by consulting the *t* table for $df = 15$, $p = 0.10$.

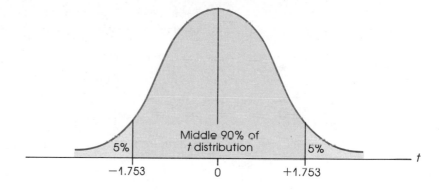

Middle 90% of *t* distribution

5%   5%

−1.753   0   +1.753   *t*

Now the estimated standard error is

$$s_{\overline{D}} = \frac{s}{\sqrt{n}} = \frac{9}{\sqrt{16}} = \frac{9}{4} = 2.25$$

To complete the estimate of μ_D, we must identify the value of *t*. We will consider the point estimate and the interval estimate separately.

Compute the point estimate To obtain a point estimate, a single value of *t* is selected to approximate the location of $\overline{D}$. Remember that the *t* distribution is symmetrical and bell-shaped with a mean of zero (see Figure 12.6). Because $t = 0$ is the most frequently occurring value in the distribution, this is the *t* value that is used for the point estimate. Using this value in the estimation formula gives

$$\mu_D = \overline{D} \pm ts_{\overline{D}}$$

$$= 21 \pm 0(2.25)$$

$$= 21$$

As noted several times before, the sample mean, $\overline{D} = 21$, provides the best point estimate of μ_D.

Construct the interval estimate The psychologist also wanted to make an interval estimate in order to be 90% confident that the interval contains the value of μ_D. To get the interval, it is necessary to determine what *t* values form the boundaries of the middle 90% of the *t* distribution. To use the *t* distribution table, we first must determine the proportion associated with the tails of this distribution. With 90% in the middle, the remaining area in both tails must be 10%, or $p = .10$. Also note that our sample has $n = 16$ scores, so the *t* statistic will have $df = n - 1 = 15$. Using $df = 15$ and $p = 0.10$ for two tails, you should find the values $+1.753$ and -1.753 in the *t* table. These values form the boundaries for the middle 90% of the *t* distribution. (See Figure 12.6.) We are confident that the *t* value for our sample is in this range because 90% of all the possible t values are there. Using these values in the estimation formula, we obtain the following: On one end of the interval,

$$\mu_D = \overline{D} - ts_{\overline{D}}$$
$$= 21 - 1.753(2.25)$$
$$= 21 - 3.94$$
$$= 17.06$$

and on the other end of the interval,

$$\mu_D = 21 + 1.753(2.25)$$
$$= 21 + 3.94$$
$$= 24.94$$

Therefore, the school psychologist can be 90% confident that the average amount of improvement in reading comprehension for the population (μ_D) will be somewhere between 17.06 and 24.94 points.

LEARNING CHECK

1. A government researcher believes that driving and automotive tips will result in energy-saving habits. A sample of nine subjects is given a brochure containing energy-saving tips and is asked to follow this advice. Before and after using the tips, the subjects maintain gasoline consumption records for their automobiles. For this sample, the average improvement in gasoline mileage (in miles per gallon) was $\overline{D} = 6.50$ with $SS = 72$. A repeated-measures t test indicated that the mean change was statistically significant. However, before the government prints millions of copies of the brochure, the researcher is requested to estimate how much mean change can be expected for the population of drivers. The investigator decides to report the 95% confidence interval. What will this interval be?

ANSWER

1. For this sample $s = 3$ and $s_{\overline{D}} = 1$. For the 95% confidence interval with $df = 8$, $t = \pm 2.306$; the 95% confidence interval for μ_D is from 4.194 to 8.806.

SECTION 12.6 **FACTORS AFFECTING THE WIDTH OF A CONFIDENCE INTERVAL**

There are two characteristics of the confidence interval that should be noted. First, notice what happens to the width of the interval when you change the level of confidence (the percent confidence). To gain more confidence in your estimate, you must increase the width of the interval. Conversely, to have a smaller interval, you must give up confidence. This is the basic trade-off between precision and confidence that was discussed earlier. In the estimation formula, the percent confidence influences the width of the interval by way of the z-score or t value. The larger the level of confidence (the percentage), the larger the z or t value, and the larger the interval. This relationship can be seen in Figure 12.6. In the figure we have identified the middle 90% of the t distribution in order to find a 90% confidence interval. It should be obvious that if we were to increase the confidence level to 95%, it would be necessary to increase the range of t values and thereby increase the width of the interval.

Second, notice what would happen to the interval width if you had a different sample size. This time, the basic rule is as follows: The bigger the sample (n), the smaller the interval. This relation is straightforward if you consider the sample size as a measure of the amount of information. A bigger sample gives you more information about the population and allows you to make a more precise estimate (a narrower interval). The sample size controls the magnitude of the standard error in the estimation formula. As the sample size increases, the standard error decreases, and the interval gets smaller.

With t statistics, the sample size has an additional effect on the width of a confidence interval. Remember that the exact shape of the t distribution depends on degrees of freedom. As the sample size gets larger, df also get larger, and the t values associated with any specific percentage of confidence get smaller. This fact simply enhances the general relation that the larger a sample, the smaller a confidence interval.

SUMMARY

1. Estimation is a procedure that uses sample data to obtain an estimate of a population mean. The estimate can be either a point estimate (single value) or an interval estimate (range of values). Point estimates have the advantage of precision, but they do not give much confidence. Interval estimates provide confidence, but you lose precision as the interval grows wider.

2. Estimation and hypothesis testing are similar processes: Both use sample data to answer questions about populations. However, these two procedures are designed to answer different questions. Hypothesis testing will tell you whether or not a treatment effect exists (yes or no). Estimation will tell you how much treatment effect there is.

3. The z-score or t formula can be used to estimate a population mean using the data from a single sample. The z-score formula is used when the population standard deviation is known and the t formula is used when σ is unknown. The two formulas are

$$\mu = \bar{X} \pm z\sigma_{\bar{X}} \quad \text{and} \quad \mu = \bar{X} \pm ts_{\bar{X}}$$

To use either formula, first calculate the sample mean and the standard error ($\sigma_{\bar{X}}$ or $s_{\bar{X}}$) from the sample data.

Next, obtain an estimate of the value of z or t by estimating the location of the sample data within the appropriate distribution. For a point estimate, use $z = 0$ or $t = 0$. For an interval estimate, first select a level of confidence (percentage) and then look up the range of z scores or t values in the appropriate table.

4. For an independent-measures experiment, the formula for estimation is

$$\mu_1 - \mu_2 = (\bar{X}_1 - \bar{X}_2) \pm ts_{\bar{X}_1 - \bar{X}_2}$$

To use this formula, you first decide on a degree of precision and a level of confidence desired for the estimate. If your primary concern is precision, use $t = 0$ to make a point estimate of the mean difference. Otherwise you select a level of confidence (percent confidence) that determines a range of t values to be used in the formula.

5. For a repeated-measures experiment, estimation of the amount of mean change for the population is accomplished by solving the t statistic formula for μ_D:

$$\mu_D = \bar{D} \pm ts_{\bar{D}}$$

For a point estimate, a t value of zero is used. A range of t values is used to construct an interval around $\overline{D}$. As in previous estimation problems, the t values that mark the interval boundaries are determined by the confidence level that is selected and by degrees of freedom.

6. The width of a confidence interval is an indication of its precision: A narrow interval is more precise than a wide interval. The interval width is influenced by sample size and the level of confidence.
   a. As sample size (n) gets larger, the interval width gets smaller (greater precision).
   b. As the percent confidence increases, the interval-width gets greater (less precision).

KEY TERMS

| estimation | point estimate | interval estimate | confidence interval |

FOCUS ON PROBLEM SOLVING

1. Although hypothesis tests and estimation are similar in some respects, you should remember that they are separate statistical techniques. A hypothesis test is used to determine whether or not there is evidence for a treatment effect. Estimation is used to determine how much effect a treatment has.

2. When students perform a hypothesis test and estimation with the same set of data, a common error is to take the z-score or t statistic from the hypothesis test and use it in the estimation formula. For estimation the z-score or t value is determined by the level of confidence and must be looked up in the appropriate table.

3. Now that you are familiar with several different formulas for hypothesis tests and estimation, one problem will be determining which formula is appropriate for each set of data. When the data consist of a single sample selected from a single population, the appropriate statistic will be either z or the single-sample t, depending on whether σ is known or unknown, respectively. For an independent-measures design you will always have two separate samples. In a repeated-measures design there is only one sample, but each individual is measured twice so that difference scores can be computed.

DEMONSTRATION 12.1   ESTIMATION WITH A SINGLE-SAMPLE t STATISTIC

A sample of $n = 16$ is randomly selected from a population with unknown parameters. For the following sample data, estimate the value of μ using point estimate and a 90% confidence interval.

Sample data: 13 10   8 13 9 14 12 10
             11 10 15 13 7   6 15 10

Note that we have a single sample and we do not know the value for σ. Thus, the single-sample t statistic should be used for these data. The formula for estimation is

$$\mu = \overline{X} \pm ts_{\overline{X}}$$

STEP 1 Compute the sample mean.

The sample mean is the basis for our estimate of μ. For these data,

$$\Sigma X = 13 + 10 + 8 + 13 + 9 + 14 + 12 + 10 +$$
$$11 + 10 + 15 + 13 + 7 + 6 + 15 + 10$$
$$= 176$$

$$\overline{X} = \frac{\Sigma X}{n} = \frac{176}{16} = 11$$

STEP 2 Compute the estimated standard error, $s_{\overline{X}}$.

To compute the estimated standard error, we must first find the value for SS and the sample standard deviation.

Sum-of-squares. We will use the definitional formula for *SS*. The following table demonstrates the computations.

X	$X - \overline{X}$	$(X - \overline{X})^2$
13	$13-11=+2$	4
10	$10-11=-1$	1
8	$8-11=-3$	9
13	$13-11=+2$	4
9	$9-11=-2$	4
14	$14-11=+3$	9
12	$12-11=+1$	1
10	$10-11=-1$	1
11	$11-11=\ \ 0$	0
10	$10-11=-1$	1
15	$15-11=+4$	16
13	$13-11=+2$	4
7	$7-11=-4$	16
6	$6-11=-5$	25
15	$15-11=+4$	16
10	$10-11=\ -1$	1

To obtain *SS*, we sum the squared deviation scores in the last column.

$$SS = \Sigma(X - \overline{X})^2 = 112$$

Standard deviation. The sample standard deviation is computed for these data.

$$s = \sqrt{\frac{SS}{n-1}} = \sqrt{\frac{112}{16-1}} = \sqrt{\frac{112}{15}} = \sqrt{7.47} = 2.73$$

Estimated standard error. The estimated standard error can now be determined.

$$s_{\overline{X}} = \frac{s}{\sqrt{n}} = \frac{2.73}{\sqrt{16}} = \frac{2.73}{4} = 0.68$$

STEP 3   Point estimate for μ.

For a point estimate, we use $t = 0$. Using the estimation formula, we obtain

$$\mu = \overline{X} \pm ts_{\overline{X}}$$
$$= 11 \pm 0(0.68)$$
$$= 11 \pm 0 = 11$$

The point estimate for the population mean is $\mu = 11$.

STEP 4   Confidence interval for μ.

For these data, we want the 90% confidence interval. Therefore, we will use a range of t values that form the middle 90% of the distribution. For this demonstration degrees of freedom is

$$df = n - 1 = 16 - 1 = 15$$

If we are looking for the middle 90% of the distribution, then 10% ($p = 0.10$) would lie in both tails outside of the interval. To find the t values, we look up $p = 0.10$, two tails, for $df = 15$ in the t distribution table. The t values for the 90% confidence interval are $t = \pm 1.753$.

Using the estimation formula, one end of the confidence interval is

$$\mu = \overline{X} - ts_{\overline{X}}$$
$$= 11 - 1.753(0.68)$$
$$= 11 - 1.19 = 9.81$$

For the other end of the confidence interval, we obtain

$$\mu = \overline{X} + ts_{\overline{X}}$$
$$= 11 + 1.753(0.68)$$
$$= 11 + 1.19 = 12.19$$

Thus, the 90% confidence interval for μ is from 9.81 to 12.19.

DEMONSTRATION 12.2   ESTIMATION WITH THE INDEPENDENT-MEASURES *t* STATISTIC

Samples are taken from two school districts and knowledge of American history is tested with a short questionnaire. For the following sample data, estimate the amount of mean difference between the students of these two districts. Specifically, provide a point estimate and a 95% confidence interval for $\mu_1 - \mu_2$.

District A scores: 18 15 24 15
District B scores: 9 12 13 6

STEP 1   Compute the sample means.

The estimate of population mean difference ($\mu_1 - \mu_2$) is based of the sample mean difference ($\overline{X}_1 - \overline{X}_2$).

For district A,

$$\Sigma X = 18 + 15 + 24 + 15 = 72$$

$$\overline{X}_1 = \frac{\Sigma X}{n} = \frac{72}{4} = 18$$

For district B,

$$\Sigma X = 9 + 12 + 13 + 6 = 40$$

$$\overline{X}_2 = \frac{\Sigma X}{n} = \frac{40}{4} = 10$$

STEP 2 Calculate the estimated standard error for mean difference, $s_{\overline{X}_1 - \overline{X}_2}$.

To compute the estimated standard error, we first need to determine the values of SS for both samples and pooled variance.

Sum-of-squares. The computations for sum-of-squares, using the definitional formula, are shown for both samples in the following tables.

	DISTRICT A	
X	$X - \overline{X}$	$(X - \overline{X})^2$
18	$18-18=\ \ 0$	0
15	$15-18=-3$	9
24	$24-18=+6$	36
15	$15-18=-3$	9

	DISTRICT B	
X	$X - \overline{X}$	$(X - \overline{X})^2$
9	$9-10=-1$	1
12	$12-10=+2$	4
13	$13-10=+3$	9
6	$6-10=-4$	16

For district A,

$$SS_1 = \Sigma(X - \overline{X})^2 = 0 + 9 + 36 + 9 = 54$$

For district B,

$$SS_2 = \Sigma(X - \overline{X})^2 = 1 + 4 + 9 + 16 = 30$$

Pooled variance. For pooled variance, we use the SS and df values from both samples. For District A, $df_1 = n_1 - 1 = 3$. For District B, $df_2 = n_2 - 1 = 3$. Pooled variance is

$$s_p^2 = \frac{SS_1 + SS_2}{df_1 + df_2} = \frac{54 + 30}{3 + 3} = \frac{84}{6} = 14$$

Estimated standard error. The estimated standard error for mean difference can now be calculated.

$$s_{\bar{X}_1 - \bar{X}_2} = \sqrt{\frac{s_p^2}{n_1} + \frac{s_p^2}{n_2}} = \sqrt{\frac{14}{4} + \frac{14}{4}} = \sqrt{3.5 + 3.5}$$

$$= \sqrt{7} = 2.65$$

STEP 3   Point estimate for $\mu_1 - \mu_2$.

For the point estimate, we use a t value of zero. Using the sample means and estimated standard error from previous steps, we obtain

$$\mu_1 - \mu_2 = (\bar{X}_1 - \bar{X}_2) \pm ts_{\bar{X}_1 - \bar{X}_2}$$

$$= (18 - 10) \pm 0(2.65)$$

$$= 8 \pm 0 = 8$$

STEP 4   Confidence interval for $\mu_1 - \mu_2$.

For the independent measures t statistic, degrees of freedom are determined by

$$df = n_1 + n_2 - 2$$

For these data df is

$$df = 4 + 4 - 2 = 6$$

With a 95% level of confidence, 5% of the distribution falls in the tails outside the interval. Therefore, we consult the t distribution table for $p = 0.05$, two tails, with $df = 6$. The t values from the table are $t = \pm 2.447$. On one end of the confidence interval, $\mu_1 - \mu_2$ is

$$\mu_1 - \mu_2 = (\bar{X}_1 - \bar{X}_2) - ts_{\bar{X}_1 - \bar{X}_2}$$

$$= (18 - 10) - 2.447(2.65)$$

$$= 8 - 6.48$$

$$= 1.52$$

On the other end of the confidence interval, the population mean difference is

$$\mu_1 - \mu_2 = (\bar{X}_1 - \bar{X}_2) + ts_{\bar{X}_1 - \bar{X}_2}$$

$$= (18 - 10) + 2.447(2.65)$$

$$= 8 + 6.48$$

$$= 14.48$$

Thus, the 95% confidence interval for population mean difference is from 1.52 to 14.48.

PROBLEMS

1. An extensive survey in 1970 revealed that preschool children spend an average of $\mu = 6.3$ hours per day watching television. The distribution of TV times is normal with $\sigma = 2$. Last year a sample of $n = 100$ preschool children gave a mean of $\overline{X} = 5.8$ hours of television per day.
   a. Use these sample data to make a point estimate of the population mean for last year.
   b. Based on your point estimate, how much change has occurred in children's television habits since 1970?
   c. Make an interval estimate of last year's population mean so you are 80% confident that the true mean is in your interval.

2. A researcher has constructed a 90% confidence interval of 87 ± 10, based on a sample of $n = 25$ scores. Note that this interval is 20 points wide (from 77 to 97). How large a sample would be needed to produce a 90% interval that is only 10 points wide?

3. Performance scores on a motor skills task form a normal distribution with $\mu = 20$ and $\sigma = 4$. A psychologist is using this task to determine the extent to which increased self-awareness affects performance. The prediction for this experiment is that increased self-awareness will reduce a subject's concentration and result in lower performance scores. A sample of $n = 16$ subjects is obtained, and each subject is tested on the motor skills task while seated in front of a large mirror. The purpose of the mirror is to make the subjects more self-aware. The average score for this sample is $\overline{X} = 15.5$.
   a. Make a point estimate of the population mean performance score with the mirror present.
   b. Make an interval estimate of the population mean so that you are 95% confident that the true mean is in your interval.

4. Researchers have developed a filament that should add to the life expectancy of light bulbs. The standard 60-watt bulb burns for an average of $\mu = 750$ hours with $\sigma = 20$. A sample of $n = 100$ bulbs is prepared using the new filament. The average life for this sample is $\overline{X} = 820$ hours.
   a. Use these sample data to make a point estimate of the mean life expectancy for the new filament.
   b. Make an interval estimate so that you are 80% confident that the true mean is in your interval.
   c. Make an interval estimate so that you are 99% confident that the true mean is in your interval.

5. A poultry farm supplies chickens to a fast-food restaurant chain. The chickens are sold by weight and average $\mu = 65$ ounces. The distribution of weights is normal with $\sigma = 4.9$ ounces. The farmer is interested in changing to a new brand of chicken food. However, the new food is more expensive and will not be economically feasible unless it results in an average weight increase of at least 3 ounces per chicken. A sample of $n = 30$ chicks is selected to be tested on the new food. At maturity, the weights for these chickens are as follows: 74, 72, 65, 79, 75, 73, 68, 75, 78, 69, 72, 75, 79, 81, 73, 63, 69, 73, 77, 73, 64, 73, 63, 78, 72, 71, 62, 72, 71, 74.
   a. Construct an 80% confidence interval for the population mean weight for chickens raised on the new feed.
   b. Based on your confidence interval, should the farmer switch to the new food? Explain your answer.

6. What factors affect the width of the confidence interval? How is the width affected by each of these factors?

7. A psychologist has developed a new personality questionnaire for measuring self-esteem and would like to estimate the population parameters for the test scores. The questionnaire is administered to a sample of $n = 25$ subjects. This sample has an average score of $\overline{X} = 43$ with $SS = 2400$.
   a. Provide an unbiased estimate for the population standard deviation.
   b. Make a point estimate for the population mean.
   c. Make an interval estimate of μ so that you are 90% confident that the value for μ is in your interval.

8. A toy manufacturer asks a developmental psychologist to test children's responses to a new product. Specifically, the manufacturer wants to know how long, on average, the toy captures children's attention. The psychologist tests a sample of $n = 9$ children and measures how long they play with the toy before they

get bored. This sample had a mean of $\bar{X} = 31$ minutes with $SS = 648$.

a. Make a point estimate for μ

b. Make an interval estimate for μ using a confidence level of 95%.

9. A random sample of $n = 11$ scores is selected from a population with unknown parameters. The scores in the sample are as follows: 12, 5, 9, 9, 10, 14, 7, 10, 14, 13, 8.

a. Provide an unbiased estimate of the population standard deviation.

b. Use the sample data to make a point estimate for μ and to construct the 95% confidence interval for μ.

10. A vocabulary skills test designed for 6-year-old children has been standardized to produce a mean score of $\mu = 50$. A researcher would like to use this test in an experiment with 5-year-old children. Before beginning the experiment, however, the researcher would like some indication of how well 5-year-olds can perform on this test. Therefore, a sample of $n = 21$ 5-year-old children is given the test. The data for this sample are as follows:

VOCABULARY TEST SCORES						
42	56	49	37	43	46	47
48	57	39	40	51	49	50
36	45	52	47	49	40	53

a. Use the data to make a point estimate of the population mean for 5-year-old children.

b. Make an interval estimate of the mean so that you are 95% confident that the true mean is in your interval.

c. On the basis of your confidence interval, can the researcher be 95% confident that the population mean for 5-year-olds is lower than the mean for 6-year-olds?

11. A curious student would like to know the average number of books owned by college professors. A random sample of 12 professors is selected, and the student counts the number of books owned by each professor. The data obtained by the student are as follows:

346, 134, 208, 640, 276, 318

211, 453, 152, 281, 109, 334

a. Use these sample data to make a point estimate of the population mean.

b. Use the data to make an interval estimate of the population mean so that you are 95% confident that the mean is in your interval.

c. Based on these data, the 80% confidence interval for the population mean extends from 229.87 to 347.13. Does this mean that 80% of all college professors own between 229.87 and 347.13 books? Explain your answer.

12. A psychologist is studying the relation between weight and hormone levels. A random sample of rats is selected, and the sample is divided into two groups of five rats each. The rats in one group are given daily injections of a "growth" hormone, and the rats in the second group are injected with a harmless salt solution. During a 2-week test period, the psychologist records the amount of weight gained by each rat. The data are as follows:

HORMONE	CONTROL
$\bar{X} = 22$	$\bar{X} = 8$
$SS = 140$	$SS = 180$

Use the data to estimate how much extra weight gain the hormone produces. Make a point estimate and an interval estimate so that you are 80% confident that the true mean difference is in your interval.

13. A psychologist would like to know how much difference there is between the problem-solving ability of 8-year-old children versus 10-year-old children. A random sample of 10 children is selected from each age group. The children are given a problem-solving test, and the results are summarized as follows:

8-YEAR-OLDS	10-YEAR-OLDS
$n = 10$	$n = 10$
$\bar{X} = 36$	$\bar{X} = 43$
$SS = 110$	$SS = 250$

a. Use the sample data to make a point estimate of the mean difference between 8-year-olds' and 10-year-olds' problem-solving ability.

b. Make an interval estimate of the mean difference so that you are 90% confident that the real difference is in your interval.

14. A developmental psychologist would like to know how much difference there is in vocabulary development between 6-year-old boys versus 6-year-old girls. Random samples of $n = 5$ boys and $n = 10$ girls are obtained, and each child is given a standardized vocabulary test. The average score for the boys is $\overline{X} = 84$ with $SS = 120$ and the average score for the girls is $\overline{X} = 91$ with $SS = 270$.

a. Use the sample data to make a point estimate of the population mean difference.

b. Make an interval estimate of the mean difference so that you are 90% confident that the true mean difference is in your interval.

15. A researcher is investigating the effectiveness of a new sleeping pill. A random sample of twenty insomniacs is obtained. Half are given the new sleeping pill to try for one week and the other half are given a placebo (sugar pill). Each person is asked to record the amount of time needed to fall asleep each evening. the average time for the $n = 10$ subjects with the real medication is $\overline{X} = 18.7$ minutes with $SS = 160$ and the average time for the placebo group is $\overline{X} = 32.5$ minutes with $SS = 200$.

a. Use the sample data to make a point estimate of the population mean difference.

b. Make an interval estimate of the mean difference so that you are 80% confident that the true mean difference is in your interval.

16. The following data were obtained from an independent-measures experiment comparing two experimental treatments.

TREATMENT 1		TREATMENT 2	
12	18	21	14
16	19	19	23
11	13	24	18
12	15	20	22

a. Use the sample data to make a point estimate of the population mean difference between the two treatments.

b. Make an interval estimate of the population mean difference so that you are 80% confident that the real mean difference is in your interval.

17. For the following studies, state whether estimation or hypothesis testing is required. Also, is an independent- or a repeated-measures t statistic appropriate?

a. An educator wants to determine how much mean difference can be expected for the population in SAT scores following an intensive review course. Two samples are selected. The first group takes the review course and the second receives no treatment. SAT scores are subsequently measured for both groups.

b. A psychiatrist would lke to test the effectiveness of a new antipsychotic medication. A sample of patients is first assessed for the severity of psychotic symptoms. Then the patients are placed on drug therapy for 2 weeks. The severity of their symptoms is assessed again at the end of the treatment.

18. A researcher is investigating the relation between reaction time and room temperature. A sample of $n = 16$ subjects is obtained and each person's reaction time is measured in a 70° room and again in a room where the temperature is 95°. On average, this sample showed a reaction time that was 45 milliseconds faster in the 70° room with SS for the difference scores equal to 6000.

a. Use the sample data to make a point estimate of the difference in reaction time produced by the change in temperature.

b. Make an interval estimate of the population mean difference so that you are 95% confident that the real population mean difference is in your interval.

19. A researcher is testing the effectiveness of a blood-pressure medication. A sample of $n = 25$ subjects is obtained, and each person's blood pressure is measured before beginning the medication. After 3 weeks, each person's blood pressure is measured again and the researcher records the amount of change for each individual. For this sample, the average blood pressure decreased by 14.6 points with $SS = 2400$.

a. Use the sample data to make a point estimate of the mean reduction in blood pressure for the general population.

b. Make an interval estimate of the population mean change so that you are 80% confident that the true mean is located in your interval.

20. A researcher would like to determine how much reaction time is impaired after drinking only four ounces of alcohol. A random sample is obtained and each person's reaction time is measured before and after drinking the alcohol. The difference scores for this sample are as follows:

24, 35, 28, 10, −1, 32, 18, 26, 34, 20, 41

a. Use the sample data to make a point estimate of the change in reaction time for the general population.

b. Make an interval estimate of the population mean difference so that you are 95% confident that the true mean is located in your interval.

21. A researcher would like to evaluate the improvement in reading speed that results from a 1-hour speed-reading course. A sample of $n = 30$ students is obtained and each person's reading speed is measured before and after the 1-hour course. For this sample, the average subject increased reading speed by 125 words per minute with $SS = 5800$. Make a point estimate and a 90% confidence interval estimate of the average improvement in reading speed for the general population.

CHAPTER 13

INTRODUCTION TO ANALYSIS OF VARIANCE

SECTION 1 3 . 1 **INTRODUCTION**

Analysis of variance (ANOVA) is a hypothesis-testing procedure used to determine if mean differences exist for two or more treatments (or populations). As with all inferential procedures, ANOVA uses sample data as the basis for drawing conclusions about populations. A diagram of a situation where analysis of variance would be used is shown in Figure 13.1.

For an independent-measures experiment, a separate sample is taken for each of the treatment conditions. Because it is very unlikely that any two samples will be identical, even if they come from the same population, we have assumed that the samples in Figure 13.1 have different scores and different means. The purpose of ANOVA is to decide whether the differences between the samples are simply due to chance (sampling error) or whether there are systematic treatment effects that have caused the scores in one group to be different from the scores in another. More precisely, the alternatives can be stated as follows:

Remember, we would expect samples to differ because of sampling error (Chapter 7).

1. The populations for all treatments are really the same (μ's for each population are identical); the mean difference between the samples occurred due to chance; that is, sampling error.

2. The populations for the treatments are different (they have different μ's); the mean difference between the samples is due to the effect of the treatment.

It may appear that analysis of variance and *t* tests are simply two different ways of doing exactly the same job: testing for mean differences. In some respects this is true—both tests use sample data to test hypotheses about population means. However, ANOVA has a tremendous advantage over *t* tests. Specifically, *t* tests are limited to situations where there are only two treatments to compare. The major advantage of ANOVA is that it can be used to compare two or more treatments.

Figure 13.1

A typical situation where ANOVA would be used. Three separate samples are obtained to evaluate the mean differences among three populations (or treatments) with unknown means.

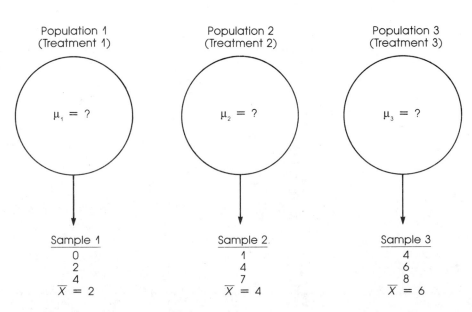

Thus, ANOVA provides researchers with much greater flexibility in designing experiments and interpreting results.

The following example will be used to introduce the statistical hypotheses for ANOVA. Suppose a psychologist examined learning performance under three temperature conditions: 50°, 70°, and 90°. Three samples of subjects are selected, one sample for each treatment condition. The purpose of the study is to determine whether room temperature affects learning performance. In statistical terms, we want to decide between two hypotheses: the null hypothesis (H_0), which says temperature has no effect, and the alternative hypothesis (H_1), which states that temperature does affect learning. In symbols, the null hypothesis states

$$H_0: \mu_1 = \mu_2 = \mu_3$$

That is, there are no differences among the means of the populations that receive the three treatments. The population means are all the same. Once again, notice that hypotheses are always stated in terms of population parameters, even though we use sample data to test them.

For the alternative hypothesis we may state that

$$H_1: \text{At least one population mean is different from the others}$$

Notice that we have not given any specific alternative hypothesis. This is because there are many different alternatives possible, and it would be tedious to list them all. One alternative, for example, would be that the first two populations are identical but that the third is different. Another alternative states that the last two means are the same but that the first is different. Other alternatives might be

$$H_1: \mu_1 \neq \mu_2 \neq \mu_3 \qquad \text{all three means are different}$$
$$H_1: \mu_1 = \mu_3 \qquad \mu_2 \text{ is different}$$

It should be pointed out that a researcher typically entertains only one (or at most a few) of these alternative hypotheses. Usually a theory or the outcomes of previous studies will dictate a specific prediction concerning the treatment effect. For the sake of simplicity, we will state a general alternative hypothesis rather than try to list all the possible specific alternatives.

SECTION 13.2 **THE LOGIC OF ANALYSIS OF VARIANCE**

The formulas and calculations required in ANOVA are somewhat complicated, but the logic that underlies the whole procedure is fairly straightforward. Therefore, this section will give a general picture of analysis of variance before we start looking at the details. We will introduce the logic of ANOVA with the help of the hypothetical data in Table 13.1. These data represent the results of an independent measures experiment comparing learning performance under three temperature conditions.

One obvious characteristic of the data in Table 13.1 is that the scores are not all the same. In everyday language, the scores are different: in statistical terms, the

Table 13.1

Hypothetical data from an experiment examining learning performance under three temperature conditions*

TREATMENT 1 50° (SAMPLE 1)	TREATMENT 2 70° (SAMPLE 2)	TREATMENT 3 90° (SAMPLE 3)
0	4	1
1	3	2
3	6	2
1	3	0
0	4	0
$\overline{X} = 1$	$\overline{X} = 4$	$\overline{X} = 1$

*Note that there are three separate samples, with $n = 5$ in each sample. The dependent variable is the number of problems solved correctly.

scores are variable. Our goal is to measure the amount of variability (the size of the differences) and to explain where it comes from.

The first step is to determine the total variability for the entire set of data. To compute the total variability, we will combine all the scores from all the separate samples to obtain one general measure of variability for the complete experiment. Once we have measured the total variability, we can begin to break it apart into separate components. The word *analysis* means dividing into smaller parts. Because we are going to analyze variability, the process is called *analysis of variance*. This analysis process divides the total variability into two basic components:

1. **Between-Treatments Variability.** Looking at the data in Table 13.1, we clearly see that much of the variability in the scores is due to general differences between treatment conditions. For example, the scores in the 70° condition tend to be much higher ($\overline{X} = 4$) than the scores in the 50° condition ($\overline{X} = 1$). We will calculate the variability between treatments to provide a measure of the overall differences between treatment conditions—that is, the differences among sample means.

2. **Within-Treatments Variability.** In addition to the general differences between treatment conditions, there is variability within each sample. Looking again at Table 13.1, the scores in the 70° condition are not all the same; they are variable. The within-treatments variability will provide a measure of the variability inside each treatment condition.

Analyzing the total variability into these two components is the heart of analysis of variance. We will now examine each of the components in more detail.

BETWEEN-TREATMENTS VARIABILITY

Whenever you compare two samples representing two treatment conditions, there are three possible explanations for the differences (variability) between sample means:

1. **Treatment Effect.** It is possible that the different treatments have caused the samples to be different. In Table 13.1, the scores in sample 1 were obtained in a 50° room, and the scores in sample 2 were obtained in a 70° room. It is possible that the difference between these two samples is due in part to the different temperatures.

Figure 13.2

The independent measures analysis of variance partitions, or analyzes, the total variability into two components: variability between treatments and variability within treatments.

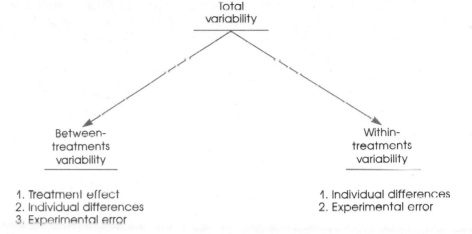

Total variability

Between-treatments variability

1. Treatment effect
2. Individual differences
3. Experimental error

Within-treatments variability

1. Individual differences
2. Experimental error

2. **Individual Differences.** Subjects enter an experiment with different backgrounds, abilities, and attitudes; that is, they are unique individuals. Whenever you compare separate samples (different groups of individuals), it is possible that the differences between samples are simply the result of individual differences.

3. **Experimental Error.** Whenever you make a measurement, there is a chance of error. The error could be caused by poor equipment, lack of attention, or unpredictable changes in the event you are measuring. This kind of uncontrolled and unexplained difference is called *experimental error,* and it can cause two samples to be different.

Thus, when we compute the variability between treatments, we are measuring differences that could be due to any of these three factors or any combination of the three.

WITHIN-TREATMENTS VARIABILITY

There are only two possible explanations for variability within a treatment condition:

1. **Individual Differences.** The scores are obtained from different individuals, which could explain why the scores are variable.

2. **Experimental Error.** There always is a chance that the differences are caused by experimental error.

Notice that the variability inside a treatment condition cannot be attributed to any treatment effect because all subjects within a treatment condition are treated exactly the same. Thus, the differences within a treatment are not systematic or predictable but rather are due to chance. The analysis, or partitioning, of variability is diagrammed in Figure 13.2.

THE *F*-RATIO: THE TEST STATISTIC FOR ANOVA

Once we have analyzed the total variability into two basic components (between treatments and within treatments), we simply compare them. The comparison is made by computing a statistic called an *F-ratio*. For the independent-measures ANOVA, the *F*-ratio has the following structure:

$$F = \frac{\text{variance between treatments}}{\text{variance within treatments}} \tag{13.1}$$

When we express each component of variability in terms of its sources (see Figure 13.2), the structure of the *F*-ratio is

$$F = \frac{\text{treatment effect} + \text{individual differences} + \text{experimental error}}{\text{individual differences} + \text{experimental error}} \tag{13.2}$$

You should note that the between treatments variability and the within treatments variability differ in only one respect: the variability (mean differences) caused by the treatment effect. This single difference between the numerator and denominator of the *F*-ratio is crucial in determining if a treatment effect has occurred. Remember, the whole purpose for doing the experiment and the analysis is to find out whether or not the treatment has any effect. Let's consider the two possibilities:

1. H_0 is true, and there is no treatment effect. In this case, the numerator and denominator of the *F*-ratio are measuring the same variance:

$$F = \frac{0 + \text{individual differences} + \text{experimental error}}{\text{individual differences} + \text{experimental error}}$$

When H_0 is true and the treatment effect is zero, the *F*-ratio is expected to equal 1.

2. If H_0 is false, then a treatment effect does exist, and the *F*-ratio becomes

$$F = \frac{\text{treatment effect} + \text{individual differences} + \text{experimental error}}{\text{individual differences} + \text{experimental error}}$$

The numerator of the ratio should be larger than the denominator, and the *F*-ratio is expected to be larger than 1.00. Ordinarily, the presence of a large treatment effect is reflected in a large value for the *F*-ratio.

In more general terms, the denominator of the *F*-ratio measures only uncontrolled and unexplained (often called *unsystematic*) variability. For this reason, the denominator of the *F*-ratio is called the *error term*. The numerator of the *F*-ratio always includes the same unsystematic variability as in the error term, but it also includes any systematic differences caused by the treatment effect. The goal of ANOVA is to find out whether or not a treatment effect exists.

DEFINITION

For ANOVA, the denominator of the *F*-ratio is called the *error term*. The error term provides a measure of the variance due to chance. When the treatment effect is zero (H_0 is true), the error term measures the same sources of variance as the numerator of the *F*-ratio, so the value of the *F*-ratio is expected to be nearly equal to 1.00. (Technically, the average value for *F*-ratios is slightly larger than 1.00 when H_0 is true.)

LEARNING CHECK

1. ANOVA is a statistical procedure that compares two or more treatment conditions for differences in variance. (True or False)

2. In ANOVA what value is expected on the average for the *F*-ratio when the null hypothesis is true?

3. What happens to the value of the *F*-ratio if differences between treatments are increased? What happens to the *F*-ratio if variability inside the treatments is increased?

4. In ANOVA, the total variability is partitioned into two parts. What are these two variability components called, and how are they used in the *F* ratio?

ANSWERS

1. False. Although ANOVA uses variability in the computations, the purpose of the test is to evaluate differences in *means* between treatments.

2. When H_0 is true, the expected value for the *F*-ratio is 1.00 because the top and bottom of the ratio are both measuring the same variance.

3. As differences between treatments increase, the *F*-ratio will increase. As variability within treatments increases, the *F*-ratio will decrease.

4. The two components are between-treatments variability and within-treatments variability. Between treatments is the numerator of the *F*-ratio and within treatments is the denominator.

SECTION 13.3 ANOVA VOCABULARY, NOTATION, AND FORMULAS

Before we introduce the notation, let's look at some special terminology that is used for ANOVA. The first term we will need from the ANOVA vocabulary is the word *factor*. This term is used in place of the words *independent variable*. Therefore, for the experiment shown in Table 13.1, the factor is temperature.

DEFINITION

In analysis of variance, a *factor* is an independent variable.

Because this experiment has only one independent variable, it is called a *single-factor experiment*. There are more complex experiments that use more than one factor. For example, a two-factor experiment has two independent variables. In this book, we will examine only single-factor experiments.

The second term you need to know is *levels*. The levels in an experiment consist of the different values used in the factor. For example, in the learning experiment (Table 13.1) we are using three values of temperature. Therefore, the temperature factor has three levels.

DEFINITION

The individual treatment conditions that make up a factor are called *levels* of the factor.

Because ANOVA most often is used to examine data from more than two treatment conditions (and more than two samples), we will need a notation system to help keep track of all the individual scores and totals. To help introduce this notational system, we will use the hypothetical data from Table 13.1 again. The data are reproduced in Table 13.2 along with some of the notation and statistics that will be described.

Table 13.2

Hypothetical data from an experiment examining learning performance under three temperature conditions*

	TEMPERATURE CONDITIONS		
1 50°	2 70°	3 90°	
0	4	1	$\Sigma X^2 = 106$
1	3	2	$G = 30$
3	6	2	$N = 15$
1	3	0	$k = 3$
0	4	0	
$T_1 = 5$	$T_2 = 20$	$T_3 = 5$	
$SS_1 = 6$	$SS_2 = 6$	$SS_3 = 4$	
$n_1 = 5$	$n_2 = 5$	$n_3 = 5$	
$\overline{X}_1 = 1$	$\overline{X}_2 = 4$	$\overline{X}_3 = 1$	

*Summary Values and Notation for an Analysis of Variance also are presented.

1. The letter k is used to identify the number of treatment conditions, that is, the number of levels of the factor. For an independent-measures experiment, k also specifies the number of separate samples. For the data in Table 13.2, there are three treatments, so $k = 3$.

2. The number of scores in each treatment is identified by a lowercase letter n. For the example in Table 13.2, $n = 5$ for all the treatments. If the samples are of different sizes, you can identify a specific sample by using a subscript. For example, n_2 is the number of scores in treatment 2.

3. The total number of scores in the entire experiment is specified by a capital letter N. When all the samples are the same size (n is constant), $N = kn$. For the data in Table 13.2, there are $n = 5$ scores in each of the $k = 3$ treatments, so $N = 3(5) = 15$.

4. The total (ΣX) for each treatment condition is identified by the capital letter T. The total for a specific treatment can be identified by adding a numerical subscript to the T. For example, the total for the second treatment in Table 13.2 is $T_2 = 20$.

5. The sum of all the scores in the experiment (the grand total) is identified by G. You can compute G by adding up all N scores or by adding up the treatment totals: $G = \Sigma T$.

6. Although there is no new notation involved, we also have computed SS and $\overline{X}$ for each sample, and we have calculated ΣX^2 for the entire set of $N = 15$ scores in the experiment. These values are given in Table 13.2 and will be important in the formulas and calculations for ANOVA.

Because ANOVA formulas require ΣX for each treatment and ΣX for the entire set of scores, we have introduced new notation (T and G) to help identify which ΣX is being used. Remember, T stands for *treatment total* and G stands for *grand total*.

ANOVA FORMULAS

Because analysis of variance requires extensive calculations and many formulas, one common problem for students is simply keeping track of the different formulas and numbers. Therefore, we will examine the general structure of the procedure and look at the organization of the calculations before we introduce the individual formulas.

Figure 13.3

The structure of ANOVA calculations.

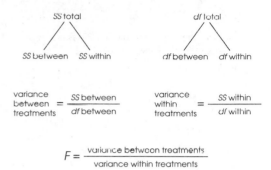

1. The final calculation for ANOVA is the *F*-ratio, which is composed of two variances:

$$F = \frac{\text{variance between treatments}}{\text{variance within treatments}}$$

2. You should recall that variance for sample data has been defined as

$$\text{sample variance} = s^2 = \frac{SS}{df}$$

Therefore, we will need to compute an *SS* and a *df* for the variance between treatments (numerator of *F*), and we will need another *SS* and *df* for the variance within treatments (denominator of *F*). To obtain these *SS* and *df* values, we must go through two separate analyses: First compute *SS* for the total experiment and analyze it into two components (between and within). Then, compute *df* for the total experiment and analyze it into two components (between and within).

Thus, the entire process of analysis of variance will require nine calculations: Three values for *SS*, three values for *df*, two variances (between and within), and a final *F*-ratio. However, these nine calculations are all logically related and are all directed toward finding the final *F*-ratio. Figure 13.3 shows the logical structure of ANOVA calculations.

ANALYSIS OF SUM OF SQUARES (SS)

The ANOVA requires that we first compute a total variability and then partition this value into two components: between treatments and within treatments. This analysis is outlined in Figure 13.4. We will examine each of the three components separately.

1. **Total Sum of Squares, SS_{total}.** As the name implies, SS_{total} is simply the sum of squares for the entire set of *N* scores. We calculate this value by using the computational formula for *SS*:

$$SS = \Sigma X^2 - \frac{(\Sigma X)^2}{N}$$

Figure 13.4

Partitioning the sum of squares *(SS)* for
the independent-measures analysis of
variance.

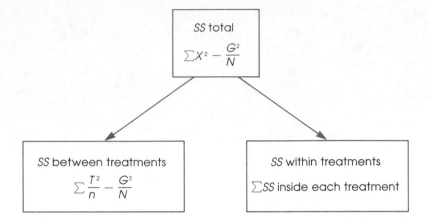

To make this formula consistent with the ANOVA notation, we substitute the
letter G in place of ΣX and obtain

$$SS_{\text{total}} = \Sigma X^2 - \frac{G^2}{N} \qquad\qquad (13.3)$$

Applying this formula to the set of data in Table 13.2, we obtain

$$SS_{\text{total}} = 106 - \frac{30^2}{15}$$

$$= 106 - 60$$

$$= 46$$

2. **Within-Treatments Sum of Squares, SS$_{\text{within}}$.** Now we are looking at the
variability inside each of the treatment conditions. We already have computed the SS within each of the three treatment conditions (Table 13.2):
$SS_1 = 6$, $SS_2 = 6$, and $SS_3 = 4$. To find the overall within treatment sum
of squares, we simply add these values together:

$$SS_{\text{within}} = \Sigma SS_{\text{inside each treatment}} \qquad\qquad (13.4)$$

For the data in Table 13.2, this formula gives

$$SS_{\text{within}} = 6 + 6 + 4$$

$$= 16$$

3. **Between-Treatments Sum of Squares, SS_{between}.** Before we introduce
the equation for SS_{between}, consider what we have found so far. The total
variability for the data in Table 13.2 is $SS_{\text{total}} = 46$. We intend to partition
this total into two parts (see Figure 13.3). One part, SS_{within}, has been
found to be equal to 16. This means that SS_{between} must be equal to 30 in
order for the two parts (16 and 30) to add up to the total (46). The equation for the between treatments sum of squares should produce a value of

---

 ALTERNATIVE FORMULA FOR SS_{within}

YOU SHOULD know that there is an alternative formula for finding SS_{within}. This formula is developed briefly in the following three steps:

1. First, recall that the two SS components add up to the total SS:

$$SS_{within} + SS_{between} = SS_{total}$$

2. By simple algebra we obtain the relation

$$SS_{within} = SS_{total} - SS_{between}$$

3. Finally, substituting the equations for SS_{total} and $SS_{between}$, we obtain

$$SS_{within} = \Sigma X^2 - \frac{G^2}{N} - \left(\Sigma \frac{T^2}{n} - \frac{G^2}{N}\right)$$

$$= \Sigma X^2 - \frac{G^2}{N} - \Sigma \frac{T^2}{n} + \frac{G^2}{N}$$

$$= \Sigma X^2 - \Sigma \frac{T^2}{n}$$

This alternative formula for SS_{within} can help simplify the calculations for ANOVA. To find all three SS values, you must compute only three numbers: ΣX^2, $\Sigma T^2/n$, and G^2/N. These three values are sufficient to satisfy the three SS formulas.

$SS_{between} = 30$. You should recall that the variability between treatments is measuring the differences between treatment means. Conceptually, the most direct way of measuring the amount of variability among the treatment means is to compute the sum of squares for the set of means but this method usually is awkward, especially when treatment means are not whole numbers. Therefore, we will use a computational formula for $SS_{between}$ that uses the treatment totals (T) instead of the treatment means.

$$SS_{between} = \Sigma \frac{T^2}{n} - \frac{G^2}{N} \tag{13.5}$$

You probably notice the general similarity between this formula and the one for SS_{total} (formula 13.3). The formula for $SS_{between}$, however, is based on squared treatment totals (T^2), and measures the variability between treatments.

Using this new formula with the data in Table 13.2, we obtain

$$SS_{between} = \frac{5^2}{5} + \frac{20^2}{5} + \frac{5^2}{5} - \frac{30^2}{15}$$

$$= 5 + 80 + 5 - 60$$

$$= 90 - 60$$

$$= 30$$

At this point of the analysis, the work may be checked to see if total SS equals between-treatments SS plus within-treatments SS.

The formula for each SS and the relationships among these three values are shown in Figure 13.4. An alternative formula for SS_{within} is developed in Box 13.1.

THE ANALYSIS OF DEGREES OF FREEDOM (df)

The analysis of degrees of freedom (df) follows the same pattern as the analysis of SS (see Figure 13.3). First, we will find df for the total set of N scores, and then we will partition this value into two components: degrees of freedom between treatments and degrees of freedom within treatments. In computing degrees of freedom, there are two important considerations to keep in mind:

1. Each df value is associated with a specific SS value.
2. Normally, the value of df is obtained by counting the number of items that were used to calculate SS and then subtracting 1. For example, if you compute SS for a set of n scores, then $df = n - 1$.

With this in mind, we will examine the degrees of freedom for each part of the analysis:

1. **Total Degrees of Freedom, df_{total}.** To find the df associated with SS_{total}, you must first recall that this SS value measures variability for the entire set of N scores. Therefore, the df value will be

$$df_{total} = N - 1 \qquad\qquad (13.6)$$

For the data in Table 13.2, the total number of scores is $N = 15$, so the total degrees of freedom would be

$$df_{total} = 15 - 1$$
$$= 14$$

2. **Within-Treatments Degrees of Freedom, df_{within}.** To find the df associated with SS_{within}, we must look at how this SS value is computed. Remember, we first find SS inside each of the treatments and then add these values together. Each of the treatment SS values measures variability for the n scores in the treatment, so each SS will have $df = n - 1$. When all these individual treatment values are added together, we obtain

$$df_{within} = \Sigma(n - 1) \qquad\qquad (13.7)$$

For the experiment we have been considering, each treatment has $n = 5$ scores. This means there are $n - 1 = 4$ degrees of freedom inside each treatment. Because there are three different treatment conditions, this gives a total of 12 for the within-treatments degrees of freedom. Notice that this formula for df simply adds up the number of scores in each treatment (the n values) and subtracts 1 for each treatment. If these two stages are done separately, you obtain

$$df_{within} = N - k \qquad\qquad (13.8)$$

(Adding up all the n values gives N. If you subtract 1 for each treatment, then altogether you have subtracted k because there are k treatments.) For the data in Table 13.2, $N = 15$ and $k = 3$, so

$$df_{within} = 15 - 3$$
$$= 12$$

3. **Between-Treatments Degrees of Freedom, $df_{between}$.** The df associated with $SS_{between}$ can be found by considering the SS formula. This SS formula measures the variability among the treatment means or totals. To find

Figure 13.5

Partitioning degrees of freedom *(df)* for the independent measures analysis of variance.

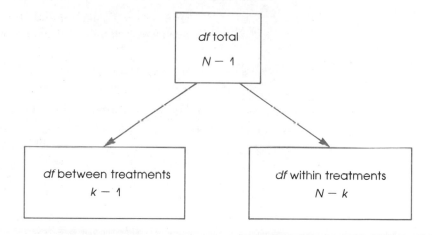

$df_{between}$, simply count the number of T values (or means) and subtract 1. Because the number of treatments is specified by the letter k, the formula for *df* is

$$df_{between} = k - 1 \tag{13.9}$$

For the data in Table 13.2, there are three different treatment conditions (three T values), so the between-treatments degrees of freedom is

$$df_{between} = 3 - 1$$

$$= 2$$

Notice that the two parts we obtained from this analysis of degrees of freedom add up to equal the total degrees of freedom:

$$df_{total} = df_{within} + df_{between}$$

$$14 = 12 + 2$$

The complete analysis of degrees of freedom is shown in Figure 13.5.

CALCULATION OF VARIANCES (*MS*) AND THE *F*-RATIO The final step in the analysis of variance procedure is to compute the variance between treatments and the variance within treatments in order to calculate the *F*-ratio (see Figure 13.3). You should recall (from Chapter 4) that variance is defined as the average squared deviation. For a sample, you compute this average by the following formula:

$$\text{variance} = \frac{SS}{n - 1} = \frac{SS}{df}$$

In ANOVA it is customary to use the term *mean square, or simply MS,* in place of the term *variance.* Note that variance is the *mean squared* deviation, so this terminology is quite sensible. For the final F-ratio you will need an MS between treatments and an MS within treatments. In each case,

$$MS = \frac{SS}{df} \tag{13.10}$$

For the data we have been considering,

$$MS_{\text{between}} = \frac{SS_{\text{between}}}{df_{\text{between}}} = \frac{30}{2} = 15$$

and

$$MS_{\text{within}} = \frac{SS_{\text{within}}}{df_{\text{within}}} = \frac{16}{12} = 1.33$$

We now have a measure of the variance (or differences) between the treatments and a measure of the variance within the treatments. The F-ratio simply compares these two variances:

$$F = \frac{MS_{\text{between}}}{MS_{\text{within}}} \tag{13.11}$$

For the experiment we have been examining, the data give an F-ratio of

$$F = \frac{15}{1.33} = 11.28$$

It is useful to organize the results of the analysis in one table called an *ANOVA summary table*. The table shows the source of variability (between-treatments, within-treatments, and total variability), *SS, df, MS,* and *F*. For the previous computations, the ANOVA summary table is constructed as follows:

SOURCE	SS	df	MS	
Between treatments	30	2	15	$F = 11.28$
Within treatments	16	12	1.33	
Total	46	14		

Although these tables are no longer commonly used in published reports, they do provide a concise method for presenting the results of an analysis. (Note that you can conveniently check your work: Adding the first two entries in the *SS* column (30 + 16) yields the total *SS*. The same applies to the *df* column.) When using analysis of variance, you might start with a blank ANOVA summary table and then fill in the values as they are calculated. With this method you will be less likely to "get lost" in the analysis, wondering what to do next.

   For this example, the obtained value of $F = 11.28$ indicates that the numerator of the F-ratio is substantially bigger than the denominator. If you recall the conceptual structure of the F-ratio as presented in formulas 13.1 and 13.2, the F value we obtained indicates that the differences between treatments are substantially greater than would be expected by chance, providing evidence that a treatment effect really exists. Stated in terms of the experimental variables, it appears that temperature does have an effect on learning performance. However, to properly evaluate the F-ratio, we must examine the F distribution.

SECTION 13.4 ## THE DISTRIBUTION OF F-RATIOS

In analysis of variance, the F-ratio is constructed so that the numerator and denominator of the ratio are measuring exactly the same variance when the null hypothesis is true (see formula 13.2). In this situation we expect the value of F to be around 1.00. The problem now is to define precisely what we mean by "around 1.00." What values are considered to be close to 1.00, and what values are far away? To answer this question, we need to look at all the possible F values, that is, the *distribution of F-ratios*.

Before we examine this distribution in detail, you should note two obvious characteristics:

1. Because F-ratios are computed from two variances (the numerator and denominator of the ratio), F values always will be positive numbers. Remember, variance is always positive.

2. When H_0 is true, the numerator and denominator of the F-ratio are measuring the same variance. In this case, the two sample variances should be about the same size, so the ratio should be near 1. In other words, the distribution of F-ratios should pile up around 1.00.

With these two factors in mind we can sketch the distribution of F-ratios. The distribution is cut off at zero (all positive values), piles up around 1.00, and then tapers off to the right (see Figure 13.6). The exact shape of the F distribution

Figure 13.6

The distribution of F-ratios with $df = 2, 12$. Of all the values in the distribution, only 5% are larger than $F - 3.88$, and only 1% are larger than $F = 6.93$.

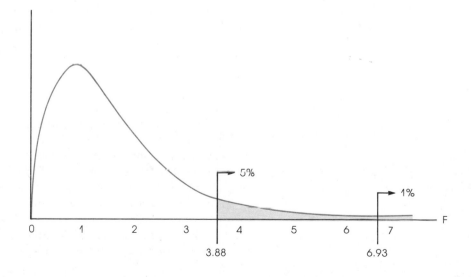

Table 13.3

A portion of the *F* distribution table. Entries in roman type are critical values for the .05 level of significance and bold type values are for the .01 level of significance.

DEGREES OF FREEDOM DENOMINATOR	DEGREES OF FREEDOM: NUMERATOR					
	1	2	3	4	5	6
10	4.96	4.10	3.71	3.48	3.33	3.22
	10.04	**7.56**	**6.55**	**5.99**	**5.64**	**5.39**
11	4.84	3.98	3.59	3.36	3.20	3.09
	9.65	**7.20**	**6.22**	**5.67**	**5.32**	**5.07**
12	4.75	3.88	3.49	3.26	3.11	3.00
	9.33	**6.93**	**5.95**	**5.41**	**5.06**	**4.82**
13	4.67	3.80	3.41	3.18	3.02	2.92
	9.07	**6.70**	**5.74**	**5.20**	**4.86**	**4.62**
14	4.60	3.74	3.34	3.11	2.96	2.85
	8.86	**6.51**	**5.56**	**5.03**	**4.69**	**4.46**

depends on the degrees of freedom for the two variances in the *F*-ratio. You should recall that the precision of a sample variance depends on the number of scores or the degrees of freedom. In general, the variance for a large sample (large *df*) provides a more accurate estimate of the population variance. Because the precision of the *MS* values depends on *df*, the shape of the *F* distribution also will depend on the *df* values for the numerator and denominator of the *F*-ratio. With very large *df* values, nearly all the *F*-ratios will be clustered very near to 1.00. With smaller *df* values, the *F* distribution is more spread out.

For analysis of variance we expect *F* near 1.00 if H_0 is true, and we expect a large value for *F* if H_0 is not true. In the *F* distribution, we need to separate those values that are reasonably near 1.00 from the values that are significantly greater than 1.00. These critical values are presented in an *F* distribution table in Appendix B, page A-28. To use the table, you must know the *df* values for the *F*-ratio (numerator and denominator), and you must know the alpha level for the hypothesis test. It is customary for an *F* table to have the *df* values for the numerator of the *F*-ratio printed across the top of the table. The *df* values for the denominator of *F* are printed in a column on the left-hand side. A portion of the *F* distribution table is shown in Table 13.3. For the temperature experiment we have been considering, the numerator of the *F*-ratio (between treatments) has *df* = 2 and the denominator of the *F*-ratio (within treatments) has *df* = 12. This *F*-ratio is said to have "degrees of freedom equal to 2 and 12." The degrees of freedom would be written as *df* = 2, 12. To use the table, you would first find *df* = 2 across the top of the table and *df* = 12 in the first column. When you line up these two values, they point to a pair of numbers in the middle of the table. These numbers give the critical cutoffs for α = .05 and α = .01. With *df* = 2, 12, for example, the numbers in the table are 3.88 and 6.93. These values indicate that the most unlikely 5% of the distribution (α = .05) begins at a value of 3.88. The most extreme 1% of the distribution begins at a value of 6.93 (see Figure 13.6).

In the temperature experiment we obtained an *F*-ratio of 11.28. According to the critical cutoffs in Figure 13.6, this value is extremely unlikely (it is in the most extreme 1%). Therefore, we would reject H_0 with α set at either .05 or .01 and conclude that temperature does have a significant effect on learning performance.

LEARNING CHECK

1. Calculate SS_{total}, $SS_{between}$, and SS_{within} for the following set of data:

TREATMENT 1	TREATMENT 2	TREATMENT 3	
$n = 10$	$n = 10$	$n = 10$	$N = 30$
$T = 10$	$T = 20$	$T = 30$	$G = 60$
$SS = 27$	$SS = 16$	$SS = 23$	$\Sigma X^2 = 206$

2. A researcher uses an ANOVA to compare three treatment conditions with a sample of $n = 8$ in each treatment. For this analysis, find df_{total}, $df_{between}$, and df_{within}.

3. With $\alpha = .05$, what value forms the boundary for the critical region in the distribution of F-ratios with $df = 2, 24$?

ANSWERS

1. $SS_{total} = 86$; $SS_{between} = 20$; $SS_{within} = 66$

2. $df_{total} = 23$, $df_{between} = 2$, and $df_{within} = 21$

3. The critical value is 3.40.

SECTION 13.5 EXAMPLES OF HYPOTHESIS TESTING WITH ANOVA

Although we have seen all the individual components of ANOVA, the following example demonstrates the complete ANOVA process using the standard four-step procedure for hypothesis testing.

EXAMPLE 13.1

The data depicted in Table 13.4 were obtained from an independent-measures experiment designed to measure the effectiveness of three pain relievers (A, B, and C). A fourth group that received a placebo (sugar pill) also was tested.

  The purpose of the analysis is to determine whether these sample data provide evidence of any significant differences among the four drugs. The dependent variable is the amount of time (in seconds) that subjects can withstand a painfully hot stimulus.

Table 13.4

The effect of drug treatment on the amount of time (in seconds) a stimulus is endured

PLACEBO	DRUG A	DRUG B	DRUG C	
0	0	3	8	$N = 12$
0	1	4	5	$G = 36$
3	2	5	5	$\Sigma X^2 = 178$
$T = 3$	$T = 3$	$T = 12$	$T = 18$	
$SS = 6$	$SS = 2$	$SS = 2$	$SS = 6$	

STEP 1 The first step is to state the hypotheses and select an alpha level:

$$H_0: \mu_1 = \mu_2 = \mu_3 = \mu_4 \quad \text{(no treatment effect)}$$

$$H_1: \text{At least one of the treatment means is different}$$

We will use $\alpha = .05$.

STEP 2 To locate the critical region for the F-ratio, we first must determine degrees of freedom for MS_{between} and MS_{within} (the numerator and denominator of F). For these data, the total degrees of freedom would be

$$df_{\text{total}} = N - 1$$
$$= 12 - 1$$
$$= 11$$

Analyzing this total into two components, we obtain

$$df_{\text{between}} = k - 1$$
$$= 4 - 1$$
$$= 3$$
$$df_{\text{within}} = N - k$$
$$= 12 - 4$$
$$= 8$$

The F-ratio for these data will have $df = 3, 8$. The distribution of all the possible F-ratios with $df = 3, 8$ is presented in Figure 13.7. Almost always (95% of the time) we should obtain an F-ratio less than 4.07 if H_0 is true.

STEP 3 We already have the data for this experiment, so it now is time for the calculations.

Analysis of SS: First we will compute the total SS and then the two components as indicated in Figure 13.3:

$$SS_{\text{total}} = \Sigma X^2 - \frac{G^2}{N}$$

$$= 178 - \frac{36^2}{12}$$

$$= 178 - 108$$

$$= 70$$

$$SS_{\text{within}} = \Sigma SS_{\text{inside each treatment}}$$

$$= 6 + 2 + 2 + 6$$

$$= 16$$

Figure 13.7

The distribution of *F*-ratios with $df = 3, 8$. The critical value for $\alpha = .05$ is $F = 4.07$.

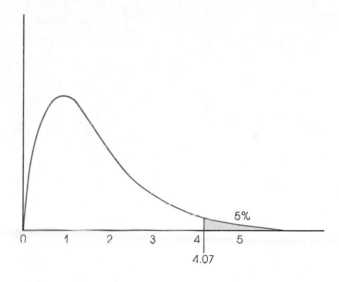

$$SS_{between} = \Sigma \frac{T^2}{n} - \frac{G^2}{N}$$

$$= \frac{3^2}{3} + \frac{3^2}{3} + \frac{12^2}{3} + \frac{18^2}{3} - \frac{36^2}{12}$$

$$= 3 + 3 + 48 + 108 - 108$$

$$= 54$$

Calculation of Mean Squares. Now we must compute the variance or *MS* for each of the two components:

$$MS_{between} = \frac{SS_{between}}{df_{between}} = \frac{54}{3} = 18$$

$$MS_{within} = \frac{SS_{within}}{df_{within}} = \frac{16}{8} = 2$$

Calculation of F. Finally, we compute the *F*-ratio:

$$F = \frac{MS_{between}}{MS_{within}} = \frac{18}{2} = 9.00$$

STEP 4 *Statistical Decision.* The *F* value we obtained, $F = 9.00$, is in the critical region (see Figure 13.7). It is very unlikely ($p < .05$) that we will obtain a value this large if H_0 is true. Therefore, we reject H_0 and conclude that there is a significant treatment effect.

Example 13.1 demonstrated the complete, step-by-step application of the ANOVA procedure. There are three additional points that can be made using this example.

First, you should look carefully at the statistical decision. We have rejected H_0 and concluded that not all the treatments are the same. But we have not determined which ones are different. Is drug A different from the placebo? Is drug A different from drug B? Unfortunately, these questions remain unanswered. We do know that at least one difference exists (we rejected H_0), but additional analysis is necessary to find out exactly where this difference is. This problem is addressed in Section 13.6.

Second, it is common in experimental reports to present the obtained F-ratio, the degrees of freedom, and the alpha level in one concise phrase. For the data in Example 13.1, this phrase would be

$$F(3, 8) = 9.00, p < .05$$

This phrase indicates that our F-ratio has $df = 3, 8$, we obtained a value of $F = 9.00$ from the data, and the F value was in the critical region with alpha equal to .05.

Third, the results can be presented in an analysis of variance summary table. The summary table for the analysis in Example 13.1 is as follows:

SOURCE	SS	df	MS	
Between treatments	54	3	18	$F = 9.00$
Within treatments	16	8	2	
Total	70	11		

AN EXAMPLE WITH UNEQUAL SAMPLE SIZES

In the previous example all the samples were exactly the same size (equal n's). However, the formulas for ANOVA can be used when the sample size varies within an experiment. With unequal sample sizes you must take care to be sure that each value of n is matched with the proper T value in the equations. You also should note that the general ANOVA procedure is most accurate when used to examine experimental data with equal sample sizes. Therefore, researchers generally try to plan experiments with equal n's. However, there are circumstances where it is impossible or impractical to have an equal number of subjects in every treatment condition. In these situations, ANOVA still provides a valid test, especially when the samples are relatively large and when the discrepancy between sample sizes is not extreme.

EXAMPLE 13.2

A psychologist conducts an experiment to compare learning performance for three species of monkeys. The animals are tested individually on a delayed-response task. A raisin is hidden in one of three containers while the animal is viewing from its cage window. A shade is then pulled over the window for 1 minute to block the view. After this delay period, the monkey is allowed to respond by tipping over one container. If its response is correct, the monkey

Table 13.5

The performance of different species of monkeys on a delayed-response task

VERVET	RHESUS	BABOON	
$n = 4$	$n = 10$	$n = 6$	$N = 20$
$\bar{X} = 9$	$\bar{X} = 14$	$\bar{X} = 4$	$G = 200$
$T = 36$	$T = 140$	$T = 24$	$\Sigma X^2 = 3400$
$SS = 200$	$SS = 500$	$SS = 320$	

is rewarded with the raisin. The number of trials it takes before the animal makes five consecutive correct responses is recorded. The experimenter used all of the available animals from each species, which resulted in unequal sample sizes (n). The data are summarized in Table 13.5.

STEP 1 *State hypothesis and select alpha.*

$H_0 : \mu_1 = \mu_2 = \mu_3$

H_1: At least one population is different from the others

$\alpha = .05$

STEP 2 *Locate the critical region.* To find the critical region, we first must determine the *df* values for the *F*-ratio:

$$df_{total} = N - 1 = 20 - 1 = 19$$
$$df_{between} = k - 1 = 3 - 1 = 2$$
$$df_{within} = N - k = 20 - 3 = 17$$

The *F*-ratio for these data will have $df = 2, 17$. With $\alpha = .05$, the critical value for the *F*-ratio is 3.59.

STEP 3 *Compute the F-ratio.* First compute *SS* for all three parts of the analysis:

$$SS_{total} = \Sigma X^2 - \frac{G^2}{N}$$
$$= 3400 - \frac{200^2}{20}$$
$$= 3400 - 2000$$
$$= 1400$$
$$SS_{between} = \Sigma \frac{T^2}{n} - \frac{G^2}{N} = \frac{T_1^2}{n_1} + \frac{T_2^2}{n_2} + \frac{T_3^2}{n_3} - \frac{G^2}{N}$$
$$= \frac{36^2}{4} + \frac{140^2}{10} + \frac{24^2}{6} - \frac{200^2}{20}$$
$$= 324 + 1960 + 96 - 2000$$
$$= 380$$
$$SS_{within} = \Sigma SS_{\text{inside each treatment}}$$
$$= 200 + 500 + 320$$
$$= 1020$$

Finally, compute the MS values and the F-ratio:

$$MS_{\text{between}} = \frac{SS}{df} = \frac{380}{2} = 190$$

$$MS_{\text{within}} = \frac{SS}{df} = \frac{1020}{17} = 60$$

$$F = \frac{MS_{\text{between}}}{MS_{\text{within}}} = \frac{190}{60} = 3.17$$

STEP 4   *Make a Decision.* Because the obtained F-ratio is not in the critical region, we fail to reject H_0 and conclude that these data do not provide evidence of significant differences among the three populations of monkeys in terms of average learning performance.

LEARNING CHECK   1. The following data sumarize the results of an experiment using three separate samples to compare three treatment conditions:

TREATMENT 1	TREATMENT 2	TREATMENT 3	
$n = 5$	$n = 5$	$n = 5$	
$T = 5$	$T = 10$	$T = 30$	$\Sigma X^2 = 325$
$SS = 45$	$SS = 25$	$SS = 50$	

Do these data provide evidence of any significant mean differences among the treatments? Test with $\alpha = .05$.

2. A researcher reports an F-ratio with $df = 2, 30$ for an independent-measures analysis of variance. How many treatment conditions were compared in the experiment? How many subjects participated in the experiment?

ANSWERS   1. The following summary table presents the results of the analysis:

SOURCE	SS	df	MS	
Between	70	2	35	$F = 3.5$
Within	120	12	10	
Total	190	14		

The critical value for F is 3.88. The obtained value for F is not in the critical region and we fail to reject H_0.

2. There were 3 treatment conditions ($df_{\text{between}} = k - 1 = 2$). A total of $N = 33$ individuals participated ($df_{\text{within}} = 30 = N - k$).

SECTION 13.6 **POST HOC TESTS**

In analysis of variance, the null hypothesis states that there is no treatment effect:

$$H_0: \mu_1 = \mu_2 = \mu_3.$$

When you reject the null hypothesis, you conclude that the means are not all the same. Although this appears to be a simple conclusion, in most cases it actually creates more questions than it answers. When there are only two treatments in an experiment, H_0 will state that $\mu_1 = \mu_2$. If you reject this hypothesis, the conclusion is quite straightforward; i.e., the two means are not equal ($\mu_1 \neq \mu_2$). However, when you have more than two treatments, the situation immediately becomes more complex. With $k = 3$, for example, rejecting H_0 indicates that not all the means are the same. Now you must decide which ones are different. Is μ_1 different from μ_2? Is μ_1 different from μ_3? Is μ_2 different from μ_3? Are all three different? The purpose of *post hoc tests* is to answer these questions.

As the name implies, post hoc tests are done after an analysis of variance. More specifically, these tests are done after ANOVA when

1. You reject H_0 and
2. There are three or more treatments ($k \geq 3$).

Rejecting H_0 indicates that at least one difference exists among the treatments. With $k = 3$ or more, the problem is to find where the differences are.

In general, a post hoc test enables you to go back through the data and compare the individual treatments two at a time. In statistical terms, this is called making *pairwise comparisons*. For example, with $k = 3$, we would compare μ_1 versus μ_2, then μ_2 versus μ_3, and then μ_1 versus μ_3. In each case, we are looking for a significant mean difference.

You might wonder why we do not perform *t* tests for all possible pairs of groups. This approach may cause a problem in avoiding Type I errors. Remember, each time you do a hypothesis test, you select an alpha level. For this reason, researchers often make a distinction between the *testwise* alpha level and the *experimentwise* alpha level. The testwise alpha level is simply the alpha level you select for each individual hypothesis test. The experimentwise alpha level is the total probability of a Type I error that is accumulated from all the separate tests in the experiment. It is the experimentwise alpha level that is most important when doing multiple comparisons between all possible pairs of groups. The more comparisons you make, the greater the experimentwise alpha level and the greater the risk of a Type I error. The problem with simply doing *t* tests for all possible pairs of treatment groups is that the experimentwise alpha level may be quite large.

Fortunately, many post hoc tests have been developed that attempt to control the experimentwise alpha level. We will examine one of these commonly used procedures, the Scheffé test.

THE SCHEFFÉ TEST

Because it uses an extremely cautious method for reducing the risk of a Type I error, the *Scheffé test* has the distinction of being one of the safest of all possible post hoc tests. The Scheffé test uses an *F*-ratio to test for a significant difference between any

Table 13.6

Pain threshold data for four different pain relievers.

	PLACEBO	DRUG A	DRUG B	DRUG C
	$n = 3$	$n = 3$	$n = 3$	$n = 3$
	$T = 3$	$T = 3$	$T = 12$	$T = 18$
	$\overline{X} = 1$	$\overline{X} = 1$	$\overline{X} = 4$	$\overline{X} = 6$

two treatment conditions. The numerator of the F-ratio is an MS between treatments that is calculated using *only the two treatments you want to compare*. The denominator is the same MS within treatments that was used for the overall ANOVA. The "safety factor" for the Scheffé test comes from the following two considerations:

1. Although you are comparing only two treatments, the Scheffé test uses the value of k from the original experiment to compute df between treatments. Thus, df for the numerator of the F-ratio is $k - 1$.

2. The critical value for the Scheffé F-ratio is the same as was used to evaluate the F-ratio from the overall ANOVA. Thus, Scheffé requires that every posttest satisfy the same criteria used for the complete analysis of variance. The following example uses the data from Example 13.1 (Table 13.6) to demonstrate the Scheffé posttest procedure.

E X A M P L E   1 3 . 3

Rather than test all the possible comparisons of the four treatment conditions shown in Table 13.6, we will begin with the largest mean difference and then test progressively smaller differences until we find one that is not significant. For these data, the largest difference is between the placebo ($T = 3$) and drug C ($T = 18$). The first step is to compute $SS_{between}$ for these two treatments.

The grand total, G, for these two treatments is found by adding the two treatment totals ($G = 3 + 18$), and N is found by adding the number of scores in the two treatments ($N = 3 + 3$).

$$SS_{between} = \Sigma \frac{T^2}{n} - \frac{G^2}{N}$$
$$= \frac{3^2}{3} + \frac{18^2}{3} - \frac{21^2}{6}$$
$$= 37.5$$

Although we are comparing only two treatments, these two were selected from an experiment consisting of $k = 4$ treatments. The Scheffé test uses the overall experiment ($k = 4$) to determine the degrees of freedom between treatments. Therefore, $df_{between} = k - 1 = 3$, and the MS between treatments is

$$MS_{between} = \frac{SS_{between}}{df_{between}} = \frac{37.5}{3} = 12.5$$

Scheffé also uses the within-treatments variance from the complete experiment, $MS_{within} = 2.00$ with $df = 8$, so the Scheffé F-ratio is

$$F = \frac{MS_{between}}{MS_{within}} = \frac{12.5}{2} = 6.25$$

With $df = 3, 8$ and $\alpha = .05$, the critical value for F is 4.07 (see Table B.4). Therefore, our F-ratio is in the critical region and we conclude that there is a significant difference between the placebo and drug C. Because the data for drug A and the placebo are equivalent (both have $T = 3$), we also conclude that drug C is significantly different from drug A.

Next, we consider the second largest mean difference for the data: Drug B ($T = 12$) versus the placebo ($T = 3$). Again, we compute $SS_{between}$ using only these two treatment groups.

$$SS_{between} = \Sigma \frac{T^2}{n} - \frac{G^2}{N}$$

$$= \frac{3^2}{3} + \frac{12^2}{3} - \frac{15^2}{6}$$

$$= 13.5$$

As before, the Scheffé test uses the overall experiment ($k = 4$) to determine df between treatments. Thus $df_{between} = k - 1 = 3$, and $MS_{between}$ for this comparison is

$$MS_{between} = \frac{SS_{between}}{df_{between}} = \frac{13.5}{3} = 4.5$$

Using $MS_{within} = 2$ with $df = 8$, we obtain a Scheffé F-ratio of

$$F = \frac{MS_{between}}{MS_{within}} = \frac{4.5}{2} = 2.25$$

With $df = 3, 8$ and $\alpha = .05$ the obtained F-ratio is less than the critical value of 4.07. Because the F-ratio is not in the critical region, our decision is that these data do not provide sufficient evidence to conclude that there is a significant difference between the placebo and drug B. Because the mean difference between the placebo and drug B is larger than any of the remaining pairs of treatments, we can conclude that none of the other pairwise comparisons would be significant with the Scheffé test.

Thus the conclusion from the Scheffé posttest is that drug C is significantly different from both the placebo and drug A. These are the only significant differences for this experiment (using Scheffé), and these differences are the source of the significant F-ratio obtained for the overall ANOVA.

SECTION 13.7 **THE RELATION BETWEEN ANOVA AND *t* TESTS**

When you have data from an independent-measures experiment with only two treatment conditions, you can use either a *t* test (Chapter 10) or independent-measures ANOVA. In practical terms, it makes no difference which you choose. These two statistical techniques always will result in the same statistical decision.

In fact, the two methods use many of the same calculations and are very closely related in several other respects. The basic relation between t statistics and F-ratios can be stated in an equation:

$$F = t^2$$

This relation can be explained by first looking at the structure of the formulas for F and t.

The structure of the t statistic compares the actual difference between the samples (numerator) with the standard difference that would be expected by chance (denominator).

$$t = \frac{\text{mean difference}}{\text{standard error}} = \frac{\text{difference between samples}}{\text{difference expected by chance}}$$

The structure of the F-ratio also compares differences between samples versus the difference due to chance or error.

$$F = \frac{\text{variability between treatments}}{\text{variability within treatments}}$$

However, the numerator and denominator of the F-ratio measure variances, or mean squared differences. Therefore, we can express the F-ratio as follows:

$$F = \frac{(\text{differences between samples})^2}{(\text{differences expected by chance})^2}$$

The fact that the t statistic is based on differences and the F-ratio is based on *squared* differences leads to the basic relation $F = t^2$.

There are several other points to consider in comparing the t statistic to the F-ratio.

1. It should be obvious that you will be testing the same hypotheses whether you choose a t test or ANOVA. With only two treatments, the hypotheses for either test are

   $$H_0: \mu_1 = \mu_2$$

   $$H_1: \mu_1 \neq \mu_2$$

2. The degrees of freedom for the t statistic and the df for the denominator of the F-ratio (df_{within}) are identical. For example, if you have two samples, each with six scores, the independent-measures t statistic will have $df = 10$, and the F-ratio will have $df = 1, 10$. In each case, you are adding the df from the first sample ($n - 1$) and the df from the second sample.

3. The distribution of t and the distribution of F-ratios match perfectly if you take into consideration the relation $F = t^2$. Consider the t distribution with $df = 18$ and the corresponding F distribution with $df = 1, 18$ that are presented in Figure 13.8. Notice the following relations:

   a. If each of the t values is squared, then all of the negative values will become positive. As a result, the whole left-hand side of the t distribu-

Figure 13.8

The distribution of *t*-scores with *df* = 18 and the corresponding distribution of *F*-ratios with *df* = 1, 18. Notice that the critical values for α = .05 are *t* = ±2.101 and that *F* = 2.101² = 4.41.

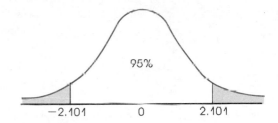

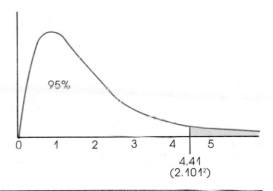

tion (below zero) will be flipped over to the positive side. This creates a nonsymmetrical, positively skewed distribution, that is, the *F* distribution.

b. For α = .05, the critical region for *t* is determined by values greater than +2.101 or less than −2.101. When these boundaries are squared, you get

$$\pm 2.101^2 = 4.41$$

Notice that 4.41 is the critical value for α = .05 in the *F* distribution. Any value that is in the critical region for *t* will end up in the critical region for *F* ratios after it is squared.

4. There are two basic assumptions that must be satisfied for the independent-measures ANOVA to be valid. The first assumption is that the population distribution for each treatment condition is normal. For the other assumption to be met, the population variances for all treatments should be equal (homogeneity of variance). These conditions are the same as those required for the independent measures *t* test (Chapter 10).

Ordinarily, researchers are not overly concerned with the assumption of normality, especially when large samples are used, unless there are strong reasons to suspect the assumption has not been satisfied. The assumption of homogeneity of variance is an important one. If a researcher suspects it has been violated, it can be tested by Hartley's *F*-max test for homogeneity of variance (Chapter 10, page 228).

LEARNING CHECK 1. The Scheffé post hoc test uses between-treatments *df* from the original ANOVA even though SS_{between} is calculated for a pair of treatments. (True or False)

2. An ANOVA produces an F-ratio with $df = 1, 34$. Could the data have been analyzed with a t test? What would be the degrees of freedom for the t statistic?

3. With $k = 2$ treatments, are post hoc tests necessary when the null hypothesis is rejected? Explain why or why not.

ANSWERS 1. True.

2. If the F-ratio has $df = 1, 34$, then the experiment compared only two treatments, and you could use a t statistic to evaluate the data. The t statistic would have $df = 34$.

3. No. Post hoc tests are used to determine which treatments are different. With only two treatment conditions, there is no uncertainty as to which two treatments are different.

SUMMARY

1. Analysis of variance is a statistical technique that is used to test for mean differences among two or more treatment conditions or among two or more populations. The null hypothesis for this test states that there are no differences among the population means. The alternative hypothesis states that at least one mean is different from the others. Although analysis of variance can be used with either an independent- or a repeated-measures experiment, this chapter examined only independent measures designs, that is, experiments with a separate sample for each treatment condition.

2. The test statistic for analysis of variance is a ratio of two variances called an F-ratio. The F-ratio is structured so that the numerator and denominator measure the same variance when the null hypothesis is true. In this way, the existence of a significant treatment effect is apparent if the data produce an "unbalanced" F-ratio. The variances in the F-ratio are called mean squares, or MS values. Each MS is computed by

$$MS = \frac{SS}{df}$$

3. For the independent-measures analysis of variance, the F-ratio is

$$F = \frac{MS_{between}}{MS_{within}}$$

The $MS_{between}$ measures differences among the treatments by computing the variability of the treatment means or totals. These differences are assumed to be produced by three factors.
a. Treatment effects (if they exist)
b. Individual differences
c. Experimental error

The MS_{within} measures variability inside each of the treatment conditions. This variability is assumed to be produced by two factors:
a. Individual differences
b. Experimental error

With these factors in mind, the F-ratio has the following structure

$$F = \frac{\text{treatment effect} + \text{individual diff's.} + \text{experimental error}}{\text{individual diff's.} + \text{experimental error}}$$

When there is no treatment effect (H_0 is true), the numerator and denominator of the F-ratio are measuring the same variance, and the obtained ratio should be near 1.00. If there is a significant treatment effect, the numerator of the ratio should be larger than the denominator, and the obtained F value should be much greater than 1.00.

4. The formulas for computing each SS, df, and MS value are presented in Figure 13.9, which also shows the general structure for the analysis of variance.

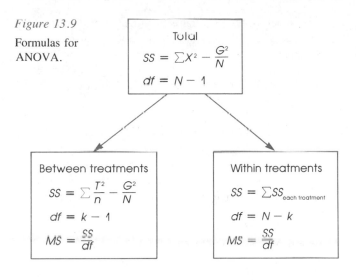

Figure 13.9
Formulas for ANOVA.

5. The *F*-ratio has two values for degrees of freedom, one associated with the *MS* in the numerator and one associated with the *MS* in the denominator. These *df* values are used to find the critical value for the *F*-ratio in the *F* distribution table.

6. When the decision from an analysis of variance is to reject the null hypothesis and when the experiment contained more than two treatment conditions, it is necessary to continue the analysis with a post hoc test such as the Scheffé test. The purpose of this test is to determine exactly which treatments are significantly different and which are not.

KEY TERMS

analysis of variance (ANOVA)	individual differences	factor	distribution of *F*-ratios
between-treatments variability	experimental error	levels	post hoc tests
within-treatments variability	*F*-ratio	mean square (*MS*)	Scheffé test
treatment effect	error term	ANOVA summary table	

FOCUS ON PROBLEM SOLVING

1. The words and labels used to describe the different components of variance can help you remember the ANOVA formulas. For example, *total* refers to the total experiment. Therefore, the SS_{total} and df_{total} values are based on the whole set of *N* scores. The word *within* refers to the variability inside (within) the treatment groups. Thus, the value for SS_{within} is based on an *SS* value from each group, computed from the scores *within* each group. Finally, *between* refers to the variability (or differences) between treatments. The $SS_{between}$ component measures the differences between treatments (T_1 versus T_2, and so on), and $df_{between}$ is simply the number of *T* values (*k*) minus one.

2. When you are computing *SS* and *df* values, always calculate all three components (total, between, and within) separately, then check your work by making sure that the *between-treatments* and *within-treatments* components add up to the *total*.

3. Because ANOVA requires a fairly lengthy series of calculations, it helps to organize your work. We suggest that you compute all of the *SS* values first, followed by the *df* values, then the two *MS* values, and finally the *F*-ratio. If you use the same system all the time (practice it!), you will be less likely to get lost in the middle of a problem.

4. The previous two focus points are facilitated by using an ANOVA summary table (for example, see page 300). The first column has the heading *source*. Listed below the heading are the three sources of variability (between, within, and total). The second and third columns have the heading *SS* and *df*. These can be filled in as you perform the appropriate computations. The last column is headed *MS* for the mean square values.

5. Remember that an *F*-ratio has two separate values for *df*: A value for the numerator and one for the denominator. Properly reported, the $df_{between}$ value is stated first. You will need both *df* values when consulting the *F* distribution table for the critical *F* value. You should recognize immediately that an error has been made if you see an *F*-ratio reported with a single value for *df*.

6. When you encounter an *F*-ratio and its *df* values reported in the literature, you should be able to recon-struct much of the original experiment. For example, if you see "$F(2, 36) = 4.80$," you should realize that the experiment compared $k = 3$ treatment groups (because $df_{between} = k - 1 = 2$), with a total of $N = 39$ subjects participating in the experiment (because $df_{within} = N - k = 36$).

7. Keep in mind that a large value for *F* indicates evidence for a treatment effect. A combination of factors will yield a large *F* value. One such factor is a large value for $MS_{between}$ in the numerator of the ratio. This will occur when there are large differences between groups, as would be expected when a treatment effect occurs. Another factor that contributes to a large *F* value would be a small value for MS_{within} on the bottom of the *F* ratio. This will occur when there is a little error variability, reflected in low variability within groups.

DEMONSTRATION 13.1   ANALYSIS OF VARIANCE

A human factors psychologist studied three computer keyboard designs. Three samples of individuals were given material to type on a particular keyboard and the number of errors committed by each subject was recorded. The data are as follows:

         Keyboard A: 0 4 0 1 0
         Keyboard B: 6 8 5 4 2
         Keyboard C: 6 5 9 4 6

Does typing performance differ significantly among the three types of keyboards?

STEP 1   State the hypotheses and specify alpha.
         The null hypothesis states that there is no difference among the keyboards in terms of number of errors committed. In symbols, we would state

H_0: $\mu_1 = \mu_2 = \mu_3$ (there is no effect of type of keyboard used)

As noted previously in this chapter, there are a number of possible statements for the alternative hypothesis. Here, we state the general alternative hypothesis.

H_1: At least one of the treatment means is different.

That is, there is an effect of the type of keyboard on typing performance. We will set alpha at $\alpha = .05$.

STEP 2   Locate the critical region.
         To locate the critical regions, we must obtain the values for $df_{between}$ and df_{within}.

$$df_{\text{between}} = k - 1 = 3 - 1 = 2$$

$$df_{\text{within}} = N - k = 15 - 3 = 12$$

The F-ratio for this problem will have $df = 2, 12$. The F distribution table is consulted for $df = 2$ in the numerator and $df = 12$ in the denominator. The critical F value for $\alpha = .05$ is $F = 3.88$. The obtained F ratio must exceed this value to reject H_0.

STEP 3 Perform the analysis.

The analysis involves the following steps:
1. Compute T and SS for each sample and obtain G and ΣX^2 for all ($N = 15$) scores.
2. Perform the analysis of SS.
3. Perform the analysis of df.
4. Calculate mean squares.
5. Calculate the F-ratio.

Compute T, SS, G and ΣX^2. We will use the computational formula for the SS of each sample. The calculations are illustrated with the following tables.

KEYBOARD A		KEYBOARD B		KEYBOARD C	
X	X^2	X	X^2	X	X^2
0	0	6	36	6	36
4	16	8	64	5	25
0	0	5	25	9	81
1	1	4	16	4	16
0	0	2	4	6	36
$\Sigma X = 5$	$\Sigma X^2 = 17$	$\Sigma X = 25$	$\Sigma X^2 = 145$	$\Sigma X = 30$	$\Sigma X^2 = 194$

For Keyboard A, T and SS are computed using only the $n = 5$ scores of this sample:

$$T_1 = \Sigma X = 0 + 4 + 0 + 1 + 0 = 5$$

$$SS_1 = \Sigma X^2 - \frac{(\Sigma X)^2}{n} = 17 - \frac{(5)^2}{5} = 17 - \frac{25}{5} = 17 - 5$$

$$= 12$$

For Keyboard B, T and SS are computed for its $n = 5$ scores:

$$T_2 = \Sigma X = 25$$

$$SS_2 = \Sigma X^2 - \frac{(\Sigma X)^2}{n} = 145 - \frac{(25)^2}{5} = 145 - \frac{625}{5} = 145 - 125$$

$$= 20$$

For the last sample, Keyboard C, we obtain:

$$T_3 = \Sigma X = 30$$

$$SS_3 = \Sigma X^2 - \frac{(\Sigma X)^2}{n} = 194 - \frac{(30)^2}{5} = 194 - \frac{900}{5} = 194 - 180$$

$$= 14$$

The grand total (G) for $N = 15$ scores is

$$G = \Sigma T = 5 + 25 + 30 = 60$$

The ΣX^2 for all $N = 15$ scores in this study can be obtained by summing the X^2 columns for the three samples. For these data we obtain

$$\Sigma X^2 = 17 + 145 + 194 = 356$$

Perform the analysis of SS. We will compute SS_{total} followed by its two components.

$$SS_{\text{total}} = \Sigma X^2 - \frac{G^2}{N} = 356 - \frac{60^2}{15} = 356 - \frac{3600}{15}$$

$$= 356 - 240 = 116$$

$$SS_{\text{within}} = \Sigma SS_{\text{inside each treatment}}$$

$$= 12 + 20 + 14$$

$$= 46$$

$$SS_{\text{between}} = \Sigma \frac{T^2}{n} - \frac{G^2}{N}$$

$$= \frac{5^2}{5} + \frac{25^2}{5} + \frac{30^2}{5} - \frac{60^2}{15}$$

$$= \frac{25}{5} + \frac{625}{5} + \frac{900}{5} - \frac{3600}{15}$$

$$= 5 + 125 + 180 - 240$$

$$= 70$$

Analyze degrees of freedom. We will compute df_{total}. Its components, df_{between} and df_{within}, were previously calculated (Step 2).

$$df_{\text{total}} = N - 1 = 15 - 1 = 14$$

$$df_{\text{between}} = 2$$

$$df_{\text{within}} = 12$$

Calculate the MS values. The values for MS_{between} and MS_{within} are determined.

$$MS_{\text{between}} = \frac{SS_{\text{between}}}{df_{\text{between}}} = \frac{70}{2} = 35$$

$$MS_{\text{within}} = \frac{SS_{\text{within}}}{df_{\text{within}}} = \frac{46}{12} = 3.83$$

Compute the F-ratio. Finally, we can compute *F*.

$$F = \frac{MS_{between}}{MS_{within}} = \frac{35}{3.83} = 9.14$$

STEP 4   Make a decision about H_0 and state a conclusion.
   The obtained *F* of 9.14 exceeds the critical value of 3.88. Therefore, we can reject the null hypothesis. The type of keyboard used has a significant effect of the number of errors committed, $F(2,12) = 9.14$, $p < .05$. The following table summarizes the results of the analysis.

SOURCE	SS	df	MS	
Between treatments	70	2	35	$F = 9.14$
Within treatments	46	12	3.83	
Total	116	14		

PROBLEMS

1. Why is the expected value for an *F*-ratio equal to 1.00 when there is no treatment effect?

2. Describe the similarities between an *F*-ratio and a *t* statistic.

3. A social psychologist would like to examine the relationship between personal appearance and authority. A special questionnaire is prepared, which requires very careful attention to instructions in order to fill it in correctly. Three random samples of college students are obtained. For the first group the psychologist dresses very causally (blue jeans and T-shirt) when the questionnaire is administered. For the second sample, the psychologist wears a suit, and for the third sample the psychologist wears a very "scientific" laboratory coat. The psychologist records the number of errors made by each individual while completing the questionnaire. These data are as follows:

BLUE JEANS	SUIT	LAB COAT	
5	3	1	
2	3	0	
2	0	1	$G = 30$
4	2	2	$\Sigma X^2 = 86$
2	2	1	
$T = 15$	$T = 10$	$T = 5$	
$SS = 8$	$SS = 6$	$SS = 2$	

Should the psychologist conclude that appearance had an influence on the amount of attention people paid to the instructions? Test at the .05 level of significance.

4. A psychologist would like to examine how the rate of presentation affects people's ability to memorize a list of words. A list of 20 words is prepared. For one group of subjects the list is presented at the rate of one word every ½ second. The next group gets one word every second. The third group has one word every 2 second, and the fourth group has one word every 3 seconds. After the list is presented, the psychologist asks each person to recall the entire list. The dependent variable is the number of errors in recall. The data from this experiment are as follows:

½ SEC.	1 SEC.	2 SEC.	3 SEC.	
4	0	3	0	
6	2	1	2	$G = 32$
2	2	2	1	
4	0	2	1	$\Sigma X^2 = 104$
$T = 16$	$T = 4$	$T = 8$	$T = 4$	
$SS = 8$	$SS = 4$	$SS = 2$	$SS = 2$	

a. Can the psychologist conclude that the rate of presentation has a significant effect on memory? Test at the .05 level.

b. Use the Scheffé test to determine which rates of presentation are statistically different and which are not.

5. The following data represent scores from three different treatment conditions.

TREATMENT 1	TREATMENT 2	TREATMENT 3	
1	3	2	$N = 12$
1	3	2	$\Sigma X^2 = 56$
1	3	2	$G = 24$
1	3	2	
$T = 4$	$T = 12$	$T = 8$	

a. Just looking at the data, describe the relative amount of variability between treatments versus within treatments.

b. Calculate SS_{total}, $SS_{between}$, and SS_{within}. You should find that all of the variability for these data comes from differences between treatments.

6. A psychologist would like to show that background noise can interfere with a student's concentration and therefore cause poorer performance on complex mental tasks. A sample of 12 students is obtained, and the psychologist randomly assigns these students to three separate groups. Each group is given a standard problem-solving task. One group works on this task under quiet conditions, one group works with soft background music, and the third group works with a loud radio tuned to a popular rock station. For each student the psychologist measures the number of errors on the task. The results from this experiment are summarized as follows:

QUIET	SOFT MUSIC	LOUD MUSIC	
$n = 4$	$n = 4$	$n = 4$	$\Sigma X^2 = 71$
$T = 4$	$T = 6$	$T = 14$	
$SS = 2$	$SS = 4$	$SS = 3$	

Can the psychologist conclude that the background noise had an effect on performance? Test at the .05 level of significance.

7. A psychologist using an independent-measures experimental design to compare different teaching methods reports an F-ratio of $F = 3.87$ with $df = 3, 28$.

a. How many teaching methods (treatments) were being compared?

b. How many subjects participated in the total experiment?

c. Were there significant differences among the teaching methods?

8. The following data represent the results of an independent-measures experiment comparing two treatment conditions.

TREATMENT 1	TREATMENT 2
1	5
2	4
2	3
4	2
1	6

a. Use an analysis of variance with $\alpha = .05$ to test for a significant difference between the two treatment means.

b. Use an independent-measures t statistic to test for a significant difference. (Remember, you should find the basic relation, $F = t^2$.)

9. Use an analysis of variance with $\alpha = .05$ to determine whether the following data provide evidence of any significant differences among the three treatments:

TREATMENT 1	TREATMENT 2	TREATMENT 3	
$n = 4$	$n = 5$	$n = 6$	$N = 15$
$T = 2$	$T = 10$	$T = 18$	$G = 30$
$SS = 13$	$SS = 21$	$SS = 26$	$\Sigma X^2 = 135$

10. A pharmaceutical company has developed a drug that is expected to reduce hunger. To test the drug, three samples of rats are selected with $n = 10$ in each sample. The first sample receives the drug every day. The second sample is given the drug once a week, and the third sample receives no drug at all. The dependent variable is the amount of food eaten by each rat over a 1-month period. These data are analyzed by an analysis of variance, and the results are reported in the following summary table. Fill in all missing values in the table. (*Hint:* Start with the *df* column.)

SOURCE	SS	df	MS	
Between treatments	24	___	___	$F =$ ___
Within treatments	___	___	2	
Total	___	___		

11. The following summary table presents the results of an ANOVA from an experiment comparing four treatment conditions with a sample of $n = 10$ in each treatment. Complete all missing values in the table.

SOURCE	SS	df	MS	
Between treatments	___	___	___	$F = 8.00$
Within treatments	72	___	___	
Total	___	___		

12. A developmental psychologist is examining problem-solving ability for grade school children. Random samples of 5-year-old, 6-year-old, and 7-year-old children are obtained with $n = 3$ in each sample. Each child is given a standardized problem-solving task, and the psychologist records the number of errors. These data are as follows:

5-YEAR-OLDS	6-YEAR-OLDS	7-YEAR-OLDS	
5	6	0	$G = 30$
4	4	1	$\Sigma X^2 = 138$
6	2	2	
$T = 15$	$T = 12$	$T = 3$	
$SS = 2$	$SS = 8$	$SS = 2$	

  a. Use these data to test whether there are any significant differences among the three age groups. Use $\alpha = .05$.
  b. Use the Scheffé test to determine which groups are different.

13. A researcher would like to know whether infants can be affected by alcohol consumed by a mother during pregnancy. A sample of 24 pregnant rats is obtained. The researcher randomly divides these rats into four groups with $n = 6$ in each group. All groups receive the same diet of rat chow but during the last 2 weeks of pregnancy one group has ¼ ounce of vodka mixed with their food. The second group receives ½ ounce, the third group receives 1 ounce, and the final group has no alcohol. One of the offspring of each rat is randomly selected to be weighed at birth. The data were examined using an ANOVA, and the results are summarized in the following table. Fill in all missing values.

SOURCE	SS	df	MS	
Between treatments	___	___	10	$F = $___
Within treatments	40	___	___	
Total	___	___		

14. A psychologist would like to demonstrate that the combination of two drugs can often produce much different effects than either of the drugs taken separately. Four random samples are selected with $n = 5$ in each sample. One group is given a sugar pill (no drug), one group is given drug A, another group is given drug B, and the final group is given drugs A and B together. Each person is then given a logic test measuring basic reasoning ability. The data are summarized as follows:

SUGAR PILL	DRUG A	DRUG B	DRUGS A AND B	
$T = 0$	$T = 5$	$T = 5$	$T = 20$	$\Sigma X^2 = 122$
$SS = 7$	$SS = 8$	$SS = 7$	$SS = 10$	

  a. Can the psychologist conclude that there are any significant differences among the treatments? Test at the .05 level.
  b. Use the Scheffé test to determine which treatments are different.

15. Several studies indicate that handedness (left-handed/right-handed) is related to differences in brain function. Because different parts of the brain are specialized for specific behaviors, this means that left- and right-handed people should show different skills or talents. To test this hypothesis, a psychologist tested pitch discrimination (a component of musical ability) for three groups of subjects: left-handed, right-handed, and ambidextrous. The data from this study are as follows:

RIGHT-HANDED	LEFT-HANDED	AMBIDEXTROUS	
6	1	2	
4	0	0	$G = 30$
3	1	0	$\Sigma X^2 = 102$
4	1	2	
3	2	1	
$T = 20$	$T = 5$	$T = 5$	
$SS = 6$	$SS = 2$	$SS = 4$	

Each score represents the number of errors during a series of pitch discrimination trials.

a. Do these-data indicate any differences among the three groups? Test with $\alpha = .05$.

b. Use the F-max test to determine whether these data satisfy the homogeneity of variance assumption (see Chapter 10).

16. In a paired-associate learning task, subjects are required to learn pairs of words. The first word in each pair is called the stimulus word, and the second is the response word. On each trial, the experimenter presents the stimulus word and asks the subject to recall the correct response. If the subject fails, the correct response word is given, and the experimenter continues through the list. The dependent variable is the number of times the experimenter must go through the entire list before the subject can recall all response words perfectly. This task often is used to demonstrate the effectiveness of mental imagery as an aid to memory. In a typical experiment, subjects in one group are instructed to form a mental image combining the two words in each pair. A second group is instructed to form a sentence that uses both of the words. A third group receives no special instructions. The data from this experiment are as follows:

NO INSTRUCTIONS			IMAGES			SENTENCES		
6	7	5	3	6	5	5	8	6
5	8	10	5	3	4	4	5	8
8	9	10	4	5	3	5	10	9

a. Compute the mean for each treatment. Draw a bar graph of these means. (See Chapter 2 for assistance.)

b. Do the data indicate significant differences among the instruction groups? Test with alpha set at .05.

c. Use the Scheffé test to determine which groups are different.

d. In a few sentences, explain what happened in this study.

17. Betz and Thomas (1979) have reported a distinct connection between personality and health. They identified three personality types who differ in their susceptibility to serious, stress-related illness (heart attack, high blood pressure, etc.). The three personality types are Alphas, who are cautious and steady; Betas, who

are carefree and outgoing; and Gammas, who tend toward extremes of behavior such as being overly cautious or very careless. Sample data representing general health scores for each of these three groups are as follows. A low score indicates poor health.

ALPHAS		BETAS		GAMMAS	
43	44	41	52	36	29
41	56	40	57	38	36
49	42	36	48	45	42
52	53	51	55	25	40
41	21	52	39	41	36

a. Compute the mean for each personality type. Do these data indicate a significant difference among the three types? Test with $\alpha = .05$.

b. Use the Scheffé test to determine which groups are different. Explain what happened in this study.

18. Do weather conditions affect people's moods? To examine this question, a researcher selected three samples of college students and administered a mood inventory questionnaire to each student. One group was tested on a dreary, overcast, and drizzly day. The second group was tested during a violent thunderstorm, and the third group was tested on a bright sunny day. The data are as follows:

DREARY		STORMY		BRIGHT	
6	9	8	12	13	10
10	12	10	6	6	13
5	7	8	9	10	8
12	8	14	10	9	12
7	10	7	7	15	11

Do these data indicate that weather has an effect on mood? Test at the .05 level of significance.

19. A psychologist is interested in the extent to which physical attractiveness can influence judgment of other personal characteristics such as intelligence or ability. The psychologist selected three groups of subjects who were to play the role of a company personnel manager. Each subject was given a stack of job applications which included a photograph of the applicant. One of these applications was previously selected as the test stimulus. For one group of subjects, this application contained a photograph of a very attractive woman. For the second group, the photograph was of an average-looking woman. For the third group, a photo of a very unattractive woman was attached to the application. The subjects were instructed to rate the quality of each job applicant (0 = "very poor" to 10 = "excellent"). The psychologist recorded the rating of the test stimulus for each subject. These data are as follows:

ATTRACTIVE			AVERAGE			UNATTRACTIVE		
5	4	4	6	5	3	4	3	1
3	5	6	6	6	7	3	1	2
4	3	8	5	4	6	2	4	3
3	5	4	8	7	8	2	1	2

a. Compute the means of the groups and draw a graph showing the results.

b. Use an ANOVA with $\alpha - .05$ to determine whether there are any significant differences among these three groups.

c. Use the Scheffé test to determine which groups are different.

d. Based on the results of the post hoc test, describe the relation between physical attractiveness and the job ratings.

20. A researcher evaluating the effects of a drug designed an experiment using three different drug doses (small, medium, and large). A separate sample of subjects was tested for each drug dose, and the researcher obtained the following scores:

SMALL	MEDIUM	LARGE
14	16	24
19	20	18
13	15	20
17	18	18
18	19	22
21	23	24

a. Use an analysis of variance to determine whether there are any significant differences among these three drug doses. Set $\alpha = .05$.

b. Use the F-max test to determine whether these data satisfy the homogeneity of variance assumption.

CHAPTER 14

CORRELATION AND REGRESSION

SECTION 14.1 **INTRODUCTION**

Correlation is a statistical technique that is used to measure and describe a relationship between two variables. Usually, the two variables are simply observed as they exist naturally in the environment—there is no attempt to control or manipulate the variables. For example, a researcher interested in the relation between nutrition and IQ could observe (and record) the dietary patterns for a group of preschool children and then measure IQ scores for the same group. Notice that the researcher is not trying to manipulate the children's diet or IQ but is simply observing what occurs naturally. You also should notice that a correlation requires two scores for each individual (one score from each of the two variables). These scores normally are identified as X and Y. The pairs of scores can be listed in a table, or they can be presented graphically in a scatterplot (see Figure 14.1). In the scatterplot, the X values are placed on the horizontal axis of a graph, and the Y values are placed on the vertical axis. Each individual is then identified by a single point on the graph so that the coordinates of the point (the X and Y values) match the individual's X score and Y score. The value of the scatterplot is that it allows you to see the nature of the relationship (see Figure 14.1).

THE CHARACTERISTICS OF A RELATIONSHIP

A correlation measures three characteristics of the relation between X and Y. These three characteristics are as follows:

1. **The Direction of the Relationship.** Correlations can be classified into two basic categories: positive and negative.

DEFINITIONS

In a *positive correlation,* the two variables tend to move in the same direction: When the X variable increases, the Y variable also increases; if the X variable decreases, the Y variable also decreases.

In a *negative correlation,* the two variables tend to go in opposite directions. As the X variable increases, the Y variable decreases. That is, it is an inverse relationship.

The direction of a relationship is identified by the sign of the correlation. A positive value ($+$) indicates a positive relationship; a negative value ($-$) indicates a negative

Figure 14.1

The same set of $n = 6$ pairs of scores (X and Y values) is shown in a table and in a scatterplot. Notice that the scatterplot allows you to see the relationship between X and Y.

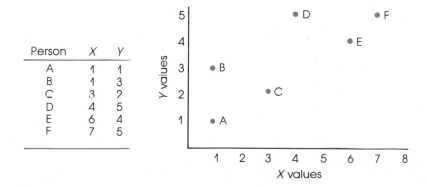

Person	X	Y
A	1	1
B	1	3
C	3	2
D	4	5
E	6	4
F	7	5

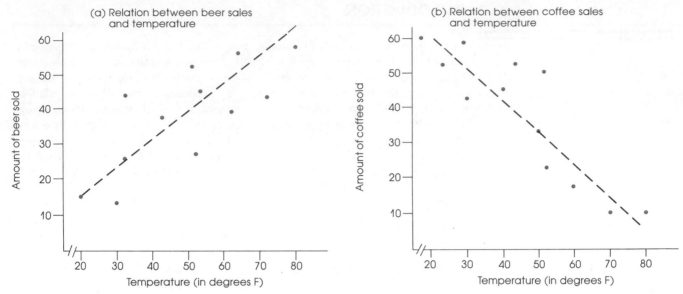

Figure 14.2

Examples of positive and negative relationships. Beer sales are positively related to
temperature, and coffee sales are negatively related to temperature.

---

relation. The following example provides a description of positive and negative
relations.

EXAMPLE 14.1 Suppose you run the drink concession at the football stadium. After several
seasons you begin to notice a relationship between the temperature at game
time and the beverages you sell. Specifically, you have noted that when the
temperature is high, you tend to sell a lot of beer. When the temperature is
low, you sell relatively little beer (see Figure 14.2). This is an example of a
positive correlation. At the same time, you have noted a relation between
temperature and coffee sales: On cold days you sell much more coffee than
on hot days (see Figure 14.2). This is an example of a negative relation.

2. **The Form of the Relation.** In the preceding coffee and beer examples, the
relationships tend to have a linear form; that is, the points in the scatterplot
tend to form a straight line. Notice that we have drawn a line through the
middle of the data points in each figure to help show the relation. The most
common use of correlation is to measure straight-line relations. However, you
should note that other forms of relationship do exist and that there are special
correlations used to measure them. For example, Figure 14.3(a) shows the
relationship between reaction time and age. In this scatterplot there is a
curved relation. Reaction time improves with age until the late teens, when it

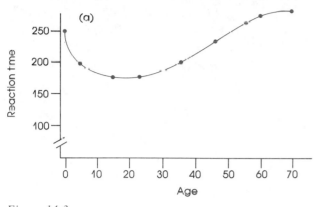

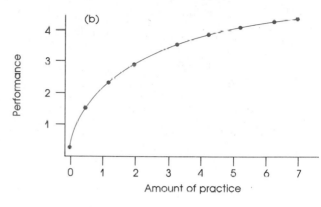

Figure 14.3

Examples of relationships that are not linear. (a) Relationship between reaction time and age. (b) Relationship between performance and amount of practice.

reaches a peak; after that, reaction time starts to get worse. Figure 14.3(b) shows the typical relation between practice and performance. Again, this is not a straight-line relationship. In the early stages of practice, performance increases rapidly. But with a great deal of practice, the improvement in performance becomes less noticeable. (Ask anyone who has taken piano lessons for 10 years.) Many different types of correlations exist. In general, each type is designed to evaluate a specific form of relationship. In this text we will concentrate on the correlation that measures linear relations.

3. **The Degree of the Relationship.** Finally, a correlation measures how well the data fit the specific form being considered. For example, a linear correlation measures how well the data points fit on a straight line. A *perfect correlation* always is identified by a correlation of 1.00, and indicates a perfect fit whereas a correlation of 0 indicates no fit at all. Intermediate values represent the degree to which the data points approximate the perfect fit. The numerical value of the correlation also reflects the degree to which there is a consistent, predictable relation between the two variables. Again, a correlation of 1.00 (or −1.00) indicates a perfectly consistent relation.

Examples of different values for linear correlations are shown in Figure 14.4. Notice that in each example we have sketched a line around the data points. This line, called an *envelope* because it encloses the data, often helps you to see the overall trend in the data.

A correlation of −1.00 also indicates a perfect fit. The direction of the relation (positive or negative) should be considered separately from the degree of the relationship.

LEARNING CHECK

1. If the world were fair, would you expect a positive or negative relationship between grade point average *(X)* and weekly studying hours *(Y)* for college students?

2. Data suggest that on average children from large families have lower IQs than children from small families. Do these data indicate a positive or negative relation between family size and average IQ?

Figure 14.4

Examples of different values for linear correlations. (a) shows a good, positive relation, approximately +.90; (b) shows a relatively poor, negative correlation, approximately −.40; (c) shows a perfect, negative correlation, −1.00; (d) shows no linear trend, .00.

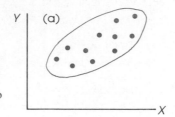

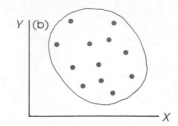

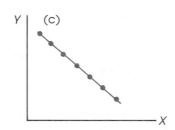

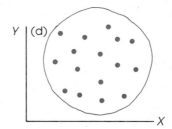

3. If you are measuring linear relationship, correlations of +.50 and −.50 are equally good in terms of how well the data fit on a straight line. (True or False)

4. It is impossible to have a correlation greater than +1.00 or less than −1.00. (True or False)

ANSWERS   1. Positive. More hours studying should be associated with higher grade point averages.

2. Negative.

3. True. The degree of fit is measured by the magnitude of the correlation independent of sign.

4. True. Correlations are always from +1.00 to −1.00.

SECTION 14.2   THE PEARSON CORRELATION

By far the most common correlation is the Pearson correlation (or the Pearson product-moment correlation).

DEFINITION   The *Pearson correlation* measures the degree and direction of linear relation between two variables.

The Pearson correlation is identified by the letter *r*. Conceptually, this correlation is computed by

$$r = \frac{\text{degree to which } X \text{ and } Y \text{ vary together}}{\text{degree to which } X \text{ and } Y \text{ vary separately}}$$

$$= \frac{\text{covariability of } X \text{ and } Y}{\text{variability of } X \text{ and } Y \text{ separately}}$$

When there is a perfect linear relation, every change in the X variable is accompanied by a corresponding change in the Y variable. In Figure 14.4(c), for example, every time the value of X increases, there is a perfectly predictable decrease in Y. The result is a perfect linear relation, with X and Y always varying together. In this case, the covariability (X and Y together) is identical to the variability of X and Y separately, and the formula produces a correlation of -1.00. At the other extreme, when there is no linear relation, a change in the X variable does not correspond to any predictable change in Y. In this case there is no covariability, and the resulting correlation is zero.

THE SUM OF PRODUCTS OF DEVIATIONS

To calculate the Pearson correlation, it is necessary to introduce one new concept: the sum of products of deviations. In the past we have used a similar concept, SS (the sum of squared deviations), to measure the amount of variability for a single variable. The *sum of products,* or *SP,* provides a parallel procedure for measuring the amount of covariability between two variables. The value for SP can be calculated with either a definitional formula or a computational formula.

The *definitional formula* for the sum of products is

$$SP = \Sigma(X - \bar{X})(Y - \bar{Y}) \tag{14.1}$$

This formula instructs you to first find the product of each X deviation and Y deviation and then add up these products. Notice that the terms in the formula define the value being calculated: the sum of the products of the deviations.

The *computational formula* for the sum of products is

Caution: The n in this formula refers to the number of pairs of scores.

$$SP = \Sigma XY - \frac{\Sigma X \Sigma Y}{n} \tag{14.2}$$

Because the computational formula uses the original scores (X and Y values), it usually results in easier calculations than those required with the definitional formula. However, both formulas will always produce the same value for SP.

You may have noted that the formulas for SP are similar to the formulas you have learned for SS (sum of squares). The relation between the two sets of formulas is described in Box 14.1. The following example demonstrates the calculation of SP with both formulas.

EXAMPLE 14.2

The same set of $n = 4$ pairs of scores will be used to calculate SP first using the definitional formula and then the computational formula.

For the definitional formula, you need deviation scores for each of the X values and each of the Y values. Note that the mean for the Xs is $\bar{X} = 3$ and that the mean for the Ys is $\bar{Y} = 5$. The deviations and the products of deviations are shown in the following table:

Caution: The signs (+ and −) are critical in determining the sum of products, *SP*.

| SCORES | | DEVIATIONS | | PRODUCTS |
X	Y	$X - \bar{X}$	$Y - \bar{Y}$	$(X - \bar{X})(Y - \bar{Y})$
1	3	−2	−2	+4
2	6	−1	+1	−1
4	4	+1	−1	−1
5	7	+2	+2	+4
				+6 = SP

For these scores, the sum of the products of the deviations is $SP = +6$.

For the computational formula, you need the sum of the *X* values, the sum of the *Y* values, and the sum of the *XY* product for each pair. These values are as follows:

X	Y	XY
1	3	3
2	6	12
4	4	16
5	7	35
12	20	66	Totals

Substituting the sums in the formula gives

$$SP = \Sigma XY - \frac{\Sigma X \Sigma Y}{n}$$

$$= 66 - \frac{12(20)}{4}$$

$$= 66 - 60$$

$$= 6$$

Note that both formulas produce the same result, $SP = 6$.

CALCULATION OF THE PEARSON CORRELATION

Note that you *multiply SS* for *X* and *SS* for *Y* in the denominator of the Pearson formula.

By using the sum of products to measure the covariability between *X* and *Y*, the formula for the Pearson correlation becomes

$$r = \frac{SP}{\sqrt{SS_X SS_Y}} \tag{14.3}$$

Notice that the variability for *X* is measured by the *SS* for the *X*-scores and the variability for *Y* is measured by *SS* for the *Y*-scores. The following example demonstrates the use of this formula with a simple set of scores.

EXAMPLE 14.3   The Pearson correlation is computed for the following set of $n = 5$ pairs of scores:

COMPARING THE *SP* AND *SS* FORMULAS

IT WILL help you to learn the formulas for *SP* if you note the similarity between the two *SP* formulas and the corresponding formulas for *SS* that were presented in Chapter 4. The definitional formula for *SS* is

$$SS = \Sigma(X - \bar{X})^2$$

In this formula, you must square each deviation, which is equivalent to multiplying it by itself. With this in mind, the formula can be rewritten as

$$SS = \Sigma(X - \bar{X})(X - \bar{X})$$

The similarity between the *SS* formula and the *SP* formula should be obvious—the *SS* formula uses squares and the *SP* formula uses products. This same relationship exists for the computational formulas. For *SS*, the computational formula is

$$SS = \Sigma X^2 - \frac{(\Sigma X)^2}{n}$$

As before, each squared value can be rewritten so that the formula becomes

$$SS = \Sigma XX - \frac{\Sigma X \Sigma X}{n}$$

Again, you should note the similarity in structure between the *SS* formula and the *SP* formula. If you remember that *SS* uses squares and *SP* uses products, the two new formulas for the sum of products should be easy to learn.

X	Y
0	1
10	3
4	1
8	2
8	3

Before starting any calculations, it is useful to put the data in a scatterplot and make a preliminary estimate of the correlation. These data have been graphed in Figure 14.5. Looking at the scatterplot, it appears that there is a very good (but not perfect) positive correlation. You should expect an approximate value of $r = +.8$ or $+.9$. To find the Pearson correlation, we will need *SP*, *SS* for X, and *SS* for Y. Each of these values is calculated using the definitional formula.

For the sum of products,

SCORES		DEVIATIONS		PRODUCTS
X	Y	$X - \bar{X}$	$Y - \bar{Y}$	$(X - \bar{X})(Y - \bar{Y})$
0	1	−6	−1	+6
10	3	+4	+1	+4
4	1	−2	−1	+2
8	2	+2	0	0
8	3	+2	+1	+2
				+14 = SP

Figure 14.5

Scatterplot of the data from Example 14.3.

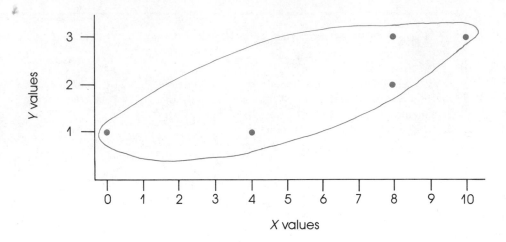

For the *X* values,

X	*X* − *X̄*	(*X* − *X̄*)²
0	−6	36
10	+4	16
4	−2	4
8	+2	4
8	+2	4
		64 = *SS* for *X*

For the *Y* values,

Y	*Y* − *Ȳ*	(*Y* − *Ȳ*)²
1	−1	1
3	+1	1
1	−1	1
2	0	0
3	+1	1
		4 = *SS* for *Y*

By using these values, the Pearson correlation is

$$r = \frac{SP}{\sqrt{SS_X SS_Y}}$$

$$= \frac{14}{\sqrt{64(4)}}$$

$$= \frac{14}{16} = +.875$$

Note that the value we obtained is in agreement with the prediction based on the scatterplot.

THE PEARSON CORRELATION AND *z*-SCORES

The Pearson correlation measures the relation between an individual's location in the *X* distribution and his or her location in the *Y* distribution. For example, a positive correlation means that individuals who score high on *X* also tend to score high on *Y*. Similarly, a negative correlation indicates that individuals with high *X* scores tend to have low *Y* scores.

You should recall from Chapter 5 that *z*-scores provide a precise way to identify the location of an individual score within a distribution. Because the Pearson correlation measures the relation between locations and because z-scores are used to specify locations, the formula for the Pearson correlation can be expressed entirely in terms of z-scores:

$$r = \frac{\Sigma z_X z_Y}{n}$$

(14.4)

In this formula, z_X identifies each individual's position within the X distribution, and z_Y identifies the position within the Y distribution. The product of the z-scores (like the product of the deviation scores) determines the strength and direction of the correlation.

Because z-scores are considered to be the best way to describe a location within a distribution, formula 14.4 often is considered to be the best way to define the Pearson correlation. However, you should realize that this formula requires a lot of tedious calculations (changing each score to a z-score), so it rarely is used to calculate a correlation.

LEARNING CHECK

1. Describe what is measured by a Pearson correlation.

2. Can SP ever have a value less than zero?

3. Calculate the sum of products of deviations (*SP*) for the following set of scores. Use the definitional formula and then the computational formula. Verify that you get the same answer with both formulas.

X	Y
1	0
3	1
7	6
5	2
4	1

Remember, it is useful to sketch a scatterplot and make an estimate of the correlation before you begin calculations.

4. Compute the Pearson correlation for the following data:

X	Y
2	9
1	10
3	6
0	8
4	2

ANSWERS

1. The Pearson correlation measures the degree and direction of linear relationship between two variables.

2. Yes. SP can be positive, negative, or zero depending on the relation between X and Y.

3. $SP = 19$

4. $r = -\dfrac{16}{20} = -.80$

SECTION 14.3 **UNDERSTANDING AND INTERPRETING THE PEARSON CORRELATION**

When you encounter correlations, there are three additional considerations that you should bear in mind:

1. Correlation simply describes a relationship between two variables. It does not explain why the two variables are related. Specifically, a correlation should not and cannot be interpreted as proof of a cause-and-effect relation between the two variables.

2. The value of a correlation can be affected greatly by the range of scores represented in the data.

3. When judging "how good" a relationship is, it is tempting to focus on the numerical value of the correlation. For example, a correlation of $+.5$ is halfway between 0 and 1.00 and therefore appears to represent a moderate degree of relation. However, a correlation should not be interpreted as a proportion. Although a correlation of 1.00 does mean that there is a 100% perfectly predictable relation between X and Y, a correlation of .5 does not mean that you can make predictions with 50% accuracy. To describe how accurately one variable predicts the other, you must square the correlation. Thus, a correlation of $r = .5$ provides only $r^2 = .5^2 = 0.25$, or 25% accuracy.

Each of these three points will now be discussed in detail.

CORRELATION AND CAUSATION

One of the most common errors in interpreting correlations is to assume that a correlation necessarily implies a cause-and-effect relation between the two variables. We constantly are bombarded with reports of relationships: Cigarette smoking is related to heart disease; alcohol consumption is related to birth defects; carrot consumption is related to good eyesight. Do these relationships mean that cigarettes cause heart disease or carrots cause good eyesight? The answer is *no*. Although there may be a causal relation, the simple existence of a correlation does not prove it. This point should become clear in the following hypothetical example.

EXAMPLE 14.4

Suppose we select a variety of different cities and towns throughout the United States and measure the number of serious crimes (X variable) and the number of churches (Y variable) for each. A scatterplot showing hypothetical data for this study is presented in Figure 14.6. Notice that this scatterplot shows a strong, positive correlation between churches and crime. You also should note that these are realistic data. It is reasonable that the smaller towns would have less crime and fewer churches and that the large cities would have large values for both variables. Does this relation mean that churches cause crime? Does it mean that crime causes churches? It should be clear that the answer is no. Although a strong correlation exists between churches and crime, the real cause of the relationship is the size of the population.

Figure 14.6

Hypothetical data showing the logical relation between the number of churches and the number of serious crimes for a sample of U.S. cities

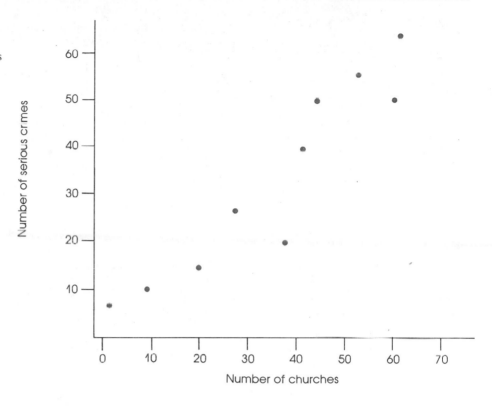

CORRELATION AND RESTRICTED RANGE

Whenever a correlation is computed from scores that do not represent the full range of possible values, you should be cautious in interpreting the correlation. Suppose, for example, you are interested in the relationship between IQ and creativity. If you select a sample of your fellow college students, your data probably would represent only a limited range of IQ scores (most likely from 110 to 130). The correlation within this restricted range could be completely different from the correlation that would be obtained from a full range of IQ scores. Two extreme examples are shown in Figure 14.7.

Figure 14.7(a) shows an example where there is strong positive relation between X and Y when the entire range of scores is considered. However, this relation is obscured when the data are limited to a *restricted range*. In Figure 14.7(b) there is no consistent relation between X and Y for the full range of scores. However, when the range of X values is restricted, the data show a strong positive relation.

To be safe, you should not generalize any correlation beyond the range of data represented in the sample. For a correlation to provide an accurate description for the general population, there should be a wide range of X and Y values in the data.

CORRELATION AND THE STRENGTH OF THE RELATION

A correlation measures the degree of relation between two variables on a scale from 0 to 1.00. Although this number provides a measure of the degree of relationship, many researchers prefer to square the correlation and use the resulting value to measure the strength of the relationship.

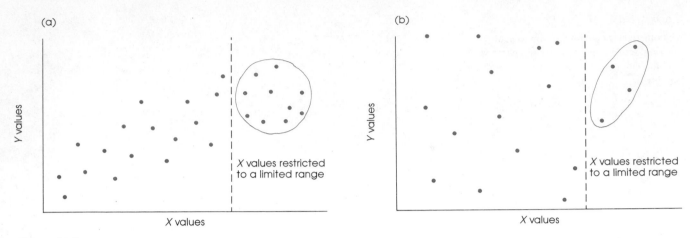

Figure 14.7

(a) An example where the full range of X and Y values show a strong, positive correlation but the restricted range of scores produces a correlation near zero. (b) An example where the full range of X and Y values show a correlation near zero but the scores in the restricted range produce a strong, positive correlation.

One of the common uses of correlation is for prediction. If two variables are correlated, you can use the value of one variable to predict the other. For example, college admissions officers do not just guess which applicants are likely to do well; they use other variables (SAT scores, high school grades, etc.) to predict which students are most likely to be successful. These predictions are based on correlations. By using correlations, the admissions officers expect to make more-accurate predictions than would be obtained by just guessing. In general, the squared correlation (r^2) measures the gain in accuracy that is obtained from using the correlation for prediction instead of just guessing.

DEFINITION   The value r^2 is called the *coefficient of determination* because it measures the proportion of variability in one variable that can be determined from the relationship with the other variable. A correlation of $r = .80$ (or $-.80$), for example, means that $r^2 = 0.64$ (or 64%) of the variability in the Y scores can be predicted from the relation with X.

Although a detailed discussion of the coefficient of determination is beyond the scope of this book, the general notion is that whenever two variables are consistently related, it is possible to use one variable to predict the values of the second variable. The amount of variability that can be predicted is determined by r^2 (see Figure 14.8).

SECTION 14.4   HYPOTHESIS TESTS WITH THE PEARSON CORRELATION

The Pearson correlation is generally computed for sample data. Quite often, however, the sample correlation is used to provide information about the entire population. For example, a psychologist would like to know whether there is a

(a) With $r = 0$, X and Y are independent. None of the Y variability can be predicted from X; $r^2 = 0$.

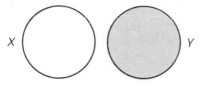

(b) With $r = 0.8$, the Y variability is partially predicted from the relation with X; $r^2 = 0.64$ or 64%.

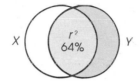

(c) With $r = 1$, all the Y variability is predicted from the relation with X; $r^2 = 1.00$ or 100%.

Figure 14.8

A graphic representation of the coefficient of determination, r^2. See text for further explanation.

relation between IQ and creativity. This is a general question concerning a population. To answer the question, a sample would be selected and the sample data would be used to compute the correlation value. You should recognize this process as an example of inferential statistics: using samples to draw inferences about populations. In the past, we have been concerned primarily with using sample means as the basis for answering questions about population means. In this section we will examine the procedures for using a sample correlation as the basis for testing hypotheses about the corresponding population correlation.

The basic question for this hypothesis test is whether or not a correlation exists in the population. The null hypothesis says "No, there is no correlation in the population," or "The population correlation is zero." The alternative hypothesis is "Yes, there is a real, nonzero, correlation in the population." Because the population correlation is traditionally represented by ρ (the Greek letter rho), these hypotheses would be stated in symbols as

Directional hypotheses for a "one-tailed" test would specify either a positive correlation ($\rho > 0$) or a negative correlation ($\rho < 0$).

$$H_0: \rho = 0 \quad \text{(no population correlation)}$$
$$H_1: \rho \neq 0 \quad \text{(there is a real correlation)}$$

The correlation from the sample data *(r)* will be used to evaluate these hypotheses. As always, samples are not expected to be identical to the populations from which they come. Specifically, you should note that it is possible to obtain a nonzero sample correlation even when the population value is zero. This is particularly true when you have a small sample (see Figure 14.9). The question for this hypothesis test is whether the obtained sample correlation provides sufficient evidence to conclude that a real, nonzero correlation exists in the population. Although it is possible to conduct this hypothesis test by calculating either a *t* statistic or an *F*-ratio, the detailed computations have been completed and are summarized in Appendix B, Table B.5. To use the table, you must know the sample size *(n)*, the magnitude of the sample correlation (independent of sign), and the alpha level. If the magnitude of the sample correlation *(r)* equals or exceeds the value given in the table, then we reject H_0 conclude that there is significant evidence for a correlation in the population. To demonstrate the use of the table, suppose you have a sample of $n = 30$ and want to test a nondirectional hypothesis about the population with $\alpha = .05$. In this case, the table indicates that your sample correlation must be greater than or equal to .361 to be significant.

The table lists critical values in terms of degrees of freedom: $df = n - 2$. Remember to subtract 2 when using this table.

Figure 14.9

Scatterplot of a population of *X* and *Y* values with a near zero correlation. However, a small sample of *n* = 3 data points from this population shows a relatively strong, positive correlation. Data points in the sample are circled.

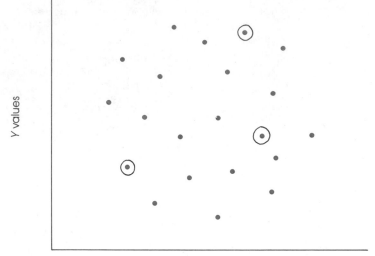

X values

---

1. A researcher obtains a correlation of $r = -.41$ for a sample of $n = 30$ individuals. Does this sample provide sufficient evidence to conclude that there is a significant, nonzero correlation in the population? Assume a nondirectional test with $\alpha = .05$.

2. For a sample of $n = 20$, how large a correlation is needed to conclude at the .05 level that there is a nonzero correlation in the population? Assume a nondirectional test.

3. As sample size gets smaller, what happens to the magnitude of the correlation necessary for significance? Explain why this occurs.

ANSWERS

1. Yes. For $n = 30$, the critical value is $r = .361$. The sample value is in the critical region.

2. For $n = 20$ the critical value is $r = .444$.

3. As the sample size gets smaller, the magnitude of the correlation needed for significance gets larger. With a small sample, it is easy to get a relatively good correlation just by chance (see Figure 14.9). Therefore, a small sample requires a very large correlation before you can be confident that there is a real (nonzero) relation in the population.

SECTION 14.5   **INTRODUCTION TO REGRESSION**

Earlier in this chapter we introduced the Pearson correlation as a technique for describing and measuring the linear relation between two variables. Figure 14.10 presents hypothetical data showing the relation between SAT scores and college

Figure 14.10

Hypothetical data showing the relation between SAT scores and GPA with a regression line drawn through the data points. The regression line defines a precise, one-to-one relation between each *X* value (SAT score) and its corresponding *Y* value (GPA).

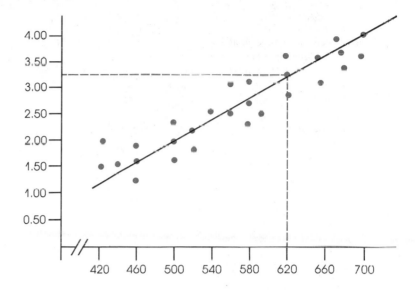

grade point average (GPA). Note that the figure shows a good, but not perfect, positive relation. Also note that we have drawn a line through the middle of the data points. This line serves several purposes:

a. The line makes the relation between SAT and GPA easier to see.

b. The line identifies the center, or "central tendency," of the relation, just as the mean describes central tendency for a set of scores. Thus the line provides a simplified description of the relation. For example, if the data points were removed, the straight line would still give a general picture of the relation between SAT and GPA.

c. Finally, the line can be used for prediction. The line establishes a precise relation between each X value (SAT score) and a corresponding Y value (GPA). For example, an SAT score of 620 corresponds to a GPA of 3.40 (see Figure 14.10). Thus, the college admissions office could use the straight line relation to predict that a student entering college with an SAT score of 620 should achieve a college GPA of approximately 3.40.

LINEAR EQUATIONS In general, a *linear relation* between two variables *X* and *Y* can be expressed by the equation $Y = bX + a$ where *b* and *a* are fixed constants.

For example, a local tennis club charges a fee of $5 per hour plus an annual membership fee of $25. With this information, the total cost of playing tennis can be computed using a *linear equation* that describes the relation between the total cost (*Y*) and the number of hours (*X*).

$$Y = 5X + 25$$

In the general linear equation, the value of *b* is called the *slope*. The slope determines how much the *Y* variable will change when *X* is increased by one point. For the tennis club example, the slope is $b = \$5$ and indicates that your total cost

Figure 14.11

Relationship between total cost and number of hours playing tennis. The tennis club charges a $25 membership fee plus $5 per hour. The relation is described by a linear equation:

Total cost = $5(number of hours) + $25

$Y = bX + a$

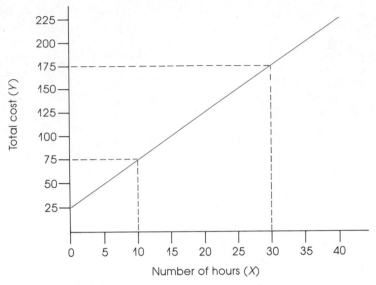

Note that a positive slope means that Y increases when X increases, and a negative slope indicates that Y decreases when X increases.

will increase by $5 for each hour you play. The value of a in the general equation is called the *Y-intercept* because it determines the value of Y when $X = 0$. (On a graph, the a value identifies the point where the line intercepts the Y-axis.) For the tennis club example, $a = \$25$; there is a $25 charge even if you never play tennis.

Figure 14.11 shows the general relation between cost and number of hours for the tennis club example. Notice that the relation results in a straight line. To obtain this graph, we picked any two values of X and then used the equation to compute the corresponding values for Y. For example,

When $X = 10$:	When $X = 30$:
$Y = bX + a$	$Y = bX + a$
$= \$5(10) + \$25$	$= \$5(30) + \$25$
$= \$50 + \$25$	$= \$150 + \$25$
$= \$75$	$= \$175$

When drawing a graph of a linear equation, it is wise to compute and plot a least three points to be certain you have not made a mistake.

Next, these two points are plotted on the graph: one point at $X = 10$ and $Y = 75$, the other point at $X = 30$ and $Y = 175$. Because two points completely determine a straight line, we simply drew the line so that it passed through these two points.

Because a straight line can be extremely useful for describing a relation between two variables, a statistical technique has been developed that provides a standardized method for determining the best fitting straight line for any set of data. The statistical procedure is regression and the resulting straight line is called the regression line.

DEFINITION

The statistical technique for finding the best-fitting straight line for a set of data is called *regression,* and the resulting straight line is called the *regression line.*

The goal for regression is to find the best-fitting straight line for a set of data. To accomplish this goal, however, it is first necessary to define precisely what is meant by "best fit." For any particular set of data it is possible to draw lots of different straight lines that all appear to pass through the center of the data points. Each of these lines can be defined by a linear equation of the form

$$Y - bX + a$$

where b and a are constants that determine the slope and Y-intercept of the line, respectively. Each individual line has its own unique values for b and a. The problem is to find the specific line that provides the best fit to the actual data points.

LEARNING CHECK   1. Identify the slope and Y-intercept for the following linear equation:

$$Y = -3X + 7$$

2. Use the linear equation $Y = 2X - 7$ to determine the value of Y for each of the following values of X.

   X values: 1, 3, 5, 10

3. If the slope constant (b) in a linear equation is positive, then a graph of the equation will be a line tilted from lower left to upper right. (True or False)

ANSWERS   1. Slope $= -3$ and Y-intercept $= +7$.

2.

X	Y
1	−5
3	−1
5	3
10	13

3. True. A positive slope indicates that Y increases (goes up in the graph) when X increases (goes to the right in the graph).

THE LEAST-SQUARES SOLUTION   To determine how well a line fits the data points, the first step is to define mathematically the distance between the line and each data point. For every X value in the data, the linear equation will determine a Y value on the line. This value is the predicted Y and is called $\hat{Y}$ ("Y hat"). The distance between this predicted value and the actual Y value in the data is determined by

$$\text{distance} = Y - \hat{Y}$$

Notice that we simply are measuring the vertical distance between the actual data point (Y) and the predicted point on the line. This distance measures the error between the line and the actual data (see Figure 14.12).

Figure 14.12.

The distance between the actual data point *(Y)* and the predicted point on the line *(Ŷ)* is defined as $Y - \hat{Y}$. The goal of regression is to find the equation for the line that minimizes these distances.

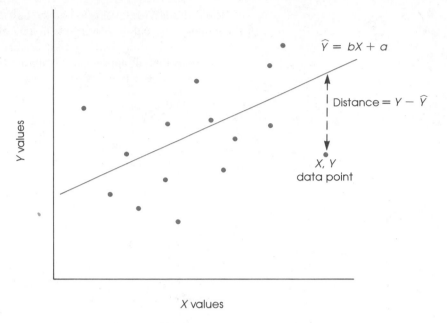

Because some of these distances will be positive and some will be negative, the next step is to square each distance in order to obtain a uniformly positive measure of error. Finally, to determine the total error between the line and the data, we sum the squared errors for all of the data points. The result is a measure of overall squared error between the line and the data:

$$\text{total squared error} = \Sigma(Y - \hat{Y})^2$$

Now we can define the *best-fitting* line as the one that has the smallest total squared error. For obvious reasons, the resulting line is commonly called the *least-squared-error* solution.

In symbols, we are looking for a linear equation of the form.

$$\hat{Y} = bX + a$$

For each value of *X* in the data, this equation will determine the point on the line *(Ŷ)* that gives the best prediction of *Y*. The problem is to find the specific values for *a* and *b* that will make this the best fitting line.

The calculations that are needed to find this equation require calculus and some sophisticated algebra, so we will not present the details of the solution. The results, however, are relatively straightforward, and the solutions for *b* and *a* are as follows:

A commonly used alternative formula for the slope is

$$b = r\frac{s_Y}{s_X}$$

where s_X and s_Y are the standard deviations for *X* and *Y*, respectively.

$$b = \frac{SP}{SS_X} \tag{14.5}$$

where *SP* is the sum of products and SS_X is the sum of squares for the *X*-scores.

$$a = \overline{Y} - b\overline{X} \tag{14.6}$$

Note that these two formulas determine the linear equation that provides the best prediction of Y values. This equation is called the regression equation for Y.

DEFINITION The *regression equation for Y* is the linear equation

$$\hat{Y} = bX + a$$

where the constants b and a are determined by formulas (14.5) and (14.6), respectively. This equation results in the least squared error between the data points and the line.

You should notice that the values of SS and SP are needed in the formulas for b and a just as they are needed to compute the Pearson correlation. An example demonstrating the calculation and use of this best fitting line is presented now.

EXAMPLE 14.5 The following table presents X and Y scores for a sample of $n = 5$ individuals. These data will be used to demonstrate the procedure for determining the linear regression equation for predicting Y values.

X	Y	$X - \bar{X}$	$Y - \bar{Y}$	$(X - \bar{X})(Y - \bar{Y})$	$(X - \bar{X})^2$
7	11	2	5	10	4
4	3	-1	-3	3	1
6	5	1	-1	-1	1
3	4	-2	-2	4	4
5	7	0	1	0	0
				$16 = SP$	$10 = SS_X$

For these data $\Sigma X = 25$, so $\bar{X} = 5$. Also, $\Sigma Y = 30$, so $\bar{Y} = 6$. These means have been used to compute the deviation scores for each X and Y value. The final two columns show the products of the deviation scores and the squared deviations for X. Based on these values,

$$SP = \Sigma(X - \bar{X})(Y - \bar{Y}) = 16$$
$$SS_X = \Sigma(X - \bar{X})^2 = 10$$

Our goal is to find the values for b and a in the linear equation so that we obtain the best fitting straight line for these data.

By using formulas 14.5 and 14.6, the solutions for b and a are

$$b = \frac{SP}{SS_X} = \frac{16}{10} = 1.6$$
$$a = \bar{Y} - b\bar{X}$$
$$= 6 - 1.6(5)$$
$$= 6 - 8$$
$$= -2$$

Figure 14.13

The scatterplot for the data in Example 14.5 is shown with the best-fitting straight line. The predicted Y values $(\hat{Y})$ are on the regression line. Unless the correlation is perfect ($+1.00$ or -1.00), there will be some error between the actual Y values and the predicted Y values. The larger the correlation, the less the error will be.

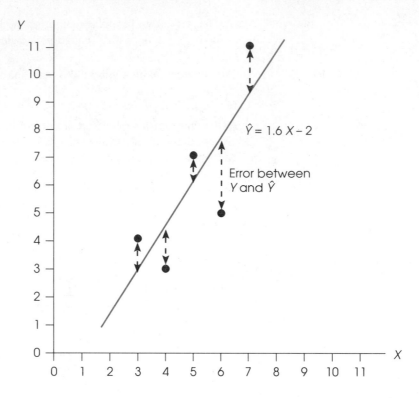

The resulting regression equation is

$$\hat{Y} = 1.6X - 2$$

The original data and the regression line are shown in Figure 14.13.

As we noted at the beginning of this section, one common use of regression equations is for prediction. For any given value of X, we can use the equation to compute a predicted value for Y. For the equation from Example 14.5, an individual with an X score of $X = 5$ would be predicted to have a Y score of

$$\hat{Y} = 1.6X - 2$$
$$= 1.6(5) - 2$$
$$= 8 - 2$$
$$= 6$$

Although regression equations can be used for prediction, there are a few cautions that should be considered whenever you are interpreting the predicted values:

1. The predicted value is not perfect (unless $r = +1.00$ or -1.00). If you examine Figure 14.13, it should be clear that the data points do not fit perfectly on the line. In general, there will be some error between the predicted Y values (on the line) and the actual data. Although the amount of error will vary from point to point, on average the errors will be directly related to the magnitude of the correlation. With a correlation near 1.00 (or -1.00) the data points will generally be close to the line (small error), but as the correlation gets nearer to zero, the magnitude of the error will increase.

2. The regression equation should not be used to make predictions for X values that fall outside the range of values covered by the original data. For Example 14.5, the X values ranged from $X = 3$ to $X = 7$ and the regression equation was calculated as the best-fitting line within this range. Because you have no information about the X-Y relation outside this range, the equation should not be used to predict Y for any X value lower than 3 or greater than 7.

LEARNING CHECK   **1.** Sketch a scatterplot for the following data, that is, a graph showing the X, Y data points:

X	Y
1	4
3	9
5	8

  a. Find the regression equation for predicting Y and X. Draw this line on your graph. Does it look like the best fitting line?

  b. Use the regression equation to find the predicted Y value corresponding to each X in the data.

ANSWERS   **1. a.** $SS_X = 8$, $SP = 8$, $b = 1$, $a = 4$.
The equation is

$$\hat{Y} = X + 4$$

  b. The predicted Y values are 5, 7, and 9.

SUMMARY

1. A correlation measures the relationship between two variables X and Y. The relationship is described by three characteristics:

  a. *Direction*. A relation can be either positive or negative. A positive relation means that X and Y vary in the same direction. A negative relation means that X and Y vary in opposite directions. The sign of the correlation ($+$ or $-$) specifies the direction.

  b. *Form*. The most common form for a relation is a straight line. However, special correlations exist for measuring other forms. The form is specified by the type of correlation used. For example, the Pearson correlation measures linear form.

  c. *Degree*. The magnitude of the correlation measures the degree to which the data points fit the specified form. A correlation of 1.00 indicates a perfect fit, and a correlation of 0 indicates no degree of fit.

2. The most commonly used correlation is the Pearson correlation, which measures the degree of linear relationship. The Pearson correlation is identified by the letter r and is computed by

$$r = \frac{SP}{\sqrt{SS_X SS_Y}}$$

In this formula, SP is the sum of products of deviations and can be calculated either with a definitional formula or a computational formula:

definitional formula: $SP = \Sigma(X - \bar{X})(Y - \bar{Y})$

computational formula: $SP = \Sigma XY - \frac{\Sigma X \Sigma Y}{n}$

3. The Pearson correlation and z-scores are closely related because both are concerned with the location of individuals within a distribution. When X and Y scores are transformed into z-scores, the Pearson correlation can be computed by

$$r = \frac{\Sigma z_X z_Y}{n}$$

4. A correlation between two variables should not be interpreted as implying a causal relation. Simply because X and Y are related does not mean that X causes Y or that Y causes X.

5. When the X or Y values used to compute a correlation are limited to a relatively small portion of the potential range, you should exercise caution in generalizing the value of the correlation. Specifically, a limited range of values can either obscure a strong relation or exaggerate a poor relation.

6. To evaluate the strength of a relation, you should square the value of the correlation. The resulting value, r^2, is called the *coefficient of determination* because it measures the portion of the variability in one variable that can be predicted using the relationship with the second variable.

7. When there is a general linear relation between two variables X and Y, it is possible to construct a linear equation that allows you to predict the Y value corresponding to any known value of X:

predicted Y value $= \hat{Y} = bX + a$

The technique for determining this equation is called regression. By using a *least-squares* method to minimize the error between the predicted Y values and the actual Y values, the best fitting line is achieved when the linear equation has

$$b = \frac{SP}{SS_X} \quad \text{and} \quad a = \bar{Y} - b\bar{X}$$

KEY TERMS

correlation	Pearson correlation	linear relationship	regression equation for Y
positive correlation	sum of products (SP)	linear equation	regression
negative correlation	restricted range	slope	regression line
perfect correlation	coefficient of determination	Y-intercept	

FOCUS ON PROBLEM SOLVING

1. A correlation always has a value from $+1.00$ to -1.00. If you obtain a correlation outside this range, then you have made a computational error.

2. When interpreting a correlation, do not confuse the sign ($+$ or $-$) with its numerical value. The sign and

numerical value must be considered separately. Remember, the sign indicates the direction of the relationship between X and Y. On the other hand, the numerical value reflects the strength of the relationship, or how well the points approximate a linear (straight-line) relationship. Therefore, correlation of $-.90$ is just as strong as a correlation of $+.90$. The signs tell us that the first correlation is an inverse relationship.

3. Before you begin to calculate a correlation, you should sketch a scatterplot of the data and make an estimate of the correlation. (Is it positive or negative? Is it near 1 or near 0?). After computing the correlation, compare your final answer with your original estimate.

4. The definitional formula for the sum of products (SP) should be used only when you have a small set (n) of scores and the means for X and Y are both whole numbers. Otherwise, the computational formula will produce quicker, easier, and more-accurate results.

5. For computing a correlation, n is number of individuals (and, therefore, the number of *pairs* of X and Y values).

6. To draw a graph from a linear equation, choose any three values for X, put each value in the equation, and calculate the corresponding values for Y. Then plot the three (X, Y) points on the graph. Its a good idea to use $X = 0$ for one of the three values because this will give you the Y-intercept. You can get a quick idea of what the graph should look like if you know the Y-intercept and the slope. Remember, the Y-intercept is the point where the line crosses the Y-axis, and the slope identifies the tilt of the line. For example, suppose the Y-intercept is 5 and the slope is -3. The line would pass through the point (0, 5), and its slope indicates that the Y value goes down 3 points each time X increases by 1.

7. Rather than memorizing the formula for the Y-intercept in the regression equation, simply remember that the graphed line of the regression equation always goes through the point ($\bar{X}$, $\bar{Y}$). Therefore, if you plug the mean value for X ($\bar{X}$) into the regression equation, the result equals the mean value for Y ($\bar{Y}$).

$$\bar{Y} = b\bar{X} + a$$

If you simply solve this equation for a, you get the formula for the Y-intercept.

$$a = \bar{Y} - b\bar{X}$$

DEMONSTRATION 14.1   CORRELATION AND REGRESSION

For the following data, calculate the Pearson correlation and find the regression equation.

PERSON	X	Y
A	0	4
B	2	1
C	8	10
D	6	9
E	4	6

STEP 1   Sketch a scatterplot.

We have constructed a scatterplot for the data (Figure 14.14) and placed an envelope around the data points to make a preliminary estimate of the correlation. Note that the envelope is narrow and elongated. This indicates that the correlation is large—perhaps 0.80 to 0.90. Also, the correlation is positive because increases in X are generally accompanied by increases in Y.

We can sketch a straight line through the middle of the envelope and data points. Now, we can roughly approximate the slope and Y-intercept of the best fit line. This is only an educated guess, but it will tell us what values are reason-

Figure 14.14

The scatterplot for the data of
Demonstration 14.1. An envelope is
drawn around the points to estimate the
magnitude of the correlation. A line is
drawn through the middle of the envelope
to roughly estimate the *Y*-intercept for the
regression equation.

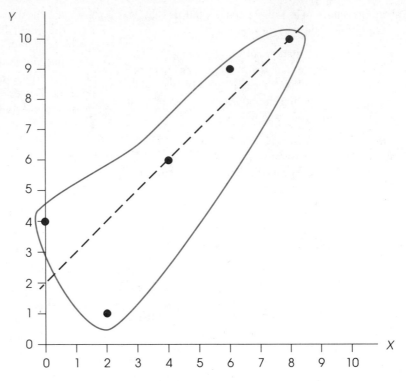

able when we actually compute the regression line. The line has a positive slope
(as *X* increases, *Y* increases) and it intersects the *Y* axis in the vicinity of +2.

STEP 2   Obtain the values for *SS* and *SP*.

To compute the Pearson correlation, we must find the values for SS_X, SS_Y,
and *SP*. These values are needed for the regression equation as well. The following table illustrates these calculations with the computational formulas for *SS* and
SP.

X	Y	X^2	Y^2	XY
0	4	0	16	0
2	1	4	1	2
8	10	64	100	80
6	9	36	81	54
4	6	16	36	24
$\Sigma X = 20$	$\Sigma Y = 30$	$\Sigma X^2 = 120$	$\Sigma Y^2 = 234$	$\Sigma XY = 160$

For SS_X, we obtain

$$SS_X = \Sigma X^2 - \frac{(\Sigma X)^2}{n} = 120 - \frac{20^2}{5} = 120 - \frac{400}{5} = 120 - 80$$

$$= 40$$

For *Y*, sum-of-squares is

$$SS_Y = \Sigma Y^2 - \frac{(\Sigma Y)^2}{n} = 234 - \frac{30^2}{5} = 234 - \frac{900}{5} = 234 - 180$$

$$= 54$$

The sum-of-products equals

$$SP = \Sigma XY - \frac{\Sigma X \Sigma Y}{n} = 160 - \frac{20(30)}{5} = 160 - \frac{600}{5} = 160 - 120$$

$$= 40$$

STEP 3 Compute the Pearson correlation.

For these data, the Pearson correlation is

$$r = \frac{SP}{\sqrt{SS_X SS_Y}} = \frac{40}{\sqrt{40(54)}} = \frac{40}{\sqrt{2160}} = \frac{40}{46.48}$$

$$= 0.861$$

In Step 1, our preliminary estimate for the correlation was between $+0.80$ and $+0.90$. The calculated correlation is consistent with this estimate.

STEP 4 Compute the values for the regression equation.

The general form of the regression equation is

$$\hat{Y} = bX + a$$

We will need to compute the values for the slope (b) of the line and the Y-intercept (a). For slope, we obtain

$$b = \frac{SP}{SS_X} = \frac{40}{40} = +1$$

The formula for the Y-intercept is

$$a = \bar{Y} - b\bar{X}$$

Thus, we will need the values for the sample means. For these data, the sample means are

$$\bar{X} = \frac{\Sigma X}{n} = \frac{20}{5} = 4$$

$$\bar{Y} = \frac{\Sigma Y}{n} = \frac{30}{5} = 6$$

Now we can compute the Y-intercept.

$$a = 6 - 1(4) = 6 - 4 = 2$$

Finally, the regression equation is

$$\hat{Y} = bX + a$$

$$= 1X + 2$$

or $\qquad \hat{Y} = X + 2$

PROBLEMS

1. For each of the following sets of scores, calculate *SP* using the definitional formula and then using the computational formula:

SET 1		SET 2		SET 3	
X	Y	X	Y	X	Y
1	3	0	7	1	5
2	6	4	3	2	0
4	4	0	5	3	1
5	7	4	1	2	6

2. For the following set of data,

DATA	
X	Y
8	2
9	2
2	4
1	5
5	2

  a. Sketch a graph showing the location of the five (X, Y) points.
  b. Just looking at your graph, estimate the value of the Pearson correlation.
  c. Compute the Pearson correlation for this data set.

3. For this problem we have used the same X and Y values that appeared in Problem 2, but we have changed the X, Y pairings:

DATA	
X	Y
8	4
9	5
2	2
1	2
5	2

  a. Sketch a graph showing these reorganized data.
  b. Estimate the Pearson correlation just by looking at your graph.
  c. Compute the Pearson correlation. (*Note:* Much of the calculation for this problem was done already in Problem 8.)

If you compare the results of Problem 2 and Problem 3, you will see that the correlation measures the relation between X and Y. These two problems use the same X and Y values, but they differ in the way X and Y are related.

4. With a very small sample, a single point can have a large influence on the magnitude of a correlation. For the following data set,

X	Y
0	1
10	3
4	1
8	2
8	3

  a. Sketch a graph showing the X, Y points.
  b. Estimate the value of the Pearson correlation.
  c. Compute the Pearson correlation.
  d. Now we will change the value of one of the points. For the first individual in the sample (X = 0 and Y = 1), change the Y value to Y = 6. What happens to the graph of the X, Y points? What happens to the Pearson correlation? Compute the new correlation.

5. In the following data there are three scores (X, Y, and Z) for each of the $n = 5$ individuals:

X	Y	Z
3	5	5
4	3	2
2	4	6
1	1	3
0	2	4

  a. Sketch a graph showing the relation between X and Y. Compute the Pearson correlation between X and Y.
  b. Sketch a graph showing the relation between Y and Z. Compute the Pearson correlation between Y and Z.
  c. Given the results of parts a and b, what would you predict for the correlation between X and Z?
  d. Sketch a graph showing the relation between X

and Z. Compute the Pearson correlation for these data.

e. What general conclusion can you make concerning relations among correlations? If X is related to Y and Y is related to Z, does this necessarily mean that X is related to Z?

6. For the following set of data,

X	Y
1	2
2	4
3	1
4	5
5	3
6	9
7	10
8	7
9	8
10	9

a. Sketch a graph showing the X, Y points.
b. Compute the Pearson correlation for the full set of data.
c. Compute the Pearson correlation using only the first five individuals in the sample (the five smallest X values).
d. Compute the Pearson correlation for the final five individuals in the sample (the five largest X values).
e. Explain why the results from parts c and d are so different from the overall correlation obtained in part b.

7. a. Compute the Pearson correlation for the following set of data:

X	Y
2	8
3	10
3	7
5	6
6	7
8	4
9	2
10	3

b. Add 5 points to each X value and compute the Pearson correlation again.

c. When you add a constant to each score, what happens to SS for X and Y? What happen to SP? What happens to the correlation between X and Y?
d. Now multiply each X in the original data by 3 and calculate the Pearson correlation once again.
e. When you multiply by a constant, what happens to SS for X and Y? What happens to SP? What happens to the correlation between X and Y?

8. A psychology instructor asked each student to report the number of hours he or she had spent preparing for the final exam. In addition, the instructor recorded the number of incorrect answers on each student's exam. These data are as follows:

HOURS	NUMBER WRONG
4	8
0	6
1	3
2	2
4	5

What is the Pearson correlation between study hours and number wrong?

9. If you obtain a random sample of $n = 2$ people and measure each person's annual salary and shoe size, what would you expect to obtain for the Pearson correlation? (Be careful. Try making up some data points to see what happens.) How would you interpret a correlation of $r = +1.00$ obtained for a sample of $n = 2$? Should you generalize this sample correlation and conclude that a strong relationship between X and Y exists in the population?

10. A psychologist would like to determine whether there is any consistent relationship between intelligence and creativity. A random sample of $n = 18$ people is obtained, and the psychologist administers a standardized IQ test and a creativity test to each individual. Using these data, the psychologist obtained a Pearson correlation of $r = +.20$ between IQ and creativity. Do these sample data provide sufficient evidence to conclude that a correlation exists in the population? Test at the .05 level of significance, one tail.

11. A high school counselor would like to know if there is a relation between mathematical skill and verbal skill. A sample of $n = 25$ students is selected, and the counselor records achievement tests scores in mathematics and English for each student. The Pear-

son correlation for this sample is $r = +.50$. Do these data provide sufficient evidence for a real relationship in the population? Test at the .05 level, two tails.

12. An educational psychologist wanted to demonstrate that scores on the SAT provide a reasonably accurate indication of how a student will perform in college. A random sample of $n = 20$ students was selected. Each student's SAT score and his or her grade point average after four semesters are as shown in the accompanying table.
   a. Calculate the Pearson correlation for these data.
   b. Is there a significant relation between the SAT and grade point average? Test at the .05 level, two tails.

STUDENT	SAT	GPA	STUDENT	SAT	GPA
1	650	3.12	11	745	3.84
2	680	3.06	12	590	2.18
3	710	3.55	13	605	2.43
4	440	1.98	14	520	2.10
5	660	3.25	15	635	2.72
6	485	2.23	16	750	3.88
7	590	2.76	17	490	2.31
8	780	4.00	18	700	3.49
9	620	3.52	19	460	2.45
10	480	3.01	20	670	3.20

13. A college professor claims that the scores on the first exam provide an excellent indication of how students will perform throughout the term. To test this claim, first-exam score and final scores were recorded for a sample of $n = 12$ students in an introductory psychology class. The data are as follows:

FIRST EXAM	FINAL GRADE
62	74
73	93
88	68
82	79
85	91
77	72
94	96
65	61
91	92
74	82
85	93
98	95

Is the professor right? Is there a significant relation between scores on the first exam and final grades? Test with $\alpha = .01$, one tail.

14. Sketch a graph showing the linear equation $Y = 3X - 2$.

15. Two major companies supply laboratory animals for psychologists. Company A sells laboratory rats for $6 each and charges a $10 fee for delivery. Company B sells rats for only $5 each but has a $20 delivery charge. In each case the delivery fee is a one-time charge and does not depend on the number of rats in the order.
   a. For each company, what is the linear equation that defines the total cost (Y) as a function of the number of rats (X)? Each equation should be of the form

   $$Y = bX + a$$

   b. What would the total cost be for an order of 10 rats from company A? From company B?
   c. If you were buying 20 rats, which company gives you the better deal?

16. For the following set of data, find the linear regression equation for predicting Y from X:

X	Y
0	9
2	9
4	7
6	3

17. a. Find the regression equation for the following data:

X	Y
1	2
4	7
3	5
2	1
5	14
3	7

b. Compute the predicted Y value for each X in the data.

18. Find the regression equation for the following data:

X	Y
3	12
0	8
4	18
2	12
1	8

19. Sternberg (1966) reported results of a human memory experiment using regression. Sternberg presented subjects with a short list of digits to hold in memory. Then he flashed a single digit, and the subjects had to decide as quickly as possible whether or not this digit was contained in the memory list. The results showed a linear relation between the number of items in memory and the reaction time; the more items in memory, the more time needed to respond. Data similar to those obtained by Sternberg are as follows:

NUMBER OF ITEMS IN MEMORY	REACTION TIME (IN MILLISECONDS)
1	430
2	471
3	505
4	543
5	578

Calculate the regression equation for predicting reaction time as a function of the number of items in memory. (Note that the slope of the regression equation corresponds to the amount of extra time needed for each additional item in memory. The Y-intercept is a measure of basic reaction time with zero items in memory.)

20. You probably have read for years about the relation between years of education and salary potential. The following hypothetical data represent a sample of $n = 10$ men who have been employed for 5 years. For each person, we report the total number of years of higher education (high school plus college) and current annual salary.

SALARY (IN $1000)	YEARS OF HIGHER EDUCATION
21.4	4
18.7	4
17.5	2
32.0	8
12.6	0
25.3	5
35.5	10
17.3	4
33.8	12
14.0	0

a. Find the regression equation for predicting salary from education.
b. How would you interpret the slope constant (b) in the regression equation?
c. How would you interpret the Y-intercept (a) in the equation?

21. The marketing division of a major breakfast cereal manufacturer prepared the following table showing the monthly advertising expenditure and sales figures for the company:

ADVERTISING EXPENDITURE (IN THOUSANDS)	SALES FIGURES (IN THOUSANDS)
14	218
23	237
27	241
17	214
29	243
15	218
19	232
25	230

a. Compute the Pearson correlation for these two variables.
b. Do these data indicate that there is a significant relation between the amount spent on advertising

and the amount of sales? Test at the .05 level of significance, two tails.

c. Next month, the company plans to spend $20,000 on advertising. Find the regression equation and then use it to predict next month's sales.

22. Data indicate that infants with low birth weight tend to lag behind in general development. The following data are infant birth weights and scholastic achievement scores at age 10 years for a sample of $n = 12$ children:

BIRTH WEIGHT	SCHOLASTIC ACHIEVEMENT	BIRTH WEIGHT	SCHOLASTIC ACHIEVEMENT
81 oz	58	127 oz	81
96 oz	65	108 oz	85
132 oz	78	76 oz	55
104 oz	76	86 oz	68
122 oz	81	113 oz	79
88 oz	62	110 oz	72

a. Calculate the Pearson correlation for these data.

b. Find the regression equation for predicting scholastic achievement from birth weight.

CHAPTER 15

THE CHI-SQUARE STATISTIC: TESTS FOR GOODNESS OF FIT AND INDEPENDENCE

SECTION 15.1   **PARAMETRIC AND NONPARAMETRIC STATISTICAL TESTS**

All the statistical tests we have examined thus far are designed to test hypotheses about specific population parameters. For example, we used t tests to assess hypotheses about μ and later about $\mu_1 - \mu_2$. In addition, these tests typically make assumptions about the shape of the population distribution and about other population parameters. Recall that for analysis of variance the population distributions are assumed to be normal and homogeneity of variance is required. Because these tests all concern parameters and require assumptions about parameters, they are called *parametric tests*.

Another general characteristic of parametric tests is that they require a numerical score for each individual in the sample. The scores then are added, squared, averaged, and otherwise manipulated using basic arithmetic. In terms of measurement scales, parametric tests require data from an interval or a ratio scale (see Chapter 1).

Often, researchers are confronted with experimental situations that do not conform to the requirements of parametric tests. In these situations it may not be appropriate to use a parametric test. Remember, when the assumptions of a test are violated, the test may lead to an erroneous interpretation of the data. Fortunately, there are several hypothesis testing techniques that provide alternatives to parametric tests. These alternatives are called *nonparametric tests*.

In this chapter, we introduce some commonly used nonparametric tests. You should notice that these nonparametric tests usually do not state hypotheses in terms of a specific parameter, and they make few (if any) assumptions about the population distribution. For the latter reason, nonparametric tests sometimes are called *distribution-free tests*. Another distinction is that nonparametric tests are well suited for data that are measured on nominal or ordinal scales. Finally, you should be warned that nonparametric tests generally are not as sensitive as parametric tests; nonparametric tests are more likely to fail in detecting a real difference between two treatments. Therefore, whenever the experimental data give you a choice between a parametric and a nonparametric test, you always should choose the parametric alternative.

SECTION 15.2   **THE CHI-SQUARE TEST FOR GOODNESS OF FIT**

Parameters such as the mean and standard deviation are the most common way to describe a population, but there are situations where a researcher has questions about the shape of a frequency distribution. For example,

How does the number of women lawyers compare with the number of men in the profession?

Of the three leading brands of soft drinks, which is preferred by most Americans? Which brands are second and third, and how big are the differences in popularity among the three?

To what extent are different ethnic groups represented in the population of your city?

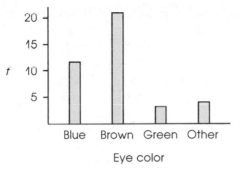

Eye color (X)	f
Blue	12
Brown	21
Green	3
Other	4

Blue	Brown	Green	Other
12	21	3	4

Figure 15.1

Distribution of eye colors for a sample of *n* = 40 individuals. The same frequency distribution is shown as a bar graph, as a table, and with the frequencies written in a series of boxes.

The name of the test comes from the Greek letter χ (chi, pronounced "kye") that is used to identify the test statistic.

Notice that each of the preceding examples asks a question about *how many*—in other words, these are all questions about frequencies. The chi-square test for goodness of fit is specifically designed to answer this type of question. In general terms, this chi-square test is a hypothesis-testing procedure that uses the frequency distribution for a sample to test hypotheses about the corresponding frequency distribution for a population.

DEFINITION

The chi-square test for *goodness of fit* determines how well the frequency distribution for a sample fits the population distribution that is specified by the null hypothesis.

You should recall from Chapter 2 that a frequency distribution is defined as a record of the number of individuals located in each category of the scale of measurement. In a frequency distribution graph, the categories that make up the scale of measurement are listed on the *X*-axis. In a frequency distribution table, the categories are listed in the first column. With chi-square tests, however, it is customary to present the scale of measurement as a series of boxes with each box corresponding to a separate category on the scale. The frequency corresponding to each category is simply presented as a number written inside the box. Figure 15.1 shows how a distribution of eye colors for a set of *n* = 40 students can be presented either as a graph, a table, or a series of boxes. Notice that the scale of measurement for this example consists of four categories of eye color (brown, blue, green, other).

THE NULL HYPOTHESIS FOR THE GOODNESS-OF-FIT TEST

For the chi-square test of goodness of fit, the null hypothesis specifies the proportion (or percentage) of the population in each category. For example a hypothesis might state that 90% of all lawyers are men and only 10% are women. The simplest way of presenting this hypothesis, is to put the hypothesized proportions in the series of boxes representing the scale of measurement:

	MEN	WOMEN
H_0:	90%	10%

Although it is conceivable that a researcher could choose any proportions for the null hypothesis, there usually is some well-defined rationale for stating a null hypothesis. Generally H_0 will fall into one of the following categories.

1. **No Preference.** The null hypothesis often states that there is no preference among the different categories. In this case, H_0 states that the population is divided equally among the categories. For example, a hypothesis stating that there is no preference among the three leading brands of soft drinks would specify a population distribution as follows:

	BRAND X	BRAND Y	BRAND Z
H_0:	$\frac{1}{3}$	$\frac{1}{3}$	$\frac{1}{3}$

2. **No Difference from a Comparison Population.** The null hypothesis can state that the frequency distribution for one population is not different from the distribution that is known to exist for another population. For example, suppose it is known that 60% of Americans favor the president's foreign policy and 40% are in opposition. A researcher might wonder if this same pattern of attitudes exists among Europeans. The null hypothesis would state that there is no difference between the two populations and specify the Europeans would be distributed as follows:

	FAVOR	OPPOSE
H_0:	60%	40%

Because the null hypothesis for the goodness-of-fit test specifies an exact distribution for the population, the alternative hypothesis (H_1) simply states that the population distribution has a different shape from that specified in H_0. If the null hypothesis stated that the population is equally divided among three categories, the alternative hypothesis would say that the population is not divided equally.

THE DATA FOR THE GOODNESS-OF-FIT TEST

The data for a chi-square test are remarkably simple. There is no need to calculate a sample mean or *SS*, you just select a sample of *n* individuals and count how many are in each category. The resulting values are called *observed frequencies*. The symbol for observed frequency is f_o. For example, the following data represent observed frequencies for a sample of $n = 40$ subjects. Each person was given a personality questionnaire and classified into one of three personality categories: A, B, or C.

CATEGORY A	CATEGORY B	CATEGORY C	
15	19	6	$n = 40$

Notice that each individual in the sample is classified into one and only one of the categories. Thus, the frequencies in this example represent three completely separate groups of individuals: 15 who were classified as category A, 19 classified as B, and 6 classified as C. Also note that the observed frequencies add up to the total sample size: $\Sigma f_o = n$.

DEFINITION

The *observed frequency* is the number of individuals from the sample who are classified in a particular category. Each individual is counted in one and only one category.

EXPECTED FREQUENCIES

The general goal of the chi-square test for goodness of fit is to compare the data (the observed frequencies) with the null hypothesis. The problem is to determine how well the data fit the distribution specified in H_0—hence the name *goodness of fit*.

The first step in the chi-square test is to determine how the sample distribution should look if the null hypothesis were exactly right. Suppose the null hypothesis states that the population is distributed in three categories with the following proportions:

CATEGORY A	CATEGORY B	CATEGORY C
25%	50%	25%

If this hypothesis is correct, how would you expect a random sample of $n = 40$ individuals to be distributed among the three categories? It should be clear that your best strategy is to predict 25% of the sample would be in category A, 50% would be in category B, and 25% would be in category C. To find the exact frequency expected for each category, multiply the sample size (n) by the proportion (or percentage) from the null hypothesis. For this example you would expect

$$25\% \text{ of } 40 = 0.25(40) = 10 \text{ individuals in category A}$$

$$50\% \text{ of } 40 = 0.50(40) = 20 \text{ individuals in category B}$$

$$25\% \text{ of } 40 = 0.25(40) = 10 \text{ individuals in category C}$$

The frequency values predicted from the null hypothesis are called *expected frequencies*. The symbol for expected frequency is f_e, and the expected frequency for each category is computed by

$$\text{expected frequency} = f_e = pn \tag{15.1}$$

where p is the proportion stated in the null hypothesis and n is the sample size.

DEFINITION

The *expected frequency* for each category is the frequency value that is predicted from the null hypothesis and the sample size (n).

THE CHI-SQUARE STATISTIC

The general purpose of any hypothesis test is to determine whether the sample data support or refute a hypothesis about the population. In the chi-square test for goodness of fit, the sample is expressed as a set of observed frequencies (f_o values), and the null hypothesis has been used to generate a set of expected frequencies (f_e values). The *chi-square statistic* simply measures how well the data (f_o) fit the

THE CHI-SQUARE FORMULA

WE HAVE seen that the chi-square formula compares observed frequencies to expected frequencies in order to assess how well the sample data match the hypothesized data. This function of the chi-square statistic is easy to spot in the numerator of the equation, $(f_o - f_e)^2$. The difference between the observed and expected frequencies is found first. The greater this difference, the more discrepancy there is between what is observed and what is expected. The difference is then squared to remove the negative signs (large discrepancies may have negative signs as well as positive signs). The summation sign in front of the equation indicates that we must examine the amount of discrepancy for every category. Why, then, must we divide the squared differences by f_e for each category before we sum the category values? Basically, we would view the $f_o - f_e$ discrepancies in a different light if f_e were very small or very large.

Suppose you were going to throw a party and you *expected* 1000 people to show up. However, at the party you counted the number of guests and *observed* that 1040 actually showed up. Forty more guests than expected are no major problem when all along you were planning for 1000. There will still probably be enough beer and potato chips for everyone. On the other hand, suppose you had a party and you expected 10 people to attend but instead 50 actually showed up. Forty more guests in this case spell big trouble. How "significant" the discrepancy is depends in part on what you were originally expecting. With very large expected frequencies, allowances are made for more error between f_o and f_e. This is accomplished in the chi-square formula by dividing the squared discrepancy for each category, $(f_o - f_e)^2$, by its expected frequency.

hypothesis (f_e). The symbol for the chi-square statistic is χ^2. The formula for the chi-square statistic is

$$\text{chi-square} = \chi^2 = \Sigma \frac{(f_o - f_e)^2}{f_e}$$

(15.2)

As the formula indicates, the value of chi-square is computed by the following steps:

1. Find the difference between f_o (the data) and f_e (the hypothesis) for each category.

2. Square the difference. This ensures that all values are positive.

3. Next, divide the squared difference by f_e. A justification for this step is given in Box 15.1.

4. Finally, sum the values from all the categories.

THE CHI-SQUARE DISTRIBUTION AND DEGREES OF FREEDOM

It should be clear from the chi-square formula that the value of chi-square is measuring the discrepancy between the observed frequencies (data) and the expected frequencies (H_0). When there are large differences between f_o and f_e the value of chi-square will be large, and we will conclude that the data do not fit the hypothesis. Thus, a large value for chi-square will lead us to reject H_0. On the other hand, when the observed frequencies are very close to the expected frequencies, chi-square will be small and we will conclude that there is a very good fit between the data and the hypothesis. Thus, a small chi-square value indicates that we should

Figure 15.2

Chi-square distributions are positively skewed. The critical region is placed in the extreme tail, which reflects large chi-square values.

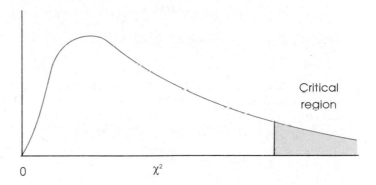

fail to reject H_0. To decide whether a particular chi-square value is "large" or "small," we must refer to a *chi-square distribution*. This distribution is the set of chi-square values for all the possible random samples when H_0 is true. Much like other distributions we have examined (t distribution, F distribution), the chi-square distribution is a theoretical distribution with well-defined characteristics. Some of these characteristics are easy to infer from the chi-square formula.

1. The formula for chi-square involves adding squared values, so you can never obtain a negative value. Thus, all chi-square values are zero or larger.

2. When H_0 is true, you expect the data (f_o values) to be close to the hypothesis (f_e values). Thus, we expect chi-square values to be small when H_0 is true.

These two factors suggest that the typical chi-square distribution will be positively skewed (see Figure 15.2). Note that small values, near zero, are expected when H_0 is true, and large values (in the right-hand tail) are very unlikely. Thus, unusually large values of chi-square will form the critical region for the hypothesis test.

Although the typical chi-square distribution is positively skewed, there is one other factor that plays a role in the exact shape of the chi-square distribution—the number of categories. You should recall that the chi-square formula requires that you sum values from every category. The more categories you have, the more likely it is that you will obtain a large sum for the chi-square value. On the average, chi-square will be larger when you are summing over 10 categories than when you are summing over only 3 categories. As a result, there is a whole family of chi-square distributions, with the exact shape of each distribution determined by the number of categories used in the study. Technically, each specific chi-square distribution is identified by degrees of freedom (*df*) rather than the number of categories. For the goodness-of-fit test, the degrees of freedom are determined by

$$df = C - 1 \tag{15.3}$$

where C is the number of categories. A brief discussion of this *df* formula is presented in Box 15.2. Figure 15.3 shows the general relation between *df* and the shape of the chi-square distribution. Note that the typical chi-square value (the mode) gets larger as the number of categories is increased.

15.2 A CLOSER LOOK AT DEGREES OF FREEDOM

DEGREES OF freedom for the chi-square test literally measure the number of free choices that exist when you are determining the null hypothesis or the expected frequencies. For example, when you are classifying individuals into three categories, you have exactly two free choices in stating the null hypothesis. You may select any two proportions for the first two categories, but then the third proportion is determined. If you hypothesize 25% in the first category and 50% in the second category, then the third category must be 25% in order to account for 100% of the population. In general, you are free to select proportions for all but one of the categories, but then the final proportion is determined by the fact that the entire set must total 100%. Thus, you have $C - 1$ free choices, where C is the number of categories: degrees of freedom, df, equals $C - 1$.

The same restriction holds when you are determining the expected frequencies. Again suppose that you have three categories and a sample of $n = 40$ individuals. If you specify expected frequencies of $f_e = 10$ for the first category and $f_e = 20$ for the second category, then you must use $f_e = 10$ for the final category.

CATEGORY A	CATEGORY B	CATEGORY C	
10	20	???	$n = 40$

As before, you may distribute the sample freely among the first $C - 1$ categories, but then the final category is determined by the total number of individuals in the sample.

Figure 15.3

The shape of the chi-square distribution for different values of *df*. As the number of categories increase, the peak (mode) of the distribution has a larger chi-square value.

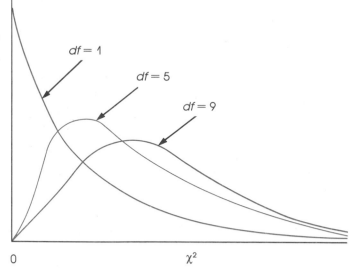

LOCATING THE CRITICAL REGION FOR A CHI-SQUARE TEST

To evaluate the results of a chi-square test, we must determine whether the chi-square statistic is large or small. Remember, an unusually large value indicates a big discrepancy between the data and the hypothesis and suggests that we reject H_0. To determine whether or not a particular chi-square value is significantly large, you first select an alpha level, typically .05 or .01. Then, you consult the table

Table 15.1

A portion of the table of critical values for the chi-square distribution

	PROPORTION IN CRITICAL REGION				
df	0.10	0.05	0.025	0.01	0.005
1	2.71	3.84	5.02	6.63	7.88
2	4.61	5.99	7.38	9.21	10.60
3	6.25	7.81	9.35	11.34	12.84
4	7.78	9.49	11.14	13.28	14.86
5	9.24	11.07	12.83	15.09	16.75
6	10.64	12.59	14.45	16.81	18.55
7	12.02	14.07	16.01	18.48	20.28
8	13.36	15.51	17.53	20.09	21.96
9	14.68	16.92	19.02	21.67	23.59

entitled The Chi-Square Distribution (Appendix B). A portion of the chi-square distribution table is shown in Table 15.1. The first column in the table lists df values for chi-square. The top row of the table lists proportions of area in the extreme right-hand tail of the distribution. The numbers in the body of the table are the critical values of chi-square. The table shows, for example, in a chi-square distribution with $df = 3$, only 5% (.05) of the values are larger than 7.81, and only 1% (.01) are larger than 11.34.

EXAMPLE OF THE CHI-SQUARE TEST FOR GOODNESS OF FIT

We will use the same step-by-step process for testing hypotheses with chi-square as we used for other hypothesis tests. In general, the steps consists of stating the hypotheses, locating the critical region, computing the test statistic, and making a decision about H_0. The following example demonstrates the complete process of hypothesis testing with the goodness-of-fit test.

EXAMPLE 15.1 A researcher is interested in the factors that are involved in course selection. A sample of 50 students is asked, "Which of the following factors is most important to you when selecting a course?" Students must choose one and only one of the following alternatives:

1. Interest in course topic
2. Ease of passing the course
3. Instructor for the course
4. Time of day course is offered

The frequency distribution of responses for this sample is summarized in Table 15.2. Do any of these factors play a greater role than others for course selection?

STEP 1 We must state the hypotheses and select a level of significance. The hypotheses may be stated as follows:

H_0: The population of students shows no preference in selecting any one of the four factors over the others. Thus, the four factors are named

Table 15.2

Part A: The most important factor in course selection (observed frequencies).

	INTEREST IN TOPIC	EASE OF PASSING	COURSE INSTRUCTOR	TIME OF DAY
f_o	18	17	7	8

It is acceptable for expected frequencies to have fractional or decimal values.

Part B: The expected frequencies for Example 15.1

	INTEREST IN TOPIC	EASE OF PASSING	COURSE INSTRUCTOR	TIME OF DAY
f_e	12.5	12.5	12.5	12.5

equally often, and the population distribution has the following proportions:

INTEREST IN TOPIC	EASE OF PASSING	COURSE INSTRUCTOR	TIME OF DAY
$\frac{1}{4}$	$\frac{1}{4}$	$\frac{1}{4}$	$\frac{1}{4}$

H_1: In the population of students, one or more of these factors plays a greater role in course selection (the factor is named more frequently by students).

The level of significance is set at a standard value, $\alpha = .05$.

STEP 2   The value for degrees of freedom is determined, and then the critical region is located. For this example, the value for degrees of freedom is

$$df = C - 1 = 4 - 1 = 3$$

For $df = 3$ and $\alpha = .05$, the table for critical values of chi-square indicates that the critical χ^2 has a value of 7.81. The critical region is sketched in Figure 15.4.

Figure 15.4

For Example 15.1, the critical region begins at a chi-square value of 7.81

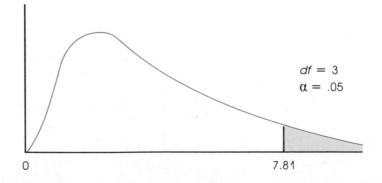

$df = 3$
$\alpha = .05$

0   7.81

STEP 3 The expected frequencies for all categories must be determined, and then the chi-square statistic can be calculated. If H_0 were true and the students display no response preference for the four alternatives, then the proportion of the population responding to each category would be ¼. Because the sample size (n) is 50, the null hypothesis predicts expected frequencies of 12.5 for all categories (Table 15.2):

$$f_e = pn = \tfrac{1}{4}(50) = 12.5$$

Using the observed and the expected frequencies from Table 15.2, the chi-square statistic may now be calculated:

$$\chi^2 = \Sigma \frac{(f_o - f_e)^2}{f_e}$$

$$= \frac{(18 - 12.5)^2}{12.5} + \frac{(17 - 12.5)^2}{12.5} + \frac{(7 - 12.5)^2}{12.5} + \frac{(8 - 12.5)^2}{12.5}$$

$$= \frac{30.25}{12.5} + \frac{20.25}{12.5} + \frac{30.25}{12.5} + \frac{20.25}{12.5}$$

$$= 2.42 + 1.62 + 2.42 + 1.62$$

$$= 8.08$$

STEP 4 The obtained chi-square value is in the critical region. Therefore, H_0 is rejected, and the researcher may conclude that the subjects mentioned some of the factors more than others in response to the question about course selection. In a research report, the investigator might state:

> The students showed a significant response preference to the question concerning factors involved in course selection, $\chi^2(3, n = 50) = 8.08$, $p < .05$.

Note that the form of reporting the chi-square value is similar to that of other statistical tests we have encountered. Degrees of freedom and the sample size are indicated in the parentheses after the χ^2 symbol. This information is followed by the obtained chi-square value and then by the probability that a Type I error has been committed.

LEARNING CHECK 1. A researcher for an insurance company would like to know if high-performance, overpowered automobiles are more likely to be involved in accidents than other types of cars. For a sample of 50 insurance claims, the investigator classifies the automobiles as high-performance, subcompact, midsize, or full-size. The observed frequencies are as follows:

Observed frequencies of insurance claims

HIGH-PERFORMANCE	SUBCOMPACT	MIDSIZE	FULL-SIZE	TOTAL
20	14	7	9	50

In determining the f_e values, assume that only 10% of the cars in the population are the high-performance variety. However, subcompacts, midsize cars, and full-size cars make up 40%, 30%, and 20%, respectively. Can the researcher conclude that the observed pattern of accidents does not fit the predicted (f_e) values? Test with $\alpha = .05$.

    a. In a few sentences, state the hypotheses.

    b. Determine the value for *df* and locate the critical region.

    c. Determine f_e values and compute chi-square.

    d. Make a decision regarding H_0.

ANSWERS **1. a.** H_0: In the population, no particular type of car shows a disproportionate number of accidents. H_1: In the population, a disproportionate number of the accidents occur with certain types of cars.

    b. $df = 3$; the critical χ^2 value is 7.81.

    c. The f_e values for high-performance, subcompact, midsize, and full-size cars are 5, 20, 15, and 10, respectively. The obtained chi-square is 51.17.

    d. Reject H_0.

SECTION 15.3 **THE CHI-SQUARE TEST FOR INDEPENDENCE**

The chi-square statistic may also be used to test whether or not there is a relationship between two varibles. In this situation, each individual in the sample is measured or classified on two separate variables. For example, a group of students could be classified in terms of personality (introvert, extrovert) and in terms of color preference (red, yellow, green, or blue). Usually the data from this classification are presented in the form of a matrix, where the rows correspond to the categories of one variable and the columns correspond to the categories of the second variable. Table 15.3 presents some hypothetical data for a sample of $n = 400$ students who have been classified by personality and color preference. The number in each box, or cell, of the matrix depicts the frequency of that particular group. In Table 15.3, for example, there are 20 introverted students who selected red as their preferred color and 180 extroverted students who preferred red. To obtain these data the researcher first selects a random sample of $n = 400$ students. Each student is then given a personality test, and each student is asked to select a preferred color from among the four choices. Notice that the classification is based on the measurements for each student, the researcher does not assign students to categories. Also notice that the data consist of frequencies, not scores, from a sample. These sample data will be used to test a hypothesis about the corresponding population frequency

Table 15.3

Color preferences according to personality types

	RED	YELLOW	GREEN	BLUE	
Introvert	20	6	30	44	100
Extrovert	180	34	50	36	300
	200	40	80	80	$n = 400$

distribution. Once again we will be using the chi-square statistic for the test, but in this case the test is called the chi-square *test for independence*.

THE NULL HYPOTHESIS

The null hypothesis for the chi-square test for independence states that there is no relationship between the two variables being measured; that is, the two variables are independent. For the example we have been considering, H_0 could be stated as

> H_0: For the general population of students, color preference is independent of personality.

The alternative hypothesis, H_1, says that there is a relation between the two variables. For this example, H_1 states that color preference does depend on personality.

OBSERVED AND EXPECTED FREQUENCIES

The chi-square test for independence uses the same basic logic that was used for the goodness-of-fit test. First, a sample is selected and each individual is classified or categorized. Because the test for independence considers two variables, every individual is classified on both variables, and the resulting frequency distribution is presented as a two-dimensional matrix (see Table 15.3). As before, the frequencies in the sample distribution are called observed frequencies and are identified by the symbol f_o.

The next step is to find the frequency distribution that would be predicted from the null hypothesis. As before, the frequencies generated from H_0 are called expected frequencies and are identified by the symbol f_e. Once the expected frequencies are obtained, we will compute a chi-square statistic to determine how well the data (observed values) fit the hypothesis (expected values). Before we get to the chi-square formula, however, we must face the relatively complex task of finding expected frequencies for the chi-square test of independence. The data in Table 15.3 will be used to help introduce the calculation of expected frequencies.

The data in Table 15.3 provide a set of observed frequencies. Our problem is to find the set of expected frequencies for this example. Remember, expected frequencies specify how the sample would be distributed if the null hypothesis were correct. Therefore, the f_e values are based on the null hypothesis and the sample size. We will begin by examining H_0. For this example, the null hypothesis would state

We could state H_0 as "personality is independent of color preference."

> H_0: Color preference is independent of personality

If this hypothesis is correct we would expect no consistent, predictable differences between the color preferences for introverts versus the color preferences for extroverts. For example, if we found that 60% of the introverts preferred red, we would expect that approximately 60% of the extroverts also would prefer red. On the other hand, a big difference in the color preference distributions for introverts versus extroverts would indicate that there is a relation between the two variables. For example, if the data showed that 60% of the extroverts chose red but only 10% of the introverts preferred red, we would probably conclude that color preference is related to personality.

In general, when two variables are independent, the distribution for one variable will not depend on the categories of the second variable. In other words, the

Table 15.4

Expected frequencies for color
preferences and personality types

Part A: An empty frequency distribution matrix showing only the row
totals and column totals. These numbers describe the basic
characteristics of the sample from Table 15.3.

	Red	Yellow	Green	Blue	
Introvert					100
Extrovert					300
	200	40	80	80	

Part B: Expected frequencies. This is the distribution that is predicted
by the null hypothesis.

	Red	Yellow	Green	Blue	
Introvert	50	10	20	20	100
Extrovert	150	30	60	60	300
	200	40	80	80	

frequency distribution for one variable will have the *same shape* (same proportions)
for all categories of the second variable.

DEFINITION

Two variables are *independent* when the frequency distribution for one
variable is not related to (or dependent on) the categories of the second
variable. As a result, the frequency distribution for one variable will have
the same shape for all categories of the second variable.

Thus, we can restate the null hypothesis for this example as follows:

H_0: The frequency distribution for color preference has the same shape
for all categories of personality.

Now, we are ready to look at the size of the sample.

The data in Table 15.3 represent a sample of $n = 400$ individuals. However, this
total sample is already divided into a set of predetermined subgroups. For example,
the sample contains 100 introverts and a separate group of 300 extroverts. Similarly,
the total sample consists of 200 people who selected red as their favorite color, 40
people who picked yellow, 80 who choose green, and 80 who preferred blue. These
subgroup sizes are crucial to the calculation of expected frequencies. Fortunately,
the subgroup numbers are easily obtained by reading the row totals and the column
totals from the data (the observed frequencies).

Part A of Table 15.4 presents an empty frequency distribution table, listing only
row totals and column totals. This empty table identifies the general characteristics
of the sample ($n = 400$, with 100 introverts, etc.). To find the expected frequencies,
we must determine how the sample should be distributed according to the null
hypothesis. In other words, our problem is to fill in the empty spaces in the table.

Once again, the null hypothesis states that the distribution of color preferences
should have the same shape for introverts as for extroverts. But what is the
"distribution of color preferences"? The best information we have about this
distribution comes from the sample data. The column totals from the sample show
the following distribution (see part A of Table 15.4):

$$200 \text{ out of } 400 \text{ choose red:} \quad \frac{200}{400} = 50\% \text{ red}$$

$$40 \text{ out of } 400 \text{ choose yellow:} \quad \frac{40}{400} = 10\% \text{ yellow}$$

$$80 \text{ out of } 400 \text{ choose green:} \quad \frac{80}{400} = 20\% \text{ green}$$

$$80 \text{ out of } 400 \text{ choose blue:} \quad \frac{80}{400} = 20\% \text{ blue}$$

If H_0 is true, we would expect to obtain this same distribution of color preferences for both introverts and extroverts. Therefore, expected frequencies can be obtained by applying the color-preference distribution equally to the set of 100 introverts and to the set of 300 extroverts. The resulting f_e values are as follows.

For the 100 introverts, we expect

$$50\% \text{ choose red:} \quad f_e = 0.50(100) = 50$$

$$10\% \text{ choose yellow:} \quad f_e = 0.10(100) = 10$$

$$20\% \text{ choose green:} \quad f_e = 0.20(100) = 20$$

$$20\% \text{ choose blue:} \quad f_e = 0.20(100) = 20$$

For the 300 extroverts, we expect

$$50\% \text{ choose red:} \quad f_e = 0.50(300) = 150$$

$$10\% \text{ choose yellow:} \quad f_e = 0.10(300) = 30$$

$$20\% \text{ choose green:} \quad f_e = 0.20(300) = 60$$

$$20\% \text{ choose blue:} \quad f_e = 0.20(300) = 60$$

These expected frequencies are shown in part B of Table 15.4. Notice that the row totals and column totals for the expected frequencies are the same as those for the original data in Table 15.3.

A SIMPLE FORMULA FOR DETERMINING EXPECTED FREQUENCIES

Although you should understand that expected frequencies are derived directly from the null hypothesis and the sample characteristics, it is not necessary to go through extensive calculations in order to find f_e values. In fact, there is a simple formula that determines f_e for any cell in the frequency distribution table.

$$f_e = \frac{f_c f_r}{n} \tag{15.4}$$

where f_c is the frequency total for the column (column total), f_r is the frequency total for the row (row total), and n is the number of individuals in the entire sample. To demonstrate this formula, we will compute the expected frequency for introverts selecting yellow in Table 15.4(A). First note that this cell is located in the top row and second column in the table. The column total is $f_c = 40$, the row total is $f_r = 100$, and the sample size is $n = 400$. Using these values in formula 15.4, we obtain

Table 15.5

Degrees of freedom and expected frequencies. Once three values have been selected, all the remaining expected frequencies are determined by the row totals and the column totals. This example has only three free choices, so $df = 3$.

	RED	YELLOW	GREEN	BLUE	
	50	10	20	?	100
	?	?	?	?	300
	200	40	80	80	

$$f_e = \frac{f_c f_r}{n} = \frac{40(100)}{400} = 10$$

Notice that this is identical to the expected frequency we obtained using percentages from the overall distribution.

THE CHI-SQUARE STATISTIC AND DEGREES OF FREEDOM

The chi-square test of independence uses exactly the same chi-square formula as the test for goodness of fit:

$$\chi^2 = \Sigma \frac{(f_o - f_e)^2}{f_e}$$

As before, the formula measures the discrepancy between the data (f_o values) and the hypothesis (f_e values). A large discrepancy will produce a large value for chi-square and will indicate that H_0 should be rejected. To determine whether a particular chi-square statistic is significantly large, you must first determine degrees of freedom (df) for the statistic and then consult the chi-square distribution in the appendix. For the chi-square test of independence, degrees of freedom are based on the number of cells for which you can freely choose expected frequencies. You should recall that the f_e values are partially determined by the sample size (n) and by the row totals and column totals from the original data. These various totals restrict your freedom in selecting expected frequencies. This point is illustrated in Table 15.5. Once three of the f_e values have been selected, all the other f_e values in the table are also determined. In general, the row totals and column totals restrict the final choices in each row and column. Thus, we may freely choose all but one expected frequency in each row and all but one f_e in each column. The total number of f_e values that you can freely choose is $(R - 1)(C - 1)$, where R is the number of rows and C is the number of columns. The degrees of freedom for the chi-square test of independence are given by the formula

$$df = (R - 1)(C - 1) \tag{15.5}$$

AN EXAMPLE OF THE CHI-SQUARE TEST FOR INDEPENDENCE

The steps for the chi-square test of independence should be familiar by now. First, the hypotheses are stated, and an alpha level is selected. Second, the value for degrees of freedom is computed, and the critical region is located. Third, expected frequencies are determined, and the chi-square statistic is computed. Finally, a decision is made regarding the null hypothesis. The following example demonstrates the complete hypothesis-testing procedure.

Table 15.6

The relationship between size of group and the type of response to the victim.

Part A. Observed frequencies

| | GROUP SIZE | | | |
	2	3	6	Totals
Assistance	11	16	4	31
No Assistance	2	10	9	21
Totals	13	26	13	

Part B: Expected frequencies.

| | GROUP SIZE | | | |
	2	3	6	Totals
Assistance	7.75	15.5	7.75	31
No Assistance	5.25	10.5	5.25	21
Totals	13	26	13	

J. M. Darley and D. Latané (1968) Bystander intervention in emergencies: Diffusion of responsibility. *Journal of Personality and Social Psychology, 8,* 377–383. Copyright (1968) by the American Psychological Association. Adapted with permission of the publisher and first author.

EXAMPLE 15.2

Darley and Latané (1968) did a study that examined the relationship between the number of observers and aid-giving behaviors. The group sizes consisted of two people (subject and victim), three people, or six people. The investigators categorized the response of a subject in terms of whether or not the observer exhibited any helping behaviors when the victim (actually another laboratory worker) staged an epileptic seizure. The data are presented in Table 15.6. Do aid-giving behaviors depend on group size?

STEP 1

State the hypotheses and select a level of significance. According to the null hypothesis, group size and helping behavior are independent of each other in the population. That is, the absence or presence of aid-giving behavior should not be related to the number of observers. The alternative hypothesis would state that the absence or presence of helping behavior is dependent on group size. The level of significance is set at $\alpha = .05$.

STEP 2

Calculate the degrees of freedom and locate the critical region. For the chi-square test of independence,

$$df = (R - 1)(C - 1)$$

Therefore, for this study.

$$df = (2 - 1)(3 - 1) = 1(2) = 2$$

With two degrees of freedom and a level of significance of .05, the critical value for χ^2 is 5.99 (see table for critical values of chi-square).

STEP 3   Determine the expected frequencies and calculate the chi-square statistic. As noted before, it is quicker to use the computational formula to determine the f_e values, rather than the percentage method. The expected frequency for each cell is as follows:

1. Group size 2 — showed aid-giving behavior:

$$f_e = \frac{f_c\, f_r}{n} = \frac{13(31)}{52} = 7.75$$

2. Group size 3 — showed aid-giving behavior:

$$f_e = \frac{26(31)}{52} = 15.5$$

3. Group size 6 — showed aid-giving behavior:

$$f_e = \frac{13(31)}{52} = 7.75$$

4. Group size 2 — no aid-giving behavior:

$$f_e = \frac{13(21)}{52} = 5.25$$

5. Group size 3 — no aid-giving behavior:

$$f_e = \frac{26(21)}{52} = 10.5$$

6. Group size 6 — no aid-giving behavior:

$$f_e = \frac{13(21)}{52} = 5.25$$

Note that the row totals and column totals for the expected frequencies are the same as the totals for the observed frequencies.

The expected frequencies are summarized in Table 15.6. Using these expected frequencies along with the observed frequencies (part A of Table 15.6), we can now calculate the value for the chi-square statistic:

$$\chi^2 = \Sigma \frac{(f_o - f_e)^2}{f_e}$$

$$= \frac{(11 - 7.75)^2}{7.75} + \frac{(16 - 15.5)^2}{15.5} + \frac{(4 - 7.75)^2}{7.75}$$

$$+ \frac{(2 - 5.25)^2}{5.25} + \frac{(10 - 10.5)^2}{10.5} + \frac{(9 - 5.25)^2}{5.25}$$

$$= 1.363 + 0.016 + 1.815 + 2.012 + 0.024 + 2.679$$

$$= 7.91$$

STEP 4   Make a decision regarding the null hypothesis. The obtained chi-square value exceeds the critical value (5.99). Therefore, the decision is to reject H_0 and conclude that there is a relationship between group size and the likelihood that someone will aid another person in trouble. For purposes of reporting the data, the researchers could state that there is a significant relationship between size of group and helping behavior, $\chi^2(2, n = 52) = 7.91$, $p < .05$. By examining the observed frequencies in part A of Table 15.6, we see that the likelihood of aid-giving behavior decreases as group size increases.

LEARNING CHECK

1. A researcher suspects that color blindness is inherited by a sex-linked gene. This possibility is examined by looking for a relationship between gender and color vision. A sample of 1000 people is tested for color blindness, and then they are classified according to their sex and color vision status (normal, red-green blind, other color blindness). Is color blindness related to gender? The data are as follows:

Observed Frequencies of Color
Vision Status According to Sex

	NORMAL COLOR VISION	RED-GREEN COLOR BLINDNESS	OTHER COLOR BLINDNESS	Totals
Male	320	70	10	400
Female	580	10	10	600
Totals	900	80	20	

   a. State the hypotheses.
   b. Determine the value for *df* and locate the critical region.
   c. Compute the f_e values and then chi-square.
   d. Make a decision regarding H_0.

ANSWERS

1. a. H_0: In the population, there is no relationship between gender and color vision.
      H_1: In the population, gender and color vision are related.
   b. $df = 2$; critical $\chi^2 = 5.99$ for $\alpha = .05$.
   c. f_e values are as follows:

Expected Frequencies

	NORMAL	RED-GREEN	OTHER
Male	360	32	8
Female	540	48	12

   Obtained $\chi^2 = 83.44$
   d. Reject H_0.

SECTION 15.4   **ASSUMPTIONS AND RESTRICTIONS FOR CHI-SQUARE TESTS**

To use a chi-square test for goodness of fit or a test of independence, several conditions must be satisfied. For any statistical test, violation of assumptions and restrictions will cast doubt on the results. For example, the probability of committing a Type I error may be distorted when assumptions of statistical tests are not satisfied. Some important assumptions and restrictions for using chi-square tests are the following:

1. **Random Sampling.** As we have seen with other inferential techniques, it is assumed that the sample under study is selected randomly from the population of interest.

2. **Independence of Observations.** This is *not* to be confused with the concept of independence between *variables* as seen in the test of independence (Section 15.3). By independence of observations, it is assumed that each observed frequency is generated by a different subject. A chi-square test would be inappropriate if a person could produce responses that can be classified in more than one category or contribute more than one frequency count to a single category.

3. **Size of Expected Frequencies.** A chi-square test should not be performed when the expected frequency of any cell is less than 5. The chi-square statistic can be distorted when f_e is very small. Consider the chi-square computations for a single cell. Suppose the cell has values of $f_e = 1$ and $f_o = 5$. The contribution of this cell to the total chi-square value is

$$\text{cell} = \frac{(f_o - f_e)^2}{f_e} = \frac{(5 - 1)^2}{1} = \frac{4^2}{1} = 16$$

Now consider another instance, where $f_e = 10$ and $f_o = 14$. The difference between the observed and expected frequency is still 4, but the contribution of this cell to the total chi-square value differs from that of the first case:

$$\text{cell} = \frac{(f_o - f_e)^2}{f_e} = \frac{(14 - 10)^2}{10} = \frac{4^2}{10} = 1.6$$

It should be clear that a small f_e value can have a great influence on the chi-square value. This problem becomes serious when f_e values are less than 5. When f_e is very small, what would otherwise be a minor discrepancy between f_o and f_e will now result in large chi-square values. The test is too sensitive when f_e values are extremely small. One way to avoid small expected frequencies is to use large samples.

SUMMARY

1. Chi-square tests are a type of nonparametric technique that tests hypotheses about the form of the entire frequency distribution. Two types of chi-square tests are the test for goodness of fit and the test for independence. The data for these tests consist of the fre-

quency of observations that fall into various categories of a variable.

2. The test for goodness of fit compares the frequency distribution for a sample to the frequency distribution that is predicted by H_0. The test determines how well the observed frequencies (sample data) fit the expected frequencies (data predicted by H_0).

3. The expected frequencies for the goodness-of-fit test are determined by

$$\text{expected frequency} = f_c = pn$$

where p is the hypothesized proportion (according to H_0) of observations falling into a category and n is the size of the sample.

4. The chi-square statistic is computed by

$$\text{chi-square} = \chi^2 = \Sigma \frac{(f_o - f_e)^2}{f_e}$$

where f_o is the observed frequency for a particular category and f_e is the expected frequency for that category. Large values for χ^2 indicate that there is a large discrepancy between the observed (f_o) and expected (f_e) frequencies and may warrant rejection of the null hypothesis.

5. Degrees of freedom for the test for goodness of fit are

$$df = C - 1$$

where C is the number of categories in the variable. Degrees of freedom measure the number of categories for which f_e values can be freely chosen. As can be seen from the formula, all but the last f_e value to be determined are free to vary.

6. The chi-square distribution is positively skewed and begins at the value of zero. Its exact shape is determined by degrees of freedom.

7. The test for independence is used to assess the relationship between two variables. The null hypothesis states that the two variables in question are independent of each other. That is, the frequency distribution for one variable does not depend on the categories of the second variable. On the other hand, if a relationship does exist, then the form of the distribution for one variable will depend on the categories of the other variable.

8. For the test for independence, the expected frequencies for H_0 can be directly calculated from the marginal frequency totals,

$$f_e = \frac{f_c f_r}{n}$$

where f_c is the total column frequency and f_r is the total row frequency for the cell in question.

9. Degrees of freedom for the test for independence are computed by

$$df = (R - 1)(C - 1)$$

where R is the number of row categories and C is the number of column categories.

10. For the test of independence, a large chi-square value means there is a large discrepancy between the f_o and f_e values. Rejecting H_0 in this test provides support for a relationship between the two variables.

11. Both chi-square tests (for goodness of fit and independence) are based on the assumption that the sample is randomly selected from the population. It is also assumed that each observation is independent of the others. That is, each observed frequency reflects a different individual, and no individual can produce a response that would be classified in more than one category or more than one frequency in a single category.

12. The chi-square statistic is distorted when f_e values are small. Chi-square tests, therefore, are restricted to situations where f_e values are 5 or greater. The test should not be performed when the expected frequency of any cell is less than 5.

KEY TERMS

goodness-of-fit test	expected frequencies	distribution of chi-square	test for independence
observed frequencies	chi-square statistic		

FOCUS ON PROBLEM SOLVING

1. The expected frequencies that you calculate must satisfy the constraints of the sample. For the goodness-of-fit test, $\Sigma f_e = \Sigma f_o = n$. For the test of independence, the row totals and column totals for the expected frequencies should be identical to the corresponding totals for the observed frequencies.

2. It is entirely possible to have fractional (decimal) values for expected frequencies. Observed frequencies, however, are always whole numbers.

3. Whenever $df = 1$, the difference between observed and expected frequencies ($f_o - f_e$) will be identical (the same value) for all cells. This makes the calculation of chi-square easier.

4. Although you are advised to compute expected frequencies for all categories (or cells), you should realize that it is not essential to calculate all f_e values separately. Remember, df for chi-square identifies the number of f_e values that are free to vary. Once you have calculated that number of f_e values, the remaining f_e values are determined. You can get these remaining values by subtracting the calculated f_e values from their corresponding row or column totals.

5. Remember, unlike previous statistical tests, the degrees of freedom (df) for a chi-square test are *not* determined by the sample size (n). Be careful!

DEMONSTRATION 15.1   TEST FOR INDEPENDENCE

A manufacturer of watches would like to examine preferences for digital versus analog watches. A sample of $n = 200$ people is selected and these individuals are classified by age and preference. The manufacturer would like to know if there is a relationship between age and watch preference. The observed frequencies (f_o) are as follows:

		PREFERENCE		
		DIGITAL	ANALOG	UNDECIDED
Age	under 30	90	40	10
	over 30	10	40	10

STEP 1 State the hypotheses and select an alpha level.

The null hypothesis states that there is no relationship between the two variables.

H_0: Preference is independent of age. That is, the frequency distribution of preferences has the same form for people under 30 as for people over 30.

The alternative hypothesis states that there is a relationship between the two variables.

H_1: Preference is related to age. That is, the type of watch preferred depends on a person's age.

We will set alpha to $\alpha = .05$.

STEP 2 Locate the critical region.

Degrees of freedom for the chi-square test for independence are determined by

$$df = (C - 1)(R - 1)$$

For these data,

$$df = (3 - 1)(2 - 1) = 2(1) = 2$$

For $df = 2$ with $\alpha = .05$, the critical chi-square value is 5.99. Thus, our obtained chi-square must exceed 5.99 to be in the critical region and to reject H_0.

STEP 3 Compute the test statistic.

Computing the chi-square statistic requires the following preliminary calculations:
1. Obtain the row and column totals
2. Calculate expected frequencies

Row and column totals. We start by determining the row and column totals from the original observed frequencies, f_o.

	DIGITAL	ANALOG	UNDECIDED	row totals
under 30	90	40	10	140
over 30	10	40	10	60
column totals	100	80	20	$n = 200$

Expected frequencies, f_e. For the test for independence, the following formula is used to obtain expected frequencies:

$$f_e = \frac{f_c f_r}{n}$$

For people under 30, we obtain the following expected frequencies.

$$f_e = \frac{100(140)}{200} = \frac{14000}{200} = 70 \text{ for digital}$$

$$f_e = \frac{80(140)}{200} = \frac{11200}{200} = 56 \text{ for analog}$$

$$f_e = \frac{20(140)}{200} = \frac{2800}{200} = 14 \text{ for undecided}$$

For individuals over 30, the expected frequencies are as follows:

$$f_e = \frac{100(60)}{200} = \frac{6000}{200} = 30 \text{ for digital}$$

$$f_e = \frac{80(60)}{200} = \frac{4800}{200} = 24 \text{ for analog}$$

$$f_e = \frac{20(60)}{200} = \frac{1200}{200} = 6 \text{ for undecided}$$

The following table summarizes the expected frequencies.

	DIGITAL	ANALOG	UNDECIDED
under 30	70	56	14
over 30	30	24	6

The chi-square statistic. The chi-square statistic is computed from the formula,

$$\chi^2 = \Sigma \frac{(f_o - f_e)^2}{f_e}$$

That is, we must
1. find the $f_o - f_e$ difference for each cell
2. square these differences
3. divide the squared differences by f_e
4. sum the results of 3

The following table summarizes these calculations.

CELL	f_o	f_e	$(f_o - f_e)$	$(f_o - f_e)^2$	$(f_o - f_e)^2/f_e$
under 30 — digital	90	70	20	400	5.71
under 30 — analog	40	56	−16	256	4.57
under 30 — undecided	10	14	−4	16	1.14
over 30 — digital	10	30	−20	400	13.33
over 30 — analog	40	24	16	256	10.67
over 30 — undecided	10	6	4	16	2.67

Finally, we can sum the last column to get the chi-square value.

$$\chi^2 = 5.71 + 4.57 + 1.14 + 13.33 + 10.67 + 2.67$$
$$= 38.09$$

STEP 4   Make a decision about H_0 and state the conclusion.
    The chi-square value is in the critical region. Therefore, we can reject the null hypothesis. There is a relationship between watch preference and age, $\chi^2(2, n = 200) = 38.09$, $p < .05$.

PROBLEMS

1. An advertising researcher is trying to determine the criteria that people use when choosing a new car. The researcher selects a sample of $n = 100$ people and asks each person to select what they consider to be the "most important factor in selecting a new car" from a list of alternatives. The data are as follows:

COST	STYLING	PERFORMANCE	RELIABILITY
30	10	20	40

On the basis of these observed frequencies, can the researcher conclude that there is any specific factor (or factors) which is most often cited as being important? Test at the .05 level of significance.

2. A researcher would like to determine if any particular age group has a greater risk of influenza-related death. A sample of 50 such cases is categorized according to the victim's age. The observed frequencies are as follows:

NUMBER OF FLU-RELATED DEATHS

UNDER 30	30 TO 60	OVER 60
5	5	40

It should be noted that in the city from which the sample was selected, 30% of the population is in the "under 30" bracket, 40% in "30 to 60," and 30% in "over 60." (This information should help in determining f_e values.) Can the investigator conclude the risk differs with age? Test with the .05 level of significance.

3. A researcher noticed that one of the laboratory rats seemed to have a strong preference for taking the right-hand branch in a T-maze. During a series of 20 trials, this rat took the right-hand branch 17 times and went left only 3 times. Explain why you should not use a chi-square goodness-of-fit test to evaluate these data.

4. A questionnaire given to last year's freshman class indicated that 30% intended to be science majors, 50% intended to major in social science or humanities, and 20% were interested in professional programs. A random sample of 100 students from the current freshman class yielded the following frequency distribution:

INTENDED MAJOR

SCIENCES	SOCIAL SCIENCE OR HUMANITIES	PROFESSIONAL
35	40	25

a. On the basis of these data, should the university officials conclude that there has been a significant change in student interests? Test at the .05 level of significance.

b. If twice as many students had been sampled with the result that the observed frequencies were doubled in each of the three categories, would there be evidence for a significant change? Again, test with $\alpha = .05$

c. How do you explain the different conclusions for parts a and b?

5. A researcher is investigating the physical characteristics that influence whether or not a person's face is judged as beautiful. The researcher selects a photograph of a woman and then creates two modifications of the photo by (1) moving the eyes slightly farther apart and (2) moving the eyes slightly closer together. The original photograph and the two modifications are then shown to a sample of $n = 150$ college students, and each student is asked to select the "most beautiful" of the three faces. The distribution of responses was as follows:

ORIGINAL PHOTO	EYES MOVED APART	EYES MOVED TOGETHER
51	72	27

Do these data indicate any significant preferences among the three versions of the photograph? Test at the .05 level of significance.

6. A marketing researcher would like to determine if a preference exists among adult readers for one of the three leading weekly news magazines. In a telephone survey, a sample of $n = 1000$ people are asked to select the magazine they like the most: *Newsweek, Time,* or *U.S. News and World Report.* The observed frequencies are as follows:

SELECTION

	NEWSWEEK	TIME	U.S. NEWS
f_o	342	355	303

Is there a significant preference? Test at the .05 level of significance.

7. It is known that blood type varies among different populations of people. In the United States, for example, types O, A, B, and AB blood make up 45%, 41%, 10%, and 4% of the population, respectively. Suppose blood type is determined for a sample of $n = 136$ individuals from a foreign country. The resulting frequency distribution is as follows:

BLOOD TYPE

	O	A	B	AB
f_o	43	38	41	14

Is there a significant difference between this distribution and what we would expect for the United States? Set alpha at .05.

8. Suppose an opinion poll taken in 1970 revealed the following data regarding the legalization of marijuana: 15% in favor of, 79% against, and 6% no opinion regarding legalization. Suppose you took a random sample of $n = 220$ people today and obtained the following data:

ATTITUDE TOWARD LEGALIZATION OF MARIJUANA

	FOR	AGAINST	NO OPINION
f_o	38	165	17

Is there a significant difference between the current data and what were obtained in 1970? Use the .05 level of significance.

9. A consumer research organization recently conducted a taste-test comparing three major brands of diet cola. A random sample of $n = 200$ people was obtained. Each person tasted all three brands and then selected his or her favorite. The frequency distribution from this study is as follows:

BRAND X	BRAND Y	BRAND Z
78	51	71

Do these data indicate any significant preferences among the three brands? Test at the .05 level of significance.

10. A psychologist would like to determine if there is a relationship between extroversion and cigarette smoking. A random sample of 150 people is selected. Each person is given a standard personality inventory to classify him or her as an introvert or extrovert. Each must also provide information about how much he or she smokes (never, less than a pack per day, more than a pack per day). The observed frequencies are as follows:

NUMBER OF CIGARETTES PER DAY

	NONE	LESS THAN A PACK	MORE THAN A PACK
Extrovert	50	12	28
Introvert	50	8	2

Can the psychologist conclude there is a relationship between these personality types and smoking behavior? Set alpha at .05.

11. A scientist would like to see if there is a relationship between handedness and eye preference. A random sample of $n = 150$ subjects is selected. For each subject the researcher determines two things: (1) whether the person is left-handed or right-handed and (2) which eye the person prefers to use when looking through a camera viewfinder. The observed frequencies are as follow:

HAND PREFERENCE

		LEFT	RIGHT
Eye Preference	Left	20	40
	Right	10	80

Is there a relationship between the two variables? Test at the .01 level of significance.

12. A researcher is interested in the relation between IQ and vocabulary for 5-year-old children.
   a. Explain how the relationship might be examined using a Pearson correlation. Specifically, describe the data that the researcher would need to collect.
   b. Explain how the relationship might be examined using a chi-square test for independence. Again, describe the data that the researcher would need to collect.

13. A random sample of 200 people is selected to determine if there is any relationship between an individual's educational background and his or her opinion concerning additional funding for higher education. Each person is classified according to the highest degree obtained and requested to give an opinion. Use the following data to determine if there is a relationship between the two variables. Set alpha at .05.

	FOR FUNDING	ATTITUDE AGAINST FUNDING	UNDECIDED
No Degree	16	26	58
High School	4	2	34
College	30	2	28

	TYPE OF POSITION		
	TEACHERS	ADMINISTRATION	COUNSELORS
Approve of Merit Raises	265	14	33
Against Merit Raises	124	37	21

Is there a relationship between the two variables? Test at the .01 level of significance.

14. The U.S. Senate recently considered a controversial amendment for school prayer. The amendment did not get the required two thirds majority, but the results of the vote are interesting when viewed in terms of the party affiliation of the senators. The data are as follows:

PRAYER AMENDMENT VOTE (MARCH 1984)

		YES	NO
Party	Democrat	19	26
	Republican	37	18

Is there a relationship between political party affiliation and prayer amendment vote? Test with $\alpha = .05$.

15. A researcher would like to know if there is a relationship between a student's gender and choice of college major. To test this hypothesis, a sample of $n = 500$ students is selected and each person's sex and college major are recorded. The resulting data are as follows:

MAJOR

	SCIENCE	HUMANITIES	ARTS	PROFESSIONAL
Male	30	10	15	45
Female	80	120	45	155

Is there a relationship between the two variables? Test at the .01 level of significance.

16. A school board would like to study a proposal to eliminate the cost-of-living raises for next year and replace them with merit raises (raises based on evaluation of performance). The board decides to assess the attitudes toward the proposal among those individuals who are working in the school system. Specifically, the school board would like to know if attitude is related to the type of position the person holds. The observed frequencies are as follows:

17. Friedman and Rosenman (1974) have suggested that personality type is related to heart disease. Specifically, type A people who are competitive, driven, pressured, and impatient, are more prone to heart disease. On the other hand, type B individuals, who are less competitive and more relaxed, are less likely to have heart disease. Suppose an investigator would like to examine the relationship between personality type and disease. For a random sample of individuals, personality type is assessed with a standardized test. These individuals are then examined and categorized according to the type of disorder they have. The observed frequencies are as follows:

TYPE OF DISORDER

	HEART	VASCULAR	HYPERTENSION	NONE
Type A Personality	38	29	43	60
Type B Personality	18	22	14	126

Is there a relationship between personality and disorder? Test at the .05 level of significance.

18. A researcher would like to determine if attitudes about career differ as a function of year in college. A random sample of college students is selected. The students fill out a questionnaire, specifying year in school and what they intend to do when they complete college. Their responses are classified and recorded in the following table:

PLANS AFTER COLLEGE

YEAR	WORK	GRADUATE SCHOOL	UNDECIDED
Freshman	22	20	48
Sophomore	37	26	29
Junior	58	31	15
Senior	56	35	9

Is there a relationship between year in college and attitude about career? Test with alpha set at .01.

19. McClelland (1961) suggested that the strength of a person's need for achievement can predict behavior in a number of situations, including risk-taking situations. This experiment is patterned after his work. A random sample of college students is given a standardized test that measures the need for achievement. On the basis of their test scores, they are classified into high achievers and low achievers. They are then confronted with a task for which they can select the level of difficulty. Their selections are classified as "cautious" (low risk of failure), "moderate" risk, or "high" risk of failure. The observed frequencies for this study are as follows:

RISK TAKEN BY SUBJECT

	CAUTIOUS	MODERATE	HIGH
High Achiever	8	24	6
Low Achiever	17	7	16

Can you conclude there is a relationship between the need for achievement and risk-taking behavior? Set alpha to .05. Describe the outcome of the study.

20. A researcher believes that people with low self-esteem will avoid situations that will focus attention on themselves. A random sample of $n = 72$ people is se- lected. Each person is given a standardized test that measures self-esteem and is classified as high, me- dium, or low in self-esteem. The subjects are then placed in a situation in which they must choose be- tween performing a task in front of other people or by themselves. The researcher notes which task is cho- sen. The observed frequencies are as follows:

TASK CHOSEN

	AUDIENCE	NO AUDIENCE
Low Self-esteem	4	16
Medium Self esteem	14	14
High Self-esteem	18	6

Is there a relationship between self-esteem and the task chosen? Use $\alpha = .05$.

21. A social psychology experiment examined the effect of success or failure on people's willingness to help others. In this experiment, individual subjects were given a task that was either very easy or impossible to perform. Thus, some subjects were guaranteed to suc- ceed, and some were doomed to fail. As subjects left the testing room, they encountered a student who was trying to reach a telephone from a wheel chair. The psychologist recorded how many subjects stopped to help. The data from this experiment are presented in the following table:

	SUCCESS	FAILURE
Help	16	11
No Help	9	14

On the basis of these data, can the psychologist con- clude that there is a significant relation between peo- ple's willingness to help and their personal experience of success or failure. Test at the .05 level of signifi- cance.

INTRODUCTION TO MINITAB*

---

*Portions of this chapter were adapted with permission from the *Minitab Primer* © copyright by Minitab, Inc. 1986, 1987. No portion of this chapter may be reproduced, stored or transmitted in any form or by any means without permission of Minitab, Inc.

SECTION 16.1 **GETTING STARTED**

Minitab is a statistical analysis program that is available for many types of computers, including PC-compatible machines. This chapter describes the fundamentals of using Minitab, including analyses from previous chapters in this book. Because there are Minitab versions for many types of computers, starting the program may vary from computer to computer. Your instructor can help you start the program. The purpose of this chapter is to familiarize you with the basic operation of the Minitab worksheet and commands. To help acquaint you with this program, we will start by introducing an example and by showing you a simple Minitab session.

EXAMPLE 16.1   A statistics instructor gives a quiz to a section of $n = 25$ students. On the quiz the students note how many hours they studied during the past week. The instructor records the hours studied and the quiz score for each student. These data are entered into the computer and saved in a file, or *worksheet*, called SECTION2. Once the data are in the computer, the instructor can use Minitab commands to review the data, transform the quiz scores into percentages, create a histogram showing the distribution of scores, and calculate statistics such as the mean or a correlation. Table 16.1 shows a Minitab session after the data were entered and stored. We have underlined the commands typed by the user to make them stand out. The remaining text is typed by the computer.

Although you may not understand all the computer printout shown in Table 16.1, it should give you some appreciation of the power of Minitab. With just seven simple commands we have instructed Minitab to perform a variety of statistical manipulations. The remainder of this chapter provides a more detailed explanation of how Minitab operates, including a complete description of the commands used in Table 16.1 as well as many other Minitab functions.

AN OVERVIEW: THE WORKSHEET
AND COMMANDS

Minitab consists of a worksheet plus commands. The worksheet is where you keep your data while you are running Minitab. The commands are used to analyze and manage (store, retrieve, edit) the data while it is in the worksheet.

The worksheet consists of rows and columns as well as constants (Table 16.2). A column is designed to hold a series of numbers for a variable, such as the quiz scores for 25 students. Columns are identified by C1, C2, C3, and so on. On the other hand, a constant holds just one number, such as the mean of the quiz scores. Constants are designated K1, K2, K3, and so on.

DEFINITIONS

The *columns* of a worksheet are used for holding data, with each variable studied assigned to a particular column. The number of *rows* in any column corresponds to the number (n) of observations made for that variable.

A *constant* on the worksheet holds a single value assigned by the user.

Table 16.1

An illustration of a Minitab session. The user entered the commands that are underlined. Text produced by the computer is not underlined.

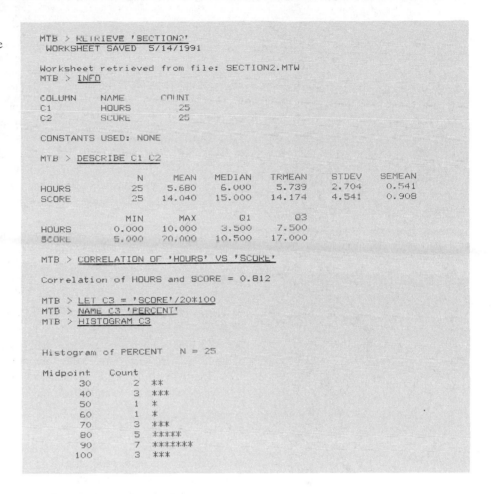

```
MTB > RETRIEVE 'SECTION2'
   WORKSHEET SAVED  5/14/1991

Worksheet retrieved from file: SECTION2.MTW
MTB > INFO

COLUMN     NAME       COUNT
C1         HOURS        25
C2         SCORE        25

CONSTANTS USED: NONE

MTB > DESCRIBE C1 C2

                N       MEAN     MEDIAN     TRMEAN     STDEV    SEMEAN
HOURS          25      5.680      6.000      5.739     2.704    0.541
SCORE          25     14.040     15.000     14.174     4.541    0.908

               MIN        MAX         Q1         Q3
HOURS        0.000     10.000      3.500      7.500
SCORE        5.000     20.000     10.500     17.000

MTB > CORRELATION OF 'HOURS' VS 'SCORE'

Correlation of HOURS and SCORE = 0.812

MTB > LET C3 = 'SCORE'/20*100
MTB > NAME C3 'PERCENT'
MTB > HISTOGRAM C3


Histogram of PERCENT    N = 25

Midpoint   Count
      30       2  **
      40       3  ***
      50       1  *
      60       1  *
      70       3  ***
      80       5  *****
      90       7  *******
     100       3  ***
```

Table 16.2

The Minitab Worksheet. Columns are numbered C1, C2, and so on. The symbol for constants is K, and they are similarly numbered K1, K2, and the like.

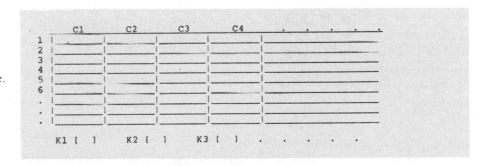

The Minitab worksheet is a temporary storage area for your data. Think of it as a scratch pad on which you can perform computations and analyses. Whenever you begin a Minitab session, a new worksheet is created. Until you enter numbers into the worksheet, it is empty and looks like the chart in Table 16.2. We must emphasize the temporary nature of the worksheet. Whenever you end a Minitab session, the worksheet and any data in it disappear. Therefore, if you have important data in the worksheet, it must be saved in a file before exiting Minitab. The command for saving data is explained in Section 16.2.

On most computers, Minitab is started by typing MINITAB and pressing the return (or Enter) key. Minitab will follow with a few introductory remarks followed by the *MTB> prompt.* You instruct Minitab to do things by typing command names after each MTB> prompt and pressing the Enter key. Most Minitab commands consist of a command name followed by an argument. Minitab will recognize approximately 180 commands names, most of which are simple English words such as READ, PLOT, and DESCRIBE. Arguments can be numerical values, columns (C1, C2, C3, and so on), constants (K1, K2, etc.), file names, or column names. For Example 16.1, the first line of the Minitab session (Table 16.1) shows the command RETRIEVE followed by a single argument, a file named SECTION2.

DEFINITIONS   *Commands* consist of a command name and usually an argument. The *command name* is a simple word instructing the computer to perform a particular task. The *argument* specifies the columns, constants, or file name on which the command will operate.

There are several shortcuts for entering commands. You can abbreviate command names by typing only their first four letters. You can add or delete text between command names and arguments as you see fit. Also, you can refer to columns by number or name (see Section 16.3 for naming columns). In Example 16.1, the third and fourth commands (Table 16.1) could have been shortened as follows (again, we have underlined the material that you enter):

MTB > DESC C1 C2
MTB > CORR C1 C2

In situations where several consecutive column numbers are specified in the argument, you can abbreviate the argument by inserting a hyphen. For example, if we wanted descriptive statistics for data in columns C1, C2, C3, and C4, the command could be written as follows:

MTB > DESCRIBE C1-C4

USING SUBCOMMANDS   Some Minitab commands can be followed by one or more *subcommands*. To tell Minitab that subcommands are to follow, end your command line with a semicolon(;). Minitab will respond with a new prompt, *SUBC>*, rather than MTB>. Each subcommand must be placed on a separate line, and all but the final subcommand must end with a semicolon. The final subcommand must end with a period. Then the command and subcommands will carry out their tasks and the MTB> prompt will return. In Example 16.1, the last command is HISTOGRAM C3, which creates a frequency distribution histogram for the percents in column C3 (Table 16.1). Notice that the distance between each midpoint in the histogram is 10 points. This distance was automatically selected by Minitab, but you can specify some other distance with the INCREMENT subcommand. Table 16.3 illustrates the use of this subcommand to set up histogram midpoints that are 5 points apart. Compare the results to those of Table 16.1.

Table 16.3

The use of the INCREMENT subcommand with HISTOGRAM. The underlined commands are entered by the user. The computer provides remaining text.

```
MTB > HISTOGRAM C1;
SUBC> INCREMENT = 5.

Histogram of PERCENT    N = 25

Midpoint    Count
  25.00       1    *
  30.00       1    *
  35.00       2    **
  40.00       1    *
  45.00       1    *
  50.00       0
  55.00       0
  60.00       1    *
  65.00       2    **
  70.00       1    *
  75.00       3    ***
  80.00       2    **
  85.00       5    *****
  90.00       2    **
  95.00       1    *
 100.00       2    **
```

ENDING YOUR SESSION

To end a Minitab session, you type STOP. This will return you to the operating system of your computer. It will also clear the worksheet for your next session. If the data in your current worksheet are important, the worksheet should be saved before the Minitab session is ended, *otherwise the data will be lost when you end the session.* Section 16.2 examines entering and saving data on the worksheet.

HELP

Minitab has a useful and very complete HELP facility that you can access at any time. To learn how to use HELP, type HELP HELP after the MTB> prompt. You can see what commands Minitab has by typing HELP COMMANDS. Finally, you can get help on a specific command by typing HELP followed by the command name. For example, to get assistance in using the command HISTOGRAM, you can type:

MTB > HELP HISTOGRAM

LEARNING CHECK

1. In the Minitab worksheet the data for each variable are assigned to a column. (True/False)

2. What is the distinction between a command name and a command argument?

3. Once data are entered into the Minitab worksheet, they are permanently stored. (True/False)

4. You can end a Minitab session by typing the command _____.

5. Assistance can be obtained during a Minitab session by using the ___ command.

ANSWERS

1. True. Each column contains the data for one variable.

2. A command name specifies the task for Minitab to perform (e.g., to make a histogram, to compute a correlation). The argument indicates the columns, variable names, or files to be used in the task.

3. False. The worksheet is temporary. Data in it are deleted when you end the Minitab session unless the worksheet is saved with a special command.

4. STOP

5. HELP

SECTION 16.2 **ENTERING AND SAVING DATA**

The first task in any Minitab session is entering data into the Minitab worksheet. This can be accomplished in three ways: directly from the keyboard, from a saved Minitab worksheet, or from a data file on your computer.

ENTERING DATA FROM THE KEYBOARD

There are two commands you can use to enter data directly from the keyboard, SET and READ. The SET command puts all the numbers you type into one column. For example, to enter numbers into C1, you type

MTB > SET C1

Minitab will respond with a new prompt, *DATA>*, and then wait for you to type in a number. For example, you might type the following:

DATA>2 4 6.5 0.2

Caution! If C1 already contains data, using SET C1 again will write over the original data.

Minitab will place these four numbers into the first four rows of C1 and once again respond with the DATA> prompt. You may continue to place numbers in this column, for example, by typing

DATA> 10 -0.1 14

These numbers are placed into the next three rows of C1. Notice that there is no special format, other than leaving at least one space between each number. You include any decimal points and negative signs that are necessary. When you have finished entering numbers in column C1, type END:

DATA> END

Minitab returns to the MTB> prompt.

The READ command enters data into several columns at once. For example, you can enter data into columns C2, C3, and C4 as follows:

MTB > READ C2-C4
DATA> 1 2 3
DATA> 4 5 6
DATA> 7 8 9
DATA> 10 11 12
DATA> END

Caution! If columns C2, C3, and C4 already contain data, then using READ C2-C4 will write over the original data.

With this example using READ, the first number entered on each DATA line goes into C2, the second number on each line is placed into C3, and the last number on each line is put in C4. Again, a space is placed between each number during entry.

Now we can look at all the data we have just entered. This is done using the PRINT command, followed by specification of the columns we want to view.

MTB > PRINT C1-C4

Minitab then displays your worksheet.

ROW	C1	C2	C3	C4
1	2	1	2	3
2	4	4	5	6
3	6.5	7	8	9
4	0.2	10	11	12
5	10			
6	-0.1			
7	14			

SAVING AND RETRIEVING A WORKSHEET

It is important to distinguish between the Minitab worksheet and a *saved worksheet*. As noted earlier, the Minitab worksheet provides temporary storage for your data. Data entered when you begin your Minitab session are deleted when you end the session. However, during the session you can permanently store your Minitab worksheet using the SAVE command followed by a worksheet name. In Example 16.1, the data were originally stored as follows

MTB > SAVE 'SECTION2'

You choose the name of the worksheet. It may contain both letters and numbers and should be placed in single quotation marks. The SAVE command takes a "snapshot" of the Minitab worksheet at a particular moment in time. Any changes made to the data later in the session will not be stored unless you use the SAVE command again. Thus it is a good idea to save your worksheet near the end of the session, even if you used the SAVE command earlier.

Saved worksheets are special (binary) files that only Minitab can access. They are very fast to store and retrieve and contain both numbers (the data) and column names. You gain access to a saved worksheet by the RETRIEVE command. For example, at the start of a Minitab session, the data from the saved worksheet SECTION2 are retrieved as follows:

MTB > RETRIEVE 'SECTION2'

It should be noted that if the SECTION2 worksheet is not located in your current directory, Minitab will respond with an error message to tell you that the requested worksheet does not exist. In that case, you will have to supply a pathname that tells Minitab where to find the saved worksheet. On microcomputers running MS-DOS (PC compatibles), you might have to type a path that resembles, for example, the following:

MTB > RETRIEVE 'C:\MINITAB\GRADES\SECTION2'

Here the computer is instructed to search drive C through the specified path for a file named SECTION2. Minitab fetches SECTION2, places its contents into the Minitab worksheet, and responds with the MTB> prompt. Note that anytime you enter a RETRIEVE command, the new data you are retrieving will replace whatever was previously in the worksheet.

ENTERING DATA FROM AN ASCII FILE

Often your data already reside in a file on your computer. Most computers use a standardized code called *ASCII*. If your data file is a standard text (or ASCII) file, you can input its contents directly into the Minitab worksheet. It is important to distinguish between these data files and the saved worksheets, which were discussed in the previous section. Data files are stored in the standard ASCII format that other software programs, such as data editors, can readily access and read. They can also be transferred easily from computer to computer. The commands READ and SET are used with these data files (note that SAVE and RETRIEVE are used with saved Minitab worksheets). Unlike saved worksheets, ASCII files do not store column numbers and names. These must be entered each time you use the file.

If all the data in your file are observations of a single variable, then you will want to put them into a single column on the worksheet. To illustrate how this is done, we will assume that the following data are stored in a standard text file named EXAMPLE:

11 22 33

44 55 66

77 88 99

To place all nine numbers from this file into C5 of your worksheet, you would use the SET command, as follows:

MTB > SET 'EXAMPLE' C5

Column C5 now contains 11, 22, 33, 44, 55, 66, 77, 88, 99. As you can see, Minitab reads the data file one row at a time from left to right.

If your data file contains observations from several variables (one observation from each variable in each row), then the data are entered with the READ command. For example, to enter the data from the EXAMPLE file into C6, C7, and C8 of the worksheet, you type

MTB > READ 'EXAMPLE' C6-C8

The Minitab worksheet now contains the following data:

ROW	C6	C7	C8
1	11	22	33
2	44	55	66
3	77	88	99

STORING DATA IN AN ASCII FILE You can store some or all of the worksheet data in an ASCII file that other software packages can read. The WRITE command is used for this purpose. For example, consider the following command statement:

MTB > <u>WRITE 'DATFIL' C1-C2</u>

Minitab creates a standard ASCII file called DATFIL and places the contents of C1 and C2 in it. The contents of any data file created with WRITE can be entered into the Minitab worksheet using READ (or SET if there is only one column of data).

LEARNING CHECK

1. Data can be entered into the worksheet with SET or READ. What is the difference between these commands?

2. You can store your entire worksheet using the _____ command and gain access to it with _____.

3. Once your worksheet is saved during a session, any changes made to the worksheet later in the session will be automatically included in the saved file. (True/False)

4. The advantage of storing data in ASCII files is that other computer software can often read these files. (True/False)

ANSWERS

1. With SET, the data are entered into one column. READ enters the data into two or more columns that are specified in the argument.

2. SAVE; RETRIEVE (the argument for each command must specify a file name).

3. False. The modified worksheet must be saved.

4. True

SECTION 16.3 SOME USEFUL COMMANDS

There are a number of useful commands that allow you to view, manipulate and edit your worksheet. A few of the most useful commands are summarized next.

CHECKING THE WORKSHEET STATUS Once you have retrieved a worksheet, you may wonder what variables and constants it contains. The easiest way to check the status of your worksheet is to use the INFO command. For Example 16.1 the status check proceeds as follows:

```
MTB > INFO

COLUMN      NAME        COUNT
C1          HOURS          25
C2          SCORE          25

CONSTANTS USED: NONE
```

As you can see, INFO lists all of the columns and constants that contain data, column names (when applicable), and the number of values in each column.

NAMING VARIABLES

Preceding sections have shown named columns. Naming columns makes your variables much easier to identify and reference and your output easier to read. In Example 16.1, the following command was used to name the columns.

MTB > NAME C1 'HOURS' C2 'SCORE'

The names you choose may be from one to eight characters in length. Once you have named a variable, you may refer to it by its name or column number. Thus the second command in Example 16.1 may be stated as

MTB > DESCRIBE C1 C2

or

MTB > DESCRIBE 'HOURS' 'SCORE'

Whenever you refer to a variable name, you must enclose the name in single quotation marks. You may change the name of a variable by issuing another NAME command for that column.

VIEWING DATA

You can view data in your worksheet anytime using the PRINT command. For Example 16.1, the PRINT command can view the contents of C1 and C2, as illustrated in Table 16.4. When the columns you are printing contain more data than will fit on a single screen, Minitab will display one screen at a time. After each screen it will ask you if you want to continue. Type the letter Y to view additional data or the letter N to return to the MTB> prompt.

Table 16.4

Using the PRINT command to view the data for Example 16.1

```
MTB > PRINT C1 C2
ROW        HOURS        SCORE
  1            8           17
  2            7           19
  3            5           15
  4            6           14
  5            5           16
  6            1            9
  7            3            7
  8            9           20
  9            3            8
 10            6           16
 11            7           17
 12            7           18
 13            4           13
 14            3           17
 15            6           13
 16            9           17
 17            6           15
 18           10           17
 19            2            7
 20            6           15

CONTINUE?
```

CORRECTING ERRORS IN DATA

There are several ways you can edit the worksheet. You can use the LET command to substitute a new value for an incorrect one. Suppose the fifteenth value in C1 (Table 16.4) should have been 8 instead of 6. You can change that value by using the LET command and the following arguments.

$$MTB > LET \ C1 \ (15) = 8$$

A new value, 8, has now been assigned to the fifteenth observation (row) of C1. Because you can always substitute a column name for a column number, you could have stated the command as follows:

$$MTB > LET \ 'HOURS' \ (15) = 8$$

Note that the row number must always be enclosed in parentheses. Also, two other commands, INSERT and DELETE, can be used to correct the worksheet. You can learn about these commands by typing HELP INSERT and HELP DELETE.

THE ON-SCREEN DATA EDITOR

Release 7 of Minitab has a new feature for the PC version. It is an *on-screen data editor* that allows you to view and edit the worksheet, much like most spreadsheet software. To activate the data editor, press the Escape (Esc) key. Minitab will then display your worksheet. Table 16.5 shows the screen display for Example 16.1 after Esc is pressed. The screen displays the columns and rows of the worksheet and any data that are in them. The first score in C1 will be highlighted by the computer (Table 16.5) and a small flashing bar, called a cursor, will be present. To change a score in the worksheet, you press the cursor arrows (↑ ↓ → ←) to move the highlighted cursor to the score you want to change. You then simply enter the new value.

DEFINITION

The *cursor* is a small flashing bar or square on the screen that indicates where a character will appear when you press a key. On some computer displays the cursor is highlighted.

Table 16.5

The screen display for the data editor, which is started by pressing the Esc key. Note that the highlighted cursor appears at the first score in C1. The data are from Example 16.1.

	HOURS C1	SCORE C2	C3	C4	C5	C6	C7	C8	C9	C10	C11	C12	C13	C14
1	8	17												
2	7	19												
3	5	15												
4	6	14												
5	5	16												
6	1	9												
7	3	7												
8	9	20												
9	3	8												
10	6	16												
11	7	17												
12	7	18												
13	4	13												
14	3	17												
15	6	13												
16	9	17												
17	6	15												
18	10	17												
19	2	7												
20	6	15												
21	0	5												
22	10	20												

Last Column: C2   Last Row: 25

Notice that the entire worksheet cannot fit on the screen. The lower right corner of the screen indicates the last column and row that contain data. In this example, the screen can fit only 22 rows, but there are actually 25 scores per column. You can display the last rows by toggling (repeatedly pressing) the down arrow (↓).

There are other useful keys that allow you to move the cursor highlight quickly. The Page Down (PgDn) key lets you view the next screen of data, and avoids the trouble of toggling the down arrow. The Page Up (PgUp) key moves the screen display in the opposite direction. The Home key moves the cursor highlight to the top of the screen, and the End key moves it to the bottom of the screen. Pressing the Control (Ctrl) key with Home or End will move the highlight to the top (C1, row 1) or bottom (last column, last row) of the entire set of data. When you have finished editing the worksheet, press the Esc key and the MTB> prompt will return to the screen. You may now enter Minitab commands to analyze the data. It is important to note that when you have edited a worksheet, the changes you have made are not permanent. You must now save the edited worksheet. This warning also applies to corrections made by the LET command.

ARITHMETIC TRANSFORMATIONS

The LET command in Example 16.1 created a new variable by computing the percent for each quiz score. The results were placed in C3 (Table 16.1). This example illustrates an arithmetic transformation. Algebraic expressions used in the LET command (for example, C3 = 'SCORE'/20*100) may contain the following operators:

+   for addition
−   for subtraction
*   for multiplication
/   for division
**   for raising to a power (exponents)

In addition, LET commands may contain functions for square root (SQRT), for computing the mean and standard deviation (MEAN, STDEV), and many others. For example, to take the square root of the data in column C2 and place the results in C4, the command would state

$$\text{MTB} > \underline{\text{LET C4} = \text{SQRT(C2)}}$$

Notice that the argument following SQRT, in this case C2, must be enclosed in parentheses. When using statistical functions that yield a single value, you may assign the result of the LET command to a constant. A few examples using the data from Example 16.1 follow:

```
MTB > LET K1 = MEAN(C1)
MTB > LET K2 = STDEV(C1)
MTB > LET K3 = MEDIAN(C1)
MTB > PRINT K1-K3
K1       5.68000
K2       2.70370
K3       6.00000
```

LEARNING CHECK

1. What information will the command INFO provide?

2. For the following commands:

    NAME C1 'AGE' C2 'GPA' C3 'SCORE'
    DESCRIBE C1 C2 C3

    a. What is the purpose of the first command?
    b. What is another way to state the DESCRIBE command?
    c. What command could you enter to view the data on this worksheet?

3. For the previous example, suppose we enter

    LET C2 (11) = 3.2
    LET K1 = MEAN(C2)

    What will these commands do?

ANSWERS
1. A list of the columns with data, variable names, number of scores in each column, and the constants used.

2. a. The worksheet columns C1, C2, and C3 are named AGE, GPA, and SCORE, respectively.
   b. DESC C1 C2 C3 or DESC 'AGE' 'GPA' 'SCORE'
   c. PRINT C1 C2 C3

3. The first command changes the 11th score in C2 to 3.2. The second command calculates the mean for C2 and stores it as constant K1.

SECTION 16.4 PLOTTING DATA

Minitab permits you to depict your data graphically in various histograms and scatterplots. Some plots summarize your data, others depict patterns in your data over time, and still others illustrate the relationship between two variables. We illustrate just a few of them in this section.

There are several ways to summarize your data in a frequency distribution. We already demonstrated the use of HISTOGRAM in Tables 16.1 and 16.3. The following example presents a similar display, a dotplot. For Example 16.1, the following command is entered:

MTB > <u>DOTPLOT C1</u>

A dotplot is constructed by Minitab for the data in column C1 (Figure 16.1). Of course, we could have used the variable name in the argument, in which case we

Figure 16.1

Minitab results for the command DOTPLOT. The data from Example 16.1 were used.

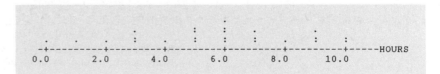

Figure 16.2

A scatterplot generated by the command PLOT for the data in Example 16.1.

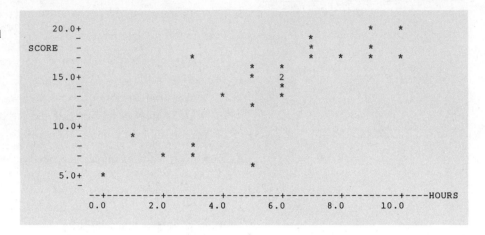

would enter DOTPLOT 'HOURS'. Each dot on the dotplot represents one score from C1. Minitab automatically selects the scales for all plots, unless you specify your own with subcommands such as INCREMENT. Typing HELP DOTPLOT will provide assistance.

You can also depict the relationship between two variables by using a scatterplot. A scatterplot is created with the PLOT command. Its argument specifies the two columns or variable names that you would like plotted. For the data in Example 16.1, the scatterplot is constructed as follows:

MTB > <u>PLOT 'SCORE' 'HOURS'</u>

The results are shown in Figure 16.2.

In the scatterplot, an asterisk is displayed for each pair of observations. If several data points are repeated, such as (6, 16) in this example, then a number appears instead of an asterisk. The number 2 on the scatterplot indicates that the coordinates (6, 16) appears twice in the data. Notice that the variable listed first in the argument of the command is plotted on the *Y*-axis (vertical axis) and the second variable is plotted on the *X*-axis (horizontal axis). Finally, Minitab has a number of subcommands for PLOT that allow you to specify the scales and labels on the axes. Type HELP PLOT to learn more about these options.

LEARNING CHECK

1. Describe the tasks that are being performed by the following command and subcommand:

    DOTPLOT 'AGE';
    INCREMENT = 5.

2. For the following command

    PLOT 'GPA' 'SCORE'

   a. What type of graph will Minitab produce?
   b. How will the axes be labeled?

ANSWERS 1. The data for the variable named AGE are presented in a dotplot. The subcommand sets up increments of 5 points on the scale of the dotplot.

2. **a.** A scatterplot is constructed.

    b. The Y- (vertical) axis is labeled GPA. The X- (horizontal) axis is labeled SCORE.

SECTION 16.5 STATISTICAL ANALYSES

Minitab can perform a wide variety of statistical analyses. In this section we illustrate analyses from previous chapters in the book. Remember, commands consist of command names and arguments. The command name specifies the analysis or operation to be done, and the arguments indicate which columns or constants are to be used. Once again, we underline the material that the user is supposed to type. Text provided by the computer is not underlined.

SIMPLE DESCRIPTIVE STATISTICS

We have previously examined several descriptive techniques for the data in Example 16.1. For example, we have seen how graphs are made using the HISTOGRAM (Tables 16.1, 16.3), DOTPLOT (Figure 16.1), and PLOT (Figure 16.2) commands. We also demonstrated (Table 16.1) the use of the DESCRIBE command to provide basic descriptive measures. Finally, we noted previously how the LET command can be used with MEAN, MEDIAN, and STDEV to obtain descriptive measures (Section 16.3).

CORRELATION AND REGRESSION

The CORRELATION command was demonstrated in Table 16.1 at the beginning of the chapter. In the argument for this command, you specify the columns (C1, C2 for example) or variable names for which the correlation is to be calculated. In Example 16.1 the command was stated as follows:

    MTB > CORRELATION OF 'HOURS' VS 'SCORE'

It could have been stated more simply as

    MTB > CORRELATION 'HOURS' 'SCORE'

or

    MTB > CORR C1 C2

If you specify more than two variables in the CORRELATION command, Minitab will provide correlations for all possible variable pairings.

    Regression is accomplished with the REGRESS command. For the data in Example 16.1, the command could be stated as

    MTB > REGRESS C2 1 C1

or

    MTB > REGRESS 'SCORE' 1 'HOURS'

Table 16.6

Minitab results for regression using
REGRESS. The data are from
Example 16.1.

```
The regression equation is
SCORE = 6.29 + 1.36 HOURS

Predictor        Coef       Stdev     t-ratio          p
Constant        6.292       1.281        4.91      0.000
HOURS          1.3641      0.2043        6.68      0.000

s = 2.707        R-sq = 66.0%     R-sq(adj) = 64.5%

Analysis of Variance

SOURCE          DF          SS          MS          F          p
Regression       1      326.46      326.46      44.56      0.000
Error           23      168.50        7.33
Total           24      494.96

Unusual Observations
Obs.    HOURS       SCORE       Fit Stdev.Fit  Residual   St.Resid
 14       3.0      17.000    10.384      0.770     6.616       2.55R
 25       5.0       6.000    13.112      0.559    -7.112      -2.69R




R denotes an obs. with a large st. resid.
```

In this command, the Y variable is specified first in the argument (SCORE in this case). Next the number of predictor variables is specified. For simple linear regression, this value will be 1. Finally, the X variable (or predictor) is specified. The results of the regression analysis are shown in Table 16.6. Notice that the results provide the regression equation. It also shows the standard error of estimate ($s = 2.707$) and r^2 (expressed as a percent). The analysis of variance summary allows one to determine how much variability is explained by the regression line and how much variability is due to error. The F-ratio tests the significance of the regression line.

HYPOTHESIS TESTS WITH THE t STATISTIC

The single-sample t test (Chapter 9) is performed by the TTEST command. Let's look at Example 16.1 again. A sample of $n = 25$ students indicated how many hours they studied statistics in a week. Suppose that the professor knows that the national average is $\mu = 4.0$ hours per course for college students. A single-sample t test can be used to determine if the sample of students differ significantly from the population (note that the value for σ is not known). The command is stated as follows:

MTB > TTEST 4.0 'HOURS'

The first part of the argument is the value for the population mean, according to H_0 ($\mu = 4.0$). The second part specifies the column or variable name for the data. The results are shown in Table 16.7.

The TWOSAMPLE command is used for the independent-measures t test (Chapter 10). Consider the following data that were used for Example 10.2, a study of the effects of imagery on memory.

Table 16.7

The results of a single-sample *t* test using the command TTEST. The professor wanted to determine if the hours spent studying by his class differ significantly from the national average, $\mu = 4$.

```
TEST OF MU = 4.000 VS MU N.E. 4.000

              N      MEAN    STDEV   SE MEAN        T    P VALUE
HOURS        25     5.680    2.704    0.541      3.11    0.0048
```

DATA FROM EXAMPLE 10.2 (Number of Words Recalled)				
Group 1	24	23	16	17	19
(No Images)	13	17	20	15	26
Group 2	18	19	23	29	30
(Images)	31	29	26	21	24

The first step is entering the data onto the worksheet. This is easily accomplished using SET.

```
MTB > SET C1
DATA> 24 23 16 17 19 13 17 20 15 26
DATA> END
MTB > SET C2
DATA> 18 19 23 29 30 31 29 26 21 24
DATA> END
```

Next, we use TWOSAMPLE to begin the analysis. Its argument indicates the two columns that contain the data for the two treatment groups. We also use the POOLED subcommand so that the estimated standard error is computed using pooled variance (Chapter 10).

```
MTB > TWOSAMPLE C1 C2;
SUBC> POOLED.
```

Remember, a semicolon is used at the end of the command statement when using subcommands. The results of the analysis are presented in Table 16.8. Notice that TWOSAMPLE provides descriptive statistics for each group, the 95% confidence interval for $\mu_1 - \mu_2$, the *t* statistic for the hypothesis test, and the probability (p) of committing a Type I error if H_0 is rejected. Of course, you would not reject H_0 unless $p < .05$.

For the repeated-measures *t* test (Chapter 11), the TTEST command is used again, only the data that are analyzed consist of difference scores (where

Table 16.8

An independent-measures *t* test using the data from Example 10.2. The command TWOSAMPLE was used with the subcommand POOLED.

```
TWOSAMPLE T FOR GROUP1 VS GROUP2
              N      MEAN    STDEV    SE MEAN
GROUP1       10     19.00    4.22      1.3
GROUP2       10     25.00    4.71      1.5

95 PCT CI FOR MU GROUP1 - MU GROUP2: (-10.2, -1.9)

TTEST MU GROUP1 = MU GROUP2 (VS NE): T= -3.00  P=0.0077  DF=  18

POOLED STDEV =       4.47
```

Table 16.9

A repeated-measures *t* test for the data in Example 11.1 was performed. The command TTEST was used for a column containing difference scores.

```
TEST OF MU = 0.000 VS MU N.E.  0.000

             N     MEAN    STDEV   SE MEAN       T   P VALUE
C3           5   -3.200    1.924    0.860    -3.72     0.020
```

$D = X_2 - X_1$). To demonstrate this analysis, let's take another look at Example 11.1. A researcher studies the effect of relaxation training on asthma attacks. The number of doses of medication needed before and after training is recorded for each subject. The data are shown in Table 11.3. First, the before-and-after data for each subject are entered in C1 and C2, respectively, using the READ command.

```
MTB > READ C1 C2
DATA> 9 4
DATA> 4 1
DATA> 5 5
DATA> 4 0
DATA> 5 1
DATA> END
```

Next, the difference scores are computed and placed in C3 using the LET command.

```
MTB > LET C3 = C2 - C1
```

Finally, the TTEST command is used to analyze the *D*-scores in C3. Because H_o states that there is no change, $\mu_D = 0$.

```
MTB > TTEST 0 C3
```

Table 16.9 shows the results of the analysis. Descriptive statistics are provided for the sample of *D*-scores as well as the obtained *t* value and probability.

One-tailed (directional) tests may be performed on any of the preceding *t* tests by using the ALTERNATIVE subcommand. If the critical region is placed in the right-hand tail, then the subcommand should state ALTERNATIVE = +1. To place the critical region on the left side of the distribution, use ALTERNATIVE = -1.

ANALYSIS OF VARIANCE (ANOVA)

A single-factor analysis of variance (ANOVA, Chapter 13) can be performed with either AOVONEWAY or ONEWAY. The difference between these two commands lies in how the data must be organized on the worksheet. For AOVONEWAY, each treatment group has its own column of data. If, for example, there are $k = 4$ treatments, enter the data from each treatment into columns C1 through C4. On the other hand, ONEWAY places all of the data in one column, say C1. A second column would contain the corresponding group number for each score. We demonstrate the use of both of these commands with the data from Example 13.1.

For AOVONEWAY, the data from Table 13.4 are entered into four separate columns, each column containing the data of one treatment group. We will demonstrate this with the SET command.

Table 16.10

The results for the AOVONEWAY command using the data from Example 13.1. ONEWAY will produce the same output.

```
ANALYSIS OF VARIANCE
SOURCE       DF         SS         MS          F          p
FACTOR        3      54.00      18.00       9.00      0.006
ERROR         8      16.00       2.00
TOTAL        11      70.00

                                     INDIVIDUAL 95 PCT CI'S FOR MEAN
                                     BASED ON POOLED STDEV
  LEVEL       N       MEAN      STDEV   --+---------+---------+---------+--
C1            3      1.000      1.732   (-------*-------)
C2            3      1.000      1.000   (-------*-------)
C3            3      4.000      1.000                   (-------*-------)
C4            3      6.000      1.732                           (-------*-------)
                                        ----+---------+---------+---------+--
POOLED STDEV =       1.414               0.0       2.5       5.0       7.5
```

```
MTB > SET C1
DATA> 0  0  3
DATA> END
MTB > SET C2
DATA> 0  1  2
DATA> END
MTB > SET C3
DATA> 3  4  5
DATA> END
MTB > SET C4
DATA> 8  5  5
DATA> END
```

The ANOVA is performed by using the AOVONEWAY command and specifying the column numbers that contain the data.

```
MTB > AOVONEWAY C1-C4
```

The results of the analysis are summarized in Table 16.10. It provides the ANOVA summary table, descriptive statistics, and 95% confidence intervals for each treatment group.

For ONEWAY, all the data are entered into one column. A second column contains the group identification number (for example, 1, 2, 3, . . ., k) for each score in the first column. First, we enter the data with the READ command. The scores are placed in C1 and the group numbers, in C2.

```
MTB > READ C1 C2
DATA> 0  1
DATA> 0  1
DATA> 3  1
DATA> 0  2
DATA> 1  2
DATA> 2  2
DATA> 3  3
DATA> 4  3
DATA> 5  3
DATA> 8  4
DATA> 5  4
DATA> 5  4
DATA> END
```

Table 16.11

The results of a chi-square test of independence for the data in Example 15.2. The CHISQUARE command was used to perform the analysis.

```
Expected counts are printed below observed counts

              C1        C2        C3     Total
   1          11        16         4        31
            7.75     15.50      7.75

   2           2        10         9        21
            5.25     10.50      5.25

 Total        13        26        13        52

ChiSq =   1.363 +   0.016 +   1.815 +
          2.012 +   0.024 +   2.679 = 7.908
 df = 2
```

Now the ONEWAY command can be used for these data. Its argument first specifies the column that contains the data, then the column with the group identifiers.

MTB > <u>ONEWAY C1 C2</u>

The results obtained with ONEWAY are identical to those of AOVONEWAY (Table 16.10).

CHI-SQUARE TEST FOR INDEPENDENCE

The chi-square test for independence (Chapter 15) is performed by CHISQUARE. The observed frequencies from a chi-square table are first entered in the worksheet with READ. Then CHISQUARE specifies the columns in which the observed frequencies are found. Minitab calculates the expected frequencies and the chi-square statistic. The following commands demonstrate this analysis using the data from Example 15.2 (Table 15.6).

MTB > <u>READ C1-C3</u>
DATA> <u>11   16   4</u>
DATA> <u> 2   10   9</u>
DATA> <u>END</u>
MTB > <u>CHISQUARE C1-C3</u>

Table 16.11 shows the results provided by Minitab. It displays the observed and expected frequencies for each cell, the computation of chi-square, and the value for *df*.

LEARNING CHECK

1. For the command

    REGRESS 'GPA' 1 'SCORE'

    which is the predictor and which is the *Y* variable?

2. Why is the POOLED subcommand used with TWOSAMPLE?

3. To do a repeated-measures *t* test, you must first calculate difference scores and store them in a column on the worksheet. (True/false)

4. What is the fundamental difference between AOVONEWAY and ONEWAY in conducting analysis of variance?

ANSWERS 1. SCORE is the predictor variable and GPA is the Y variable.

2. TWOSAMPLE performs an independent measures t test. The POOLED subcommand computes the standard error with pooled variance, the method recommended in this textbook.

3. True

4. For AOVONEWAY, the data from each treatment group are entered in their own column. For ONEWAY, one column contains all the data from the study and a second column contains the group identification numbers.

SECTION 16.6 **SENDING OUTPUT TO THE PRINTER**

When you work through a Minitab session, your results are displayed on the screen in front of you. You can also produce a permanent record of the results of an analysis by sending the output to the printer. This is accomplished by entering the following command:

MTB > PAPER

All the commands you enter after the PAPER command, as well as the results or analyses of those commands, are sent to the printer and to your screen simultaneously. Although simultaneous printing will occur on the PC version, on some computers the output is sent to a temporary print file instead of directly to a printer. When you exit Minitab, this file is automatically printed and then deleted.

If you want a complete record of your entire Minitab session, its commands and results, then PAPER should be used at the beginning of your session. Also, you can produce a page advance (form feed) on your printer anytime by entering the following command:

MTB > NEWPAGE

When you want to stop sending output to a printer, enter

MTB > NOPAPER

During a single Minitab session, you can start and stop sending output to a printer as many times as you wish by alternating between PAPER and NOPAPER.

KEY TERMS

worksheet	MTB> prompt	SUBC> prompt	ASCII file
column	command	DATA> prompt	on-screen editor
row	argument	saved worksheet	cursor
constant	subcommand		

LIST OF COMMANDS

Data Management	Graphs and Descriptive Statistics	Inferential Statistics	Printer Command
SET	DOTPLOT	TTEST	PAPER
END	PLOT	TWOSAMPLE	NEWPAGE
READ	HISTOGRAM	AOVONEWAY	NOPAPER
PRINT	DESCRIBE	ONEWAY	
SAVE		CHISQUARE	Miscellaneous
RETRIEVE	Measures of Relationship		HELP
WRITE			STOP
NAME	CORRELATION		INFO
LET	REGRESS		

PROBLEMS

Data Set 1

The following data set consists of attitude scores for an opinion survey given to college students. Problems 1–3 pertain to these data.

		Attitude Scores			
9	73	62	52	14	46
31	26	74	61	13	5
79	58	16	62	7	55
77	43	30	18	23	11
42	78	10	66	72	25

1. For Data Set 1, construct a histogram and a dotplot.

2. Obtain descriptive statistics for the distribution of attitude scores.

3. The general population has an average attitude score of $\mu = 52$. Use a *t* test to determine whether or not the college students differ significantly from the general population.

Data Set 2

For each subject in this study, blood alcohol concentration (BAC) and reaction time (RT) were measured. Problems 4–7 refer to these data.

BAC	RT
0.07	235
0.00	205
0.10	250
0.15	244
0.05	230
0.14	263
0.12	250
0.00	190
0.06	228
0.05	233
0.03	211
0.08	233
0.10	250
0.04	214

A final note: This chapter summarized the fundamentals of Minitab, focusing on basic procedures that are relevant to the topics in this textbook. However, Minitab is capable of much more, and there are many other commands and subcommands in this software. For those that wish to delve into Minitab's full capabilities, we refer you to the *Minitab Reference Manual,* Release 7 (1989) published by Minitab, Inc.

4. Obtain descriptive statistics for BAC and RT.

5. Construct a scatterplot for these data. Place BAC on the X-axis.

6. Compute the correlation for these variables.

7. Use regression to obtain the equation for the best-fitting line, with BAC as the predictor for RT.

Data Set 3
The following data are from an independent-measures study. These data are used in problems 8–10.

Treatment 1			Treatment 2		
62	45	52	42	12	37
63	63	59	28	21	33
58	68	38	51	14	26
66	67	61	15	47	18
59	60	68	33	22	28
53	51	67	39	56	19
30	48		20	16	

8. Provide descriptive statistics for both treatments in Data Set 3.

9. Construct dotplots for both groups.

10. Perform a t test to determine if there is a difference between the two treatments. Use pooled variance in the analysis.

Data Set 4
These data are from a repeated-measures study in which subjects were tested before and after receiving a treatment. Problems 11–13 use these data.

Before	After
46	74
52	58
56	90
35	64
53	39
71	65
50	75
72	85
53	79
39	82
88	90
61	77

11. Construct separate histograms for the BEFORE and AFTER data.

12. Obtain descriptive statistics for data taken before and after treatment.

13. Is there a significant change following treatment?

Data Set 5
In this study, four samples of subjects were used to test the effect of several treatments. These data are used for problems 14–16.

Control	Treatment A	Treatment B	Treatment C
12	15	15	34
20	19	6	21
15	24	9	17
17	28	19	15
15	26	5	32
9	14	11	38
10	30	4	33
19	26	6	20
15	10	20	34
18	22	7	24

14. Provide descriptive statistics for each group.

15. Construct a dotplot for each group.

16. Perform an analysis of variance to see if there is a significant effect.

BASIC MATHEMATICS REVIEW

SECTION A.1 **SKILLS ASSESSMENT**

This appendix reviews some of the basic math skills that are necessary for the statistical calculations presented in this book. Many students already will know some or all of this material. Others will need to do extensive work and review. To help you assess your own skills, we are including a skills assessment exam here. You should allow approximately 30 minutes to complete the test. When you finish, grade your test using the answer key on page A-20.

Notice that the test is divided into four sections. If you miss more than three questions in any section of the test, you probably need help in that area. Turn to the section of this appendix that corresponds to your problem area. In each section, you will find a general review, some examples, and some additional practice problems. After reviewing the appropriate section and doing the practice problems, turn to the end of the appendix. You will find another version of the skills assessment exam. If you still miss more than three questions in any section of the exam, continue studying. Get assistance from an instructor or tutor if necessary. At the end of this appendix is a list of recommended books for individuals who need a more extensive review than can be provided here. We must stress that mastering this material now will make the rest of the course much easier.

SKILLS ASSESSMENT EXAM

SECTION 1
(corresponding to Sections A.2 and A.3 of the appendix)

1. The fraction $\frac{3}{4}$ corresponds to a percentage of _____.
2. Express 30% as a fraction.
3. Convert $\frac{12}{40}$ to a decimal.
4. $\frac{2}{13} + \frac{8}{13} = ?$
5. $1.375 + .25 = ?$
6. $\frac{2}{5} \times \frac{1}{4} = ?$
7. $\frac{1}{8} + \frac{2}{3} = ?$
8. $3.5 \times .4 = ?$
9. $\frac{1}{5} \div \frac{3}{4} = ?$

10. $3.75/.5 = ?$

11. In a group of 80 students, 20% are psychology majors. How many psychology majors are in this group?

12. A company reports that two-fifths of its employees are women. If there are 90 employees, how many are women?

SECTION 2
(corresponding to Section A.4 of this appendix)

1. $3 + (-2) + (-1) + 4 = ?$
2. $6 - (-2) = ?$
3. $-2 - (-4) = ?$
4. $6 + (-1) - 3 - (-2) - (-5) = ?$
5. $4 \times (-3) = ?$
6. $-2 \times (-6) = ?$
7. $-3 \times 5 = ?$
8. $-2 \times (-4) \times (-3) = ?$
9. $12 \div (-3) = ?$
10. $-18 \div (-6) = ?$
11. $-16 \div 8 = ?$
12. $-100 \div (-4) = ?$

SECTION 3
(corresponding to Section A.5 of this appendix)

For each equation, find the value of X.

1. $X + 6 = 13$
2. $X - 14 = 15$
3. $5 = X - 4$
4. $3X = 12$
5. $72 = 3X$
6. $X/5 = 3$

7. $10 = X/8$
8. $3X + 5 = -4$
9. $24 = 2X + 2$
10. $(X + 3)/2 = 14$
11. $(X - 5)/3 = 2$
12. $17 = 4X - 11$

SECTION 4
(corresponding to Section A.6 of this appendix)

1. $4^3 = ?$
2. $\sqrt{25 - 9} = ?$
3. If $X = 2$ and $Y = 3$, then $XY^3 = ?$
4. If $X = 2$ and $Y = 3$, then $(X + Y)^2 = ?$
5. If $a = 3$ and $b = 2$, then $a^2 + b^2 = ?$
6. $-3^3 = ?$
7. $-4^4 = ?$
8. $\sqrt{4} \times 4 = ?$
9. $36/\sqrt{9} = ?$
10. $(9 + 2)^2 = ?$
11. $5^2 + 2^3 = ?$
12. If $a = 3$ and $b = -1$, then $a^2b^3 = ?$

The answers to the skills assessment exam are at the end of the appendix (page A-20).

Table A.1

SYMBOL	MEANING	EXAMPLE
+	Addition	$5 + 7 = 12$
−	Subtraction	$8 - 3 = 5$
×, ( )	Multiplication	$3 \times 9 = 27$, $3(9) = 27$
:, /	Division	$15 \div 3 = 5$, $15/3 = 5$, $\frac{15}{3} = 5$
>	Greater than	$20 > 10$
<	Less than	$7 < 11$
≠	Not equal to	$5 \neq 6$

SECTION A.2 **SYMBOLS AND NOTATION**

Table A.1 presents the basic mathematical symbols that you should know, and it provides examples of their use. Statistical symbols and notation will be introduced and explained throughout this book as they are needed. Notation for exponents and square roots is covered separately at the end of this appendix.

Parentheses are a useful notation because they specify and control the order of computations. Everything inside the parentheses is calculated first. For example,

$$(5 + 3) \times 2 = 8 \times 2 = 16$$

Changing the placement of the parentheses also changes the order of calculations. For example,

$$5 + (3 \times 2) = 5 + 6 = 11$$

SECTION A.3 **PROPORTIONS: FRACTIONS, DECIMALS, AND PERCENTAGES**

A proportion is a part of a whole and can be expressed as a fraction, or a decimal or a percentage. For example, in a class of 40 students, only 3 failed the final exam.

The proportion of the class that failed can be expressed as a fraction,

$$\text{fraction} = \frac{3}{40}$$

or as a decimal value

$$\text{decimal} = .075$$

or a percentage

$$\text{percentage} = 7.5\%$$

In a fraction, the bottom value (the denominator) indicates the number of equal pieces the whole is split up into. Here the "pie" is split up into four equal pieces:

If the denominator has a larger value, say 8, then each piece of the whole pie is smaller:

A larger denominator indicates a smaller fraction of the whole.

The value on top of the fraction (the numerator) indicates how many pieces of the whole are being considered. Thus, the fraction $\frac{3}{4}$ indicates that the whole is split evenly into four pieces and that three of them are being used:

A fraction is simply a concise way of stating a proportion: "Three out of four" is equivalent to $\frac{3}{4}$. To convert the fraction to a decimal, you divide the numerator by the denominator:

$$\frac{3}{4} = 3 \div 4 = .75$$

To convert the decimal to a percentage, simply multiply by 100 and place a percent sign (%) after the answer:

$$.75 \times 100 = 75\%$$

The U.S. money system is a convenient way of illustrating the relationship between fractions and decimals. "One quarter," for example, is one-fourth $\left(\frac{1}{4}\right)$ of a dollar, and its decimal equivalent is .25. Other familiar equivalencies are as follows:

	DIME	QUARTER	50-CENT PIECE	75 CENTS
Fraction	$\frac{1}{10}$	$\frac{1}{4}$	$\frac{1}{2}$	$\frac{3}{4}$
Decimal	.10	.25	.50	.75
Percentage	10%	25%	50%	75%

FRACTIONS 1. **Finding equivalent fractions**   The same proportional value can be expressed by many equivalent fractions. For example,

$$\frac{1}{2} = \frac{2}{4} = \frac{10}{20} = \frac{50}{100}$$

To create equivalent fractions, you can multiply the numerator and denominator by the same value. As long as both the numerator and denominator of the fraction are multiplied by the same value, the new fraction will be equivalent to the original. For example,

$$\frac{3}{10} = \frac{9}{30}$$

because both the numerator and denominator of the original fraction have been multiplied by 3. Dividing the numerator and denominator of a fraction by the same value will also result in an equivalent fraction. By using division, you can reduce a fraction to a simpler form. For example,

$$\frac{40}{100} = \frac{2}{5}$$

because both the numerator and denominator of the original fraction have been divided by 20.

You can use these rules to find specific equivalent fractions. For example, find the fraction that has a denominator of 100 and is equivalent to $\frac{3}{4}$. That is,

$$\frac{3}{4} = \frac{?}{100}$$

Notice that the denominator of the original fraction must be multiplied by 25 to produce the denominator of the desired fraction. For the two fractions to be equal, both the numerator and the denominator must be multiplied by the same number. Therefore, we also multiply the top of the original fraction by 25 and obtain

$$\frac{3 \times 25}{4 \times 25} = \frac{75}{100}$$

2. Multiplying fractions   To multiply two fractions, you first multiply the numerators and then multiply the denominators. For example,

$$\frac{3}{4} \times \frac{5}{7} = \frac{3 \times 5}{4 \times 7} = \frac{15}{28}$$

3. Dividing fractions   To divide one fraction by another, you invert the second fraction and then multiply. For example,

$$\frac{1}{2} \div \frac{1}{4} = \frac{1}{2} \times \frac{4}{1} = \frac{1 \times 4}{2 \times 1} = \frac{4}{2}$$

4. Adding and subtracting fractions   Fractions must have the same denominator before you can add or subtract them. If the two fractions already have a common denominator, you simply add (or subtract as the case may be) *only* the values in the numerators. For example,

$$\frac{2}{5} + \frac{1}{5} = \frac{3}{5}$$

Suppose you divided a pie into five equal pieces (fifths). If you first ate two-fifths of the pie and then another one-fifth, the total amount eaten would be three-fifths of the pie:

If the two fractions do not have the same denominator, you must first find equivalent fractions with a common denominator before you can add or subtract. The product of the two denominators will always work as a common denominator for equivalent fractions (although it may not be the lowest common denominator). For example,

$$\frac{2}{3} + \frac{1}{10} = ?$$

Because these two fractions have different denominators, it is necessary to convert each into an equivalent fraction and find a common denominator. We will use $3 \times 10 = 30$ as the common denominator. Thus the equivalent fraction of each is

$$\frac{2}{3} = \frac{20}{30} \quad \text{and} \quad \frac{1}{10} = \frac{3}{30}$$

Now the two fractions can be added:

$$\frac{20}{30} + \frac{3}{30} = \frac{23}{30}$$

5. Comparing the size of fractions   When comparing the size of two fractions with the same denominator, the larger fraction will have the larger numerator. For example,

$$\frac{5}{8} > \frac{3}{8}$$

The denominators are the same, so the whole is partitioned into pieces of the same size. Five of these pieces is more than three of them:

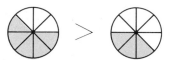

When two fractions have different denominators, you must first convert them to fractions with a common denominator to determine which is larger. Consider the following fractions:

$$\frac{3}{8} \quad \text{and} \quad \frac{7}{16}$$

If the numerator and denominator of $\frac{3}{8}$ are multiplied by 2, the resulting equivalent fraction will have a denominator of 16:

$$\frac{3}{8} = \frac{3 \times 2}{8 \times 2} = \frac{6}{16}$$

Now a comparison can be made between the two fractions:

$$\frac{6}{16} < \frac{7}{16}$$

Therefore,

$$\frac{3}{8} < \frac{7}{16}$$

DECIMALS

1. Converting decimals to fractions   Like a fraction, a decimal represents part of the whole. The first decimal place to the right of the decimal point indicates how many tenths are used. For example,

$$.1 - \frac{1}{10} \qquad .7 - \frac{7}{10}$$

The next decimal place represents $\frac{1}{100}$, the next $\frac{1}{1000}$, the next $\frac{1}{10,000}$, and so on. To change a decimal to a fraction, just use the number without the decimal point for the numerator. Use the denominator that the last (on the right) decimal place represents. For example,

$$.32 = \frac{32}{100}$$
$$.5333 = \frac{5333}{10,000}$$
$$.05 = \frac{5}{100}$$
$$.001 = \frac{1}{1000}$$

2. Addition and subtraction   To add and subtract decimals, the only rule is that you must keep the decimal points in a straight vertical line. For example,

$$
\begin{array}{r}
.27 \\
+\ 1.326 \\
\hline
1.596
\end{array}
\qquad
\begin{array}{r}
3.595 \\
-\ .67 \\
\hline
2.925
\end{array}
$$

3. Multiplying decimals   To multiply two decimal values, you first multiply the two numbers ignoring the decimal points. Then you position the decimal point in the answer so that the number of digits to the right of the decimal point is equal to the total number of decimal places in the two numbers being multiplied. For example,

$$
\begin{array}{rl}
1.73 & \text{(two decimal places)} \\
\times\ \ .251 & \text{(three decimal places)} \\
\hline
173 & \\
865 & \\
346 & \\
\hline
.43423 & \text{(five decimal places)}
\end{array}
$$

$$
\begin{array}{rl}
.25 & \text{(two decimal places)} \\
\times\ \ .005 & \text{(three decimal places)} \\
\hline
125 & \\
00 & \\
00 & \\
\hline
.00125 & \text{(five decimal places)}
\end{array}
$$

4. Dividing decimals   The simplest procedure for dividing decimals is based on the fact that dividing two numbers is identical to expressing them as a fraction:

$$.25 \div 1.6 \text{ is identical to } \frac{.25}{1.6}$$

You now can multiply both the numerator and denominator of the fraction by 10, 100, 1000, or whatever number is necessary to remove the decimal places. Remember, multiplying both the numerator and denominator of a fraction by the *same* value will create an equivalent fraction. Therefore,

$$\frac{.25}{1.6} = \frac{.25 \times 100}{1.6 \times 100} = \frac{25}{160}$$

The result is a division problem without any decimal places in the two numbers.

PERCENTAGES

1. Converting a percentage to a fraction or decimal   To convert a percentage to a fraction, remove the percent sign, place the number in the numerator, and use 100 for the denominator. For example,

$$52\% = \frac{52}{100} \qquad 5\% = \frac{5}{100}$$

To convert a percentage to a decimal, remove the percent sign and divide by 100, or simply move the decimal point two places to the left. For example,

$$83\% = 83. \ = .83$$
$$14.5\% = 14.5 = .145$$
$$5\% = 5. \ = .05$$

2. Arithmetic operations with percentages   There are situations when it is best to change percent values into decimals in order to perform certain arithmetic operations. For example, what is 45% of 60? This question may be stated as

$$45\% \times 60 = ?$$

The 45% should be converted to decimal form to find the solution to this question. Therefore,

$$.45 \times 60 = 27$$

LEARNING CHECK

1. Convert $\frac{3}{25}$ to a decimal.

2. Convert $\frac{3}{8}$ to a percentage.

3. Next to each set of fractions, write ''true'' if they are equivalent and ''false'' if they are not:

   a. $\frac{3}{8} = \frac{9}{24}$ _____

   b. $\frac{7}{9} = \frac{17}{19}$ _____

   c. $\frac{2}{7} = \frac{4}{14}$ _____

4. Compute the following:

   a. $\frac{1}{6} \times \frac{7}{10}$ **b.** $\frac{7}{8} - \frac{1}{12}$ **c.** $\frac{9}{10} \div \frac{2}{3}$ **d.** $\frac{7}{22} + \frac{2}{3}$

5. Identify the larger fraction of each pair:

   a. $\frac{7}{10}, \frac{21}{100}$ **b.** $\frac{3}{4}, \frac{7}{12}$ **c.** $\frac{22}{3}, \frac{19}{3}$

6. Convert the following decimals into fractions:

   a. .012 **b.** .77 **c.** .005

7. $2.59 \times .015 = ?$

8. $1.8 \div .02 = ?$

9. What is 28% of 45?

ANSWERS **1.** .12 **2.** 37.5% **3. a.** True **b.** False **c.** True **4.a.** $\frac{7}{60}$ **b.** $\frac{3}{8}$ **c.** $\frac{27}{20}$ **d.** $\frac{65}{66}$

5. a. $\frac{7}{10}$ **b.** $\frac{3}{4}$ **c.** $\frac{22}{3}$ **6. a.** $\frac{12}{1000}$ **b.** $\frac{77}{100}$ **c.** $\frac{5}{1000}$ **7.** .03885 **8.** 90 **9.** 12.6

SECTION A.4 NEGATIVE NUMBERS

Negative numbers are used to represent values less than zero. Negative numbers may occur when you are measuring the difference between two scores. For example, a researcher may want to evaluate the effectiveness of a propaganda film by measuring people's attitude with a test both before and after viewing the film:

	BEFORE	AFTER	AMOUNT OF CHANGE
Person A	23	27	+4
Person B	18	15	−3
Person C	21	16	−5

Notice that the negative sign provides information about the direction of the difference: a plus sign indicates an increase in value, and a minus sign indicates a decrease.

Because negative numbers are frequently encountered, you should be comfortable working with these values. This section reviews basic arithmetic operations using negative numbers. You should also note that any number without a sign (+ or −) is assumed to be positive.

1. Addition with negative numbers When adding numbers that include negative values, simply interpret the negative sign as subtraction. For example,

$$3 + (-2) + 5 = 3 - 2 + 5 = 6$$

When adding a long string of numbers, it often is easier to add all the positive values to obtain the positive sum and then add all of the negative values to obtain the negative sum. Finally, you subtract the negative sum from the positive sum. For example,

$$-1 + 3 + (-4) + 3 + (-6) + (-2)$$

positive sum = 6   negative sum = 13

Answer: $6 - 13 = -7$

2. Subtraction with negative numbers   To subtract a negative number, change it to positive and add. For example,

$$4 - (-3) = 4 + 3 = 7$$

This rule is easier to understand if you think of subtraction as "taking away." In the preceding example, if you substitute $7 - 3$ in place of the original 4 (note that $7 - 3 = 4$), you obtain

$$4 - (-3)$$

$$7 - 3 - (-3) \qquad \text{(substitution of } 7 - 3 \text{ for 4)}$$

$$7 - 3 \text{ "take away" } -3 \qquad (-3 \text{ "take away" } -3 \text{ is zero)}$$

$$7 \qquad \text{(7 is the remainder)}$$

3. Multiplying and dividing negative numbers   When the two numbers being multiplied (or divided) have the same sign, the result is a positive number. When the two numbers have different signs, the result is negative. For example,

$$3 \times (-2) = -6$$

$$-4 \times (-2) = +8$$

The first example is easy to explain by thinking of multiplication as repeated addition. In this case,

$$3 \times (-2) = (-2) + (-2) + (-2) = -6$$

You take three negative 2s, which result in a total of negative 6. In the second example, we are multiplying by a negative number. This amounts to repeated subtraction. That is,

$$-4 \times (-2) = -(-2) - (-2) - (-2) - (-2)$$

$$= 2 + 2 + 2 + 2 = 8$$

By using the same rule for both multiplication and division, we ensure that these two operations are compatible. For example,

$$-6 \div 3 = -2$$

which is compatible with

$$3 \times (-2) = -6$$

Also,

$$8 \div (-4) = -2$$

which is compatible with

$$-4 \times (-2) = +8$$

LEARNING CHECK   **1.** Complete the following calculations:

   a. $3 + (-8) + 5 + 7 + (-1) + (-3)$
   b. $5 - (-9) + 2 - (-3) - (-1)$
   c. $3 - 7 - (-21) + (-5) - (-9)$
   d. $4 - (-6) - 3 + 11 - 14$
   e. $9 + 8 - 2 - 1 - (-6)$
   f. $9 \times (-3)$
   g. $-7 \times (-4)$
   h. $-6 \times (-2) \times (-3)$
   i. $-12 \div (-3)$
   j. $18 \div (-6)$

ANSWERS   **1. a.** 3   **b.** 20   **c.** 21   **d.** 4   **e.** 20
             f. −27   **g.** 28   **h.** −36   **i.** 4   **j.** −3

SECTION A.5   **BASIC ALGEBRA: SOLVING EQUATIONS**

An equation is a mathematical statement which indicates that two quantities are identical. For example,

$$12 = 8 + 4$$

Often an equation will contain an unknown (or variable) quantity that is identified with a letter or symbol rather than a number. For example,

$$12 = 8 + X$$

In this event, your task is to find the value of X that makes the equation "true," or balanced. For this example, an X value of 4 will make a true equation. Finding the value of X is usually called *solving the equation*.

   To solve an equation, there are two points to be kept in mind:

1. Your goal is to have the unknown value *(X)* isolated on one side of the equation. This means that you need to remove all of the other numbers and symbols that appear on the same side of the equation as the X.

2. The equation will remain balanced provided you treat both sides exactly the same. For example, you could add 10 points to *both* sides, and the solution (the X value) for the equation would be unchanged.

FINDING THE SOLUTION   We will consider four basic types of equations and the operations needed to solve
FOR AN EQUATION   them.

1. When X has a value added to it   An example of this type of equation is

$$X + 3 = 7$$

Your goal is to isolate X on one side of the equation. Thus, you must remove the $+3$ on the left-hand side. The solution is obtained by subtracting 3 from *both* sides of the equation:

$$X + 3 - 3 = 7 - 3$$
$$X = 4$$

The solution is $X = 4$. You should always check your solution by returning to the original equation and replacing X with the value you obtained for the solution. For this example,

$$X + 3 = 7$$
$$4 + 3 = 7$$
$$7 = 7$$

2. When X has a value subtracted from it   An example of this type of equation is

$$X - 8 = 12$$

In this example, you must remove the -8 from the left-hand side. Thus, the solution is obtained by adding 8 to *both* sides of the equation:

$$X - 8 + 8 = 12 + 8$$
$$X = 20$$

Check the solution

$$X - 8 = 12$$
$$20 - 8 = 12$$
$$12 = 12$$

3. When X is multiplied by a value   An example of this type of equation is

$$4X = 24$$

In this instance, it is necessary to remove the 4 that is multiplied by X. This may be accomplished by dividing both sides of the equation by 4:

$$\frac{4X}{4} = \frac{24}{4}$$
$$X = 6$$

Check the solution:

$$4X = 24$$

$$4(6) = 24$$

$$24 = 24$$

4. When X is divided by a value   An example of this type of equation is

$$\frac{X}{3} = 9$$

Now the X is divided by 3, so the solution is obtained by multiplying by 3. Multiplying both sides yields

$$3\left(\frac{X}{3}\right) = 9(3)$$

$$X = 27$$

For the check,

$$\frac{X}{3} = 9$$

$$\frac{27}{3} = 9$$

$$9 = 9$$

SOLUTIONS FOR MORE-COMPLEX EQUATIONS

More-complex equations can be solved by using a combination of the preceding simple operations. Remember, at each stage you are trying to isolate X on one side of the equation. For example,

$$3X + 7 = 22$$

$$3X + 7 - 7 = 22 - 7 \qquad \text{(remove +7 by subtracting 7 from both sides)}$$

$$3X = 15$$

$$\frac{3X}{3} = \frac{15}{3} \qquad \text{(remove 3 by dividing both side by 3)}$$

$$X = 5$$

To check this solution, return to the original equation and substitute 5 in place of X:

$$3X + 7 = 22$$

$$3(5) + 7 = 22$$

$$15 + 7 = 22$$

$$22 = 22$$

Following is another type of complex equation that is frequently encountered in statistics:

$$\frac{X + 3}{4} = 2$$

First, remove the 4 by multiplying both sides by 4:

$$4\left(\frac{X + 3}{4}\right) = 2(4)$$

$$X + 3 = 8$$

Now remove the +3 by subtracting 3 from both sides:

$$X + 3 - 3 = 8 - 3$$

$$X = 5$$

To check this solution, return to the original equation and substitute 5 in place of X:

$$\frac{X + 3}{4} = 2$$

$$\frac{5 + 3}{4} = 2$$

$$\frac{8}{4} = 2$$

$$2 = 2$$

LEARNING CHECK 1. Solve for X and check the solutions:

   a. $3X = 18$ **b.** $X + 7 = 9$ **c.** $X - 4 = 18$ **d.** $5X - 8 = 12$

   e. $\dfrac{X}{9} = 5$ **f.** $\dfrac{X + 1}{6} = 4$ **g.** $X + 2 = -5$ **h.** $\dfrac{X}{5} = -5$

   i. $\dfrac{2X}{3} = 12$ **j.** $\dfrac{X}{3} + 1 = 3$

ANSWERS 1. **a.** $X = 6$ **b.** $X = 2$ **c.** $X = 22$ **d.** $X = 4$ **e.** $X = 45$
   f. $X = 23$ **g.** $X = -7$ **h.** $X = -25$ **i.** $X = 18$ **j.** $X = 6$

SECTION A . 6 **EXPONENTS AND SQUARE ROOTS**

EXPONENTIAL NOTATION A simplified notation is used whenever a number is being multiplied by itself. The notation consists of placing a value, called an exponent, on the right-hand side of and raised above another number called a base. For example,

$$7^3 \leftarrow \text{exponent}$$
$$\uparrow$$
$$\text{base}$$

The exponent indicates how many times the base is multiplied by itself. Some examples are the following:

$7^3 = 7(7)(7)$ (read "7 cubed" or "7 raised to the third power")

$5^2 = 5(5)$ (read "5 squared")

$2^5 = 2(2)(2)(2)(2)$ (read "2 raised to the fifth power")

There are a few basic rules about exponents that you will need to know for this course. They are outlined here.

1. Numbers raised to one or zero Any number raised to the first power equals itself. For example,

$$6^1 = 6$$

Any number (except zero) raised to the zero power equals 1. For example,

$$9^0 = 1$$

2. Exponents for multiple terms The exponent applies only to the base that is just in front of it. For example,

$$XY^2 = XYY$$
$$a^2b^3 = aabbb$$

3. Negative bases raised to an exponent If a negative number is raised to a power, then the result will be positive for exponents that are even and negative for exponents that are odd. For example,

$$-4^3 = -4(-4)(-4)$$
$$= 16(-4)$$
$$= -64$$

and

$$-3^4 = -3(-3)(-3)(-3)$$
$$= 9(-3)(-3)$$
$$= 9(9)$$
$$= 81$$

4. Exponents and parentheses If an exponent is present outside of parentheses, then the computations within the parentheses are done first, and the exponential computation is done last:

$$(3 + 5)^2 = 8^2 = 64$$

Notice that the meaning of the expression is changed when each term in the parentheses is raised to the exponent individually:

$$3^2 + 5^2 = 9 + 25 = 34$$

Therefore,

$$X^2 + Y^2 \neq (X + Y)^2$$

5. Fractions raised to a power If the numerator and denominator of a fraction are each raised to the same exponent, then the entire fraction can be raised to that exponent. That is,

$$\frac{a^2}{b^2} = \left(\frac{a}{b}\right)^2$$

For example,

$$\frac{3^2}{4^2} = \left(\frac{3}{4}\right)^2$$

$$\frac{9}{16} = \frac{3}{4}\left(\frac{3}{4}\right)$$

$$\frac{9}{16} = \frac{9}{16}$$

SQUARE ROOTS The square root of a value equals a number which when multiplied by itself yields the original value. For example, the square root of 16 equals 4, because 4 times 4 equals 16. The symbol for the square root is called a radical, $\sqrt{}$. The square root is taken for a number under the radical. For example,

$$\sqrt{16} = 4$$

The square root is the inverse of raising a number to the second power (squaring). Thus,

$$\sqrt{a^2} = a$$

For example,

$$\sqrt{3^2} = \sqrt{9} = 3$$

Also,

$$(\sqrt{b}\,)^2 = b$$

For example,

$$(\sqrt{64})^2 = 8^2 = 64$$

Computations under the same radical are performed *before* the square root is taken. For example,

$$\sqrt{9 + 16} = \sqrt{25} = 5$$

Note that with addition (or subtraction) separate radicals yield a different result:

$$\sqrt{9} + \sqrt{16} = 3 + 4 = 7$$

Therefore,

$$\sqrt{X} + \sqrt{Y} \neq \sqrt{X + Y}$$

$$\sqrt{X} - \sqrt{Y} \neq \sqrt{X - Y}$$

If the numerator and denominator of a fraction each have a radical, then the entire fraction can be placed under a single radical:

$$\frac{\sqrt{16}}{\sqrt{4}} = \sqrt{\frac{16}{4}}$$

$$\frac{4}{2} = \sqrt{4}$$

$$2 = 2$$

Therefore,

$$\frac{\sqrt{X}}{\sqrt{Y}} = \sqrt{\frac{X}{Y}}$$

Also, if the square root of one number is multiplied by the square root of another number, then the same result would be obtained by taking the square root of the product of both numbers. For example,

$$\sqrt{9} \times \sqrt{16} = \sqrt{9 \times 16}$$

$$3 \times 4 = \sqrt{144}$$

$$12 = 12$$

Therefore,

$$\sqrt{a} \times \sqrt{b} = \sqrt{ab}$$

LEARNING CHECK 1. Perform the following computations:

a. -6^3

b. $(3 + 7)^2$

c. a^3b^2 when $a = 2$ and $b = -5$

d. a^4b^3 when $a = 2$ and $b = 3$

e. $(XY)^2$ when $X = 3$ and $Y = 5$

f. $X^2 + Y^2$ when $X = 3$ and $Y = 5$

g. $(X + Y)^2$ when $X = 3$ and $Y = 5$

h. $\sqrt{5} + 4$

i. $(\sqrt{9})^2$

j. $\dfrac{\sqrt{16}}{\sqrt{4}}$

ANSWERS 1. **a.** -216 **b.** 100   **c.** 200   **d.** 432   **e.** 225
f. 34   **g.** 64   **h.** 3   **i.** 9   **j.** 2

PROBLEMS FOR APPENDIX A   Basic Mathematics Review

1. Convert $\frac{7}{20}$ to a decimal.

2. Express $\frac{9}{25}$ as a percentage.

3. Convert .91 to a fraction.

4. Express .0031 as a fraction.

5. Next to each set of fractions, write "true" if they are equivalent and "false" if they are not:

a. $\dfrac{4}{1000} = \dfrac{2}{100}$ _____

b. $\dfrac{5}{6} = \dfrac{52}{62}$ _____

c. $\dfrac{1}{8} = \dfrac{7}{56}$ _____

6. Perform the following calculations:

a. $\dfrac{4}{5} \times \dfrac{2}{3} = ?$

b. $\dfrac{7}{9} \div \dfrac{2}{3} = ?$

c. $\dfrac{3}{8} + \dfrac{1}{5} = ?$

d. $\dfrac{5}{18} - \dfrac{1}{6} = ?$

7. $2.51 \times .017 = ?$

8. $3.88 \times .0002 = ?$

9. $3.17 + 17.0132 = ?$

10. $5.55 + 10.7 + .711 + 3.33 + .031 = ?$

11. $2.04 \div .2 = ?$

12. $.36 \div .4 = ?$

13. $5 + 3 - 6 - 4 + 3 = ?$

14. $9 - (-1) - 17 + 3 - (-4) + 5 = ?$

15. $5 + 3 - (-8) - (-1) + (-3) - 4 + 10 = ?$

16. $8 \times (-3) = ?$

17. $-22 \div (-2) = ?$

18. $-2(-4) \times (-3) = ?$

19. $84 \div (-4) = ?$

Solve the equations in Problems 20–27 for X.

20. $X - 7 = -2$

21. $9 = X + 3$

22. $\dfrac{X}{4} = 11$

23. $-3 = \dfrac{X}{3}$

24. $\dfrac{X + 3}{5} = 2$

25. $\dfrac{X + 1}{3} = -8$

26. $6X - 1 = 11$

27. $2X + 3 = -11$

28. $-5^2 = ?$

29. $-5^3 = ?$

30. If $a = 4$ and $b = 3$, then $a^2 + b^1 = ?$

31. If $a = -1$ and $b = 4$, then $(a + b)^2 = ?$

32. If $a = -1$ and $b = 5$, then $ab^2 = ?$

33. $\dfrac{18}{\sqrt{4}} = ?$

34. $\sqrt{\dfrac{20}{5}} = ?$

SKILLS ASSESSMENT EXAM A   Follow-up Test

SECTION 1

1. Express $\frac{14}{80}$ as a decimal.

2. Convert $\frac{6}{25}$ to a percentage.

3. Convert 18% to a fraction.

4. $\frac{3}{5} \times \frac{2}{3} = ?$

5. $\frac{5}{24} + \frac{5}{6} = ?$

6. $\frac{7}{12} \div \frac{5}{6} = ?$

7. $\frac{5}{9} - \frac{1}{3} = ?$

8. $6.11 \times .22 = ?$

9. $.18 \div .9 = ?$

10. $8.742 + .76 = ?$

11. In a statistics class of 72 students, three eighths of the students received a *B* on the first test. How many *B*s were earned?

12. What is 15% of 64?

SECTION 2

1. $3 - 1 - 3 + 5 - 2 + 6 = ?$

2. $-8 - (-6) = ?$

3. $2 - (-7) - 3 + (-11) - 20 = ?$

4. $-8 - 3 - (-1) - 2 - 1 = ?$

5. $8(-2) = ?$

6. $-7(-7) = ?$

7. $-3(-2)(-5) = ?$

8. $-3(5)(-3) = ?$

9. $-24 \div (-4) = ?$

10. $36 \div (-6) = ?$

11. $-56/7 = ?$

12. $-7/(-1) = ?$

SECTION 3

Solve for X.

1. $X + 5 = 12$

2. $X - 11 = 3$

3. $10 = X + 4$

4. $4X = 20$

5. $\dfrac{X}{2} = 15$

6. $18 = 9X$

7. $\dfrac{X}{5} = 35$

8. $2X + 8 = 4$

9. $\dfrac{X + 1}{3} = 6$

10. $4X + 3 = -13$

11. $\dfrac{X + 3}{3} = -7$

12. $23 = 2X - 5$

SECTION 4

1. $5^3 = ?$

2. $-4^3 = ?$

3. $-2^5 = ?$

4. $-2^6 = ?$

5. If $a = 4$ and $b = 2$, then $ab^2 = ?$

6. If $a = 4$ and $b = 2$, then $(a + b)^3 = ?$

7. If $a = 4$ and $b = 2$, then $a^2 + b^2 = ?$

8. $(11 + 4)^2 = ?$

9. $\sqrt{7^2} = ?$

10. If $a = 36$ and $b = 64$, the $\sqrt{a + b} = ?$

11. $\dfrac{25}{\sqrt{25}} = ?$

12. If $a = -1$ and $b = 2$, then $a^3b^4 = ?$

A N S W E R   K E Y Skills Assessment Exams

EXAM FROM SECTION A.1 (P. A-1)

SECTION 1

1. 75% **2.** $\dfrac{30}{100}$ or $\dfrac{3}{10}$ **3.** .3 **4.** $\dfrac{10}{13}$ **5.** 1.625 **6.** $\dfrac{2}{20}$

7. $\dfrac{19}{24}$ **8.** 1.4 **9.** $\dfrac{4}{15}$ **10.** 7.5 **11.** 16 **12.** 36

SECTION 2

1. 4 **2.** 8 **3.** 2 **4.** 9 **5.** -12 **6.** 12

7. -15 **8.** -24 **9.** -4 **10.** 3 **11.** -2 **12.** 25

SECTION 3

1. $X = 7$ **2.** $X = 29$ **3.** $X = 9$ **4.** $X = 4$ **5.** $X = 24$ **6.** $X = 15$

7. $X = 80$ **8.** $X = -3$ **9.** $X = 11$ **10.** $X = 25$ **11.** $X = 11$ **12.** $X = 7$

SECTION 4

1. 64 **2.** 4 **3.** 54 **4.** 25 **5.** 13 **6.** -27

7. 256 **8.** 8 **9.** 12 **10.** 121 **11.** 33 **12.** -9

FOLLOW-UP EXAM

SECTION 1

1. .175 **2.** 24% **3.** $\dfrac{18}{100}$ or $\dfrac{9}{50}$ **4.** $\dfrac{6}{15}$ **5.** $\dfrac{25}{24}$ **6.** $\dfrac{42}{60}$ or $\dfrac{7}{10}$

7. $\dfrac{2}{9}$ **8.** 1.3442 **9.** .2 **10.** 9.502 **11.** 27 **12.** 9.6

SECTION 2

1. 8 **2.** -2 **3.** -25 **4.** -13 **5.** -16 **6.** 49

7. -30 **8.** 45 **9.** 6 **10.** -6 **11.** -8 **12.** 7

SECTION 3

1. $X = 7$ **2.** $X = 14$ **3.** $X = 6$ **4.** $X = 5$ **5.** $X = 30$ **6.** $X = 2$

7. $X = 175$ **8.** $X = -2$ **9.** $X = 17$ **10.** $X = -4$ **11.** $X = -24$ **12.** $X = 14$

SECTION 4

1. 125	**2.** −64	**3.** −32	**4.** 64	**5.** 16	**6.** 216
7. 20	**8.** 225	**9.** 7	**10.** 10	**11.** 5	**12.** −16

SOLUTIONS TO SELECTED PROBLEMS ● APPENDIX A   Basic Mathematics Review

1. .35   **2.** 36%   **4.** $\dfrac{31}{10,000}$ **5. b.** False   **6. a.** $\dfrac{8}{15}$ **b.** $\dfrac{21}{18}$ **c.** $\dfrac{23}{40}$ **7.** 0.4267

9. 20.1832   **12.** .9   **14.** 5   **16.** −24   **17.** 11   **20.** $X = 5$

23. $X = -9$ **25.** $X = -25$ **26.** $X = 2$ **29.** −125   **31.** 9   **32.** −25

34. 2

SUGGESTED REVIEW BOOKS

There are many basic mathematics review books available if you need a more extensive review than this appendix can provide. The following books are but a few of the many that you may find helpful:

Barker, V. C., and Aufmann, R. N. (1982). *Essential Mathematics*. Boston: Houghton Mifflin.

Falstein, L. D. (1986). *Basic Mathematics* 2d ed. Reading, Mass.: Addison Wesley.

Washington, A. J. (1984). *Arithmetic and Beginning Algebra*. Menlo Park, Calif.: Benjamin/Cummings.

APPENDIX B   **STATISTICAL TABLES**

T A B L E B . 1   **The unit normal table***

*Column A lists the z-score values.
Column B provides the proportion of area between the mean and the z-score value.
Column C provides the proportion of area beyond the z-score.

Note: Because the normal distribution is symmetrical, areas for negative z-scores are the same as those for positive z-scores.

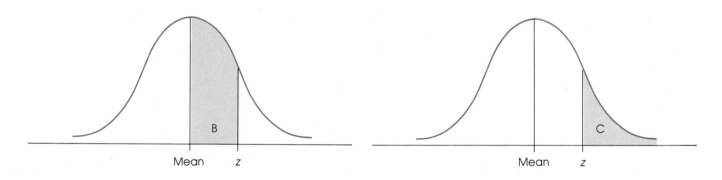

(A)	(B) AREA BETWEEN MEAN AND z	(C) AREA BEYOND z	(A)	(B) AREA BETWEEN MEAN AND z	(C) AREA BEYOND z	(A)	(B) AREA BETWEEN MEAN AND z	(C) AREA BEYOND z
z			z			z		
0.00	.0000	.5000	0.10	.0398	.4602	0.20	.0793	.4207
0.01	.0040	.4960	0.11	.0438	.4562	0.21	.0832	.4168
0.02	.0080	.4920	0.12	.0478	.4522	0.22	.0871	.4129
0.03	.0120	.4880	0.13	.0517	.4483	0.23	.0910	.4090
0.04	.0160	.4840	0.14	.0557	.4443	0.24	.0948	.4052
0.05	.0199	.4801	0.15	.0596	.5505	0.25	.0987	.4013
0.06	.0239	.4761	0.16	.0636	.4364	0.26	.1026	.3974
0.07	.0279	.4721	0.17	.0675	.4325	0.27	.1064	.3936
0.08	.0319	.4681	0.18	.0714	.4286	0.28	.1103	.3897
0.09	.0359	.4641	0.19	.0753	.4247	0.29	.1141	.3859

T A B L E   B . 1   continued

(A) z	(B) AREA BETWEEN MEAN AND z	(C) AREA BEYOND z	(A) z	(B) AREA BETWEEN MEAN AND z	(C) AREA BEYOND z	(A) z	(B) AREA BETWEEN MEAN AND z	(C) AREA BEYOND z
0.30	.1179	.3821	0.75	.2734	.2266	1.20	.3849	.1151
0.31	.1217	.3783	0.76	.2764	.2236	1.21	.3869	.1131
0.32	.1255	.3745	0.77	.2794	.2206	1.22	.3888	.1112
0.33	.1293	.3707	0.78	.2823	.2177	1.23	.3907	.1093
0.34	.1331	.3669	0.79	.2852	.2148	1.24	.3925	.1075
0.35	.1368	.3632	0.80	.2881	.2119	1.25	.3944	.1056
0.36	.1406	.3594	0.81	.2910	.2090	1.26	.3962	.1038
0.37	.1443	.3557	0.82	.2939	.2061	1.27	.3980	.1020
0.38	.1480	.3520	0.83	.2967	.2033	1.28	.3997	.1003
0.39	.1517	.3483	0.84	.2995	.2005	1.29	.4015	.0985
0.40	.1554	.3446	0.85	.3023	.1977	1.30	.4032	.0968
0.41	.1591	.3409	0.86	.3051	.1949	1.31	.4049	.0951
0.42	.1628	.3372	0.87	.3078	.1922	1.32	.4066	.0934
0.43	.1664	.3336	0.88	.3106	.1894	1.33	.4082	.0918
0.44	.1700	.3300	0.89	.3133	.1867	1.34	.4099	.0901
0.45	.1736	.3264	0.90	.3159	.1841	1.35	.4115	.0885
0.46	.1772	.3228	0.91	.3186	.1814	1.36	.4131	.0869
0.47	.1808	.3192	0.92	.3212	.1788	1.37	.4147	.0853
0.48	.1844	.3156	0.93	.3238	.1762	1.38	.4162	.0838
0.49	.1879	.3121	0.94	.3264	.1736	1.39	.4177	.0823
0.50	.1915	.3085	0.95	.3289	.1711	1.40	.4192	.0808
0.51	.1950	.3050	0.96	.3315	.1685	1.41	.4207	.0793
0.52	.1985	.3015	0.97	.3340	.1660	1.42	.4222	.0778
0.53	.2019	.2981	0.98	.3365	.1635	1.43	.4236	.0764
0.54	.2054	.2946	0.99	.3389	.1611	1.44	.4251	.0749
0.55	.2088	.2912	1.00	.3413	.1587	1.45	.4265	.0735
0.56	.2123	.2877	1.01	.3438	.1562	1.46	.4279	.0721
0.57	.2157	.2843	1.02	.3461	.1539	1.47	.4292	.0708
0.58	.2190	.2810	1.03	.3485	.1515	1.48	.4306	.0694
0.59	.2224	.2776	1.04	.3508	.1492	1.49	.4319	.0681
0.60	.2257	.2743	1.05	.3531	.1469	1.50	.4332	.0668
0.61	.2291	.2709	1.06	.3554	.1446	1.51	.4345	.0655
0.62	.2324	.2676	1.07	.3577	.1423	1.52	.4357	.0643
0.63	.2357	.2643	1.08	.3599	.1401	1.53	.4370	.0630
0.64	.2389	.2611	1.09	.3621	.1379	1.54	.4382	.0618
0.65	.2422	.2578	1.10	.3643	.1357	1.55	.4394	.0606
0.66	.2454	.2546	1.11	.3665	.1335	1.56	.4406	.0594
0.67	.2486	.2514	1.12	.3686	.1314	1.57	.4418	.0582
0.68	.2517	.2483	1.13	.3708	.1292	1.58	.4429	.0571
0.69	.2549	.2451	1.14	.3729	.1271	1.59	.4441	.0559
0.70	.2580	.2420	1.15	.3749	.1251	1.60	.4452	.0548
0.71	.2611	.2389	1.16	.3770	.1230	1.61	.4463	.0537
0.72	.2642	.2358	1.17	.3790	.1210	1.62	.4474	.0526
0.73	.2673	.2327	1.18	.3810	.1190	1.63	.4484	.0516
0.74	.2704	.2296	1.19	.3830	.1170	1.64	.4495	.0505

- one tail
.05

TABLE B.1   continued

(A)	(B) AREA BETWEEN	(C) AREA BEYOND	(A)	(B) AREA BETWEEN	(C) AREA BEYOND	(A)	(B) AREA BETWEEN	(C) AREA BEYOND
z	MEAN AND z	z	z	MEAN AND z	z	z	MEAN AND z	z
1.65	.4505	.0495	2.10	.4821	.0179	2.55	.4946	.0054
1.66	.4515	.0485	2.11	.4826	.0174	2.56	.4948	.0052
1.67	.4525	.0475	2.12	.4830	.0170	2.57	.4949	.0051
1.68	.4535	.0465	2.13	.4834	.0166	2.58	.4951	.0049
1.69	.4545	.0455	2.14	.4838	.0162	2.59	.4952	.0048
1.70	.4554	.0446	2.15	.4842	.0158	2.60	.4953	.0047
1.71	.4564	.0436	2.16	.4846	.0154	2.61	.4955	.0045
1.72	.4573	.0427	2.17	.4850	.0150	2.62	.4956	.0044
1.73	.4582	.0418	2.18	.4854	.0146	2.63	.4957	.0043
1.74	.4591	.0409	2.19	.4857	.0143	2.64	.4959	.0041
1.75	.4599	.0401	2.20	.4861	.0139	2.65	.4960	.0040
1.76	.4608	.0392	2.21	.4864	.0136	2.66	.4961	.0039
1.77	.4616	.0384	2.22	.4868	.0132	2.67	.4962	.0038
1.78	.4625	.0375	2.23	.4871	.0129	2.68	.4963	.0037
1.79	.4633	.0367	2.24	.4875	.0125	2.69	.4964	.0036
1.80	.4641	.0359	2.25	.4878	.0122	2.70	.4965	.0035
1.81	.4649	.0351	2.26	.4881	.0119	2.71	.4966	.0034
1.82	.4656	.0344	2.27	.4884	.0116	2.72	.4967	.0033
1.83	.4664	.0336	2.28	.4887	.0113	2.73	.4968	.0032
1.84	.4671	.0329	2.29	.4890	.0110	2.74	.4969	.0031
1.85	.4678	.0322	2.30	.4893	.0107	2.75	.4970	.0030
1.86	.4686	.0314	2.31	.4896	.0104	2.76	.4971	.0029
1.87	.4693	.0307	2.32	.4898	.0102	2.77	.4972	.0028
1.88	.4699	.0301	2.33	.4901	.0099	2.78	.4973	.0027
1.89	.4706	.0294	2.34	.4904	.0096	2.79	.4974	.0026
1.90	.4713	.0287	2.35	.4906	.0094	2.80	.4974	.0026
1.91	.4719	.0281	2.36	.4909	.0091	2.81	.4975	.0025
1.92	.4726	.0274	2.37	.4911	.0089	2.82	.4976	.0024
1.93	.4732	.0268	2.38	.4913	.0087	2.83	.4977	.0023
1.94	.4738	.0262	2.39	.4916	.0084	2.84	.4977	.0023
1.95	.4744	.0256	2.40	.4918	.0082	2.85	.4978	.0022
1.96	.4750	.0250	2.41	.4920	.0080	2.86	.4979	.0021
1.97	.4756	.0244	2.42	.4922	.0078	2.87	.4979	.0021
1.98	.4761	.0239	2.43	.4925	.0075	2.88	.4980	.0020
1.99	.4767	.0233	2.44	.4927	.0073	2.89	.4981	.0019
2.00	.4772	.0228	2.45	.4929	.0071	2.90	.4981	.0019
2.01	.4778	.0222	2.46	.4931	.0069	2.91	.4982	.0018
2.02	.4783	.0217	2.47	.4932	.0068	2.92	.4982	.0018
2.03	.4788	.0212	2.48	.4934	.0066	2.93	.4983	.0017
2.04	.4793	.0207	2.49	.4936	.0064	2.94	.4984	.0016
2.05	.4798	.0202	2.50	.4938	.0062	2.95	.4984	.0016
2.06	.4803	.0197	2.51	.4940	.0060	2.96	.4985	.0015
2.07	.4808	.0192	2.52	.4941	.0059	2.97	.4985	.0015
2.08	.4812	.0188	2.53	.4943	.0057	2.98	.4986	.0014
2.09	.4817	.0183	2.54	.4945	.0055	2.99	.4986	.0014

Handwritten annotations: ".05 Two Tailed" (circling 1.96 row); "One Tail .01" (circling 2.33 row); "Two Tail .01" (circling 2.58 row).

T A B L E   B . 1   continued

(A) z	(B) AREA BETWEEN MEAN AND z	(C) AREA BEYOND z	(A) z	(B) AREA BETWEEN MEAN AND z	(C) AREA BEYOND z	(A) z	(B) AREA BETWEEN MEAN AND z	(C) AREA BEYOND z
3.00	.4987	.0013	3.11	.4991	.0009	3.22	.4994	.0006
3.01	.4987	.0013	3.12	.4991	.0009	3.23	.4994	.0006
3.02	.4987	.0013	3.13	.4991	.0009	3.24	.4994	.0006
3.03	.4988	.0012	3.14	.4992	.0008	3.30	.4995	.0005
3.04	.4988	.0012	3.15	.4992	.0008	3.40	.4997	.0003
3.05	.4989	.0011	3.16	.4992	.0008	3.50	.4998	.0002
3.06	.4989	.0011	3.17	.4992	.0008	3.60	.4998	.0002
3.07	.4989	.0011	3.18	.4993	.0007	3.70	.4999	.0001
3.08	.4990	.0010	3.19	.4993	.0007	3.80	.49993	.00007
3.09	.4990	.0010	3.20	.4993	.0007	3.90	.49995	.00005
3.10	.4990	.0010	3.21	.4993	.0007	4.00	.49997	.00003

TABLES

TABLE B.2   The *t* distribution

df	0.25	0.10	0.05	0.025	0.01	0.005
			PROPORTION IN ONE TAIL			
	0.50	0.20	0.10	0.05	0.02	0.01
			PROPORTION IN TWO TAILS			
1	1.000	3.078	6.314	12.706	31.821	63.657
2	0.816	1.886	2.920	4.303	6.965	9.925
3	0.765	1.638	2.353	3.182	4.541	5.841
4	0.741	1.533	2.132	2.776	3.747	4.604
5	0.727	1.476	2.015	2.571	3.365	4.032
6	0.718	1.440	1.943	2.447	3.143	3.707
7	0.711	1.415	1.895	2.365	2.998	3.499
8	0.706	1.397	1.860	2.306	2.896	3.355
9	0.703	1.383	1.833	2.262	2.821	3.250
10	0.700	1.372	1.812	2.228	2.764	3.169
11	0.697	1.363	1.796	2.201	2.718	3.106
12	0.695	1.356	1.782	2.179	2.681	3.055
13	0.694	1.350	1.771	2.160	2.650	3.012
14	0.692	1.345	1.761	2.145	2.624	2.977
15	0.691	1.341	1.753	2.131	2.602	2.947
16	0.690	1.337	1.746	2.120	2.583	2.921
17	0.689	1.333	1.740	2.110	2.567	2.898
18	0.688	1.330	1.734	2.101	2.552	2.878
19	0.688	1.328	1.729	2.093	2.539	2.861
20	0.687	1.325	1.725	2.086	2.528	2.845
21	0.686	1.323	1.721	2.080	2.518	2.831
22	0.686	1.321	1.717	2.074	2.508	2.819
23	0.685	1.319	1.714	2.069	2.500	2.807
24	0.685	1.318	1.711	2.064	2.492	2.797
25	0.684	1.316	1.708	2.060	2.485	2.787
26	0.684	1.315	1.706	2.056	2.479	2.779
27	0.684	1.314	1.703	2.052	2.473	2.771
28	0.683	1.313	1.701	2.048	2.467	2.763
29	0.683	1.311	1.699	2.045	2.462	2.756
30	0.683	1.310	1.697	2.042	2.457	2.750
40	0.681	1.303	1.684	2.021	2.423	2.704
60	0.679	1.296	1.671	2.000	2.390	2.660
120	0.677	1.289	1.658	1.980	2.358	2.617
∞	0.674	1.282	1.645	1.960	2.326	2.576

TABLE B.3   Critical values for the *F*-max statistic*

*The critical values for $\alpha = .05$ are in lightface type, and for $\alpha = .01$ they are in boldface type.

	k = NUMBER OF SAMPLES										
$n - 1$	2	3	4	5	6	7	8	9	10	11	12
4	9.60	15.5	20.6	25.2	29.5	33.6	37.5	41.4	44.6	48.0	51.4
	23.2	**37.**	**49.**	**59.**	**69.**	**79.**	**89.**	**97.**	**106.**	**113.**	**120.**
5	7.15	10.8	13.7	16.3	18.7	20.8	22.9	24.7	26.5	28.2	29.9
	14.9	**22.**	**28.**	**33.**	**38.**	**42.**	**46.**	**50.**	**54.**	**57.**	**60.**
6	5.82	8.38	10.4	12.1	13.7	15.0	16.3	17.5	18.6	19.7	20.7
	11.1	**15.5**	**19.1**	**22.**	**25.**	**27.**	**30.**	**32.**	**34.**	**36.**	**37.**
7	4.99	6.94	8.44	9.70	10.8	11.8	12.7	13.5	14.3	15.1	15.8
	8.89	**12.1**	**14.5**	**16.5**	**18.4**	**20.**	**22.**	**23.**	**24.**	**26.**	**27.**
8	4.43	6.00	7.18	8.12	9.03	9.78	10.5	11.1	11.7	12.2	12.7
	7.50	**9.9**	**11.7**	**13.2**	**14.5**	**15.8**	**16.9**	**17.9**	**18.9**	**19.8**	**21.**
9	4.03	5.34	6.31	7.11	7.80	8.41	8.95	9.45	9.91	10.3	10.7
	6.54	**8.5**	**9.9**	**11.1**	**12.1**	**13.1**	**13.9**	**14.7**	**15.3**	**16.0**	**16.6**
10	3.72	4.85	5.67	6.34	6.92	7.42	7.87	8.28	8.66	9.01	9.34
	5.85	**7.4**	**8.6**	**9.6**	**10.4**	**11.1**	**11.8**	**12.4**	**12.9**	**13.4**	**13.9**
12	3.28	4.16	4.79	5.30	5.72	6.09	6.42	6.72	7.00	7.25	7.48
	4.91	**6.1**	**6.9**	**7.6**	**8.2**	**8.7**	**9.1**	**9.5**	**9.9**	**10.2**	**10.6**
15	2.86	3.54	4.01	4.37	4.68	4.95	5.19	5.40	5.59	5.77	5.93
	4.07	**4.9**	**5.5**	**6.0**	**6.4**	**6.7**	**7.1**	**7.3**	**7.5**	**7.8**	**8.0**
20	2.46	2.95	3.29	3.54	3.76	3.94	4.10	4.24	4.37	4.49	4.59
	3.32	**3.8**	**4.3**	**4.6**	**4.9**	**5.1**	**5.3**	**5.5**	**5.6**	**5.8**	**5.9**
30	2.07	2.40	2.61	2.78	2.91	3.02	3.12	3.21	3.29	3.36	3.39
	2.63	**3.0**	**3.3**	**3.5**	**3.6**	**3.7**	**3.8**	**3.9**	**4.0**	**4.1**	**4.2**
60	1.67	1.85	1.96	2.04	2.11	2.17	2.22	2.26	2.30	2.33	2.36
	1.96	**2.2**	**2.3**	**2.4**	**2.4**	**2.5**	**2.5**	**2.6**	**2.6**	**2.7**	**2.7**

T Test

$\bar{x} = \frac{\sum x}{n}$

I. H_0

II. $df = n-1$

III. $S = \sqrt{\frac{SS}{n-1}}$

$SS = \sum (x - \bar{x})^2$

IV. $S_{\bar{x}} = \frac{S}{\sqrt{n}}$

V. $t = \frac{\bar{x} - U}{S_{\bar{x}}}$

TABLE B.4   The *F* distribution*

*Table entries in lightface type are critical values for the .05 level of significance. Boldface type values are for the .01 level of significance.

Critical
F

DEGREES OF FREEDOM: DENOMINATOR	DEGREES OF FREEDOM: NUMERATOR															
	1	2	3	4	5	6	7	8	9	10	11	12	14	16	20
1	161	200	216	225	230	234	237	239	241	242	243	244	245	246	248
	4052	**4999**	**5403**	**5625**	**5764**	**5859**	**5928**	**5981**	**6022**	**6056**	**6082**	**6106**	**6142**	**6169**	**6208**
2	18.51	19.00	19.16	19.25	19.30	19.33	19.36	19.37	19.38	19.39	19.40	19.41	19.42	19.43	19.44
	98.49	**99.00**	**99.17**	**99.25**	**99.30**	**99.33**	**99.34**	**99.36**	**99.38**	**99.40**	**99.41**	**99.42**	**99.43**	**99.44**	**99.45**
3	10.13	9.55	9.28	9.12	9.01	8.94	8.88	8.84	8.81	8.78	8.76	8.74	8.71	8.69	8.66
	34.12	**30.82**	**29.46**	**28.71**	**28.24**	**27.91**	**27.67**	**27.49**	**27.34**	**27.23**	**27.13**	**27.05**	**26.92**	**26.83**	**26.69**
4	7.71	6.94	6.59	6.39	6.26	6.16	6.09	6.04	6.00	5.96	5.93	5.91	5.87	5.84	5.80
	21.20	**18.00**	**16.69**	**15.98**	**15.51**	**15.22**	**14.98**	**14.80**	**14.66**	**14.54**	**14.45**	**14.37**	**14.24**	**14.15**	**14.02**
5	6.61	5.79	5.41	5.19	5.05	4.95	4.88	4.82	4.78	4.74	4.70	4.68	4.64	4.60	4.56
	16.26	**13.27**	**12.06**	**11.39**	**10.97**	**10.67**	**10.45**	**10.27**	**10.15**	**10.05**	**9.96**	**9.89**	**9.77**	**9.68**	**9.55**
6	5.99	5.14	4.76	4.53	4.39	4.28	4.21	4.15	4.10	4.06	4.03	4.00	3.96	3.92	3.87
	13.74	**10.92**	**9.78**	**9.15**	**8.75**	**8.47**	**8.26**	**8.10**	**7.98**	**7.87**	**7.79**	**7.72**	**7.60**	**7.52**	**7.39**
7	5.59	4.47	4.35	4.12	3.97	3.87	3.79	3.73	3.68	3.63	3.60	3.57	3.52	3.49	3.44
	12.25	**9.55**	**8.45**	**7.85**	**7.46**	**7.19**	**7.00**	**6.84**	**6.71**	**6.62**	**6.54**	**6.47**	**6.35**	**6.27**	**6.15**
8	5.32	4.46	4.07	3.84	3.69	3.58	3.50	3.44	3.39	3.34	3.31	3.28	3.23	3.20	3.15
	11.26	**8.65**	**7.59**	**7.01**	**6.63**	**6.37**	**6.19**	**6.03**	**5.91**	**5.82**	**5.74**	**5.67**	**5.56**	**5.48**	**5.36**
9	5.12	4.26	3.86	3.63	3.48	3.37	3.29	3.23	3.18	3.13	3.10	3.07	3.02	2.98	2.93
	10.56	**8.02**	**6.99**	**6.42**	**6.06**	**5.80**	**5.62**	**5.47**	**5.35**	**5.26**	**5.18**	**5.11**	**5.00**	**4.92**	**4.80**
10	4.96	4.10	3.71	3.48	3.33	3.22	3.14	3.07	3.02	2.97	2.94	2.91	2.86	2.82	2.77
	10.04	**7.56**	**6.55**	**5.99**	**5.64**	**5.39**	**5.21**	**5.06**	**4.95**	**4.85**	**4.78**	**4.71**	**4.60**	**4.52**	**4.41**
11	4.84	3.98	3.59	3.36	3.20	3.09	3.01	2.95	2.90	2.86	2.82	2.79	2.74	2.70	2.65
	9.65	**7.20**	**6.22**	**5.67**	**5.32**	**5.07**	**4.88**	**4.74**	**4.63**	**4.54**	**4.46**	**4.40**	**4.29**	**4.21**	**4.10**
12	4.75	3.88	3.49	3.26	3.11	3.00	2.92	2.85	2.80	2.76	2.72	2.69	2.64	2.60	2.54
	9.33	**6.93**	**5.95**	**5.41**	**5.06**	**4.82**	**4.65**	**4.50**	**4.39**	**4.30**	**4.22**	**4.16**	**4.05**	**3.98**	**3.86**
13	4.67	3.80	3.41	3.18	3.02	2.92	2.84	2.77	2.72	2.67	2.63	2.60	2.55	2.51	2.46
	9.07	**6.70**	**5.74**	**5.20**	**4.86**	**4.62**	**4.44**	**4.30**	**4.19**	**4.10**	**4.02**	**3.96**	**3.85**	**3.78**	**3.67**
14	4.60	3.74	3.34	3.11	2.96	2.85	2.77	2.70	2.65	2.60	2.56	2.53	2.48	2.44	2.39
	8.86	**6.51**	**5.56**	**5.03**	**4.69**	**4.46**	**4.28**	**4.14**	**4.03**	**3.94**	**3.86**	**3.80**	**3.70**	**3.62**	**3.51**
15	4.54	3.68	3.29	3.06	2.90	2.79	2.70	2.64	2.59	2.55	2.51	2.48	2.43	2.39	2.33
	8.68	**6.36**	**5.42**	**4.89**	**4.56**	**4.32**	**4.14**	**4.00**	**3.89**	**3.80**	**3.73**	**3.67**	**3.56**	**3.48**	**3.36**

TABLE B.4   continued

DEGREES OF FREEDOM: DENOMINATOR	DEGREES OF FREEDOM: NUMERATOR														
	1	2	3	4	5	6	7	8	9	10	11	12	14	16	20
16	4.49	3.63	3.24	3.01	2.85	2.74	2.66	2.59	2.54	2.49	2.45	2.42	2.37	2.33	2.28
	8.53	6.23	5.29	4.77	4.44	4.20	4.03	3.89	3.78	3.69	3.61	3.55	3.45	3.37	3.25
17	4.45	3.59	3.20	2.96	2.81	2.70	2.62	2.55	2.50	2.45	2.41	2.38	2.33	2.29	2.23
	8.40	6.11	5.18	4.67	4.34	4.10	3.93	3.79	3.68	3.59	3.52	3.45	3.35	3.27	3.16
18	4.41	3.55	3.16	2.93	2.77	2.66	2.58	2.51	2.46	2.41	2.37	2.34	2.29	2.25	2.19
	8.28	6.01	5.09	4.58	4.25	4.01	3.85	3.71	3.60	3.51	3.44	3.37	3.27	3.19	3.07
19	4.38	3.52	3.13	2.90	2.74	2.63	2.55	2.48	2.43	2.38	2.34	2.31	2.26	2.21	2.15
	8.18	5.93	5.01	4.50	4.17	3.94	3.77	3.63	3.52	3.43	3.36	3.30	3.19	3.12	3.00
20	4.35	3.49	3.10	2.87	2.71	2.60	2.52	2.45	2.40	2.35	2.31	2.28	2.23	2.18	2.12
	8.10	5.85	4.94	4.43	4.10	3.87	3.71	3.56	3.45	3.37	3.30	3.23	3.13	3.05	2.94
21	4.32	3.47	3.07	2.84	2.68	2.57	2.49	2.42	2.37	2.32	2.28	2.25	2.20	2.15	2.09
	8.02	5.78	4.87	4.37	4.04	3.81	3.65	3.51	3.40	3.31	3.24	3.17	3.07	2.99	2.88
22	4.30	3.44	3.05	2.82	2.66	2.55	2.47	2.40	2.35	2.30	2.26	2.23	2.18	2.13	2.07
	7.94	5.72	4.82	4.31	3.99	3.76	3.59	3.45	3.35	3.26	3.18	3.12	3.02	2.94	2.83
23	4.28	3.42	3.03	2.80	2.64	2.53	2.45	2.38	2.32	2.28	2.24	2.20	2.14	2.10	2.04
	7.88	5.66	4.76	4.26	3.94	3.71	3.54	3.41	3.30	3.21	3.14	3.07	2.97	2.89	2.78
24	4.26	3.40	3.01	2.78	2.62	2.51	2.43	2.36	2.30	2.26	2.22	2.18	2.13	2.09	2.02
	7.82	5.61	4.72	4.22	3.90	3.67	3.50	3.36	3.25	3.17	3.09	3.03	2.93	2.85	2.74
25	4.24	3.38	2.99	2.76	2.60	2.49	2.41	2.34	2.28	2.24	2.20	2.16	2.11	2.06	2.00
	7.77	5.57	4.68	4.18	3.86	3.63	3.46	3.32	3.21	3.13	3.05	2.99	2.89	2.81	2.70
26	4.22	3.37	2.98	2.74	2.59	2.47	2.39	2.32	2.27	2.22	2.18	2.15	2.10	2.05	1.99
	7.72	5.53	4.64	4.14	3.82	3.59	3.42	3.29	3.17	3.09	3.02	2.96	2.86	2.77	2.66
27	4.21	3.35	2.96	2.73	2.57	2.46	2.37	2.30	2.25	2.20	2.16	2.13	2.08	2.03	1.97
	7.68	5.49	4.60	4.11	3.79	3.56	3.39	3.26	3.14	3.06	2.98	2.93	2.83	2.74	2.63
28	4.20	3.34	2.95	2.71	2.56	2.44	2.36	2.29	2.24	2.19	2.15	2.12	2.06	2.02	1.96
	7.64	5.45	4.57	4.07	3.76	3.53	3.36	3.23	3.11	3.03	2.95	2.90	2.80	2.71	2.60
29	4.18	3.33	2.93	2.70	2.54	2.43	2.35	2.28	2.22	2.18	2.14	2.10	2.05	2.00	1.94
	7.60	5.42	4.54	4.04	3.73	3.50	3.33	3.20	3.08	3.00	2.92	2.87	2.77	2.68	2.57
30	4.17	3.32	2.92	2.69	2.53	2.42	2.34	2.27	2.21	2.16	2.12	2.09	2.04	1.99	1.93
	7.56	5.39	4.51	4.02	3.70	3.47	3.30	3.17	3.06	2.98	2.90	2.84	2.74	2.66	2.55
32	4.15	3.30	2.90	2.67	2.51	2.40	2.32	2.25	2.19	2.14	2.10	2.07	2.02	1.97	1.91
	7.50	5.34	4.46	3.97	3.66	3.42	3.25	3.12	3.01	2.94	2.86	2.80	2.70	2.62	2.51
34	4.13	3.28	2.88	2.65	2.49	2.38	2.30	2.23	2.17	2.12	2.08	2.05	2.00	1.95	1.89
	7.44	5.29	4.42	3.93	3.61	3.38	3.21	3.08	2.97	2.89	2.82	2.76	2.66	2.58	2.47
36	4.11	3.26	2.86	2.63	2.48	2.36	2.28	2.21	2.15	2.10	2.06	2.03	1.98	1.93	1.87
	7.39	5.25	4.38	3.89	3.58	3.35	3.18	3.04	2.94	2.86	2.78	2.72	2.62	2.54	2.43
38	4.10	3.25	2.85	2.62	2.46	2.35	2.26	2.19	2.14	2.09	2.05	2.02	1.96	1.92	1.85
	7.35	5.21	4.34	3.86	3.54	3.32	3.15	3.02	2.91	2.82	2.75	2.69	2.59	2.51	2.40
40	4.08	3.23	2.84	2.61	2.45	2.34	2.25	2.18	2.12	2.07	2.04	2.00	1.95	1.90	1.84
	7.31	5.18	4.31	3.83	3.51	3.29	3.12	2.99	2.88	2.80	2.73	2.66	2.56	2.49	2.37
42	4.07	3.22	2.83	2.59	2.44	2.32	2.24	2.17	2.11	2.06	2.02	1.99	1.94	1.89	1.82
	7.27	5.15	4.29	3.80	3.49	3.26	3.10	2.96	2.86	2.77	2.70	2.64	2.54	2.46	2.35
44	4.06	3.21	2.82	2.58	2.43	2.31	2.23	2.16	2.10	2.05	2.01	1.98	1.92	1.88	1.81
	7.24	5.12	4.26	3.78	3.46	3.24	3.07	2.94	2.84	2.75	2.68	2.62	2.52	2.44	2.32

TABLE B.4   continued

DEGREES OF FREEDOM: DENOMINATOR	DEGREES OF FREEDOM: NUMERATOR														
	1	2	3	4	5	6	7	8	9	10	11	12	14	16	20
46	4.05	3.20	2.81	2.57	2.42	2.30	2.22	2.14	2.09	2.04	2.00	1.97	1.91	1.87	1.80
	7.21	**5.10**	**4.24**	**3.76**	**3.44**	**3.22**	**3.05**	**2.92**	**2.82**	**2.73**	**2.66**	**2.60**	**2.50**	**2.42**	**2.30**
48	4.04	3.19	2.80	2.56	2.41	2.30	2.21	2.14	2.08	2.03	1.99	1.96	1.90	1.86	1.79
	7.19	**5.08**	**4.22**	**3.74**	**3.42**	**3.20**	**3.04**	**2.90**	**2.80**	**2.71**	**2.64**	**2.58**	**2.48**	**2.40**	**2.28**
50	4.03	3.18	2.79	2.56	2.40	2.29	2.20	2.13	2.07	2.02	1.98	1.95	1.90	1.85	1.78
	7.17	**5.06**	**4.20**	**3.72**	**3.41**	**3.18**	**3.02**	**2.88**	**2.78**	**2.70**	**2.62**	**2.56**	**2.46**	**2.39**	**2.26**
55	4.02	3.17	2.78	2.54	2.38	2.27	2.18	2.11	2.05	2.00	1.97	1.93	1.88	1.83	1.76
	7.12	**5.01**	**4.16**	**3.68**	**3.37**	**3.15**	**2.98**	**2.85**	**2.75**	**2.66**	**2.59**	**2.53**	**2.43**	**2.35**	**2.23**
60	4.00	3.15	2.76	2.52	2.37	2.25	2.17	2.10	2.04	1.99	1.95	1.92	1.86	1.81	1.75
	7.08	**4.98**	**4.13**	**3.65**	**3.34**	**3.12**	**2.95**	**2.82**	**2.72**	**2.63**	**2.56**	**2.50**	**2.40**	**2.32**	**2.20**
65	3.99	3.14	2.75	2.51	2.36	2.24	2.15	2.08	2.02	1.98	1.94	1.90	1.85	1.80	1.73
	7.04	**4.95**	**4.10**	**3.62**	**3.31**	**3.09**	**2.93**	**2.79**	**2.70**	**2.61**	**2.54**	**2.47**	**2.37**	**2.30**	**2.18**
70	3.98	3.13	2.74	2.50	2.35	2.23	2.14	2.07	2.01	1.97	1.93	1.89	1.84	1.79	1.72
	7.01	**4.92**	**4.08**	**3.60**	**3.29**	**3.07**	**2.91**	**2.77**	**2.67**	**2.59**	**2.51**	**2.45**	**2.35**	**2.28**	**2.15**
80	3.96	3.11	2.72	2.48	2.33	2.21	2.12	2.05	1.99	1.95	1.91	1.88	1.82	1.77	1.70
	6.96	**4.88**	**4.04**	**3.56**	**3.25**	**3.04**	**2.87**	**2.74**	**2.64**	**2.55**	**2.48**	**2.41**	**2.32**	**2.24**	**2.11**
100	3.94	3.09	2.70	2.46	2.30	2.19	2.10	2.03	1.97	1.92	1.88	1.85	1.79	1.75	1.68
	6.90	**4.82**	**3.98**	**3.51**	**3.20**	**2.99**	**2.82**	**2.69**	**2.59**	**2.51**	**2.43**	**2.36**	**2.26**	**2.19**	**2.06**
125	3.92	3.07	2.68	2.44	2.29	2.17	2.08	2.01	1.95	1.90	1.86	1.83	1.77	1.72	1.65
	6.84	**4.78**	**3.94**	**3.47**	**3.17**	**2.95**	**2.79**	**2.65**	**2.56**	**2.47**	**2.40**	**2.33**	**2.23**	**2.15**	**2.03**
150	3.91	3.06	2.67	2.43	2.27	2.16	2.07	2.00	1.94	1.89	1.85	1.82	1.76	1.71	1.64
	6.81	**4.75**	**3.91**	**3.44**	**3.14**	**2.92**	**2.76**	**2.62**	**2.53**	**2.44**	**2.37**	**2.30**	**2.20**	**2.12**	**2.00**
200	3.89	3.04	2.65	2.41	2.26	2.14	2.05	1.98	1.92	1.87	1.83	1.80	1.74	1.69	1.62
	6.76	**4.71**	**3.88**	**3.41**	**3.11**	**2.90**	**2.73**	**2.60**	**2.50**	**2.41**	**2.34**	**2.28**	**2.17**	**2.09**	**1.97**
400	3.86	3.02	2.62	2.39	2.23	2.12	2.03	1.96	1.90	1.85	1.81	1.78	1.72	1.67	1.60
	6.70	**4.66**	**3.83**	**3.36**	**3.06**	**2.85**	**2.69**	**2.55**	**2.46**	**2.37**	**2.29**	**2.23**	**2.12**	**2.04**	**1.92**
1000	3.85	3.00	2.61	2.38	2.22	2.10	2.02	1.95	1.89	1.84	1.80	1.76	1.70	1.65	1.58
	6.66	**4.62**	**3.80**	**3.34**	**3.04**	**2.82**	**2.66**	**2.53**	**2.43**	**2.34**	**2.26**	**2.20**	**2.09**	**2.01**	**1.89**
∞	3.84	2.99	2.60	2.37	2.21	2.09	2.01	1.94	1.88	1.83	1.79	1.75	1.69	1.64	1.57
	6.64	**4.60**	**3.78**	**3.32**	**3.02**	**2.80**	**2.64**	**2.51**	**2.41**	**2.32**	**2.24**	**2.18**	**2.07**	**1.99**	**1.87**

TABLE B.5 Critical values for the Pearson correlation

df = n − 2	LEVEL OF SIGNIFICANCE FOR ONE-TAILED TEST			
	.05	.025	.01	.005
	LEVEL OF SIGNIFICANCE FOR TWO-TAILED TEST			
	.10	.05	.02	.01
1	.988	.997	.9995	.9999
2	.900	.950	.980	.990
3	.805	.878	.934	.959
4	.729	.811	.882	.917
5	.669	.754	.833	.874
6	.622	.707	.789	.834
7	.582	.666	.750	.798
8	.549	.632	.716	.765
9	.521	.602	.685	.735
10	.497	.576	.658	.708
11	.476	.553	.634	.684
12	.458	.532	.612	.661
13	.441	.514	.592	.641
14	.426	.497	.574	.623
15	.412	.482	.558	.606
16	.400	.468	.542	.590
17	.389	.456	.528	.575
18	.378	.444	.516	.561
19	.369	.433	.503	.549
20	.360	.423	.492	.537
21	.352	.413	.482	.526
22	.344	.404	.472	.515
23	.337	.396	.462	.505
24	.330	.388	.453	.496
25	.323	.381	.445	.487
26	.317	.374	.437	.479
27	.311	.367	.430	.471
28	.306	.361	.423	.463
29	.301	.355	.416	.456
30	.296	.349	.409	.449
35	.275	.325	.381	.418
40	.257	.304	.358	.393
45	.243	.288	.338	.372
50	.231	.273	.322	.354
60	.211	.250	.295	.325
70	.195	.232	.274	.302
80	.183	.217	.256	.283
90	.173	.205	.242	.267
100	.164	.195	.230	.254

TABLE B.6   The chi-square distribution*

*The table entries are critical values of χ^2.

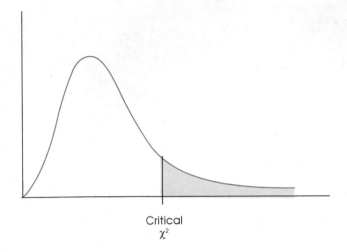

Critical
χ^2

$$f_e = \frac{f_c \times f_r}{n}$$

$$\chi^2 = \sum \frac{(f_0 - f_e)}{f_e}$$

$$df = (r-1)(c-1)$$

I. H_0
   H_1
II. df + & determine rejection region
III. $f_e = \frac{f_c + f_r}{n}$ + find χ^2
IV. determine if χ^2 falls in rejection region.

	PROPORTION IN CRITICAL REGION				
df	0.10	0.05	0.025	0.01	0.005
1	2.71	3.84	5.02	6.63	7.88
2	4.61	5.99	7.38	9.21	10.60
3	6.25	7.81	9.35	11.34	12.84
4	7.78	9.49	11.14	13.28	14.86
5	9.24	11.07	12.83	15.09	16.75
6	10.64	12.59	14.45	16.81	18.55
7	12.02	14.07	16.01	18.48	20.28
8	13.36	15.51	17.53	20.09	21.96
9	14.68	16.92	19.02	21.67	23.59
10	15.99	18.31	20.48	23.21	25.19
11	17.28	19.68	21.92	24.72	26.76
12	18.55	21.03	23.34	26.22	28.30
13	19.81	22.36	24.74	27.69	29.82
14	21.06	23.68	26.12	29.14	31.32
15	22.31	25.00	27.49	30.58	32.80
16	23.54	26.30	28.85	32.00	34.27
17	24.77	27.59	30.19	33.41	35.72
18	25.99	28.87	31.53	34.81	37.16
19	27.20	30.14	32.85	36.19	38.58
20	28.41	31.41	34.17	37.57	40.00
21	29.62	32.67	35.48	38.93	41.40
22	30.81	33.92	36.78	40.29	42.80
23	32.01	35.17	38.08	41.64	44.18
24	33.20	36.42	39.36	42.98	45.56
25	34.38	37.65	40.65	44.31	46.93
26	35.56	38.89	41.92	45.64	48.29
27	36.74	40.11	43.19	46.96	49.64
28	37.92	41.34	44.46	48.28	50.99
29	39.09	42.56	45.72	49.59	52.34
30	40.26	43.77	46.98	50.89	53.67

TABLE B.6 continued

df	PROPORTION IN CRITICAL REGION				
	0.10	0.05	0.025	0.01	0.005
40	51.81	55.76	59.34	63.69	66.77
50	63.17	67.50	71.42	76.15	79.49
60	74.40	79.08	83.30	88.38	91.95
70	85.53	90.53	95.02	100.42	104.22
80	96.58	101.88	106.63	112.33	116.32
90	107.56	113.14	118.14	124.12	128.30
100	118.50	124.34	129.56	135.81	140.17

ACKNOWLEDGMENTS

The statistical tables in Appendix B have been adapted or reprinted, with permission, from the following sources:

TABLE B.1 Appendix 2 of R. Clarke, A. Coladarci, and J. Caffrey, *Statistical Reasoning and Procedures*. Columbus, Ohio: Charles E. Merrill Publishing, 1965.

TABLE B.2 Table III of R. A. Fisher and F. Yates, *Statistical Tables for Biological, Agricultural and Medical Research*, 6th ed. London: Longman Group Ltd., 1974 (previously published by Oliver and Boyd Ltd., Edinburgh).

TABLE B.3 Table 31 of E. Pearson and H. O. Hartley, *Biometrika Tables for Statisticians*, 2nd ed. New York: Cambridge University Press, 1958. Adapted and reprinted by permission of the Biometrika trustees.

TABLE B.4 Table A14 of *Statistical Methods*, 7th ed. by George W. Snedecor and William G. Cochran, Copyright © 1980 by the Iowa State University Press, 2121 South State Avenue, Ames, Iowa 50010.

TABLE B.5 Table VI of R. A. Fisher and F. Yates, *Statistical Tables for Biological, Agricultural and Medical Research*, 6th ed. London: Longman Group Ltd., 1974 (previously published by Oliver and Boyd Ltd., Edinburgh).

TABLE B.6 Table 8 of E. Pearson and H. Hartley, *Biometrika Tables for Statisticians*, 3d ed. New York: Cambridge University Press, 1966. Adapted and reprinted with permission of the Biometrika trustees.

SOLUTIONS FOR PROBLEMS IN THE TEXT

Many of the problems in the text require several stages of computation. At each stage there is an opportunity for rounding answers. Depending on the exact sequence of operations used to solve a problem, different individuals will round their answers at different times and in different ways.

Also, problems worked on a computer will not be rounded at each stage. As a result, you may obtain answers that are slightly different from those presented here. As long as those differences are small, they probably can be attributed to rounding error and should not be a matter for concern.

CHAPTER 1 INTRODUCTION TO STATISTICS

1. Scientific study is based on data collected from observation rather than hunches or feelings.

3. Correlations do not determine the cause and effect nature of a relationship.

5. The independent variable is the type of pill (sleeping drug or placebo). The dependent variable is the time needed to fall asleep.

7. **a.** The researcher could simply find two different offices, one with music and one without, and measure productivity.
   b. The researcher could select one office and measure productivity for one month with music, then for one month without music.
   c. The independent variable is the presence/absence of music. The dependent variable is office productivity.

9. A nominal scale simply names the categories of measurement. An ordinal scale names and orders the categories. Order of finish is an ordinal measurement. Sex of jockeys is a nominal measurement.

11. A ratio scale has a zero point that represents "none" of the variable being measured. An interval scale does not have an absolute zero point.

13. A construct is a hypothetical concept. An operational definition defines a construct in terms of a measurement procedure.

15. **a.** $\Sigma X = 11$
   b. $\Sigma Y = 15$
   c. $\Sigma X + \Sigma Y = 26$
   d. $\Sigma(X + Y) = 26$
   e. $\Sigma XY = 28$
   f. $\Sigma X \Sigma Y = 165$

17. Adding 3 points to each of $N = 10$ scores will add 30 points (10 times 3) to the total.

19. **a.** $\Sigma X = 24$
   b. $\Sigma X^2 = 146$
   c. $\Sigma Y = 30$
   d. $\Sigma Y^2 = 250$
   e. $\Sigma XY = 115$
   f. $\Sigma X \Sigma Y = 720$

21. **a.** $\Sigma(X + 3)$
   b. $\Sigma(X^2 - 1)$
   c. $\Sigma(X - 2)^2$
   d. $(\Sigma X)^2 + 10$

23. **a.** $\Sigma X = 5$
   b. $\Sigma(X + 2) = 17$
   c. $\Sigma X^2 = 95$

CHAPTER 2 **FREQUENCY DISTRIBUTIONS**

1. With a range of only 15 points a regular table listing all the scores would be relatively simple and would provide complete information about the distribution. If there are space limitations, you could use a grouped table with an interval width of 2, but the grouped table would lose some of the detailed information about specific scores.

3. In a grouped table you cannot determine the exact value of each score. For example, you may know that f = 7 individuals had scores in the interval from 80 to 89, but you do not know the values for the actual scores.

5.

X	f
6	2
5	4
4	3
3	2
2	1
1	1

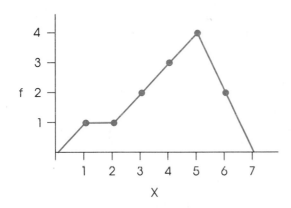

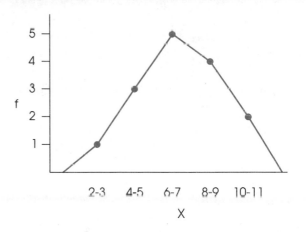

7.

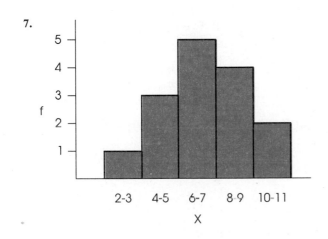

9. The scores range from 112 to 816 and should be presented in a grouped table.

X	f
800–899	1
700–799	3
600–699	4
500–599	6
400–499	5
300–399	3
200–299	1
100–199	1

11.

X	f	X	f
30–31	1	30–34	1
28–29	2	25–29	5
26–27	2	20–24	12
24–25	3	15–19	8
22–23	5	10–14	2
20–21	5		
18–19	5		
16–17	3		
14–15	1		
12–13	1		

13. a.

X	f (I)	f (II)
95–99	0	1
90–94	2	5
85–89	3	7
80–84	5	3
75–79	7	4
70–74	5	3
65–69	4	3
60–64	3	1
55–59	1	1

b. The distribution for section I is relatively symmetrical and the distribution for section II is negatively skewed. The scores in section II are generally higher than the scores in section I.

15. a.

X	f
85–89	2
80–84	0
75–79	3
70–74	4
65–69	6
60–64	6
55–59	2
50–54	3
45–49	3
40–44	1

b.

X	f
80–89	2
70–79	7
60–69	12
50–59	5
40–49	4

17.

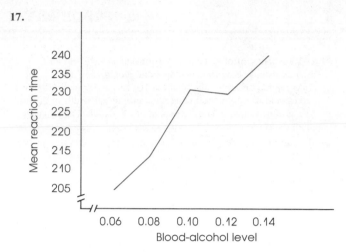

19.

X	f	p	%
6	2	.08	8%
5	3	.12	12%
4	3	.12	12%
3	4	.16	16%
2	5	.20	20%
1	8	.32	32%

The distribution is positively skewed.

CHAPTER 3 **CENTRAL TENDENCY**

1. If you compute the distance between each X and μ, the sum of the distances above the mean will equal the sum of the distances below the mean. If the X-axis were a weightless beam and the scores were blocks piled on the beam, the beam would balance at the mean.

3. N = 8

5. The old $\Sigma X = 432$ with n = 18. The new $\Sigma X = 500$ with n = 20. The new mean is 500/20 = 25.

7. The median divides the set of scores into two equal groups. Exactly 50% are less than the median.

9. The mode is used when the scores are measured on a nominal scale. The mean and median cannot be computed with a nominal scale.

11. Mean = 3
Median = 2.5
Mode = 1

13. Positively skewed. The mean is more displaced toward the tail of the distribution.

15. Mean = 25/8 = 3.125
Median = 3.5
Mode = 4

17. a. Mean = 19, Median = 19.5, Mode = 21.
b. The distribution is negatively skewed.

19. Use the median. The mean cannot be computed with undetermined scores.

21. For Section I $\Sigma X = 1890$. For Section II $\Sigma X = 5460$. For the combined group n = 100, $\Sigma X = 7350$, and $\overline{X} = 73.50$.

23. a. $\overline{X} = 4.71$
b. After adding 20 points to each score, $\overline{X} = 24.71$.

25. For the morning class, $\Sigma X = 2690.1$. For the afternoon class $\Sigma X = 1710.2$. For the combined group n = 95, $\Sigma X = 4400.3$, and the mean is 46.32.

27. $\overline{X} = 0.973$. Median = 0.967

29. $\overline{X} = 7.18$. This class is slightly above the national norm.

CHAPTER 4 **VARIABILITY**

1. a. SS is the sum of squared deviation scores.
   b. Variance is the mean squared deviation.
   c. Standard deviation is the square root of the variance. It provides a measure of the standard distance from the mean.

3. Range = 12 points. Q1 = 3.5 and Q3 = 8.5. Semi-interquartile range = 2.5. SS = 120, s = 3.30.

5. a. SS = 48.67
   b. SS = $(-3.33)^2 + (-2.33)^2 + (5.67)^2 = 48.67$

7. a. Sample B covers a wider range.
   b. For sample A: $\overline{X} = 9.17$ and s = 1.72.
   c. For sample B: $\overline{X} = 9.00$ and s = 5.66.

9. a. Any set of four scores that sum to zero.
   b. Answer will depend on student's scores.
   c. Each score is its own deviation, so $\Sigma X^2 = $ SS.

11. The scores range from 1 to 7, and the mean must be within this range. Thus, no score can deviate from the mean by more than 6 points, so the standard deviation must be less than 6.

13. $\overline{X} = 433$, SS = 24, $s^2 = 4$, and s = 2.

15. a.

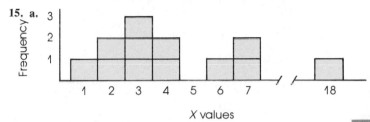

b. $\overline{X} = 5$ and s = 4.53
c. Median = 3.5. Semi-interquartile range = 2 (Q1 = 2.5 and Q3 = 6.5)
d. The majority of the scores are clustered around X = 3 or 4, so the median and semi-interquartile range provide a better description. The extreme score of X = 18 distorts the mean and standard deviation.

17. SS cannot be less than zero because it is computed by adding squared deviations. Squared deviations are always greater than or equal to zero.

19. a. For set A the mean is 2.5. For set B the mean is 8.
   b. The definitional formula for SS is appropriate when the mean is a whole number (as in set B).

21. a. College students $\overline{X} = 40.6$ and Business Men $\overline{X} = 40.1$. On average, both groups are very accurate.
   b. College students s = 9.22 and Business Men s = 2.56. Age estimates for the business men are generally close to the correct value. The estimates for the college students are much more scattered.

23. a.

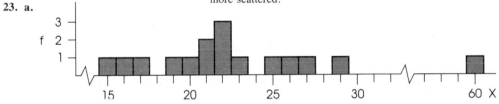

b. $\overline{X} = 24.06$; s = 10.33
c. Median = 21.83; Q3 = 25.5 and Q1 = 19.5. The semi-interquartile range is 6/2 = 3.
d. The mean and standard deviation are more affected by the single extreme score. The median and semi-interquartile range are more descriptive.

CHAPTER 5 **Z-SCORES**

1. A z-score describes a precise location within a distribution. The sign of the z-score tells whether the location is above (+) or below (−) the mean, and the magnitude tells the distance from the mean in terms of the number of standard deviations.

3. Tom's z-score indicates that he scored far above average for this class. This means that he knows a lot relative to the rest of the students, but it does not mean that he knows a lot about developmental psychology in absolute terms.

5. Because the score, X = 55, is above the mean, $\mu = 45$, it must have a positive z-score. Therefore, z = −2.00 cannot be correct.

7. a.

X	z	X	z
27	+0.40	28	+0.60
31	+1.20	34	+1.80
29	+0.80	33	+1.60
17	−1.60	19	−1.20
15	−2.00	22	−0.60

b.

X	z	X	z
27	+0.40	32	+1.40
30	+1.00	23	−0.40
10	−3.00	18	−1.40
39	+2.80	35	+2.00

9. a. For this population, $\mu = 7$ and $\sigma = 4$.

b.

X	z	X	Z
14	1.75	5	−0.50
11	1.00	8	0.25
1	−1.50	7	0
4	−0.75	3	−1.00
12	1.25	5	−0.50

11.

X	z	X	z
65	+2.50	53	+0.50
56	+1.00	38	−2.00
32	−3.00	50	0
42	−1.33	47	−0.50
41	−1.50		

13. $\mu = 240$

15. $\sigma = 20$

17. With $\sigma = 2$, $z = −.50$. This is the higher value.

19. Your z-score is +1.50 which is better than your friend's z-score of +1.10.

21. The numerator of the z-score formula is a deviation score, $X − \mu$. Deviation scores always sum to zero.

23. a. $\mu = 4.4$ and $\sigma = 2.15$

b.

X	z
1	−1.58
3	−0.65
5	+0.28
6	+0.74
7	+1.21

c. For the z-scores the mean is zero and the standard deviation is 1.

d. With a mean of zero the sign indicates direction above or below the mean. With a standard deviation of one, the magnitude of a z-score indicates the number of standard deviations away from the mean.

CHAPTER 6 **PROBABILITY**

1. a. $p = 45/60 = 0.75$
   b. $p = 25/60 = 0.42$
   c. $p = 5/60 = 0.08$

3. a. 0.3085
   b. 0.0401
   c. 0.0668
   d. 0.4013

5. a. $z = +0.25$, $p = 0.4013$
   b. $z = −0.50$, $p = 0.6915$
   c. $z = +1.00$, $p = 0.8413$
   d. $z = −1.50$, $p = 0.0668$

7. a. $z = +0.25$, $X = 125$
   b. $z = +1.28$, $X = 145.6$ or greater
   c. z between $−0.84$ and $+0.84$, X between 103.2 and 136.8.

9. a. $p = 0.6915$
   b. $p = 0.0668$
   c. $p = 0.9772$
   d. $p = 0.8664$

11. Converted to z-scores, the correct order is:
   John $z = +0.75$ highest
   Tom $z = +0.50$ middle
   Mary $= +0.25$ lowest

13. You cannot find the probability. You cannot use the Unit Normal Table because the distribution is not normal.

15. a. Bill's z-score is $z = +0.92$ and his rank is 82.12%. If he were in the pre-engineering section his z-score would $z = +0.25$ and his rank would be 59.87%.

   b. A rank of 40% corresponds to $z = −0.25$ or $X = 70$. In the humanities section a score of $X = 70$ corresponds to $z = +0.58$ and a rank of 71.90%.
   c. Mary's score is $X = 66$. Jane's score is $X = 68$.

17. a. $z = +0.84$ or $X = 116.8$
   b. $z = +0.40$ so the percentage is 34.46%

19. a. $z = −0.33$ so $p = .6293$
   b. $z = −0.38$ so $p = .6480$
   c. Students with scores between 450 and 470 were admitted last year but would have been rejected by this year's standard. These students account for .0855 of the total population last year, or $p = .0855/.6293 = .1359$ of the students who were admitted last year.
   d. Students with scores between 450 and 470 were rejected this year but would have been admitted by last year's standard. These students account for .0877 of the total population this year, or $p = .0877/.3520 = .2491$ of the students who were rejected this year.

21. a. $z = 1.04$, $X = 68.32$
   b. $z = 0.25$, $X = 62$
   c. $z = −0.84$, $X = 53.28$

23. a. $z = −1.04$, $X = 104.4$
   b. $z = 1.18$, $X = 137.7$
   c. $z = 1.47$, rank = 92.92%
   d. $z = −1.20$, rank = 11.51%
   e. $z = 0$, rank = 50%
   f. semi-interquartile range = 10 points

CHAPTER 7 PROBABILITY AND SAMPLES: THE DISTRIBUTION OF SAMPLE MEANS

1. **a.** The distribution of sample means is the set of all possible sample means for random samples of a specific size (n) from a specific population.
   b. The expected value of $\overline{X}$ is the mean of the distribution of sample means (μ).
   c. The standard error of $\overline{X}$ is the standard deviation of the distribution of sample means ($\sigma_{\overline{X}} = \sigma/\sqrt{n}$).

3. The larger sample (n = 30) will have the smaller standard error. On average, $\overline{X}$ from the larger sample will be closer to μ.

5. **a.** Standard error = $100/\sqrt{4} = 50$
   b. Standard error = $100/\sqrt{25} = 20$
   c. Standard error = $100/\sqrt{100} = 10$

7. **a.** $z = -0.50$, p = 0.3085
   b. Standard error = 1; z = -1.00; p = 0.1587

9. **a.** $z = +1.00$, p = 0.1587
   b. $z = -2.00$, p = 0.0228

11. **a.** Standard error = 6, z = -1.00, p = 0.1587 (more likely)
    b. Standard error = 2, z = 1.50, p = 0.0668

13. **a.** n > 4
    b. n > 16
    c. n > 400

15. **a.** $\mu = 4.5$, $\sigma = 2.87$
    b. With n = 8, $\sigma_X = 1.01$, z = 1.73, and $P(\overline{X} > 6.25) = 0.0418$
    c. With n = 12, $\sigma_{\overline{X}} = 0.83$, z = -0.40, and $P(\overline{X} > 4.17) = 0.6554$

17. To total 600 screws, the mean must be at least 120. With n = 5, $\sigma_{\overline{X}} = 2.68$, z = 1.87, and $P(\overline{X} > 120) = .0307$.

19. **a.** $z = \pm 0.31$, p = 0.2434
    b. $z = \pm 0.70$, p = 0.5160
    c. $z = \pm 0.99$, p = 0.6778

21. **a.** The distribution is normal with $\mu = 85$ and $\sigma_{\overline{X}} = 4.74$.
    b. z scores corresponding to -1.96 to +1.96 and sample means from 75.71 to 94.29.
    c. z scores corresponding to -2.58 to +2.58 and sample means from 72.77 to 97.23.

CHAPTER 8 INTRODUCTION TO HYPOTHESIS TESTING

1. **a.** Dependent variable is reaction time and independent variable is the position of the indicator light.
   b. The position of the indicator light has no effect on reaction time.
   c. H_0: $\mu = 200$
   H_1: $\mu \neq 200$

   Where μ refers to the mean reaction time with the light at eye level.

   d. The distribution of sample means is normal with $\mu = 200$ and $\sigma_{\overline{X}} = 4$. The critical region corresponds to z-score values greater than +1.96 or less than -1.96.
   e. $\overline{X} = 195$ corresponds to z = -1.25. Fail to reject H_0.
   f. With n = 100, $\sigma_{\overline{X}} = 2$ and $\overline{X} = 195$ corresponds to z = -2.50. Reject H_0. With the larger sample there is less error so that 5 point difference is sufficient to reject the null hypothesis.

3. **a.** $\overline{X} - \mu$ measures the difference between the sample data and the null hypothesis.
   b. A sample mean is not expected to be identical to the population mean. The standard error indicates how much difference between $\overline{X}$ and μ is expected by chance.

5. With inferential reasoning it is easier to demonstrate that a hypothesis is false than to prove it is true. The null hypothesis states that there is no effect and we try to show that this hypothesis is false.

7. The null hypothesis states that the price change has no effect on weekly sales. For these data, $\overline{X} = 161.75$, the standard error is

8.13, and the z-score statistic is -2.86. Reject the null hypothesis and conclude that there has been a significant change in weekly sales.

9. **a.** If there is not change and the population mean is still $\mu = 8.4$, this sample mean corresponds to z = -5.65. This is a very unlikely value so reject the null hypothesis and conclude that there has been a change in homework time.
   b. With n = 20 the standard error would be 0.74 and the z-score for this sample would be z = -1.76. In this case you would fail to reject the null hypothesis.

11. H_0: $\mu = 98.6$ (no change during withdrawal)
    H_1: $\mu \neq 98.6$ (there is a change)
    The critical region consists of z-score values greater than +2.58 or less than z = -2.58. For these data, z = 6.06 which is in the critical region so we reject the null hypothesis and conclude that there is a significant change in temperature during withdrawal.

13. **a.** H_0: $\mu = 55$ (patients' scores are not different from the normal population). The critical region consists of z-scores greater than +2.58 or less than -2.58. For these data, $\overline{X} = 76.62$ and z = 8.25. Reject the null hypothesis. Scores for depressed patients are significantly different from scores for normal individuals on this test.

15. The null hypothesis states that birth weights for infants of smoking mothers are not different from birth weights in the general population. For these data, $\overline{X} = 2.38$, the standard error is 0.17, and the z-score statistic is z = -3.06. Reject H_0, and

conclude that infants of smoking mothers are significantly different from infants in the general population.

17. The analyses are contradictory. The critical region for the two-tailed tests consists of the extreme 2.5% in each tail of the distribution. The two-tailed conclusion indicates that the data were not in this critical region. However, the one-tailed test indicates that the data were in the extreme 1% of one tail. Data cannot be in the extreme 1% and at the same time fail to be in the extreme 2.5%.

19. **a.** H_0: $\mu \leq 100$ (not above average), and H_1: $\mu > 100$ (above average). For these data the standard error is 1.875 and the z-score is z = 2.61. Reject H_0.

CHAPTER 9 INTRODUCTION TO THE t STATISTIC

1. The t statistic is used when the population standard deviation is unknown. You use the sample data to estimate the standard deviation and the standard error.

3. The t statistic assumes random sampling from a normal distribution.

5. As df increases the t distribution becomes less variable (less spread out) and more like a normal distribution. For $\alpha = .05$, the critical t values move toward ± 1.96 as df increases.

7. **a.** H_0: $\mu \geq 20$ (not better)
    H_1: $\mu < 20$ (better − fewer trials)
    The null hypothesis states that watching other animals will not result in fewer trials needed to solve the problem. H_1 states that performance will improve with watching.
   b. In the distribution of t scores with df = 3, the critical region consists of values less than −4.541.
   c. $t(3) = -5/5 = -1.00$
   d. Fail to reject H_0. These data do not provide sufficient evidence to conclude that animals perform significantly better after viewing others.

9. H_0: $\mu = 62$. For these data, $\overline{X} = 48.86$, s = 16.79, the standard error is 3.17, and the t statistic is t = −4.15. Reject H_0.

11. H_0: $\mu = 7.80$. $\overline{X} = 6.98$ and s = 0.61, the standard error is 0.22, and $t(7) = -3.73$. Reject H_0 and conclude that pay for the nonunion workers is significantly different from the union standard.

13. H_0: $\mu \leq 166$ (not heavier), H_1: $\mu > 166$ (heavier). The critical boundary is t = 2.528. $\overline{X} = 188.86$ and s = 20.54. The standard error is 4.48 and $t(20) = 5.10$. Reject H_0 and conclude that the patients are significantly heavier than average.

15. H_0: $\mu = 10$. $\overline{X} = 9.16$ and s = 1.43. The standard error is 0.37 and $t(14) = -2.27$. Reject H_0 and conclude that the rats eat significantly less with high humidity.

17. H_0: $\mu = 5.0$. $\overline{X} = 6.3$ and s = 2.03. The standard error is 0.11 and $t(326) = 11.82$. Reject H_0.

CHAPTER 10 HYPOTHESIS TESTS WITH TWO INDEPENDENT SAMPLES

1. **a.** A single-sample t would be used.
   b. An independent-measures hypothesis test to examine the difference between two populations.
   c. An independent-measures t would be used to evaluate the difference between the two treatments.

3. The homogeneity of variance assumption specifies that $\sigma_1^2 = \sigma_2^2$ for the two populations from which the samples are obtained. If this assumption is violated, the t statistic can cause misleading conclusions for a hypothesis test.

5. Pooled variance = 500, $t(18) = -1.30$. Fail to reject H_0. There is no evidence of a significant difference between the two age groups.

7. **a.** H_0: $\mu = 60$ (no effect). The data from sample 1 produce a t statistic of $t(8) = -2.00$. Fail to reject H_0. The mean for Treatment A is not significantly different from 60.
   b. H_0: $\mu = 60$ (no effect). The data from sample 2 produce a t statistic of $t(8) = 2.00$. Fail to reject H_0. The mean for Treatment B is not significantly different from 60.
   c. H_0: $\mu_1 - \mu_2 = 0$ (no difference between treatments A and B). The pooled variance is 9 and the test statistic is $t(16) =$ −2.84. Reject H_0 and conclude that there is a significant difference between the two treatments.
   d. The results are not contradictory. Treatment A produces a mean that is less than 60, but not enough to be significantly less. Treatment B produces a mean greater than 60, but not enough to be significantly greater. Each treatment appears to have a small (nonsignificant) effect, and the effects are in opposite directions. When the two small effects are combined in the independent-measures test, the result is a significant difference.

9. **a.** For experiment I, pooled variance = 10 and $t(8) = 2.50$. Reject H_0. For experiment II, pooled variance = 40 and $t(8) = 1.25$. Fail to reject H_0. For experiment III, pooled variance = 10 and $t(8) = 1.00$. Fail to reject H_0.
   b. Experiment II has greater variability which produces a larger standard error. In this experiment the 5 point mean difference is not sufficient to reject H_0.
   c. In experiment III there is only a 2 point difference between the sample means. This difference is not sufficient to reject H_0.

11. H_0: $(\mu_1 - \mu_2) \leq 0$ (no increase). H_1: $(\mu_1 - \mu_2) > 0$ (increase). Pooled variance = 30 and $t(13) = 3.67$. Reject H_0 and conclude that fatigue has a significant effect.

13. Pooled variance = 540 and $t(28) = -3.67$. Reject H_0 and conclude that pollution has a significant effect on life expectancy.

15. a.

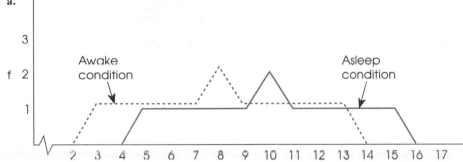

   b. For the asleep group, $\overline{X} = 10$ and SS = 110. For the awake group, $\overline{X} = 8$ and SS = 110. The standard error is 1.29 and $t(22) = 1.55$. Fail to reject H_0.

   c. The data in this problem are much more variable than the data in problem 14. The increased variability produces a larger standard error and reduces the value of the t statistic.

17. For the regular course, $\overline{X} = 4.07$ and SS = 10.93. For the programmed course, $\overline{X} = 3.00$ and SS = 14. The standard error is 0.34 and $t(28) = 3.15$. Reject H_0 and conclude that there is a significant difference in the level of enjoyment between the two courses.

19. For the first questionnaire $\overline{X} = 56.8$ and SS = 590.4. For the second questionnaire $\overline{X} = 49$ and SS = 270. The pooled variance is 30.73, the standard error is 2.02, and $t(28) = 3.86$. Reject H_0.

21. a. For treatment 1, $\overline{X} = 2.83$ with SS = 1.04. For treatment 2, $\overline{X} = 2.03$ with SS = 0.64. The pooled variance = .093 and the standard error is 0.136. $t(18) = 5.88$. Reject H_0 and conclude that there is a significant difference between the two treatments.

   b. When each score is multiplied by 60, the sample means and the sample standard deviations also will be multiplied by 60. However, the t statistic and the statistical decision should not change because the data have not actually been changed.

   c. You should still obtain $t(18) = 5.88$.

CHAPTER 11 HYPOTHESIS TESTS WITH RELATED SAMPLES

1. a. This is an independent measures experiment with two separate samples.

   b. This is repeated measures. The same sample is measured twice.

   c. This is a matched subjects design. The repeated measures t statistic is appropriate.

3. a. For these data, s = 10 and $t(24) = -2.50$. Reject H_0 and conclude that imprisonment changes personality.

   b. With $\alpha = .01$ the decision would be to fail to reject H_0.

5. The researcher expects the beer to increase the time required to respond. Thus, X_2 should be larger than X_1. The hypotheses would be: H_0: $\mu_D \leq 0$ (no increase), H_1: $\mu_D > 0$ (increase).

7. s = 18, the standard error is 4.65, and $t(14) = -2.75$. Reject H_0 and conclude that the drug significantly reduced blood pressure.

9. H_0: $\mu_D \leq 0$ (no improvement), and H_1: $\mu_D > 0$ (improved scores). For these data, $\overline{D} = 37.19$, s = 42.25, the standard error is 10.56 and $t(15) = 3.52$. Reject H_0 and conclude that there are a significant improvement in SAT scores.

11. For these data $\overline{D} = 0.90$, s = 0.74, the standard error is 0.22 and $t(10) = 4.09$. Reject H_0 and conclude that the drug has a significant effect.

13. For these data $\overline{D} = 7.33$, s = 5.87, and $t(11) = 4.33$. Reject H_0 and conclude that Ritalin significantly improves performance for hyperkinetic children.

15. For these data, $\overline{D} = 0.50$, s = 2.02, and $t(11) = 0.86$. Fail to reject H_0. There is no evidence for a significant difference between the two books.

17. For these data, $\overline{D} = 1.13$, s = 2.36, and $t(14) = 1.86$. Fail to reject H_0. The evidence is not sufficient to conclude that the drug has a significant effect.

CHAPTER 12 **ESTIMATION**

1. a. Use $\overline{X} = 5.8$ for the point estimate of μ.
  b. The amount of change is the difference between 6.3 hours and 5.8 hours. Children are watching TV 0.5 hours less now than in 1970.
  c. Estimate μ between 5.544 and 6.056 hours per day.

3. a. Use $\overline{X} = 15.5$ as the point of estimate of μ.
  b. With increased self-awareness the population mean is estimated to be between 13.54 and 17.46.

5. a. The sample mean is 72.1 with a standard error is 0.89. The 80% confidence interval extends from 70.96 ounces to 73.24 ounces.
  b. Yes. A 3 ounce increase would produce a mean weight of 68 ounces. The confidence interval indicates that the new mean should be even larger than this.

7. a. $s = 10$
  b. Use $\overline{X} = 43$ to estimate μ.
  c. With 90% confidence, use $t = \pm 1.711$ and estimate μ between 39.578 and 46.422.

9. a. $s = 2.91$ and the standard error is 0.88.
  b. Use $\overline{X} = 10.09$ for the point estimate. The 95% confidence interval uses $t = \pm 2.228$ and extends from 8.13 to 12.03.

11. a. Use $\overline{X} = 288.5$ as the point estimate.
  b. df = 11 and t = ± 2.201. SS = 244281 and the estimated standard error is 43.02, the 95% confidence interval extends from 193.81 to 383.19.
  c. No. The confidence interval estimates the value of the population mean. It does not estimate what values would be obtained for other samples.

13. a. Use the sample mean difference, $43 - 36 = 7$ to estimate the population mean difference.
  b. The standard error is 2. With 90% confidence use $t = \pm 1.734$ to estimate the mean difference between 3.532 and 10.468.

15. a. The sample mean difference, 13.8 minutes, is used to estimate the population difference.
  b. Pooled variance = 20 and standard error = 2. With 80% confidence, $t = 1.330$ and the population mean difference is estimated to be between 11.14 and 16.46.

17. a. With two separate samples, use an independent measures t statistic to estimate how much difference there is between the review course and control conditions.
  b. This is a repeated measures hypothesis testing situation. The researcher wants to determine whether or not the medication is effective.

19. a. For the point estimate, use the sample mean difference, 14.6.
  b. For these data, s = 10 and the standard error = 2. With 80% confidence, $t = \pm 1.318$ and the population mean difference is estimated to be between 11.964 and 17.236.

21. The sample mean $\overline{D} = 125$, is used for the point estimate. The sample standard deviation is 14.14 and the standard error is 2.58. With 90% confidence, $t = \pm 1.699$ and the population mean difference is estimated to be between 120.62 and 129.38.

CHAPTER 13 **INTRODUCTION TO ANALYSIS OF VARIANCE**

1. When there is no treatment effect, the numerator and the denominator of the F-ratio are both measuring the same sources of variability (individual differences and experimental error). In this case, the F-ratio is balanced and should have a value near 1.00.

3.

SOURCE	SS	df	MS	
Between Treatments	10	2	5.00	$F(2,12) = 3.75$
Within Treatments	16	12	1.33	
Total	26	14		

Fail to reject H_0. These data do not provide evidence that appearance influenced performance.

5. a. You should recognize that there is no variability within treatments for these data. However, the treatment means are different so there is some variability between treatments.
  b. $SS_{total} = 8$, $SS_{Between} = 8$, $SS_{Within} = 0$

7. a. k = 4
  b. N = 32

c. Yes, F = 3.87 is in the critical region at the .05 level of significance.

9.

SOURCE	SS	df	MS	
Between Treatments	15	2	7.5	$F(2,12) = 1.50$
Within Treatments	60	12	5	
Total	75	14		

Fail to reject H_0. No evidence of any significant differences.

11.

SOURCE	SS	df	MS	
Between Treatments	48	3	16	$F(3,36) = 8.00$
Within Treatments	72	36	2	
Total	120	39		

13.

SOURCE	SS	df	MS	
Between Treatments	30	3	10	$F(3,20) = 5.00$
Within Treatments	40	20	2	
Total	70	23		

15. a.

SOURCE	SS	df	MS	
Between Treatments	30	2	15	$F(2,12) = 15.00$
Within Treatments	12	12	1	
Total	42	14		

Reject H_0 and conclude that there are significant differences among the three groups.

b. Of the three samples the largest variance is for the right-handed subjects ($s^2 = 1.50$) and the smallest is for the left-handed subjects ($s^2 = 0.50$). F-max $= 3.00$ which is not significant. The homogeneity assumption is satisfied.

17. a. The means and SS values are:

Alphas	Betas	Gammas
$\overline{X} = 44.2$	$\overline{X} = 47.1$	$\overline{X} = 36.8$
SS = 865.6	SS = 500.9	SS = 325.6

The analysis of variance produces:

SOURCE	SS	df	MS	
Between Treatments	564.2	2	282.10	$F(2,27) = 4.50$
Within Treatments	1692.1	27	62.67	
Total	2256.3	29		

Reject H_0. There are significant differences among the three groups.

b. Beginning with the largest mean difference, the Scheffe test results are:

Betas versus Gammas: $F(2,27) = 4.23$ (significant)
Alphas versus Gammas: $F(2,27) = 2.18$
(not significant)

The only significant difference is between the Betas and the Gammas. The Alphas are an intermediate group, not significantly different from either extreme.

19. a. The means and SS values for these data are

Attractive	Average	Unattractive
$\overline{X} = 4.50$	$\overline{X} = 5.92$	$\overline{X} = 2.33$
SS = 23.00	SS = 24.92	SS = 12.67

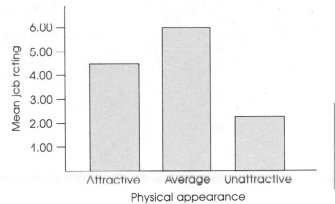

b.

SOURCE	SS	df	MS	
Between Treatments	78.17	2	39.08	$F(2,33) = 21.24$
Within Treatments	60.59	33	1.84	
Total	138.76	35		

c. Beginning with the largest difference between samples, the Scheffe comparisons and F-ratios are as follows:
Average vs Unattract. $F(2, 33) = 20.94$ (significant)
Attract vs Unattract. $F(2, 33) = 7.65$ (significant)
Attract vs Average $F(2, 33) = 3.27$ (not significant)

d. An average appearance produces the highest job rating. Individuals who are too attractive or too unattractive are rated lower, although the difference between average and attractive was not significant.

CHAPTER 14 CORRELATION AND REGRESSION

1. Set I SP = 6; Set II SP = -16; Set III SP = -4

3. a.

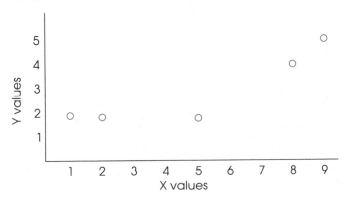

b. Estimate a strong positive correlation, probably $+.8$ or $+.9$.
c. $SS_X = 50$, $SS_Y = 8$, SP = 18, r = $+0.90$.

5. a. The correlation between X and Y is r = $+0.60$.
b. The correlation between Y and Z is r = $+0.60$.
c. Based on the answers to part a and part b you might expect a fairly strong positive correlation between X and Z.
d. The correlation between X and Z is r = $-.20$.
e. Simply because two variables are both related to a third variable does not necessarily imply that they are related to each other.

7. a. $SS_X = 63.5$, $SS_Y = 50.875$, SP = -51.25, and r = $-.902$.
b. The correlation is still r = $-.902$
c. Adding a constant does not change SS or SP or the correlation.
d. The correlation is still r = $-.902$.
e. Multiplying each score by 3 will cause all the SS and SP values to be multiplied by 9. However, this multiplication

cancels out in the correlation formula, so the correlation is unchanged.

9. With a sample of n = 2, the two data points always will fit perfectly on a straight line. Therefore, the correlation will be +1.00 or −1.00. With a sample of only n = 2 the correlation is meaningless.

11. With n = 25 the correlation must be greater than 0.396 to be significant at the .05 level. Reject H_0 and conclude that these data provide evidence for a non-zero correlation in the population.

13. SS_X = 1385.67, SS_Y = 1586, and SP = 920. r = +0.621 which is smaller than the critical value of 0.658. Fail to reject H_0. The data do not provide sufficient evidence to conclude that there is a significant relationship.

15. a. For company A, Y = 6X + 10. For company B, Y = 5X + 20.
   b. For company A the cost is $70, and for company B the cost is $70.

c. An order of 20 rats would be less money from company B ($120 versus $130).

17. a. $\hat{Y}$ = 3X − 3
   b. For each X, the predicted Y value would be,

X	$\hat{Y}$
1	0
4	9
3	6
2	3
5	12
3	6

19. $\hat{Y}$ = 36.8X + 395

21. a. SS_X = 224.88, SS_Y = 880.87, SP = 400.88, r = +0.901
   b. With n = 8 and α = .05, the critical value is 0.707. Reject H_0 and conclude that there is a significant relationship.
   c. The regression equation is $\hat{Y}$ = 1.78X + 191.47. For X = 20 thousand, the predicted Y value is 227.07 thousand.

CHAPTER 15 CHI-SQUARE TESTS

1. H_0: The four factors are equally important, p = .25 for each factor. The expected frequency is 25 for all four categories. Chi-square = 20. Reject H_0 and conclude that the four factors are not equally important.

3. The chi-square test requires that each observed frequency represent a separate and independent observation. Usually this requires that each individual be counted once and only once. For example, a sample of n = 20 observations usually requires a sample of n = 20 individuals. In this problem the same rat is observed over and over again, and it is not reasonable to assume that the different observations are independent.

5. The null hypothesis states that there is no preference among the three photographs; p = 1/3 for all categories. The expected frequencies are f_e = 50 for all categories, and chi-square = 20.28. Reject H_0 and conclude that there are significant preferences.

7. The null hypothesis states that the distribution of blood types in the foreign country is the same as in the United States. The expected frequencies are:

TYPE O	TYPE A	TYPE B	TYPE AB
61.20	55.76	13.60	5.44

Chi-square = 79.74. Reject H_0.

9. The null hypothesis states that there is no preference among the three colas, expected frequencies are 66.67 for each brand. Chi-square = 5.89. Fail to reject H_0 and conclude there is not enough evidence to show significant preferences.

11. The null hypothesis states that there is no relation between handedness and eye preference. The expected frequencies for

left handed subjects are 12 left eye and 18 right eye. For right handed subjects the expected frequencies are 48 for left eye and 72 for right eye. Chi-square = 11.11. There is a significant relation between hand and eye preference.

13. The null hypothesis states that there is no relation between education and opinion. The expected frequencies are:

	FOR	AGAINST	UNDECIDED
No degree	25	15	60
High School	10	6	24
College	15	9	36

Chi-square = 44.03. Reject H_0.

15. The null hypothesis states that there is no relation between gender and college major. The expected frequencies are:

	SCIENCE	HUMANITIES	ARTS	PROFESSIONAL
Male	22	26	12	40
Female	88	104	48	160

Chi-square = 17.66. Reject H_0.

17. The null hypothesis states that there is no relation between personality and heart disease. The expected frequencies are:

	HEART	VASCULAR	HYPERTENSION	NONE
Type A	27.20	24.77	27.69	90.34
Type B	28.80	26.23	29.31	95.66

Chi-square = 46.02. Reject H_0.

19. The null hypothesis states that there is no relation between need for achievement and risk. The expected frequencies are:

	CAUTIOUS	MODERATE	HIGH
High	12.18	15.10	10.72
Low	12.82	15.90	11.28

Chi-square = 17.08. Reject H_0.

21. The null hypothesis states that helping behavior is independent of success and failure. The expected frequencies are:

	SUCCESS	FAILURE
Help	13.5	13.5
No Help	11.5	11.5

For these data, chi-square = 2.01. Fail to reject H_0. There is no significant relationship.

CHAPTER 16 INTRODUCTION TO MINITAB

1.
```
MTB > NOTE  *PROBLEM 1*
MTB > HISTOGRAM C1


Histogram of C1   N = 30

Midpoint    Count
      10        7    *******
      20        3    ***
      30        4    ****
      40        2    **
      50        2    **
      60        5    *****
      70        4    ****
      80        3    ***

MTB > DOTPLOT C1
```

3.
```
MTB > NOTE  *PROBLEM 3*
MTB > TTEST 52 C1


TEST OF MU = 52.000 VS MU N.E. 52.000

          N      MEAN     STDEV    SE MEAN         T    P VALUE
C1       30    41.267    25.430      4.643     -2.31      0.028
```

5.

```
MTB > PLOT 'RT' 'BAC'


RT       -                                                                    *
         -
         -
      250+                                              2            *
         -                                                                   *
         -
         -                        *       *       *
         -                        *    *
      225+
         -
         -             *
         -          *
         - *
      200+
         -
         - *
         -
         +---------+---------+---------+---------+---------+-----BAC
      0.000     0.030     0.060     0.090     0.120     0.150
```

7.

```
MTB > REGRESS 'RT' 1 'BAC'
```

The regression equation is
RT = 203 + 395 BAC

Predictor	Coef	Stdev	t-ratio	p
Constant	203.245	4.183	48.59	0.000
BAC	394.51	49.77	7.93	0.000

s = 8.460   R-sq = 84.0%   R-sq(adj) = 82.6%

Analysis of Variance

SOURCE	DF	SS	MS	F	p
Regression	1	4496.9	4496.9	62.83	0.000
Error	12	858.8	71.6		
Total	13	5355.7			

Unusual Observations

Obs.	BAC	RT	Fit	Stdev.Fit	Residual	St.Resid
4	0.150	244.00	262.42	4.55	-18.42	-2.58R

R denotes an obs. with a large st. resid.

9.

```
MTB > DOTPLOT C1 C2
```

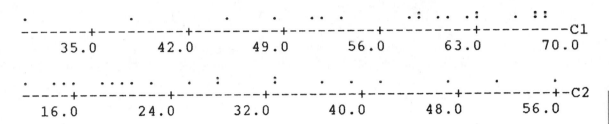

11.

```
MTB > HISTOGRAM 'BEFORE' 'AFTER'
```

```
Histogram of BEFORE    N = 12

Midpoint    Count
      35        1    *
      40        1    *
      45        1    *
      50        2    **
      55        3    ***
      60        1    *
      65        0
      70        2    **
      75        0
      80        0
      85        0
      90        1    *


Histogram of AFTER    N = 12

Midpoint    Count
      40        1    *
      45        0
      50        0
      55        0
      60        1    *
      65        2    **
      70        0
      75        3    ***
      80        2    **
      85        1    *
      90        2    **
```

13.

```
MTB > LET C3=C2-C1

MTB > TTEST 0 C3

TEST OF MU =  0.000 VS MU N.E.  0.000

            N      MEAN     STDEV    SE MEAN         T     P VALUE
C3          12    16.833    17.130     4.945      3.40     0.0059
```

15.

```
MTB > DOTPLOT C1-C4
```

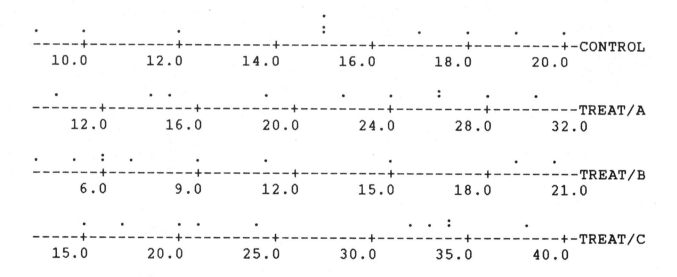

APPENDIX D INTRODUCTION TO MYSTAT

MYSTAT is a data analysis program that allows you to enter data into the computer and perform a wide range of statistical computations. To use MYSTAT you first must type your data into the computer and save it in a computer "file." Once your data are saved in the computer, you may type in a variety of computer commands that will instruct MYSTAT to perform different statistical calculations and print out the results. This appendix will provide a basic set of instructions for using MYSTAT to perform most of the statistical procedures covered in this book. Please note that we will not attempt to describe all of the capabilities of MYSTAT; for more detailed instructions, please refer to the MYSTAT booklet that came with your program disk.

The information in this appendix is divided into four sections.

1. **Getting started.** This section outlines the procedure for starting the MYSTAT program on most PC compatible computers. The next two sections correspond to the two major components of the MYSTAT program.

2. **The editor.** One major portion of the MYSTAT program is dedicated to entering data into the computer. The Editor allows you to type in data, to edit data, and to use a set of Editor commands to modify or transform your data prior to analysis.

3. **Statistical analysis.** The second major portion of the MYSTAT program contains the set of commands that are used to perform the different statistical techniques that MYSTAT permits you to do.

4. **Summary of MYSTAT commands.** A complete summary of the MYSTAT commands is presented at the end of this appendix.

SECTION D.1 GETTING STARTED

The exact sequence of commands for starting MYSTAT will vary from one computer system to another. However, the following sequence of commands will start MYSTAT for most systems. Please note that we are assuming that the MYSTAT program is "installed" on your computer—that is, you have created a working copy of MYSTAT and a data disk for a floppy disk system or you have installed MYSTAT on your hard disk. If this is the very first time MYSTAT is being used on your computer, please refer to the INSTALLATION instructions in the MYSTAT booklet.

If you have a *floppy disk* system, insert a DOS boot disk and turn on the computer. At the A> prompt, remove the DOS disk, put in your working copy of MYSTAT, and type MYSTAT and press Return or Enter. When you see the MYSTAT logo, press Enter and you will see the command menu which lists all of the commands you can use (see Figure D–1).

If you have a *hard disk* system, turn on the computer and continue to press Enter until you get the C> prompt. Then type

>CD\SYSTAT

>MYSTAT

pressing Enter after each command. When you see the MYSTAT logo, press Enter and you will see the command menu which lists all of the MYSTAT commands (see Figure D–1).

HELP   In the following sections we will introduce and describe most of the MYSTAT commands. Before we start, however, we would like to call attention to the HELP command. Whenever the command menu is on the screen, you can use the HELP command to obtain more information about all of MYSTAT's commands. Type HELP to obtain a brief description of each command. For more detailed information about a specific command, type HELP followed by the command name. For example, to obtain detailed information about the EDIT command, simply type HELP EDIT.

SECTION D.2 THE EDITOR

When you first turn on the MYSTAT program you will find yourself looking at the main command menu (see Figure D–1). This menu is the starting point for most of MYSTAT's statistical analysis procedures. However, before you can perform any statistical procedure, you must enter your data into the computer. To accomplish this, you must leave the main command menu and enter The Editor portion of the program where you can enter, edit, and modify data.

Figure D–1

The main command menu for MYSTAT.

```
MYSTAT --- An Instructional Version of SYSTAT

┌──────────┬──────────┬───────────┬────────────┬───────────┬────────────┐
│ DEMO     │ EDIT     │ MENU      │ PLOT       │ STATS     │ MODEL      │
│ HELP     │          │ NAMES     │ BOX        │ TABULATE  │ CATEGORY   │
│ SYSTAT   │ USE      │ LIST      │ HISTOGRAM  │ TTEST     │ ANOVA      │
│          │ SAVE     │ FORMAT    │ STEM       │ PEARSON   │ COVARIATE  │
│          │ PUT      │ NOTE      │ TPLOT      │           │ ESTIMATE   │
│          │ SUBMIT   │           │            │           │            │
│          │          │           │            │           │            │
│ QUIT     │ OUTPUT   │ SORT      │ CHARSET    │ SIGN      │            │
│          │          │ RANK      │            │ WILCOXON  │            │
│          │          │ WEIGHT    │            │ FRIEDMAN  │            │
└──────────┴──────────┴───────────┴────────────┴───────────┴────────────┘

>
```

CREATING A DATA FILE   The first step in using the MYSTAT program is entering your data into the computer. This is accomplished by using the following set of commands:

1. When the command menu is on the screen, type EDIT and press return. An empty data file will appear on the screen (see Figure D–2). Each row of the data file represents an individual or a "case" and each column corresponds to a variable. For example, if you have measurements of Age, Sex, and IQ for a sample of n = 8 individuals, then you would enter each individual's Age in column #1, Sex in column #2, and IQ score in column #3.

2. Before you can start entering data, you first must enter names for the variables in the top row. The cursor is already positioned in the first cell in the top row so you are ready to type in your first variable name. The following rules apply to variable names:

   a. Each name must be surrounded by single or double quotation marks.

   b. Each name must start with a letter and can be no more than 8 characters long.

   c. If the variable values consists of words or letters, the variable name must end with a dollar sign ($). For example, one of our variables is Sex and will consist of letter values (M for male and F for female).

   For this example, our variables are Age, Sex, and IQ. To name these variables, type

   'AGE'   (and press Enter)

   'SEX$'   (and press Enter)

   'IQ'   (and press Enter)

   The cursor moves automatically to the next variable when you press the Enter key. Notice that when entering variable names, each name is surrounded by quotation marks. Also notice that we have used a dollar sign at the end of the Sex variable because the values for this variable will be letters (not numbers).

3. When you have named each variable, press the Home key to move the cursor to the first data cell. (For most computers, the Home key is 7 on the

MYSTAT

Figure D–2

An empty data file for MYSTAT. Variable names are entered in the top row and the values for each variable are entered beneath the variable names in rows 1, 2, 3, etc. for each individual case.

```
MYSTAT Editor
   Case
     1
     2
     3
     4
     5
     6
     7
     8
     9
    10
    11
    12
    13
    14
    15
```

number keypad. If pressing this key types a 7 instead of moving the cursor, press the NumLock key and try again.) The following rules apply to entering data values:

a. If the value is a number, simply type the number and press return. If the number is very large or very small (more than 12 characters) you may use scientific notation. For example, the value 0.000000000023 would be entered as 2.3E-11.

b. If the value is a letter or a word, it must be surrounded by single or double quotation marks. For example, you must type 'M' if you are entering M for male. Press Enter after each value. Again, a value cannot be longer than 12 characters.

c. If you have missing data, enter a decimal (.) in place of the missing numeric value.

MYSTAT will move automatically to the next position in the data file when you press the Enter key.

EDITING DATA (CORRECTING MISTAKES)

You can use the arrow keys to move the cursor around in the data file. Also, the Home key will move to the first cell in the first row, the End key will move to the last cell in the last row, and the PgUp and PgDn keys will produce large moves if your data file is larger than the screen display.

To change a variable value or a variable name, move to the cell you want, type the new value, and press Enter.

USING EDITOR COMMANDS

When you have completed entering and editing your data, you exit the data file by pressing the ESC key. The cursor will move out of the data file to the bottom of the screen and present the command prompt (>). At this point you are ready to use other Editor commands.

If you want to return to the data file, press the Esc key again and the cursor will move back into the data file. Alternate presses of the Esc key will move you out of the data file or back into it.

ERASING ENTIRE ROWS OR COLUMNS

You can delete an entire row by typing DELETE and the row number. For example.

>DELETE 3   deletes the third row

>DELETE 5–10   deletes rows 5 through 10

You can erase a column by typing DROP and the variable name. For example,

>DROP SEX$ deletes the Sex variable (column)

NAMING AND SAVING YOUR DATA FILE

After you have completed entering and editing your data file, you must save the file so that it can be used for statistical analysis. This process is accomplished as follows:

1. Leave the data file by pressing the Esc key. The cursor will move to the bottom of the screen and present the command prompt (>).

2. Select a name for your data file. In order to save the data (and to call it back later) your file must have a name. File names can be up to 8 characters long and must begin with a letter.

3. To save the file, simply type SAVE followed by the file name you have selected. For example, if you want to name your data file EXAMPLE, then type

>SAVE EXAMPLE   (and press Enter)

Note: If you want to save your file on a work disk in the B drive, type SAVE B:EXAMPLE (and press Enter). To retrieve this file later for editing, you would type EDIT B:EXAMPLE.

EDITING AN EXISTING DATA FILE

If you have already created and saved a data file, you can retrieve it and edit it by typing EDIT followed by the name of the file. For example, if you have created and saved a data file named DATA, you can retrieve the file and have it available for editing (add new data or correct mistakes) by typing

EDIT DATA

Note: This command can be used only when the computer is displaying the main command menu (Figure D–1).

Note: If the file has been saved on a work disk on drive B, type EDIT B:DATA

EXAMPLES OF DATA FILES

For most statistical procedures, your data file will have one of the following three structures. These three types of data files correspond to the most common experimental designs and are appropriate for the most common statistical techniques.

1. **A single set of scores** For example, suppose you have a sample of n = 15 quiz scores and want to present them in a histogram, or compute the mean and standard deviation.

   For this type of data, you create a data file consisting of only one column of scores. Use the EDIT command to enter a variable name, and then type in the individual scores. An example of this type of data file is shown in Table D–1. Note that we have named this file ONESAMPL and will use it later to help demonstrate other MYSTAT commands.

Table D–1

The ONESAMPL data file with n = 15 quiz scores.

		QUIZ
CASE	1	1.000
CASE	2	3.000
CASE	3	2.000
CASE	4	5.000
CASE	5	1.000
CASE	6	2.000
CASE	7	4.000
CASE	8	0.000
CASE	9	3.000
CASE	10	4.000
CASE	11	5.000
CASE	12	2.000
CASE	13	4.000
CASE	14	3.000
CASE	15	3.000

Table D–2

The REPDATA data file showing Sex, Score1, Score2, and Difference score for each n = 12 individuals.

		SEX\$	SCORE1	SCORE2	DIFF
CASE	1	M	14.000	18.000	4.000
CASE	2	M	12.000	19.000	7.000
CASE	3	F	17.000	15.000	-2.000
CASE	4	M	13.000	16.000	3.000
CASE	5	F	17.000	21.000	4.000
CASE	6	M	21.000	20.000	-1.000
CASE	7	F	16.000	17.000	1.000
CASE	8	F	16.000	22.000	6.000
CASE	9	F	13.000	13.000	0.000
CASE	10	F	15.000	26.000	11.000
CASE	11	M	11.000	14.000	3.000
CASE	12	F	17.000	19.000	2.000

2. **A single set of individuals with several scores for each individual** An example would be data from a repeated-measures experiment where you have obtained 2 (or more) scores for each subject. Other examples would be data for a correlation (X and Y scores for each individual) or data from a survey where each individual has answered a series of questions.

For this type of data, you create a data file where each individual corresponds to a row in the data file, and each variable corresponds to a column. Type in the variables names (column headings), and then type in the scores. Remember that you type in the row of scores for each individual, then the computer automatically moves to the next row where you enter the scores for the next individual. An example of this type of data file is shown in Table D–2. We have named this file REPDATA and we will use it later to help demonstrate other MYSTAT commands.

3. **Separate sets of data from separate groups of individuals** For example, you may have data from an independent-measures experiment with a separate sample for each treatment condition. Or, you may have data from two or more different populations (males vs females, 8-year-olds versus 10-year-olds, etc.). Usually these data would be used for an independent-measure t test, an analysis of variance, or a chi-square test for independence.

For this type of data, the file must contain at least one column that designates the group in which each individual belongs. Table D–3 shows an example of this type of data file. We have named this file INDEPDAT and we will use it later to demonstrate other MYSTAT commands. Notice that we have included two different grouping variables, one using numeric values and one using letters:

a) The first column identifies the treatment condition to which the subject has been assigned (Treatment 1 or Treatment 2). Notice that the treatments are identified by numeric values, 1 or 2.

b) The second column identifies the sex of the subject (M for male and F for female). Remember, when you are using letters or words for the variable values, you must enter the values surrounded by quotation marks and you must use a dollar sign (\$) at the end of the variable name.

OTHER EDITOR COMMANDS   There are two other editor commands that are very useful for creating new variables out of the existing variables in your data file.

Table D-3

The INDEPDAT data file for n = 20 individuals. The TREAT variable identifies one of two treatment conditions for each individual. The Sex and Score are recorded for each individual. The final two columns list the scores from Treatment 1 and Treatment 2 respectively.

		TREAT	SEX$	SCORE	X1	X2
CASE	1	1.000	M	20.000	20.000	.
CASE	2	1.000	M	16.000	16.000	.
CASE	3	1.000	F	21.000	21.000	.
CASE	4	1.000	M	13.000	13.000	.
CASE	5	1.000	F	15.000	15.000	.
CASE	6	1.000	M	17.000	17.000	.
CASE	7	1.000	F	22.000	22.000	.
CASE	8	1.000	M	19.000	19.000	.
CASE	9	1.000	M	20.000	20.000	.
CASE	10	1.000	M	16.000	16.000	.
CASE	11	2.000	F	23.000	.	23.000
CASE	12	2.000	F	19.000	.	19.000
CASE	13	2.000	M	24.000	.	24.000
CASE	14	2.000	F	22.000	.	22.000
CASE	15	2.000	F	24.000	.	24.000
CASE	16	2.000	M	20.000	.	20.000
CASE	17	2.000	F	24.000	.	24.000
CASE	18	2.000	F	26.000	.	26.000
CASE	19	2.000	M	21.000	.	21.000
CASE	20	2.000	F	18.000	.	18.000

1. The LET command can be used to transform existing variables or to create new variables. The following format is used with the LET command:

LET (newvariable) = (expression)

where "newvariable" is the variable you are creating (new column in the data file), and "expression" is the combination or transformation of old variables that you desire.

For example, suppose you have data from a repeated measures experiment consisting of two scores for each individual (see Table D-2). If the original scores are named SCORE1 and SCORE2, you can create a new column of *difference scores* by using the command

>LET DIFF = SCORE2 − SCORE1   (press Enter)

As soon as you execute this command, the computer will automatically add a new column named DIFF that contains the difference between the two original scores for each subject. This command was used to create the DIFF column in the REPDATA file shown in Table D-2.

Commonly used expressions and examples of how they can be used with the LET command are as follows:

+ addition	LET SUM = SCORE1+SCORE2
− subtraction	LET DIFF = SCORE2−SCORE1
* multiplication	LET PRODUCT = SCORE1*SCORE2
/ division	LET QUOTIENT = SCORE1/SCORE2
^ exponentation	LET SQUARE = SCORE1^2

2. The IF-THEN command is used to create new variables in situations where you want to specify the conditions under which a new value is needed. For example, Table D-3 shows a data file where individuals are grouped into Treatment 1 and

Treatment 2. You can use the IF-THEN command to create a column listing *only* the scores from Treatment 1. The command

>IF TREAT=1 THEN LET X1=SCORE

will create a column named X1 that lists only the scores for individuals for whom the TREAT variable is equal to 1. In the same way you can create a column containing only the scores from Treatment 2 by using the command

>IF TREAT=2 THEN LET X2=SCORE

These commands were used to create the final two columns (X1 and X2) in the INDEPDAT file shown in Table D–3. Notice that the missing values in the X1 and X2 columns are marked with decimals. Using this procedure to create separate columns for each individual treatment condition can be very useful because it allows you to compute statistics (mean, standard deviation, etc.) for each treatment condition separately.

QUITTING THE EDITOR AND PREPARING FOR DATA ANALYSIS

To leave the EDITOR, use the QUIT command at the command prompt:

>QUIT   (and press Enter)

Be sure that you have saved the final version of your data file before you quit. When you QUIT the EDITOR, you will be returned to the main command menu and you will have access to all the MYSTAT data analysis commands.

SECTION D.3 STATISTICAL ANALYSIS

Before you begin any data analysis procedures, there are two special commands you should know.

First, you *must* tell MYSTAT which data file you want to analyze. This is accomplished with the USE command. For example, if you want to examine or analyze the scores in the ONESAMPL file, you would type

>USE ONESAMPL

Note: If you have saved your data file on a work disk in the B drive, you would retrieve it by typing

>USE B:ONESAMPL

Remember, it is essential that you begin any analysis with the USE command. MYSTAT must know which file you are using before you can do any statistics.

The second useful command is LIST. The LIST command simply presents a complete listing of the data file you have selected. This provides you with an opportunity to view the data file and be sure it is the one you want before you start any statistical analysis.

PRINTING OUTPUT

The MYSTAT program will present the results of all analyses on the computer screen. To obtain printed copies of your results, you can direct MYSTAT to use the printer by typing

>OUTPUT@

After this command, all output will be sent to the printer and shown on the screen. To stop the printer and have output appear on the screen only, type

>OUTPUT *

After this command, all output will appear on the screen only.

DESCRIPTIVE STATISTICS

The STATS command provides basic descriptive statistics for all numerical variables in your data file: number of cases, maximum score, minimum score, mean, and standard deviation. For example to obtain statistics for the data in the ONESAMPL file (Table D–1), type

>USE ONESAMPL

>STATS

The resulting output appears as follows:

TOTAL OBSERVATIONS: 15

QUIZ

N OF CASES	15
MINIMUM	0.000
MAXIMUM	5.000
MEAN	2.800
STANDARD DEV	1.474

If you want statistics for only one or two of the variables in your file, you can specify which variable(s) after the STATS command. For example, to obtain statistics for each of the two separate samples in the INDEPDAT file (Table D–3), type

>USE INDEPDAT

>STATS X1 X2

The resulting output appears as follows:

TOTAL OBSERVATIONS: 20

	X1	X2
N OF CASES	10	10
MINIMUM	13.000	18.000
MAXIMUM	22.000	26.000
MEAN	17.900	22.100
STANDARD DEV	2.923	2.558

Note: The standard deviation computed by MYSTAT is the *sample* standard deviation using n−1 in the formula (see Chapter 4).

---

t TESTS

The TTEST command does either the independent-measures t test (Chapter 10) or the related-samples t test (Chapter 11).

To do an independent-measures test, you must designate which variable (column) contains the scores and you must designate which variable (column) identifies the different treatments or populations being compared. In the INDEPDAT file (Table D−3), for example, the actual scores are listed in the SCORE column, and the two treatment conditions are identified in the TREAT column. To perform the t test, type

>USE INDEPDAT   (and press Enter)

>TTEST SCORE*TREAT   (and press Enter)

The resulting output appears as follows:

```
INDEPENDENT SAMPLES T-TEST ON     SCORE     GROUPED BY     TREAT

      GROUP          N       MEAN           SD
      1.000         10      17.900         2.923
      2.000         10      22.100         2.558
   POOLED VARIANCES T  =      3.419 DF =     18 PROB = .003
```

Note: For the independent-measures t test, the first variable identified in the command statement must be the dependent variable (scores) and the second variable must be the independent variable with values that identify the two separate groups being compared.

Using the same data file (INDEPDAT), you can perform an independent-measures t test comparing the Males versus the Females by using the command

>TTEST SCORE*SEX$ (and press Enter)

The resulting output appears as follows:

```
INDEPENDENT SAMPLES T-TEST ON     SCORE     GROUPED BY     SEX$

      GROUP          N       MEAN           SD
  M                 10      18.600         3.134
  F                 10      21.400         3.273
     POOLED VARIANCES T  =      1.954 DF =     18 PROB = .066
```

For a *related-samples* t test, your data file must have two scores for each individual. To perform a related samples t test using the data in the REPDATA file (Table D−2), for example, you type

>USE REPDATA   (and press Enter)

>TTEST SCORE1 SCORE2 (and press Enter)

The resulting output appears as follows:

```
PAIRED SAMPLES T-TEST ON    SCORE1      VS    SCORE2      WITH      12 CASES

MEAN DIFFERENCE =         -3.167
SD DIFFERENCE =           3.639
T =         3.014 DF =      11 PROD =  .012
```

ANALYSIS OF VARIANCE

To perform a single-factor, independent-measures ANOVA (Chapter 13), your data file must contain two variables. First, the file must contain an independent variable with values that identify the group or treatment condition for each individual. Second, the file must contain a column listing the dependent variable (score) for each individual. For example, the INDEPDATA file (Table D–3) contains a TREAT variable that specifies whether the individual is assigned to Treatment 1 or Treatment 2, and a SCORE variable that contains the score for each individual.

A series of three separate commands is used to perform the ANOVA:

1. The CATEGORY command is used to identify the independent variable and the number of levels (number of separate samples or k).
2. The ANOVA command is used to identify the dependent variable (scores).
3. The ESTIMATE command is used to start the analysis.

For example, to perform an ANOVA comparing Treatment 1 versus Treatment 2 for the INDEPDAT file (Table D–3), the complete sequence of commands would be

>USE INDEPDAT

>CATEGORY TREAT=2

>ANOVA SCORE

>ESTIMATE

The resulting output appears as follows:

```
DEP VAR:    SCORE      N:   20    MULTIPLE R:   .627    SQUARED MULTIPLE R:    .394
```

ANALYSIS OF VARIANCE

SOURCE	SUM-OF-SQUARES	DF	MEAN-SQUARE	F-RATIO	P
TREAT	88.200	1	88.200	11.691	0.003
ERROR	135.800	18	7.544		

PEARSON CORRELATION AND REGRESSION

To compute a Pearson correlation (Chapter 14) your data file must contain at least two scores for each individual. The PEARSON command computes the Pearson correlation for all numeric variables in the data file. The results are presented in a correlation matrix.

MYSTAT

For example, the REPDATA file (Table D–2) contains three variables (SCORE1, SCORE2, and DIFF). To compute all of the Pearson correlations for these variables, type

>USE REPDATA

>PEARSON

The resulting printout appears as follows:

```
PEARSON CORRELATION MATRIX

                        SCORE1        SCORE2        DIFF

        SCORE1          1.000
        SCORE2          0.389         1.000
          DIFF         -0.365         0.716         1.000


NUMBER OF OBSERVATIONS:    12
```

To find the correlation between any two variables, locate the first variable name across the top row of the matrix and the second variable name in the first column. The correlation between these two variables is found in the corresponding row and column position within the matrix. For example, the correlation between SCORE1 and SCORE2 is r = 0.389. Notice that the computer calculates *every possible* correlation including the self-correlations (for example, the correlation between SCORE1 and SCORE1 is r = 1.00). The self-correlations (all r = 1) appear across the diagonal of the matrix.

MYSTAT also can be used to compute the linear regression equation for predicting Y values from X values. Again, your data file must have at least two variables (two scores for each individual subject). The process of linear regression requires two MYSTAT commands. First, the MODEL command is used to identify the Y variable, the X variable, and the general form of the linear equation. Second, the ESTIMATE command is used to execute the regression program.

Using the data in the REPDATA file (Table D–2), the process for computing the regression equation for predicting SCORE2 (Y) from SCORE1 (X) would be as follows:

>USE REPDATA
>MODEL SCORE2 = CONSTANT + SCORE1
>ESTIMATE

The resulting printout appears as follows:

```
DEP VAR:  SCORE2      N:   12     MULTIPLE R:   .389     SQUARED MULTIPLE R:    .151
ADJUSTED SQUARED MULTIPLE R:   .066      STANDARD ERROR OF ESTIMATE:        3.553


    VARIABLE     COEFFICIENT     STD ERROR    STD COEF  TOLERANCE      T    P(2 TAIL)
    CONSTANT         10.478         5.980       0.000     .          1.752    0.110
      SCORE1          0.518         0.388       0.389  .100E+01      1.333    0.212



                              ANALYSIS OF VARIANCE


      SOURCE     SUM-OF-SQUARES    DF    MEAN-SQUARE     F-RATIO        P


    REGRESSION         22.444       1        22.444       1.778       0.212
      RESIDUAL        126.223      10        12.622
```

Note: In this printout, the information relevant to the regression equation appears under the heading COEFFICIENT. The CONSTANT portion of the equation is 10.478 and the coefficient for the SCORE1 variable is 0.518. Thus, the regression equation is

$$\text{SCORE2} = 0.518(\text{SCORE1}) + 10.478$$

CHI-SQUARE TEST FOR INDEPENDENCE

The TABULATE command can be used to construct the frequency matrix for two variables and to compute the chi-square value for the test for independence (Chapter 15). To use this chi-square test, each individual must be classified on two variables (two scores for each individual). Therefore, the data file must include two columns (variables) and each variable must have at least two different values. For example, the INDEPDAT file (Table D–3) has a TREAT variable and a SEX$ variable and each individual is classified into one of two treatments (1 or 2) and is identified as either M (male) or F (female). To construct the frequency distribution matrix for these two variables and to compute the chi-square value, type

>USE INDEPDAT

>TABULATE TREAT*SEX$

The resulting printout appears as follows:

```
TABLE OF      TREAT      (ROWS) BY      SEX$      (COLUMNS)
FREQUENCIES
                  F          M        TOTAL

    1.000         3          7          10

    2.000         7          3          10

  TOTAL          10         10          20
```

```
TEST STATISTIC                          VALUE      DF       PROB
  PEARSON CHI-SQUARE                     3.200       1       .074
  LIKELIHOOD RATIO CHI-SQUARE           3.291       1       .070
  MCNEMAR SYMMETRY CHI-SQUARE            .000       1      1.000
  YATES CORRECTED CHI-SQUARE            1.800       1       .180
  FISHER EXACT TEST (TWO-TAIL)                              .179
```

(Note: Additional, irrelevant printout is not shown.)
Note: The relevant information concerning the chi-square statistic is contained in the row labeled PEARSON CHI-SQUARE. For these data, chi-square = 3.200 with df = 1 and a probability (alpha level) of p = .074.

FREQUENCY DISTRIBUTIONS

MYSTAT can be used to construct either a frequency distribution histogram or a frequency distribution table. The HISTOGRAM command will construct a separate graph for each of the numeric variables in the data file. For example, the INDEPDAT file (Table D–3) contains five variables (TREAT, SEX$, SCORE, X1 and X2), and the HISTOGRAM command will construct four separate graphs (no graph for SEX$ because it is not a numeric variable).

If you want a histogram for a single variable, specify the variable after the HISTOGRAM command. For example, to produce a histogram showing the frequency distribution for the SCORE variable in the INDEPDAT file, type

>USE INDEPDAT

>HISTOGRAM SCORE

The resulting printout is shown in Figure D–3:

Figure D–3

Printout from HISTOGRAM command.

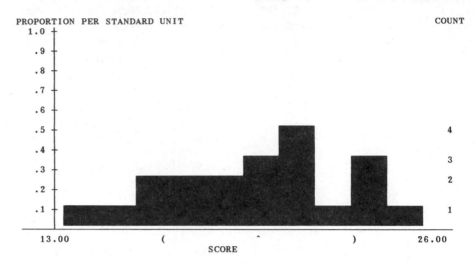

Note: The histograms generated by MYSTAT show the general shape of the frequency distribution. They do not list each individual score and show every frequency. Also, if your scores cover a wide range of values, the HISTOGRAM command will automatically group the scores into class intervals before constructing the histogram.

To obtain the exact frequency count for each individual score you can use the TABULATE command. This command will list each individual score and its frequency for all of the variables in your data file.

If you want a tabulated frequency distribution for only one variable, simple specify the variable name after the TABULATE command. For example, to obtain the frequency distribution for the SCORE variable in the INDEPDAT file (Table D–3), type

>USE INDEPDAT

>TABULATE SCORE

The resulting printout appears as follows:

TABLE OF VALUES FOR   SCORE
FREQUENCIES

13.000	15.000	16.000	17.000	18.000	19.000	
1	1	2	1	1	2	

20.000	21.000	22.000	23.000	24.000	26.000	TOTAL
3	2	2	1	3	1	20

SCATTERPLOTS The PLOT command creates a scatterplot showing the relationship between two variables. Your data file must have at least two numeric variables.

For example, the REPDATA file (Table D–2) contains the variables SCORE1, SCORE2, and DIFF. To generate a scatterplot showing the relation between SCORE1 and SCORE2, type

>USE REPDATA

>PLOT SCORE1*SCORE2

The resulting printout is shown in Figure D–4:

Figure D–4

Printout from PLOT command showing the relation between SCORE1 and SCORE2.

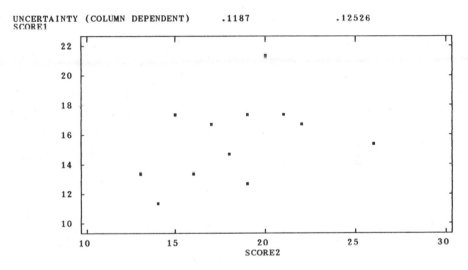

Note: The variable after the asterisk is plotted on the X-axis.

The PLOT command also can be used to show two different scatterplots in the same graph. For example, to show the relation between SCORE1 and SCORE2 along with the relationship between DIFF and SCORE2, type

>USE REPDATA

>PLOT SCORE1 DIFF*SCORE2/SYMBOL='1','2'

The resulting printout is shown in Figure D–5:

Figure D–5

Printout from PLOT command showing the relationship between SCORE1 and SCORE2 and the relation between DIFF and SCORE2 in one scatterplot.

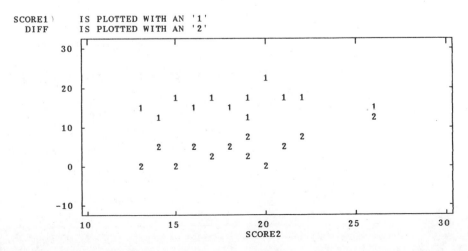

Note: The SCORE1 points will be shown as 1s in the graph and the DIFF points will be shown as 2s. Also note that you must use the same variable on the X-axis for both plots.

SECTION D.4 **SUMMARY OF MYSTAT COMMANDS**

EDITOR COMMANDS

1. EDIT moves you from the main command menu into the data file.
2. Within the data file, the arrow keys, Home, End, PgUp and PgUp move to a new cursor position.
3. Esc moves you out of the data file to the Editor command prompt (>). Pressing Esc again moves you back into the data file.
4. DELETE erases a row or rows of data.
5. DROP erases a column or columns of data.
6. LET creates a new variable by combining or transforming existing variables.
7. IF...THEN LET creates a new variable contingent on the specified conditions.
8. SAVE saves the data file.
9. QUIT moves you from the Editor back to the main command menu.

STATISTICAL ANALYSIS COMMANDS

1. USE selects the data file to be examined or analyzed.
2. LIST presents a complete copy of the data file.
3. EDIT moves you from the main command menu into an empty data file. EDIT FILENAME moves you into the file specified.
4. OUTPUT @ sends output to the printer and the screen.
5. OUTPUT * sends output to the screen only.
6. STATS presents basic descriptive statistics for the data file.
7. TTEST VARIABLE1*VARIABLE2 performs an independent-measures t test where VARIABLE1 contains the scores and VARIABLE2 identifies the two groups.
8. TTEST VARIABLE1 VARIABLE2 performs a related-samples t test.
9. CATEGORY, ANOVA, and ESTIMATE are used in sequence to perform an analysis of variance.
10. TABULATE VARIABLE1*VARIABLE2 presents a frequency distribution matrix for the two variables and computes the chi-square test for independence.

11. PEARSON computes the Pearson correlation between all pairs of numeric variables in the data file.

12. MODEL Y=CONSTANT+X and ESTIMATE are used in sequence to compute a linear regression equation for predicting variable Y from variable X.

13. HISTOGRAM presents a frequency distribution histogram for all numeric variables in the data file.

14. TABULATE presents a frequency distribution for all variables in the data file.

15. PLOT VARIABLE1*VARIABLE2 presents a scatterplot showing the relation between the two variables with VARIABLE2 on the X-axis.

MYSTAT

REFERENCES

Betz, B. J., and Thomas, C. B. (1979). Individual temperament as a predictor of health or premature disease. *The Johns Hopkins Medical Journal, 144,* 81–89.

Bransford, J. D., and Johnson, M. K. (1972). Contextual prerequisites for understanding: Some investigations of comprehension and recall. *Journal of Verbal Learning and Verbal Behavior, 11,* 717–726.

Cowles, M., and Davis, C. (1982). On the origins of the .05 level of statistical significance. *American Psychologist, 37,* 553–558.

Darley, J. M., and Latané, B. (1968). Bystander intervention in emergencies: Diffusion of responsibility. *Journal of Personality and Social Psychology, 8,* 377–383.

Friedman, M., and Rosenman, R. H. (1974). *Type A behavior and your heart.* New York: Knopf.

McClelland, D. C. (1961). *The achieving society.* Princeton, N.J.: Van Nostrand.

Rosenthal, R. (1963). On the social psychology of the psychological experiment: The experimenter's hypothesis as unintended determinant of experimental results. *American Scientist, 51,* 268–283.

Rosenthal, R., and Fode, K. L. (1963). The effect of experimenter bias on the performance of the albino rat. *Behavioral Science, 8,* 183–189.

Scaife, M. (1976). The response to eye-like shapes by birds. I. The effect of context: A predator and a strange bird. *Animal Behaviour, 24,* 195–199.

Sternberg, S. (1966). High-speed scanning in human memory. *Science, 153,* 652–654.

Tversky, A., and Kahneman, D. (1974). Judgment under uncertainty: Heuristics and biases. *Science, 185,* 1124–1131.

INDEX